Philosophy of Logic
An Anthology

Edited by

Dale Jacquette

Copyright © Blackwell Publishers Ltd 2002
Editorial matter and organization copyright © Dale Jacquette 2002

First published 2002

2 4 6 8 10 9 7 5 3 1

Blackwell Publishers Inc.
350 Main Street
Malden, Massachusetts 02148
USA

Blackwell Publishers Ltd
108 Cowley Road
Oxford OX4 1JF
UK

Library of Congress Cataloging-in-Publication Data

Philosophy of logic: an anthology / edited by Dale Jacquette.
     p. cm. — (Blackwell philosophy anthologies; 14)
    Includes bibliographical references and index.
    ISBN 0-631-21867-X (alk. paper) — ISBN 0-631-21868-8 (pb. : alk. paper)
    1. Logic. I. Jacquette, Dale. II. Series.

BC71 .P55 2002
160—dc21

                        2001018476

British Library Cataloguing in Publication Data

A CIP catalogue record for this book is available from the British Library.

Typeset in 9 on 11 pt Ehrhardt
by Kolam Information Services Pvt Ltd, Pondicherry, India

Printed in Great Britain by MPG Books Ltd, Bodmin, Cornwall
This book is printed on acid-free paper.

Philosophy of Logic

BLACKWELL PHILOSOPHY ANTHOLOGIES

Each volume in this outstanding series provides an authoritative and comprehensive collection of the essential primary readings from philosophy's main fields of study. Designed to complement the *Blackwell Companions to Philosophy* series, each volume represents an unparalleled resource in its own right, and will provide the ideal platform for course use.

Contents

Contents

Contents

Preface

The essays in this anthology include some of the most important recent scholarship in philosophy of logic. I have deliberately avoided republishing papers that are readily available in other anthologies, or that are more closely related to philosophy of language or philosophy of mathematics, regardless of their influence in contemporary work in logic. My intention has been to make this volume a more unique distinctive resource that will complement rather than duplicate other selections of readings currently available. Although some of the papers are more technical than others, all are intended for and can be read with good understanding by beginning students in philosophy who have completed a first course in symbolic logic.

My choice of papers has been guided by a sense of major issues in philosophy of logic that have shaped recent discussion and contributed to ongoing research programs in theoretical and applied philosophical logic. To this end, I have organized the papers thematically rather than chronologically, to give the best overview of philosophical issues connected with logical analysis and the development of formal systems of symbolic logic. The papers range from general topics in classical logic to specialized investigations of the concept of meaning and truth, the interpretation of

quantifiers in predicate logic, the theory of valid inference and logical entailment, and problems of alethic modality, intensionality, and propositional attitude. These are undoubtedly among the central problems of philosophical logic reflecting some of the most intriguing new directions in the field, but they by no means exhaust the possibilities.

Additional writings related to the philosophy of logic can be found in my Blackwell collection *Philosophy of Mathematics: An Anthology*. Newly commissioned papers on additional topics, concerning the metatheory of logic, logical and semantic paradoxes, nonstandard logics of many different sorts, fuzzy logic, relevance logics, paraconsistent logics, free logics, monotonic versus nonmonotic systems, applied logics in mathematics, science, probability theory, formal semantics, linguistic modeling, computer and cognitive applications, ethics, epistemology, and time, are collected in my Blackwell *Companion to Philosophical Logic*. The present book will serve its purpose if it helps provide readers at all levels with the necessary background and a sufficient sense of interest in its subject to continue philosophical inquiry and pursue advanced study of the methods, uses and longstanding problems in the philosophy of logic.

Acknowledgments

I thank the Alexander von Humboldt-Stiftung for supporting work on this project during my Research Fellowship at the Franz Brentano Forschung of the Bayerische-Julius-Maximilians-Universität-Würzburg, Germany. I am indebted to the Brentano Forschung for its hospitality, and to its Director, my friend Wilhelm Baumgartner, for graciously hosting my research visit during the academic term 2000 to 2001, when this volume was in preparation. I am grateful to Michael Jarrett and Brian Armstrong for their professional scholarly editorial assistance. Finally, I thank Steve Smith and the excellent team at Blackwell for inviting me to edit this project, and for smooth and professional handling of all production aspects. This book is dedicated to the memory of Henry W. Johnstone, Jr.

The editor and publishers wish to thank the following for permission to reprint copyrighted materials:

Anderson, Alan Ross, and Nuel D. Belnap, Jr., "The Pure Calculus of Entailment," *The Journal of Philosophical Logic*, 27 (1962), pp. 19–52, reprinted by permission of Association for Symbolic Logic, Vassar College, New York. All rights reserved. The reproduction is by special permission for this publication only.

Baldwin, Thomas, "Interpretations of Quantifiers," *Mind*, 88 (1979), pp. 215–40, reprinted by permission of Oxford University Press, Oxford.

Bealer, George, "Propositions," *Mind*, 107 (1998), pp. 1–32, reprinted by permission of Oxford University Press, Oxford.

Davidson, Donald, "Truth and Meaning," *Synthese*, 17 (1967), pp. 304–23, reprinted by permission of Kluwer Academic Publishers, Dordrecht, The Netherlands.

Etchemendy, John, "Tarski on Truth and Logical Consequence," *The Journal of Symbolic Logic*, 53 (1988), pp. 51–79, reprinted by permission of Association for Symbolic Logic, Vassar College, New York. All rights reserved. The reproduction is by special permission for this publication only.

Field, Hartry, "Tarski's Theory of Truth," *The Journal of Philosophy*, 69, 13 (1972), pp. 347–75, reprinted by permission of *The Journal of Philosophy*, Columbia University.

Føllesdal, Dagfin, "Interpretation of Quantifiers," from *Logic, Methodology and Philosophy of Science III*. Proceedings of the Third International Congress for Logic, Methodology and Philosophy of Science, Amsterdam, 1967. (North-Holland Publishing Company, Amsterdam, 1968.)

Forbes, Graeme, "Substitutivity and the Coherence of Quantifying In," from *Philosophical Review*, 105 (1996), pp. 337–72. Copyright 1996 Cornell University. Reprinted by permission of the publisher and the author.

George, Rolf, "Bolzano's Concept of Consequence," *The Journal of Philosophy*, 83, 10 (1956), pp. 558–64, reprinted by permission of *The Journal of Philosophy*, Columbia University.

Gödel, Kurt, "Russell's Mathematical Logic," from *The Philosophy of Bertrand Russell* (ed. Paul Arthur Schilpp) (Tudor Publishing Company, New York, 1951), pp. 125–53.

Hintikka, Jaakko, "Language Games for Quantifiers," from *Studies in Logical Theory* (ed. Nicholas Rescher) (Blackwell Publishers, Oxford, 1968).

Jubien, Michael, "The Intensionality of Ontological Commitment," *Nôus*, 51 (1972), pp. 378–87, reprinted by permission of Blackwell Publishers.

Kaplan, David, "Quantifying In," *Synthese*, 19 (1968–9), pp. 178–214, reprinted by permission of Kluwer Academic Publishers, Dordrecht, The Netherlands.

Kripke, Saul A., "Outline of a Theory of Truth," *The Journal of Philosophy*, 72, 19 (1975), pp. 690–716, reprinted by permission of *The Journal of Philosophy*, Columbia University.

Lejewski, Czeslaw, "Logic and Existence," from *British Journal for the Philosophy of Science*, 5, 18 (1954), pp. 104–19, reprinted by permission of Oxford University Press, Oxford.

Lewis, David, "Counterpart Theory and Quantified Modal Logic," *The Journal of Philosophy*, 65, 5 (1968), pp. 113–26, reprinted by permission of *The Journal of Philosophy*, Columbia University.

Marcus, Ruth Barcan, "Nominalism and the Substitutional Quantifier," *The Monist*, 61, 3 (1978), pp. 351–62.

Marcus, Ruth Barcan, "A Backward Look at Quine's Animadversions on Modalities," from *Perspectives on Quine* (ed. Robert B. Barrett and Roger F. Gibson) (Blackwell Publishers, Oxford, 1990).

Nolt, John E., "What are Possible Worlds," *Mind*, 95 (1986), pp. 432–45, reprinted by permission of Oxford University Press, Oxford.

Pap, Arthur, "The Laws of Logic," from *An Introduction to the Philosophy of Science* (The Free Press, New York, 1962). Reprinted with the permission of The Free Press, a Division of Simon & Schuster, Inc. from *An Introduction to the Philosophy of Science* by Arthur Pap. Copyright © 1962 by The Free Press.

Parsons, Charles, "A Plea for Substitutional Quantification," *The Journal of Philosophy*, 68, 8 (1971), pp. 231–7, reprinted by permission of *The Journal of Philosophy*, Columbia University.

Popper, Karl, "What Can Logic Do for Philosophy?," from *Logical Positivism and Ethics*. The Symposia Read at the Joint Session of the Aristotelian Society and the Mind Association at Durham, July 9–11, 1948.

Quine, W. V., "Quantifiers and Propositional Attitudes," *The Journal of Philosophy*, 53, 5 (1956), pp. 177–87, reprinted by permission of *The Journal of Philosophy*, Columbia University.

Read, Stephen, "Formal and Material Consequence," *Journal of Philosophical Logic*, 23 (1994), pp. 247–65, reprinted by permission of Kluwer Academic Publishers, Dordrecht, The Netherlands.

Sommers, Fred, "Types and Ontology," from *Philosophical Review*, 72 (1963), pp. 327–63. Copyright © 1963 Cornell University. Reprinted by permission of the publisher.

Tarski, Alfred, "On the Concept of Logical Consequence," from *Logic, Semantics, Metamathematics: Papers from 1923 to 1938* (trans. J. H. Woodger) (Clarendon Press, Oxford, 1956, reprinted by permission of Oxford University Press, Oxford).

Tharp, Leslie H., "Which Logic is the Right Logic?," *Synthese*, 31 (1975), pp. 1–21, reprinted by permission of Kluwer Academic Publishers, Dordrecht, The Netherlands.

Every effort has been made to trace copyright holders. The publishers apologize for any errors or omissions in the above list and will be pleased to make the necessary arrangement at the first opportunity.

Introduction: Logic and Philosophy of Logic

Dale Jacquette

Logic and Philosophy

The relation between logic and philosophy is complex. Logic has been a part of philosophy since its inception. Although Aristotle is generally credited as the inventor of syllogistic logic, a proto-formal systematization of deductively valid inference, it is clear that Plato and the Presocratics were aware of the difference between logically correct and logically incorrect reasoning, and hence of at least some informal aspects of logic. During the middle ages, logic was taught along with grammar and rhetoric as part of the liberal arts, as the three most basic studies needed for advanced work in arithmetic, geometry, music, and astronomy.

Immanuel Kant in his (1787) *Critique of Pure Reason*, was able to report that "It is remarkable . . . that to the present day this [Aristotelian] logic has not been able to advance a single step, and is thus to all appearance a closed and completed body of doctrine" (Bviii). To the extent that Kant is justified in his pronouncement, he reports a stagnancy that was not improved until the following century with the algebraic treatment of logic in Augustus DeMorgan's (1847) *Formal Logic, or The Calculus of Inference, Necessary and Probable*, coincidentally in the same year as George Boole's (1847) logical algebra, *The Mathematical Analysis of Logic: Being an Essay Towards a Calculus of Deductive Reasoning*, followed in 1854 by Boole's *An Investigation of the Laws of Thought on Which Are Founded the Mathematical Theories of Logic and Probabilities*. The torch then passed to Gottlob Frege, who in his (1879) *Begriffsschrift* and

(1893, 1903) *Grundgesetze der Arithmetik*, moved beyond the symbolization of syllogistic logic and Boolean relations to develop a precursor of modern propositional and predicate logic, much at the same time that Charles Sanders Peirce in scattered sources now found in his *Collected Papers* offered similar results in the theory of relations, laying the groundwork for modern set theory.

The trend toward the mathematization of logic begun by DeMorgan, Boole, Frege, and Peirce culminated in the three-volume *Principia Mathematica* of Alfred North Whitehead and Bertrand Russell (1910; 2nd edition, 1925–7). In the century following the publication of Whitehead and Russell's monumental system, there has been a proliferation of logical systems that have both developed the original insights of these formal theories, and extended basic logical methods in many new directions, some of which at least are inconsistent with what has come to be known as classical logic. It is nevertheless significant that all of the logicians who were founding figures in the discovery of mathematical logic were also philosophers, or, in DeMorgan's and Boole's case, although primarily mathematicians, also had philosophical interests in philosophical psychology.

Logic has recently become so specialized that some of its branches are primarily the province of mathematicians, creating an occasion for the distinction between mathematical logic and philosophical logic. Yet it remains true that many if not most of the ongoing work in logic continues to be done by philosophers. The explanation of this fact is only partly a historical accident of the sociology of professional disciplines. There is good justification for such a division of labor, because philosophers are specially concerned with the nature of reasoning, for which logic is sometimes defined as the theory of correct reasoning. Unlike natural scientists, who also use logic and rely on sound reasoning, philosophical methodology involves an almost exclusive reliance on argument, so that philosophers are naturally also the researchers most directly concerned with and in some ways most qualified to investigate the principles of correct inference.

The role of logic in philosophy has featured its potential both as a tool for the precise expression of arguments and a source of philosophical puzzles and paradoxes. Philosophers interested in logic are concerned among other questions with the correct interpretation of logical expressions, with the formal semantics and ontology of logic, the metaphysical status of objects, properties, relations, propositions, and functions and operators referred to in logic, and with the paradoxes that can be formulated by means of particular logical notations, their significance and the innovations to which they can give rise in the effort to solve or avoid them. New symbolisms make possible the formulation of more ingenious paradoxes, and the cycle of refinement of logic in light of more sophisticated criticisms and formal antinomy spirals indefinitely, to the improvement of logic and the philosopher's understanding of logical relations.

One Logic or Many Logics?

Kant's observation of the lack of progress in logic from Aristotle's time is not an unqualified complaint about the inactivity of logicians in the intervening years of logic's history. Kant prefaces his remark with the pronouncement that: "That logic has already, from the earliest times, proceeded upon this sure path is evidenced by the fact that since Aristotle it has not required to retrace a single step, unless, indeed, we care to count as improvements the removal of certain needless subtleties or the clearer exposition of its recognized teaching, features which concern the elegance rather than the certainty of this science" (Bviii). The clear implication is that Aristotle had largely arrived at the correct theory, so that if there had been no significant movement in the science of logic, it was primarily because there was little need for improvement.

When we fast-forward to logic in the early twenty-first century, the situation is radically different from Kant's time. It is an extraordinary fact about the state of the art in logical investigations today, by comparison with Kant's perspective in the late eighteenth century, that there is no longer a single logic, whatever its form, to which all logicians assent. Instead, there are families upon families of logics, some of which are in open conflict as competing formalizations of the same body of discourse, while others live together in harmony as specialized formal theories of distinct but compatible types of inference, like powerful animals that happen to survive on different parts of the food chain. There are modal logics, many-valued logics and logics that recognize truth value gaps, a wide variety of logics that offer alternative formal modelings of deductively valid inference or entailment, logics of highly particularized types of relations in distinct subject matters, even logics that disagree about whether syntactical inconsistencies discredit a logical system, or whether or not quantification in a predicate logic presupposes or implies that objects must exist in order to be referred to and have properties truly predicated of them. If Aristotle had a corner on the logical inference market from the ancient Greek world until Kant's day, it appears that not long afterward free competitive entrepreneurship in the field has gone about as wild as a festival bazaar. Why should this be, and what does it mean?

Of course, it is no more true today than for Aristotle that absolutely anything goes in philosophical logic. Even paraconsistent logics that tolerate logical inconsistencies without inferential explosion, that accommodate contradictions but do not authorize the logically valid deduction of any and every proposition, do so according to strict rules, as strict as the rules that govern Aristotle's syllogisms. If the rules themselves are different, there might yet be something in common between logical rules by virtue of which multiple sets of rules each constitute a logic, and whatever this underlying essential element of logical rules turns out to be is logic in the true singular sense of the word, perhaps even in the sense which Aristotle and other absolutists in the theory of logic have sought but only partially glimpsed in proposing particular logical systems. It is conceivable, but no one has so far identified the characteristics that uniquely belong to all and only logical rules that would qualify all the apparently different systems of logics as manifestations of a universal logic. Among the difficult problems to be addressed include finding properties that make the rules of apparently diverse and even mutually contradictory logical systems logical rules in a univocal universal sense, while at the same time different from mathematical rules or the rules of chess or safe boating.

There is often said to be a distinction between regulative and constitutive rules in rule-following activities of all kinds. The distinction divides rules that must be followed in order for the activity to take place at all, versus rules that serve as guidelines for improving the activity, but that if violated do not disqualify the activity as an activity of the kind. Moving the rook diagonally in what had otherwise appeared to be a game of chess turns the activity into something other than chess, into no game at all or an improvised invention of a new game that will require a different set of constitutive rules. For the movement of tokens on a board of 64 squares of alternating color is not a game of chess unless the tokens are moved according to very precisely specified rules. By contrast, driving a car while violating traffic rules can be more difficult and dangerous, but it is still driving a car. Similarly with respect to many kinds of rules.

Are the rules of logic constitutive or regulative? This, too, is not as easy a question to answer as may first appear. To consider the possibility of interpreting universal logical rules as regulative in the first place, we can say that such rules are unique to logic in that they specifically concern the correct form of reasoning in the sense of licensing only deductive valid derivation of conclusions from assumptions. But there is a problem. If I violate the rules of deductively valid logical inference by deliberately or inadvertently committing a fallacy, am I no longer reasoning at all, or am I just reasoning badly, invalidly, or fallaciously? We speak of fallacious reasoning, but it is not clear whether this phrase qualifies a special category of reasoning, namely reasoning that has the property of being fallacious, or whether fallacious reasoning is no more genuine reasoning than, as Alice was reluctant to believe in Lewis Carroll's *Alice's Adventures in Wonderland*, mock turtle soup is a kind of soup made from mock turtles. The disadvantages of treating fallacious reasoning as a type or species of reasoning seem to preclude the possibility of treating logical rules as regulative. But the alternative encounters a more serious obstacle. If we try to say that logical rules are constitutive, they cannot in any event constitute all of the distinct systems of logic whose differences and unifying traits we are trying to explain, which are not plausibly described merely as different ways of following a common set of logical rules. Such a conclusion would appear to stretch the concept of a constitutive rule beyond recognition, and at best it does not shed light on the main issue in the search for the essence of logic. A constitutive universal concept of logical rules would have to be whatever is required in order to constitute a system of logic, or to constitute a rule as a logical rule, as opposed to this or that particular system of logic, or this or that particular logical rule. This is the very elusive concept at issue in the question of whether in truth there is only one fundamental logic or many distinct and ultimately irreducible logics.

Classical Logic Naturally Leads to Nonclassical Logics

All things considered, it may be best for the time being to leave open questions about the unity of logic or multiplicity of logics. The answer might be forthcoming at some future time if a revolutionary simplification of the variety of logics is achieved in which the contemporary opulence of logical system is reduced to a common core.

To the extent that any such reductions are possible, as has happened repeatedly in the history of mathematics, then we will have enhanced our understanding of what is and is not essential to logical inference. In the meantime, we must try to appreciate the diversity of logical systems, and recognize the propagation of logics as a fact of the historical development of the formalization of reasoning. A healthy tolerance of the many systems of logic may be the only sane choice, except where it is possible to refute particular systems as incompetently formalized or inappropriately conceived. But I think it will not do to take an arch conservative stance, and hold that some version of classical logic is the one and only true or correct logic, and that all the others are no more logic than a pretender to the throne is a monarch of the realm. Nor will it do to take sides with any particular alternative choice of nonclassical logic, say, relevant or paraconsistent or free logic or fuzzy logic, as the one and only true or correct logic.

The reason is that the thin edge of the wedge in the exuberant burgeoning of logics is inevitable, if we are to understand and try to formalize the conspicuous logical features even of classical logic. Alethic modality, the logic of necessity and possibility and of the necessary or possible truth of propositions, is deeply implicated in the standard concept of deductive validity, embodied not only in classical logics modeled after Frege and Whitehead and Russell, but even in Aristotle's syllogistic logic. The definition of a deductively valid inference states alternatively and equivalently that an inference is deductively valid just in case if its assumptions are true then its conclusions must, in the sense of logical necessity, also be true, or such that it is logically impossible for the assumptions of a deductively valid inference to be true and its conclusions false. The alethic modality of deductive validity on anything like the classical conception makes it unavoidable eventually to investigate the nature of alethic modality in a thorough formalization of whatever concepts are essential to a classical logical framework.

Once logic recognizes the need to rigorously articulate the modality of deductively valid inference, there is no turning back. For modal logic by its very nature is not monolithic, but fragmented into multiple systems of modal qualifications, reflected in the plurality of accessibility relations on modal model structures or logically possible worlds in the model set theoretical semantics for standard modal logics. We are overwhelmed by the multiplicity of modal logics that bubble up when we open the floodgates to alethic modality in the classical logical concept of deductive validity. How, after all, can anyone prevent the natural curiosity of symbolic logicians from taking this turn? And why should anyone want to? Conservative logicians have tried to hold the line against modal logics or at least against quantified modal logics. The image this logical conservatism irresistibly calls forth is that of the legendary Dutch boy with his finger in the dike, trying to keep back the water at a tiny hole, which is sure to split apart the defensive wall if given half a chance.

Unlike the little Dutch boy, logicians and philosophers of logic cannot simply plug up the leaks through which they fear the onrush of nonclassical logics. They must put forward good arguments to persuade more adventurous logicians that it is unpromising, unprofitable, or even theoretically dangerous to advocate nonclassical alternatives in logic. The historical fact is that while the authority of some of these bulwarks had a limited and temporary effect in restraining the entrenchment of new logics, their arguments were deemed unconvincing in light of the need for such systems, given the fact that even the classical concept of deductive validity is saturated with modality. Of late, even some of the most prestigious objectors to quantified modal logic have softened their position and admitted its claim to a legitimate place in logic. The situation is similar in many ways to the rise of non-Euclidean geometries in mathematics, and the resistance they first met, before being incorporated into the mainstream of mathematical symbolisms. The success of non-Euclidean geometries may either have provided an indirect inspiration for a parallel expansion among nonclassical logics, or the two might be different expressions of the intellectual forces that characterize the modern *Zeitgeist*.

Whatever the explanation of the flowering of nonclassical logics in recent times, the balanced philosophical response to the phenomenon is arguably to be found in a mean between extremes. We should avoid both a radical syncretism that uncritically accepts and tries to assimilate any and all formalisms that purport to represent the logic of a given subject, and the radical conservatism that refuses to acknowledge that there could possibly be more than one logic, that the very idea of there being logics is itself somehow logically incoherent. By remaining open-minded to the potential value of nonclassical logics while at the same time subjecting contending systems to the same level of rigorous criticism that prevails in the best examples of classical logic and mathematics, logic and the philosophy of logic can only hope to gain.

Truth, Existence, and Intensionality

The course of philosophical logic in recent years has not only taken new logical symbolisms under its wings, but has applied methods of formal symbolic logic to clarify and investigate problems in the theory of meaning, metaphysics and ontology, and the philosophy of language. The philosophy of logic in these ways has become an adjunct to related philosophical subdisciplines into which it sometimes merges imperceptibly. There is reciprocation between logic and philosophy of logic, in that conceptual housekeeping in the philosophy of logic about, among other things, the semantics of truth, existence, and the delineation of intensional and extensional linguistic expressions, has contributed directly to refinements in the foundations and superstructure of symbolic logic.

The way philosophy of logic influences these studies is illustrated by recent work in the theory of truth and meaning, questions of logic and existence in connection with interpretations of quantifiers in predicate logic, and the intensionality of propositional attitude contexts. All related topics have been prominently debated in contemporary philosophy of logic, and are important not only because of their intrinsic interest, but because they represent a vital intersection of philosophical problems in semantics, ontology, and philosophy of language. It may be worthwhile to describe in some detail one of the major divisions and general directions of philosophical dispute, that is not only a hotbed of contention, but that divides philosophy of logic and philosophy of language along one of its most fundamental faultlines.

There are, roughly speaking, two camps in philosophy of logic: extensionalists and intensionalists. Extensionalists have held the field during most of modern logic's history. They believe that quantifiers in predicate logic presuppose the existence of whatever objects can be referred to by constants or bound variables, or enter into true predications of properties. Thus, if a proposition in predicate logic that object a has property F is interpreted extensionally, then, in order for the proposition to be true, object a must exist, and it must belong to the *extension* of predicate "F," consisting of all and only the existent objects that have property F. It is a seldom noticed difficulty in this style of philosophical semantics that it seems to involve a blatant circularity. For, in order for the proposition "Fa" to be interpreted as true, we must know that object a belongs to the extension of predicate "F," and, in order to know what the extension of predicate "F" is and whether in fact object a belongs or does not belong to or fall under its extension, we must already know which objects belong to the extension. In other words, in order to know whether "Fb" is true, in an extensionalist semantics, we need to know whether "Fa" is true, whether "Fb" is true, and so on, for "Fc" and all other predications of property F to all the existent objects in the logic's semantic domain.

Defenders of extensionalist semantics will likely reply that the theory is not meant to be a practical epistemic procedure for determining whether or not a particular proposition is true or false, but rather a statement of the conditions that must obtain in order for a proposition to be true or false. Whether and to what extent this solution avoids circularity in an extensionalist semantics is

another issue for another occasion. More interesting is the fact that in an extensionalist semantics, only existent objects can be referred to, and only sets of existent objects can enter into the extensions of predicates by which the possession of a property by an object is determined as true or false. But why should this be? What difference can it make to logic whether or not quarks or vortices or demons or unicorns happen to exist or not exist?

In everyday thought and discourse we regularly and apparently without undue confusion speak about nonexistent objects, and about their properties or lack of properties, which we suppose are truly or falsely expressed in propositions in which nonexistent objects are designated. As examples, we can turn not only to mythology and the characters of fiction in literature, but to numerous scientific theories that falsely hypothesize the existence of objects that in the end have turned out not to exist, including, for all we know, some or even many of the theories we may currently believe to be true. It has appeared to some thinkers in the philosophy of logic that either an extensionalist semantics is inadequate, or that we are wrong to suppose that Sherlock Holmes truly is a detective, or that Pegasus truly is a winged horse, that Holmes is not his friend and associate Watson, and that Watson is not Holmes, but that these are different nonexistent objects, each, despite being nonexistent, with its own distinct identity predicated on its possession of uniquely distinguishing properties and characteristics.

The problem of nonexistent objects highlights the difference between extensionalism and intensionalism. But the distinction arises even without considering the semantics needed for fiction, mythology, and false scientific theories. Intensionalism represents another way of thinking about the meaning and truth conditions of propositions, the interpretation of quantifiers in predicate logic, and the complementarity between intensional and extensional linguistic contexts, yet to be explained. The leading alternative to extensionalist semantics and philosophy of logic is intensionalism, according to which the meaning of a proposition is determined by the properties an object possesses. There are several types of intensionalism, all of which recognize the properties of objects as conceptually basic, and some of which allow nonexistent objects to be referred to in logic as truly possessing properties in the same or at least in some sense as existent entities, identified as particular objects distinct from others by virtue of the unique sets of properties with which they are correlated.

The thesis of the intensionality of reference is originally owing to Frege, in a central assumption of his otherwise extensionalist philosophy of language, that the sense of a proper name or sentence determines its reference. This is in effect to say that for Frege intension determines extension. The idea is that the possession of properties by an object is logically more fundamental than its membership in a particular set, such as the extension of a predicate, and possibly even more fundamental than the question of whether or not the object exists. An object must first satisfy identity requirements, which it does by virtue of the properties it has, and then it can be considered as belonging to a set of other objects with some or all of the same properties. The appearance of circularity in extensionalist semantics is thereby avoided under the intensionalist alternative. In that case, we do not to say that the truth of a predication of property F to object a depends on whether or not object a is included in the extension of predicate "F," which is the source of trouble. We can maintain instead in a version of the correspondence theory of truth that Fa is true just in case object a in fact has property F.

The conflict of intuitions driving some logicians toward extensionalism rather than intensionalism is so basic, and the disagreement between these categories of semantics in the philosophy of logic is so deeply entrenched, that is unlikely for agreement ever to be reached among the factions by means of argument and persuasion. There is only the predominance of one theory over the contrary theory in an influential majority of thinkers, or the reverse in other places in the philosophical community or at other times. How, extensionalists rhetorically ask, voicing their commitment to a position against which they can imagine no satisfactory answer, could an object actually have properties if the object does not actually exist? An intensionalist, by contrast, typically has no conceptual impediment in thinking of nonexistent objects actually possessing properties. How is it, they will ask from their diametrically opposed position, that a nonexistent object like Pegasus can fail to exist unless Pegasus truly has the property of being a winged horse, where it happens to be the case that no existent object has that property?

As a final example of the issues involved in the dispute between extensionalism and intensionalism, consider the intensionality or referential opacity of certain linguistic contexts. There are several categories of intensional contexts, including indirect discourse in quotation and mention versus use, modal qualifications, and propositional attitudes. Intensional contexts generally are said not to support the intersubstitution of coreferential terms or logically equivalent expressions *salva veritate*, preserving the truth value of a proposition in which the substitution is made. Here are three instances: (1) Tom said "Sue is charming" (suppose it is true that he says this); Susan is identical with, the very same person as, Sue (suppose that this is also true); therefore, Tom said "Susan is charming" (false, where this is not word-for-word what Tom is correctly quoted as saying). (2) The name "Susan" contains five letters of the alphabet (true); Susan is identical with Sue (true); therefore, the name "Sue" contains five letters of the alphabet (false). (3) Susan believes that Mark Twain wrote *Huckleberry Finn* (suppose that this is true); Mark Twain is identical with Samuel Clemens (true); therefore, Susan believes that Samuel Clemens wrote *Huckleberry Finn* (false, where Susan does not happen to know that Mark Twain is the pen name of Samuel Clemens, or has never even heard of Samuel Clemens).

The intensionality of certain linguistic contexts in the philosophy of mind is frequently remarked by philosophers interested in the logic of intentional states like belief, doubt, desire, expectation, love, hate, hope, fear, and so on. To suppose that these contexts can be eliminated or ignored in a purely extensionalist philosophy of logic is to suppose either that these psychological states do not exist or that the meaning of sentences that ostensibly refer to propositional attitudes and related phenomena ordinarily expressed by means of intensional contexts can be fully reduced to sentences whose meaning can be completely explained in a purely extensional logic. The program to eliminate or reduce intentional states and with them the intensional contexts in which they are described in so-called folk psychology is the aim of scientific and philosophical theories of eliminative or reductive behaviorism, materialism, functionalism, computationalism, and the hard psychological and cognitive sciences. There is a close connection between the opposition of extensionalist versus intensionalist philosophy of logic and eliminativist or reductivist versus folk psychological and intentionalist philosophy of mind. The philosophy of logic in this and unlimitedly many other ways reaches beyond the boundaries of formal syntax to directly engage in longstanding philosophical controversies.

PART I

Classical Logic

Introduction to Part I

What has come to be known as classical logic is not so much a matter of chronology as of doctrine. Classical logic is roughly the logic of Whitehead and Russell's *Principia Mathematica*, with its offshoots and developments, and the limiting metatheorems in the work of Kurt Gödel, Alonzo Church, and others, that have come to be associated with it, and its historical precedents. A classical logic is sometimes defined negatively as a logic that is not modal or many-valued or that involves no nonstandard concepts of deductive validity. More positively, classical logic is a bivalent or two-valued system of propositional and predicate logic, in which all propositions are either true or false exclusively, and in which the predicate fragment is purely extensional and existence-presuppositional, in the sense that it involves quantifications over a semantic domain consisting of existent objects only, in which reference and true predications of properties are interpreted exclusively as applying to existent objects.

Classical logic is an appropriate place to begin studying the philosophy of logic. It is the natural, but not inevitable way for logic to have established itself in the late nineteenth and early twentieth century. It is, so to speak, the most conservative development of symbolic logic that might be projected. This also makes it predictable that the developers of classical logic should be loyal to it and energetic in its defense, even to the extent of considering some preferred version of classical logic to be the only correct logic, and to opposing upstart efforts to devise nonclassical logics either for the sake of experimenting with alternative formalisms, or in order to correct perceived defects in classical systems. Although classical logic is the foundation of contemporary logical theory, the trend has now largely turned against classical logic as formally and philosophically satisfactory for all analytic purposes.

If classical logic is the proper starting place in understanding and working toward new contributions in symbolic logic, it is essential background to much of contemporary philosophy of logic. Interesting explorations have gone significantly beyond the characteristic tenets of classical logic, exploiting the possibilities of rejecting, denying, or otherwise working around its most cherished principles. Where classical logic requires all propositions to be true or false, nonclassical logics have flourished by questioning this assumption and formulating symbolisms in which there are three or unlimitedly many more truth values. There are also nonclassical fuzzy logics with indefinitely many probability values, and logics that have truth value gaps for propositions that have no truth value at all, or, as in paraconsistent logics, that can be both true and false without thereby validly entailing any and all propositions so as to trivialize deductive inference.

Where classical logic holds that deductive inference requires that if a valid argument's assumptions are true then its conclusions must also be true, nonclassical logics have explored alternative conceptions of entailment. Where classical predicate logic presupposes the existence of objects for true predications of properties, interpreted in terms of the extensions of predicates, nonclassical free logics have proposed that logic be liberated from existence presuppositions, and that true quantifications not depend on the existence of particular objects in a semantic domain, or, indeed, on the existence of any objects. Logics of nonexistent objects have gone even further in this direction, permitting the reference and true predication of properties to objects regardless of their ontological status, whether existent or nonexistent. Where classical logic interprets predicate and quantificational expressions in terms of extensions of predicates consisting entirely of existent objects, intensional logics have examined interpretational strategies that are based instead on sets of properties associated with objects in a logic's domain, and articulate formalisms for intensional contexts in which it is possible to intersubstitute coreferential terms without preserving the proposition's truth value. Finally, specialized nonclassical logics have emerged for purposes of formally modeling structural features of thought and discourse that transcend the limits of classical logic in modal systems of many types, for alethic propositional necessity and possibility, logics of belief, knowledge, moral obligation and permission, among others, logics of questions, commands, quantum phenomena in microparticle physics, and logics of space and time, many of which are also considered to be intensional logics.

All of modern logic nevertheless continues to take its bearings from classical logic, which is the foundation for contemporary studies even when they diverge most radically. The papers presented in this first section offer a unique perspective on the scope and limits of classical logic. We begin with Arthur Pap's "The Laws of Logic," in which logical principles are identified with tautologies, necessary logical truths such as "Either p or not-p," "Not both p and not-p," and "If p, then p." Pap argues that logical laws as tautologies are *a priori* necessary truths, but not merely by convention. In the realist spirit of classical logic which his essay represents, Pap upholds the mind-independence of logical laws as known to be true by discovery rather than stipulation by means of objective decision procedures.

Kurt Gödel's brilliant study of "Russell's Mathematical Logic," in the second selection, offers one of the most insightful expositions of Russell's contributions to classical symbolic logic with his coauthor Whitehead in *Principia Mathematica*. Gödel is most famous for his own 1931 logical metatheorems limiting the deductive completeness of classical logics similar to Whitehead and Russell's

Principia that are powerful enough to formalize the axioms of infinitary arithmetic. Gödel's first incompleteness metatheorem is generally acknowledged as having defeated the logicist program represented by Whitehead and Russell's efforts to reduce mathematics to logic, together with some of the elements of a set theory and special arguably extralogical assumptions. Gödel explains the philosophical background and formal logical significance of classical logic in nontechnical terms, and more critically points out the need for greater clarification of some vital primitive concepts of Russell's system.

Leslie H. Tharp, in "Which Logic is the Right Logic," presents a metatheoretical assessment of classical logic as a basis for arithmetic. The analysis sheds further light on the strengths and limitations of standard symbolic logic with respect to a particular aspect of an important mathematical application. Tharp uses Lindström's Theorem to show that classical elementary logic is adequate for most of these purposes, suggesting that to such an extent logic *per se* can be identified with classical logic. The idea is to consider the minimally necessary resources available in the semantic domain of a classical logic, given some important metatheoretical results about the cardinality or size of a logic's domain in comparison with the cardinality of the logic's subject matter, the objects whose properties the logic represents. The details are clearly provided in the paper, which is perhaps the most technical in this section. Tharp concludes that if a logic contains classical elementary or propositional logic, and is either complete or compact, then if the logic has the Löwenheim–Skolem property, then the logic is equivalent to elementary logic. To be complete, a logic must be such that any well-formed formula recognized by the logic's decision methods (truth tables, truth trees, or the like) as a tautology is interpreted as false. The Löwenheim–Skolem property applies to any logic which is such that every nonempty class of the logic has a countable member. Finally, for a nonempty class of a classical logic to have a countable member means that the class includes a member that can be put in one-one correspondence with any set of entities whose cardinality is less than or equal to the lowest order of infinity, such as the set of all whole numbers or positive integers. Tharp argues that while Lindström's Theorem proves that classical logic is adequate for arithmetic generally, a full logic of relations might require a more complex second-order logic, in which it is possible not only to predicate properties of objects but of other properties.

Karl Popper, distinguished philosopher of science, in his provocative chapter, "What Can Logic Do For Philosophy?", completes the discussion. Popper maintains that logic can usefully clarify philosophical problems, especially in the examples he handpicks in metaphysics and the philosophy of religion, relying on standard logical features of classical logic. He argues that there are logical connections in the concepts of the necessity of causal connection with implications for the philosophical issue of free will versus determinism, and for St. Thomas Aquinas's so-called "second way" of proving the existence of God in his *Summa Theologiae*. Causal connections, contrary to David Hume's conclusions in *A Treatise of Human Nature*, according to Popper, are logically necessary in the sense that they follow deductively once we assert the appropriate natural law. The form of such an inference, which Popper does not spell out in quite this way, is something like: An event of type C has occurred. But whenever an event of type C occurs, an event of type E later occurs (this is the statement of scientific law correlating causes and effects). Therefore, an event of type E later occurs. A defender of Hume on the contingency of causal connections might nevertheless object that although the inference is deductively valid, and to that extent carries necessity from assumptions to conclusion, the conclusion itself is not necessary unless the assumptions are also logically necessary, and that no scientific laws correlating causes and effects – this is really the point of Hume's philosophical inquiry into the origin of the idea of causation – are logically necessary. Popper anticipates the objection, but still insists that the relation of the events relative to the law in question remains necessary. Again, it might be questioned whether the logical necessity obtaining between the assumptions and conclusion of a valid inference about real world events necessarily qualifies or attaches to the events themselves, which is arguably what an effort to show the relevance of logic to metaphysics would need to establish.

Popper is somewhat more convincingly in his second main illustration concerning Aquinas's cosmological proof for the existence of God. The argument is that causation of events cannot extend infinitely backward in time, so that God must exist as a first cause. Popper criticizes Aquinas on the grounds that the proof involves a logical inconsistency in assuming that the universal laws of nature are given, precluding the possibility that God is the author responsible for creating all natural laws. Here too it is unclear whether Popper may not have conflated Aquinas's appeal to natural laws as an assumption in an argument for the sake of demonstrating a conclusion or confirming belief in the existence of God as opposed to supposing that in reality natural laws both precede God and are created by God. Aquinas, presumably, will not allow that anything comes before God, even when it is expedient for epistemic argumentative purposes to make assumptions about the laws of nature in order to infer that God exists, and even if God should turn out to be responsible for the order in causal laws through which God's existence can be proved. Popper in any case powerfully indicates the potential for classical logical conceptions of valid inference, logical consistency, and the like, to help answer longstanding philosophical problems.

Further Reading

Carnap, Rudolf. 1967: *The Logical Structure of the World*. Rolf George (trans.). Berkeley: University of California Press.

Grayling, A. C. 1982: *An Introduction to Philosophical Logic*. Sussex: Harvester Books.

Haack, Susan. 1978: *Philosophy of Logics*. Cambridge: Cambridge University Press.

Hunter, Geoffrey. 1971: *Metalogic: An Introduction to the Metatheory of Standard First Order Logic*. Berkeley and Los Angeles: University of California Press.

Kneale, William and Kneale, Martha. 1962: *The Development of Logic*. Oxford: Clarendon Press.

Nagel, Ernest and Newman, J. R. 1971: *Gödel's Proof*. London: Routledge.

Quine, Willard Van Orman. 1986: *Philosophy of Logic*. 2nd edn. Cambridge: Harvard University Press.

Read, Stephen. 1994: *Thinking About Logic: an Introduction to the Philosophy of Logic*. Oxford: Oxford University Press.

Russell, Bertrand. 1903: *Principles of Mathematics*. Cambridge: Cambridge University Press.

Wittgenstein, Ludwig. 1922: *Tractatus Logico-Philosophicus*. C. K. Ogden (ed.). London: Routledge & Kegan Paul.

The Laws of Logic

Arthur Pap

Tautologies and Analytic Statements

The statement that arithmetic is, with the help of adequate definitions, reducible to logic hardly clarifies the nature of arithmetic as long as we do not know what a logical truth is. The philosophers of science who have contributed the lion's share to the clarification of mathematics, logic, and the relation of these formal sciences to experience, are the logical positivists. And it is one of their characteristic tenets that the laws or truths of logic are tautologies and thus have no "factual content"; another terminology often used to make the same claim is that they are "analytic," in contrast to the synthetic propositions established by the factual sciences. It is also not uncommon to pass from this assertion to the conclusion that the allegedly inexorable necessity of the laws of logic is somehow reducible to linguistic conventions. The latter thesis is sometimes called *logical conventionalism*. In order to make up our minds about its merits, we must first attend carefully to the meanings of the key terms in this important controversy in the philosophy of science – "tautology" and "analytic."

The simple prototype of a tautology is any statement of the form "*p* or not *p*," where "*p*" represents a statement; such as "that man is a banker, or else he isn't." Such a statement is obviously true regardless of whether its component statement "*p*"

Arthur Pap, The Laws of Logic. *An Introduction to the Philosophy of Science*. New York: Free Press, 1962. 94–106.

is true or false. For a disjunction, i.e., a statement of the form "*p* or *q*," is true provided at least one component statement is true. So, if "*p*" is true, "*p* or not *p*" is true; and if "*p*" is false, then by the very meaning of "not," "not-*p*" is true, so again the disjunction is true. Generalizing from this simple example, we call a tautology any compound statement that is true regardless of whether its component statements be true or false. Sometimes the computation that establishes that a given compound statement is a tautology is quite complicated, just as it may be complicated to prove that a mathematical equation reduces to an identity. The appropriate methods of computation are explained in numerous textbooks of symbolic logic; hence they need not be explained here in detail. Let us just illustrate this concept of tautology in terms of a slightly more complicated example: If *p*, and (if *p*, then *q*), then *q*. This statement form corresponds to the principle of deduction, "Whatever statement is implied by true statements, is itself true." In order to show that any compound statement of that form must be true, regardless of the truth-values of the statements replacing the variables "*p*" and "*q*," we show that it could not possibly be false. In order for it to be false, the antecedent "*p* and (if *p*, then *q*)" – which corresponds to the two premises of a deductive argument of that form – would have to be true while the consequent "*q*" is false. But in order for the antecedent to be true "*p*" must be true, and "if *p*, then *q*" must be true. But if "*p*" is true and "*q*" false, then "if *p*, then *q*" cannot be true. In other words, if the consequent is false, the antecedent is bound to be false – which is equivalent to saying that if the antecedent is true, the consequent is bound to be true.

By contrast, consider: If q, and (if p, then q), then p. It is possible for a true implication to have a false antecedent, hence it is possible that q and (if p, then q) be true and p be false. Hence it is possible for the above complex implication to be false, hence it is not a tautology. Again, "If not-q and (if p, then q), then not-p" is a tautology because in order for the implication to be false p would have to be true while q is false (i.e., not-q true) and (if p, then q) true, which is impossible. It may be left to the reader to apply the same method to establish that "If not-p, and (if p, then q), then not-q" is *not* a tautology.

These illustrations bring out an important connection between the concept *tautology* and the concept *valid deductive argument:* suppose that an implication "If P_1 and P_2 and ... and P_n, then C" is a tautology in the explained sense; then an argument (or inference) whose premises are $P_1, P_2, \ldots, P_n$ and whose conclusion is C, is valid, in the sense that C must be true if $P_1, P_2, \ldots, P_n$ are all true. The converse of this conditional statement, however, does not hold. Thus, consider a valid syllogism, say, one of the form "All M are P, all S are M, therefore all S are P." Here the corresponding implication is not a tautology. For, since the three statements here do not have statements, but rather terms, as parts, each is to be represented by a simple statement variable and the corresponding implication has the form: If p and q, then r. And clearly not all implications of this form are true. Generally speaking, the tautological character of a compound statement depends upon the meanings of the logical connectives, which are particles used to form compound statements out of statements that do not contain statements as parts: "not," "if-then," "or," "and" (and certain others that are definable on the basis of these). The validity of a syllogism, as well as of many other forms of deductive inference, does not, however, depend just on the meanings of logical connectives. Here the logical constants whose meanings are decisive are "all," "some," and "are" as used to express inclusion of one class in another.

In the light of this distinction, the statement that the laws of logic are simply tautologies must be condemned as either false or trivial. It is false if "tautology" is meant in the restricted sense explained above. Let us add an example of a law

of logic that is not a tautology in the restricted sense, and which moreover is beyond the scope of Aristotelian logic, which dealt exclusively with syllogistic reasoning: Whatever relation R may be, if something has R to everything else, then everything has the converse of R to something or other (where the converse of R is that relation which x has to y if and only if y has R to x). However, since all tautologies are formal truths, and it is often uncritically assumed that all formal truths are tautologies, the word, "tautology" has also come to be used in the broader sense of "formal truths." But since "formal truth" in any precise sense turns out to be synonymous with "law of logic" (or "logical truth") it is then trivial to say that all laws of logic are tautologies. A "formal truth" or a "law of logic" is a statement that is true by virtue of its logical form, and this means that its truth depends only on the meanings of the *logical constants* it contains, not on the meanings of the *descriptive* terms. "John is tall or John is not tall": clearly you can replace "John" by "Plato" and "tall" by "fat," and the resulting statement will be just as true. Similarly, any statement of the form "If all M are P and some S are M, then some S are P" is true, regardless of what descriptive terms may be substituted for "M," "P," and "S" (provided, of course, that no equivocation is committed). What is usually called a "law of logic" is a purely abstract, universal statement devoid of descriptive constants, such as: For all classes M, P, and S, if all M are P and some S are M, then some S are P. A substitution instance of a law of logic, such as "if all African–Americans have black skin and some Americans are African–Americans, then some Americans have black skin," is called a *logically true* statement.

Teachers of elementary logic explain to their students that one of the most frequent sources of fallacious reasoning is illicit conversion: from all A are B it does not follow that all B are A. Although philosophers are supposed to know elementary logic, they too sometimes commit illicit conversions. Passing from "all tautologies are formal truths, and hence logical truths," to "All logical truths are tautologies" is one illustration. Another instance of illicit conversion is the argument leading from the valid premise "all logical truths are true by sole virtue of the meanings of their constituent terms (in particular of the logical constants)" to the thesis that all statements that are true just by virtue of the meanings of the terms (hence, that do not require empirical verification and that cannot be empirically falsified) are logical truths. Obviously, "All bachelors are unmarried" is true by virtue of the meaning of "Bachelor," but since the word "bachelor" does not belong to the vocabulary of logic, the statement is not logically true. Now, this counterinstance is relatively trivial, since with the help of the definition "A bachelor is an unmarried man" (which fairly accurately expresses the meaning of "bachelor" in English) the above statement is translatable into a logically true statement: All unmarried men are unmarried. Such statements, which are translatable into logically true statements with the help of definitions that express the ordinary meanings of the defined terms, we call *strictly analytic*.

But not all statements that are commonly accepted as necessary, or a priori, truths, are strictly analytic. For example: No event precedes itself. That this is not a logical truth is evident from the fact that the verb "to precede" does not belong to the vocabulary of logic – it designates something we find in the world, a temporal relation – and yet it occurs essentially in the statement, i.e., you cannot substitute in the universal statement "For any event *x*, *x* does not precede *x*" any other grammatically admissible expression for "precede" without changing the truth-value of the statement. For example, if we substitute "occur at the same place as" we obtain a plain falsehood. In other words, the statement has the form: For any *x*, *not-(xRx)*, and since some statements of that form are false, the statement in question is not a formal, or logical, truth. Now, it yet might be strictly analytic. It would be strictly analytic if it were possible to analyze the familiar relation of temporal precedence in such a way that the statement could be translated into a logically true statement – in somewhat the way in which "All uncles have siblings" can be revealed as analytic by the definition "An uncle is a human male who has a sibling who is a parent. "But precedence seems to be a simple relation that does not admit of further analysis. And if so, we have here a *synthetic* statement that is necessarily true (a priori). It has empirical content, if you wish, in the sense that it is about an empirically given relation – unlike logical truths, which do not contain descriptive terms essentially, and in that sense are not "about" the world of experience. But it is not an empirical statement, because an empirical statement, as we use this term, is a statement whose truth or falsehood depends on facts of experience. To be sure, a being who never experienced temporal succession could not possibly understand the meaning of such words as "before," "earlier," "to precede." It does not follow that the assertion we make about this nonlogical relation when we say that it is irreflexive and asymmetrical (and, for that matter, transitive) is subject to the test of experience.

Tautologies and Linguistic Conventions

We have seen that the claim of logical positivism, which derives from Wittgenstein, that systems of logic are systems of tautologies, must be taken with at least one grain of salt. But let us assume, for the sake of argument, that all the laws of logic, including those of the so-called theory of quantification, are in some way reducible to tautologies, as was believed by Wittgenstein. Why did this seem to have great philosophical significance to the logical positivists, as well as to some of their critics? Because it was believed that a tautology owes its *necessity* to the force of linguistic conventions, and that therefore such a reduction would *explain* logical necessity without any metaphysical assumptions. Consider again the prototype of tautology, "*p* or not-*p*," which corresponds to the law of the excluded middle: For any proposition *p*, either *p* or the negation of *p* is true. That any statement of this form must be true follows from the definitions of "or" and "not," given in the form of statements of the truth-conditions of disjunctions and negations. Similarly, the principle of deductive inference, that whatever proposition is implied by true proposition is itself true, would seem to owe its validity to the very rule governing the use of "implies": to say that *p* implies *q* though *p* is true and *q* false, is just as self-contradictory as to say that *X* is a bachelor and married at the same time. If so, it looks as though the compulsion we feel to assent to these laws of logic is simply the ingrained habit of abiding by the linguistic conventions we were educated to conform to when we were taught the language. But linguistic conventions, after all, *may* be changed. Therefore, say the logical conventionalists, systems of logic may be changed; there is no absolute logical necessity; the logical necessity of a proposition is entirely relative to linguistic conventions, which it is possible to change.

The test of tautology by means of truth tables consists in computing the truth-values of the statement-form in question corresponding to all possible combinations of truth-values of the elementary statements. If and only if the statement-form comes out true in all cases, then it (or its substitution instances) is a tautology. But the outcome of the computation depends, of course, on the definitions of the connectives, such as "or," "and," "if, then." Thus, having laid down for "or," "and," "if, then" the truth-conditions tabulated in tables 1.1, 1.2 and 1.3, we find in table 1.4 that "If [p and (if p, then q)], then q" is a tautology but suppose

Table 1.1		Table 1.2		Table 1.3*	
p q	p or q	p q	p and q	p q	If p, then q
T T	T	T T	T	T T	T
T F	T	T F	F	T F	F
F T	T	F T	F	F T	T
F F	F	F F	F	F F	T

*This table defines the so-called material, or truth-functional, meaning of "if, then."

Table 1.4

p	q	p and (if p, then q)	If [p and (if p, then q)], then q
T	T	T	T
T	F	F	T
F	T	F	T
F	F	F	T

we defined "If p, then q" as a compound statement that is true if p is false and q is true, and false in all other cases. On the basis of this definition, "If [p, and (if p, then q)], then q" would not express a tautology, as shown by table 1.5. More obviously still, if we defined "not" as

Table 1.5

p	q	If p, then q	p and (if p, then q)	If [p and (if p, then q)], then q
T	T	F	F	T
T	F	F	F	F
F	T	T	F	T
F	F	F	F	F

signifying a contrary, not the contradictory, of the proposition on which it operates, the law of the excluded middle would cease to be a tautology: since contrary propositions (such as "All alcoholics are unhappy" and "No alcoholics are unhappy") may both be false, "p" and "not-p" may now both be false, in which case "p or not-p" would likewise

be false. And so on, for any law of logic that might be cited.

If by saying that no law of logic has *absolute* validity we mean that whether or not a given formula or sentence expresses a law of logic (in either the narrower sense, viz. truth-functional tautology, or the broader sense of "formal truth") depends on the interpretation of the logical constants, the claim is undoubtedly correct. But once it is clearly understood that the truth or falsehood of *any* sentence depends on its interpretation, such a "relativism" appears to be quite innocuous. At any rate, in this light the controversy between the conventionalist and the rationalist regarding the necessity of the laws of logic appears rather futile. What one ascribes truth to, be it formal or empirical truth, is never a bare sentence (string of marks, or sequence of noises), but a statement that is made by means of a given sentence, and what that statement is depends on the *meanings* that are assigned to the constituent symbols. Clearly the truth of a statement I am making by the use of a sentence p cannot be converted into falsehood by putting upon some symbol contained in p an interpretation different from the one I intended. And this is the case whether the statement be necessary or contingent. What I mean by saying "There are no squares that are not equilateral" is necessarily true and will remain so even if the word "square" should come to be used in the sense in which "triangle" is used at present. If at such a later time, at which we are supposing the relevant linguistic conventions to be different, the same words were used in accordance with what were then the linguistic conventions, they would be used to make a false statement. But that does not mean that the statement I am *now* making by means of that sentence would have been falsified.

It is hard to believe that the conventionalist interpretation of the laws of logic, which has been advocated by acute, sophisticated philosophers, amounts to just a gross failure to distinguish between a bare sentence (a certain kind of sequence of linguistic signs) and an assertion made by means of a sentence. Some conventionalists have meant to say, indeed have said explicitly, that the rationalists err in regarding the traditional laws of logic as necessary truths apprehended by reason, because they are "laws" in a prescriptive rather than a descriptive sense. When we speak of the laws of nature, such as the law of freely falling bodies, the law of gravitation, the laws of chemistry, we mean universal statements that *describe* the world, the course of nature as it happens to be. Now, the laws of logic do not describe any contingent features of the world that can be conceived to be different. They do not even describe mental phenomena, e.g., men's habits of drawing such and such conclusions from such and such premises. For if we find a man reasoning fallaciously, i.e., inferring from propositions assumed to be true a proposition that just does not follow from them, we do not say that the relevant law of logic has been refuted. We are prepared to describe conceivable observations that would refute certain presumed laws of nature, including laws of mental association, but it would be even absurd to suppose that any observations, whether of physical or of psychological facts, might ever refute a law such as "If a thing has either property P or property Q, and it does not have P, then it has Q." According to the conventionalist's diagnosis of rationalism, the rationalist has been led to postulate a mysterious realm of necessary truths apprehended by reason because, while realizing that the valid sentences of logic do not describe empirical facts, he makes the mistaken assumption that they do describe facts of some kind. But, says the conventionalist, they are not descriptive sentences at all, they are *rules*. In particular, they are rules for the use of logical constants. Naturally, a rule cannot be refuted by any facts, because it does not make sense to speak of "refuting" a rule; a rule can only be violated.

In order to understand this conception of laws of logic as linguistic rules, we should reflect on the method of specifying the meanings of logical constants, i.e., such expressions as "and," "or," "not," "if, then," "all," which are involved in scientific discourse about any subject-matter. The validity of a statement of logic depends only on the meanings of logical constants, but how are the latter to be specified? Explicit definition is not possible. Some logical constants, on the other hand, can be contextually defined in terms of others. Examples:

all things have property
$P = not\text{-}(some$ things do *not* have $P)$
p *and* $q = not\text{-}(not\text{-}p$ *or* $not\text{-}q)$
p *or* $q = if$ $not\text{-}p, then$ q

Let us assume that in our logical system the logical constants here used to define contextually "all," "and," and "or," viz. "some," "not," and "if, then," occur as primitives. How are we to explain their meanings, their rules of usage? Superficially it seems that this can easily be done (at least for "not" and "if, then") by means of truth tables which stipulate the conditions under which statements of the forms "not-p" and "if p, then q" are true. The truth table for "not" is very simple:

p	not-p
T	F
F	T

Here "T" means true, and "F" false, and the table is to be read from left to right as follows: if p is true, then not-p is false, and if p is false, then not-p is true. But as a definition this is circular if "p is false" is in turn defined as "p is not true." More obviously still, it would be circular to attempt to explain the meaning of "if, then" by means of a truth table. Quite apart from the consideration that the truth of a conditional statement (i.e., statement of the form "If p, then q") does not just depend on the truth-values of the component statements, but rather on their meanings [technically this is expressed by saying that "if, then" is, in most uses, not a truth-functional connective], it is clear that we use "if, then" in interpreting any truth table. For a truth table says that a given kind of compound statement, such as conjunction, disjunction, negation, is true *if* the combinations of truth-values of the component statements are such and such. We must have recourse, then, to another method of formulating the rules of use of the primitive logical constants. The method in question differs fundamentally from *definition* in the usual sense, i.e., formulation of rules of substitution or translation by virtue of which the defined expression is theoretically eliminable. It is the method of *postulates*.

Thus we might explain "if, then" by stipulating that all statements of the following forms are to be true (note that this is different from *asserting* that all such statements *are* true, for according to ordinary usage of "assert," "I assert that p is true" makes sense only if it makes sense to doubt whether p is true, but such doubt is senseless if "p" just serves to specify, partially, the meanings of constituent terms):[1] if (if p, then q), then, if (if q, then r), then (if p, then r); if p, then, if (if p, then q), then q. Then we might add postulates introducing "not" along with "if, then": if p, then not-(not-p); if not-q, then, if (if p, then q), then not-p; if p, then (if not-p, then q). We have postulated, then, that all statements derivable from these schemas by substituting statements for the statement variables (in such a way that the same statement replaces the same variable within a given schema, though the same statement may be substituted for different variables) are to be true. The schemas correspond to the following principles of logic: the principle of the hypothetical syllogism (corresponding to *barbara* in the theory of categorical syllogisms); a statement implied by a true statement is true (*modus ponens*); the principle of noncontradiction; a statement that implies a false statement is false (*modus tollens*); from a contradiction any proposition follows.

The conventionalist, now, maintains that it is senseless to speak, in the manner of rationalists, of insight into the necessary truth of such principles, because they are nothing but conventional assignments of meanings to the logical constants "if, then" and "not." It does not make sense to ask how we know, indeed know for certain, that every substitution instance of these schemas is true, because no cognitive claim is involved in stipulations of rules of usage. You can say, "I do not wish to use 'if, then' in such a way that every substitution instance of this schema is true," but it would be nonsense to say, "I do not believe that all substitution instances of this schema are true." In the same way, if one were to stipulate, "'Green' is to be used to designate the color of these objects," he might be opposed by one who, for whatever reason, did not wish to use the word "green" that way. But one cannot sensibly counter: "Before accepting your rule I want to make sure that those objects really are green."

To be sure, if the expression for which a rule of usage is laid down already has a prior use, one can sensibly ask whether the rule conforms to that prior use. In the case of our logical schemata, it is clear that if any logician were to "postulate" them (in the explained sense), he would be guided by his familiarity with the already existing rules of usage of the logical constants. He would not, for example, postulate that all substitution instances of "If q, then (if p, then q), then p" are to be true, because if he did, he would require us to use "if, then" differently from the way it is in fact used. In other words, according to the actual use of "if, then" in English not all substitution instances of this schema are true. Whether or not the stipulations accord with actual linguistic usage is a question of empirical fact. But what the conventionalist is out to refute is the view that our knowledge of logical

truths amounts to a priori knowledge of necessary propositions. Our knowledge that, say, the logical constants "if, then" and "not" are so used by English-speaking people that all substitution instances of, say, "If p, then not-(not-p)" are true, is just plain empirical knowledge. It is, of course, conceivable that a man might deny a statement of that form, but in that case we would just have to conclude that his speech habits are different: perhaps he uses "if, then" the way "either-or" is ordinarily used, for example. But to tell him "You cannot deny it, *because it is necessarily true*" is, according to the conventionalist, like saying "You must speak the way we speak, because you have to speak that way."

Yet, the conventionalist cannot get around the admission that there is such a thing as a priori knowledge of logical truths, which is in no intelligible sense reducible to stipulation of, or acquaintance with, linguistic rules. In the first place, it is a meaningful question to ask whether it is possible, say, to define "if, then" on the basis of "not" and "or" in such a way that (*a*) the definition accords approximately with ordinary usage, (*b*) our postulates are transformed into truth-functional tautologies if "not" and "or" are defined as truth-functional connectives in the usual way. The definition that fulfills these requirements is: If p, then q = not-p or q. We know, for example, on the basis of truth-table analysis, that any statement of the form "not-p or not-(not-p or q) or q" (the transform into primitive notation of "if p, then, if (if p, then q), then q") is a tautology. Surely it does not make sense to say *it is a linguistic rule* that in a language containing the mentioned rules for the use of "not" and "or" any statement of the above form is a tautology. Indeed, this metastatement is a necessary statement, not a contingent statement about linguistic usage. That is, it is inconceivable that, while the rules for the use of "not" and "or" remain the same, a statement of the above form should fail to be a tautology.

Secondly, logicians usually lay down their postulates, not in order to prescribe a usage for logical constants or to describe how they are in fact used, but in order to construct a system, and this means that they intend to deduce a lot of theorems from the postulates. These deductions are, of course, guided by rules of deduction. Two of the most important rules of deduction (whether or not they be absolutely indispensable) are the rule of substitution and the rule of detachment (or "modus ponens"). The rule of substitution says with reference to our postulates: any formula obtainable from a postulate by substituting for a statement variable another statement variable or a truth-function of a statement variable, the same substitution being made for each occurrence of a given variable, is a theorem (and any formula derivable from a theorem in the same manner is also a theorem). The rule of detachment says: if A and (if A, then B) are postulates or theorems, then B is a theorem (here A and B are syntactic variables ranging over formulae of the system). Without raising the question of the justification of these rules of deductive proof, we wish to insist on the following simple point: a metastatement to the effect that such and such a formula is a theorem in the system that is characterized by such and such postulates and such and such rules of deduction is not a "rule" of any kind. It is, if true, *necessarily true*. It is a fact that cannot be altered by changing rules, that in a deductive system with specified formation rules, postulates, and rules of deduction, such and such a formula is a theorem whose proof involves such and such a minimal number of elementary steps. That the discovery of such "facts" by mathematicians and logicians involves the manipulation of symbols in accordance with rules is entirely consistent with its being an intellectual discovery – even if it is a proposition about symbols and not about intangible and invisible abstract entities. Even if algebra were construed as a science whose subject-matter consists of symbols, not of abstract entities such as numbers, it would be a meaningful question whether, say, Fermat's "last theorem" (for $n > 2$, there are no solutions for the equation: $x^n + y^n = z^n$) is really a theorem in such and such a system of algebra. Mathematicians have not found the answer yet, but most of them regard it as a serious and meaningful question. And the proposition in question is either necessary or impossible; it is not an empirical proposition. It

would be silly to say that the question here is whether such and such rules ought to be adopted. The question is not like the question whether there is a number that satisfies the equation "$x^2 = 2$"; it is rather like the question whether there is a rational number that satisfies that equation. It was, indeed, no discovery that there is an irrational number that satisfies it. This was a matter of decision, of deciding to broaden, by fiat, the extension of the term "number," whatever the reasons motivating the decision may have been. But Euclid did not *stipulate* that the equation has no rational solution; he *discovered* it by a well-known indirect proof.

We conclude that though logical conventionalists have rendered a valuable service in focusing attention on the role played by linguistic conventions in the acquisition of logical and mathematical knowledge, they have not shown that there is no such thing as a priori knowledge of necessary propositions and that the necessity of the laws of logic "depends" in some intelligible sense on linguistic conventions. In particular, to say of a certain complicated statement that it is a tautology, is not to deny that it is necessarily true nor that it makes sense to speak of "discovering" its truth; it is rather to explicate what the necessity and its discovery consist in. The thesis of Whitehead and Russell that all mathematical propositions are tautologies is still acutely controversial; and the thesis that all necessary propositions are tautologies is certainly false. But whether it be true or false has no bearing whatever on the question whether there is such a thing as purely intellectual discovery of necessary truths. Of course there is such discovery. And the discovery by means of some mechanical decision procedure (such as the use of "truth tables") that a certain complicated form of deductive argument is valid because the corresponding implication is a tautology is not the least useful and respectable among such intellectual discoveries.

Note

1   Readers who are untrained in formal logic will find it easier to grasp the sense of these postulates if they occasionally replace "if p, then q" by "p implies q" – though this is technically inaccurate inasmuch as grammar requires "p" and "q" to be quoted when they are connected by "implies." The first postulate, for example, is then recognizable as the principle of the hypothetical syllogism in the form: if "p" implies "q," then, if "q" implies "r," then "p" implies "r."

Selected Readings

Carnap, R., *Meaning and Necessity* (Chicago, 1956).

——, "The Old and the New Logic," in A. J. Ayer (ed.), *Logical Positivism* (New York, 1959).

Ewing, A. C., "The Linguistic Theory of A Priori Propositions," *Aristotelian Society Proceedings*, 1940.

Goodman, N., "On Likeness of Meaning," *Analysis*, 1949–50. [Reprinted in M. Macdonald (ed.), *Philosophy and Analysis* (Oxford, 1954).]

Grice, H. P., and P. F. Strawson, "In Defense of a Dogma," *Philosophical Review*, 1956.

Hahn, H., "Logic, Mathematics, and Knowledge of Nature," in A. J. Ayer (ed.), *Logical Positivism* (New York, 1959).

Hardie, C. D., "The Necessity of A Priori Propositions," *Aristotelian Society Proceedings*, 1937.

Kneale, W., "Are Necessary Truths True by Convention?," *Aristotelian Society Proceedings*, supp., 1947.

——"The Truths of Logic," *Aristotelian Society Proceedings*, 1945–6.

Lewis, C. I., *An Analysis of Knowledge and Valuation* (La Salle, Ill., 1946), chap. 5.

Malcolm, N., "Are Necessary Propositions Really Verbal?," *Mind*, 1940.

——, "The Nature of Entailment," *Mind*, 1940.

Mises, R. von, *Positivism: A Study in Human Understanding* (Cambridge, Mass., 1951).

Nagel, E., "Some Theses in the Philosophy of Logic," *Philosophy of Science*, 1938.

——, "Logic without Ontology," in H. Feigl and W. Sellars (eds.), *Readings in Philosophical Analysis* (New York, 1949); and in E. Nagel, *Logic without Metaphysics* (New York, 1957).

Pap, A., *Semantics and Necessary Truth* (New Haven, Conn., 1958), chs. 5–8.

Quine, W. V., "Truth by Convention," in H. Feigl and W. Sellars (eds.), *Readings in Philosophical Analysis* (New York, 1949).

——, "Two Dogmas of Empiricism," in W. V. Quine, *From a Logical Point of View* (Cambridge, 1953).

Waismann, F., "Analytic-Synthetic, I–VI," *Analysis*, 1949–53.

White, M. G., "The Analytic and the Synthetic: An Untenable Dualism," in S. Hook (ed.), *John Dewey: Philosopher of Science and Freedom* (New York, 1950). [Reprinted in L. Linsky (ed.), *Semantics and the Philosophy of Language* (Urbana, Ill., 1952).]

Wittgenstein, L., *Tractatus Logico-Philosophicus* (London, 1922).

2

Russell's Mathematical Logic

Kurt Gödel

Mathematical logic, which is nothing else but a precise and complete formulation of formal logic, has two quite different aspects. On the one hand, it is a section of Mathematics treating of classes, relations, combinations of symbols, etc., instead of numbers, functions, geometric figures, etc. On the other hand, it is a science prior to all others, which contains the ideas and principles underlying all sciences. It was in this second sense that Mathematical Logic was first conceived by Leibniz in his *Characteristica universalis*, of which it would have formed a central part. But it was almost two centuries after his death before his idea of a logical calculus really sufficient for the kind of reasoning occurring in the exact sciences was put into effect (in some form at least, if not the one Leibniz had in mind) by Frege and Peano.[1] Frege was chiefly interested in the analysis of thought and used his calculus in the first place for deriving arithmetic from pure logic. Peano, on the other hand, was more interested in its applications within mathematics and created an elegant and flexible symbolism, which permits expressing even the most complicated mathematical theorems in a perfectly precise and often very concise manner by single formulas.

It was in this line of thought of Frege and Peano that Russell's work set in. Frege, in consequence of his painstaking analysis of the proofs, had not gotten beyond the most elementary properties of

Kurt Gödel, Russell's Mathematical Logic. *The Philosophy of Bertrand Russell*. Ed. Paul Arthur Schilpp. New York: Tudor Publishing Company, 1951. 125–53.

the series of integers, while Peano had accomplished a big collection of mathematical theorems expressed in the new symbolism, but without proofs. It was only in *Principia Mathematica* that full use was made of the new method for actually deriving large parts of mathematics from a very few logical concepts and axioms. In addition, the young science was enriched by a new instrument, the abstract theory of relations. The calculus of relations had been developed before by Peirce and Schröder, but only with certain restrictions and in too close analogy with the algebra of numbers. In *Principia* not only Cantor's set theory but also ordinary arithmetic and the theory of measurement are treated from this abstract relational standpoint.

It is to be regretted that this first comprehensive and thorough going presentation of a mathematical logic and the derivation of Mathematics from it is so greatly lacking in formal precision in the foundations (contained in *1–*21 of *Principia*), that it presents in this respect a considerable step backwards as compared with Frege. What is missing, above all, is a precise statement of the syntax of the formalism. Syntactical considerations are omitted even in cases where they are necessary for the cogency of the proofs, in particular in connection with the "incomplete symbols." These are introduced not by explicit definitions, but by rules describing how sentences containing them are to be translated into sentences not containing them. In order to be sure, however, that (or for what expressions) this translation is possible and uniquely determined and that (or to what extent) the rules of inference apply also to the new kind of expressions, it is necessary to have a survey of all possible expressions, and this can be furnished only by syntactical considerations. The matter is especially doubtful for the rule of substitution and of replacing defined symbols by their *definiens*. If this latter rule is applied to expressions containing other defined symbols it requires that the order of elimination of these be indifferent. This however is by no means always the case ($\varphi!\hat{u} = \hat{u}[\varphi!u]$, e.g., is a counter-example). In *Principia* such eliminations are always carried out by substitutions in the theorems corresponding to the definitions, so that it is chiefly the rule of substitution which would have to be proved.

I do not want, however, to go into any more details about either the formalism or the mathematical content of *Principia*, but want to devote the subsequent portion of this essay to Russell's work concerning the analysis of the concepts and axioms underlying mathematical logic. In this field Russell has produced a great number of interesting ideas some of which are presented most clearly (or are contained only) in his earlier writings. I shall therefore frequently refer also to these earlier writings, although their content may partly disagree with Russell's present standpoint.

What strikes one as surprising in this field is Russell's pronouncedly realistic attitude, which manifests itself in many passages of his writings. "Logic is concerned with the real world just as truly as zoology, though with its more abstract and general features," he says, e.g., in his *Introduction to Mathematical Philosophy* (edition of 1920, p. 169). It is true, however, that this attitude has been gradually decreasing in the course of time[2] and also that it always was stronger in theory than in practice. When he started on a concrete problem, the objects to be analyzed (e.g., the classes or propositions) soon for the most part turned into "logical fictions." Though perhaps this need not necessarily mean [according to the sense in which Russell uses this term] that these things do not exist, but only that we have no direct perception of them.

The analogy between mathematics and a natural science is enlarged upon by Russell also in another respect (in one of his earlier writings). He compares the axioms of logic and mathematics with the laws of nature and logical evidence with sense perception, so that the axioms need not necessarily be evident in themselves, but rather their justification lies (exactly as in physics) in the fact that they

make it possible for these "sense perceptions" to be deduced; which of course would not exclude that they also have a kind of intrinsic plausibility similar to that in physics. I think that (provided "evidence" is understood in a sufficiently strict sense) this view has been largely justified by subsequent developments, and it is to be expected that it will be still more so in the future. It has turned out that (under the assumption that modern mathematics is consistent) the solution of certain arithmetical problems requires the use of assumptions essentially transcending arithmetic, i.e., the domain of the kind of elementary indisputable evidence that may be most fittingly compared with sense perception. Furthermore it seems likely that for deciding certain questions of abstract set theory and even for certain related questions of the theory of real numbers new axioms based on some hitherto unknown idea will be necessary. Perhaps also the apparently unsurmountable difficulties which some other mathematical problems have been presenting for many years are due to the fact that the necessary axioms have not yet been found. Of course, under these circumstances mathematics may lose a good deal of its "absolute certainty;" but, under the influence of the modern criticism of the foundations, this has already happened to a large extent. There is some resemblance between this conception of Russell and Hilbert's "supplementing the data of mathematical intuition" by such axioms as, e.g., the law of excluded middle which are not given by intuition according to Hilbert's view; the borderline however between data and assumptions would seem to lie in different places according to whether we follow Hilbert or Russell.

An interesting example of Russell's analysis of the fundamental logical concepts in his treatment of the definite article "the." The problem is: what do the so-called descriptive phrases (i.e., phrases as, e.g., "the author of *Waverley*" or "the king of England") denote or signify[3] and what is the meaning of sentences in which they occur? The apparently obvious answer that, e.g., "the author of *Waverley*" signifies Walter Scott, leads to unexpected difficulties. For, if we admit the further apparently obvious axiom, that the signification of a composite expression, containing constituents which have themselves a signification, depends only on the signification of these constituents (not on the manner in which this signification is expressed), then it follows that the sentence "Scott is the author of *Waverley*" signifies the same thing as "Scott is Scott;" and this again leads almost inevitably to the conclusion that all true sentences have the same signification (as well as all false ones).[4] Frege actually drew this conclusion; and he meant it in an almost metaphysical sense, reminding one somewhat of the Eleatic doctrine of the "One." "The True" – according to Frege's view – is analyzed by us in different ways in different propositions; "the True" being the name he uses for the common signification of all true propositions.[5]

Now according to Russell, what corresponds to sentences in the outer world is facts. However, he avoids the term "signify" or "denote" and uses "indicate" instead (in his earlier papers he uses "express" or "being a symbol for"), because he holds that the relation between a sentence and a fact is quite different from that of a name to the thing named. Furthermore, he uses "denote" (instead of "signify") for the relation between things and names, so that "denote" and "indicate" together would correspond to Frege's "*bedeuten*." So, according to Russell's terminology and view, true sentences "indicate" facts and, correspondingly, false ones indicate nothing.[6] Hence Frege's theory would in a sense apply to false sentences, since they all indicate the same thing, namely nothing. But different true sentences may indicate many different things. Therefore this view concerning sentences makes it necessary either to drop the above mentioned principle about the signification (i.e., in Russell's terminology the corresponding one about the denotation and indication) of composite expressions or to deny that a descriptive phrase denotes the object described. Russell did the latter[7] by taking the viewpoint that a descriptive phrase denotes nothing at all but has meaning only in context; for example, the sentence "the author of *Waverley* is Scotch," is defined to mean: "There exists exactly one entity who wrote *Waverley* and whoever wrote *Waverley* is Scotch." This means that a sentence involving the phrase "the author of *Waverley*" does not (strictly speaking) assert anything about Scott (since it contains no constituent denoting Scott), but is only a roundabout way of asserting something about the concepts occurring in the descriptive phrase. Russell adduces chiefly two arguments in favor of this view, namely (1) that a descriptive phrase may be meaningfully employed even if the object described does not exist (e.g., in the sentence: "The present king of France does not exist"). (2) That one may very well understand a sentence containing a descriptive phrase without being acquainted with the object described; whereas it seems impossible to understand a sentence without being acquainted with the objects about which something is being asserted. The fact that Russell does not consider this whole question of the interpretation of descriptions as a matter of mere linguistic conventions, but rather as a question of right and wrong, is another example of his realistic attitude, unless perhaps he was aiming at a merely psychological investigation of the actual processes of thought. As to the question in the logical sense, I cannot help feeling that the problem raised by Frege's puzzling conclusion has only been evaded by Russell's theory of descriptions and that there is something behind it which is not yet completely understood.

There seems to be one purely formal respect in which one may give preference to Russell's theory of descriptions. By defining the meaning of sentences involving descriptions in the above manner, he avoids in his logical system any axioms about the particle "the," i.e., the analyticity of the theorems about "the" is made explicit; they can be shown to follow from the explicit definition of the meaning of sentences involving "the." Frege, on the contrary, has to assume an axiom about "the," which of course is also analytic, but only in the implicit sense that it follows from the meaning of the undefined terms. Closer examination, however, shows that this advantage of Russell's theory over Frege's subsists only as long as one interprets definitions as mere typographical abbreviations, not as introducing names for objects described by the definitions, a feature which is common to Frege and Russell.

I pass now to the most important of Russell's investigations in the field of the analysis of the concepts of formal logic, namely those concerning the logical paradoxes and their solution. By analyzing the paradoxes to which Cantor's set theory had led, he freed them from all mathematical technicalities, thus bringing to light the amazing fact that our logical intuitions (i.e., intuitions concerning such notions as: truth, concept, being, class, etc.) are self-contradictory. He then investigated where and how these common sense assumptions of logic are to be corrected and came to the conclusion that the erroneous axiom consists in assuming that for every propositional function there exists the class of objects satisfying it, or that every propositional function exists "as a separate entity;"[8] by which is meant something separable from the argument (the idea being that propositional functions are abstracted from propositions which are primarily given) and also something distinct from the combination of symbols expressing the propositional function; it is then what one may call the notion or concept defined by it.[9] The existence of this concept already suffices for the paradoxes in their "intensional" form, where the concept of "not applying to itself" takes the place of Russell's paradoxical class.

Rejecting the existence of a class or concept in general, it remains to determine under what further hypotheses (concerning the propositional function) these entities do exist. Russell pointed out (loc. cit.) two possible directions in which one may look for such a criterion, which he called the zig-zag theory and the theory of limitation of size, respectively, and which might perhaps more significantly be called the intensional and the extensional theory. The second one would make the existence of a class or concept depend on the extension of the propositional function (requiring that it be not too big), the first one on its content or meaning (requiring a certain kind of "simplicity," the precise formulation of which would be the problem).

The most characteristic feature of the second (as opposed to the first) would consist in the non-existence of the universal class or (in the intensional interpretation) of the notion of "something" in an unrestricted sense. Axiomatic set theory as later developed by Zermelo and others can be considered as an elaboration of this idea as far as classes are concerned.[10] In particular the phrase "not too big" can be specified (as was shown by J. v. Neumann[11]) to mean: not equivalent with the universe of all things, or, to be more exact, a propositional function can be assumed to determine a class when and only when there exists no relation (in intension, i.e., a propositional function with two variables) which associates in a one-to-one manner with each object, an object satisfying the propositional function and vice versa. This criterion, however, does not appear as the basis of the theory but as a consequence of the axioms and inversely can replace two of the axioms (the axioms of replacement and that of choice).

For the second of Russell's suggestions too, i.e., for the zig-zag theory, there has recently been set up a logical system which shares some essential features with this scheme, namely Quine's system.[12] It is, moreover, not unlikely that there are other interesting possibilities along these lines.

Russell's own subsequent work concerning the solution of the paradoxes did not go in either of the two afore-mentioned directions pointed out by himself, but was largely based on a more radical idea, the "no-class theory," according to which classes or concepts never exist as real objects, and sentences containing these terms are meaningful only to such an extent as they can be interpreted as a façon de parler, a manner of speaking about other things. Since in Principia and elsewhere, however, he formulated certain principles discovered in the course of the development of this theory as general logical principles without mentioning any longer their dependence on the no-class theory, I am going to treat of these principles first.

I mean in particular the vicious circle principle, which forbids a certain kind of "circularity" which is made responsible for the paradoxes. The fallacy in these, so it is contended, consists in the circumstance that one defines (or tacitly assumes) totalities, whose existence would entail the existence of certain new elements of the same totality, namely elements definable only in terms of the whole totality. This led to the formulation of a principle which says that "no totality can contain members definable only in terms of this totality, or members involving or presupposing this totality" [vicious circle principle]. In order to make this principle applicable to the intensional paradoxes, still another principle had to be assumed, namely that "every propositional function presupposes the totality of its values" and therefore evidently also the totality of its possible arguments.[13] [Otherwise the concept of "not applying to itself" would presuppose no totality (since it involves no quantifications),[14] and the vicious circle principle would not prevent its application to itself.] A corresponding vicious circle principle for propositional functions which says that nothing defined in terms of a propositional function can be a possible argument of this function is then a consequence.[15] The logical system to which one is led on the basis of these principles is the theory of orders in the form adopted, e.g., in the first edition of Principia, according to which a propositional function which either contains quantifications referring to propositional functions of order n or can be meaningfully asserted of propositional functions of order n is at least of order $n + 1$, and the range of significance of a propositional function as well as the range of a quantifier must always be confined to a definite order.

In the second edition of Principia, however, it is stated in the Introduction (pp. XI and XII) that "in a limited sense" also functions of a higher order than the predicate itself (therefore also functions defined in terms of the predicate as, e.g., in p 'κ ε κ) can appear as arguments of a predicate of functions; and in appendix B such things occur constantly. This means that the vicious circle principle for propositional functions is virtually dropped. This change is connected with the new axiom that functions can occur in propositions only "through their values," i.e., extensionally, which has the consequence that any propositional function can take as an argument any function of appropriate type, whose extension is defined (no matter what order of quantifiers is used in the definition of this extension). There is no doubt that these things are quite unobjectionable even from the constructive standpoint, provided that quantifiers are always restricted to definite orders. The paradoxes are avoided by the theory of simple types,[16] which in *principia* is combined with the theory of orders (giving as a result the "ramified hierarchy") but is entirely independent of it and has nothing to do with the vicious circle principle.

Now as to the vicious circle principle proper, it is first to be remarked that, corresponding to the phrases "definable only in terms of," "involving," and "presupposing," we have really three different principles, the second and third being much more plausible than the first. It is the first form which is of particular interest, because only this one makes impredicative definitions[17] impossible and thereby destroys the derivation of mathematics from logic, effected by Dedekind and Frege, and a good deal of modern mathematics itself. It is demonstrable that the formalism of classical mathematics does not satisfy the vicious circle principle in its first form, since the axioms imply the existence of real numbers definable in this formalism only by reference to all real numbers. Since classical mathematics can be built up on the basis of *Principia* (including the axiom of reducibility), it follows that even *Principia* (in the first edition) does not satisfy the vicious circle principle in the first form, if "definable" means "definable within the system" and no methods of defining outside the system (or outside other systems of classical mathematics) are known except such as involve still more comprehensive totalities than those occurring in the systems.

I would consider this rather as a proof that the vicious circle principle is false than that classical mathematics is false, and this is indeed plausible

also on its own account. For, first of all one may, on good grounds, deny that reference to a totality necessarily implies reference to all single elements of it or, in other words, that "all" means the same as an infinite logical conjunction. One may, e.g., follow Langford's and Carnap's[18] suggestion to interpret "all" as meaning analyticity or necessity or demonstrability. There are difficulties in this view; but there is no doubt that in this way the circularity of impredicative definitions disappears.

Secondly, however, even if "all" means an infinite conjunction, it seems that the vicious circle principle in its first form applies only if the entities involved are constructed by ourselves. In this case there must clearly exist a definition (namely the description of the construction) which does not refer to a totality to which the object defined belongs, because the construction of a thing can certainly not be based on a totality of things to which the thing to be constructed itself belongs. If, however, it is a question of objects that exist independently of our constructions, there is nothing in the least absurd in the existence of totalities containing members, which can be described (i.e., uniquely characterized)[19] only by reference to this totality.[20] Such a state of affairs would not even contradict the second form of the vicious circle principle, since one cannot say that an object described by reference to a totality "involves" this totality, although the description itself does; nor would it contradict the third form, if "presuppose" means "presuppose for the existence" not "for the knowability."

So it seems that the vicious circle principle in its first form applies only if one takes the constructivistic (or nominalistic) standpoint[21] toward the objects of logic and mathematics, in particular toward propositions, classes and notions, e.g., if one understands by a notion a symbol together with a rule for translating sentences containing the symbol into such sentences as do not contain it, so that a separate object denoted by the symbol appears as a mere fiction.[22]

Classes and concepts may, however, also be conceived as real objects, namely classes as "pluralities of things" or as structures consisting of a plurality of things and concepts as the properties and relations of things existing independently of our definitions and constructions.

It seems to me that the assumption of such objects is quite as legitimate as the assumption of physical bodies and there is quite as much reason to believe in their existence. They are in the same sense necessary to obtain a satisfactory system of mathematics as physical bodies are necessary for a satisfactory theory of our sense perceptions and in both cases it is impossible to interpret the propositions one wants to assert about these entities as propositions about the "data," i.e., in the latter case the actually occurring sense perceptions. Russell himself concludes in the last chapter of his book on *Meaning and Truth*, though "with hesitation," that there exist "universals," but apparently he wants to confine this statement to concepts of sense perceptions, which does not help the logician. I shall use the term "concept" in the sequel exclusively in this objective sense. One formal difference between the two conceptions of notions would be that any two different definitions of the form $\alpha(x) = \varphi(x)$ can be assumed to define two different notions α in the constructivistic sense. (In particular this would be the case for the nominalistic interpretation of the term "notion" suggested above, since two such definitions give different rules of translation for propositions containing α.) For concepts, on the contrary, this is by no means the case, since the same thing may be described in different ways. It might even be that the axiom of extensionality[23] or at least something near to it holds for concepts. The difference may be illustrated by the following definition of the number two: "Two is the notion under which fall all pairs and nothing else." There is certainly more than one notion in the constructivistic sense satisfying this condition, but there might be one common "form" or "nature" of all pairs.

Since the vicious circle principle, in its first form does apply to constructed entities, impredicative definitions and the totality of all notions or classes or propositions are inadmissible in constructivistic logic. What an impredicative definition would require is to construct a notion by a combination of a set of notions to which the notion to be formed itself belongs. Hence if one tries to effect a retranslation of a sentence containing a symbol for such an impredicatively defined notion in turns out that what one obtains will again contain a symbol for the notion in question.[24] At least this is so if "all" means an infinite conjunction; but Carnap's and Langford's idea would not help in this connection, because "demonstrability," if introduced in a manner compatible with the constructivistic standpoint towards notions, would have to be split into a hierarchy of orders, which would prevent one from obtaining the desired results.[25] As Chwistek has shown,[26] it is even

possible under certain assumptions admissible within constructivistic logic to derive an actual contradiction from the unrestricted admission of impredicative definitions. To be more specific, he has shown that the system of simple types becomes contradictory if one adds the "axiom of intensionality" which says (roughly speaking) that to different definitions belong different notions. This axiom, however, as has just been pointed out, can be assumed to hold for notions in the constructivistic sense.

Speaking of concepts, the aspect of the question is changed completely. Since concepts are supposed to exist objectively, there seems to be objection neither to speaking of all of them nor to describing some of them by reference to all (or at least all of a given type). But, one may ask, isn't this view refutable also for concepts because it leads to the "absurdity" that there will exist properties φ such that $\varphi(a)$ consists in a certain state of affairs involving all properties (including φ itself and properties defined in terms of φ), which would mean that the vicious circle principle does not hold even in its second form for concepts or propositions? There is no doubt that the totality of all properties (or of all those of a given type) does lead to situations of this kind, but I don't think they contain any absurdity.[27] It is true that such properties φ [or such propositions $\varphi(a)$] will have to contain themselves as constituents of their content [or of their meaning], and in fact in many ways, because of the properties defined in terms of φ; but this only makes it impossible to construct their meaning (i.e., explain it as an assertion about sense perceptions or any other non-conceptual entities), which is no objection for one who takes the realistic standpoint. Nor is it self-contradictory that a proper part should be identical (not merely equal) to the whole, as is seen in the case of structures in the abstract sense. The structure of the series of integers, e.g., contains itself as a proper part and it is easily seen that there exist also structures containing infinitely many different parts, each containing the whole structure as a part. In addition there exist, even within the domain of constructivistic logic, certain approximations to this self-reflexivity of impredicative properties, namely propositions which contain as parts of their meaning not themselves but their own formal demonstrability.[28] Now formal demonstrability of a proposition (in case the axioms and rules of inference are correct) implies this proposition and in many cases is equivalent to it. Furthermore, there doubtlessly exist sentences referring to a totality of sentences to which they themselves belong as, e.g., the sentence: "Every sentence (of a given language) contains at least one relation word."[29]

Of course this view concerning the impredicative properties makes it necessary to look for another solution of the paradoxes, according to which the fallacy (i.e., the underlying erroneous axiom) does not consist in the assumption of certain self-reflexivities of the primitive terms but in other assumptions about these. Such a solution may be found for the present in the simple theory of types and in the future perhaps in the development of the ideas sketched on pp. 24 and 31. Of course, all this refers only to concepts. As to notions in the constructivistic sense there is no doubt that the paradoxes are due to a vicious circle. It is not surprising that the paradoxes should have different solutions for different interpretations of the terms occurring.

As to classes in the sense of pluralities or totalities it would seem that they are likewise not created but merely described by their definitions and that therefore the vicious circle principle in the first form does not apply. I even think there exist interpretations of the term "class" (namely as a certain kind of structures), where it does not apply in the second form either.[29] But for the development of all contemporary mathematics one may even assume that it does apply in the second form, which for classes as mere pluralities is, indeed, a very plausible assumption. One is then led to something like Zermelo's axiom system for set theory, i.e., the sets are split up into "levels" in such a manner that only sets of lower levels can be elements of sets of higher levels (i.e., xεy is always false if x belongs to a higher level than y). There is no reason for classes in this sense to exclude mixtures of levels in one set and transfinite levels. The place of the axiom of reducibility is now taken by the axiom of classes [Zermelo's *Aussonderungsaxiom*] which says that for each level there exists for an arbitrary propositional function φ (x) the set of those x of this level for which φ (x) is true, and this seems to be implied by the concept of classes as pluralities.

Russell adduces two reasons against the extensional view of classes, namely the existence of (1.) the null class, which cannot very well be a collection, and (2.) the unit classes, which would have to be identical with their single elements. But it seems to me that these arguments could, if anything, at most prove that the null class and the unit classes (as distinct from their only element) are fictions (introduced to simplify the calculus like the points at infinity in geometry), not that all classes are fictions.

But in Russell the paradoxes had produced a pronounced tendency to build up logic as far as possible without the assumption of the objective existence of such entities as classes and concepts. This led to the formulation of the aforementioned "no class theory," according to which classes and concepts were to be introduced as a *façon de parler*. But propositions, too, (in particular those involving quantifications)[30] were later on largely included in this scheme, which is but a logical consequence of this standpoint, since e.g., universal propositions as objectively existing entities evidently belong to the same category of idealistic objects as classes and concepts and lead to the same kind of paradoxes, if admitted without restrictions. As regards classes this program was actually carried out; i.e., the rules for translating sentences containing class names or the term "class" into such as do not contain them were stated explicitly; and the basis of the theory, i.e, the domain of sentences into which one has to translate is clear, so that classes can be dispensed with (within the system *Principia*), but only if one assumes the existence of a concept whenever one wants to construct a class. When it comes to concepts and the interpretation of sentences containing this or some synonymous term, the state of affairs is by no means as clear. First of all, some of them (the primitive predicates and relations such as "red" or "colder") must apparently be considered as real objects;[31] the rest of them (in particular according to the second edition of *Principia*, all notions of a type higher than the first and therewith all logically interesting ones) appear as something constructed (i.e., as something not belonging to the "inventory" of the world); but neither the basic domain of propositions in terms of which finally everything is to be interpreted, nor the method of interpretation is as clear as in the case of classes (see below).

This whole scheme of the no-class theory is of great interest as one of the few examples, carried out in detail, of the tendency to eliminate assumptions about the existence of objects outside the "data" and to replace them by constructions on the basis of these data.[32] The result has been in this case essentially negative; i.e., the classes and concepts introduced in this way do not have all the properties required for their use in mathematics, unless one either introduces special axioms about the data (e.g., the axiom of reducibility), which in essence already mean the existence in the data of the kind of objects to be constructed, or makes the fiction that one can form propositions of infinite (and even non-denumerable) length,[33] i.e., operates with truth-functions of infinitely many arguments, regardless of whether or not one can construct them. But what else is such an infinite truth-function but a special kind of an infinite extension (or structure) and even a more complicated one than a class, endowed in addition with a hypothetical meaning, which can be understood only by an infinite mind? All this is only a verification of the view defended above that logic and mathematics (just as physics) are built up on axioms with a real content which cannot be "explained away."

What one can obtain on the basis of the constructivistic attitude is the theory of orders; only now (and this is the strong point of the theory) the restrictions involved do not appear as *ad hoc* hypotheses for avoiding the paradoxes, but as unavoidable consequences of the thesis that classes, concepts, and quantified propositions do not exist as real objects. It is not as if the universe of things were divided into orders and then one were prohibited to speak of all orders; but, on the contrary, it is possible to speak of all existing things; only, classes and concepts are not among them; and if they are introduced as a *façon de parler*, it turns out that this very extension of the symbolism gives rise to the possibility of introducing them in a more comprehensive way, and so on indefinitely. In order to carry out this scheme one must, however, presuppose arithmetic (or something equivalent) which only proves that not even this restricted logic can be built up on nothing.

In the first edition of *Principia*, where it was a question of actually building up logic and mathematics, the constructivistic attitude was, for the most part, abandoned, since the axiom of reducibility for types higher than the first together with the axiom of infinity makes it absolutely necessary that there exist primitive predicates of arbitrarily high types. What is left of the constructive attitude is only: (1) The introduction of classes as a *façon de parler*; (2) the definition of $\sim$, v, ., etc., as applied to propositions containing quantifiers (which incidentally proved its fecundity in a consistency proof for arithmetic); (3) the step by step construction of functions of orders higher than 1, which, however, is superfluous owing to the axiom

of reducibility; (4) the interpretation of definitions as mere typographical abbreviations, which makes every symbol introduced by definition an incomplete symbol (not one naming an object described by the definition). But the last item is largely an illusion, because, owing to the axiom of reducibility, there always exist real objects in the form of primitive predicates, or combinations of such, corresponding to each defined symbol. Finally also Russell's theory of descriptions is something belonging to the constructivistic order of ideas.

In the second edition of *Principia* (or to be more exact, in the introduction to it) the constructivistic attitude is resumed again. The axiom of reducibility is dropped and it is stated explicitly that all primitive predicates belong to the lowest type and that the only purpose of variables (and evidently also of constants) of higher orders and types is to make it possible to assert more complicated truth-functions of atomic propositions,[34] which is only another way of saying that the higher types and orders are solely a *façon de parler*. This statement at the same time informs us of what kind of propositions the basis of the theory is to consist, namely of truth-functions of atomic propositions.

This, however, is without difficulty only if the number of individuals and primitive predicates is finite. For the opposite case (which is chiefly of interest for the purpose of deriving mathematics) Ramsey (*loc. cit.*) took the course of considering our inability to form propositions of infinite length as a "mere accident," to be neglected by the logician. This of course solves (or rather cuts through) the difficulties; but it is to be noted that, if one disregards the difference between finite and infinite in this respect, there exists a simpler and at the same time more far reaching interpretation of set theory (and therewith of mathematics). Namely, in case of a finite number of individuals, Russell's *aperçu* that propositions about classes can be interpreted as propositions about their elements becomes literally true, since, e.g., "$x\varepsilon m$" is equivalent to "$x = a_1$, v $x = a_2$v ... v $x = a_k$" where the a_i are the elements of m; and "there exists a class such that..." is equivalent to "there exist individuals $x_1, x_2, \ldots x_n$ such that...,"[35] provided n is the number of individuals in the world and provided we neglect for the moment the null class which would have to be taken care of by an additional clause. Of course, by an iteration of this procedure one can obtain classes of classes, etc., so that the logical system obtained would resemble the theory of simple types except for the circumstance that mixture of types would be possible. Axiomatic set theory appears, then, as an extrapolation of this scheme for the case of infinitely many individuals or an infinite iteration of the process of forming sets.

Ramsey's viewpoint is, of course, everything but constructivistic, unless one means constructions of an infinite mind. Russell, in the second edition of *Principia*, took a less metaphysical course by confining himself to such truth-functions as can actually be constructed. In this way one is again led to the theory of orders, which, however, appears now in a new light, namely as a method of constructing more and more complicated truth-functions of atomic propositions. But this procedure seems to presuppose arithmetic in some form or other (see next paragraph).

As to the question of how far mathematics can be built up on this basis (without any assumptions about the data–i.e., about the primitive predicates and individuals – except, as far as necessary, the axiom of infinity), it is clear that the theory of real numbers in its present form cannot be obtained.[36] As to the theory of integers, it is contended in the second edition of *Principia* that it can be obtained. The difficulty to be overcome is that in the definition of the integers as "those cardinals which belong to every class containing o and containing $x + 1$ if containing x," the phrase "every class" must refer to a given order. So one obtains integers of different orders, and complete induction can be applied to integers of order n only for properties of order n; whereas it frequently happens that the notion of integer itself occurs in the property to which induction is applied. This notion, however, is of order $n + 1$ for the integers of order n. Now, in Appendix B of the second edition of *Principia*, a proof is offered that the integers of any order higher than 5 are the same as those of order 5, which of course would settle all difficulties. The proof as it stands, however, is certainly not conclusive. In the proof of the main lemma *89.16, which says that every subset α (of arbitrary high order)[37] of an inductive class β of order 3 is itself an inductive class of order 3, induction is applied to a property of β involving α [namely $\alpha - \beta \neq \Lambda$, which, however, should read $\alpha - \beta \sim \varepsilon$ Induct$_2$ because (3) is evidently false]. This property, however, is of an order > 3 if α is of an order > 3. So the question whether (or to what extent) the theory of integers can be obtained on the basis of the ramified hierarchy must be considered as unsolved at the present time. It is to be noted, however, that,

even in case this question should have a positive answer, this would be of no value for the problem whether arithmetic follows from logic, if propositional functions of order n are defined (as in the second edition of *Principia*) to be certain finite (though arbitrarily complex) combinations (of quantifiers, propositional connectives, etc.), because then the notion of finiteness has to be presupposed, which fact is concealed only by taking such complicated notions as "propositional function of order n" in an unanalyzed form as primitive terms of the formalism and giving their definition only in ordinary language. The reply may perhaps be offered that in *Principia* the notion of a propositional function of order n is neither taken as primitive nor defined in terms of the notion of a finite combination, but rather quantifiers referring to propositional functions of order n (which is all one needs) are defined as certain infinite conjunctions and disjunctions. But then one must ask: Why doesn't one define the integers by the infinite disjunction: $x = o \vee x = o + 1 \vee x = o + 1 + 1 \vee \ldots .ad\ infinitum$, saving in this way all the trouble connected with the notion of inductiveness? This whole objection would not apply if one understands by a propositional function of order n one "obtainable from such truth-functions of atomic propositions as presuppose for their definition no totalities except those of the propositional functions of order $< n$ and of individuals;" this notion, however, is somewhat lacking in precision.

The theory of orders proves more fruitful if considered from a purely mathematical standpoint, independently of the philosophical question whether impredicative definitions are admissible. Viewed in this manner, i.e., as a theory built up within the framework of ordinary mathematics, where impredicative definitions are admitted, there is no objection to extending it to arbitrarily high transfinite orders. Even if one rejects impredicative definitions, there would, I think, be no objection to extending it to such transfinite ordinals as can be constructed within the framework of finite orders. The theory in itself seems to demand such an extension since it leads automatically to the consideration of functions in whose definition one refers to all functions of finite orders, and these would be functions of order ω. Admitting transfinite orders, an axiom of reducibility can be proved. This, however, offers no help to the original purpose of the theory, because the ordinal α – such that every propositional function is extensionally equivalent to a function of order α – is so great, that it presupposes impredicative totalities. Nevertheless, so much can be accomplished in this way, that all impredicativities are reduced to one special kind, namely the existence of certain large ordinal numbers (or, well ordered sets) and the validity of recursive reasoning for them. In particular, the existence of a well ordered set, of order type ω_1 already suffices for the theory of real numbers. In addition this transfinite theorem of reducibility permits the proof of the consistency of the Axiom of Choice, of Cantor's Continuum-Hypothesis and even of the generalized Continuum-Hypothesis (which says that there exists no cardinal number between the power of any arbitrary set and the power of the set of its subsets) with the axioms of set theory as well as of *Principia*.

I now come in somewhat more detail to the theory of simple types which appears in *Principia* as combined with the theory of orders; the former is, however, (as remarked above) quite independent of the latter, since mixed types evidently do not contradict the vicious circle principle in any way. Accordingly, Russell also based the theory of simple types on entirely different reasons. The reason adduced (in addition to its "consonance with common sense") is very similar to Frege's, who, in his system, already had assumed the theory of simple types for functions, but failed to avoid the paradoxes, because he operated with classes (or rather functions in extension) without any restriction. This reason is that (owing to the variable it contains) a propositional function is something ambiguous (or, as Frege says, something unsaturated, wanting supplementation) and therefore can occur in a meaningful proposition only in such a way that this ambiguity is eliminated (e.g., by substituting a constant for the variable or applying quantification to it). The consequences are that a function cannot replace an individual in a proposition, because the latter has no ambiguity to be removed, and that functions with different kinds of arguments (i.e., different ambiguities) cannot replace each other; which is the essence of the theory of simple types. Taking a more nominalistic viewpoint (such as suggested in the second edition of *Principia* and in *Meaning and Truth*) one would have to replace "proposition" by "sentence" in the foregoing considerations (with corresponding additional changes). But in both cases, this argument clearly belongs to the order of ideas of the "no class" theory, since it considers the notions (or propositional functions) as something constructed out of propositions or sentences by leaving one or several constituents of them undetermined. Propositional functions in this sense are so to speak "fragments" of propositions, which have no meaning in themselves, but only in so far as one can use them for forming propositions by combining several of them, which is possible only if they "fit together," i.e., if they are of appropriate types. But, it should be noted that the theory of simple types (in contradistinction to the vicious circle principle) cannot in a strict sense follow from the constructive standpoint, because one might construct notions and classes in another way, e.g., as indicated on p. 28, where mixtures of types are possible. If on the other hand one considers concepts as real objects, the theory of simple types is not very plausible, since what one would expect to be a concept (such as, e.g., "transitivity" or the number two) would seem to be something behind all its various "realizations" on the different levels and therefore does not exist according to the theory of types. Nevertheless, there seems to be some truth behind this idea of realizations of the same concept on various levels, and one might, therefore, expect the theory of simple types to prove useful or necessary at least as a stepping-stone for a more satisfactory system, a way in which it has already been used by Quine.[38] Also Russell's "typical ambiguity" is a step in this direction. Since, however, it only adds certain simplifying symbolic conventions to the theory of types, it does not *de facto* go beyond this theory.

It should be noted that the theory of types brings in a new idea for the solution of the paradoxes, especially suited to their intensional form. It consists in blaming the paradoxes not on the axiom that every propositional function defines a concept or class, but on the assumption that every concept gives a meaningful proposition, if asserted for any arbitrary object or objects as arguments. The obvious objection that every concept can be extended to all arguments, by defining another one which gives a false proposition whenever the original one was meaningless, can easily be dealt with by pointing out that the concept "meaningfully applicable" need not itself be always meaningfully applicable.

The theory of simple types (in its realistic interpretation) can be considered as a carrying through of this scheme, based, however, on the following additional assumption concerning meaningfulness:

"Whenever an object x can replace another object y in one meaningful proposition, it can do so in every meaningful proposition."[39] This of course has the consequence that the objects are divided into mutually exclusive ranges of significance, each range consisting of those objects which can replace each other; and that therefore each concept is significant only for arguments belonging to one of these ranges, i.e., for an infinitely small portion of all objects. What makes the above principle particularly suspect, however, is that its very assumption makes its formulation as a meaningful proposition impossible,[40] because x and y must then be confined to definite ranges of significance which are either the same or different, and in both cases the statement does not express the principle or even part of it. Another consequence is that the fact that an object x is (or is not) of a given type also cannot be expressed by a meaningful proposition.

It is not impossible that the idea of limited ranges of significance could be carried out without the above restrictive principle. It might even turn out that it is possible to assume every concept to be significant everywhere except for certain "singular points" or "limiting points," so that the paradoxes would appear as something analogous to dividing by zero. Such a system would be most satisfactory in the following respect: our logical intuitions would then remain correct up to certain minor corrections, i.e., they could then be considered to give an essentially correct, only somewhat "blurred," picture of the real state of affairs. Unfortunately the attempts made in this direction have failed so far;[41] on the other hand, the impossibility of this scheme has not been proved either, in spite of the strong inconsistency theorems of Kleene and Rosser.[42]

In conclusion I want to say a few words about the question whether (and in which sense) the axioms of *Principia* can be considered to be analytic. As to this problem it is to be remarked that analyticity may be understood in two senses. First, it may have the purely formal sense that the terms occurring can be defined (either explicitly or by rules for eliminating them from sentences containing them) in such a way that the axioms and theorems become special cases of the law of identity and disprovable propositions become negations of this law. In this sense even the theory of integers is demonstrably non-analytic, provided that one requires of the rules of elimination that they allow one actually to carry out the elimination

in a finite number of steps in each case.[43] Leaving out this condition by admitting, e.g., sentences of infinite (and non-denumerable) length as intermediate steps of the process of reduction, all axioms of *Principia* (including the axioms of choice, infinity and reducibility) could be proved to be analytic for certain interpretations.[44] But this observation is of doubtful value, because the whole of mathematics as applied to sentences of infinite length has to be presupposed in order to prove this analyticity, e.g., the axiom of choice can be proved to be analytic only if it is assumed to be true.

In a second sense a proposition is called analytic if it holds, "owing to the meaning of the concepts occurring in it," where this meaning may perhaps be undefinable (i.e., irreducible to anything more fundamental).[45] It would seem that all axioms of *Principia*, in the first edition, (except the axiom of infinity) are in this sense analytic for certain interpretations of the primitive terms, namely if the term "predicative function" is replaced either by "class" (in the extensional sense) or (leaving out the axiom of choice) by "concept," since nothing can express better the meaning of the term "class" than the axiom of classes and the axiom of choice, and since, on the other hand, the meaning of the term "concept" seems to imply that every propositional function defines a concept.[46] The difficulty is only that we don't perceive the concepts of "concept" and of "class" with sufficient distinctness, as is shown by the paradoxes. In view of this situation, Russell took the course of considering both classes and concepts (except the logically uninteresting primitive predicates) as nonexistent and of replacing them by constructions of our own. It cannot be denied that this procedure has led to interesting ideas and to results valuable also for one taking the opposite viewpoint. On the whole, however, the outcome has been that only fragments of Mathematical Logic remain, unless the things condemned are reintroduced in the form of infinite propositions or by such axioms as the axiom of reducibility which (in case of infinitely many individuals) is demonstrably false unless one assumes either the existence of classes or of infinitely many "*qualitates occultae*." This seems to be an indication that one should take a more conservative course, such as would consist in trying to make the meaning of the terms "class" and "concept" clearer, and to set up a consistent theory of classes and concepts as objectively existing entities. This is the course which the actual development of

Mathematical Logic has been taking and which Russell himself has been forced to enter upon in the more constructive parts of his work. Major among the attempts in this direction (some of which have been quoted in this essay) are the simple theory of types (which is the system of the first edition of *Principia* in an appropriate interpretation) and axiomatic set theory, both of which have been successful at least to this extent, that they permit the derivation of modern mathematics and at the same time avoid all known paradoxes. Many symptoms show only too clearly, however, that the primitive concepts need further elucidation.

It seems reasonable to suspect that it is this incomplete understanding of the foundations which is responsible for the fact that Mathematical Logic has up to now remained so far behind the high expectations of Peano and others who (in accordance with Leibniz's claims) had hoped that it would facilitate theoretical mathematics to the same extent as the decimal system of numbers has facilitated numerical computations. For how can one expect to solve mathematical problems sys-tematically by mere analysis of the concepts occurring, if our analysis so far does not even suffice to set up the axioms? But there is no need to give up hope. Leibniz did not in his writings about the *Characteristica universalis* speak of a utopian project; if we are to believe his words he had developed this calculus of reasoning to a large extent, but was waiting with its publication till the seed could fall on fertile ground.[47] He went even so far[48] as to estimate the time which would be necessary for his calculus to be developed by a few select scientists to such an extent "that humanity would have a new kind of an instrument increasing the powers of reason far more than any optical instrument has ever aided the power of vision." The time he names is five years, and he claims that his method is not any more difficult to learn than the mathematics or philosophy of his time. Furthermore, he said repeatedly that, even in the rudimentary state to which he had developed the theory himself, it was responsible for all his mathematical discoveries; which, one should expect, even Poincaré would acknowledge as a sufficient proof of its fecundity.[49]

Notes

1 Frege has doubtless the priority, since his first publication about the subject, which already contains all the essentials, appeared ten years before Peano's.

2 The above quoted passage was left out in the later editions of the *Introduction*.

3 I use the term "signify" in the sequel because it corresponds to the German word "*bedeuten*" which Frege, who first treated the question under consideration, used in this connection.

4 The only further assumptions one would need in order to obtain a rigorous proof would be: 1) that "φ (a)" and the proposition "a is the object which has the property φ and is identical with a" mean the same thing and 2) that every proposition "speaks about something," i.e., can be brought to the form φ (a). Furthermore one would have to use the fact that for any two objects a. b. there exists a true proposition of the form φ (a, b) as, e.g., a ≠ b or a = a. b = b.

5 Cf. "Sinn und Bedeutung," *Zeitschrift für Philosophie und philosophische Kritik*, Vol. 100 (1892), p. 35.

6 From the indication (*Bedeutung*) of a sentence is to be distinguished what Frege called its meaning (*Sinn*) which is the conceptual correlate of the objectively existing fact (or "the True"). This one should expect to be in Russell's theory a possible fact (or rather the possibility of a fact), which would exist also in the case of a false proposition. But Russell, as he says, could never believe that such "curious shadowy" things really exist. Thirdly, there is also the psychological correlate of the fact which is called "signification." "Sentence" in contradistinction to "proposition" is used to denote the mere combination of symbols.

7 He made no explicit statement about the former; but it seems it would hold for the logical system of *Principia*, though perhaps more or less vacuously.

8 In Russell's first paper about the subject: "On Some Difficulties in the Theory of Transfinite Numbers and Order Types," *Proc. London Math. Soc.*, Second Series, Vol. 4, 1906, p. 29. If one wants to bring such paradoxes as "the liar" under this viewpoint, universal (and existential) propositions must be considered to involve the class of objects to which they refer.

9 "Propositional function" (without the clause "as a separate entity") may be understood to mean a proposition in which one or several constituents are designated as arguments. One might think that the pair consisting of the proposition and the argument could then for all purposes play the rôle of the "propositional function as a separate entity," but it is to be noted that this pair (as one entity) is again a set or a concept and therefore need not exist.

10 The intensional paradoxes can be dealt with e.g. by the theory of simple types or the ramified hierarchy, which do not involve any undesirable restrictions if applied to concepts only and not to sets.

11 Cf. "Über eine Widerspruchsfreiheitsfrage in der axiomatischen Mengenlehre," *Journal für reine und angewandte Mathematik*, Vol. 160, 1929, p. 227.

12 Cf. "New Foundations for Mathematical Logic," *Amer. Math. Monthly*, Vol. 44, p. 70.

13 Cf. *Principia Mathematica*, Vol. I, p. 39.

14 Quantifiers are the two symbols ($\exists$ x) and (x) meaning respectively, "there exists an object x" and "for all objects x." The totality of objects x to which they refer is called their range.

15 Cf. *Principia Mathematica*, Vol. I, p. 47, section IV.

16 By the theory of simple types I mean the doctrine which says that the objects of thought (or, in another interpretation, the symbolic expressions) are divided into types, namely: individuals, properties of individuals, relations between individuals, properties of such relations, etc. (with a similar hierarchy for extensions), and that sentences of the form: "a has the property φ," "b bears the relation R to c," etc. are meaningless, if a, b, c, R, φ are not of types fitting together. Mixed types (such as classes containing individuals and classes as elements) and therefore also transfinite types (such as the class of all classes of finite types) are excluded. That the theory of simple types suffices for avoiding also the epistemological paradoxes is shown by a closer analysis of these. (Cf. F. P. Ramsey's paper, quoted in note 20, and A. Tarski, *Der Wahrheitsbegriff in den formalisierten Sprachen, Stud. phil.*, Vol. I, Lemberg, 1935, p. 399.)

17 These are definitions of an object α by reference to a totality to which α itself (and perhaps also things definable only in terms of α) belong. As, e.g., if one defines a class α as the intersection of all classes satisfying a certain condition φ and then concludes that α is a subset also of such classes u as are defined in terms of α (provided they satisfy φ).

18 See Rudolf Carnap in *Erkenntnis*, Vol. 2, p. 103, and *Logical Syntax of Language*, p. 162, and C. H. Langford, *Bulletin American Mathematical Society*, Vol. 33 (1927), p. 599.

19 An object a is said to be described by a propositional function φ (x) if φ (x) is true for x = a and for no other object.

20 Cf. F. P. Ramsey, "The Foundations of Mathematics," in *Proc. London Math Soc.*, Series 2, Vol. 25 (1926), p. 338. (Reprinted in *The Foundations of Mathematics*, New York and London, 1931, p. 1.)

21 I shall use in the sequel "constructivism" as a general term comprising both these standpoints and also such tendencies as are embodied in Russell's "no class" theory.

22 One might think that this conception of notions is impossible, because the sentences into which one translates must also contain notions so that one would get into an infinite regress. This, however, does not preclude the possibility of maintaining the above viewpoint for all the more abstract notions, such as those of the second and higher types, or in fact for all notions except the primitive terms which might be only a very few.

23 I.e., that no two different properties belong to exactly the same things, which, in a sense, is a counterpart to Leibniz's *Principium identitatis indiscernibilium*, which says no two different things have exactly the same properties.

24 Cf. Carnap, *loc. cit.*, note 18 above.

25 Nevertheless the scheme is interesting because it again shows the constructibility of notions which can be meaningfully asserted of notions of arbitrarily high order.

26 See *Erkenntnis*, Vol. 3, p. 367.

27 The formal system corresponding to this view would have, instead of the axiom of reducibility, the rule of substitution for functions described, e.g., in Hilbert-Bernays, *Grundlagen der Mathematik*, Vol. 1 (1934), p. 90, applied to variables of any type, together with certain axioms of intensionality required by the concept of property which, however, would be weaker than Chwistek's. It should be noted that this view does not necessarily imply the existence of concepts which cannot be expressed in the system, if combined with a solution of the paradoxes along the lines indicated on p. 149.

28 Cf. my paper in *Monatshefte für Mathematik und Physik*, Vol. 38 (1931), p. 173, or R. Carnap, *Logical Syntax of Language*, § 35.

29 Ideas tending in this direction are contained in the following papers by D. Mirimanoff: "Les antinomies de Russell et de Buraliforte et le problème fondamental de la théorie des ensembles," *L'Enseignment mathematique*, Vol. 19 (1917), V. 37–52, and "Remarques sur la théorie des ensembles et les antinomies Cantoriennes," *L'Enseignment mathematique*, Vol. 19 (1917), pp. 209–217 and Vol. 21 (1920), pp. 29–52. Cf. in particular Vol. 19, p. 212.

30 Cf. "Les paradoxes de la logique," *Rev. de Metaph. et de Morale*, Vol. 14 (1906), p. 627.

31 In Appendix C of *Principia* a way is sketched by which these also could be constructed by means of certain similarity relations between atomic propositions, so that these latter would be the only ones remaining as real objects.

32 The "data" are to be understood in a relative sense here, i.e., in our case as logic without the assumption of the existence of classes and concepts.

33 Cf. Ramsey, *loc. cit.*, note 20 above.

34 I.e., propositions of the form S(a), R(a,b), etc., where S, R are primitive predicates and a, b individuals.

35 The x_i may, of course, as always, be partly or wholly identical with each other.

36 As to the question how far it is possible to build up the theory of real numbers, presupposing the integers, cf. Hermann Weyl, *Das Kontinuum*, reprinted, 1932.

37 That the variable α is intended to be of undetermined order is seen from the later applications of *89.17 and from the note to *89.17. The main application is in line (2) of the proof of *89.24, where the lemma under consideration is needed for α's of arbitrarily high orders.

38 *Loc. cit.*, cf. note 12 above.

39 Russell formulates a somewhat different principle with the same effect, in *Principia*, Vol. I, p. 95.

40 This objection does not apply to the symbolic interpretation of the theory of types, spoken of earlier, because there one does not have objects but only symbols of different types.

41 A formal system along these lines is Church's (cf. "A Set of Postulates for the Foundation of Logic," *Annals of Mathematics*, Vol. 33 (1932), p. 346 and Vol. 34 (1933), p. 839), where, however, the underlying idea is expressed by the somewhat misleading statement that the law of excluded middle is abandoned. However, this system has been proved to be inconsistent. See note 42.

42 Cf. S. C. Kleene and J. B. Rosser, "The Inconsistency of Certain Formal Logics," *Annals of Math.*, Vol. 36 (1935), p. 630.

43 Because this would imply the existence of a decision-procedure for all arithmetical propositions. Cf. A. M. Turing, *Proc. Lond. Math. Soc.*, Vol. 42 (1936), p. 230.

44 Cf. also F. P. Ramsey, *loc. cit.*, (note 21), where, however, the axiom of infinity cannot be obtained, because it is interpreted to refer to the individuals in the world.

45 The two significations of the term *analytic* might perhaps be distinguished as tautological and analytic.

46 This view does not contradict the opinion defended above that mathematics is based on axioms with a real content, because the very existence of the concept of e.g., "class" constitutes already such an axiom; since, if one defined e.g., "class" and "ε" to be "the concepts satisfying the axioms," one would be unable to prove their existence. "Concept" could perhaps be defined in terms of "proposition" (although I don't think that this would be a natural procedure); but then certain axioms about propositions, justifiable only with reference to the undefined meaning of this term, will have to be assumed. It is to be noted that this view about analyticity makes it again possible that every mathematical proposition could perhaps be reduced to a special case of a = a, namely if the reduction is effected not in virtue of the definitions of the terms occurring, but in virtue of their meaning, which can never be completely expressed in a set of formal rules.

47 *Die philosophischen Schriften von G. W. Leibniz*, herausgegeben von C. J. Gerhardt, Vol. 7 (1890), p. 12. Cf. also G. Vacca, "La logica di Leibniz" (section VII), *Riv. di Mat.*, Vol. 8 (1902–06), p. 72, and the preface in the first volume of the first series of *Leibniz's Sämtliche Briefe und Schriften*, herausgegeben von der Preussischen Akademie der Wissenschaften (1923–).

48 Leibniz, *Philosophische Schriften* (ed. Gerhardt), Vol. 7, p. 187.

49 I wish to express my thanks to Professor Alonzo Church of Princeton University, who helped me to find the correct English expressions in a number of places.

3

Which Logic is the Right Logic?

Leslie H. Tharp

Introduction

It has been generally accepted in the philosophy of mathematics that elementary logic (*EL*), also known as *the predicate calculus*, or *first order logic*, yields a stable and distinguished body of truths, those which are instances of its valid formulas. I am concerned with presenting and examining evidence relevant to such a claim. In sentential logic there is a simple proof that all truth functions, of any number of arguments, are definable from (say) "not" and "and". Thus one has not overlooked any truth-functional connectives, even though one started with the few which naturally presented themselves. Operators such as "for infinitely many x", or for an arbitrary cardinal $\aleph$, "for at least $\aleph$ x", are in some ways analogous to the standard quantifier "for at least one x". If these operators are counted as quantifiers, there are many more such quantifiers than there are formulas of elementary logic; so on rather trivial grounds, there can be no theorem that all possible quantifiers are already definable in *EL*. This observation does not, however, rule out the possibility that there might be a narrower notion of quantifier for which such a theorem holds. If so, and to the extent that the narrower notion is significant, one will have evidence that *EL* is no arbitrary stopping point. I will argue that natural and satisfying criteria are suggested by the standard quantifiers which characterize arbitrary for-

Leslie H. Tharp, Which Logic is the Right Logic?
Synthese, 31 (1975): 1–21.

mulas of elementary monadic logic. The full logic of relations, however, appears to be more problematical.

Background

Whether or not it is a satisfactory picture of interpreted language, we shall retain the analysis which resolves interpreted language into a semantical part (models), a syntactical part (formulas), and the relation of a model satisfying (or being a model of) a formula. We do not contemplate altering the notion of model as it is used in elementary logic. A model still consists of a universe and a finite sequence of relations over the universe (for simplicity we shall ignore constants and functions). What we do contemplate is enriching the set of formulas, and thereby of course extending the satisfaction relation. Let us suppose that the set of formulas of a possible logic is a countably infinite set, and that each formula contains only finitely many letters. Restrictions of effectiveness will be introduced when they are relevant. It hardly needs to be argued that these are reasonable conditions to impose on any potential competitor of elementary logic.

As a concrete example, let us take elementary logic and define a new logic $L(I)$ by adding the symbol (Ix) which is read "for infinitely many x". It is clear how to define the resulting set of formulas, and the corresponding satisfaction relation. This logic extends *EL* in a definite sense, since the class of models satisfying $\neg (Ix) (x = x)$ is just the class of all models with finite universes, which cannot be defined by a formula of EL. (We are taking EL and other logics to contain identity.) We can also characterize the natural numbers with a formula of $L(I)$, since we can say that each number has finitely many predecessors.

These examples suggest a general framework for comparing logics. Without specifying the inner workings of a logic L, we may take it to be a collection of L-classes; each L-class may be thought of as a class of models of the form $\{M: MSat_L \mathscr{A}$ where $\mathscr{A}$ is a (closed) formula of L and Sat_L is the satisfaction relation for L.[1] Then we may say that a logic L_1 is contained in L_2 if every L_1-class is an L_2-class. The relations of equivalence and (proper) extension are then defined in the obvious way from containment. In the previous example EL is contained in $L(I)$, but they are not equivalent, since a certain $L(I)$-class is not an EL-class.

Within this framework one can define, for a given logic L, a notion of logical implication between a set of formulas X and a formula $\mathscr{A}$. X logically implies $\mathscr{A}$ (X1.i. $\mathscr{A}$, for short) in case all models satisfying all members of X satisfy $\mathscr{A}$. This is the concept, going back to Bolzano, which is dealt with by Tarski in "On the Concept of Logical Consequence",[2] and which we take to be a satisfactory formulation of the notion of a formula $\mathscr{A}$ following from X on "purely logical grounds". It should be remarked that our overall concern is basically the problem discussed by Tarski towards the end of his paper: Is there a sharp division of terms into logical and extra-logical?

Elementary logic is *axiomatizable*. That is, there is a proof procedure $\vdash$ such that X 1.i. $\mathscr{A}$ if and only if $X \vdash \mathscr{A}$. The proof procedure is such that a proof can involve only finitely many formulas, so if $X \vdash \mathscr{A}$ then $\Gamma \vdash \mathscr{A}$ of X. That $\vdash$ provides an axiomatization is equivalent to the conjunction of two conditions which are frequently singled out. The first is that $\vdash$ is *complete* in the sense that the formulas which are valid (i.e. true in all models) are exactly those which are provable without hypotheses. In other words, to say $\vdash$ is complete is to say ϕ 1.i. $\mathscr{A}$ if and only if $\phi \vdash \mathscr{A}$. It follows easily from completeness that for finite sets of formulas Γ, Γ 1.i. $\mathscr{A}$ if and only if $\Gamma \vdash \mathscr{A}$. The second condition is *compactness*, which says that if every finite subset of X has a model, then X has a model. Compactness is equivalent to saying that if X 1.i. $\mathscr{A}$ then, for some finite subset Γ of X, Γ 1.i. $\mathscr{A}$. Putting completeness and compactness together, one has axiomatizability. The reader should be warned that we have chosen terminology convenient for our purposes but which is by no means universally adopted. For example, "axiomatizability" is frequently used to mean our completeness.

The notions above were defined for the logic EL, and we wish to formulate them for other logics. Compactness is a purely model-theoretic notion, and, as stated, it clearly makes sense for the most general logics. Completeness can also be defined in a fairly general setting. Identify the formulas with a recursive set of natural numbers and take completeness to mean that the valid formulas are effectively enumerable. Then define a proof procedure $\vdash$ for the logic: $\{\mathscr{B}_1 \ldots, \mathscr{B}_n\} \vdash \mathscr{A}$ in case $\mathscr{B}_1 \to (\mathscr{B}_2 \to \ldots \ldots (\mathscr{B}_n \to \mathscr{A}) \ldots)$ is in the enumeration of valid formulas; for an arbitrary set of formulas X, let $X \vdash \mathscr{A}$ in case $\Gamma \vdash \mathscr{A}$ for some finite Γ included in X. (We are assuming that the logic has effective constructions corresponding to the sentential connectives.) Again in the general case compactness and completeness give axiomatizability: X 1.i $\mathscr{A}$ if and only if $X \vdash \mathscr{A}$.

A very elegant proof of axiomatizability for EL, due to Henkin, shows that every consistent set of formulas has a model. Since in fact the model produced is countable (i.e. finite or countably infinite), one has a further corollary: If X has a model, X has a countable model. This corollary is one version of a well known and somewhat controversial theorem, the Löwenheim–Skolem theorem. As a special case, if a single formula $\mathscr{A}$ has a model, then $\mathscr{A}$ has a countable model. We take this special case[3] and say that a logic L has the Löwenheim–Skolem property if every nonempty L-class has a countable member.

This leads us to the first basic technical result, an intrinsic characterization of elementary logic due to Lindström:[4] Suppose L contains EL and is either complete or compact; then if L has the Löwenheim–Skolem property, L is equivalent to EL. As an example, the logic $L(I)$ mentioned before is easily shown to have the Löwenheim–Skolem property, using the submodel proof of Tarski and Vaught.[5] Thus since $L(I)$ is not equivalent to EL, $L(I)$ is neither complete nor compact. (Of course, to show that $L(I)$ was different from EL we in effect pointed out that it was not compact.) In Lindström's theorem one does have to make a few general assumptions about the logic L. For example the L-classes must be closed under intersection and complement. This of course means that L has the sentential connectives. It is not necessary, however, to assume that L has something like quantification.[6] A few more basic restrictions are needed, e.g., that isomorphic models lie in the same L-classes. Also, for completeness one needs to bring in the obvious stipulations of effectiveness.

What Must a Logic Do?

Lindström's result gives an exceedingly sharp characterization of elementary logic as a maximal solution to certain general conditions. Elementary logic has for many years been taken as the standard logic, with little explicit justification for this role. Since it appears not to go beyond what one would call logic, the problem evidently is whether it can be extended. Thus one is tempted to look to Lindström's theorem for a virtual proof that logic must be identified with elementary logic. The success of this enterprise obviously depends on the extent to which one can justify, as necessary characteristics of logic, the hypotheses needed in the theorem, principally completeness (or compactness) and the Löwenheim–Skolem property.

A complete logic has an effective enumeration of the valid formulas. The proof procedures proposed for elementary logic were clearly *sound* in the sense that they proved only valid formulas. Gödel established completeness by showing that all valid formulas were provable by a standard proof procedure. Second-order logic, which is an extension of *EL* formed by allowing quantification over predicate letters, is a classical example of a logic with sound proof procedures, but which demonstrably admits no complete proof procedure. That is, there is no proof procedure complete with respect to the intended semantics. The standard proof procedures can be shown complete with respect to certain semantics – but such nonstandard semantics have little independent interest.

Soundness would seem to be an essential requirement of a proof procedure, since there is little point in proving formulas which may turn out false under some interpretations. But it is trivial to provide sound proof procedures: take the null procedure, or take some finite set of valid formulas. Of course the proof procedures suggested for logics such as second order logic enumerate an infinite number of valid formulas, and perhaps appear to yield, in some further sense,

a large and useful set of valid formulas; in particular one may incorporate the comprehension schema which says, for each formula $\mathscr{A}(x)$, that there exists the class of those individuals x such that $\mathscr{A}(x)$.

The question is, should one demand that a logic have a complete proof procedure? In order to answer this, it seems essential to be somewhat more precise about the role logic is expected to play. One can distinguish at least two quite different senses of logic.[7] The first is, as an instrument of demonstration, and the second can perhaps be described as an instrument for the characterization of structures. In the present context, a logic L will have this latter ability if, for example, there are L-classes consisting, up to isomorphism, of a single structure of mathematical interest. Second order logic is striking in this respect. Such central theories as number theory and the theory of the real numbers seem to involve in their concepts a quantifier over all subsets of the domain of elements, and in fact they can be characterized up to isomorphism in second order logic. Even rather large portions of set theory can be described categorically by this logic.

Interesting as such a notion of logic is, it seems perfectly reasonable to distinguish the other sense of logic as a theory of deduction.[8] Elementary logic cannot characterize the usual mathematical structures, but rather seems to be distinguished by its completeness. Thus one is inevitably led to ask whether it is a necessary stopping point, or whether it can be extended to a richer logic which is still a theory of deduction in the same sense. Completeness, after all, is not just another nice property of a system. When a deductive system of whatever sort is presented, one of the most immediate questions is whether it is (in the relevant sense) complete. If all valid (or true) formulas can be proven by the rules, then apart from practical limitations such as length and complexity, they can be *known* to be valid (or true). This seems to be as interesting and significant a criterion as one could propose. Until the modern development of logic, it was generally assumed that mathematical systems had this property. One now knows from Gödel's work that the condition is too stringent even for number theory, and it is conceivable that it could have been too stringent for logic. Thus one should not claim to see *a priori* that a logic must be complete in order to be a theory of deduction. The point is rather that when it is discovered that the best known candidate satisfies such a condition, that tends to establish a sense of logic and a standard to be applied to competitors.

Two points concerning completeness should be mentioned. The mere existence of an effective enumeration of the valid formulas does not, by itself, provide knowledge. For example, one might be able to prove that there is an effective enumeration, without being able to specify one. Normally one will exhibit axioms known to be valid and rules known to preserve truth; preferably these axioms and rules will be more or less self-evident. Unfortunately these further conditions do not appear amenable to exact treatment. A second point, frequently noted, is that the completeness proof for *EL* actually shows that a somewhat vague intuitive notion, "valid *EL* formula", coincides with formal provability. It appears from inspection of the axioms and rules that formally provable formulas are intuitively valid; and intuitively valid formulas are certainly true in (say) all arithmetical models. Since the completeness theorem demonstrates that all formulas true in all arithmetical models are provable in *EL*, one must conclude that all three notions coincide in extension.

It is not out of the question that even in a theory of deduction completeness might be sacrificed for other advantages, such as greater expressive power. The strongest example historically is perhaps second order logic. One might claim that this is in some sense an acceptable theory of deduction, since in particular it yields all of the inferences of *EL*. But in fact it is not accepted as the basic logic. The expressive power of this logic, which is too great to admit a proof procedure, is adequate to express set-theoretical statements. Typical open questions, such as the continuum hypothesis or the existence of big cardinals, are easily stated as questions of the validity of second order formulas. Thus the principles of this logic are part of an active and somewhat esoteric area of mathematics. There seems to be a justifiable feeling that this theory should be considered mathematics, and that logic – one's theory of inference – is supposed to be more self-evident and less open.

Of course not all incomplete extensions of *EL* are as strong as second order logic. But the other known examples also tend not to look as natural, and they, like second order logic, invite further extension. In general, if completeness fails there is no algorithm to list the valid formulas; so one can expect many of the principles of the logic to be unknowable, or determinable only by means of *ad*

hoc or inconclusive arguments. Clearly one will hesitate to substitute other desirable features for completeness in a theory of deduction. The negative evidence, together with the epistemological appeal of the completeness condition, make it seem reasonable to suppose that completeness is essential to an important sense of logic.

Strangely, compactness seems to be frequently ignored in discussions of the philosophy of logic. It is strange since the most important theories have infinitely many axioms. With only completeness it seems possible, *a priori*, that a logic might not prove all logical consequences of these theories. Compactness amounts to the condition that if X l.i. $\mathscr{A}$ then Γ l.i. $\mathscr{A}$ for some finite subset Γ of X. Since completeness ensures that if Γ l.i. $\mathscr{A}$ then $\Gamma \vdash \mathscr{A}$, one may conclude that if the system is both compact and complete, all logical consequences of a set of hypotheses are provable. We claim that that is the philosophical point at issue: if something follows, it can be known to follow.

However, the primary question is whether compactness by itself can be given a better justification than was given for completeness, since we are concerned to justify Lindström's hypotheses which require either completeness or compactness (plus the Löwenheim–Skolem condition). It seems to me that it is not all clear that compactness, *per se*, can be defended. The compactness condition in effect states that if $\mathscr{A}$ is implied by an infinite set of assumptions, $\mathscr{A}$ is already implied by a finite subset. The notion of implication here is of course the semantical one, not provability. The condition thus seems to state some weakness of the logic (as if it were futile to add infinitely many hypotheses), without yielding a compensating reward – such as knowledge that $\mathscr{A}$ is implied. To look at it another way, compactness also immediately entails that formalizations of (say) arithmetic will admit non-standard models.

A second question, not strictly relevant to the present purpose, is whether, having accepted completeness, compactness can be seen to be an essential property of a theory of deduction. Perhaps one should first remark that to some extent completeness implies compactness,[9] so in many cases the question is dissolved, if not answered. We have noted that compactness is *sufficient* in conjunction with completeness to yield the desired consequence: if X l.i. $\mathscr{A}$ then $X \vdash \mathscr{A}$. It would appear that if one had a proof procedure of the usual sort the natural further condition to demand would be compactness, in order to get a reduction from an infinite set of hypotheses to a finite subset. The trouble is, it is not quite clear that one need divide the labor in exactly this way. For example, one might have a condition like: if X l.i. $\mathscr{A}$ then $\exists e(W_e \subseteq X$ and W_e l.i. $\mathscr{A})$, where W_e are the recursively enumerable sets (in a standard coding). If one also had an effective method for enumerating the pairs $\langle e, \mathscr{A} \rangle$ such that W_e l.i. $\mathscr{A}$, these two properties would do much the same work as completeness plus compactness. However, it is easy to show that they in fact imply compactness. This is no proof that compactness is necessary, but it seems highly likely that if completeness is required, compactness will be accepted. As for the main point, though, compactness by itself seems much less defensible than completeness.

This leaves the Löwenheim–Skolem property to be considered. On the face of it, this property seems to be undesirable, in that it states a limitation concerning the distinctions the logic is capable of making. Such a logic fails to make those distinctions intended in the usual theories, for example that there are uncountably many reals ("Skolem's paradox"). It is true that completeness also entails a limitation on the power of a logic to discern structures – a complete logic cannot, for example, determine the natural numbers by a single formula. But unlike completeness, the Löwenheim–Skolem condition does not express any clearly desirable property of a theory of deduction. It might follow from some other conditions which express desirable properties; in that case, it would be those conditions which one should attempt to defend. As it happens, it does follow from certain conditions which I shall attempt to justify (The existence of true but unprovable sentences in arithmetic is undesirable; it follows, however, from a defensible condition, namely that the axiom system be effective.)

There are positions, perhaps some kinds of finitism or countabilism, where the Löwenheim–Skolem property is, if not desirable, simply true. Obviously, under the general assumptions we have made, this neatly resolves the question of what logic is. However these positions are not merely minority positions, but positions which ignore, or drastically reinterpret, the overall body of science and mathematics. Further, I doubt whether the arguments that there are only countably many things are very cogent in their own right. I cannot pursue a discussion of these related positions here, but will simply accept mathematics as it exists, and

conclude that there is no *a priori* reason to impose the Löwenheim–Skolem condition on a logic.

Some Complete Competitors

Two examples of axiomatizable logics have been discussed in the literature. The first, call it $L\,(U)$, adds an additional quantifier (Ux), which is read "for uncountably many x". Some time after the logic was known to be axiomatizable, Keisler[10] proved that the following elegant set of axioms is adequate:

0   Axioms of EL.
1   $(\forall x)(\forall y)\neg(Uz)(z = x \lor z = y)$,   "The uncountable is bigger than 2".
2   $(\forall x)(\mathscr{A} \to \mathscr{B}) \to [(Ux)\mathscr{A} \to (Ux)\mathscr{B}]$, "If all $\mathscr{A}$s are $\mathscr{B}$s, and there are uncountably many $\mathscr{A}$s, then there are uncountably many $\mathscr{B}$s."
3   $(Ux)\mathscr{A}(x) \leftrightarrow (Uy)\mathscr{A}(y)$,   "Changing variables".
4   $(Ux)\,(\exists y)\mathscr{A} \to [(\exists y)\,(Ux)\mathscr{A} \lor (Uy)\,(\exists x)\mathscr{A}]$, "If uncountably many things are put into boxes, either some box gets uncountably many members, or else uncountably many boxes are used".

Modus ponens and generalization are the rules of inference. Notice that all of the axioms remain valid if the quantifier "for infinitely many x" is substituted for (Ux). It is easy, however, to show that there are formulas valid under this interpretation which are not valid under the original interpretation. Also note that the axioms do not assert that there are uncountably many things.

By considering the contrapositive of Axiom (4), one sees that it expresses the principle that a countable union of countable sets is countable. This may be considered a weak form of the axiom of choice. Dropping choice, one can give models for Zermelo–Fraenkel set theory in which a countable union of countable sets is uncountable. On the other hand, if one assumes certain forms of the axiom of choice, such as the principle that a countable set of nonempty sets has a choice function, then (4) follows readily.

Since a version of the axiom of choice is expressed by the validity of a formula of $L\,(U)$, if one accepts $L\,(U)$ one accepts this form of the axiom of choice as a principle of logic. This is especially interesting in view of the rather controversial history of this axiom. The objections against it, however, now seem simply mistaken. Probably the main objection was that it was supposed that the choice function had to be given by some law or definition. But since sets are completely arbitrary collections, this requirement is irrelevant. Except for formalists, who regard it as meaningless, set theorists generally regard the axiom of choice as true, and indeed practically obvious. Whether or not it may be taken as a logical principle is another matter – its infinitistic nature might give pause.

The second example, L (C), has the quantifier (Cx), the Chang quantifier:[11] (Cx) $\mathscr{A}(x)$ is satisfied in a model just in case $\{x : \mathscr{A}(x)\text{is satisfied}\}$ has the same cardinality as the universe of the model. This logic, however, is complete and compact only if one rules out finite models. One does not have a simple and explicit axiom system for the Chang quantifier, but there is one for this logic with identity deleted.[12] Curiously, it too assumes a form of the axiom of choice. It would be interesting to know whether there is some deeper connection between axiomatizable extensions of EL and the axiom of choice. It is possible to give rather trivial extensions of EL and prove them complete and compact without using the axiom of choice. Whether this is true for any interesting extensions seems to be an open question.

Recently other examples of axiomatizable logics have been found which serve also to illustrate another generalization of quantifiers. Besides quantifiers of one argument, one might want quantifiers of two arguments. For example (Wx, y) $\mathscr{A}(x, y)$ might mean that $\mathscr{A}(x, y)$ defines a well ordering. This is a useful concept, but like (Ix), it will enable one to characterize arithmetic categorically and so cannot give a complete logic. Shelah[13] has shown that there is a whole category of quantifiers similar to (Wx, y) which give axiomatizable logics. Unfortunately they involve technical notions of set theory: for any regular cardinal λ let $(S^\lambda x, y)$ $\mathscr{A}(x, y)$ mean that $\mathscr{A}(x, y)$ defines a linear ordering of cofinality λ. The quantifiers S^λ give axiomatizable logics, and moreover one can generalize to certain sets of cardinals, and to the quantifiers "confinality less than λ", and still get axiomatizable logics.

One result to hope for is that there might be a maximum logic L, that is, an axiomatizable logic containing all others. This is immediately seen to be impossible since any logic L has only countably many L-classes, while the various logics of Shelah define an unlimited number (i.e. a proper class in

number) of classes of models. More interesting is the observation that our first two examples are incompatible: L (U) and L (C) have no common extension.[14]

One might wonder how these extended logics could or would be used. Consider number theory. An obvious axiom to state using (Ux) is that there are only countably many numbers. Or, using the Chang quantifier, one can say that the set of predecessors of a number is of smaller cardinality than the universe. It seems possible that these axioms might yield new theorems in the original language of number theory, but they do not. The proof is easy for the first axiom, but is not at all trivial for the second.[15] In number theory there is no reason to suppose that all such proposals will yield conservative extensions. However, in set theory it is clear that one will never get new theorems, at least if the axioms of the logic are set theoretical principles. This is because any proof in the strong logic can be translated into an ordinary proof which uses principles of set theory. Although it is conceivable that some logical axiom independent of set theory could be seen to be true, it is probable that it would be clearly a set theoretical principle. Thus extended logics are probably best regarded as changes in the boundary which demarcates as logic a part of set theory.

Can the Competitors Be Rejected?

There is a serious objection against the quantifier "for uncountably many x". One would expect that if this were a legitimate quantifier, the quantifier "for infinitely many x" would also be acceptable; but no complete logic can contain the latter quantifier. Specifically, the cardinal $\aleph_1$ plays a role in the model theory of any complete logic containing the quantifier (Ux) which cannot be played by the smaller cardinal $\aleph_0$. One can say "The universe has cardinality less than $\aleph_1$", but one cannot say "The universe has cardinality less than $\aleph_0$". One cannot even have a formula, using various predicate letters, which is satisfiable exactly in finite universes. The fact that one can say so much more about $\aleph_1$ than $\aleph_0$ seems to me to be a state of affairs sufficiently unnatural to discredit (Ux) as a logical notion.

If the uncountable is no logical notion, a line of argument is suggested which invokes Lindström's theorem. This theorem entails that any complete extension of elementary logic must have something like an "axiom of uncountability", that is, it must have a formula with uncountable models but no countable models. If the uncountable is no logical concept, one is tempted to regard this consequence as a proof that there are no complete logics extending elementary logic. However that would be a mistake. Elementary logic already has "axioms of infinity" in a similar sense. That is, there are formulas with models of all infinite cardinalities but with no finite models, even though "infinite" is not a logical concept in the sense of there being a quantifier expressing "for infinitely many x".

Being able to distinguish the uncountable by means of axioms of uncountability is evidently a much weaker property than having a quantifier "for uncountably many x". Further, if one allows even weaker criteria, elementary logic is already able to distinguish the uncountable from the countable. Call a theory with infinite models categorical in the cardinal $\aleph$ if all models of cardinality $\aleph$ are isomorphic. It is known that there also theories categorical in $\aleph_0$ but in no uncountable cardinal. There are also theories categorical in all uncountable cardinals but not in $\aleph_0$; theories categorical in all infinite cardinals; and theories categorical in no infinite cardinals. Morley's theorem demonstrates that for infinite cardinals, these are the only possible categories. In this sense, elementary logic cannot distinguish two uncountable cardinals, although it can distinguish the countably infinite from the uncountably infinite.

From this extensional viewpoint, Shelah's quantifier "cofinality ω" fares considerably better than the quantifier (Ux). One has axioms of uncountability in precisely the same sense one has axioms of infinity, namely formulas with predicate letters satisfiable in, and only in, the uncountable universes. Other gross properties seem reasonable also: just as one cannot have formulas satisfiable exactly in finite universes, this logic has no formulas satisfiable exactly in countable universes. The obvious objection against the Shelah logic is that one would never have supposed that a technical notion like cofinality was a logical concept. Unless it could be shown equivalent to some more palatable notion, this must remain a serious objection.

Continuity of the Standard Quantifiers

If one considers, instead of the entire logic EL, the standard quantifiers, it would appear that there must be some sense in which $\forall$ and $\exists$ are very simple and primitive. It may be possible to state some natural condition which expresses this simplicity, and which, at the same time, rules out quantifiers one feels are no part of logic. To start with, $\forall$ and $\exists$ may be regarded as extrapolations of the truth functional connectives $\land$ and $\lor$ to infinite domains. To see how one can make such extrapolations, take the infinite list of sentential letters $P_0, P_1, P_2, \ldots$, and suppose one is given an arbitrary truth assignment t, that is, a function which assigns a truth value $t(P_i)$ to each letter P_i. By the truth table rules, t may be extended to assign a value $t(\mathscr{A})$ to each formula $\mathscr{A}$ of sentential logic.

Consider, for increasing n, the values $t(P_0 \land P_1 \land \ldots \land P_n)$ assigned to the finite conjunctions. One sees at once that no matter what assignment t is, the limit $\lim n \to \infty \, t(P_0 \land P_1 \land \ldots \land P_n)$ has a clear value: there is a finite point N such that the conjunction $(P_0 \land P_1 \land \ldots \land P_N)$ is assigned a value $t(P_0 \land P_1 \land \ldots \land P_N)$, and for all m greater than N, $t(P_0 \land P_1 \land \ldots \land P_m)$ is the same as $t(P_0 \land P_1 \land \ldots \land P_N)$. It is easily seen that exactly the same property is true of finite disjunctions.

Compare another familiar binary connective, the biconditional $\leftrightarrow$. It is also commutative and associative so that parentheses may be dropped, and $(P_0 \leftrightarrow P_1 \leftrightarrow \ldots \leftrightarrow P_n)$ considered to be a formula. However, in this case there is no evident limit of the values $t(P_0 \leftrightarrow P_1 \leftrightarrow \ldots \leftrightarrow P_n)$ as n increases. This is not merely due to the unfamiliarity of the construction. If, for example, $t(P_i)$ is $\perp$ (falsehood) for all i, then the value of $t(P_0 \leftrightarrow P_1 \leftrightarrow \ldots \leftrightarrow P_n)$ is $\top$ for n even, and $\perp$ for n odd. There is simply no well-defined limit value to be used for an infinite quantification.

These considerations can be restated in the language of quantifiers and predicates. Suppose a model M is given which interprets a one-place letter F. In each finite submodel $\mathcal{J}$ with universe $\{a_0, \ldots, a_n\}$, $\forall x F(x)$ has a truth value, the same value as $(F(a_0) \land F(a_1) \land \ldots \land F(a_n))$ has in $\mathcal{J}$. $\forall$ is continuous in the sense that for each model M there is a finite submodel $\mathcal{J}$, in which $\forall x F(x)$ takes a truth value and holds that truth value for all submodels K between $\mathcal{J}$ and M, including M. Thus if one thinks of the model M as being revealed step by step, there is a finite portion at which $\forall x F(x)$ assumes a truth value, and holds that truth value no matter how much the model is further revealed, and even if it is totally revealed.

This is the continuity condition we wish to isolate, and of course the quantifier $\exists$, as well as

$\forall$, is continuous in this sense. However if (Qx) is any quantifier such that $(Qx)F(x)$ agrees with $(F(a_0) \leftrightarrow F(a_1) \leftrightarrow \ldots \leftrightarrow\leftrightarrow F(a_n))$ in models with universe $\{a_0, a_1, \ldots, a_n\}$, then (Qx) must exhibit a sort of discontinuity: For certain M, $(Qx)\ F(x)$ will oscillate back and forth in truth value as one considers larger and larger finite submodels, and the value of $(Qx)\ F(x)$ in infinite models will be no direct extrapolation of its value in finite submodels. It should be noted in passing that there is another possible kind of discontinuity which occurs, for example, with the quantifier "for infinitely many x". Since $(Ix)\ (x = x)$ comes out false in all finite models, it has a definite limiting value – the trouble is that its value in an infinite model is not equal to this limit.

We have exhibited a type of continuity for the basic quantifiers $\forall$ and $\exists$ in terms of the behavior of the formulas $\forall x F(x)$ and $\exists x F(x)$, where F is any one-place letter. Not only are the basic quantifiers continuous, but every formula of elementary monadic logic, which is the subsystem of EL using one-place relations, is continuous in this sense. Moreover one has an exact converse: Given any quantifier[16] of monadic type, if it is continuous in the sense sketched above, it is definable in elementary monadic logic.

It is clear that the standard quantifiers can be *tested* for truth in certain ways. Let us examine more closely the exact sense in which $\exists$ has operational meaning. Suppose one has an intuitively decidable one-place predicate F, interpreted (say) as "is a frog". One wants to determine the truth of $\exists x F(x)$ in the standard model – the actual world. One proceeds along, examining specimens, and at some finite point one reaches a portion of the model in which $\exists x F(x)$ comes out true; and at that point one knows that it is true in the whole model no matter what the rest of the model is like. (We are assuming, for purposes of the example, that the world is infinite.) It is easy to formulate this criterion precisely and show that any such quantifier is continuous.[17]

This test does not work for $\forall$; instead, if $\forall x F(x)$ is ultimately false, its falsehood can be known at a finite point. Another way to put it is that one has only half a test for $\exists$: if $\exists x F(x)$ is true, one can actually find it out in finitely many steps; but if $\exists x F(x)$ is false, one may never be sure, short of exhausting the entire model. One might consider the stronger demand that the correct truth value always be ascertainable at a finite point, even though $\forall$ and $\exists$ do not satisfy such a stringent

condition. But it is easy to show that only trivial quantifiers result.

In summary, those quantifiers which are partially decidable in the same sense as $\exists$ are all continuous; their complements are the quantifiers partially decidable in the same sense as $\forall$, and are also continuous. The notion of continuous quantifier seems to be the most natural symmetrical condition containing both $\forall$ and $\exists$. We have remarked that any continuous *monadic* quantifier is definable in elementary monadic logic, hence in EL. For non-monadic continuous quantifiers, however, one must appeal to completeness of the resulting logic to conclude that they are definable in EL. In fact, one can give binary quantifiers which are partially decidable in the same sense as $\exists$, but which give incomplete logics. It would seem, in conclusion, that the major properties of the standard quantifiers of epistemic significance can be precisely captured, and any such quantifier shown to be definable in EL, invoking completeness only for non-monadic quantifiers.[18]

What about Complex Formulas?

One sees at once that no such simple criteria as continuity apply to an arbitrary formula of the full elementary logic of relations. For example, there is a formula $\mathscr{A}$, with a single binary letter G, which says G is a linear ordering without last element. $\mathscr{A}$ has only infinite models, so given a model M of $\mathscr{A}$, $\mathscr{A}$ must be false in each finite submodel of M. One can also exhibit other kinds of discontinuity: There is a formula $\mathscr{B}$ which says that G is a function mapping part of the universe one-one onto the remainder; $\mathscr{B}$ has infinite models, and for any such model N, $\mathscr{B}$ will be true in some finite submodels, and false in others.

Continuity does not apply to arbitrary complex formulas of EL, and the best one can say is that a complete logic based on continuous quanti fiers does not extend EL. Whether this formulation is good enough is open to question. How does one, for example, know that a given logic can be defined by adjoining quantifiers to EL? Put this way, the question does not pose a problem. We have taken a quantifier to be an arbitrary class of models of a fixed type, closed under isomorphism of models, which amounts to saying that a totally arbitrary formula can be taken to be a quantifier (see note 18). The assumption that the logic be based on quantifiers seems to involve no great restriction, for, given a logic L, one can take each formula of L as a quantifier and adjoin it to EL, getting $L*$. Trivially, $L \subseteq L*$, and it is reasonable to suppose $L = L*$, because otherwise L would not be closed under the familiar constructions with connectives and the iteration of quantifiers.

The problem, then, is not that it is unreasonable to assume a given logic L is constructed by adjoining quantifiers to EL. Rather, the problem is to give some intrinsic justification for the particular method by which complex formulas are built up from the primitives. That is, suppose one is presented with a logic L, defined by adjoining quantifiers to EL, but which cannot be defined by the adjunction of continuous quantifiers to EL. How does one know that there might not be some other acceptable way of generating the logic from simple quantifiers? Second order logic is in a sense generated from the standard quantifiers – but one applies them to predicate letters as well as to individual variables.

Complex formulas with relations no longer have the operational simplicity of the basic quantifiers, or the finitistic nature of monadic formulas. Thus it is not easy to see a suitable criterion to apply directly to arbitrary formulas. And, in the absence of such a criterion, it is not easy to predict what primitives and operations might have a clear enough meaning to be used in constructing a logic.

These seem to me to be serious objections which pinpoint the weakness in this argument for the primacy of EL. I do not know how to overcome them, nor am I confident that there is a completely watertight argument for EL. Everything considered, I think it must be conceded that the considerations which gave a rather satisfactory characterization of elementary monadic logic do not provide a comparably definitive characterization of the full logic. But they do, I believe, give some insight into the reasons EL has been taken as standard, and the reasons it appears natural and primitive in comparison with the known extensions.

Logic and Ontology

The reasons for taking elementary logic as standard evidently have to do also with certain imprecise – but I think *vital* – criteria, such as the fact that it easily codifies many inferences of ordinary language and of informal mathematics, and the fact that stronger quantifiers can be fruitfully analyzed

in set theory, a theory of EL. It is not surprising that in practice elementary logic has been taken as logic. Yet the criteria which justify this choice do not justify the use to which elementary logic is frequently put. It should be recalled that a tremendous amount of weight has been thrown on the alleged distinction between logic (i.e. elementary logic) and mathematics. Perhaps the most extreme example is Skolem,[19] who deduces from the Löwenheim–Skolem theorem that "the absolutist conceptions of Cantor's theory" are "illusory". I think it clear that this conclusion would not follow even if elementary logic were in some sense the true logic, as Skolem tacitly assumed. From the absolutist standpoint, elementary logic is not able to preserve in the new structure all significant features of the initial structure. For example, the power set of ω is intended to contain *all* sets of integers. It should also be noted that one has a similar problem for ordinary number theory, and even for certain weak decidable subtheories of number theory: there are nonstandard models, countable as well as uncountable.

Elementary logic has also been invoked in connection with ontology by Quine, who has argued that one is to look to the range of the quantifiers to uncover one's ontological commitments. There are difficulties in interpreting this prescription which we shall not dwell on here, but at a very basic level one can question his doctrine by proposing different logics. One challenge he considers[20] is a logic due to Henkin, which has formulas with "branching quantifiers" such as $\genfrac{}{}{0pt}{}{\forall u \exists v}{\forall x \exists y} F(u, v, x, y)$, which is to be interpreted, using Skolem functions, as $\exists f \exists g \forall u \forall x F(u, fu, x, gx)$. This looks very much like the Skolem form of a formula of EL, the difference being that v is a function of u alone, and y is a function of x alone. To express such a formula in EL one naturally quantifies over functions. Thus such a formula as $\genfrac{}{}{0pt}{}{\forall u \exists v}{\forall x \exists y} F(u, v, x, y)$ appears to blur the distinction between those objects which are quantified over, and those which are not. Quine rejects the Henkin logic primarily[21] because it is not complete (it turns out, surprisingly, that in it one can express the quantifier "for infinitely many x"). But we have a number of "deviant" logics which are axiomatizable and allow us to do exactly this sort of thing: we can say that there are countably many helium atoms without quantifying over anything except physical objects. Quine does concede that some extensions of EL are complete, and mentions the example of a logic which adds finitely many valid formulas. However, no indication is given how the complete extensions of *EL* are to be ruled out.

To go to another extreme, one can formulate *EL* with modus ponens as the sole rule of inference. By means of a simple translation one may consider *EL*, and theories based on it, to be theories in *sentential* logic. Sentential logic certainly has many attractive technical properties to recommend it. And perhaps one's ontological commitment would be to the two truth values.

This is clearly an implausible suggestion, and it is not hard to see why. Evidently our conceptual scheme is such that we think of the world in terms of objects and relations. Sentential logic deals with whole sentences and, unlike *EL*, suppresses this prior analysis and *prior commitment*. Of course *EL* has quantifiers as well as individual variables and relation letters. The particular choice of quantifiers must be explained, and we have attempted to give illuminating reasons why the standard quantifiers are singularly primitive. One can consider stronger quantifiers, but one does not have as clear a grasp of their meaning, and they usually seem to demand further explanation.

This is not to claim that it is impossible to operate with certain quantifiers, such as "for infinitely many *x*", or equivalently, "for finitely many *x*". It is true that in this case the resulting logic is not complete and invites further extension. These are good reasons to conclude that the logic is not as satisfactory as *EL*, but they do not seem to bear on the ontological issue. Perhaps one could understand "for finitely many *x*" in some intuitive sense as a primitive notion and work quite well within this logic. Many of the rules would be sufficiently clear – for example if $\mathscr{A}(x)$ and $\mathscr{B}(x)$ are each true of finitely many *x*, so are $(\mathscr{A}(x) \wedge \mathscr{B}(x))$ and $(\mathscr{A}(x) \vee \mathscr{B}(x))$. The user of this logic might not have in mind any particular analysis of "finite". If so, it would seem incorrect to attribute to him some such analysis in terms of an ontology of sets, or of numbers and functions. Which of several possible analyses should be attributed to him?

It may even be fair to say that mathematicians in effect used such quantifiers before the development of set theory. Since Cantor and Dedekind, one has a reasonably clear and quite general theory of "finite", "infinite", and related notions. In view of the existence of such a general theory, there is little point in taking notions such as "finite" as primitive. The conceptual scheme of set theory deals with objects (sets), relations (membership and identity), and uses the standard quantifiers. Formulas of *EL* directly codify this scheme, and, so interpreted, they reflect ontological assumptions correctly. But to appeal to criteria such as completeness to justify the logic, and then mechanically use the logic to "assess a theory's ontological demands", seems to stand the matter on its head. It also leads, via the Löwenheim–Skolem theorem, to pointless puzzles about ontological reduction. These, however, have been discussed at length elsewhere.[22]

Notes

I am heavily indebted to Jonathan Lear, D. A. Martin and Hao Wang with whom I discussed many of these matters. I also wish to express thanks to a number of other colleagues and students who contributed valuable criticism and comments.

1 An *L*-class has models of a fixed finite type, e.g., with one binary and four ternary relations.

2 See A. Tarski, *Logic, Semantics, Metamathematics*, Clarendon Press, Oxford, 1956, pp. 409–20.

3 For monadic logics it does matter whether one assumes the Löwenheim–Skolem property for single formulas or for infinite sets of formulas. See my paper, "The Characterization of Monadic Logic", *The Journal of Symbolic Logic* 38 (1973), 481–8.

4 See Per Lindström "On Extensions of Elementary Logic", *Theoria* 35 (1969), 1–11. It should be noted that Harvey Friedman later rediscovered these theorems and pointed out their philosophical interest.

5 See "Arithmetical Extensions of Relational Systems", *Compositio Mathematica* 13 (1957), 81–102.

6 Something like quantification is used with regard to the "upward Löwenheim–Skolem property" (Theorem 3) and in Corollary 2 of Lindström's paper cited above.

7 D. A. Martin has emphasized this distinction to me. Of course there are other senses of logic, for example, as "a science prior to all others, which contains the ideas and principles underlying all sciences". See Kurt Gödel, "Russell's Mathematical Logic", in *Philosophy of Mathematics*, Benacerraf and Putnam (eds.), Prentice-Hall, Englewood Cliffs, N.J., 1964, p. 211.

8 I concentrate only on certain gross features of a theory of deduction. This is not to deny that finer structure – the particular rules of inference and axioms – may be highly important.

9 Lindström has shown in unpublished work that for a wide class of logics, if the logic is complete it is compact for recursively enumerable sets of formulas. The result holds for logics using finitely many "generalized quantifiers". Lindström's "First Order Predicate Logic with Generalized Quantifiers" (*Theoria* 32 (1966), 186–95) discusses such quantifiers; see also note 17 below.

10 See H. J. Keisler, "Logic with the Quantifier 'There Exist Uncountably Many'", *Annals of Mathematical Logic* 1 (1970), 1–93. This logic is *countably* compact; this is the sense in which we are using "compact", since sets of formulas are taken to be countable.

11 Named after C. C. Chang. It is sometimes called the "equicardinal quantifier", but this suggests the quantifier (Qx) which operates on a pair of formulas, $(Qx) [\mathscr{A} (x); \mathscr{B} (x)]$ being true in M just in case $\mathscr{A} (x)$ and $\mathscr{B} (x)$ are true of the same number of things in M. Although similar to (Cx), this quantifier is too strong to be axiomatizable. This follows because one can say, "G is a linear ordering with no last element, and any two distinct points have a distinct number of predecessors". This formula characterizes the ordering of the natural numbers.

12 See Bell and Slomson, *Models and Ultraproducts*, North-Holland, Amsterdam, 1969, p. 283.

13 Personal communication. These results are related to his "On Models with Power-Like Orderings", *The Journal of Symbolic Logic* 37 (1972), 247–67.

14 To prove $L(U)$ and $L(C)$ have no common extension, consider the formula which says "G is a linear ordering with no last element and $(\forall x)\neg(Cy)$ $G(y, x)$". The only countable model of this formula is isomorphic to $\langle\omega, \langle\rangle$. Since one can say "the universe is countable" in $L(U)$, any logic containing $L(C)$ and $L(U)$ characterizes $\langle\omega, \langle\rangle$. Martin pointed out that one can modify the quantifier C to a quantifier C' which is C in universes of cardinality $\leq \aleph_1$, and is $\forall$ in larger universes. The generalized continuum hypothesis was used to prove only special cases of the axiomatizability of C, and it turns out it is not needed for C'. Also C' is axiomatizable without restriction to infinite models. Our argument above still holds for $L(U)$ and $L(C')$.

15 See Bell and Slomson, *op. cit.*, pp. 284–5.

16 A *type* is a finite sequence of predicate letters; a *monadic* type has only monadic letters. A *quantifier* $\mathscr{Q}$ is a class of models of some fixed type, such that if $M \in \mathscr{Q}$ and N is isomorphic to M, then $N \in \mathscr{Q}$. For example, suppose $\mathscr{Q}$ is the class of models of type $\langle G \rangle$, where G is binary and is interpreted in the model as a well-ordering of the universe. One adjoins this $\mathscr{Q}$ to EL by introducing a symbol Q, and adding to the definition of formula the clause: $Q_i, v_j \mathscr{A}(v_i, v_j)$ is a formula if $\mathscr{A}(v_i, v_j)$ is. $M \models Q v_i, v_j \mathscr{A}(v_i, v_j)$ is defined to mean $M* \in \mathscr{Q}$ where the universe of $M*$ is the universe of M, and the binary relation of $M*$ is $\{\langle x_i, x_j\rangle : M \models \mathscr{A}(x_i, x_j)\}$. Thus $M \models Q v_i, v_j \ \mathscr{A}(v_i, v_j)$ just in case $\mathscr{A}(v_i, v_j)$ defines a well ordering over the universe of M; this Q is just the quantifier W mentioned in passing in Section 3. For further discussion see my "Continuity and Elementary Logic", *The Journal of Symbolic Logic* 39 (1974), 700–16.

17 Let $\mathscr{P}$ be a class of finite models satisfying: if $M \in \mathscr{P}$ and N is isomorphic to M then $N \in \mathscr{P}$. A continuous quantifier $\mathscr{Q}$ is defined by: $M \in \mathscr{Q} \Leftrightarrow (\exists \mathscr{J})[\mathscr{J} \subseteq M \wedge \mathscr{J} \in \mathscr{P}]$. To bring in considerations of effectiveness, encode each finite model $\mathscr{J}$ with universe $\{0, 1, \ldots, n\}$ as a number $\# (\mathscr{J})$. Given a recursive set R, define $\mathscr{P} = \{K : (\exists \mathscr{J}) [K$ is isomorphic to $\mathscr{J}$ and $\# (\mathscr{J}) \in R]\}$, and define $\mathscr{Q}$ as above. Then given a model M, suppose that one examines finite submodels K, checking whether there is an isomorphic $\mathscr{J}$ with $\#(\mathscr{J})$ in R. M is in $\mathscr{Q}$ if and only if this procedure eventually leads to a positive answer. Conversely, any quantifier which is partially decidable in the same sense as $\exists$ appears to fall under this definition, for suitably chosen recursive R.

18 A logic based on continuous quantifiers satisfies the Löwenheim–Skolem condition, so if it is complete, it is *EL*. Note that if one demands a uniform finite bound (uniform continuity) one need not invoke completeness. See especially theorems 2, 4, 5 and 7 of my paper cited in note 17.

19 See p. 47 of Thoralf Skolem, *Abstract Set Theory* (Notre Dame Mathematical Lectures No. 8, Notre Dame, 1962).

20 See pp. 89–91 of W. V. Quine, *Philosophy of Logic*, Prentice-Hall, Englewood Cliffs, N.J., 1970.

21 However, in an earlier paper Quine also notes that a certain typical construction which one would formulate with the Henkin quantifier "is not after all very ordinary language; its grammar is doubtful". See p. 112 of "Existence and Quantification", in *Ontological Relativity and Other Essays*, Columbia University Press, New York, 1969.

22 See my "Ontological Reduction", *The Journal of Philosophy* 68 (1971), 151–64.

What Can Logic Do for Philosophy?

Karl Popper

The aim of this chapter is to show, with the help of a few examples, that certain very simple logical considerations can throw some light upon philosophical problems, including some of the traditional problems of metaphysics and theology. One of my main points will be to establish by way of these examples, that there are such things as philosophical problems – not only pseudo-problems. Another point will be that we may apply to them simple methods of logical analysis which have little or nothing to do with an analysis in terms of our elementary experiences (sense-data, perceptions, or what not) or with an analysis of the meaning of words. The methods I have in mind are, rather, those of constructing, or analysing, or criticizing, arguments, and ways of approaching the problem.

One of my main difficulties in preparing this paper was that of selecting my examples, that is, of selecting philosophical problems; especially in view of the fact that the most obvious and important source of examples – the philosophy of language – is one which is to be discussed in another symposium, and therefore better left aside. I have tried hard to select examples which I think are both representative and interesting; but I fear that I have not quite succeeded. I thought, further, that since in a short paper like this it is impossible to go very deeply into

Karl Popper, What Can Logic Do for Philosophy?
Logical Positivism and Ethics. The Symposia Read at
the Joint Session of the Aristotelian Society and the
Mind Association at Durham, July 9–11, 1948.
London: Harrison and Sons, 1948. 141–54.

the analysis of any one problem, it will be better to select a number from various representative fields, including what is usually called metaphysics and ethics, and to be frankly sketchy. On the other hand, I have tried to introduce at least some slight degree of coherence into my somewhat mixed collection of problems which ranges from the problem of the existence of philosophy and the problems of causality and determinism to those of the role of experience in ethics.

1

Let us begin with a brief discussion of an extremely general philosophical problem – the much discussed question whether there is anything which may be called "philosophy."

I have always felt much sympathy with Kant, the positivists and all others who, repelled by the extravagant claims of some philosophical system builders, began to doubt whether there was anything at all in philosophy. I have only admiration for those who reacted against apriorism – the attitude of possessing, if not all fundamental knowledge, at least the key to it – and against empty verbalism. But it is interesting to observe the fate of these brave fighters against apriorism and against verbalism.

The positivists who were mainly anti-apriorists, that is to say, those who believed that there is no room for a third realm of studies besides the empirical sciences on the one hand and knowledge of logic and mathematics on the other, found themselves nearly immediately in difficulties when asked to give a criterion of empirical knowledge. Their answers were, very often, naive and mistaken. But this is not my main point here. What was so striking was what I may call a strong aprioristic character of their answers. Their attempts to characterise empirical knowledge led them to the construction of fairly complicated philosophical systems, such as the sense-data theories or phenomenalism – systems which were perhaps not so very different from those against which they originally reacted. And these systems, in spite of paying lip-service to anti-apriorism, took up more and more the strange character of the old aprioristic systems; one felt quite clearly that their defenders had an axe to grind, and that they were much more interested in this philosophical axe-grinding than in learning from experience.

A similar fate befell those positivists who reacted not so much against philosophical apriorism but rather against philosophical verbalism. To them, philosophy was "mere words" – meaningless verbiage. But when confronted with the task to explain the criterion of meaningful language, as opposed to meaningless verbiage, they got into very serious difficulties, proposing, for example, criteria in terms which turned out to be themselves meaningless. They discovered that they had started from a naive philosophy of language; and they were soon surrounded by difficulties which they found practically unsurmountable. To these difficulties they reacted by giving up arguing about problems; instead, these philosophers, who had started by denouncing philosophy as merely verbal, and who had demanded that, instead of attempting to solve them, we should turn away from the verbal problems to those which are real and empirical, found themselves bogged up in the thankless and apparently endless task of analysing and unmasking verbal pseudo problems.

This is how I see the recent history of a movement with which I thoroughly sympathise, as far as its starting points are concerned – the revolt against apriorism and philosophical verbiage. It has shown, I believe, that there exist, at the very least, two kinds of philosophical problems – the philosophy of the empirical sciences, which tries to analyse what makes the empirical sciences empirical, and the philosophy of language, including the theory of meaning.

But where does logic come in here?

The parallelism in the fate of the two revolts, against apriorism and against verbiage, does not seem to be accidental. And I believe that the development could have been, to a certain extent, foreseen. The reason is that an assertion like "there cannot exist statements besides those of the natural sciences and of logic," is very similar to the paradox of the liar, since it is certainly no statement of the natural sciences, and hardly one of logic (since it is about logic). Thus one way in which logic, and especially the analysis of paradoxes, might help us is by warning us against such sweeping aprioristic assertions and positions, and by making us a little more modest.

2

But does this mean that there must be a "science of philosophy" or a philosophical system? I do not know, and I think rather not.

I believe that most of us think too much in terms of subject-matters or disciplines – physics, chemistry, biology, etc. Admittedly, we have in some of these unified theoretical systems. But these may or may not be found. In any case, we find them in our attempts, not so much to build up a coherent "body of knowledge" (a particularly silly expression), but to solve certain definite problems. Our subject matters or disciplines or "bodies of knowledge" are, I think, largely didactic devices designed to help in the organisation of teaching. The scientist – the man who does not only teach but adds to our knowledge – is, I believe, fundamentally a *student of problems*, not of subject matters.

Now problems often cut through all these subject matters. A problem of neuro-physiology, for example, may need, for its solution, bits from practically all the sciences known to us. And the fact that it needs mathematics, for its solution does not make it a mathematical problem or one of physics.

From this point of view, there is no particular difficulty in admitting the existence of philosophical problems. They may turn up in all sorts of contexts, and may need all sorts of considerations – empirical, logical, mathematical – for their solution. They can be called "philosophical" either because of certain historical associations, or because of the fact that they are of a *second-storey character* – connected with questions *about* science, or *about* mathematics, or *about* art, etc.

There seems to be *one* great difficulty to this view, from the point of view of those anti-aprioristic tendencies which I share: how do we *test* an answer to a philosophical problem? An answer to a scientific problem, it seems, can be tested by experience; but what about the status of an answer which is neither purely logical nor testable by empirical science?

The proper reply to this is, I suppose, on the following lines: philosophical answers must always remain tentative. There is no reason, it seems, why we should reach agreement on them. But this is no reason to deny the existence of philosophical problems. It is an aprioristic dogma (held by some positivists) that only such problems are real problems to which we can ("in principle") find a definite, established answer. This dogma must be given up. Even in the empirical sciences, our answers are, as a rule, tentative. They have in the past often changed, and we cannot know whether in future they will not continue to do so. Admittedly, the situation in philosophy is worse, owing to the absence of empirical tests, and those who find this situation distressing should better turn to some other field. Nevertheless, we sometimes make some progress – for example, we may discover that some progress – for example, we may discover that some proposed theory does not really answer the question which it is supposed to answer. This may not be much of a success, but it is something; and it is the kind of thing which is achieved, mainly, with the help of logic.

3

I shall turn to the philosophy of philosophy at the end of this paper. Meanwhile I intended to discuss a series of slightly more concrete problems; and I take as my first example the problem of *causality*, because it is an example of a problem where logical analysis can help us even in a mildly constructive way.

In this section, I shall sketch[1] an analysis of what may be called the logical mechanism of causal explanation; and I shall apply the analysis to some questions raised by Hume, and by some theists.

A scientific explanation of a certain singular event E (i.e. an event that happens in a certain place at a certain time) always consists of a number of statements from which a singular statement e, describing the event E, can be deduced. These premises or explanatory statements are of two kinds, universal statements u (or laws), and singu-

lar statements i which state what may be called the initial conditions.

In other words, an explanation of an event E consists of a deductive inference,

$$\frac{\begin{array}{c} u \\ i \end{array}}{e}$$

in which from universal laws u and initial conditions i the statement e describing the event E (which is to be explained) is deduced.

Trivial premises are, of course, often taken for granted, or "suppressed."

In order that the explanation should be acceptable or satisfactory, the statements u and i must be well tested (*independently* of the event E in question; see below).

In the natural sciences, we usually do not use any longer the vague terms "cause" and "effect"; but I shall now show that the logical mechanism just analysed can be interpreted as covering what may be called a "causal explanation," and that what is usually called "cause" is described, in a causal explanation, by the initial conditions i, and the "effect" by e.

Take, as an example, that the event E which we wish to explain causally is the death of Mr. X. Somebody may suggest that the cause of his death is that he took a spoonful of potassium cyanide; and if we can find evidence that he did, we shall accept this as "cause" of his death. But why? We may also find that he ate, immediately before, a bar of chocolate. Why do we say that his taking potassium cyanide caused his death rather than his taking chocolate? Obviously because we assume the truth of the universal law that everybody who takes a spoonful of potassium cyanide dies at once, while we do not believe that a corresponding law holds for bars of chocolate. In other words, we accept the suggested cause only because we believe in the truth of a certain universal law u ("Everybody who takes a spoonful of potassium cyanide dies at once"), which, together with the description of the cause, i.e., with the initial condition i ("Mr. X took a spoonful of potassium cyanide"), allows us to deduce the statement e ("Mr. X died") which describes the effect which is to be explained.

A fairly important point in our analysis is that we must have good evidence in favour of u and i, *independently* of the fact that e is true; that is to say, u and i must be well tested, and we must not count the fact that X died after taking potassium cyanide as evidence in favour of *u*, nor the fact that *u* and *e* are established as evidence in favour of *i*.

I do not, of course, believe that this simple analysis is exhaustive. Undoubtedly there are cases which conform to our analysis but which we should hesitate to call causal explanations. For example, the famous syllogism "All men are mortal. Socrates is a man. Socrates is mortal" conforms to our scheme. Nevertheless, it is certainly a bit awkward to say that the fact that Socrates is a man is the cause of his being mortal. And we should be even more reluctant to call a certain day the cause of the following night, even though we believe in the truth of the universal law which allows us to deduce (or predict) the arrival of the particular night in question from the statement that it was daytime. I believe that it is possible to augment our analysis in such a way as to allow for the difference between such cases of deductive explanations or predictions and the other cases which we may feel inclined to accept as truly causal explanations. But I shall not go into this matter here. For our present purposes it is sufficient to note that all causal explanations fall under our scheme, even though other things may fall under our scheme as well. In fact, all that we need at present is this:

If anybody says that a certain singular event *I* is the cause of a certain singular event *E*, then he tacitly assumes that there is an independently testable universal law *u* such that from *u* and *i* (i.e. the statement describing *I*) we can deduce *e* (the statement describing *e*). Or more briefly, to say that *I* is the cause of *E* is to assume the truth of a universal law *u* such that, in its presence, *e* follows from *i*.

To be sure, in most cases of ordinary experience, *u* is "suppressed," that is to say, *u* is taken to be so trivial that we do not mention it. For example, if we say that my holding a match to it was the cause of this fire's beginning to burn, or when we say that the cause of the death of Charles I was that his head had been cut off, then we are, as a rule, not conscious of the fact that we assumed, in each case, the truth of a universal law. But if we had reason to believe that people whose heads had been cut off usually are the better for this operation, then we certainly should not accept the explanation which historians offer for the death of Charles I.

All this is very trivial; but it can throw some light on well known philosophical problems.

Let us first take Hume's problem whether there is a *necessary* connection between a cause and the effect which it produces. Hume's answer is negative. Ours, I think, must be affirmative.

It must be affirmative because whenever we consider *I* to be the cause of *E*, we do so in view of a (usually suppressed) law *u* in the presence of which *e follows* from *i*; and since we may take it that the relationship of deducibility may be described as a "necessary" one, we may say that the connection between *I* and *E* is a necessary one (although not "absolutely necessary," but only "necessary relative to *u*.")

Hume sees only *I* and *E*, and overlooking the suppressed *u*, he thinks that there is no connection between them – nothing beyond the fact that events similar to *I* have been, as a rule, followed by events similar to *E*. He does not notice that, if we formulate this fact in form of a universal law, the dependence of *E* upon *I* becomes, relative to this law, logically necessary. And he does not see that, even if we introduce the universal law in question merely as a tentative hypothesis, this means that we assume – tentatively and hypothetically – that the relationship between *I* and *E* is a necessary one, in the sense described.

I shall not here discuss Hume's attempt causally to explain a belief in a regularity or law by habit, although I think that this particular attempt at causally explaining away causality can be easily shown to be completely mistaken; I only wish to point out that he overlooked that a belief in a universal law *u* – whether or not causally explicable in terms of habits or associations – is, rationally, identical with a belief in a *necessary* connection between the corresponding *I*'s and *E*'s. We need not believe in the necessity or even in the truth of *u* in order to see that, given *u*, *e* can be logically obtained from *i*. Accordingly, we may describe the situation in this way: in the same degree in which we believe in *u* or doubt *u* or disbelieve in *u*, in the same degree do we believe or doubt or disbelieve that there holds a kind of *necessary* connection between *I* and *E* – a connection such that, given *I*, *E* must follow.

Our simple and somewhat trivial logical analysis thus allows us to explain certain psychological attitudes, and it does so perhaps better than the psychological analysis employed by Hume.

A second application of our analysis is to the cosmological proof of the existence of God (Aquina's "Second Way.") This argument has often been criticised, from many points of view, and it has recently been reformulated by Whittaker. It seems to be based on the intuitive idea that, if we can ask for the cause of an event, we can also ask for the cause of this cause. In this way we obtain a regressive chain of causes, and, if the regress is to be finite, a first cause, which we may call "God"; or more precisely (since a cause is not a person or thing but an event or fact), the fact of the existence of God.

I shall not discuss that aspect of this argument which I consider the only one which is philosophically relevant (viz., that this argument, even if successful, could at best prove the existence of a God who is good). I shall only point out that the regress from one "cause" to a preceding one is always relative to one or another *universal law*, and that, accordingly, the argument from causation assumes the universal laws of nature to be given. It therefore cannot conceive God as the creator of universal laws, or of order in nature, and must clash with the design argument (St. Thomas's "Fifth Way"), especially in the form proffered by Jeans and Whittaker (in which the fact that some natural laws can be conveniently formulated in a mathematical language is taken to indicate that God must be a mathematician).

4

I now turn to the problem of determinism. It is easy enough to visualise the world in the way the determinist sees it – as a kind of clockwork or planetary system or as an electro-chemical machine. It is more difficult to analyse in words the determinist's faith.

I think the following formulation may be satisfactory.

Every future event, the determinist may say, can be predicted with any desired degree of precision, provided we can measure all the relevant initial conditions (with an appropriate degree of precision), and provided we have completed the discovery of the relevant natural laws.

According to quantum mechanics, this statement is either not relevant or not true; but I shall neglect this aspect. Even without quantum mechanics, we can see that the statement is very unsatisfactory. Any more complicated and more distant event will defeat us; we simply cannot obtain the knowledge of the initial conditions which we would need; and we even cannot, as a rule, find out, from the formulation of the problem – the event to be predicted – what the initial conditions are which will be relevant to the prob-

lem, and to which degree of exactness they must be known. (The only exception to this seems to be that misleading case, the planetary system – a simple mechanism which is as well insulated as a clockwork, and not at all characteristic of the physical world in general). Thus we shall probably never be able to predict the weather in London with any precision even for a month ahead.

But apart from the very important and insurmountable difficulties which are connected with the initial conditions, there is no reason to believe that we shall ever have a complete knowledge of the universal laws of nature. We operate with hypotheses, and we find again and again that we have to improve upon them. And even if this process would come to an end, we could not know that it has come to an end.

Thus the determinist's programme is, at best, a pious wish, for a kind of divine omniscience; but it may be something worse – a completely misleading idea. (This is suggested by two aspects of scientific method which, it appears, is always one of bold oversimplifications. We have reason to believe, first that most of our so-called natural laws are lucky oversimplifying guesses; secondly that our experimental method involves interference with the things we study: we construct artificial, oversimplified cases – cases for study. One may even put it, perhaps, like this: the natural sciences do not deal so much with hard facts as with *interpretations* of facts, in the light of our theories, guesses, prejudices).

This discussion of determinism is completely independent of any problem of ethics. But it may clear the ground for one simple logical consideration in the field of ethics.

I shall discuss the question:

When do people consider human behaviour as praiseworthy or blameworthy action and when do they consider it not so?

I suggest a rough and very simple answer:

If people believe that under the same initial conditions, *as far as they can be independently ascertained or tested*, all or most people would act in this way, in other words, if they think that the behaviour can be satisfactorily (i.e., without the help of *ad hoc* hypotheses) *causally explained* with the help of independently established initial conditions and universal laws ("All men – or most men – in such circumstances act in this way"), then they do not think that it is either praiseworthy or blameworthy. Or in other words, they think it praiseworthy or blameworthy or, as we may say, "morally free," to the degree in which it is not causally explicable, on independently ascertainable initial conditions. They may then say, if they are determinists, that the action flows from the personality or from early influences, etc.; that is to say, they postulate hidden initial conditions. Or they may say if they are indeterminists, that the action was due to the free will of the individual. But both agree, roughly, that if ascertainable initial conditions – those for which we can obtain independent evidence – can be considered as sufficient "causes," and to the degree to which they can be so considered, the action is not one to be morally judged.

This is just another suggestion about the way in which our very simple scheme of causal explanation may contribute a little towards certain philosophical problems.

5

Our analysis of causal explanation can be applied to other and, in my opinion, more important problems – to problems of the philosophy of society, and of history. I have more especially, one problem in mind — the problem whether there are what may be called "natural laws of social life" or "sociological laws"; that is to say, laws which describe regularities of social life which are not produced by legislation, or by religious or moral custom.

The problem mentioned is, of course, of fundamental interest for the student of the methods of the social sciences. Nevertheless, it is not merely a methodological problem. It is of great significance for our whole attitude towards society and politics. We enter, as it were, into a new world – the world of purposes, of rational actions which pursue ends, and, of course, of irrational actions also. Has this world a similar structure as the world of physics and, say, physiology? The question is certainly of philosophical interest, even if it turns out to be a simple question of empirical fact. But it hardly is a question of empirical fact: at least it is not one on which social scientists have reached agreement. (Even in the natural sciences, we are constantly dealing with *interpretations*, rather than with hard facts. In the social sciences, this seems to be so to a higher degree).

The question whether there exist sociological laws has often been answered, both in the affirmative and in the negative, in a way which I consider

mistaken. People have asserted, for example, that there are laws of social evolution. I do not think that there are good reasons to believe that such laws exist, either in the field studied by biology or in that of sociology. Others have denied the existence of sociological laws altogether, the field of economics included. (This would make practically all rational political action impossible, since it does make impossible to predict the consequences of changed conditions). Many people seem still to believe in the view of Comte and Mill – that there are two kinds of laws, "laws of succession" (or of evolution) and "laws of coexistence."

I think that nearly all these views are mistaken and mainly because of misunderstandings of a logical character.

It is impossible for me here to go into these interesting questions of social philosophy in detail, and unnecessary because I have done so elsewhere.[2] I shall confine myself to a story: A friend of mine, an economist, recently expressed his scepticism concerning his science. In his opinion, economic laws did not exist. Economics was only a system of empty definitions, without empirical content. He illustrated this by an example. "If asked by the Government what policy they should adopt in order to have full employment without inflation, I could not answer; indeed, I suspect, that there is no answer." I pointed out to him that he had, in order to illustrate the absence of economic laws, just formulated one: The statement "There does not exist a policy which allows us to have full employment without inflation" (whether this is true is another question) is indeed a model of a sociological law. In order to see this clearly, we have only to apply some of the simplest logical rules to it – the equivalence of universal statements to negated existential ones. On the basis of this equivalence, all universal laws can be expressed in "There-does-not-exist" form. For example, the second law of thermodynamics by "There does not exist a machine which is one hundred per cent efficient." The similarity with the economic hypothesis mentioned above is obvious."

6

Another example of the significance of logic for ethics.

Perhaps the simplest and the most important point about ethics is purely logical. I mean the impossibility to derive non-tautological ethical rules – imperatives: principles of policy; aims; or however we may describe them – from statements of facts.

Only if this fundamental logical position is realised can we begin to formulate the real problems of moral philosophy, and to appreciate their difficulty.

As one of the most central problems of the theory of ethics, I consider the following: If ethical rules (aims, principles of policy, etc.) cannot be derived from facts – how then can we explain that we can learn about these matters from experience?

We can also put the question in this way: if aims cannot be derived from facts, can we do more than see that our system of aims is coherent? And if it is, can we do more than try to alter the facts, to "reform" them – in such a way that they conform to our aims?

The simple answer is, I believe, that not all the facts which can be altered can be altered in conformity with every preconceived and internally coherent system of aims. To take the example mentioned above. We may know that certain facts – such as unemployment, or inflation – can be altered. We may aim, on moral grounds, to avoid both. But we may learn from our attempt to do so that our system of aims, although internally coherent, does not cohere with some of the laws of economics, previously unknown to us.

7

To close with a general remark.

A number of philosophical problems can be shown, it appears, to be composed of an empirical and of a logical component. The analysis into these components, together with the claim that there is no further problem left, do not, if successful, establish that the original problem was a pseudo problem; on the contrary, it shows that there is a problem, and the way in which it can be solved.

Notes

1 See my *Logik der Forschung*, section 12, pp. 26ff; *The Poverty of Historicism* III (*Economica*, N.S. XII), section 28, pp. 75ff, and *The Open Society* II, note 9 to ch. 25.

2 See especially my *Poverty of Historicism* (*Economica* N.S. XI and XIII).

PART II

Truth, Propositions, and Meaning

Introduction to Part II

The semantic concept of truth and the meaning of propositions are central to the philosophy of logic. Truth is often described as a relation of correspondence between a proposition asserting that a state of affairs exists and actual conditions in the world. If the state of affairs described by the proposition exists or obtains, then the proposition is true, and is otherwise false. But there are many difficult questions connected with the concept of truth as it relates specifically to propositions in symbolic logic.

There are formal semantic paradoxes that can be formulated in logic that cast doubt on the universality of some of the more straightforward, or possibly naive, ideas of truth. The liar sentence states in effect that "This sentence is false." As with formal paradoxes generally, there is a construction of a proposition or inference that denies of itself a logically or semantically interesting property, and a dilemma that arises by virtue of the construction. The dilemma based on the liar sentence is that, classically, the liar sentence must either be true or false. If the liar sentence is true, then, since it says of itself that it is false, it is true that it is false; while if the liar sentence is false, then, since again it says of itself that it is false, it is false that it is false, which is to say that it is true. Thus, the liar sentence appears to be true if and only if it is false, an evident and classically intolerable paradox.

Puzzles like the liar paradox raise challenging questions for the philosophy of logic. Is the liar sentence a proposition? If it is not, then the problem posed by the liar paradox simply disappears, since it is only propositions that according to classical logic are supposed to be exclusively true or false. To discredit the liar sentence as nonpropositional rescues classical bivalent logic, but at a certain conceptual cost, since the liar sentence in other ways certainly looks like other propositions. There is no apparent logical inconvenience in the sentence, "This sentence is true," which to all intents and purposes seems to be a genuine proposition that does not support the same kind of dilemma as the liar sentence. But if "This sentence is true" is a genuine proposition, then its negation, the liar sentence, should also be a genuine proposition, with the opposite truth value, a choice that has already been eliminated as paradoxical. The moral seems to be that if we are going to solve the liar paradox by concluding that the liar sentence is not a genuine proposition, then we must propose an adequate theory of propositions.

This is the approach of Alfred Tarski's theory of truth in formalized languages. Tarski argues that in a correct logical notation no proposition can express its own truth value, whether true or false, as in both the liar sentence and its negation. Instead, Tarski holds that truth predications and denials can only be made in a meta-language or language about another language, such as an object language or lower-level meta-language, in an unending hierarchy of object languages, meta-languages, meta-meta-languages, and so on, indefinitely. Tarski's theory of truth forestalls the liar paradox in a stratification of languages and languages about languages. But some philosophers have found Tarski's method objectionable. In the first place, Tarski's hierarchy of languages and meta-languages rules out not only the liar sentence, but the negation of the liar sentence, which seems logically inoffensive. Secondly, Tarski's hierarchy seems to preclude the definite characterization of truth or the truth determination of certain propositions. We never arrive at an idea of truth for propositions generally, but only for propositions at a certain level within the hierarchy of languages and meta-languages that recedes for any chosen propositions into an infinite regress. The problem is that if in language L_0 a sentence S_0 is true, this cannot be said in L_0 itself, but only in the next higher meta-language L_1. Language L_1 contains another sentence S_1 in which the truth of sentence S_0 is asserted. But the truth of S_0 is expressed by S_1 only if S_1 is true, which is a truth value pronouncement that cannot be made in language L_1 about a sentence it contains, but only in yet another higher-order meta-language L_2, in the form of another sentence S_2 about the truth of S_1, and so on, indefinitely, to S_3, S_4, S_5, etc., with no final definite true statement of the truth even of the original sentence S_0. Tarski's theory of truth has nevertheless exerted an enormous influence on contemporary philosophy of logic, philosophy of language, and philosophical semantics, in the conventions by which truth and meaning are determined for propositions in logic.

Other efforts to avoid the contradiction of the liar include acknowledging the liar sentence as a proposition, but revising classical logic so that the liar sentence does not result in a contradiction, either because the liar sentence is neither true nor false but has some other third or higher truth value, or lacks truth value altogether in a so-called gap logic. Another alternative is to develop a formalism in which contradictions can be tolerated as true or otherwise logically harmless, in particular by restricting the valid deduction of any and every proposition from an assumption set including a contradiction. The constructability of the liar sentence within the notation of a logic nevertheless motivates some sort of philosophical response about the concept of truth or the conception of proposition or both. The traditional definition of a proposition as a true or false sentence or the abstract true or false meaning or thought expressed by a true or false sentence, is evidently under siege by such philosophical problems as the liar paradox and the dilemma that arises from the liar sentence. The semantic theory by which the meaning of propositions is interpreted is as much a part of logic as its syntactical structures, the mathematical language of symbolic logic. Philosophers

continue to address these questions about the semantics of logic in many different ways; the principal contemporary approaches among which are represented by the essays in this section.

Donald Davidson, in his influential paper, "Truth and Meaning," identifies the central task of a theory of meaning in philosophical semantics as explaining how language users can determine the meaning of an arbitrary expression. He believes that the characterization of a truth predicate provides the required structure for this purpose with a clear and testable criterion of an adequate semantics for natural language in which defining the concept of truth is an essential first step toward establishing an expression's meaning. Davidson makes this initial move, but acknowledges difficulties in a truth–predicate oriented semantic program.

Hartry Field examines the theory of truth underlying the T-conventions in Davidson's semantics owing to Alfred Tarski. Field in "Tarski's Theory of Truth" argues that the received conception of Tarski as having reduced truth to more acceptable concepts is misleading. Tarski, according to Field, can at most be said to have reduced truth to other semantic concepts, and that as a result Tarski's definition of the concept of truth for formalized languages is acceptable only if the semantic concepts to which he reduces truth are themselves acceptable. Field insists that this distinction is not trivial but important, and that it contradicts what most commentators have assumed. In the course of advancing his interpretation, Field offers useful perspectives on Tarski's theory of truth, situated in a broader philosophical context.

Saul A. Kripke's "Outline of a Theory of Truth" argues that Tarski's theory on its own is inadequate to solve the liar paradox. In an important searching discussion of the problem, Kripke proposes to combine a nonclassical semantics of truth value gaps with a modified Tarskian stratification of object and metalanguages, in which there are transfinitely ramified occurrences of metalanguages within each level of a Tarskian hierarchy. Kripke diagnoses the logical ailment of the liar sentence as a failure of "grounding", since the sentence seems to flip-flop between truth and falsehood without reaching any settled semantic value.

A related topic is explored in Fred Sommers's valuable paper, "Types and Ontology." Sommers explains and extends Russell's theory of types to applications for natural language. Russell's theory of types was originally designed to forestall logical paradoxes like the liar. What is common in this large family of paradoxes is the denial of a proposition in which some term asserts a logical or semantic property of itself. The liar sentence, for example, denies its own truth, which can be represented informally as a sentence saying of itself that it is false. Russell hoped to eliminate such constructions from the symbolic logic of *Principia Mathematica* by restricting the well-formed formulas of the logic to those in which only terms of a higher type can legitimately be attached to terms of a lower type. Object terms, constants and variables, are typed as 0, predicates that attach to object terms as 1 (hence the name first-order logic for classical propositional and predicate symbolic logic, in which properties can only be predicated of objects and not of other properties), predicates of predicates as 2, and so on, indefinitely. Sommers regards ontology or the metaphysics of being as a mapping of a logic's semantic domain of existent entities onto set theory. In the process, logic just like ontology discriminates between different sorts of things, which Sommers construes as the natural language equivalent of Russell's types. Russell's program for ontology to be defined by a logically correct (typed) language is thereby reinstated in Sommer's view, in defense of which he answers objections and illustrates the method with several independently interesting examples.

Finally, George Bealer in his essay, "Propositions" defends a traditional theory of propositions against two kinds of objections, both of which he claims are tied to fundamental misconceptions about how the theory of propositions should be developed. The opposition at issue is between efforts to reduce propositions to extensional entities, which is to say sets of objects with specific properties, by contrast with intensional concepts of fine-grained propositional identity conditions, which distinguish propositions and propositional content on the basis of the properties attributed to objects. Bealer wants to break through the traditional impasse in the philosophy of logic over these two methods by means of a nonreductive algebraic approach in which propositional content is distinguished by means of intensionalization functions as they apply to the behavior of logical operations on the elements of a logic's semantic domain.

The idea is that whether we are extensionalists, traditional intensionalists, or nonreductivists like Bealer, we expect to begin with the same domain. The question is how thereafter we should best think of the identity conditions for propositions. The extensionalist method is too crude, because we cannot infer from the fact that the extensions of the predicates "chordate" (having a central nervous system) and "renate" (having a kidney) are identical that therefore the proposition "All chordates are herbaceous" is the same proposition as "All renates are herbaceous," even though all vertebrates are renates and conversely. The content of the propositions is not the same. On the other hand, many distinct objections have been offered against the traditional intensionalist alternative, which Bealer considers in detail. He regards both of these approaches as reductionist in different ways, and recommends in their place a more constructive solution, in which we begin with the elements in the semantic domain and consider how distinct intensionally fine-grained propositions can be built up from them by particular kinds of logical operations. The essay concludes with a selection of five applications of the theory to difficult problems in the theory of meaning involving propositional identity conditions.

Further Reading

Barwise, Jon and Etchemendy, John. 1987: *The Liar: An Essay on Truth and Circularity*. New York: Oxford University Press.

Blackburn, Simon. 1975: *Meaning, Reference and Necessity*. Cambridge: Cambridge University Press.

Cartwright, Richard. 1962: "Propositions", in *Analytical Philosophy, First Series*: 81–103. R. J. Butler (ed.). Oxford: Blackwell. ·

Davidson, Donald. 1984: *Inquiries into Truth and Interpretation*. Oxford: Oxford University Press.

Evans, Gareth and McDowell, John (eds). 1976: *Truth and Meaning: Essays in Semantics*. Oxford: Oxford University Press.

Grice, P. H. 1989: *Studies in the Way of Words*. Cambridge: Harvard University Press.

Hacking, Ian. 1975: *Why Does Language Matter to Philosophy?* Cambridge: Cambridge University Press.

Lepore, Ernest (ed.). 1986: *Truth and Interpretation: Perspectives on the Philosophy of Donald Davidson*. Oxford and New York: Blackwell.

Sher, Gila. 1991: *The Bounds of Logic*. Cambridge: MIT Press.

Wright, Crispin. 1993: *Realism, Meaning and Truth*. Oxford: Blackwell.

5

Truth and Meaning

Donald Davidson

It is conceded by most philosophers of language, and recently even by some linguists, that a satisfactory theory of meaning must give an account of how the meanings of sentences depend upon the meanings of words. Unless such an account could be supplied for a particular language, it is argued, there would be no explaining the fact that we can learn the language: no explaining the fact that, on mastering a finite vocabulary and a finitely stated set of rules, we are prepared to produce and to understand any of a potential infinitude of sentences. I do not dispute these vague claims, in which I sense more than a kernel of truth.[1] Instead I want to ask what it is for a theory to give an account of the kind adumbrated.

One proposal is to begin by assigning some entity as meaning to each word (or other significant syntactical feature) of the sentence; thus we might assign Theaetetus to 'Theaetus' and the property of flying to 'flies' in the sentence 'Theaetetus flies'. The problem then arises how the meaning of the sentence is generated from these meanings. Viewing concatenation as a significant piece of syntax, we may assign to it the relation of participating in or instantiating; however, it is obvious that we have here the start of an infinite regress. Frege sought to avoid the regress by saying that the entities corresponding to predicates (for example) are 'unsaturated' or 'incomplete' in contrast to the entities that correspond to names,

but this doctrine seems to label a difficulty rather than solve it.

The point will emerge if we think for a moment of complex singular terms, to which Frege's theory applies along with sentences. Consider the expression 'the father of Annette'; how does the meaning of the whole depend on the meaning of the parts? The answer would seem to be that the meaning of 'the father of' is such that when this expression is prefixed to a singular term the result refers to the father of the person to whom the singular term refers. What part is played, in this account, by the unsaturated or incomplete entity for which 'the father of' stands? All we can think to say is that this entity 'yields' or 'gives' the father of x as value when the argument is x, or perhaps that this entity maps people onto their fathers. It may not be clear whether the entity for which 'the father of' is said to stand performs any genuine explanatory function as long as we stick to individual expressions; so think instead of the infinite class of expressions formed by writing 'the father of' zero or more times in front of 'Annette'. It is easy to supply a theory that tells, for an arbitrary one of these singular terms, what it refers to: if the term is 'Annette' it refers to Annette, while if the term is complex, consisting of 'the father of' prefixed to a singular term t, then it refers to the father of the person to whom t refers. It is obvious that no entity corresponding to 'the father of' is, or needs to be, mentioned in stating this theory.

It would be inappropriate to complain that this little theory *uses* the words 'the father of' in giving

Donald Davidson, Truth and Meaning. *Synthese,* 17 (1967): 304–23.

the reference of expressions containing those words. For the task was to give the meaning of all expressions in a certain infinite set on the basis of the meanings of the parts; it was not in the bargain also to give the meanings of the atomic parts. On the other hand, it is now evident that a satisfactory theory of the meanings of complex expressions may not require entities as meanings of all the parts. It behooves us then to rephrase our demand on a satisfactory theory of meaning so as not to suggest that individual words must have meanings at all, in any sense that transcends the fact that they have a systematic effect on the meanings of the sentences in which they occur. Actually, for the case at hand we can do better still in stating the criterion of success: what we wanted, and what we got, is a theory that entails every sentence of the form 't refers to x' where 't' is replaced by a structural description[2] of a singular term, and 'x' is replaced by that term itself. Further, our theory accomplishes this without appeal to any semantical concepts beyond the basic 'refers to'. Finally, the theory clearly suggests an effective procedure for determining, for any singular term in its universe, what that term refers to.

A theory with such evident merits deserves wider application. The device proposed by Frege to this end has a brilliant simplicity: count predicates as a special case of functional expressions, and sentences as a special case of complex singular terms. Now, however, a difficulty looms if we want to continue in our present (implicit) course of identifying the meaning of a singular term with its reference. The difficulty follows upon making two reasonable assumptions: that logically equivalent singular terms have the same reference; and that a singular term does not change its reference if a contained singular term is replaced by another with the same reference. But now suppose that 'R' and 'S' abbreviate any two sentences alike in truth value. Then the following four sentences have the same reference:

(1) R

(2) $\hat{x}(x = x.R) = \hat{x}(x = x)$

(3) $\hat{x}(x = x.S) = \hat{x}(x = x)$

(4) S

For (1) and (2) are logically equivalent, as are (3) and (4), while (3) differs from (2) only in contain-

ing the singular term '$\hat{x}(x = x.S)$' where (2) contains '$\hat{x}(x = x.R)$' and these refer to the same thing if S and R are alike in truth value. Hence any two sentences have the same reference if they have the same truth value.[3] And if the meaning of a sentence is what it refers to, all sentences alike in truth value must be synonymous – an intolerable result.

Apparently we must abandon the present approach as leading to a theory of meaning. This is the natural point at which to turn for help to the distinction between meaning and reference. The trouble, we are told, is that questions of reference are, in general, settled by extra-linguistic facts, questions of meaning not, and the facts can conflate the references of expressions that are not synonymous. If we want a theory that gives the meaning (as distinct from reference) of each sentence, we must start with the meaning (as distinct from reference) of the parts.

Up to here we have been following in Frege's footsteps; thanks to him, the path is well known and even well worn. But now, I would like to suggest, we have reached an impasse: the switch from reference to meaning leads to no useful account of how the meanings of sentences depend upon the meanings of the words (or other structural features) that compose them. Ask, for example, for the meaning of 'Theaetetus flies'. A Fregean answer might go something like this: given the meaning of 'Theaetetus' as argument, the meaning of 'flies' yields the meaning of 'Theaetetus flies' as value. The vacuity of this answer is obvious. We wanted to know what the meaning of 'Theaetetus flies' is; it is no progress to be told that it is the meaning of 'Theaetetus flies'. This much we knew before any theory was in sight. In the bogus account just given, talk of the structure of the sentence and of the meanings of words was idle, for it played no role in producing the given description of the meaning of the sentence.

The contrast here between a real and pretended account will be plainer still if we ask for a theory, analogous to the miniature theory of reference of singular terms just sketched, but different in dealing with meanings in place of references. What analogy demands is a theory that has as consequences all sentences of the form 's means m' where 's' is replaced by a structural description of a sentence and 'm' is replaced by a singular term that refers to the meaning of that sentence; a theory, moreover, that provides an effective method for arriving at the meaning of an arbitrary sentence structurally described. Clearly some more articulate way of referring to meanings than any we have seen is essential if these criteria are to be met.[4] Meanings as entities, or the related concept of synonymy, allow us to formulate the following rule relating sentences and their parts: sentences are synonymous whose corresponding parts are synonymous ('corresponding' here needs spelling out of course). And meanings as entities may, in theories such as Frege's, do duty, on occasion as references, thus losing their status as entities distinct from references. Paradoxically, the one thing meanings do not seem to do is oil the wheels of a theory of meaning – at least as long as we require of such a theory that it non-trivially give the meaning of every sentence in the language. My objection to meanings in the theory of meaning is not that they are abstract or that their identity conditions are obscure, but that they have no demonstrated use.

This is the place to scotch another hopeful thought. Suppose we have a satisfactory theory of syntax for our language, consisting of an effective method of telling, for an arbitrary expression, whether or not it is independently meaningful (i.e., a sentence), and assume as usual that this involves viewing each sentence as composed, in allowable ways, out of elements drawn from a fixed finite stock of atomic syntactical elements (roughly, words). The hopeful thought is that syntax, so conceived, will yield semantics when a dictionary giving the meaning of each syntactic atom is added. Hopes will be dashed, however, if semantics is to comprise a theory of meaning in our sense, for knowledge of the structural characteristics that make for meaningfulness in a sentence, plus knowledge of the meanings of the ultimate parts, does not add up to knowledge of what a sentence means. The point is easily illustrated by belief sentences. Their syntax is relatively unproblematic. Yet, adding a dictionary does not touch the standard semantic problem, which is that we cannot account for even as much as the truth conditions of such sentences on the basis of what we know of the meanings of the words in them. The situation is not radically altered by refining the dictionary to indicate which meaning or meanings an ambiguous expression bears in each of its possible contexts; the problem of belief sentences persists after ambiguities are resolved.

The fact that recursive syntax with dictionary added is not necessarily recursive semantics has been obscured in some recent writing on linguistics by the intrusion of semantic criteria into the discussion of purportedly syntactic theories. The matter would boil down to a harmless difference over terminology if the semantic criteria were clear; but they are not. While there is agreement that it is the central task of semantics to give the semantic interpretation (the meaning) of every sentence in the language, nowhere in the linguistic literature will one find, so far as I know, a straightforward account of how a theory performs this task, or how to tell when it has been accomplished. The contrast with syntax is striking. The main job of a modest syntax is to characterize *meaningfulness* (or sentencehood). We may have as much confidence in the correctness of such a characterization as we have in the representativeness of our sample and our ability to say when particular expressions are meaningful (sentences). What clear and analogous task and test exist for semantics?[5]

We decided a while back not to assume that parts of sentences have meanings except in the ontologically neutral sense of making a systematic contribution to the meaning of the sentences in which they occur. Since postulating meanings has netted nothing, let us return to that insight. One direction in which it points is a certain holistic view of meaning. If sentences depend for their meaning on their structure, and we understand the meaning of each time in the structure only as an abstraction from the totality of sentences in which it features, then we can give the meaning of any sentence (or word) only by giving the meaning of every sentence (and word) in the language. Frege said that only in the context of a sentence does a word have meaning; in the same vein he might have added that only in the context of the language does a sentence (and therefore a word) have meaning.

This degree of holism was already implicit in the suggestion that an adequate theory of meaning must entail *all* sentences of the form '*s* means *m*'. But now, having found no more help in meanings of sentences than in meanings of words, let us ask whether we can get rid of the troublesome singular terms supposed to replace '*m*' and to refer to meanings. In a way, nothing could be easier: just write '*s* means that *p*', and imagine '*p*' replaced by a sentence. Sentences, as we have seen, cannot name meanings, and sentences with 'that' prefixed are not names at all, unless we decide so. It looks as though we are in trouble on another count, however, for it is reasonable to expect that in wrestling with the logic of the apparently non-extensional 'means that' we will encounter problems as hard as, or perhaps identical with, the problems our theory is out to solve.

The only way I know to deal with this difficulty is simple, and radical. Anxiety that we are enmeshed in the intensional springs from using the words 'means that' as filling between description of sentence and sentence, but it may be that the success of our venture depends not on the filling but on what it fills. The theory will have done its work if it provides, for every sentence s in the language under study, a matching sentence (to replace 'p') that, in some way yet to be made clear, 'gives the meaning' of s. One obvious candidate for matching sentence is just s itself, if the object language is contained in the metalanguage; otherwise a translation of s in the metalanguage. As a final bold step, let us try treating the position occupied by 'p' extensionally: to implement this, sweep away the obscure 'means that', provide the sentence that replaces 'p' with a proper sentential connective, and supply the description that replaces 's' with its own predicate. The plausible result is

(T) s is T if and only if p.

What we require of a theory of meaning for a language L is that without appeal to any (further) semantical notions it place enough restrictions on the predicate 'is T' to entail all sentences got from schema T when 's' is replaced by a structural description of a sentence of L and 'p' by that sentence.

Any two predicates satisfying this condition have the same extension,[6] so if the metalanguage is rich enough, nothing stands in the way of putting what I am calling a theory of meaning into the form of an explicit definition of a predicate 'is T'. But whether explicitly defined or recursively characterized, it is clear that the sentences to which the predicate 'is T' applies will be just the true sentences of L, for the condition we have placed on satisfactory theories of meaning is in essence Tarski's Convention T that tests the adequacy of a formal semantical definition of truth.[7]

The path to this point has been tortuous, but the conclusion may be stated simply: a theory of meaning for a language L shows 'how the meanings of sentences depend upon the meanings of words' if it contains a (recursive) definition of truth-in-L. And, so far at least, we have no other

idea how to turn the trick. It is worth emphasizing that the concept of truth played no ostensible role in stating our original problem. That problem, upon refinement, led to the view that an adequate theory of meaning must characterize a predicate meeting certain conditions. It was in the nature of a discovery that such a predicate would apply exactly to the true sentences. I hope that what I am doing may be described in part as defending the philosophical importance of Tarski's semantical concept of truth. But my defense is only distantly related, if at all, to the question whether the concept Tarski has shown how to define is the (or a) philosophically interesting conception of truth, or the question whether Tarski has cast any light on the ordinary use of such words as 'true' and 'truth'. It is a misfortune that dust from futile and confused battles over these questions has prevented those with a theoretical interest in language – philosophers, logicians, psychologists, and linguists alike – from recognizing in the semantical concept of truth (under whatever name) the sophisticated and powerful foundation of a competent theory of meaning.

There is no need to suppress, of course, the obvious connection between a definition of truth of the kind Tarski has shown how to construct, and the concept of meaning. It is this: the definition works by giving necessary and sufficient conditions for the truth of every sentence, and to give truth conditions is a way of giving the meaning of a sentence. To know the semantic concept of truth for a language is to know what it is for a sentence – any sentence – to be true, and this amounts, in one good sense we can give to the phrase, to understanding the language. This at any rate is my excuse for a feature of the present discussion that is apt to shock old hands: my freewheeling use of the word 'meaning', for what I call a theory of meaning has after all turned out to make no use of meanings, whether of sentences or of words. Indeed since a Tarski-type truth definition supplies all we have asked so far of a theory of meaning, it is clear that such a theory falls comfortably within what Quine terms the 'theory of reference' as distinguished from what he terms the 'theory of meaning'. So much to the good for what I call a theory of meaning, and so much, perhaps, against my so calling it.[8]

A theory of meaning (in my mildly perverse sense) is an empirical theory, and its ambition it to account for the workings of a natural language. Like any theory, it may be tested by comparing some of its consequences with the facts. In the present case this is easy, for the theory has been characterized as issuing in an infinite flood of sentences each giving the truth conditions of a sentence; we only need to ask, in selected cases, whether what the theory avers to be the truth conditions for a sentence really are. A typical test case might involve deciding whether the sentence 'Snow is white' *is* true if and only if snow is white. Not all cases will be so simple (for reasons to be sketched), but it is evident that this sort of test does not invite counting noses. A sharp conception of what constitutes a theory in this domain furnishes an exciting context for raising deep questions about when a theory of language is correct and how it is to be tried. But the difficulties are theoretical, not practical. In application, the trouble is to get a theory that comes close to working; anyone call tell whether it is right.[9] One can see why this is so. The theory reveals nothing new about the conditions under which an individual sentence is true; it does not make those conditions any clearer than the sentence itself does. The work of the theory is in relating the known truth conditions of each sentence to those aspects ('words') of the sentence that recur in other sentences, and can be assigned identical roles in other sentences. Empirical power in such a theory depends on success in recovering the structure of a very complicated ability – the ability to speak and understand a language. We can tell easily enough when particular pronouncements of the theory comport with our understanding of the language; this is consistent with a feeble insight into the design of the machinery of our linguistic accomplishments.

The remarks of the last paragraph apply directly only to the special case where it is assumed that the language for which truth is being characterized is part of the language used and understood by the characterizer. Under these circumstances, the framer of a theory will as a matter of course avail himself when he can of the built-in convenience of a metalanguage with a sentence guaranteed equivalent to each sentence in the object language. Still, this fact ought not to con us into thinking a theory any more correct that entails ' "Snow is white" is true if and only if snow is white' than one that entails instead:

(S)   'Snow is white' is true if and only if grass is green,

provided, of course, we are as sure of the truth of (S) as we are of that of its more celebrated pre-decessor. Yet (S) may not encourage the same confidence that a theory that entails it deserves to be called a theory of meaning.

The threatened failure of nerve may be counter-acted as follows. The grotesqueness of (S) is in itself nothing against a theory of which it is a consequence, provided the theory gives the correct results for every sentence (on the basis of its structure, there being no other way). It is not easy to see how (S) could be party to such an enterprise, but if it were – if, that is, (S) followed from a characterization of the predicate 'is true' that led to the invariable pairing of truths with truths and falsehoods with falsehoods – then there would not, I think, be anything essential to the idea of meaning that remained to be captured.

What appears to the right of the biconditional in sentences of the form '*s* is true if and only if *p*' when such sentences are consequences of a theory of truth plays its role in determining the meaning of *s* not by pretending synonymy but by adding one more brush-stroke to the picture which, taken as a whole, tells what there is to know of the meaning of *s*; this stroke is added by virtue of the fact that the sentence that replaces '*p*' is true if and only if *s* is.

It may help to reflect that (S) is acceptable, if it is, because we are independently sure of the truth of 'Snow is white' and 'Grass is green'; but in cases where we are unsure of the truth of a sentence, we can have confidence in a characterization of the truth predicate only if it pairs that sentence with one we have good reason to believe equivalent. It would be ill advised for someone who had any doubts about the color of snow or grass to accept a theory that yielded (S), even if his doubts were of equal degree, unless he thought the color of the one was tied to the color of the other. Omniscience can obviously afford more bizarre theories of meaning than ignorance; but then, omniscience has less need of communication.

It must be possible, of course, for the speaker of one language to construct a theory of meaning for the speaker of another, though in this case the empirical test of the correctness of the theory will no longer be trivial. As before, the aim of theory will be an infinite correlation of sentences alike in truth. But this time the theory-builder must not be assumed to have direct insight into likely equivalences between his own tongue and the alien. What he must do is find out, however he can, what sentences the alien holds true in his own tongue (or better, to what degree he holds them true). The linguist then will attempt to construct a characterization of truth-for-the-alien which yields, so far as possible, a mapping of sentences held true (or false) by the alien onto sentences held true (or false) by the linguist. Supposing no perfect fit is found, the residue of sentences held true translated by sentences held false (and vice versa) is the margin for error (foreign or domestic). Charity in interpreting the words and thoughts of others is unavoidable in another direction as well: just as we must maximize agreement, or risk not making sense of what the alien is talking about, so we must maximize the self-consistency we attribute to him, on pain of not understanding *him*. No single principle of optimum charity emerges; the constraints therefore determine no single theory. In a theory of radical translation (as Quine calls it) there is no completely disentangling questions of what the alien means from questions of what he believes. We do not know what someone means unless we know what he believes; we do not know what someone believes unless we know what he means. In radical translation we are able to break into this circle, if only incompletely, because we can sometimes tell that a person accedes to a sentence we do not understand.[10]

In the past few pages I have been asking how a theory of meaning that takes the form of a truth definition can be empirically tested, and have blithely ignored the prior question whether there is any serious chance such a theory can be given for a natural language. What are the prospects for a formal semantical theory of a natural language? Very poor, according to Tarski; and I believe most logicians, philosophers of language and linguists agree.[11] Let me do what I can to dispel the pessimism. What I can in a general and programmatic way, of course; for here the proof of the pudding will certainly be in the proof of the right theorems.

Tarski concludes the first section of his classic essay on the concept of truth in formalized languages with the following remarks, which he italicizes:

The very possibility of a consistent use of the expression 'true sentence' which is in harmony with the laws of logic and the spirit of everyday language seems to be very questionable, and consequently the same doubt attaches to the possibility of constructing a correct definition of this expression.[12]

Late in the same essay, he returns to the subject:

the concept of truth (as well as other semantical concepts) when applied to colloquial language in conjunction with the normal laws of logic leads inevitably to confusions and contradictions. Whoever wishes, in spite of all difficulties, to pursue the semantics of colloquial language with the help of exact methods will be driven first to undertake the thankless task of a reform of this language. He will find it necessary to define its structure, to overcome the ambiguity of the terms which occur in it, and finally to split the language into a series of languages of greater and greater extent, each of which stands in the same relation to the next in which a formalized language stands to its metalanguage. It may, however be doubted whether the language of everyday life, after being 'rationalized' in this way, would still preserve its naturalness and whether it would not rather take on the characteristic features of the formalized languages.[13]

Two themes emerge: that the universal character of natural languages leads to contradiction (the semantic paradoxes), and that natural languages are too confused and amorphous to permit the direct application of formal methods. The first point deserves a serious answer, and I wish I had one. As it is, I will say only why I think we are justified in carrying on without having disinfected this particular source of conceptual anxiety, The semantic paradoxes arise when the range of the quantifiers in the object language is too generous in certain ways. But it is not really clear how unfair to Urdu or to Hindi it would be to view the range of their quantifiers as insufficient to yield an explicit definition of 'true-in-Urdu' or 'true-in-Hindi'. Or, to put the matter in another, if not more serious way, there may in the nature of the case always be something we grasp in understanding the language of another (the concept of truth) that we cannot communicate to him. In any case, most of the problems of general philosophical interest arise within a fragment of the relevant natural language that may be conceived as containing very little set theory. Of course these comments do not meet the claim that natural languages are universal. But it seems to me this claim, now that we know such universality leads to paradox, is suspect.

Tarski's second point is that we would have to reform a natural language out of all recognition before we could apply formal semantical methods. If this is true, it is fatal to my project, for the task of a theory of meaning as I conceive it is not to change, improve or reform a language, but to describe and understand it. Let us look at the positive side. Tarski has shown the way to giving a theory for interpreted formal languages of various kinds; pick one as much like English as possible. Since this new language has been explained in English and contains much English we not only may, but I think must, view it as part of English for those who understand it. For this fragment of English we have, *ex hypothesi*, a theory of the required sort. Not only that, but in interpreting this adjunct of English in old English we necessarily gave hints connecting old and new. Wherever there are sentences of old English with the same truth conditions as sentences in the adjunct we may extend the theory to cover them. Much of what is called for is just to mechanize as far as possible what we now do by art when we put ordinary English into one or another canonical notation. The point is not that canonical notation is better than the rough original idiom, but rather that if we know what idiom the canonical notation is canonical *for*, we have as good a theory for the idiom as for its kept companion.

Philosophers have long been at the hard work of applying theory to ordinary language by the device of matching sentences in the vernacular with sentences for which they have a theory. Frege's massive contribution was to show how 'all', 'some', 'every', 'each', 'none', and associated pronouns, in some of their uses, could be tamed; for the first time, it was possible to dream of a formal semantics for a significant part of a natural language. This dream came true in a sharp way with the work of Tarski. It would be a shame to miss the fact that as a result of these two magnificent achievements, Frege's and Tarski's, we have gained a deep insight into the structure of our mother tongues. Philosophers of a logical bent have tended to start where the theory was and work out towards the complications of natural language. Contemporary linguists, with an aim that cannot easily be seen to be different, start with the ordinary and work toward a general theory. If either party is successful, there must be a meeting. Recent work by Chomsky and others is doing much to bring the complexities of natural languages within the scope of serious semantic theory. To give an example: suppose success in giving the truth conditions for some significant range of sentences in the active voice. Then with a formal procedure for transforming each such sentence into a corresponding sentence in the passive voice, the theory of truth could be extended in an obvious way to this new set of sentences.[14]

One problem touched on in passing by Tarski does not, at least in all its manifestations, have to be solved to get ahead with theory: the existence in natural languages of 'ambiguous terms'. As long as ambiguity does not affect grammatical form, and can be translated, ambiguity for ambiguity, into the metalanguage, a truth definition will not tell us any lies. The trouble, for systematic semantics, with the phrase 'believes that' in English is not its vagueness, ambiguity, or unsuitability for incorporation in a serious science: let our metalanguage be English, and all *these* problems will be translated without loss or gain into the metalanguage. But the central problem of the logical grammar of 'believes that' will remain to haunt us.

The example is suited to illustrating another, and related, point, for the discussion of belief sentences has been plagued by failure to observe a fundamental distinction between tasks: uncovering the logical grammar or form of sentences (which is in the province of a theory of meaning as I construe it), and the analysis of individual words or expressions (which are treated as primitive by the theory). Thus Carnap, in the first edition of *Meaning and Necessity*, suggested we render 'John believe that the earth is round' as 'John responds affirmatively to 'the earth is round' as an English sentence'. He gave this up when Mates pointed out that John might respond affirmatively to one sentence and not to another no matter how close in meaning. But there is a confusion here from the start. The semantic structure of a belief sentence, according to this idea of Carnap's, is given by a three-place predicate with places reserved for expressions referring to a person, a sentence, and a language. It is a different sort of problem entirely to attempt an analysis of this predicate, perhaps along behavioristic lines. Not least among the merits of Tarski's conception of a theory of truth is that the purity of method it demands of us follows from the formulation of the problem itself, not from the self-imposed restraint of some adventitious philosophical puritanism.

I think it is hard to exaggerate the advantages to philosophy of language of bearing in mind this distinction between questions of logical form or grammar, and the analysis of individual concepts. Another example may help advertise the point.

If we suppose questions of logical grammar settled, sentences like 'Bardot is good' raise no special problems for a truth definition. The deep differences between descriptive and evaluative (emotive, expressive, etc.) terms do not show here. Even if we hold there is some important sense in which moral or evaluative sentences do not have a truth value (for example, because they cannot be 'verified'), we ought not to boggle at ' "Bardot is good" is true if and only if Bardot is good'; in a theory of truth, this consequence should follow with the rest, keeping track, as must be done, of the semantic location of such sentences in the language as a whole – of their relation to generalizations, their role in such compound sentences as 'Bardot is good and Bardot is foolish', and so on. What is special to evaluative words is simply not touched: the mystery is transferred from the word 'good' in the object-language to its translation in the metalanguage.

But 'good' as it features in 'Bardot is a good actress' is another matter. The problem is not that the translation of this sentence is not in the metalanguage – let us suppose it is. The problem is to frame a truth definition such that ' "Bardot is a good actress" is true if and only if Bardot is a good actress' – and all other sentences like it – are consequences. Obviously 'good actress' does not mean 'good and an actress'. We might think of taking 'is a good actress' as an unanalyzed predicate. This would obliterate all connection between 'is a good actress' and 'is a good mother', and it would give us no excuse to think of 'good', in these uses, as a word or semantic element. But worse, it would bar us from framing a truth definition at all, for there is no end to the predicates we would have to treat as logically simple (and hence accommodate in separate clauses in the definition of satisfaction): 'is a good companion to dogs', 'is a good 28-years old conversationalist', and so forth. The problem is not peculiar to the case: it is the problem of attributive adjectives generally.

It is consistent with the attitude taken here to deem it usually a strategic error to undertake philosophical analysis of words or expressions which is not preceded by or at any rate accompanied by the attempt to get the logical grammar straight. For how can we have any confidence in our analyses of words like 'right', 'ought', 'can', and 'obliged', or the phrases we use to talk of actions, events and causes, when we do not know what (logical, semantical) parts of speech we have to deal with? I would say much the same about

studies of the 'logic' of these and other words, and the sentences containing them. Whether the effort and ingenuity that has gone into the study of deontic logics, modal logics, imperative and erotetic logics has been largely futile or not cannot be known until we have acceptable semantic analyses of the sentences such systems purport to treat. Philosophers and logicians sometimes talk or work as if they were free to choose between, say, the truth-functional conditional and others, or free to introduce non-truth-functional sentential operators like 'Let it be the case that' or 'It ought to be the case that'. But in fact the decision is crucial. When we depart from idioms we can accomodate in a truth definition, we lapse into (or create) language for which we have no coherent semantical account – that is, no account at all of how such talk can be integrated into the language as a whole.

To return to our main theme: we have recognized that a theory of the kind proposed leaves the whole matter of what individual words mean exactly where it was. Even when the metalanguage is different from the object language, the theory exerts no pressure for improvement, clarification or analysis of individual words, except when, by accident of vocabulary, straightforward translation fails. Just as synonymy, as between expressions, goes generally untreated, so also synonymy of sentences, and analyticity. Even such sentences as 'A vixen is a female fox' bear no special tag unless it is our pleasure to provide it. A truth definition does not distinguish between analytic sentences and others, except for sentences that owe their truth to the presence alone of the constants that give the theory its grip on structure: the theory entails not only that these sentences are true but that they will remain true under all significant rewritings of their non-logical parts. A notion of logical truth thus given limited application, related notions of logical equivalence and entailment will tag along. It is hard to imagine how a theory of meaning could fail to read a logic into its object language to this degree; and to the extent that it does, our intuitions of logical truth, equivalence and entailment may be called upon in constructing and testing the theory.

I turn now to one more, and very large, fly in the ointment: the fact that the same sentence may at one time or in one mouth be true and at another time or in another mouth be false. Both logicians and those critical of formal methods here seem largely (though by no means universally) agreed that formal semantics and logic are incompetent to deal with the disturbances caused by demonstratives. Logicians have often reacted by downgrading natural language and trying to show how to get along without demonstratives; their critics react by downgrading logic and formal semantics. None of this can make me happy: clearly demonstratives cannot be eliminated from a natural language without loss or radical change, so there is no choice but to accommodate theory to them.

No logical errors result if we simply treat demonstratives as constants,[15] neither do any problems arise for giving a semantic truth definition. ' "I am wise" is true if and only if I am wise', with its bland ignoring of the demonstrative element in 'I' comes off the assembly line along with ' "Socrates is wise" is true if and only if Socrates is wise' with *its* bland indifference to the demonstrative element in 'is wise' (the tense).

What suffers in this treatment of demonstratives is not the definition of a truth predicate, but the plausibility of the claim that what has been defined is truth. For this claim is acceptable only if the speaker and circumstances of utterance of each sentence mentioned in the definition is matched by the speaker and circumstances of utterance of the truth definition itself. It could also be fairly pointed out that part of understanding demonstratives is knowing the rules by which they adjust their reference to circumstance; assimilating demonstratives to constant terms obliterates this feature. These complaints can be met, I think, though only by a fairly far-reaching revision in the theory of truth. I shall barely suggest how this could be done, but bare suggestion is all that is needed: the idea is technically trivial, and quite in line with work being done on the logic of the tenses.[16]

We could take truth to be a property, not of sentences, but of utterances, or speech acts, or ordered triples of sentences, times and persons; but it is simplest just to view truth as a relation between a sentence, a person, and a time. Under such treatment, ordinary logic as now read applies as usual, but only to sets of sentences relativized to the same speaker and time; further logical relations between sentences spoken at different times and by different speakers may be articulated by new axioms. Such is not my concern. The theory of meaning undergoes a systematic but not puzzling change: corresponding to each expression with a demonstrative element there must in the theory be a phrase that relates the truth conditions of sentences in which the expression occurs to changing times and speakers. Thus the theory will entail sentences like the following:

'I am tired' is true as (potentially) spoken by p at t if and only if p is tired at t.
'That book was stolen' is true as (potentially) spoken by p at t if and only if the book demonstrated by p at t is stolen prior to t.[17]

Plainly, this course does not show how to eliminate demonstratives; for example, there is no suggestion that 'the book demonstrated by the speaker' can be substituted ubiquitously for 'that book' salva veritate. The fact that demonstratives are amenable to formal treatment ought greatly to improve hopes for a serious semantics of natural language, for it is likely that many outstanding puzzles, such as the analysis of quotations or sentences about propositional attitudes, can be solved if we recognize a concealed demonstrative construction.

Now that we have relativized truth to times and speakers, it is appropriate to glance back at the problem of empirically testing a theory of meaning for an alien tongue. The essence of the method was, it will be remembered, to correlate held-true sentences with held-true sentences by way of a truth definition, and within the bounds of intelligible error. Now the picture must be elaborated to allow for the fact that sentences are true, and held true, only relative to a speaker and a time. The real task is therefore to translate each sentence by another that is true for the same speakers at the same times. Sentences with demonstratives obviously yield a very sensitive test of the correctness of a theory of meaning, and constitute the most direct link between language and the recurrent macroscopic objects of human interest and attention.[18]

In this paper I have assumed that the speakers of a language can effectively determine the meaning or meanings of an arbitrary expression (if it has a meaning), and that it is the central task of a theory of meaning to show how this is possible. I have argued that a characterization of a truth predicate describes the required kind of structure, and provides a clear and testable criterion of an adequate semantics for a natural language. No doubt there are other reasonable demands that may be put on a theory of meaning. But a theory that does no more than define truth for a language comes far closer to

Donald Davidson

constituting a complete theory of meaning than superficial analysis might suggest; so, at least, I have urged.

Since I think there is no alternative, I have taken an optimistic and programmatic view of the possibilities for a formal characterization of a truth predicate for a natural language. But it must be allowed that a staggering list of difficulties and conundrums remains. To name a few: we do not know the logical form of counterfactual or subjunctive sentences; nor of sentences about probabilities and about causal relations; we have no

good idea what the logical role of adverbs is, nor the role of attributive adjectives; we have no theory for mass terms like 'fire', 'water' and 'snow', nor for sentences about belief, perception and intention, nor for verbs of action that imply purpose. And finally, there are all the sentences that seem not to have truth values at all: the imperatives, optatives, interrogatives, and a host more. A comprehensive theory of meaning for a natural language must cope successfully with each of these problems.

Notes

An earlier version of this paper was read at the Eastern Division meeting of the American Philosophical Association in December, 1966; the main theme traces back to an unpublished paper delivered to the Pacific Division of the American Philosophical Association in 1953. Present formulations owe much to John Wallace, with whom I have discussed these matters since 1962. My research was supported by the National Science Foundation.

1 Elsewhere I have urged that it is a necessary condition, if a language is to be learnable, that it have only a finite number of semantical primitives: see 'Theories of Meaning and Learnable Languages', in *Proceedings of the 1964 International Congress for Logic, Methodology and Philosophy of Science*, North-Holland Publishing Company, Amsterdam, 1965, pp. 383–94.

2 A 'structural description' of an expression describes the expression as a concatention of elements drawn from a fixed finite list (for example of words or letters).

3 The argument is essentially Frege's. See A. Church, *Introduction to Mathematical Logic*, Vol. I, Princeton 1956, pp. 24–25. It is perhaps worth mentioning that the argument does not depend on any particular identification of the entities to which sentences are supposed to refer.

4 It may be thought that Church, in 'A Formulation of the Logic of Sense and Denotation', in *Structure, Method and Meaning: Essays in Honor of H. M. Sheffer* (ed. by Henle, Kallen and Langer), Liberal Arts Press, New York, 1951, pp. 3–24, has given a theory of meaning that makes essential use of meanings as entities. But this is not the case: Church's logics of sense and denotation are interpreted as being about meanings, but they do not mention expressions and so cannot of course be theories of meaning in the sense now under discussion.

5 For a recent and instructive statement of the role of semantics in linguistics, see Noam Chomsky, 'Topics in the Theory of Generative Grammer', in

Current Trends in Linguistics (ed. by Thomas A. Sebeok), Vol. III, The Hague 1966. In this article, Chomsky (1) emphasizes the central importance of semantics in linguistic theory, (2) argues for the superiority of transformational grammers over phrase structure grammars largely on the grounds that, although phrase structure grammars may be adequate to define sentencehood for (at least) some natural languages, they are inadequate as a foundation for semantics, and (3) comments repeatedly on the 'rather primitive state' of the concepts of semantics and remarks that the notion of semantic interpretation 'still resists any deep analysis'.

6 Assuming, of course, that the extension of these predicates is limited to the sentences of *L*.

7 Alfred Tarski, 'The Concept of Truth in Formalized Languages', in *Logic, Semantics, Metamathematics*, Oxford 1956, pp. 152–278.

8 But Quine may be quoted in support of my usage: '. . . in point of *meaning* . . . a word may be said to be determined to whatever extent the truth or falsehood of its contexts is determined.' 'Truth by Convention', first published in 1936; now in *The Ways of Paradox*, New York 1966, p. 82. Since a truth definition determines the truth value of every sentence in the object language (relative to a sentence in the metalanguage), it determines the meaning of every word and sentence. This would seem to justify the title Theory of Meaning.

9 To give a single example: it is clearly a count in favor of a theory that it entails ' "Snow is white" is true if and only if snow is white'. But to contrive a theory that entails this (and works for all related sentences) is not trivial. I do not know a theory that succeeds with this very case (the problem of 'mass terms').

10 This sketch of how a theory of meaning for an alien tongue can be tested obviously owes its inspiration to Quine's account of radical translation in Chapter II of *Word and Object*, New York 1960. In suggesting

that an acceptable theory of radical translation take the form of a recursive characterization of truth, I go beyond anything explicit in Quine. Toward the end of this paper, in the discussion of demonstratives, another strong point of agreement will turn up.

11 So far as I am aware, there has been very little discussion of whether a formal truth definition can be given for a natural language. But in a more general vein, several people have urged that the concepts of formal semantics be applied to natural language. See, for example, the contributions of Yehoshua Bar-Hillel and Evert Beth to *The Philosophy of Rudolph Carnap* (ed. by Paul A. Schilpp), La Salle, Ill., 1963, and Bar-Hillel's 'Logical Syntax and Semantics', *Language* 30, 230–7.

12 Tarski, *ibid.*, p. 165.

13 *Ibid.*, p. 267.

14 The rapprochement I prospectively imagine between transformational grammar and a sound theory of meaning has been much advanced by a recent change in the conception of transformational grammar described by Chomsky in the article referred to above (note 5). The structures generated by the phrase-structure part of the grammar, it has been realized for some time, are those suited to semantic interpretation; but this view is inconsistent with the idea, held by Chomsky until recently, that recursive operations are introduced only by the transformation rules. Chomsky now believes the phrase-structure rules are recursive. Since languages to which formal semantic methods directly and naturally apply are ones for which a (recursive) phrase-structure grammar is appropriate, it is clear that Chomsky's present picture of the relation between the structures generated by the phrase-structure part of the grammar, and the sentences of the language, is very much like the picture many logicians and philosophers have had of the relation between the richer formalized languages and ordinary language. (In these remarks I am indebted to Bruce Vermazen.)

15 Quine has good things to say about this in *Methods of Logic*, New York 1950. See § 8.

16 For an up-to-date bibliography, and discussion, see A. N. Prior, *Past, Present, and Future*, Oxford 1967.

17 There is more than an intimation of this approach to demonstratives and truth in Austin's 1950 article 'Truth', reprinted in *Philosophical Papers*, Oxford 1961. See pp. 89–90.

18 These remarks clearly derive from Quine's idea that 'occasion sentences' (those with a demonstrative element) must play a central role in constructing a translation manual.

6

Outline of a Theory of Truth

Saul A. Kripke

The Problem

Ever since Pilate asked, 'What is truth?' (*John* XVIII, 38), the subsequent search for a correct answer has been inhibited by another problem, which, as is well known, also arises in a New Testament context. If, as the author of the Epistle to Titus supposes (*Titus* I, 12), a Cretan prophet, 'even a prophet of their own,' asserted that 'the Cretans are always liars,' and if 'this testimony is true' of all other Cretan utterances, then it seems that the Cretan prophet's words are true if and only if they are false. And any treatment of the concept of truth must somehow circumvent this paradox.

The Cretan example illustrates one way of achieving self-reference. Let $P(x)$ and $Q(x)$ be predicates of sentences. Then in some cases empirical evidence establishes that the sentence '$(x)(P(x) \supset Q(x))$' [or '$(\exists x)(P(x) \wedge Q(x))$', or the like] itself satisfies the predicate $P(x)$; sometimes the empirical evidence shows that it is the *only* object satisfying $P(x)$. In this latter case, the sentence in question 'says of itself' that it satisfies $Q(x)$. If $Q(x)$ is the predicate[1] 'is false', the Liar paradox results. As an example, let $P(x)$ abbreviate the predicate 'has tokens printed in copies of the *Journal of Philosophy*, November 6, 1975, p. 691, line 5'. Then the sentence:

$$(x)(P(x) \supset Q(x))$$

Saul A. Kripke, Outline of a Theory of Truth. *The Journal of Philosophy*, 72, 19 (1975): 690–716.

leads to paradox if $Q(x)$ is interpreted as falsehood.

The versions of the Liar paradox which use empirical predicates already point up one major aspect of the problem: *many, probably most, of our ordinary assertions about truth and falsity are liable, if the empirical facts are extremely unfavorable, to exhibit paradoxical features.* Consider the ordinary statement, made by Jones:

(1)   Most (i.e., a majority) of Nixon's assertions about Watergate are false.

Clearly, nothing is intrinsically wrong with (1), nor is it ill-formed. Ordinarily the truth value of (1) will be ascertainable through an enumeration of Nixon's Watergate-related assertions, and an assessment of each for truth or falsity. Suppose, however, that Nixon's assertions about Watergate are evenly balanced between the true and the false, except for one problematic case,

(2)   Everything Jones says about Watergate is true.

Suppose, in addition, that (1) is Jones's sole assertion about Watergate, or alternatively, that all his Watergate-related assertions except perhaps (1) are true. Then it requires little expertise to show that (1) and (2) are both paradoxical: they are true if and only if they are false.

The example of (1) points up an important lesson: it would be fruitless to look for an *intrinsic* criterion that will enable us to sieve out – as meaningless, or ill-formed – those sentences which lead to paradox. (1) is, indeed, the paradigm of an ordinary assertion involving the notion of falsity; just such assertions were characteristic of our recent political debate. Yet no syntactic or semantic feature of (1) guarantees that it is unparadoxical. Under the assumptions of the previous paragraph, (1) leads to paradox.[2] Whether such assumptions hold depends on the empirical facts about Nixon's (and other) utterances, not on anything intrinsic to the syntax and semantics of (1). (Even the subtlest experts may not be able to avoid utterances leading to paradox. It is said that Russell once asked Moore whether he always told the truth, and that he regarded Moore's negative reply as the sole falsehood Moore had ever produced. Surely no one had a keener nose for paradox than Russell. Yet he apparently failed to realize that if, as he thought, all Moore's *other* utterances were true, Moore's negative reply was not simply false but paradoxical.[3]) The moral: an adequate theory must allow our statements involving the notion of truth to be *risky*: they risk being paradoxical if the empirical facts are extremely (and unexpectedly) unfavorable. There can be no syntactic or semantic 'sieve' that will winnow out the 'bad' cases while preserving the 'good' ones.

I have concentrated above on versions of the paradox using empirical properties of sentences, such as being uttered by particular people. Gödel showed essentially that such empirical properties are dispensable in favor of purely syntactic properties: he showed that, for each predicate $Q(x)$, a syntactic predicate $P(x)$ can be produced such that the sentence $(x)(P(x) \supset Q(x))$ is demonstrably the only object satisfying $P(x)$. Thus, in a sense, $(x)(P(x) \supset Q(x))$ 'says of itself' that it satisfies $Q(x)$. He also showed that elementary syntax can be interpreted in number theory. In this way, Gödel put the issue of the legitimacy of self-referential sentences beyond doubt; he showed that they are as incontestably legitimate as arithmetic itself. But the examples using empirical predicates retain their importance: they point up the moral about riskiness.

A simpler, and more direct, form of self-reference uses demonstratives or proper names: Let 'Jack' be a name of the sentence 'Jack is short', and we have a sentence that says of itself that it is short. I can see nothing wrong with 'direct' self-reference of this type. If 'Jack' is not already a name in the language,[4] why can we not introduce it as a name of any entity we please? In particular, why can it not be a name of the (uninterpreted) finite sequence of marks 'Jack is short'? (Would it be permissible to call this sequence of marks 'Harry,' but not 'Jack'? Surely prohibitions on naming are arbitrary here.) There is no vicious circle in our procedure, since we need not *interpret* the sequence of marks 'Jack is short' before we name it. Yet if we name it 'Jack,' it at once becomes meaningful and true. (Note that I am speaking of self-referential sentences, not self-referential propositions.[5])

In a longer version, I would buttress the conclusion of the preceding paragraph not only by a more detailed philosophical exposition, but also by a mathematical demonstration that the simple kind of self-reference exemplified by the 'Jack is short' example could actually be used to prove the Gödel incompleteness theorem itself (and also, the Gödel–Tarski theorem on the undefinability of truth). Such a presentation of the proof of the Gödel theorem might be more perspicuous to the beginner than is the usual one. It also dispels the impression that Gödel was forced to replace direct self-reference by a more circumlocutory device. The argument must be omitted from this outline.[6]

It has long been recognized that some of the intuitive trouble with Liar sentences is shared with such sentences as

(3)   (3) is true.

which, though not paradoxical, yield no determinate truth conditions. More complicated examples include a pair of sentences each one of which says that the other is true, and an infinite sequence of sentences $\{P_i\}$, where P_i says that P_{i+1} is true. In general, if a sentence such as (1) asserts that (all, some, most, etc.) of the sentences of a certain class C are true, its truth value can be ascertained if the truth values of the sentences in the class C are ascertained. If some of these sentences themselves involve the notion of truth, their truth value in turn must be ascertained by looking at *other* sentences, and so on. If ultimately this process terminates in sentences not mentioning the concept of truth, so that the truth value of the original statement can be ascertained, we call the original sentence *grounded*; otherwise, *ungrounded*.[7] As the example of (1) indicates, whether a sentence is grounded is not in general an intrinsic (syntactic or semantic) property of a sentence, but usually depends on the empirical facts. We make utterances which we hope will turn out to be grounded. Sentences such as (3), though not paradoxical, are

Saul A. Kripke

ungrounded. The preceding is a rough sketch of the usual notion of groundedness and is not meant to provide a formal definition: the fact that a formal definition can be provided will be a principal virtue of the formal theory suggested below.[8]

Previous Proposals

Thus far the only approach to the semantic paradoxes that has been worked out in any detail is what I will call the 'orthodox approach,' which leads to the celebrated hierarchy of languages of Tarski,[9] Let L_0 be a formal language, built up by the usual operations of the first-order predicate calculus from a stock of (completely defined) primitive predicates, and adequate to discuss its own syntax (perhaps using arithmetization). (I omit an exact characterization.) Such a language cannot contain its own truth predicate, so a metalanguage L_1 contains a truth (really satisfaction) predicate $T_1(x)$ for L_0. (Indeed, Tarski shows how to define such a predicate in a higher-order language.) The process can be iterated, leading to a sequence $\{L_0, L_1, L_2, L_3, \ldots\}$ of languages, each with a truth predicate for the preceding.

Philosophers have been suspicious of the orthodox approach as an analysis of our intuitions. Surely our language contains just one word 'true', not a sequence of distinct phrases $\ulcorner true_n \urcorner$, applying to sentences of higher and higher levels. As against this objection, a defender of the orthodox view (if he does not dismiss natural language altogether, as Tarski inclined to do) may reply that the ordinary notion of truth is systematically ambiguous: its 'level' in a particular occurrence is determined by the context of the utterance and the intentions of the speaker. The notion of differing truth predicates, each with its own level, seems to correspond to the following intuitive idea, implicit in the discussion of 'groundedness' above. First, we make various utterances, such as 'snow is white', which do not involve the notion of truth. We then attribute truth values to these, using a predicate 'true$_1$'. ('True$_1$' means – roughly – 'is a true statement not itself involving truth or allied notions.') We can then form a predicate 'true$_2$' applying to sentences involving 'true$_1$', and so on. We may assume that, on each occasion of utterance, when a given speaker uses the word 'true', he attaches an implicit subscript to it, which increases as, by further and further reflec-

tion, he goes higher and higher in his own Tarski hierarchy.[10]

Unfortunately this picture seems unfaithful to the facts. If someone makes such an utterance as (1), he does *not* attach a subscript, explicit or implicit, to his utterance of 'false', which determines the 'level of language' on which he speaks. An implicit subscript would cause no trouble if we were sure of the 'level' of *Nixon's* utterances; we could then cover them all, in the utterance of (1) or even of the stronger

(4)   All of Nixon's utterances about Watergate are false.

simply by choosing a subscript higher than the levels of any involved in Nixon's Watergate-related utterances. Ordinarily, however, a speaker *has no way of knowing the 'levels' of Nixon's relevant utterances*. Thus Nixon may have said, 'Dean is a liar,' or 'Haldeman told the truth when he said that Dean lied,' etc., and the 'levels' of these may yet depend on the levels of Dean's utterances, and so on. If the speaker is forced to assign a 'level' to (4) in advance [or to the word 'false' in (4)], he may be unsure how high a level to choose; if, in ignorance of the 'level' of Nixon's utterances, he chooses too low, his utterance (4) will fail of its purpose. The idea that a statement such as (4) should, in its normal uses, have a 'level' is intuitively convincing. It is, however, equally intuitively obvious that the 'level' of (4) should not depend on the form of (4) alone (as would be the case if 'false' – or, perhaps, 'utterances' – were assigned explicit subscripts), nor should it be assigned in advance by the speaker, but rather its level should depend on the empirical facts about what Nixon has uttered. The higher the 'levels' of Nixon's utterances happen to be, the higher the 'level' of (4). This means that in some sense a statement should be allowed to seek its own level, high enough to say what it intends to say. It should not have an intrinsic level fixed in advance, as in the Tarski hierarchy.

Another situation is even harder to accommodate within the confines of the orthodox approach. Suppose Dean asserts (4), while Nixon in turn asserts

(5)   Everything Dean says about Watergate is false.

Dean, in asserting the sweeping (4), wishes to include Nixon's assertion (5) within its scope (as one of the Nixonian assertions about Watergate which is said to be false); and Nixon, in asserting (5), wishes to do the same with Dean's (4). Now on any theory that assigns intrinsic 'levels' to such statements, so that a statement of a given level can speak only of the truth or falsity of statements of lower levels, it is plainly impossible for both to succeed: if the two statements are on the same level, neither can talk about the truth or falsity of the other, while otherwise the higher can talk about the lower, but not conversely. Yet intuitively, we can often assign unambiguous truth values to (4) and (5). Suppose Dean has made at least one true statement about Watergate [other than (4)]. Then, independently of any assessment of (4), we can decide that Nixon's (5) is false. If all Nixon's other assertions about Watergate are false as well, Dean's (4) is true; if one of them is true, (4) is false. Note that in the latter case, we could have judged (4) to be false without assessing (5), but in the former case the assessment of (4) as true depended on a *prior* assessment of (5) as false. Under a different set of empirical assumptions about the veracity of Nixon and Dean, (5) would be true [and its assessment as true would depend on a prior assessment of (4) as false]. It seems difficult to accommodate these intuitions within the confines of the orthodox approach.

Other defects of the orthodox approach are more difficult to explain within a brief outline, though they have formed a substantial part of my research. One problem is that of transfinite levels. It is easy, within the confines of the orthodox approach, to assert

(6)   Snow is white.

to assert that (6) is true, that '(6) is "true" is true,' that '(6) is "true" "is true"' is true, etc.; the various occurrences of 'is true' in the sequence are assigned increasing subscripts. It is much more difficult to assert that all the statements in the sequence just described are true. To do this, we need a metalanguage of transfinite level, above all the languages of finite level. To my surprise, I have found that the problem of defining the languages of transfinite level presents substantial technical difficulties which have never seriously been investigated.[11] (Hilary Putnam and his students essentially investigated – under the guise of a superficially completely different description and mathematical motivation – the problem for the special case where we start at the lowest level

with the language of elementary number theory.) I have obtained various positive results on the problem, and there are also various negative results; they cannot be detailed here. But in the present state of the literature, it should be said that if the 'theory of language levels' is meant to include an account of transfinite levels, then one of the principal defects of the theory is simply the *nonexistence* of the theory. The existing literature can be said to define 'Tarski's hierarchy of languages' only for *finite* levels, which is hardly adequate. My own work includes an extension of the orthodox theory to transfinite levels, but it is as yet incomplete. Lack of space not only prevents me from describing the work; it prevents me from mentioning the mathematical difficulties that make the problem highly nontrivial.

Other problems can only be mentioned. One surprise to me was the fact that the orthodox approach by no means obviously guarantees groundedness in the intuitive sense mentioned above. The concept of truth for $\sum_1$ arithmetical statements is itself $\sum_1$, and this fact can be used to construct statements of the form of (3). Even if unrestricted truth definitions are in question, standard theorems easily allow us to construct a *descending* chain of first-order languages $L_0, L_1, L_2, \ldots$, such that L_i contains a truth predicate for L_{i+1}. I don't know whether such a chain can engender ungrounded sentences, or even quite how to state the problem here; some substantial technical questions in this area are yet to be solved.

Almost all the extensive recent literature seeking alternatives to the orthodox approach – I would mention especially the writings of Bas van Fraassen and Robert L. Martin[12] – agrees on a single basic idea: there is to be only one truth predicate, applicable to sentences containing the predicate itself; but paradox is to be avoided by allowing truth-value gaps and by declaring that paradoxical sentences in particular suffer from such a gap. These writings seem to me to suffer sometimes from a minor defect and almost always from a major defect. The minor defect is that some of these writings criticize a strawmannish version of the orthodox approach, not the genuine article.[13] The major defect is that these writings almost invariably are mere suggestions, not genuine theories. Almost never is there any precise semantical formulation of a language, at least rich enough to speak of its own elementary syntax (either directly or via arithmetization) and containing its own truth predicate. Only if such a language were set up with formal precision could it be said that a theory of the semantic paradoxes has been presented. Ideally, a theory should show that the technique can be applied to arbitrarily rich languages, no matter what their 'ordinary' predicates other than truth. And there is yet another sense in which the orthodox approach provides a theory while the alternative literature does not. Tarski shows how, for a classical first-order language whose quantifiers range over a set, he can give a *mathematical definition* of truth, using the predicates of the object language plus set theory (higher-order logic). The alternative literature abandons the attempt at a mathematical definition of truth, and is content to take it as an intuitive primitive. Only one paper in the 'truth-gap' genre that I have read – a recent paper by Martin and Peter Woodruff[14] – comes close even to beginning an attempt to satisfy any of these desiderata for a theory. Nevertheless the influence of this literature on my own proposal will be obvious.[15]

The Present Proposal

I do not regard any proposal, including the one to be advanced here, as definitive in the sense that it gives *the* interpretation of the ordinary use of 'true', or *the* solution to the semantic paradoxes. On the contrary, I have not at the moment thought through a careful philosophical justification of the proposal, nor am I sure of the exact areas and limitations of its applicability. I do hope that the model given here has two virtues: first, that it provides an area rich in formal structure and mathematical properties; second, that to a reasonable extent these properties capture important intuitions. The model, then, is to be tested by its technical fertility. It need not capture every intuition, but it is hoped that it will capture many.

Following the literature mentioned above, we propose to investigate languages allowing truth-value gaps. Under the influence of Strawson,[16] we can regard a sentence as an attempt to make a statement, express a proposition, or the like. The meaningfulness or well-formedness of the sentence lies in the fact that there are specifiable circumstances under which it has determinate truth conditions (expresses a proposition), not that it always does express a proposition. A sentence such as (1) is always *meaningful*, but under various circumstances it may not 'make a statement' or 'express

a proposition.' (I am not attempting to be philosophically completely precise here.)

To carry out these ideas, we need a semantical scheme to handle predicates that may be only partially defined. Given a nonempty domain D, a monadic predicate $P(x)$ is interpreted by a pair (S_1, S_2) of disjoint subsets of D. S_1 is the *extension* of $P(x)$ and S_2 is its *anti-extension*. $P(x)$ is to be true of the objects in S_1, false of those in S_2, undefined otherwise. The generalization to n-place predicates is obvious.

One appropriate scheme for handing connectives is Kleene's strong three-valued logic. Let us suppose that $\sim P$ is true (false) if P is false (true), and undefined if P is undefined. A disjunction is true if at least one disjunct is true regardless of whether the other disjunct is true, false, or undefined[17]; it is false if both disjuncts are false; undefined, otherwise. The other truth functions can be defined in terms of disjunction and negation in the usual way. (In particular, then, a conjunction will be true if both conjuncts are true, false if at least one conjunct is false, and undefined otherwise.) $(\exists x)A(x)$ is true if $A(x)$ is true for some assignment of an element of D to x; false if $A(x)$ is false for all assignments to x, and undefined otherwise. $(x)A(x)$ can be defined as $\sim (\exists x) \sim A(x)$. It therefore is true if $A(x)$ is true for all assignments to x, false if $A(x)$ is false for at least one such assignment, and undefined otherwise. We could convert the preceding into a more precise formal definition of satisfaction, but we won't bother.[18]

We wish to capture an intuition of somewhat the following kind. Suppose we are explaining the word 'true' to someone who does not yet understand it. We may say that we are entitled to assert (or deny) of any sentence that it is true precisely under the circumstances when we can assert (or deny) the sentence itself. Our interlocutor then can understand what it means, say, to attribute truth to (6) ('snow is white') but he will still be puzzled about attributions of truth to sentences containing the word 'true' itself. Since he did not understand these sentences initially, it will be equally nonexplanatory, initially, to explain to him that to call such a sentence 'true' ('false') is tantamount to asserting (denying) the sentence itself.

Nevertheless, with more thought the notion of truth as applied even to various sentences themselves containing the word 'true' can gradually become clear. Suppose we consider the sentence,

(7) Some sentence printed in the *New York Daily News*, October 7, 1971, is true.

(7) is a typical example of a sentence involving the concept of truth itself. So if (7) is unclear, so still is

(8) (7) is true.

However, our subject, if he is willing to assert 'snow is white', will according to the rules be willing to assert '(6) is true'. But suppose that among the assertions printed in the *New York Daily News*, October 7, 1971, is (6) itself. Since our subject is willing to assert '(6) is true', and also to assert '(6) is printed in the *New York Daily News*, October 7, 1971', he will deduce (7) by existential generalization. Once he is willing to assert (7), he will also be willing to assert (8). In this manner, the subject will eventually be able to attribute truth to more and more statements involving the notion of truth itself. There is no reason to suppose that *all* statements involving 'true' will become decided in this way, but most will. Indeed, our suggestion is that the 'grounded' sentences can be characterized as those which eventually get a truth value in this process.

A typically ungrounded sentence such as (3) will, of course, receive no truth value in the process just sketched. In particular, it will never be called 'true.' But the subject cannot express this fact by saying, '(3) is not true.' Such an assertion would conflict directly with the stipulation that he should deny that a sentence is true precisely under the circumstances under which he would deny the sentence itself. In imposing this stipulation, we have made a deliberate choice (see below).

Let us see how we can give these ideas formal expression. Let L be an interpreted first-order language of the classical type, with a finite (or even denumerable) list of primitive predicates. It is assumed that the variables range over some nonempty domain D, and that the primitive n-ary predicates are interpreted by (totally defined) n-ary relations on D. The interpretation of the predicates of L is kept fixed throughout the following discussion. Let us also assume that the language L is rich enough so that the syntax of L (say, via arithmetization) can be expressed in L, and that some coding scheme codes finite sequences of elements of D into elements of D. We do not attempt to make these ideas rigorous; Y. N. Moschovakis's notion of an 'acceptable' structure would do so.[19] I

should emphasize that a great deal of what we do below goes through under much weaker hypotheses on L.[20]

Suppose we extend L to a language $\mathfrak{L}$ by adding a monadic predicate $T(x)$ whose interpretation need only be partially defined. An interpretation of $T(x)$ is given by a 'partial set' (S_1, S_2), where S_1, as we said above, is the *extension* of $T(x)$, S_2 is the *antiextension* of $T(x)$, and $T(x)$ is undefined for entities outside $S_1 \smile S_2$. Let $\mathfrak{L}(S_1, S_2)$ be the interpretation of $\mathfrak{L}$ which results from interpreting $T(x)$ by the pair (S_1, S_2), the interpretation of the other predicates of L remaining as before.[21] Let S_1' be the set of (codes of)[22] true sentences of $\mathfrak{L}$ (S_1, S_2), and let S_2' be the set of all elements of D which either are not (codes of) sentences of $\mathfrak{L}(S_1, S_2)$ or are (codes of) false sentences of $\mathfrak{L}(S_1, S_2)$. S_1' and S_2' are uniquely determined by the choice of (S_1, S_2). Clearly, if $T(x)$ is to be interpreted as truth for the very language L containing $T(x)$ itself, we must have $S_1 = S_1'$ and $S_2 = S_2'$. [This means that if A is any sentence, A satisfies (falsifies) $T(x)$ iff A is true (false) by the evaluation rules.]

A pair (S_1, S_2) that satisfies this condition is called a *fixed point*. For a given choice of (S_1, S_2) to interpret $T(x)$, set $\phi((S_1, S_2)) = (S_1', S_2')\phi$ then is a unary function defined on all pairs (S_1, S_2) of disjoint subsets of D, and the 'fixed points' (S_1, S_2) are literally the fixed points of ϕ; i.e., they are those pairs (S_1, S_2) such that $\phi((S_1, S_2)) = (S_1, S_2)$. If (S_1, S_2) is a fixed point, we sometimes call $\mathfrak{L}(S_1, S_2)$ a fixed point also. Our basic task is to prove the existence of fixed points, and to investigate their properties.

Let us first construct a fixed point. We do so by considering a certain 'hierarchy of languages.' We start by defining the interpreted language $\mathfrak{L}_0$ as $\mathfrak{L}(\Lambda, \Lambda)$, where Λ is the empty set; i.e., $\mathfrak{L}_0$ is the language where $T(x)$ is completely undefined. (It is never a fixed point.) For any integer α, suppose we have defined $\mathfrak{L}_\alpha = \mathfrak{L}(S_1, S_2)$. Then set $\mathfrak{L}_{\alpha+1} = \mathfrak{L}(S_1', S_2')$, where as before S_1' is the set of (codes of) true sentences of $\mathfrak{L}_\alpha$, and S_2' is the set of all elements of D which either are not (codes of) sentences of $\mathfrak{L}_\alpha$ or are (codes of) false sentences of $\mathfrak{L}_\alpha$.

The hierarchy of languages just given is analogous to the Tarski hierarchy for the orthodox approach. $T(x)$ is interpreted in $\mathfrak{L}_{\alpha+1}$ as the truth predicate for $\mathfrak{L}_\alpha$. But an interesting phenomenon, detailed in the following paragraphs, arises on the present approach.

Let us say that $(S_1{}^\dagger, S_2{}^\dagger)$ *extends* (S_1, S_2) [symbolically, $(S_1{}^\dagger, S_2{}^\dagger) \geq (S_1, S_2)$ or $(S_1, S_2) \leq (S_1{}^\dagger, S_2{}^\dagger)$] iff $S_1 \subseteq S_1{}^\dagger, S_2 \subseteq S_2{}^\dagger$. Intuitively this means that if $T(x)$ is interpreted as $(S_1{}^\dagger, S_2{}^\dagger)$, the interpretation agrees with the interpretation by (S_1, S_2) in all cases where the latter is defined; the only difference is that an interpretation by $(S_1{}^\dagger, S_2{}^\dagger)$ may lead $T(x)$ to be defined for some cases where it was undefined when interpreted by (S_1, S_2). Now a basic property of our valuation rules is the following: ϕ is a monotone (order-preserving) operation on $\leq$: that is, if $(S_1, S_2) \leq (S_1{}^\dagger, S_2{}^\dagger), \phi ((S_1, S_2)) \leq \phi ((S_1{}^\dagger, S_2{}^\dagger))$. In other words, *if* $(S_1, S_2) \leq (S_1{}^\dagger, S_2{}^\dagger)$, *then any sentence that is true (or false) in* $\mathfrak{L}(S_1, S_2)$ *retains its truth value in* $\mathfrak{L}(S_1{}^\dagger, S_2{}^\dagger)$. What this means is that *if the interpretation of $T(x)$ is extended by giving it a definite truth value for cases that were previously undefined, no truth value previously established changes or becomes undefined*; at most, certain previously undefined truth values become defined. This property – technically, the monotonicity of ϕ – is crucial for all our constructions.

Given the monotonicity of ϕ, we can deduce that for each α, *the interpretation of $T(x)$ in $\mathfrak{L}_{\alpha+1}$ extends the interpretation of $T(x)$ in $\mathfrak{L}_\alpha$*. The fact is obvious for $\alpha = 0$: since, in $\mathfrak{L}_0$, $T(x)$ is undefined for all x, any interpretation of $T(x)$ automatically extends it. If the assertion holds for $\mathfrak{L}_\beta$ – that is, if the interpretation of $T(x)$ in $\mathfrak{L}_{\beta+1}$ extends that of $T(x)$ in $\mathfrak{L}_\beta$ – then any sentence true or false in $\mathfrak{L}_\beta$ remains true or false in $\mathfrak{L}_{\beta+1}$. If we look at the definitions, *this says that the interpretation of $T(x)$ in $\mathfrak{L}_{\beta+2}$ extends the interpretation of $T(x)$ in $\mathfrak{L}_{\beta+1}$. We have thus proved by induction that the interpretation of $T(x)$ in $\mathfrak{L}_{\alpha+1}$ always extends the interpretation of $T(x)$ in $\mathfrak{L}_\alpha$ for all finite α. It follows that the predicate $T(x)$ increases, in both its extension and its antiextension, as α increases. More and more sentences get declared true or false as α increases; but once a sentence is declared true or false, it retains its truth value at all higher levels.*

So far, we have defined only *finite* levels of our hierarchy. For finite α, let $(S_{1,\alpha}, S_{2,\alpha})$ be the interpretation of $T(x)$ in $\mathfrak{L}_\alpha$. Both $S_{1,\alpha}$ and $S_{2,\alpha}$ increase (as sets) as α increases. Then there is an obvious way of defining the first 'transfinite' level – call it '$\mathfrak{L}_\omega$.' Simply define $\mathfrak{L}_\omega = \mathfrak{L}(S_{1,\omega}, S_{2,\omega})$, where $S_{1,\omega}$ is the union of all $S_{1,\alpha}$ for finite α, and $S_{2,\omega}$ is similarly the union of $S_{2,\alpha}$ for finite α. Given $\mathfrak{L}_\omega$, we can then define $\mathfrak{L}_{\omega+1}$, $\mathfrak{L}_{\omega+2}$, $\mathfrak{L}_{\omega+2}$, etc., just as we did for the finite levels. When we get again to a 'limit' level, we take a union as before.

Formally, we define the languages $\mathfrak{L}_\alpha$ for each ordinal α. If α is a successor ordinal ($\alpha = \beta + 1$), let $\mathfrak{L}_\alpha = \mathfrak{L}(S_{1,\alpha}, S_{2,\alpha})$, where $S_{1,\alpha}$ is the set of (codes of) true sentences of $\mathfrak{L}_\beta$, and $S_{2,\alpha}$ is the set consisting of all elements of D which either are (codes of) false sentences of $\mathfrak{L}_\beta$ or are not (codes of) sentences of $\mathfrak{L}_\beta$. If λ is a limit ordinal, $\mathfrak{L}_\lambda = \mathfrak{L}(S_{1,\lambda}, S_{2,\lambda})$, where $S_{1,\lambda} = \cup_\beta < \lambda S_{1,\beta}$, $S_{2,\lambda} = \cup_{\beta<\lambda} S_{2,\beta}$. So at 'successor' levels we take the truth predicate over the previous level, and, at limit (transfinite) levels, we take the union of all sentences declared true or false at previous levels. *Even with the transfinite levels included, it remains true that the extension and the antiextension of $T(x)$ increase with increasing α.*

It should be noted that 'increase' does not mean 'strictly increase'; we have asserted that $S_{i,\alpha} \subseteq S_{i,\alpha+1}(i = 1, 2)$, which allows equality. Does the process go on forever with more and more statements being declared true or false, or does it eventually stop? That is to say, is there an ordinal level σ for which $S_{1,\sigma} = S_{1,\sigma+1}$ and $S_{2,\sigma} = S_{2,\sigma+1}$, so that no 'new' statements are declared true or false at the next level? The answer must be affirmative. The sentences of $\mathfrak{L}$ form a set. If new sentences of $\mathfrak{L}$ were being decided at each level, we would eventually exhaust $\mathfrak{L}$ at some level and be unable to decide any more. This can easily be converted to a formal proof (the technique is elementary and is well known to logicians) that there is an ordinal level σ such that $(S_{1,\sigma}, S_{2,\sigma}) = (S_{1,\sigma+1}, S_{2,\sigma+1})$. But since $(S_1, \sigma + 1, S_{2,\sigma+1}) = \phi((S_{1,\sigma}, S_{2,\sigma}))$, *this means that $(S_{1,\sigma}, S_{2,\sigma})$ is a fixed point*. It can also be proved that it is a 'minimal' or 'smallest' fixed point: *any fixed point extends $(S_{1,\sigma}, S_{2,\sigma})$*. That is, if a sentence is valuated as true or false in $\mathfrak{L}_\sigma$, it has the same truth value in *any* fixed point.

Let us relate the construction of a fixed point just given to our previous intuitive ideas. At the initial stage $(\mathfrak{L}_0)$, $T(x)$ is completely undefined. This corresponds to the initial stage at which the subject has no understanding of the notion of truth. Given a characterization of truth by the Kleene valuation rules, the subject can easily ascend to the level of $\mathfrak{L}_1$. That is, he can evaluate various statements as true or false without knowing anything about $T(x)$ – in particular, he can evaluate all those sentences not containing $T(x)$. Once he has made the evaluation, he extends $T(x)$, as in $\mathfrak{L}_1$. Then he can use the new interpretation of $T(x)$ to evaluate more sentences as true or false and ascend to $\mathfrak{L}_2$, etc. Eventually, when the process becomes 'saturated,' the subject reaches the fixed point $\mathfrak{L}_\sigma$. (*Being a fixed point*, $\mathfrak{L}_\sigma$ *is a language that contains its own truth predicate.*) So the formal definition just given directly parallels the intuitive constructions stated previously.[23]

We have been talking of a language that contains its own truth predicate. Really, however, it would be more interesting to extend an arbitrary language to a language containing its own *satisfaction* predicate. If L contains a name for each object in D, and a denotation relation is defined (if D is non-denumerable, this means that L contains nondenumerably many constants), the notion of satisfaction can (for most purposes) effectively be replaced by that of truth: e.g., instead of talking of $A(x)$ being satisfied by an object a, we can talk of $A(x)$ becoming true when the variable is replaced by a name of a. Then the previous construction suffices. Alternatively, if L does not contain a name for each object, we can extend L to $\mathfrak{L}$ by adding a binary satisfaction predicate $Sat(s,x)$ where s ranges over finite sequences of elements of D and x ranges over formulas. We define a hierarchy of languages, parallel to the previous construction with truth, eventually reaching a fixed point – a language that contains its own satisfaction predicate. If L is denumerable but D is not, the construction with truth alone closes off at a countable ordinal, but the construction with satisfaction may close off at an uncountable ordinal. Below we will continue, for simplicity of exposition, to concentrate on the construction with truth, but the construction with satisfaction is more basic.[24]

The construction could be generalized so as to allow more notation in L than just first-order logic. For example, we could have a quantifier meaning 'for uncountably many x,' a 'most' quantifier, a language with infinite conjunctions, etc. There is a fairly canonical way, in the Kleene style, to extend the semantics of such quantifiers and connectives so as to allow truth–value gaps, but we will not give details.

Let us check that our model satisfies some of the desiderata mentioned in the previous sections. It is clearly a theory in the required sense: any language, including those containing number theory or syntax, can be extended to a language with its own truth predicate, and the associated concept of truth is *mathematically* defined by set-theoretic techniques. There is no problem about the languages of transfinite level in the hierarchy.

Given a sentence A of $\mathfrak{L}$, let us define A to be *grounded* if it has a truth value in the smallest fixed point $\mathfrak{L}_\sigma$; otherwise, *ungrounded*. What hitherto has been, as far as I know, an intuitive concept with no formal definition, becomes a precisely defined concept in the present theory. If A is grounded, define the *level* of A to be the smallest ordinal α such that A has a truth value in $\mathfrak{L}_\alpha$.

There is no problem, if $\mathfrak{L}$ contains number theory or syntax, of constructing Gödelian sentences that 'say of themselves' that they are false (Liar sentences) or true [as in (3)]; all these are easily shown to be ungrounded in the sense of the formal definition. If the Gödelian form of the Liar paradox is used, for example, the Liar sentence can get the form

$$(9) \qquad (x)(P(x) \supset \sim T(x))$$

where $P(x)$ is a syntactic (or arithmetical) predicate uniquely satisfied by (the Gödel number of) (9) itself. Similarly (3) gets the form

$$(10) \qquad (x)(Q(x) \supset T(x))$$

where $Q(x)$ is uniquely satisfied by (the Gödel number of) (10). It is easy to prove, under these hypotheses, by induction on α, that neither (9) nor (10) will have a truth value in any $\mathfrak{L}_\alpha$, that is, that they are ungrounded. Other intuitive cases of ungroundedness come out similarly.

The feature I have stressed about ordinary statements, that there is no intrinsic guarantee of their safety (groundedness) and that their 'level' depends on empirical facts, comes out clearly in the present model. Consider, for example, (9) again, except that now $P(x)$ is an empirical predicate whose extension depends on unknown empirical facts. If $P(x)$ turns out to be true only of (9) itself, (9) will be ungrounded as before. If the extension of $P(x)$ consists entirely of grounded sentences of levels, say, 2, 4, and 13, (9) will be grounded with level 14. If the extension of $P(x)$ consists of grounded sentences of arbitrary finite level, (9) will be grounded with level ω. And so on.

Now let us consider the cases of (4) and (5). We can formalize (4) by (9), interpreting $P(x)$ as 'x is a sentence Nixon asserts about Watergate.' [Forget for simplicity that 'about Watergate' introduces a semantic component into the interpretation of $P(x)$.] Formalize (5) as

$$(11) \qquad (x)(Q(x) \supset \sim T(x))$$

interpreting $Q(x)$ in the obvious way. To complete the parallel with (4) and (5), suppose that (9) is in the extension of $Q(x)$ and (11) is in the extension of $P(x)$. Now nothing guarantees that (9) and (11) will be grounded. Suppose, however, parallel to the intuitive discussion above, that some true grounded sentence satisfies $Q(x)$. If the lowest level of any such sentence is α, then (11) will be false and grounded of level $\alpha + 1$. If in addition all the sentences other than (11) satisfying $P(x)$ are false, (9) will then be grounded and true. The level of (9) will be at least $\alpha + 2$, because of the level of (11). On the other hand, if some sentence satisfying $P(x)$ is grounded and true, then (9) will be grounded and false with level $\beta + 1$, where β is the lowest level of any such sentence. It is crucial to the ability of the present model to assign levels to (4) and (5) [(9) and (11)] that the levels depend on empirical facts, rather than being assigned in advance.

We said that such statements as (3), though ungrounded, are not intuitively paradoxical either. Let us explore this in terms of the model. The smallest fixed point $\mathfrak{L}_\sigma$ is not the only fixed point. Let us formalize (3) by (10), where $Q(x)$ is a *syntactic* predicate (of L) true of (10) itself alone. Suppose that, instead of starting out our hierarchy of languages with $T(x)$ completely undefined, we had started out by letting $T(x)$ be true of (10), undefined otherwise. We then can continue the hierarchy of languages just as before. It is easy to see that if (10) is true at the language of a given level, it will remain true at the next level [using the fact that $Q(x)$ is true of (10) alone, false of everything else]. From this we can show as before that the interpretation of $T(x)$ at each level extends all previous levels, and that at some level the construction closes off to yield a fixed point. The difference is that (10), which lacked truth value in the smallest fixed point, is now *true*.

This suggests the following definition: a sentence is *paradoxical* if it has not truth value in *any* fixed point. That is, a paradoxical sentence A is such that if $\phi(S_1, S_2)) = (S_1, S_2)$, then A is neither an element of S_1 nor an element of S_2.

(3) [or its formal version (10)] is ungrounded, but not paradoxical. This means that we *could* consistently use the predicate 'true' so as to give (3) [or (10)] a truth value, though the minimal process for assigning truth values does not do so. Suppose, on the other hand, in (9), that $P(x)$ is true of (9) itself and false of everything else, so that (9) is a Liar sentence. Then the argument of the Liar

paradox easily yields a proof that (9) cannot have a truth value in any fixed point. So (9) is paradoxical in our technical sense. Notice that, if it is merely an empirical fact that $P(x)$ is true of (9) and false of everything else, the fact that (9) is paradoxical will itself be empirical. (We could define notions of 'intrinsically paradoxical', 'intrinsically grounded', etc., but will not do so here.)

Intuitively, the situation seems to be as follows. Although the smallest fixed point is probably the most natural model for the intuitive concept of truth, and is the model *generated* by our instructions to the imaginary subject, the other fixed points never *conflict* with these instructions. We *could* consistently use the world 'true' so as to give a truth value to such a sentence as (3) without violating the idea that a sentence should be asserted to be true precisely when we would assert the sentence itself. The same does not hold for the paradoxical sentences.

Using Zorn's Lemma, we can prove that *every fixed point can be extended to a maximal fixed point*, where a maximal fixed point is a fixed point that has no proper extension that is also a fixed point. Maximal fixed points assign 'as many truth values as possible'; one could not assign more consistently with the intuitive concept of truth. Sentences like (3), though ungrounded, have a truth value in every maximal fixed point. Ungrounded sentences exist, however, which have truth values in some but not all maximal fixed points.

It is as easy to construct fixed points which make (3) false as it is to construct fixed points which make it true. So the assignment of a truth value to (3) is *arbitrary*. Indeed any fixed point which assigns no truth value to (3) can be extended to fixed points which make it true and to fixed points which make it false. Grounded sentences have the same truth value in all fixed points. There are ungrounded and unparadoxical sentences, however, which have the same truth value in all the fixed points where they have a truth value. An example is:

(12) Either (12) or its negation is true.

It is easy to show that there are fixed points which make (12) true and none which make (12) false. Yet (12) is ungrounded (has no truth value in the minimal fixed point).

Call a fixed point *intrinsic* iff it assigns no sentence a truth value conflicting with its truth value in any other fixed point. That is, a fixed point

(S_1, S_2) is intrinsic iff there is no other fixed point $(S_1^\dagger, S_2^\dagger)$ and sentence A of L' such that $A\varepsilon(S_1 \cap S_2^\dagger) \cup (S_2 \cap S_1^\dagger)$. We say that a sentence has *an intrinsic truth value* iff some intrinsic fixed point gives it a truth value; i.e., A has an intrinsic truth value iff there is an intrinsic fixed point (S_1, S_2) such that $A\varepsilon S_1 \cup S_2$. (12) is a good example.

There are unparadoxical sentences which have the same truth value in all fixed points where they have truth value but which nevertheless lack an intrinsic truth value. Consider $P \vee \sim P$, where P is any ungrounded unparadoxical sentence. Then $P \vee \sim P$ is true in some fixed points (namely, those where P has a truth value) and is false in none. Suppose, however, that there are fixed points that make P true and fixed points that make P false. [For example, say, P is (3).] Then $P \vee \sim P$ cannot have a truth value in any intrinsic fixed point, since, by our valuation rules, it cannot have a truth value unless some disjunct does.[25]

There is no 'largest' fixed point that extends every other; indeed, any two fixed points that give different truth values to the same formula have no common extension. However, it is not hard to show that there is a largest intrinsic fixed point (and indeed that the intrinsic fixed points form a complete lattice under $\leq$). The largest intrinsic fixed point is the unique 'largest' interpretation of $T(x)$ which is consistent with our intuitive idea of truth and makes no arbitrary choices in truth assignments. It is thus an object of special theoretical interest as a model.

It is interesting to compare 'Tarski's hierarchy of languages' with the present model. Unfortunately, this can hardly be done in full generality without introducing the transfinite levels, a task omitted from this sketch. But we can say something about the finite levels. Intuitively, it would seem that Tarski predicates true_n are all special cases of a single truth predicate. For example, we said above that 'true_1' means 'is a true sentence not involving truth.' Let us carry this idea out formally. Let $A_1(x)$ be a syntactic (arithmetical) predicate true of exactly the formulas of $\mathfrak{L}$ not involving $T(x)$, i.e., of all formulas of L. $A_1(x)$, being syntactic, is itself a formula of L, as are all other syntactic formulas below. Define '$T_1(x)$' as '$T(x) \wedge A_1(x)$'. Let $A_2(x)$ be a syntactic predicate applying to all those formulas whose atomic predicates are those of L plus '$T_1(x)$'. [More precisely the class of such formulas can be defined as the least class including all formulas of L and

$T(x_i) \wedge A_1(x_i)$, for any variable x_i, and closed under truth functions and quantification.] Then define $T_2(x)$ as $T(x) \wedge A_2(x)$. In general, we can define $A_{n+1}(x)$ as a syntactic predicate applying precisely to formulas built out of the predicates of L and $T_n(x)$, and $T_{n+1}(x)$ as $T(x) \wedge A_{n+1}(x)$. Assume that $T(x)$ is interpreted by the smallest fixed point (or any other). Then it is easy to prove by induction that each predicate $T_n(x)$ is totally defined, that the extension of $T_0(x)$ consists precisely of the true formulas of L, while that of $T_{n+1}(x)$ consists of the true formulas of the language obtained by adjoining $T_n(x)$ to L. This means that *all the truth predicates of the finite Tarski hierarchy are definable within $\mathfrak{L}_\sigma$, and all the languages of that hierarchy are sublanguages of $\mathfrak{L}_\sigma$.*[26] This kind of result could be extended into the transfinite if we had defined the transfinite Tarski hierarchy.

There are converse results, harder to state in this sketch. It is characteristic of the sentences in the Tarski hierarchy that they are safe (intrinsically grounded) and that their level is intrinsic, given independently of the empirical facts. It is natural to conjecture that any grounded sentence with intrinsic level n is in some sense 'equivalent' to a sentence of level n in the Tarski hierarchy. Given proper definitions of 'intrinsic level', 'equivalent', and the like, theorems of this kind can be stated and proved and even extended into the transfinite.

So far we have assumed that truth gaps are to be handled according to the methods of Kleene. It is by no means necessary to do so. Just about any scheme for handling truth-value gaps is usable, provided that the basic property of the monotonicity of ϕ is preserved; that is, provided that extending the interpretation of $T(x)$ never changes the truth value of any sentence of $\mathfrak{L}$, but at most gives truth values to previously undefined cases. Given any such scheme, we can use the previous arguments to construct the minimal fixed point and other fixed points, define the levels of sentences and the notions of 'grounded', 'paradoxical', etc.

One scheme usable in this way is van Fraassen's notion of *supervaluation*.[27] For the language $\mathfrak{L}$, the definition is easy. Given an interpretation (S_1, S_2) of $T(x)$ in $\mathfrak{L}$, call a formula A true (false) iff it comes out true (false) by the ordinary classical valuation under every interpretation $(S_1^\dagger, S_2^\dagger)$ which extends (S_1, S_2) and is *totally defined*, i.e., is such that $S_1^\dagger \cup S_2^\dagger = D$. We can then define the hierarchy $\{\mathfrak{L}_\alpha\}$ and the minimal fixed point $\mathfrak{L}_\sigma$ as before. Under the supervaluation interpretation, all formulas provable in classical quantification theory become true in $\mathfrak{L}_\sigma$; under the Kleene valuation, one could say only that they were true whenever they were defined. Thanks to the fact that $\mathfrak{L}_\sigma$ contains its own truth predicate, we need not express this fact by a schema, or by a statement of a metalanguage. If $PQT(x)$ is a syntactic predicate true exactly of the sentences of $\mathfrak{L}$ provable in quantification theory, we can assert:

(13) $(x)(PQT(x) \supset T(x))$

and (13) will be true in the minimal fixed point.

Here we have used supervaluations in which *all* total extensions of the interpretation of $T(x)$ are taken into account. It is natural to consider restrictions on the family of total extensions, motivated by intuitive properties of truth. For example, we could consider only *consistent* interpretations $(S_1^\dagger, S_2^\dagger)$, where $(S_1^\dagger, S_2^\dagger)$ is consistent iff S_1 contains no sentence together with its negation. Then we could define A to be true (false) with $T(x)$ interpreted by (S_1, S_2) iff A is true (false) classically when A is interpreted by any *consistent* totally defined extension of (S_1, S_2).

(14) $(x) \sim (T(x) \wedge T(\text{neg}(x)))$

will be true in the minimal fixed point. If we restricted the admissible total extensions to those defining *maximal* consistent sets of sentences, in the usual sense, not only (14) but even

$(x)(Sent(x) \supset T(x) \vee T(\text{neg}(x)))$

will come out true in the minimal fixed point.[28] The last-mentioned formula, however, must be interpreted with caution, since it is still not the case, even on the supervaluation interpretation in question, that there is any fixed point that makes every formula or its negation true. (The paradoxical formulas still lack truth value in all fixed points.) The phenomenon is associated with the fact that that, on the supervaluation interpretation, a disjunction can be true without it following that some disjunct is true.

It is not the purpose of the present work to make any particular recommendation among the Kleene strong three-valued approach, the van Fraassen supervaluation approaches, or any other scheme (such as the Fregean weak three-valued logic, preferred by Martin and Woodruff, though I am in fact tentatively inclined to consider the latter excessively cumbersome). Nor is it even my present purpose to make any firm recommendation between the minimal fixed point of a particular valuation scheme and the various other fixed points.[29] Indeed, without the nonminimal fixed points we could not have defined the intuitive difference between 'grounded' and 'paradoxical'. My purpose is rather to provide a family of flexible instruments which can be explored simultaneously and whose fertility and consonance with intuition can be checked.

I am somewhat uncertain whether there is a definite factual question as to whether natural language handles truth-value gaps – at least those arising in connection with the semantic paradoxes – by the schemes of Frege, Kleene, van Fraassen, or perhaps some other. Nor am I even *quite* sure that there is a definite question of fact as to whether natural language should be evaluated by the minimal fixed point or another, given the choice of a scheme for handling gaps.[30] We are not at the moment searching for *the* correct scheme.

The present approach can be applied to languages containing model operators. In this case, we do not merely consider truth, but we are given, in the usual style of modal model theory, a system of possible worlds, and evaluate truth and $T(x)$ in each possible world. The inductive definition of the languages $\mathfrak{L}_\alpha$ approximating to the minimal fixed point must be modified accordingly. We cannot give details here.[31]

Ironically, the application of the present approach to languages with modal operators may be of some interest to those who dislike intensional operators and possible worlds and prefer to take modalities and propositional attitudes as predicates true of sentences (or sentence tokens). Montague and Kaplan have pointed out, using elementary applications of Gödelian techniques, that such approaches are likely to lead to semantic paradoxes, analogous to the Liar.[32] Though the difficulty has been known for some time, the extensive literature advocating such treatments has usually simply ignored the problem rather than indicating how it is to be solved (say, by a hierarchy of languages?). Now, if a necessity operator and a truth predicate are allowed, we could define a necessity predicate $Nec(x)$ applied to sentences, either by $T(x)$ or $T(\text{nec}(x))$ according to taste,[33] and treat it according to the possible-world scheme sketched in the preceding paragraph. (I do think that any necessity predicate of sentences should intuitively be regarded as derivative, defined in terms of an operator and a truth predicate. I also think the same holds for propositional attitudes.) We can even 'kick away the ladder' and take $Nec(x)$ as primitive, treating it in a possible-world scheme *as if* it were defined by an operator plus a truth predicate. Like remarks apply to the propositional attitudes, if we are willing to treat them, using possible worlds, like modal operators. (I myself think that such a treatment involves considerable philosophical difficulties). It is possible that the present approach can be applied to the supposed predicates of sentences in question without using either intensional operators or possible worlds, but at present I have no idea how to do so.

It seems likely that many who have worked on the truth-gap approach to the semantic paradoxes have hoped for a universal language, one in which everything that can be stated at all can be expressed. (The proof by Gödel and Tarski that a language cannot contain its own semantics applied only to languages without truth gaps.) Now the languages of the present approach contain their own truth predicates and even their own satisfaction predicates, and thus to this extent the hope has been realized. Nevertheless the present approach certainly does not claim to give a universal language, and I doubt that such a goal can be achieved. First, the induction defining the minimal fixed point is carried out in a set-theoretic meta-language, not in the object language itself. Second, there are assertions we can make about the object language which we cannot make in the object language. For example, Liar sentences are *not true* in the object language, in the sense that the inductive process never makes them true; but we are precluded from saying this in the object language by our interpretation of negation and the truth predicate. If we think of the minimal fixed point, say under the Kleene valuation, as giving a model of natural language, then the sense in which we can say, in natural language, that a Liar sentence is not true must be thought of as associated with some later stage in the development of natural language, one in which speakers reflect on the generation process leading to the minimal fixed point. It is not itself a part of that process. The necessity to ascend to a metalanguage may be one of the weaknesses of the present theory. The ghost of the Tarski hierarchy is still with us.[34]

The approach adopted here has presupposed the following version of Tarski's 'Convention T', adapted to the three-valued approach: If 'k' abbreviates a name of the sentence A, $T(k)$ is to be true, or false, respectively iff A is true, or false. This captures the intuition that $T(k)$ is to have the same truth conditions as A itself; it follows that $T(k)$ suffers a truth-value gap if A does. An alternate intuition[35] would assert that, if A is either false or undefined, then A is *not true* and $T(k)$ should be *false*, and its negation *true*. On this view, $T(x)$ will be a totally defined predicate and there are no truth-value gaps. Presumably Tarski's Convention T must be restricted in some way.

It is not difficult to modify the present approach so as to accommodate such an alternate intuition. Take any fixed point $L'(S_1, S_2)$. Modify the interpretation of $T(x)$ so as to make it false of any sentence outside S. [We call this 'closing off' $T(x)$.] A modified version of Tarski's Convention T holds in the sense of the conditional $T(k) \vee T$ (neg(k) $\cdot \supset \cdot A \equiv T(k)$. In particular, if A is a paradoxical sentence, we can now assert $\sim T(k)$. Equivalently, if A had a truth value before $T(x)$ was closed off, then $A \equiv T(k)$ is true.

Since the object language obtained by closing off $T(x)$ is a classical language with every predicate totally defined, it is possible to define a truth predicate for that language in the usual Tarskian manner. This predicate will *not* coincide in extension with the predicate $T(x)$ of the object language, and it is certainly reasonable to suppose that it is really the metalanguage predicate that expresses the 'genuine' concept of truth for the closed-off object language; the $T(x)$ of the closed-off language defines truth for the fixed point *before* it was closed off. So we still cannot avoid the need for a metalanguage.

On the basis of the fact that the goal of a universal language seems elusive, some have concluded that truth-gap approaches, or any approaches that attempt to come closer to natural language than does the orthodox approach, are fruitless. I hope that the fertility of the present approach, and its agreement with intuitions about natural language in a large number of instances, cast doubt upon such negative attitudes.

There are mathematical applications and purely technical problems which I have not mentioned in this sketch; they would be beyond the scope of a paper for a philosophical journal. Thus there is the question, which can be answered in considerable generality, of characterizing the ordinal σ at which the construction of the minimal fixed point closes off. If L is the language of first-order arithmetic, it turns out that σ is ω_1, the first nonrecursive ordinal. A set is the extension of a formula with one free variable in $\mathfrak{L}_\sigma$ iff it is Π_1^1, and it is the extension of a totally defined formula iff it is hyperarithmetical. The languages $\mathfrak{L}_\alpha$ approximating to the minimal fixed point give an interesting 'notation-free' version of the hyperarithmetical hierarchy. More generally, if L is the language of an acceptable structure in the sense of Moschovakis, and the Kleene valuation is used, a set is the extension of a monadic formula in the minimal fixed point iff it is inductive in the sense of Moschovakis.[36]

Notes

Originally it was understood that I would present this paper orally without submitting a prepared text. At a relatively late date, the editors of this journal requested that I submit at least an 'outline' of my paper. I agreed that this would be useful. I received the request while already committed to something else, and had to prepare the present version in tremendous haste, without even the opportunity to revise the first draft. Had I had the opportunity to revise, I might have expanded the presentation of the basic model so as to make it clearer. The text shows that a great deal of the formal and philosophical material, and the proofs of results, had to be omitted.

Abstracts of the present work were presented by title at the spring, 1975, meeting of the Association for Symbolic Logic held in Chicago. A longer version was presented as three lectures at Princeton University, June, 1975.

1 I follow the usual convention of the 'semantic' theory of truth in taking truth and falsity to be predicates true of sentences. If truth and falsity primarily apply to propositions or other nonlinguistic entities, read the predicate of sentences as 'expresses a truth.'

I have chosen to take sentences as the primary truth vehicles *not* because I think that the objection that truth is primarily a property of propositions (or 'statements') is irrelevant to serious work on truth or to the semantic paradoxes. On the contrary, I think that ultimately a careful treatment of the problem may well need to separate the 'expresses' aspect (relating sentences to propositions) from the 'truth' aspect (putatively applying to propositions). I have not investigated whether the semantic paradoxes present problems when directly applied to propositions. The main reason I apply the truth predicate directly to linguistic objects is that for such objects a mathematical theory of self-reference has been developed. (See also note 32.)

Further, a more developed version of the theory would allow languages with demonstratives and ambiguities and would speak of utterances, sentences under a reading, and the like, as having truth value. In the informal exposition this paper does not attempt to be precise about such matters. Sentences are the official truth vehicles, but informally we occasionally talk about utterances, statements, assertions, and so on. Occasionally we may speak as if every utterance of a sentence in the language makes a statement, although below we suggest that a sentence may fail to make a statement if it is paradoxical or ungrounded. We are precise about such issues only when we think that imprecision may create confusion or misunderstanding. Like remarks apply to conventions about quotation.

2 Both Nixon and Jones may have made their respective utterances without being aware that the empirical facts make them paradoxical.

3 On an ordinary understanding (as opposed to the conventions of those who state Liar paradoxes), the question lay in the sincerity, not the truth, of Moore's utterances. Paradoxes could probably be derived on this interpretation also.

4 We assume that 'is short' *is* already in the language.

5 It is *not* obviously possible to apply this technique to obtain 'directly' self-referential *propositions*.

6 There are several ways of doing it, using either a nonstandard Gödel numbering where statements can contain numerals designating their own Gödel numbers, or a standard Gödel numbering, plus added constants of the type of 'Jack'.

7 If a sentence asserts, e.g., that all sentences in class C are true, we allow it to be false and grounded if one sentence in C is false, irrespective of the groundedness of the other sentences in C.

8 Under that name, groundedness seems to have been first explicitly introduced into the literature in Hans Hertzberger, 'Paradoxes of Grounding in Semantics,' *Journal of Philosophy*, XVII, 6 (March 26, 1970): 145–67. Hertzberger's paper is based on unpublished work on a 'groundedness' approach to the semantic paradoxes undertaken jointly with Jerrold J. Katz. The intuitive notion of groundedness in semantics surely was part of the folklore of the subject much earlier. As far as I know, the present work gives the first rigorous definition.

9 By an 'orthodox approach', I mean any approach that works within classical quantification theory and requires all predicates to be totally defined on the range of the variables. Various writers speak as if the 'hierarchy of languages' or Tarskian approach *prohibited* one from forming, for example, languages

with certain kinds of self-reference, or languages containing their own truth predicates. On my interpretation, there are no *prohibitions*; there are only *theorems* on what can and cannot be done within the framework of ordinary classical quantification theory. Thus Gödel *showed* that a classical language can talk about its own syntax; using restricted truth definitions and other devices, such a language can say a great deal about its own semantics. On the other hand, Tarski *proved* that a classical language cannot contain its own truth predicate, and that a higher-order language can define a truth predicate for a language of lower order. None of this came from any a priori restrictions on self-reference other than those deriving from the restriction to a classical language, all of whose predicates are totally defined.

10   Charles Parsons, 'The Liar Paradox,' *Journal of Philosophical Logic*, III, 4 (October 1974): 380–412, may perhaps be taken as giving an argument like the one sketched in this paragraph. Much of his paper, however, may be regarded as confirmed rather than refuted by the present approach. See in particular his fn 19, which hopes for a theory that avoids explicit subscripts. The minimal fixed point (see sec. III below) avoids explicit subscripts but nevertheless has a notion of level; in this respect it can be compared with standard set theory as opposed to the theory of types. The fact that the levels are not intrinsic to the sentences is peculiar to the present theory and is additional to the absence of explicit subscripting.

The orthodox assignment of intrinsic levels guarantees freedom from 'riskiness' in the sense explained in sec. I above. For (4) and (5) below, the very assignment of intrinsic levels which would eliminate their riskiness would also prevent them from 'seeking their own levels' (see pp. 695–7). *If we wish to allow sentences to seek their own levels apparently we must also allow risky sentences.* Then we must regard sentences as *attempting* to express propositions, and allow truth–value gaps. See below.

11   The problem of transfinite levels is perhaps not too difficult to solve in a canonical way at level ω, but it becomes increasingly acute at higher ordinal levels.

12   See Martin, ed., *The Paradox of the Liar* (New Haven: Yale, 1970) and the references given there.

13   See note 9 above. Martin, for example, in his papers 'Toward a Solution to the Liar Paradox,' *Philosophical Review*, LXXVI, 3 (July 1967): 279–311, and 'On Grelling's Paradox,' *ibid.*, LXXVII, 3 (July 1968): 325–31, attributes to 'the theory of language levels' all kinds of restrictions on self-reference which must be regarded as simply refuted, even for classical languages, by Gödel's work. Perhaps there are or have been some theorists who believed that *all* talk of an object language must take place in a distinct metalanguage. This hardly matters; the main issue is: what constructions can be

carried out within a classical language, and what require truth-value gaps? Almost all the cases of self-reference Martin mentions can be carried out by orthodox Gödelian methods without any need to invoke partially defined predicates or truth-value gaps. In fn 5 of his second paper Martin takes some notice of Gödel's demonstration that sufficiently rich languages contain their own syntax, but he seems not to realize that this work makes most of his polemics against 'language levels' irrelevant.

At the other extreme, some writers still seem to think that some kind of general ban on self-reference is helpful in treating the semantic paradoxes. In the case of self-referential *sentences*, such a position seems to me to be hopeless.

14   In the terminology of the present paper, the paper by Martin and Woodruff proves the existence of *maximal* fixed points (not the minimal fixed point) in the context of the weak three-valued approach. It does not develop the theory much further. I believe the paper is as yet unpublished, but is forthcoming in a volume dedicated to Yehoshua Bar-Hillel. Although it partially anticipates the present approach, it was unknown to me when I did the work.

15   Actually I was familiar with relatively little of this literature when I began work on the approach given here. Even now I am unfamiliar with a great deal of it, so that tracing connections is difficult. Martin's work seems, in its formal consequences if not its philosophical basis, to be closest to the present approach.

There is also a considerable literature on three-valued or similar approaches to the set-theoretical paradoxes, with which I am not familiar in detail but which seems fairly closely related to the present approach. I should mention Gilmore, Fitch, Feferman.

16   I am interpreting Strawson as holding that 'the present king of France is bald' fails to make a statement but is still meaningful, because it gives directions (conditions) for making a statement. I apply this to the paradoxical sentences, without committing myself on his original case of descriptions. It should be stated that Strawson's doctrine is somewhat ambiguous and that I have chosen a preferred interpretation, which I think Strawson also prefers today.

17   Thus the disjunction of 'snow is white' with a Liar sentence will be true. If we had regarded a Liar sentence as *meaningless*, presumably we would have had to regard any compound containing it as meaningless also. Since we don't regard such a sentence as meaningless, we can adopt the approach taken in the text.

18   The valuation rules are those of S. C. Kleene, *Introduction to Metamathematics* (New York: Van Nos-

trand, 1952), sec. 64, pp. 332–40. Kleene's notion of regular tables is equivalent (for the class of valuations he considers) to our requirement of the monotonicity of ϕ below.

I have been amazed to hear my use of the Kleene valuation compared occasionally to the proposals of those who favor abandoning standard logic 'for quantum mechanics,' or positing extra truth values beyond truth and falsity, etc. Such a reaction surprised me as much as it would presumably surprise Kleene, who intended (as I do here) to write a work of standard mathematical results, provable in conventional mathematics. 'Undefined' is not an *extra* truth value, any more than – in Kleene's book – u is an extra *number* in sec. 63. Nor should it be said that 'classical logic' does not generally hold, any more than (in Kleene) the use of partially defined functions invalidates the commutative law of addition. *If certain sentences express propositions, any tautological truth function of them expresses a true proposition.* Of course formulas, even with the forms of tautologies, which have components that do not express propositions may have truth functions that do not express propositions either. (This happens under the Kleene valuation, but not under the van Fraassen.) Mere conventions for handling terms that do not designate numbers should not be called changes in arithmetic; conventions for handling sentences that do not express propositions are not in any philosophically significant sense 'changes in logic.' The term 'three-valued logic', occasionally used here, should not mislead. All our considerations can be formalized in a classical metalanguage.

19 *Elementary Induction on Abstract Structures* (Amsterdam: North-Holland, 1974). The notion of an acceptable structure is developed in chap. 5.

20 It is unnecessary to suppose, as we have for simplicity, that all the predicates in L are totally defined. The hypothesis that L contain a device for coding finite sequences is needed only if we are adding satisfaction rather than truth to L. Other hypotheses can be made much weaker for most of the work.

21 $\mathfrak{L}$ is thus a language with all predicates but the single predicate $T(x)$ interpreted, but $T(x)$ is uninterpreted. The languages $\mathfrak{L}(S_1, S_2)$ and the languages $\mathfrak{L}_\alpha$ defined below are languages obtained from $\mathfrak{L}$ by specifying an interpretation of $T(x)$.

22 I parenthetically write 'codes of' or 'Gödel numbers of' in various places to remind the reader that syntax may be represented in L by Gödel numbering or some other coding device. Sometimes I lazily drop the parenthetical qualification, identifying expressions with their codes.

23 A comparison with the Tarski hierarchy:
The Tarski hierarchy uses a new truth predicate at each level, always changing. The limit levels of the Tarski hierarchy, which have not been defined in the literature, but have been to some extent in my own work, are cumbersome to characterize.

The present hierarchy uses a single truth predicate, ever increasing with increasing levels until the level of the minimal fixed point is reached. The limit levels are easily defined. The languages in the hierarchy are not the primary object of interest, but are better and better approximations to the minimal language with its own truth predicate.

24 Consider the case where L has a canonical name for every element of D. We can then consider pairs (A, T), (A, F), where A is true, or false, respectively. The Kleene rules correspond to closure conditions on a set of such pairs: e.g., if $(A(a), F)$ ε S for each name of a element of D, put $((\exists x)A(x), F))$ in S; if $((A(a), T)$ ε S, put $((\exists x)A(x), T)$ in S, etc. Consider the least set S of pairs closed under the analogues of the Kleene rules, containing (A, T) $((A, F))$ for each true (false) atomic A of L, and closed under the two conditions: (i) if (A, T) ε S, $(T(k), T)$ ε S; (ii) if (A, F) ε S, $(T(k), F)$ ε S, where 'k' abbreviates a name of A. It is easily shown that the set S corresponds (in the obvious sense) to the minimal fixed point [thus, it is closed under the converses of (i) and (ii).] I used this definition to show that the set of truths in the minimal fixed point (over an acceptable structure), is inductive in Moschovakis's sense. It is probably simpler than the definition given in the text. The definition given in the text has, among others, the advantages of giving a definition of 'level', facilitating a comparison with the Tarski hierarchy, and easy generalization to valuation schemes other than Kleene's.

25 If we use the supervaluation technique instead of the Kleene rules, $P \vee \sim P$ will always be grounded and true, and we must change the example.

26 We suppose that the Tarski hierarchy defines $L_0 = L, L_{n+1} = L + T_{n+1}(x)$ (truth, or satisfaction, for L_n). Alternatively, we might prefer the inductive construction $L_0 = L, L_{n+1} = L_n + T_{n+1}(x)$ where the language of each new level contains all the previous truth predicates. It is easy to modify the construction in the text so as to accord with the second definition. The two alternative hierarchies are equivalent in expressive power at each level.

27 See his 'Singular Terms, Truth-value Gaps, and Free Logic,' *Journal of Philosophy*, 63, 17 (Sept. 15, 1966): 481–95.

28 A version of the Liar paradox due to H. Friedman shows that there are limits to what can be done in this direction.

29 Though the minimal fixed point certainly is singled out as natural in many respects.

30 I do not mean to *assert* that there are no definite questions of fact in these areas, or even that I myself may not favor some valuation schemes over others. But my personal views are less important than the variety of tools that are available, so for the purposes of this sketch I take an agnostic position. (I remark

that if the viewpoint is taken that logic applies primarily to propositions, and that we are merely formulating conventions for how to handle sentences that do not express propositions, the attractiveness of the supervaluation approach over the Kleene approach is somewhat decreased. See note 18.)

31 Another application of the present techniques is to 'impredicative' substitutional quantification, where the terms of the substitution class themselves contain substitutional quantifiers of the given type. (For example, a language containing substitutional quantifiers with arbitrary sentences of the language itself as substituends.) It is impossible in general to introduce such quantifiers into classical languages without truth-value gaps.

32 Richard Montague, 'Syntactical Treatments of Modality, with Corollaries on Reflection Principles and Finite Axiomatizability,' *Acta Philosophica Fennica, Proceedings of a Colloquium on Model and Many Valued Logics*, 1963: 153–67; David Kaplan and Montague, 'A Paradox Regained,' *Notre Dame Journal of Formal Logic*, I, 3 (July 1960): 79–90.

At present the problems are *known* to arise only if modalities and attitudes are predicates applied to sentences or their tokens. The Montague-Kaplan arguments do not apply to standard formalizations taking modalities or propositional attitudes as intensional operators. Even if we wish to quantify over objects of belief, the arguments do not apply if the objects of belief are taken to be propositions and the latter are identified with sets of possible worlds.

However, if we quantify over propositions, paradoxes may arise in connection with propositional attitudes given appropriate empirical premises. [See, e.g., A. N. Prior, 'On a Family of Paradoxes,' *Notre Dame Journal of Formal Logic*, II 1 (January 1961): 16–32.] Also, we may wish (in connection with propositional attitudes but not modalities), to individuate propositions more finely than by sets of possible worlds, and it is possible that such a 'fine structure' may permit the application of Gödelian arguments of the type used by Montague and Kaplan directly to propositions.

33 As a formalization of the concept intended by those who speak of modalities and attitudes as predicates of sentences, the second version is generally better. This is true especially for the propositional attitudes.

34 Note that the metalanguage in which we write this paper can be regarded as containing no truth gaps. A sentence either does or does not have a truth value in a given fixed point.

Such semantical notions as 'grounded,' 'paradoxical,' etc. belong to the metalanguage. This situation seems to me to be intuitively acceptable; in contrast to the notion of truth, none of these notions is to be found in natural language in its pristine purity, before philosophers reflect on its semantics (in particular, the semantic paradoxes). If we give up the goal of a universal language, models of the type presented in this paper are plausible as models of natural language at a stage before we reflect on the generation process associated with the concept of truth, the stage which continues in the daily life of nonphilosophical speakers.

35 I think the primacy of the first intuition can be defended philosophically, and for this reason I have emphasized the approach based on this intuition. The alternate intuition arises only after we have reflected on the process embodying the first intuition. See above.

Tarski's Theory of Truth

Hartry Field

In the early 1930s there was prevalent, among scientifically minded philosophers, the view that semantic notions such as the notions of truth and denotation were illegitimate: that they could not or should not be incorporated into a scientific conception of the world. But when Tarski's work on truth became known, all this changed. "As a result of Tarski's teaching, I no longer hesitate to speak of 'truth' and 'falsity'," wrote Popper[1]; and Popper's reaction was widely shared.[2]

A philosopher who shared Popper's reaction to Tarski's discoveries would presumably argue as follows. "What Tarski did was to define the term 'true', using in his definitions only terms that are clearly acceptable. In particular, he did not employ any undefined semantic terms in his definitions. So Tarski's work should make the term 'true' acceptable even to someone who is initially suspicious of semantic terms."

This contention has an initial plausibility, but I will argue that it is radically wrong. My contrary claim will be that Tarski succeeded in reducing the notion of truth *to certain other semantic notions*; but that he did not in any way explicate these other notions, so that his results ought to make the word 'true" acceptable only to someone who already regarded these other semantic notions as acceptable.

By claiming that Tarski merely reduced truth to other semantic notions, I don't mean to suggest that his results on truth are trivial. On the con-

trary, I think that they are extremely important, and have applications not only to mathematics but also to linguistics and to more directly 'philosophical" problems about realism and objectivity. I think, however, that the real value of Tarski's discoveries for linguistics and philosophy is widely misunderstood, and I hope to eradicate the most central misunderstandings by clarifying and defending the claim that Tarski merely reduced truth to other semantic notions.

I

I believe that Tarski presented his semantic theory in a very misleading way, one which has encouraged the misinterpretations just alluded to. In this section I will present Tarski's theory as I think he should have presented it. However, I do not expect instant agreement that this new way is better than the old, and so I will use the name 'Tarski*' for a logician who gave the sort of semantic theory I will now sketch. Later in the paper I will compare Tarski*s semantics to the semantics that the real Tarski actually gave; by doing this I will cast light on the issues raised in my introductory paragraphs.

In sketching Tarski*s theory, I will focus my attention on a particular object language L. The language L that I choose will be a quantificational language with names ('c_1', 'c_2', ...), one-place function symbols ('f_1', 'f_2', ...), and one-place predicates ('p_1', 'p_2', ...). The language of course cannot be viewed as an "uninterpreted" language,

Hartry Field, Tarski's Theory of Truth. *The Journal of Philosophy*, 69, 13 (1972): 347–75.

i.e., as just a bunch of strings of meaningless marks, for then there would be no truth to worry about. Instead, the language should be regarded as something that people actually speak or write; and it is because the speakers speak or write the way they do that the words of the language have the meaning they have.[3]

Initially I will follow Tarski in supposing that in L "the sense of every expression is unambiguously determined by its form,"[4] i.e., that whenever two speakers use the same name (or one speaker uses it on two occasions) they are referring to the same thing, that whenever two speakers use the same sentence either both are saying something true or neither is, etc. In these circumstances it makes sense to speak of the names of the language denoting things (a name denotes whatever the users of the name refer to) and the sentences being true or false (true when speakers who use it say something true by so doing). The more general situation, in which there are expressions whose "sense" is not determined wholly by their form, will be dealt with later. (We'll see that it is one of the advantages of Tarski*s semantics that it can easily handle this more general situation.)

The syntax of L can be given by two recursive definitions: first we define the *singular terms* by saying that all names and variables are singular terms, and a function symbol followed by a singular term is a singular term; then we define the *formulas* by saying that a predicate followed by a singular term is a formula, as is the negation of a formula, the conjunction of two formulas, and the universal quantification of a formula with any variable. The *sentences*, or *closed formulas*, are then singled out in the usual way.

Now we can proceed to Tarski*s semantics. Rather than characterize truth directly, we characterize it relative to some assignment of objects to the variables, say s_k to 'x_k'. The idea is going to be to treat the variables, or at least the free variables, as sort of "temporary names" for the objects assigned to them. So we proceed by fixing a sequence $s = \langle s_1, s_2, \ldots \rangle$ of objects, to be assigned to 'x_1', 'x_2', ..., respectively; and we want to say what it is for a formula to be true, i.e., true relative to the assignment s. As a preliminary we say what it is for a term to denote, an object, i.e., to denote it relative to the assignment s. The denotation of 'x_k' relative to s is evidently s_k, for this is the object assigned to 'x_k'. But what is the denotation relative to s of 'c_k'? Evidently what objects are assigned to the variables here is irrelevant, and the denotation

of 'c_k', is some fixed object that users of the language refer to when they use the name 'c_k'. Just what this object is depends on facts we have not yet been given about the use of 'c_k'. Similarly there are facts we have not yet been given about the use of 'p_k', and 'f_k', which we need in order to fix the truth value of sentences containing them. For 'p_k' the relevant facts concern the extension of the predicate – what objects the predicate *applies to* – for it is this which affects the truth value of all utterances containing 'p_k'. For 'f_k', the relevant facts concern what pairs of objects *fulfill* that function symbol – in the sense that the pair ⟨ John Adams, John Quincy Adams ⟩ and every other father-son pair fulfill the function symbol "father of".

With these points in mind it is now easy to give an inductive characterization of denotation$_s$:

> T1 (A) 1. 'x_k' denotes$_s$ s_k.
>
> 2. 'c_k' denotes$_s$ what it denotes.
>
> 3. $\ulcorner f_k(e) \urcorner$ denotes$_s$ an object a if and only if
>   (i) there is an object b that e denotes$_s$
>   and (ii) 'f_k' is fulfilled by $\langle a, b \rangle$.

(Here 'e' is a variable ranging over expressions of L.) Similarly we define 'true$_s$' for formulas – what Tarski calls satisfaction of a formula by s:

> (B) 1. $\ulcorner p_k(e) \urcorner$ is true$_s$ if and only if
>   (i) there is an object a that e denotes$_s$ and (ii) 'p_k' applies to a.
>
> 2. $\ulcorner \sim e \urcorner$ is true$_s$ if and only if e is not true$_s$.
>
> 3. $\ulcorner e_1 \wedge e_2 \urcorner$ is true$_s$ if and only if e_1 is true$_s$ and so is e_2.
>
> 4. $\ulcorner \forall x_k(e) \urcorner$ is true$_s$ if and only if for each sequence s^* that differs from s at the kth place at most, e is true.$_s^*$

This completes the characterization of truth relative to an assignment of objects to the variables. In the case of sentences it is easily seen that we get the same results whatever such assignment we pick; we can say

(C) A sentence is true if and only if its is true$_s$ for some (or all) s.

This completes my elaboration of Tarski*s "truth definition" T1 for L – or his *truth characterization* (TC), as I prefer to call it. What is its philosophical significance? The obvious answer, and the correct one, I think, is that the TC reduces one semantic notion to three others. It explains what it is for a sentence to be true in terms of certain semantic features of the primitive components of the sentence: in terms of what it is for a name to denote something, what it is for a predicate to apply to something, and what it is for a function symbol to be fulfilled by some pair of things. It is convenient to introduce the expression 'primitively denotes' as follows: every name *primitively denotes* what it denotes; every predicate and every function symbol *primitively denotes* what it applies to or is fulfilled by; and no complex expression primitively denotes anything. In this terminology, what T1 does is to explain truth in terms of primitive denotation. Similarly we can explain denotation for arbitrary closed singular terms [such as '$f_1(c_1)$'] in terms of primitive denotation, i.e., in terms of the semantic features of the names and function symbols from which the complex singular term is composed – we merely say that a closed singular term denotes an object a if it denotes$_s$ a for some (or all) s, where denotation$_s$ is defined as before. We see then that *Tarski's semantics explains the semantic properties of complex expressions* (e.g., truth value for sentences, denotation for complex singular terms) *in terms of semantic properties of their primitive components.*

To explain truth in terms of primitive denotation is, I think, an important task. It certainly doesn't answer *every* question that anyone would ever want answered about truth, but for many purposes it is precisely what we need. For instance, in model theory we are interested in such questions as: given a set Γ of sentences, is there any way to choose the denotations of the primitives of the language so that every sentence of Γ will come out true given the usual semantics for the logical connectives?[5] For questions such as this, what we need to know is how the truth value of a whole sentence depends on the denotations of its primitive nonlogical parts, and that is precisely what T1 tells us. So *at least for model-theoretic purposes*, Tarski's TC is precisely the kind of explication of truth we need.

I want now to return to a point I mentioned earlier, about Tarski's restriction to languages in which "the sense of every expression is unambiguously determined by its form." Natural languages are full of expressions that do not meet this requirement. For instance, different tokens of 'John takes grass' can differ in "sense" – e.g.,

one token may be uttered in saying that John Smith smokes marijuana, and another may be uttered in saying that John Jones steals lawn material, and these differences may give rise to differences of truth value in the tokens. (I say that a complete[6] token of a sentence is true if the person who spoke or wrote that token said something true by so doing; I also say that a name token denotes an object if the person who spoke or wrote the token referred to the object by so doing.) The prevalence of such examples in natural languages raises the question of whether Tarski's type of semantic theory is applicable to languages in which the sense is *not* determined by the form; for if the answer is no, then Davidson's very worth while project[7] of giving truth characterizations for natural languages seems doomed from the start.

It seems clear that if we stick to the kind of TC that Tarski actually gave (see next section), there is no remotely palatable way of extending TC's to sentences like 'John takes grass'. But if we use TC's like T1 there is no difficulty at all. The only point about languages containing 'John' or 'grass' or 'I' or 'you' is that for such languages 'true', 'denotes', and other semantic terms make no clear sense as applied to expression types; they make sense only as applied to tokens. For this reason we have to interpret clause (B)2 of T1 as meaning

A token of $\lceil \bar{e} \rceil$ is true$_s$ if and only if the token of e that it contains is not true$_s$.

and similarly for the other clauses. Once we interpret our TC in this way in terms of tokens, i.e., individual occasions of utterance, that TC works perfectly: someone who utters 'John is sick' (or 'I am sick') says something true if and only if his token of 'sick' applies to the person he refers to by 'John' (or by 'I'); and the fact that other speakers (or this speaker on other occasions) sometimes refer to different things when they use 'John' (or 'I') is beside the point.

This analysis leaves entirely out of account the ways in which 'I' and 'John' differ: it leaves out of account, for instance, the fact that a token of 'I' always denotes the speaker who produced it. But that is no objection to the analysis, for the analysis purports merely to explain truth in terms of primitive denotation; it does not purport to say anything about primitive denotation, and the differences between 'I' and 'John' (or their analogues in a language like L) are purely differences of how they denote. (The word 'I' denotes according to the simple rule mentioned two sentences back; 'John' denotes according to much more complex rules that I have no idea how to formulate.)

Of course, the fact that a theory of denotation for a word like 'I' is so simple and obvious, makes it possible to alter the TC so that the theory of denotation for such a word is built into the TC itself – such a course is adopted, for instance, by Davidson at the end of "Truth and Meaning." I myself prefer to preserve the analogies of the word 'I' to words that function less systematically, e.g., 'we', 'she', and 'John'. How one treats 'I' is more or less a matter of taste; but the less systematic words I've just mentioned cannot be handled in the way that Davidson handles 'I', and the only reasonable way I can see to handle them is the way I have suggested: use a truth characterization like T1 (except stated in terms of tokens rather than types), and leave it to a separate theory of primitive denotation to explain the relevant differences between tokens of 'John' that denote John Adams and tokens of 'John' that denote John Lennon, and between tokens of 'bank' that apply to things along rivers and tokens of 'bank' that apply to the Chase Manhattan.[8]

There are other advantages to T1 besides its ability to handle ambiguous sentences, i.e., sentences for which the sense is not determined by the form. For instance, Tarski required that the vocabulary of the language be fixed once and for all; but if we decide to give truth characterizations of type T1, this is unnecessary: all that is required is that the general structure of the language be fixed, e.g., that the semantic categories[9] (name, one-place predicate, etc.) be held constant. In other words, if a language already contained proper names, the invention of a new name to baptize an object will not invalidate the old TC; though introduction of a name into a hitherto nameless language will.

To show this, we have merely to reformulate the given TC so that it does not rely on the actual vocabulary that the language contains at a given time, but works also for sentences containing new names, one-place predicates, etc., that speakers of the language might later introduce. To do this is trivial: we define denotation$_s$ by

1 The kth variable denotes$_s$ s_k.
2 If e_1 is a name, it denotes$_s$ what it denotes.

3 If e_1 is a singular term and e_2 is a function symbol, then $\lceil e_2(e_1) \rceil$ denotes$_s$ a if and only if
   (i) as before,
   and (ii) e_2 is fulfilled by $\langle a, b \rangle$.

and we can generalize the definition of truth$_s$ in a similar manner.[10] This shows that, in giving a TC, there is no need to utilize the particular vocabulary used at one temporal stage of a language, for we can instead give a more general TC which can be incorporated into a diachronic theory of the language (and can also be applied directly to other languages of a similar structure). *If*, that is, we accept the modification of Tarski proposed in this section.

II

The kind of truth characterization advocated in the previous section differs from the kind of TC Tarski offered in one important respect. Tarski stated the policy "I shall not make use of any semantical concept if I am not able previously to reduce it to other concepts" (CTFL 152/3), and this policy is flagrantly violated by T1: T1 utilizes unreduced notions of proper names denoting things, predicates applying to things, and function symbols being fulfilled by things.

Tarski's truth characterizations, unlike T1, accorded with his stated policy: they did not contain any semantic terms like 'applies to' or 'denotes'. How did Tarski achieve this result? Very simply: first, he translated every name, predicate, and function symbol of L into English; then he utilized these translations in order to reformulate clauses 2 and 3 (ii) of part (A) of the definition and clause 1 (ii) of part (B). For simplicity, let's use '$\bar{c}_1$', '$\bar{c}_2$', etc. as abbreviations for the English expressions that are the translations of the words 'c_1', 'c_2', ... of L: e.g.: if L is simplified German and 'c_1' is "Deutschland', then '$\bar{c}_1$' is an abbreviation for 'Germany'. Similarly, let '$\bar{f}_1$' abbreviate the translation into English of the word 'f_1' of L, and let '$\bar{p}_1$' abbreviate the translation of 'p_1' into English. Then Tarski's reformulated truth definition will read as follows:

T2 (A) 1. as before
       2. 'c_k' denotes$_s$ $\bar{c}_k$
       3. $\lceil f_k(e) \rceil$ denotes$_s$ a if and only if
           (i) as before
           (ii) a is $\bar{f}_k(b)$

(B) 1. $\ulcorner pk(e) \urcorner$ is true$_s$, if and only if
    (i) as before
    (ii) $\bar{p}_k(a)$
2–4. as before
(C) as before

What T2 is like depends of course on the precise character of the translations of the primitives that are utilized. For instance, if we translate 'c_1' as 'the denotation of 'c_1' ', translate 'p_1' as 'is something that 'p_1' applies to', etc., then T2 becomes identical with T1. This of course is *not* what Tarski intended. What Tarski intended is that T2 not contain unexplicated semantic terms, and if we are to get this result we must not employ any semantic terms in our translations.[11]

But other restrictions on translations are also necessary: if we were to translate 'Deutschland' as 'Bertrand Russell', a truth characterization T2 that was based on this translation would grossly misrepresent L. In order to state the matter more generally, I introduce the term 'coreferential': two singular terms are coreferential if they denote the same thing; two predicative expressions are coreferential if they have the same extension, i.e., if they apply to the same things; and two functional expressions are coreferential if they are fulfilled by the same pairs. It is then easily seen that any departure from coreferentiality in translation will bring errors into T2. For instance, suppose we translate the foreign predicate 'glub' as "yellow", and suppose 'glub' and yellow are not *precisely* coreferential; then clause (B)$_1$ will say falsely that 'glub (x)' is true of just those objects which are yellow.

Let us say, then, that

(1)   An adequate translation of a primitive e_1 of *L* into English is an expression e_2 of English such that
        (i) e_1 and e_2 are coreferential, and
        (ii) e_2 contains no semantic terms.

This notion of an adequate translation is of course a semantic notion that Tarski did not reduce to nonsemantic terms. But that is no objection to his characterization T2 (at least, it isn't obviously an objection), for the notion of an adequate translation is never built into the truth characterization and is not, properly speaking, part of a theory of truth. On Tarski's view we need to adequately translate the object language into the metalanguage in order to give an adequate theory of truth for the object language; this means that the notion of an adequate translation is employed in the methodology of giving truth theories, but it is not employed in the truth theories themselves.

In what follows I shall assume that the language L with which we are dealing is so related to English that all its primitives *can* be adequately translated into English, according to the standards of adequacy set forth in (1). (This is another restriction that we avoid if we give TC's of the type T1; quite a significant restriction, I think.) If we then suppose that the translation given ('$\bar{c}_1$' for 'c_1', etc.) is one of the adequate translations, then T2, like T1, is a correct recursive characterization of truth for the language L. There is, of course, a simple procedure for transforming recursive characterizations such as these into explicit characterizations. To carry the procedure through in these cases would be pretty complicated, but it could be done; so we could regard T1 (or T2) as implicitly specifying a metalinguistic formula '$A_1(e)$' (or '$A_2(e)$'), and saying that an utterance e of L is true if and only if $A_1(e)$ (or $A_2(e)$). If we regard T1 and T2 as written in this form, then the key difference between them is that '$A_1(e)$' *contains semantic terms* and '$A_2(e)$' *does not*. The question then arises: is the fact that '$A_2(e)$' does not contain semantic terms an advantage of T2 over T1? If so, then *why* is it an advantage?

In order to discuss the possible advantages of T2 over T1, I think we have to go beyond mathematical considerations and focus instead on linguistic and other "philosophical" matters. It is not enough to say that T2 *defines* truth without utilizing semantic terms, whereas T2 defines it only in other semantic terms: this is not enough until we say something more about the purpose of definition. If the purpose of giving a "definition" of truth is to enable you to do model theory, then the elimination of semantic terms from T1 gives no advantage. For what purpose do we want definitions for which the elimination of semantic terms is useful?

One purpose to which definitions are sometimes put is in explaining the meaning of a word. This of course is very vague, but I think it is clear enough to enable us to recognize that neither T1 nor T2 has very much to do with explaining the meaning of the word 'true'. This is especially obvious for T2: a T2-type truth definition works for a single language only, and so if it "explains the meaning of" the word 'true' as applied to that language, then for *any* two languages L_1 and L_2, the word 'true' means something different when applied to utterances of L_1 than it means when applied to utterances of L_2! I make this point not in criticism of T2, but in criticism of the idea that the significance of T2 can be explained by saying that it "gives the meaning of" the word 'true'.

We still need to know what purpose a truth characterization like T1 or T2 could serve that would give someone reason to think that a TC with unexplicated semantic terms would be better than a TC without unexplicated semantic terms. Tarski hints at such a purpose in one place in his writings, where he is discussing the importance of being able to define the word 'true', as opposed to merely introducing axioms to establish the basic properties of truth. If a definition of semantic notions such as truth could not be given, Tarski writes,

> it would then be difficult to bring [semantics] into harmony with the postulates of the unity of science and of physicalism (since the concepts of semantics would be neither logical nor physical concepts).[12]

This remark seems to me to be of utmost importance in evaluating the philosophical significance of Tarski's work, and so I will now say something about the general philosophical issues it raises. When this is done we will be in a better position to understand Tarski's choice of T2 over T1.

III

In the early 1930s many philosophers believed that the notion of truth could not be incorporated into a scientific conception of the world. I think that the main rationale for this view is hinted at in the remark of Tarski's that I quoted at the end of the last section, and what I want to do now is to elaborate a bit on Tarski's hint.

In the remark I have quoted, Tarski put a heavy stress on the doctrine of physicalism: the doctrine that chemical facts, biological facts, psychological facts, and semantical facts, are all explicable (in principle) in terms of physical facts. The doctrine of physicalism functions as a high-level empirical hypothesis, a hypothesis that no small number of experiments can force us to give up. It functions, in other words, in much the same way as the doctrine of mechanism (that all facts are explicable

in terms of *mechanical* facts) once functioned: this latter doctrine has now been universally rejected, but it was given up only by the development of a well-accepted theory (Maxwell's) which described phenomena (electromagnetic radiation and the electromagnetic field) that were very difficult to account for mechanically, and by amassing a great deal of experiment and theory that together made it quite conclusive that mechanical explanations of these phenomena (e.g., by positing "the ether") would never get off the ground. Mechanism has been empirically refuted; its heir is physicalism, which allows as "basic" not only facts about mechanics, but facts about other branches of physics as well.[13] I believe that physicists a hundred years ago were justified in accepting mechanism, and that, similarly, physicalism should be accepted until we have convincing evidence that there is a realm of phenomena it leaves out of account. Even if there *does* turn out to be such a realm of phenomena, the only way we'll ever come to know that there is, is by repeated efforts and repeated failures to explain these phenomena in physical terms.

That's my view, anyway, but there are philosophers who think that it is in order to reject physicalism now. One way of rejecting physicalism is called "vitalism": it is the view that there are irreducibly biological facts, i.e., biological facts that aren't explicable in nonbiological terms (and hence, not in physical terms). Physicalism and vitalism are incompatible, and it is because of this incompatibility that the doctrine of physicalism has the methodological importance it has for biology. Suppose, for instance, that a certain woman has two sons, one hemophilic and one not. Then, according to standard genetic accounts of hemophilia, the ovum from which one of these sons was produced must have contained a gene for hemophilia, and the ovum from which the other son was produced must not have contained such a gene. But now the doctrine of physicalism tells us that there must have been a *physical* difference between the two ova that explains why the first son had hemophilia and the second one didn't, if the standard genetic account is to be accepted. We should not rest content with a special biological predicate 'has-a-hemophilic-gene' – rather, we should look for nonbiological facts (chemical facts; and ultimately, physical facts) that underlie the correct application of this predicate. That at least is what the principle of physicalism tells us, and it can hardly be doubted that this principle has motivated a great deal of very profitable research into the chemical foundations of genetics.

So much for vitalism; now let us turn to other irreducibility doctrines that are opposed to physicalism. One such irreducibility doctrine is Cartesianism: it is the doctrine that there are irreducibly mental facts. Another irreducibility doctrine has received much less attention than either vitalism or Cartesianism, but it is central to our present concerns: this doctrine, which might be called "semanticalism," is the doctrine that there are irreducibly semantic facts. The semanticalist claims, in other words, that semantic phenomena (such as the fact that 'Schnee' refers to snow) must be accepted as primitive, in precisely the way that electromagnetic phenomena are accepted as primitive (by those who accept Maxwell's equations and reject the ether); and in precisely the way that biological phenomena and mental phenomena are accepted as primitive by vitalists and Cartesians. Semanticalism, like Cartesianism and vitalism, posits nonphysical primitives, and as a physicalist I believe that all three doctrines must be rejected.

There are two general sorts of strategy that can be taken in rejecting semanticalism, or Cartesianism, or vitalism. One strategy, illustrated two paragraphs back in discussing vitalism, is to try to explicate the terms of a biological theory in nonbiological terms. But there is another possible strategy, which is to argue that the biological terms are illegitimate. The second strategy seems reasonable to adopt in dealing with the following predicate of (reincarnationist) biology: 'x has the same soul as y'. A physicalist would never try to find physical or chemical facts that underlie reincarnation; rather, he would reject reincarnation as a myth.

Since biological theory is as well developed as it is, we usually have a pretty good idea which biological terms require explication and which require elimination. When we turn to psychology and semantics, however, it is often not so obvious which strategy is the more promising. Thus in semantics, physicalists agree that all *legitimate* semantic terms must be explicable nonsemantically – they think in other words that there are no irreducibly semantic facts – but they disagree as to which semantic terms are legitimate. That disagreement has become fairly clear in recent years in the theory of meaning, with the work of Quine: the disagreement is between those physicalists who would look for a nonsemantic basis for terms in the theory of meaning, and those who would follow Quine in simply throwing out those terms. Our concern, however, is not with the theory of meaning, but with the theory of reference, and here the disagreement has been less clear, since there haven't been many physicalists who openly advocate getting rid of terms like 'true' and 'denotes'. There were such physicalists in the early 1930s; part of the importance of Tarski's work was to persuade them that they were on the wrong track, to persuade them that we should explicate notions in the theory of reference nonsemantically rather than simply get rid of them.

The view that we should just stop using semantic terms (here and in the rest of this paper, I mean terms in the theory of reference, such as 'true' and 'denotes' and 'applies to') draws its plausibility from the apparent difficulty of explicating these terms nonsemantically. People utter the sounds 'Electrons have rest mass but photons don't', or 'Schnee ist weiss und Gras ist grün', and we apply the word 'true' to their utterances. We don't want to say that it is a primitive and inexplicable fact about these utterances that they are true, a fact that cannot be explicated in nonsemantic terms; this is as unattractive to a physicalist as supposing that it is a primitive and inexplicable fact about an organism at a certain time that it is in pain. But how could we ever explicate in nonsemantic terms the alleged fact that these utterances are true? *Part* of the explication of the truth of 'Schnee ist weiss und Gras ist grün', presumably, would be that snow is white and grass is green. But this would only be part of the explanation, for still missing is the connection between snow being white and grass being green on the one hand, and the German utterance being true on the other hand. It is this connection that seems so difficult to explicate in a way that would satisfy a physicalist, i.e., in a way that does not involve the use of semantic terms.

If, in face of these difficulties, we were ever to conclude that it was *impossible* to explicate the notions of truth and denotation in non-semantic terms, we would have either to give up these semantic terms or else to reject physicalism. It seems to me that that is essentially what Tarski is saying in the quotation at the end of the last section, and I have tried to make it plausible by sketching analogies to areas other than semantics. Tarski's view, however, was that, for certain languages at least, semantic terms *are* explicable nonsemantically, and that truth definitions like T2 provide the required explication. It is understandable that as far as *philosophical* purposes go Tarski should think that T1 leaves something to be desired: after all, it merely explicates truth in terms of other semantic concepts; but what good does that do if those other concepts can't be explicated nonsemantically? T2, then, has a strong prima facie advantage over T1. In the next section I will show that it is not a genuine advantage.

IV

The apparent advantage of T2 over T1, I have stressed, is that it appears to reduce truth to non-semantic terms; and I *think* this is why Tarski wanted to give a truth definition like T2 rather than like T1. This interpretation makes sense of Tarski's remark about physicalism, and it also explains why someone who was certainly not interested in "meaning analysis" as that is usually conceived would have wanted to give "definitions" of truth and would emphasize that, in these "definitions," "I will not make use of any semantical concept if I am not able previously to reduce it to other concepts." In any case, the problem of reducing truth is a very important problem, one which T1 and T2 provide a partial solution to, and one which T2 *might* be thought to provide a full solution to; and it is not at all clear what *other* interesting problems T2 could be thought to solve better than T1.

In Tarski's own exposition of his theory of truth, Tarski put very little stress on the problem of reduction or on any other problem with a clear philosophical or mathematical motivation; instead, he set up a formal criterion of adequacy for theories of truth without any serious discussion of whether or why this formal criterion is reasonable. Roughly, the criterion was this:[14]

(M) Any condition of the form
$$(2) \qquad (\forall_e)[e \text{ is true} \equiv B(e)]$$
should be accepted as an adequate definition of truth if and only if it is correct and '$B(e)$' is a well-formed formula containing no semantic terms. (The quantifiers are to be taken as ranging over expressions of one particular language only.)

The "only if" part of condition M is not something I will contest.

It rules out the possibility of T1 *by itself* being an adequate truth definition; and it is right to do so, if the task of a truth definition is to reduce truth to nonsemantic terms, for T1 provides only a *partial* reduction. (To complete the reduction we need to reduce primitive denotation to nonsemantic terms.) T2, on the other hand, meets condition M; so either T2 is superior to T1 as a reduction, or else condition M is too weak and the "if" part of it must be rejected. My own diagnosis is the latter, but the other possibility seems initially reasonable. After all, how could condition M be strengthened? We might try requiring that '$B (e)$' be not only *extensionally* equivalent to 'e is true', but *intensionally* equivalent to it; but this clearly won't do, for even if we grant that there is an intelligible notion of intensional equivalence, our concern is not with analyzing the meaning of the word "true" but with performing a reduction. A clear and useful standard of equivalence that is stronger than extensional equivalence but not so strong as to rule out acceptable reductions is unknown at the present time, so I know no way to improve on condition M. My view is that we have a rough but useful concept of reduction which we are unable to formulate precisely; but I must admit that the alternative view, that extensional equivalence is adequate, has an initial appeal.

A closer look, however, will reveal quite conclusively that extensional equivalence is not a sufficient standard of reduction. This can be seen by looking at the concept of valence. The valence of a chemical element is an integer that is associated with that element, which represents the sort of chemical combinations that the element will enter into. What I mean by the last phrase is that it is possible – roughly, at least – to characterize which elements will combine with which others, and in what proportions they will combine, merely in terms of their valences. Because of this fact, the concept of valence is a physically important concept, and so if physicalism is correct it ought to be possible to explicate this concept in physical terms – e.g., it ought to be possible to find structural properties of the atoms of each element that determine what the valence of that element will be. Early in the twentieth century (long after the notion of valence had proved its value in enabling chemists to predict what chemical combinations there would be) this reduction of the concept of valence to the physical properites of atoms was established; the notion of valence was thus shown to be a physicalistically acceptable notion.

Now, it would have been easy for a chemist, late in the last century, to have given a "valence definition" of the following form:

(3) $(\forall E)(\forall n)$ (E has valence $n \equiv E$ is potassium and n is +1, or... or E is sulphur and n is -2)

where in the blanks go a list of similar clauses, one for each element. But, though this is an extensionally correct definition of valence, it would not have been an acceptable reduction; and had it turned out that nothing else was possible – had all efforts to explain valence in terms of the structural properties of atoms proved futile – scientists would have eventually had to decide either (a) to give up valence theory, or else (b) to replace the hypothesis of physicalism by another hypothesis (chemicalism?). It is part of scientific methodology to resist doing (b); and I also think it is part of scientific methodology to resist doing (a) as long as the notion of valence is serving the purposes for which it was designed (i.e., as long as it is proving useful in helping us characterize chemical compounds in terms of their valences). But the methodology is not to resist (a) and (b) by giving lists like (3); the methodology is to look for a real reduction. This is a methodology that has proved extremely fruitful in science, and I think we'd be crazy to give it up in linguistics. *And I think we are giving up this fruitful methodology, unless we realize that we need to add theories of primitive reference to T1 or T2 if we are to establish the notion of truth as a physicalistically acceptable notion.*

I certainly haven't yet given much argument for this last claim. I *have* argued that the standard of extensional equivalence doesn't guarantee an acceptable reduction; but T2 is obviously not trivial to the extent that (3) is. What *is* true, however, is roughly that T2 minus T1 is as trivial as (3) is. One way in which this last claim can be made more precise is by remembering that really we often apply the term 'valence' not only to elements, but also to configurations of elements (at least to stable configurations that are not compounds, i.e., to radicals). Thus, if we abstract from certain physical limitations on the size of possible configurations of elements (as, in linguistics, we usually abstract from the limitations that memory, etc., impose on the lengths of possible utterances), there is an infinite number of entities to which the term 'valence' is applied. But it is an important fact about valence that the valence of a configuration of elements is determined from the valences of the elements that make it up, and from the way they're put together. Because of this, we might try to give a recursive characterization of valence. First of all, we would try to characterize all the different *structures* that configurations of elements can have (much as we try to characterize all the different grammatical structures before we give a truth definition like T1 or T2). We would then try to find rules that would enable us to determine what the valence of a complicated configuration would be, given the valences of certain less complicated configurations that make it up and the way they're put together. If we had enough such rules, we could determine the valence of a given configuration given only its structure and the valences of the elements that make it up. And if we like, we can transform our recursive characterization of valence into an explicit characterization, getting

V1 $(\forall c)$ $(\forall n)$ (c has valence $n \equiv B(c, n)$)

The formula '$B(c, n)$' here employed will still contain the term 'valence', but it will contain that term only as applied to elements, not as applied to configurations. Thus our "valence definition' V1 would characterize the valence of the complex *in terms of the valences of the simple.*

It would now be possible to eliminate the term 'valence' from '$B(c, n)$', in either of two ways. One way would be to employ a genuine reduction of the notion of valence for elements to the structural properties of atoms. The other way would be to employ the pseudo-reduction (3). It is clear that we could use (3) to give a trivial reformulation V2 of V1, which would have precisely the "advantages" as a reduction that T2 has over T1. (V2, incidentally, would also have one of the disadvantages over V1 that T2 has over T1: V1 does not need to be overhauled when you discover or synthesize new elements, whereas V2 does.)

That is a sketch of one way that the remark I made two paragraphs back about "T2 minus T1" could be made more precise. But it is somewhat more fruitful to develop the point slightly differently: doing this will enable me to make clearer that there is unlikely to be *any* purpose that T2 serves better than T1 (not merely that T2 is no better at reduction).

To get this result I'll go back to my original use of the term 'valence', where it applies to elements only and not to configurations. And what I will do is compare (3) not to Tarski's theory of *truth*, but to Tarski's theory of *denotation* for names; the effect of this on his theory of truth will then be considered. Tarski states his theory of denotation for names in a footnote, as follows:

> To say that the name *x* denotes a given object *a* is the same as to stipulate that the object *a* ... satisfies a sentential function of a particular type. In colloquial language it would be a function which consists of three parts in the following order: a variable, the word "is" and the given name *x* (CTFL 194).

This is actually only part of the theory, the part that defines denotation in terms of satisfaction; to see what the theory looks like when all semantic terms are eliminated, we must see how satisfaction is defined. The definition is given by the (A) and (B) clauses of T2, for, as I've remarked, 'satisfaction' is Tarski's name for what I've called "truth$_s$". What Tarski's definition of satisfaction tells us is this: for any name N, an object a satisfies the sentential function $\lceil x_1 \text{is} N \rceil$ if and only if a is France and N is 'France' or ... or a is Germany and N is 'Germany'. Combining this definition of satisfaction (for sentential functions of form $\lceil x_1 \text{is} N \rceil$) with the earlier account of denotation in terms of satisfaction, we get:

(DE):   To say that the name N denotes a given object a is the same as to stipulate that either a is France and N is "France", or ... or a is Germany and N is "Germany".

This is Tarski's account of denotation for English proper names. For foreign proper names, the definition of denotation in terms of satisfaction needs no modification (except that the 'is' must be replaced by a name of a foreign word, say 'ist' for German). Combining this with the definition (again given by T2) of satisfaction for foreign sentential functions like $\lceil x_1 \text{ is } N \rceil$, we get:

(DG):   To say that the name N denotes a given object a is the same as to stipulate that either a is France and N is 'Frankreich', or ..., or a is Germany and N is 'Deutschland'.

DE and DG have not received much attention in commentaries on Tarski, but in fact they play a key

role in his semantic theory; and it was no aberration on Tarski's part that he offered them as theories of denotation for English and German names, for *they satisfy criteria of adequacy exactly analogous to the criteria of adequacy that Tarski accepted for theories of truth*.[15] Nevertheless, it seems clear that DE and DG do not really reduce truth to nonsemantic terms, any more than (3) reduces valence to nonchemical terms. What would a real explication of denotation in nonsemantic terms be like? The "classical" answer to this question (Russell's) is that a name like 'Cicero' is "analytically linked" to a certain description (such as 'the denouncer of Catiline'); so to explain how the name 'Cicero' denotes what it does you merely have to explain

(i)   the process by which it is linked to the description (presumably you bring in facts about how it was learned by its user, or facts about what is going on in the user's brain at the time of the using)

and

(ii)   how the description refers to what it does

Because of (ii), of course, the project threatens circularity: the project is to explain how names refer in terms of how descriptions refer; but the natural way to explain how descriptions refer is in terms of how they're built up from their significant parts,[16] and how those significant parts refer (or apply, or are fulfilled), and those significant parts will usually include names. But Russell recognized this threat of circularity, and carefully avoided it: he assumed that the primitives of the language were to be partially ordered by a relation of "basicness," and that each name except a most basic ("logically proper") name was to be analytically linked to a formula containing only primitives more basic than it. The most basic primitives were to be linked to the world without the intervention of other words, by the relation of acquaintance.

This classical view of how names (and other primitives) latch onto their denotations is extremely implausible in many ways (e.g., it says you can refer only to things that are definable from "logically proper" primitives; it requires that there be certain statements, such as 'If Cicero existed then Cicero denounced Catiline', which are analytic in the sense that they are guaranteed by linguistic rules and are immune to revision by future discoveries). I conjecture that it is because of the difficulties with this classical theory, which was the only theory available at the time that Tarski wrote, that Tarski's pseudo-theories DE and DG seemed reasonable – they weren't exciting, but if you wanted something exciting you got logically proper names. The diagnosis that any attempt to explain the relation between words and the things they are about must inevitably lead to either a wildly implausible theory (like Russell's) or a trivial theory (like Tarski's) seems to be widely accepted still; but I think that the diagnosis has become less plausible in recent years through the development of *causal* theories of denotation by Saul Kripke[17] and others. According to such theories, the facts that 'Cicero' denotes Cicero and that 'muon' applies to muons are to be explained in terms of certain kinds of causal networks between Cicero (muons) and our uses of 'Cicero' ('muon'): causal connections both of a social sort (the passing of the word 'Cicero' down to us from the original users of the name, or the passing of the word 'muon' to laymen from physicists) and of other sorts (the evidential causal connections that gave the original users of the name "access" to Cicero and gave physicists "access" to muons). I don't think that Kripke or anyone else thinks that *purely* causal theories of primitive denotation can be developed (even for proper names of past physical objects and for natural-kind predicates); this however should not blind us to the fact that he has suggested a kind of factor involved in denotation that gives new hope to the idea of explaining the connection between language and the things it is about. It seems to me that the possibility of *some such* theory of denotation (to be deliberately very vague) is essential to the joint acceptability of physicalism and the semantic term 'denotes', and that denotation definitions like DE and DG merely obscure the need for this.

It might be objected that the purpose of DE and DG was not reduction; but what was their purpose? One answer might be that (DE) and (DG) enable us to eliminate the word 'denote' whenever it occurs. ("To explain is to show how to eliminate.") For instance,

(4) No German name now in use denotes something that does not yet exist.

would become

(4') For any name N now in use, if N is 'Frankreich' then France already exists,

and..., and if N is 'Deutschland' then Germany already exists.

provided that (DG) is a correct and complete list of the denotations of all those German proper names that have denotations. It seems reasonably clear that we could specify a detailed procedure for transforming sentences like (4) into materially equivalent sentences like (4'). A similar claim could be made for the "valence definition" (3). Such a valence definition makes it possible to eliminate the word 'valence' from a large class of sentences containing it, and in a uniform way. For instance,

(5) For any elements A and B, if one atom of A combines with two of B, then the valence of A is -2 times that of B.

is materially equivalent to

(5') For any elements A and B, if one atom of A combines with two of B, then either A is sodium and B is sodium and $+1 = -2$ $(+1)$, or..., or A is sulphur and B is sodium and $-2 = -2(+1)$, or...

provided that (3) is a correct and complete list of valences. So if anyone ever wants to eliminate the word 'denote" or the word 'valence" from a large class of English sentences by a uniform procedure, denotation definitions and valence definitions are just the thing he needs. There are, however, sentences from which these words are not eliminable by the sketched procedure. For instance, in semantics and possibly in chemistry there are problems with counterfactuals, e.g., 'If "Germany" had been used to denote France, then...'. Moreover, there are special problems affecting the case of semantics, arising from the facts

(i) that the elimination procedure works only for languages in which nothing is denoted that cannot be denoted (without using semantic terms) in one's own language,

(ii) that it works only for languages that contain no ambiguous names,

and

(iii) that the denotation definitions provide no procedure for eliminating 'denote" from sentences where it is applied to more than one language; e.g., it gives no way of handling sentences like " 'Glub' denotes different things in different languages."

But, subject to these three qualifications (plus perhaps that involving counterfactuals), the elimination procedure for 'denote' is every bit as good as that for 'valence'!

What value did Tarski attach to such transformations? Unfortunately he did not discuss the one about valences, but he did discuss the one that transforms "Smith used a proper name to denote Germany" into something logically equivalent to "Smith uttered 'Deutschland'." And it is clear that to this definition he attached great philosophical importance. After defining semantics as "the totality of considerations concerning those concepts which, roughly speaking, express certain connexions between the expressions of a language and the objects and states of affairs referred to by those expressions" (ESS 401), he says that with his definitions, "the problem of establishing semantics on a scientific basis is completely solved" (ESS 407). In other places his claims are almost as extravagant. For instance, the remark about physicalism that I quoted at the end of section II is intended to apply to denotation as well as to truth: if definitions of denotation like DE and DG could not be given, "it would ... be impossible to bring [semantics] into harmony with ... physicalism" (ESS 406); but because of these definitions, the compatibility of the semantic concept of denotation with physicalism is established. By similar standards of reduction, one might prove that witchcraft is compatible with physicalism, as long as witches cast only a finite number of spells: for then 'cast a spell' can be defined without use of any of the terms of witchcraft theory, merely by listing all the witch-and-victim pairs.

In other places Tarski makes quite different claims for the value of his denotation definitions. For example:

We desire semantic terms (referring to the object language) to be introduced into the meta-language only by definition. For, if this postulate is satisfied, the definition of truth, or of any other semantic concept [including denotation, which Tarski had already specifically mentioned to be definable], will fulfill what we intuitively expect from every definition; that is, it will explain the meaning of the term being defined in terms whose meaning appears to be completely clear and unequivocal.[18]

But it is no more plausible that DE "explains the meaning of" 'denote' as applied to English, or that DG "explains the meaning of" "denote" as applied to German, than that (3) "explains the meaning of" 'valence' – considerably *less* so in fact, since for 'valence' there is no analogue to the conclusions that "denote" means something different when applied to English than it means when applied to German. In fact, it seems pretty clear that denotation definitions like DE and DG have no philosophical interest whatever. But what conclusions can we draw from this about Tarski's *truth* definitions like T2? I think the conclusion to draw is that *T2 has no philosophical interest whatever that is not shared by T1*. How this follows I will now explain.

We have seen that Tarski advocated theories of denotation for names that had the form of mere lists: examples of his denotation definitions were DE and DG, and for language L his denotation definition would take the following form:

D2 $(\forall e)\ (\forall a)\ [e$ is a name that denotes $a \equiv (e$ is 'c_1' and a is $c_1)$ or $(e$ is 'c_2' and a is $c_2)$ or ...]

where into the dots go analogous clauses for every name of L. Similarly, we can come up with definitions of application and fulfillment which are acceptable according to Tarski's standards, and which also have the form of mere lists. The definition of application runs:

A2 $(\forall e)\ (\forall a)\ [e$ is a predicate that applies to $a \equiv (e$ is 'p_1' and $p_1(a))$ or $(e$ is 'p_2' and $p_2(a))$ or ...].

Similarly, we can formulate a list-like characterization F2 of fulfillment for the function symbols. Clearly neither A2 nor F2 is of any more theoretical interest than D2.

Tarski, I have stressed, accepted D2 as part of his semantic theory, and would also have accepted A2 and F2; and this fact is quite important, since D2, A2, and F2 together with T2 imply T1. In other words, T1 is simply a weaker version of Tarski's semantic theory; it is a logical consequence of Tarski's theory. Now, an interesting question is what you have to add to T1 to get the rest of Tarski's semantic theory. Suppose we can find a formula R that we can argue to be of no interest whatever, such that Tarski's semantic theory (T2 ∧ D2 ∧ A2 ∧ F2) is logically equivalent to T1 ∧ R. It will then follow that the whole interest of Tarski's semantic theory lies in T1 – the rest of his semantic theory results simply by adding to it the formula R, which (I have assumed) has no interest whatever. And if there is nothing of interest in the conjunction T2 ∧ D2 ∧ A2 ∧ F2 beyond T1, certainly there can be nothing of interest in T2 alone beyond T1.

An example of such a formula R is D2 ∧ A2 ∧ F2: it is obvious that Tarski's semantic theory is logically equivalent to T1 ∧ D2 ∧ A2 ∧ F2. Because of this, *any interest in Tarski's semantic theory over* T1 *must be due to an interest in* D2 *or* A2 *or* F2 *(or to confusion): in this sense* D2 ∧ A2 ∧ F2 *is* "T2 *minus* T1". But I've already argued that D2, A2, and F2 have no theoretical interest whatever, and so that establishes that T2 has no theoretical interest whatever that is not shared by T1.

V

Much of what I've said in this paper gains plausibility by being put in a wider perspective, and so I now want to say a little bit about why we want a notion of truth. The notion of truth serves a great many purposes, but I suspect that its original purpose – the purpose for which it was first developed – was to aid us in utilizing the utterances of others in drawing conclusions about the world. To take an extremely simple example, suppose that a friend reports that he's just come back from Alabama and that there was a foot of snow on the ground there. Were it not for his report we would have considered it extremely unlikely that there was a foot of snow on the ground in Alabama – but the friend knows snow when he sees it and is not prone to telling us lies for no apparent reason, and so after brief deliberation we conclude that probably there *was* a foot of snow in Alabama. What we did here was first to use our evidence about the person and his situation to decide that he probably said something true when he made a certain utterance, and then to draw a conclusion from the truth of his utterance to the existence of snow in Alabama. In order to make such inferences, we have to have a pretty good grasp of (i) the circumstances under which what another says is likely to be true, and (ii) how to get from a belief

in the truth of what he says to a belief about the extralinguistic world.

If this idea is right, then two features of truth that are intimately bound up with the purposes to which the notion of truth are put are (I) the role that the attempt to tell the truth and the success in doing so play in social institutions, and (II) the fact that normally one is in a position to assert of a sentence that it is true in just those cases where one is in a position to assert the sentence or a paraphrase of it. It would then be natural to expect that what is involved in communicating the meaning of the word 'true' to a child or to a philosopher is getting across to him the sorts of facts listed under (I) and (II); for those are the facts that it is essential for him to have an awareness of if he is to put the notion of truth to its primary use (child) or if he is to get a clear grasp of what its primary use is (philosopher).

I think that this natural expectation is correct, and that it gives more insight than was given in sections II and IV into why it is that neither T1 nor T2 can reasonably be said to explain the meaning of the term 'true' – even when a theory of primitive reference is added to them. First consider (I). The need of understanding the sort of thing alluded to in (I), if we are to grasp the notion of truth, has been presented quite forcefully in Michael Dummett's article "Truth,"[19] in his analogy between speaking the truth and winning at a game. It is obvious that T1 and T2 don't explain anything like this (and in fact Dummett's fourth paragraph, on Frege-style truth definitions, can be carried over directly to T1 and T2).

The matter might perhaps be expressed in terms of assertibility conditions that one learns in learning to use the word 'true': part of what we learn, in learning to use this word, is that in cases like that involving the friend from Alabama there is some prima facie weight to be attached to the claim that the other person is saying something true. But there are also *other* assertibility conditions that one learns in learning the word 'true', assertibility conditions which have received considerable attention in the philosophical literature on truth. To begin with, let's note one obvious fact about how the word 'true' is standardly learned: we learn how to apply it to utterances of our own language first, and when we later learn to apply it to other languages it is by conceiving the utterances of another language more or less on the model of utterances our own language. The obvious model of the first stage of this process is that we learn to assert all instances of the schema

(T) X is true if and only if p.

where 'X' is replaced by a quotation-mark name of an English sentence S and 'p' is replaced by S. This must be complicated to deal with ambiguous and truth-value-less sentences, but let's ignore them. Also let's ignore the fact that certain pathological instances of (T) – the Epimenides-type paradoxical sentences – are logically refutable. Then there is a sense in which the instances of (T) that we've learned to assert determine a unique extension for the predicate 'true' as applied to sentences of our own language.[20] Our views about what English sentences belong to this unique extension may be altered, but as long as we stick to the instances of (T) they cannot consistently be altered without also altering our beliefs in what those sentences express. This fact is extremly important to the functions that the word 'true' serves (as the Alabama example illustrates).

In stressing the assertibility conditions for simple sentences containing the word 'true', I have followed Quine (*ibid*. 138); for, like him, I believe that such assertibility conditions are enough to make the term 'true' reasonably clear. But now it might be asked, "Then why do we need causal (etc.) theories of reference? The words 'true' and 'denotes' are made perfectly clear by schemas like (T). To ask for more than these schemas – to ask for causal theories of reference to nail language to reality – is to fail to recognize that we are at sea on Neurath's boat: we have to work *within* our conceptual scheme, we can't glue it to reality from the outside."

I suspect that this would be Quine's diagnosis – it is strongly suggested by §6 of *Word and Object*, especially when that is taken in conjunction with some of Quine's remarks about the inscrutibility of reference and truth value, the underdetermination of theories, and the relativity of ontology. It seems to me, however, that the diagnosis is quite wrong. In looking for a theory of truth and a theory of primitive reference we *are* trying to explain the connection between language and (extralinguistic) reality, but we are *not* trying to step outside of our theories of the world in order to do so. Our accounts of primitive reference and of truth are not to be thought of as something that could be given by philosophical reflection prior to scientific information – on the contrary, it seems likely that

such things as psychological models of human beings and investigations of neurophysiology will be very relevant to discovering the mechanisms involved in reference. *The reason why accounts of truth and primitive reference are needed is not to tack our conceptual scheme onto reality from the outside; the reason, rather, is that without such accounts our conceptual scheme breaks down from the inside.* On our theory of the world it would be extremely surprising if there were some non-physical connection between words and things. Thus if we could argue from our theory of the world that the notion of an utterer's saying something true, or referring to a particular thing, cannot be made sense of in physicalist terms (say, by arguing that any semantic notion that makes physicalistic sense *can* be explicated in Skinnerian terms, and that the notions of truth and reference *can't* be explicated in Skinnerian terms), then to the extent that such an argument is convincing we ought to be led to conclude that, if we are to remain physicalists, the notions of truth and reference must be abandoned. No amount of pointing out the clarity of these terms helps enable us to escape this conclusion: 'valence' and 'gene' were perfectly clear long before anyone succeeded in reducing them, but it was their reducibility and not their clarity before reduction that showed them to be compatible with physicalism.

The clarity of 'valence' and 'gene' before reduction – and even more, their *utility* before reduction – did provide physicalists with substantial reason to think that a reduction of these terms was possible, and, as I remarked earlier, a great deal of fruitful work in physical chemistry and chemical genetics was motivated by the fact. Similarly, insofar as semantic notions like 'true' are useful, we have every reason to suspect that they will be reducible to non-semantic terms, and it is likely that progress in linguistic theory will come by looking for such reductions. (In fact, the fruitfulness of Tarski's work in aiding us to understand language is already some sign of this, even though it represents only a partial reduction.) Of course, this sort of argument for the prospects of reducing semantic notions is only as powerful as our arguments for the utility of semantic terms; and it is clear that the question of the utility of the term 'true' – the purposes it serves, and the extent to which those purposes could be served by less pretentious notions such as warranted assertibility – needs much closer investigation.

All these remarks require one important qualification. The notion of valence, it must be admitted, is *not* reducible to nonchemical terms on the *strictest* standards of reduction, but is only *approximately* reducible; yet, in spite of this, we don't want to get rid of the notion, since it is still extremely useful in those contexts where its approximate character isn't too likely to get in the way and where if we did not approximate we'd get into quantum-mechanical problems far too complex for anyone to solve. (Moreover, considerations about the purposes of the notion of valence were sufficient to show that the notion of valence would only be approximately reducible: for the utility of the notion of valence is that it aids us in approximately characterizing which elements will combine with which and in what proportions; yet it is obvious that no *precise* such characterization is possible.)

Similarly, it may well be that a detailed investigation into the purposes of the notion of truth might show that these purposes require only an approximate reduction of the notion of truth. Still, to require an approximate reduction is to require quite a bit; after all, 'is a reincarnation of' isn't even approximately reducible to respectable biology, and 'electromagnetic field' is not approximately reducible to mechanics. Obviously the notion of approximate reduction needs to be made more precise (as in fact does the notion of strict, or nonapproximate, reduction); but even without making it so, I think we can see that T2 is no more of an approximate reduction than is V2, since D2 ∧ A2 ∧ F2 is no more of an approximate reduction than is (3). In other words, the main point of the paper survives when we replace the ideal of strict reduction by the ideal of approximate reduction.

It should be kept carefully in mind that the Quinean view that all we need do is clarify the term 'true', in the sense that this term is clarified by schema T (or by schema T plus a theory of translation to handle foreign languages; or by schema T plus the sort of thing alluded to in connection with Dummett), is *not* Tarski's view. Tarski's view is that we have to provide a truth characterization like T2 (which, when we choose as our object language L a "nice" fragment of our own language, can be shown correct merely by assuming that all instances of schema T are valid – cf. note 14; and such a truth characterization does much more than schema T does. It does not do everything that Tarski ever claimed for it, for Tarski attached much too much importance to the pseudo-theories D2, A2, and F2; but even when we "subtract" such trivialities from his truth characterization T2, we still get the very interesting and important truth characterization T1. T1, I believe, adequately represents Tarski's real contribution to the theory of truth, and in doing this it has a number of positive advantages over T2 (in addition to the important negative advantage I've been stressing, of preventing extravagant claims based on the fact that T2 contains no semantic terms). First of all, T1, unlike T2, is applicable to languages that contain ambiguities and languages that contain terms not adequately translatable into English. Second, T1, unlike T2, can be used in diachronic linguistics: it doesn't need overhauling as you add new words to the language, provided those new words belong to the same semantic category as words already in the language. Third, I think that the reason why Tarski's theory of truth T2 has seemed so uninteresting to so many people is that it contains the vacuous semantic theories D2, A2, and F2 for the primitives of the language. By expressing the really important features of Tarski's results on truth, and leaving out the inessential and uninteresting "theories" of the semantics of the primitives, T1 should make the philosophical importance of Tarski's work more universally recognized.

Notes

This paper grew out of a talk I gave at Princeton in the fall of 1970, where I defended T1 over T2. Donald Davidson and Gilbert Harman – and later, in private conversation, John Wallace – all came to the defense of T2, and their remarks have all been of help to me in writing the paper. I have also benefited from advice given by Michael Devitt, Paul Benacerraf, and especially David Hills.

1 *Logic of Scientific Discovery* (New York: Basic Books, 1968), p. 274.

2 Cf. Carnap's "Autobiography," in P. A. Schilpp, ed., *The Philosophy of Rudolf Carnap* (Lasalle, Ill.: Open Court, 1963), p. 61.

3 It is sometimes claimed that Tarski was interested in languages considered in abstraction from all speakers and writers of the language; that the languages he was dealing with are abstract entities to be specified by giving their rules. This seems incorrect: Tarski was interested in giving the semantics of

languages that mathematicians had been writing for years; and only as a result of Tarski's work was it then possible for philosophers like Carnap to propose that the clauses of a Tarski-type truth definition for such languages be called rules of the languages and be used in defining the languages as abstract entities.

4 "The Concept of Truth in Formalized Languages" (CTFL), in *Logic, Semantics, and Metamathematics (LSM)* (New York: Oxford, 1956), p. 166.

5 Actually in model theory we are interested in allowing a slightly unusual semantics for the quantifiers: we are willing to allow that the quantifier not range over everything. We could build this generalization into our truth definition, by stipulating that in addition to the denotations of the nonlogical symbols we specify a universe U, and then reformulating clause (B) 4 by requiring that the kth member of s^* belong to U. If we did this, then it would be the range of the quantifiers as well as the denotations of the nonlogical primitives that we would have explained truth in terms of.

6 An *incomplete* sentence token is a sentence token which [like the occurrence of '$2 + 2 = 4$' inside '$(2 + 2 = 4)$'] is part of a larger sentence token.

7 "Truth and Meaning," *Synthese*, XVII, 3 (September, 1967): 304–23, pp. 314/15.

8 Note that the claims I've been making are intended to apply only to cases where different tokens have different semantic features; they are not intended to apply to cases of indeterminacy, i.e., to cases where a particular name token or predicate token has no determinate denotation or extension. To deal with indeterminacy requires more complex devices than I employ in this paper.

9 The notion of a semantic category is Tarski's: cf. CTFL, p. 215.

10 To do so in the obvious way requires that we introduce semantic categories of negation symbol, conjunction symbol, and universal-quantification symbol; though by utilizing some ideas of Frege it could be shown that there is really no need of a separate semantic category for each logical operator. The use of semantic categories in the generalized truth characterization raises important problems which I have had to suppress for lack of space in this paper.

11 For simplicity, I have assumed that L itself contains no semantic terms.

12 "This Establishment of Scientific Semantics" (ESS) in *LSM*, p. 406.

13 This, of course, is very vague, but most attempts to explicate the doctrine of physicalism more precisely result in doctrines that are very hard to take seriously [e.g., the doctrine that for every acceptable predicate '$P(x)$' there is a formula '$B(x)$' containing only terminology from physics, such that '$\forall x(P(x) \equiv B(x))$' is true]. Physicalism should be understood as the doctrine (however precisely it is to be characterized) that guides science in the way I describe.

14 Tarski actually gives a different formulation, the famous Convention T, evidently because he does not think that the word "correct" ought to be employed in stating a criterion of adequacy. First of all Tarski writes:

> we shall accept as valid every sentence of the form
> [T] the sentence x is true if and only p
> where 'p' is to be replaced by any sentence of the language under investigation and 'x' by any individual name of that sentence provided this name occurs in the metalanguage (ESS 404).

Is Tarski's policy of accepting these sentences as "valid" (i.e., true) legitimate? It seems to me that it is, in a certain special case. The special case is where

I. The object language is a proper part of the metalanguage (here, English).

II. The object language contains no paradoxical or ambiguous or truth-value-less sentences.

In this special case – and it was the case that Tarski was primarily concerned with – I think it will be generally agreed that all instances of Schema T hold. From this, together with the fact that only grammatical sentences are true, we can argue that, if a necessary and sufficient condition of form (2) has the following consequences:

(a) Every instance of Schema T

(b) The sentence '$(\forall x)$ (x is true $\supset S(x)$)', where '$S(x)$' formulates (correct) conditions for an utterance of L to be a sentence

then that necessary and sufficient condition is correct. Let's say that a "truth definition" for L (a necessary and sufficient condition of truth in L) *satisfies Convention T* if it has all the consequences listed under (a) and (b). Then, restating: when L is a language for which I and II hold, then any truth definition satisfying Convention T is correct; and since only quite uncontroversial assumptions about truth are used in getting this result, anyone will admit to the correctness of a truth characterization satisfying Convention T. If we use the term 'formally correct definition' for a sentence of form (2) in which '$B(e)$' contains no semantic terms, this means that a formally correct definition that satisfies Convention T is bound to satisfy Condition M (when the language L satisfies I and II). As far as I can see, this is the only motivation for Convention T.

Tarski sometimes states a more general form of Convention T, which applies to languages that do not meet restriction I: it is what results when one allows as instances of Schema T the results of replacing 'p' by a *correct translation* of the sentence that the name substituted for 'x' denotes (in some sense of 'correct translation' in which correctness requires preservation of truth value). But then the advantage of the ungeneralized form of Convention T (viz., that anything satisfying it wears its correctness on its face, or more accurately, on the faces of its logical consequences) is lost.

15 A sentence of the form '$(\forall N)$ $(\forall x)$ [N denotes $x \equiv B(N, x)$]' *satisfies convention* D if it has as consequences every instance of the schema 'y denotes z', in which 'y' is to be replaced by a quotation-mark name for a name N, and 'z' is to be replaced by (an adequate translation of N into English, i.e.) a singular term of English that contains no semantic terms and that denotes the same thing that N denotes. Clearly DE and DG are not only extensionally correct, they also satisfy Convention D. Presumably philosophers who are especially impressed with Convention T will be equally impressed with this fact, but they owe us a reason why satisfying Convention D is of any interest.

16 For example, by extending our definition of denotation$_s$ to descriptions by:

$\lceil \imath x_k(e) \rceil$ denotes$_s$ a if and only if [for each sequence s^* which differs from s at the kth place at most, e is true$_s^*$ if and only if the kth member of s^* is a].

and then defining denotation in terms of denotation$_s$ by stipulating that a closed term denotes an object if and only if it denotes$_s$ that object for some (or all) s.

17 Some of Kripke's work on names will be published shortly in Davidson and Harman, eds., *Semantics of Natural Language* (Dordrecht: Reidel, 1971). What I've said about Russell's view is influenced by some of Kripke's lectures on which his paper there is based.

18 "The Semantic Conception of Truth and the Foundations of Semantics," *Philosophy and Phenomenological Research*, IV, 3 (March 1944): 341–75, p. 351.

19 *Proceedings of the Aristotelian Society*, LIX (1958/9): 141–62.

20 Cf. W. V. Quine, *From a Logical Point of View* (New York: Harper & Row, 1961), p. 136.

8

Types and Ontology

Fred Sommers

In this chapter[1] I shall be examining several notions of *types* which have important application in natural languages. I shall show that one of Russell's definitions of a type can be combined with one of Ryle's to give us two other and more powerful type conceptions which are free of the criticisms advanced against each of the former. The results cast considerable light on the relation of "a language" to the sorts of things one can use the language to make statements about; for example, it becomes clear that the number of "sorts of things" discriminated by any natural language is always finite. But far more important, the new type concepts enable us to exhibit formally the type structure of any natural language. It is this structure which determines the way the language discriminates different sorts of things. Since the question of ontology is "What sorts of things are there?" the results may be construed as a formal ontology. The old Russell program for an ontology which is defined by a logically correct (or corrected) language is thereby reinstated, though in a revised form. That program has foundered on the type problem for natural languages. Black, for example, has brought out grave difficulties in Russell's type theory as it applies to natural languages, and he used those difficulties to promote skepticism about the Russell program. But if I am right, a simple and adequate theory of types governs natural language and dictates its ontological commitments to different sorts of things.

Fred Sommers, Types and Ontology. *Philosophical Review*, 72 (1963): 327–63.

I

The difference between the ordinary class notion and the notion of a "sort" or a type is essential for an understanding of what ontologists are interested in. The ontologist says that the three classes of men, odd numbers, and even numbers are contained in two "sorts" of things. It might be said that the ontologist has in mind a more general kind of class. (Thus Quine appears to think that the difference between the zoologist and the ontologist is only breadth of interest.)[2] But that leaves open the crucial question: what kind of generality interests the ontologist? Of course a "sort" is a class, but what *kind* of class?

In asking that question we are asking for certain logical characteristics which distinguish types or sorts from other classes. Categories, types, sorts – all these terms have been used by philosophers – are classes of a special kind. We might call such a class an ontological class; but this would only add to the list of obscure synonyms even if it did serve to remind us that a clarification of the type question will help us to understand ontology as a branch of philosophy. In the early sections of this paper I shall use the word "type." The advantage of dealing with "type" (over "sort," "category," "ontological class," and so forth) lies in the fact that recent literature has given "type" some precise technical meanings.

One clear answer to the question "What is a type?" comes from Russell:

The definition of a logical type is as follows: A and B are of the same logical type if, and only if, given any fact of which A is a constituent, there is a corresponding fact which has B as a constituent, which either results by substituting B for A or is the negation of what so results. To take an illustration, Socrates and Aristotle are of the same type, because "Socrates was a philosopher" and "Aristotle was a philosopher" are both facts; Socrates and Caligula are of the same type, because "Socrates was a philosopher" and "Caligula was not a philosopher" are both facts. To love and to kill are of the same type, because "Plato loved Socrates" and "Plato did not kill Socrates" are both facts.[3]

Russell here defines a type as a class of things or relations. I shall ignore relations.

Confining ourselves to the criterion for type sameness as it applies to things, we have the following: Two things are of the same type with respect to a monadic predicate P, if and only if P is significantly (that is, truly or falsely but not absurdly) predicable of both. All the things of which it makes sense to predicate P belong to the same type. When $P = $ "is a philosopher," Julius Caesar and Socrates are of the same type with respect to P, but Julius Caesar and the Industrial Revolution are not of the same type with respect to P.

Since, as we shall see, Russell's type concept is only one of four fundamental type notions, it will be convenient to designate a set of things which meet Russell's specifications for a type by some special name. We shall call such a set an "α-type." Also, we shall say that every member of an α-type is "spanned" by the predicate which defines it. (A predicate will be said to span a thing if it is predicated of it either truly or falsely but not absurdly.) Thus an α-type may be defined as a set of all and only those things that are spanned by some (monadic) predicate.

A second and different notion of types is to be found in Ryle's idea of a type or category mistake. Where Russell's formulation is material, Ryle's is formal or syntactical. A type or category mistake is made by any sentence which conjoins two expressions (predicates) that are not both significantly applicable to the same thing. Thus "a sedan chair" and "a flood of tears" cannot both be applied to the same thing. We cannot, for example, say that both expressions apply to what a young lady came home in: "She came home in a sedan chair and a flood of tears" is therefore a type

mistake. But this is true of any category mistake. "Vanity" and "feeling" are expressions which cannot both apply to some one thing together; the same is true of "itch" and "mood." In calling "Vanity is a feeling" and "An itch is a mood" type mistakes, Ryle is evidently using "type" for a class of *expressions*.

Confining ourselves once again to monadic predicates, we can arrive at a formulation. If P and Q are monadic predicates which can both be significantly applied to any one thing, then a sentence (P, Q) is not a type mistake; that is, P and Q are expressions of the same type. And in general, if t is some given thing, then the set of all and only all those predicates which span (are significantly predicable of) t form a type. We shall call this sort of predicate-set a "B-type."

Where Russell has defined a type to be a set of things spanned by a given predicate, Ryle's type concept is that of a set of expressions which span some given thing. Russell's α-type and Ryle's B-type suffer from this relativity to some specific predicate or thing. And it is hardly surprising that Black's criticism of Russell can easily be generalized to apply to Ryle's conception of a B-type.

For Black in his criticism of Russell[4] showed that the notion of an α-type renders the relation of "being of the same type" a nontransitive relation. Thus if a and b are things of the same α-type, while b and c are also of the same α-type, it does not follow that a and c are of the same α-type. For a and b may be of the same α-type with respect to P, while b and c may be of the same α-type with respect to Q. For example, let $a = $ Aristotle, $b = $ Bertrand Russell, $c = $ continuity, $P = $ (is) a philosopher and $Q = $ (is) thought about. Ryle's criterion for types of expressions suffers similarly from the nontransitivity of the relation "being of the same B-type." For suppose "(is) a philosopher" and "(is) thought about" are of the same B-type since both span Plato, while "is thought about" and "even prime" are of the same B-type since both span the second natural number. It does not follow that "(is) a philosopher" and "(is) an even prime" are of the same B-type. Here again it is the introduction of those "high" predicates – like "(is) interesting," "(is) thought about" – which exposes the difficulty. We may therefore put Black's criticism in its general form: the existence of high predicates like "is interesting," and so forth renders Russell's and Ryle's criteria for type sameness inadequate. *We require type notions that retain transitivity for the relation "is of the same type."*

Russell's α-types are sets of things; Ryle's *B*-types are sets of predicates. Corresponding to Russell's α-types we want now to define a type of thing for which "being of the same type" is transitive without qualification. We shall call such a set of things a "*β*-type." Similarly, corresponding to Ryle's *B*-types we shall define a set of predicates – which we shall call an *A*-type – for which type sameness is transitive. More specifically, we use the concept of a *B*-type to define *β*-types while the notion of a α-type is used to define an *A*-type.

Consider some one thing *t* and the set of all those predicates such that any member of the set is predicable significantly of *t*. Such a predicate set we are calling a *B*-type. For example, let *t* = Thales. Then in the *B*-type of *t* there will be predicate expressions like "happy," "married," "bachelor," "carpenter," "weighs one hundred pounds," "brown," and so forth. Outside the set there will be predicates like "holiday," "prime number," "legal," and so forth. It is evident that the same *B*-type will be unique for other individuals besides Thales. Thus using the *B*-type, we can define a set of things (a *β*-type) any one of which entertains predication by all and only all of the members of that *B*-type. More formally:

1 Two things are of the same *β*-type if the *B*-types for both are identical.
2 A *β*-type is a set of things all of whose members are spanned by predicates of some *B*-type and none of whose members is spanned by any predicate outside of that *B*-type.

It is obvious that for *β*-types, the relation "being of the same type" is transitive. Also on the criterion for *β*-type sameness, it is clear that Russell and continuity are of different types, since while they share some spanning predicates (such as "is thought about"), they do not share all. On the other hand, Socrates and Julius Caesar *are* of the same type since whatever spans one spans the other and nothing which spans one fails to span the other.

The three type concepts so far defined are:

1 α-types: a set of *things* constitutes an α-type with respect to a predicate *P* if and only if *P* spans all of the things in the set and nothing outside the set.
2 *B*-types: a set of *predicates* constitutes a *B*-type with respect to an individual *t* if and only if *t* is spanned by every member of the set and by no predicate outside the set.
3 *β*-types: a set of things constitutes a *β*-type if and only if every member of the set is spanned by every member of the same *B*-type and no member of the set is spanned by any predicate outside of that *B*-type.

Our fourth type concept is therefore:

4 *A*-types: a set of predicates constitutes an *A*-type if and only if every member of the set spans every member of some α-type and no member of the set spans a thing outside of that α-type.[5]

The notion of spanning is fundamental to all four type concepts; essentially they are defined in terms of it. It is evident that for any language of finite vocabulary – and every natural language is finite in that sense – the number of α-types spanned by the predicates is finite. The number of *β*-types is even smaller than the number of α-types and it too is finite. We may therefore conclude that the sorts of things (in either of the above senses of "sorts") discriminated by any natural language is finite. Whether we define a sort or type of thing by what is spanned by a single predicate, or whether we define it by what is spanned by a set of predicates (and the combinatory possibilities for unique sets is limited for a finite vocabulary), we cannot have more than a finite number of sorts of things talked about by the same language.

Finally, by the above definitions the number of *A*-types corresponds exactly to the number of α-types, and the number of *B*-types corresponds exactly to the number of *β*-types, so that for all four senses of "type" the number of types in any natural language is finite.

II

We have so far used the semantic concept of spanning to define *B*-types. But *B*-types can very usefully be defined in syntactical terms. Consider a set of expressions, $A', B', C' \ldots K'$, that can serve as grammatical predicates in subject predicate sentences. Thus A' might be "is Socrates," B' might be "is a philosopher," C' might be "is an even prime," and so on. We shall speak of a corresponding set of $A, B, C \ldots K$ as a set of *terms*. Where $A' =$ "is Socrates," $A =$ "Socrates"; where

Fred Sommers

B' = "is a philosopher," B = "philosopher"; and so on for the rest of the terms of the set.

Now let any pair of terms (X, Y) represent some sentence which conjoins the terms X and Y. Thus (X, Y) will be a sentence like "X is Y," "Some Y is X," "All non-Y is X" and so on for all the logical forms of sentences conjoining the two terms X and Y. Let us suppose that $(X, Y)_i$ represents some one sentence with X and Y and that $(X, Y)_j$ represents some other sentence whose logical form differs from that of $(X, Y)_i$. We now state the syntactical equivalence. For any term X and Y and for any forms i and j:

$$(X, Y)_i \text{ is significant} \equiv (X, Y)_j \text{ is significant.}$$

This equivalence expresses the simple fact that when a sentence (X, Y) is significant it remains significant under all the normal logical operations such as conversion, negation, contraposition, and so forth. And, similarly, if the sentence is category nonsense, then all such transformations are also nonsensical.

The significance or nonsignificance of a sentence $(X, Y)_i$ is therefore independent of the omnibus operator "i." Whether the sentence is significant depends only on what X and Y are. We may therefore ignore the logical form of the sentence and concentrate only on the compatibility or lack of compatibility of the two terms.

Let us say that two terms which can be used together to form significant sentences are U-related terms. To indicate this we prefix the value U to the pair of terms.[6] The U-relation may be defined thus:

$$(X, Y)_i \text{ is not a category mistake} \equiv U(X, Y)_{df}.$$

$$(X, Y)_i \text{ is a category mistake} \equiv N(X, Y)$$
$$\equiv \text{not-}U(X, Y)_{df}.$$

For example, the value for the pair (tall, philosopher) is U and we therefore say: U (philosopher, tall). And if we are given a set of terms – "Socrates," "philosopher," "even prime," "tall," "fence" – we would write down the following ten values for the pairs: $U(S, P)$, (S, E), $U(S, T)$, $N(S, F)$, $N(P, E)$, $U(P, T)$, $N(P, F)$, $N(E, T)$, $U(T, F)$, $N(E, F)$.

The properties of the U and N relations form the formal heart of the theory of types. For X and Y to be U-related means that they are significantly conjoinable. And (1) assures us of the symmetry of the U-relation, that is, $U(X, Y) = U(Y,$

$X)$. Clearly the U-relation is also reflexive so that $U(X, X)$ holds for any term in the language. We shall see that one major source of trouble concerns the question whether the U-relation is transitive. But our immediate task is the definition of B-types in terms of the U-relation. This we can now do.

A set of terms S *constitutes a* B-*type of a language if all the terms of* S *are mutually* U-*related so that any pair of terms in* S *has the value* U *and there is no larger set* S' *in* L *whose terms are mutually* U-*related and such that* S *is included in* S'.

In other words, the B-types of a language are the largest sets of mutually U-related terms. And to say that two terms are of the same B-type is equivalent to saying that they are U-related.

The notion of a set of terms having mutual use may be found in Black as well as in Ryle. It underlies his tentative formulation of a "negative criterion" for establishing that two expressions are of different types. Black's formulation, like Ryle's, is wider since he intends his criterion to apply to all sorts of expressions, not merely those expressions we here call terms or monadic predicates. But if we confine Black's remarks to terms, we see him making use of the idea of a set of mutually U-related terms. We must, says Black,

> interpret the theory of types negatively as essentially an instrument for establishing *differences* of type. . . . The new procedure consists in asserting that two typographically distinct words are syntactically *dissimilar* if there is *at least one* context in which one cannot be substituted for the other without generating nonsense [italics his].[7]

Thus let C be some linguistic context (. . . , C). We can, says Black, establish that two terms A and B are of different types if we notice that $U(A, C)$ while $N(B, C)$.

Black uses the notion of a mutual U-set of terms for a negative criterion because he does not – as we do – consider mutual U-relatedness to be a sufficient condition for establishing that two terms are of the same type. On our definition of a B-type it is, for example, sufficient to know that U (philosopher, tall) in order for us to say that "philosopher" and "tall" belong to the same B-type. But for Black, this is to ignore the fact that U (fence, tall) will also establish that "tall" and "fence" are of the same type, and yet we should not wish to go on to say that "philosopher" and "fence" are of the same type. For this reason Black ignores the notion of type sameness and uses the notion of mutually U-related terms as a necessary condition for not being of different types.

We may put Black's syntactical criterion symbolically:

$U(X, Y)$ and $\mathcal{N}(X, Z)$ implies that Y and Z are of different types.

Black's formula appears to override an important distinction. Look at the following two cases which apply it:

1 U (Russell, philosopher) and $\mathcal{N}$ (prime number, philosopher) implies "Russell" and "prime number" are syntactically dissimilar.
2 U (Russell, thought about) and $\mathcal{N}$ (Russell, continuity) implies that "thought about" and "continuity" are syntactically dissimilar.

Does Black wish to consider the type difference in the consequent of (i) to be on a par with the type difference in the consequent of (ii)? The terms of the consequent of (ii) are U-related while the terms of the consequent of (i) are $\mathcal{N}$-related. And if there exists a difference of type between the second two terms, it is quite a different difference from the type difference between the terms of (i).z

Yet Black cannot be accused of overlooking the difference between the two cases. For Black denies that the formal type theorist can *have* three terms with the values: $U(X, Y)$, $\mathcal{N}(X, Z)$ $U(Y, Z)$. In other words, every time we have $U(X, Y)$ and $\mathcal{N}(X, Z)$ this implies that $\mathcal{N}(Y, Z)$. Therefore, if we *do* have U (Russell, thought about), $\mathcal{N}$ (Russell, continuity), and U (continuity thought about), *this can only mean* that "thought about" has *two* senses in its two significant occurrences with "Russell" and "continuity." And in general, if A and B are known to be of different types, then $\mathcal{N}(A, B)$:

> Thus the application of the theory of types to ordinary language is a more complex undertaking than Russell's own account would suggest. A single attempt at substitution may establish that "A" is not of the same type as "B." Suppose that two sentences are typographically identical except in containing "A" in place of "B" then the corresponding symbols, in spite of typographical identity must be considered as belonging to different types.[8]

And this, says Black:

> requires the two occurrences of "thinking" in "I am thinking about Russell" and "I am think-

ing about continuity" to be construed as instances of *two* words belonging to different syntactical types.[9]

Thus Black is not only saying:

(1) $U(X, Y)$ and $\mathcal{N}(X, Z)$ implies Y and Z are syntactically dissimilar.

He is also saying:

(2) $U(X, Y)$ and $\mathcal{N}(X, Z)$ implies $\mathcal{N}(Y, Z)$ or – what is the same thing – $U(X, Y)$ and $U(Y, Z)$ implies $U(X, Z)$.

It is because Black maintains (2) that he need not consider case (ii) above. In that case, "thought about" is equivocal. If it were not equivocal, then we should really say "I am thinking about continuity" is nonsense. And Russell, too, in his *Reply* agrees with Black in saying that unless "thought about" is equivocal in the two sentences "I am thinking about Russell" and "I am thinking about continuity," one of these two sentences is nonsensical.[10]

Both Black and Russell, it is clear, consider U to be a *transitive* relation. And Ryle in his paper, *Categories*, also maintains a position which in effect adopts (2) as a syntactical rule. Since these philosophers maintain the rule, it will be necessary to see why they do so. Important philosophical questions turn on its acceptance or rejection. I shall show that the rule must be rejected. But for the moment I wish to show how its acceptance has disastrous consequences for the fourfold distinction of types which has been formulated above. And to do this it will be helpful to introduce an important notion in a formal way, namely "the use of a term."

Let $U(X)$ be a set of terms any one of which is U-related to X. We call such a set the "use of the term X" since it contains all those terms with which X can be paired to form significant sentences. For example, in the set, U (philosopher) – "the use of 'philosopher'" – we would have the terms "philosopher," "Socrates," "tall," "happy," and so on; any term is in its own use since for any term X, it is never the case that $\mathcal{N}(X, X)$. Using the notion of the use of a term, we can syntactically define A-types in a convenient way: *a set of terms* S *constitutes an A-type in* L *if and only if all the terms of* S *have the same use and there is no larger set* S' *such that all the terms of* S' *have the same use and* S' *includes* S.

The difference between A-types and B-types in the two syntactical definitions may be made clear by considering any two U-related terms X and Y. According to the syntactical formulation of a B-type it is clear that: $U(X, Y) \equiv X$ and Y are of the same B-type. On the other hand, given $U(X, Y)$, we do *not* know that X and Y are of the same A-type. For it may be that there is a term Z such that $U(X, Z)$ and $\mathcal{N}(Y, Z)$, or such that $U(Y, Z)$ and $\mathcal{N}(X, Z)$. If there is, then the use of X will not be the same as the use of Y.

But now, if the transitivity rule (2) holds, it follows that there can *never* be such a term Z, since $U(X, Y)$ and $U(Y, Z)$ always implies that $U(X, Z)$ and, similarly, $U(X, Y)$ and $U(X, Z)$ implies $U(Y, Z)$. In short, for any two terms X and Y, $U(X, Y) \equiv X$ and Y are of the same A-type, and the distinction between A-and B-types is obliterated in favor of the former. A-types as we defined them are indeed transitive with respect to type sameness. But for those who maintain the transitivity of the U-relation, B-types, like A-types, become transitive, and indeed there is no meaning any longer to the distinction between the two kinds of types. Since this undercuts the whole principle underlying the fourfold distinction of types, it will be necessary to deal the formula (2) a decisive blow. It is not an overstatement to say that the adoption of (2) as a syntactical rule is responsible for the lack of an adequate type theory for natural languages. Black, using the rule, comes to the conclusion that any formal type theory for natural languages leads to ever finer differences and shades of meaning which one would never wish to make, a *reductio ad absurdum* for any attempt to apply formal techniques to natural languages. For whenever we come across a triad of sentences – $U(X, Y)$, $U(X, Z)$, $\mathcal{N}(Y, Z)$ – we are forced to split the meaning of X in order to avoid violating the transitivity rule. We saw this happen for "thought about" in the case of U (Russell, thought about), U (continuity, thought about), $\mathcal{N}$ (Russell, continuity).

> The consistent elaboration of this leading idea involves the making of ever finer distinctions of "meaning" between words not customarily regarded as ambiguous.[11]

The source of all the difficulties, Black believes, is to be found in the Russell program itself. Formal techniques, techniques which seek the structure of arguments without regard to meaning but with strict regard to rules and substitution possibilities, ought not to be applied to natural language, or at any rate ought to be applied only "on occasion":

> The demonstration of distinctions of type, defined in terms of mutual substitution of words, is on occasion a valuable technique for exhibiting operative ambiguity whose removal is relevant for the solution of philosophical disputes. But the consequences of an attempt to apply such techniques universally may be regarded as a *reductio ad absurdum* of a point of view which seeks to apply to ordinary language segregatory criteria appropriate to an artificially constructed calculus. And this in turn can be traced back to the inclination to regard the relation between the world and language exclusively in the light of identity of structure.[12]

The idea that a logical "formal" correction of natural language can be ontologically revealing is central to the Russell program. So far as a theory of types is concerned, Black's use of the transitivity principle leads to a principled skepticism about the possibility of such a formal ontology. But may it not be the case that this *reductio* ought to be turned on itself? It is, after all, the rule of transitivity which leads into skepticism. This reflects on this "rule," not on the search for a rule. It is because Black, Russell, Ryle, and others have unquestioningly accepted the assumption that any "theory" of types requires that type sameness must be transitive, that formal type theory has so far been futile. If Ryle and Black have turned to "informal logic" using "techniques" only on the proper occasions (but when is an occasion proper?) it is because they have found the transitivity of the U-relation too strong an assumption. And if Russell is reduced to a hope for a good theory of types, and to the lame acceptance of the "ever finer distinctions" which Black has shown to be required, this too is due to his unquestioning acceptance of the transitivity rule. We are thus left with only two alternatives. Accept the unwelcome consequences and make all the fine distinctions called for by the use of the rule, or drop the attempt to use formal techniques for natural languages.

It is evident that we need a type theory which does not lead to the making of counterintuitive distinctions of sense, a theory which dispenses with the rule of transitivity as a formal type rule, yet one which uses a formal type rule and applies it *universally* to natural language. But first we ought to see why philosophers have been seduced by the transitivity rule to such an extent that they did not believe in the possibility of any type theory which dispenses with it.

A serious reason appears legitimately to dictate the acceptance of transitivity for the U-relation. In any natural language it is possible to formulate interesting and sometimes funny sorts of Rylean sentences known as zeugmas. Examples are "She came home in a sedan chair and a flood of tears," "The chair and question were hard," "Some periods are punctuation marks while others are vacations." Each of the two sentences "The chair is hard" and "The question is hard" is significant, yet "The chair and the question were hard" is a category mistake. If we assume transitivity, this becomes quite clear: we have U (chair, hard) and U (question, hard), while $\mathcal{N}$ (question, chair). Since that would violate transitivity, we are *forced* to say that "hard" has two senses in those two sentences. Thus the transitivity rule shows us that "hard" must have two senses. And for this reason the sentence "The chair and question are hard" is a category mistake. In a *single* sentence, we have no opportunity to make the necessary distinction called for by the use of the transitivity rule.

One tempting way to avoid accepting the transitivity rule to account for zeugmas must be stoutly resisted by the formalist: he may not say that the ambiguity in "hard" is not known by means of a rule. He cannot appeal to the "obviousness" of the equivocation. If he does that he gives the case away to the informalist. Thus he is apparently presented with the dilemma which confronted Russell: accept the transitivity rule and you generate ambiguity where you don't want it, or reject transitivity and you fail to account for it where you ought to. The case of U (hard, chair), U (hard, question), $\mathcal{N}$ (question, chair) is an example of the second sort. The case of U (Russell, thought about), U (continuity, thought about), $\mathcal{N}$ (Russell, continuity) is an example of the first sort.

The fact that zeugmas suggest the transitivity principle is not overlooked by Ryle. He uses the principle to establish that "exist" has several senses in its use with "prime numbers" and "Wednesdays" and "navies."

A man would be thought to be making a poor joke who said that three things are now rising, namely, the tide, hopes, and the average age of death. It would be just as good or bad a joke to say that there exist prime numbers and Wednesdays and public opinions and navies; or that there exist both bodies and minds.[13]

Ryle is arguing that "exists" cannot univocally be used with prime numbers and navies because they are of different types. And just as $\mathcal{N}$ (hopes, tides), $\mathcal{N}$ U (hopes, rising), and U (tides, rising) "shows" us that "rising" is equivocal, so too $\mathcal{N}$ (prime numbers, navies), U (exist, navies), and U (exist, prime numbers) "show" us that "exists" is equivocal. The existence of zeugmas, in short, is supposed to indicate to us that there can be no three terms X, Y, and Z such that $U(X, Y)$, $U(X, Z)$ and $\mathcal{N}(Y, Z)$. Yet Ryle himself uses this principle only "as a valuable technique for exhibiting operative ambiguity whose removal is relevant to the solution of philosophical problems"; he does so only "on occasion." It is Ryle who coined the phrase "informal logic."

Anyone using the transitivity principle "on occasion" is bound to use it in an informal spirit. The consequences of applying it universally are, as Black has shown, too severe. Yet a technique which is applicable only on occasion for "exhibiting operative ambiguity" cannot be employed to enforce ambiguity in those cases where it is in doubt. And surely the ambiguity or univocity of "exists" is here in doubt.

Unless both Black and Ryle are prepared to employ their technique universally – which in view of the unwelcome consequences they are not – they cannot do more than account for the zeugmatic character of *known* zeugmas; the informalist spirit oversteps its bounds when it attempts to enforce a judgment of zeugma on a dubious case. Indeed, the whole idea of using a logical technique only in certain cases (however obvious and "operative"), and refraining from using it in others, is quite inadmissible. It is as much of a *reductio* as the unwelcome consequences which threaten us when we seek to apply the transitivity rule universally. But it may be that I have not yet caught the full spirit of this approach.

In any case, we have before us three alternatives: (1) Use the transitivity rule "on occasion," for example, in accounting for "obvious" zeugmas. (2) Accept transitivity and face the "unwelcome consequences" of generating ambiguity in counterintuitive instances. (3) Reject transitivity and face the consequences of being unable to account even for obvious zeugmas. The first way is adopted by those who despair of the second two formalistic alternatives. Black and Ryle are its representatives. The formalist must reject it or surrender to Black's criticism. It is interesting that Russell, like Ryle, stoutly maintains that existence is equivocal. And of course he is forced to say this if he accepts transitivity in the formal spirit. On the other hand, any formalistic philosopher who maintains that existence is univocal is forced to accept the third alternative. A striking and belligerent case is Quine.

Quine, for well-known reasons of his own, rejects Ryle's and Russell's view that "existence" is equivocal, and with his usual boldness he does not shirk the consequences. For if we insist on the univocity of existence, we thereby deprive ourselves of the use of the transitivity assumption to enforce ambiguity. Since Quine does not wish to employ the transitivity rule for existence (for example, for ambiguity in the sentences "chair exists" and "question exists"), he cannot avail himself of this rule for "hard" either.

Why not say that chairs and questions, however unlike, are hard in a single inclusive sense of the word? There is an air of zeugma about "The chair and question were hard" but is it not due merely to the dissimilarity of chairs and questions? Are we not in effect calling "hard" ambiguous if at all, just because it is true of some very unlike things?

Essentially this same question comes up in instances that are taken seriously. There are philosophers who stoutly maintain that 'true' said of logical or mathematical laws and 'true' said of weather predictions or suspects' confessions are two usages of an ambiguous term 'true.' There are philosophers who stoutly maintain that 'exists' said of numbers, classes, and the like, and "exists" said of material objects are two usages of an ambiguous term 'exists.' What mainly baffles me is the stoutness of their maintenance. What can they possibly count as evidence? Why not view 'true' as unambiguous but very general, and recognize the difference between true logical laws and true confessions as a difference merely between logical laws and confessions? And correspondingly for existence?[14]

Having ruled out the transitivity rule as a method for enforcing a judgment of ambiguity, Quine finds "no evidence" for calling "existence" and "truth" and "hard" ambiguous when predicated of things of different types. But the evidence for the rule appears clear enough. The *Oxford English Dictionary* gives us an example of a zeugma: "She came home in a flood of tears and a bath chair." If the rule of transitivity is rejected why is that a zeugma? Why not say that "what she came home in" has a single general sense which applies univocally to bath chairs and floods of tears? Indeed, all so-called zeugmas can be treated in the way Quine suggests. The existence of zeugmas *suggests* the rule of transitivity. Zeugmas appear incorrect because they embody an allegedly univocal use of a term in a way which violated the rule of transitivity. If Quine rejects the transitivity rule he is faced with the question "Why is 'hard' univocal while 'what she came home in' is not?" He evidently does not wish to validate *all* zeugmas; he must therefore supply some criterion for distinguishing between ambiguous and univocal predicates that are used with things of different types. On such a criterion, it should turn out that "hard" is ambiguous while "exists" need not be. We shall later see that this is indeed the case. On any such criterion, "what she came home in" ought to turn out to be ambiguous.

Quine is in fact correct in ruling out the transitivity rule as a method for enforcing ambiguity. But since the existence of zeugmas apparently suggests the existence of a transitivity rule, we are left with the two intolerable "formalist" alternatives: accept the transitivity rule and enforce ambiguity in words "not customarily regarded as ambiguous," or reject the rule and find "no evidence" for enforcing distinctions in words that are not customarily regarded as univocal. I shall confine myself now to showing that the rule must be rejected. Another rule, to be stated later, supplies the needed criterion which takes us between the horns of the dilemma.

III

Is it in fact a rule that for any three univocal expressions, $U(X, Y)$ and $U(X, Z)$ implies $U(Y, Z)$? To show, on *purely formal* grounds, that this *cannot* be a rule is the task now before us.

The "grounds," however, consist of answers to two important questions which have not been explicitly considered by most philosophers of natural language. We speak very often of a term as being a term of a given language. It is obvious that in order for a given term $\mathfrak{T}$ to be part of a language L, it must have some use in L. Furthermore, if every sentence containing $\mathfrak{T}$ were a category mistake, then, though $\mathfrak{T}$ had grammatical use, it could not be considered as a part of the language L. Or at any rate, it would have no "meaning" in L, and we are concerned with the meaningful terms of L. Thus our first question is: what use conditions must a term fulfill in order to have meaning in (be a term of) a given language? And our answer to this question must be that it is at least a necessary condition that $\mathfrak{T}$ be U-related to at least one other expression of L, in order for $\mathfrak{T}$ to be in L. We shall need no more than the knowledge of this necessary condition for our purpose.

But a second question immediately poses itself: what conditions of *mutual* use must a *set* of terms fulfill in order that the set be the terms of a given language? For example, we often say that a given group of predicates is in the *same* language as another group. What (besides purely grammatical rules which allow for substitutions) use conditions hold for this? A formal restatement, employing the "U-relation," will enable us to deal with this question.

We consider a model natural language $\mathcal{N}L$ containing terms A, B, $C \ldots K$. Any pair of these terms will have a sense value (U or $\mathcal{N}$) depending on whether the terms in the pair are U-related or not. Since this is a natural language some of the pairs will be $\mathcal{N}$ in value. Thus if $A =$ "angry," $B =$ "bold," $C =$ "crime," $D =$ "drowsy," we might have values $U(A, B)$, $\mathcal{N}(C, D)$, $U(B, C)$, and so forth.

The use condition already stated requires that the sense values for the pairs of terms of $\mathcal{N}L$ must be such that every term appear at least once in a pair which has the value U. But now suppose that the use condition is met with the following values for the terms of $\mathcal{N}L$, all other pairs except those listed having the value $\mathcal{N}$.

$$(1)\ U(A, B), U(A, C), U(C, D), U(E, F), U(E, G),$$
$$U(E, H), U(E, I), U(E, \mathfrak{J}), U(E, \mathfrak{R}).$$

Given these values, every term has some use with at least one other term of $\mathcal{N}L$. We notice, however, that the language may be divided in two since none of the terms A, B, C, D has any connection in use with any of the terms of the set E, F, G, H, I, $\mathfrak{J}$, $\mathfrak{R}$. So far as their use with one another is concerned we have indeed no reason to consider the first group of

terms to be in the same language with the second group. Thus the answer to our second question is that for a set of terms to be terms of the *same* language, it is a necessary condition that all the terms of the set be connected through mutual use with one another. This does not mean that all of them must be mutually U-related with one another. The fact that we have the value $\mathcal{N}(B, C)$ does not mean that B and C are not connected. Their connection may be assured by the U-values for the pairs (A, B) and (A, C). Thus the terms of the subset A, B, C, D are connected with one another but they are all unconnected with the terms of the second group. To be part of a language is to have some use. To be a group of terms in the same language is to have connected use.

The connectedness condition may be more formally stated. Using "$con(X, Y)$" to mean the X and Y are in the same language, the following two relations hold:

(i) $U(X, Y)$ and $U(X, Z)$ implies $con(Y, Z)$.

(ii) $con(Y, Z)$ and $con(W, Z)$ implies $con(Y, W)$.

We can now say that if a set of terms $A, B, C \ldots K$ are terms of the same language, then any two of them are connected through the use of the terms in the language. The values given in (1) above do not assure the connectedness of all the terms. If we changed the value of $(B, \mathfrak{J})$ from $\mathcal{N}$ to U, however, all the terms would then be connected.

The two conditions just stated – the use condition for a *single* term to be in a given language and the connectedness condition for a *group* of terms to be terms of the *same* language – are fundamental. I shall refer to them as linguistic conditions since no language *is* a language unless it satisfies them. They are, of course, only necessary conditions, but they suffice for our immediate purposes.

We are now assuming that every natural language is *connected through use*. But now let us suppose that sameness of type is transitive. This, we recall, is (2): for any three terms X, Y, and Z, $U(X, Y)$ and $U(X, Z)$ implies $U(Y, Z)$. Since the language is connected, (2) would enable us to prove that any two terms are U-related. For example, suppose our language contained only four terms and the values $U(A, B)$, $U(A, C)$, $U(B, C)$, $U(C, D)$, $\mathcal{N}(A, D)$, $\mathcal{N}(B, D)$. These values satisfy the linguistic conditions of the use and connectedness. But now by applying (2) we could show that (A, D) and (B, D) must *also* be U since $U(A, C)$

and $U(C, D)$ implies $U(A, D)$, and $U(A, D)$ and $U(A, B)$ implies $U(B, D)$. In other words, for any connected language, the use of the transitivity rule insures that *all* possible pairs of the language are U in value. But this means that the language contains no type mistakes and hence *no type distinctions*. The very meaning of the sense value U is obliterated if there can be no pairs with the value $\mathcal{N}$. Thus we have shown that any connected language containing type distinctions (that is, *any natural language*) cannot use (2) to enforce distinctions of sense. The transitivity rule is, therefore, not a possible rule for a natural language.

We noted the dilemma in which we are placed by the lack of a rule of transitivity for type sameness. Without this rule, which we have now found to be contralinguistic, we can have $U(A, B)$, $U(A, C)$, and $\mathcal{N}(B, C)$, and when we do, we have no warrant for a judgment of ambiguity for the term A. Quine and others who maintain that "exists" is univocal in the pairs (chair, exists) and (question, exists) are thereby free to hold this position. But we noted also the price they pay. We do need an ambiguity rule. Quine says that "hard," too, is univocal in (chair, hard) and (question, hard). He finds "no evidence" for a judgment of ambiguity. But this can go too far. There is also no evidence for a judgment of ambiguity in the pairs (period, vacation) and (period, smudged), no evidence for ambiguity in (rational, number) and (rational, man) and in general no evidence for the ambiguity of *any* term that has heterotypical uses.

Though the transitivity rule is unavailable, this does not mean we cannot find some *other formal* way of proving ambiguity. It must be acknowledged that Quine's request for "evidence" is quite legitimate. Any term is univocal until proven equivocal. But what sort of proof is appropriate? The correct answer to this question is of fundamental importance.

One basic requirement for any criterion for enforcing a judgment of ambiguity is that the criterion enable us to do this *whether or not we understand the meaning or meanings of the term* in question. Indeed, we cannot be said to know the meaning of a term whose univocity is in question. Thus it must be possible to show that the term has two meanings (or more) and to show that this is so *whatever the term may mean*. A criterion which requires a knowledge of the meaning or meanings of the term is not admissible. Those who approach philosophy in the ordinary language spirit, with no more than a better than average intuitive discern-

ment of the nuances and senses of the terms they wish to analyze or clarify, are bound to violate this fundamental requirement. Philosophy, in large part, is the technique of making important and needed distinctions of sense for crucial terms. For this reason it is necessary to be clear about what happens when clarifying distinctions are made. Problems about the logic of clarification are as old as Plato's *Meno* and as recent as the so-called paradox of analysis. In the attempt to be clear about clarification, the spirit of the Russell program is a far better guide than the "informalist" spirit of the later Wittgenstein. Any clarification procedure, any logical procedure for showing that a given expression has different meanings in two or more of its occurrences, ought, ideally, to be one which enforces those distinctions in a truly logical way, that is, independently of the "meaning" or "meanings" the particular expression may have. Moreover, the Russell spirit demands that we consider a term to be thus equivocal *for no other reason* than the fact that a given clarification rule *requires* that the term has two senses and not one. If one cannot prove a term to be equivocal, it is not equivocal. We never merely discern it to be. This is only another way of saying that ambiguity is not a fact in language; it is the result of the application of a "clarification procedure." There is no such fact as ambiguity which the procedure enables us to discern. It is the procedure which forces us to consider an expression ambiguous. And it does so independently of the "meanings" we then discern.

By a clarification procedure I mean a procedure which we use implicitly or explicitly to detect a meaning distinction or, better, to *enforce* a judgment that an expression which recurs in two or more contexts has more than one meaning. The *whole* context containing the recurrent expression I shall call a linguistic sequence. A sequence may be a sentence or longer.

A linguistic sequence may be correct or incorrect in different ways. I shall consider three such ways by way of illustrating the general character of clarification. A sequence may be grammatical or ungrammatical, it may be category correct or category mistaken, it may be consistent or inconsistent. We may call these ways of being correct or incorrect "levels of rectitude." The reason for calling them levels is that a sequence which is incorrect in one way must be correct in other ways and the ways it must be correct are therefore "lower" than, because presupposed by, the way it is incorrect. Also, an incorrect sequence is neither correct nor incorrect with respect to other ways, and these ways are "higher" since they presuppose the rectitude of the sequence. For example, an ungrammatical sentence is not a sentence at all; it cannot therefore make a category mistake. Thus the incorrectness we call a category mistake presupposes the grammaticalness of the sentence. Again, a category mistake is neither consistent nor inconsistent. If I say "his anger was triangular and not triangular" I have not contradicted myself; I have said nothing and retracted nothing. An inconsistent sentence is neither true nor false empirically. Thus inconsistency as a way of being incorrect presupposes both the grammaticalness *and* the category correctness of the sequence. Again, empirical falsity presupposes that the sequence is grammatical, category correct, *and* consistent. In short, any sequence which is incorrect at one level of rectitude must be correct at all lower levels and is neither correct nor incorrect at any higher level.

A given sequence contains ambiguity if and only if:

1 it is incorrect at some level of rectitude if all terms are taken univocally;
2 there are pragmatic reasons to consider the sequence to be correct at that level;
3 the sequence is correct if some recurrent expression is treated as if it were nonrecurrent.

Consider a sequence which violates grammatical rules. A foreigner who knows very little English hears someone say "I peer at the peer." This sentence sounds ungrammatical (1) since if "peer" has only one meaning the sentence lacks a verb phrase. Since he hears the sequence spoken by a native speaker he has reason to consider it grammatically correct (2). He therefore doctors the sentence and says to himself (as it were): "Whatever this word 'peer' means, it has two meanings in this sentence. In its first occurrence it is a verb, in its second it is a noun."

The clarification procedure involved here does not require a knowledge of the meaning of the term judged to be ambiguous. The procedure can be applied to any similar case (I *x* the *x*., for example, "I saw the saw," and so forth).

We have so far no clarification procedure for the category level of rectitude. The discarded transitivity rule, however, is the *sort* of thing we want. With that rule one need not know the meaning of

the word "period" to declare it ambiguous in the sequence "the period was my vacation." ... "The period was smudged." All one needs to know is the fact that (vacation, smudged) cannot be used together. If we have any reason to accept the sentences embodying "period" as category correct, we could then use the transitivity rule to doctor them, giving "period" two meanings. This rule, however, is now unavailable to us. We have therefore to look for something *like* the transitivity rule which can do the job we need done. The new rule and its use as a clarification procedure will be presently illustrated.

Inconsistency is a common enforcer of ambiguity. If I hear someone say "It is raining and it isn't" I recognize a violation of inconsistency (1). I nevertheless have good reason to consider the sentence consistent (2). I therefore construe the sentence with two meanings of "raining" (3). In connection with inconsistency as a clarification procedure, it is worth nothing that there are probably no tautologies in ordinary language. When someone says "Boys will be boys," "War is war," "What will be will be," "Business is business," it is always acceptable to deny the statement and then to use inconsistency to enforce the ambiguity intended in the original assertion.

A clarification procedure is nothing but a language rule applied in a certain way. Any language rule, when it is violated, can be used in one of two ways. (1) We can throw out the offending sequence, or (2) we can use the rule to introduce ambiguity in such a way that the rule is no longer violated by the sequence. In artificial languages the rules are used only in the first way; in natural languages we often use a rule to "clarify." It is sometimes said by those favoring constructed languages that the natural language is shot through with ambiguity because it is anarchical, not governed by rules. The opposite is true; the ambiguity is a product of the rules. It is due to their satisfaction.

Enough has now been said about clarification procedures as such. In what follows, a rule for the category "level of rectitude" will be stated and a proof of the rule will be offered. Its application for clarification will then be illustrated.

IV

The main object of the ensuing analysis is to tie together several seemingly disparate topics. These include: (a) a theory of types (that is, a theory describing the *way* terms are conjoined to form category correct statements in a natural language); (b) a formal theory of ontological categories and ontological features; (c) a theory of *predication* (that is, a theory accounting for the subject-predicate distinction and one which provides certain formal characteristics of the binary relation "is predicable of"); (d) a procedure for enforcing ambiguity.

The results of the analysis support the main features of the Russell program. I take these to be that (a) clarification of natural language is ontologically revealing and discriminatory of the sorts of things there are; (b) linguistic structures and ontological structures are isomorphic. The meaning of "ontology" in what immediately follows is "the science of categories."

We have noted that whenever a predicate P is significantly applicable to a thing, then so is its complement non-P. Now this gives us the right to treat predicates as having no "sign" *for purposes of a type analysis*. Thus, any predicate P can be construed as $|P|$ or "the absolute 'value' of P, by which we mean that P spans the things that are either P or non-P but does not span things which are neither P nor non-P. For example, if $P =$ philosopher, then $|P|$ defines the class of things which are either philosophers or nonphilosophers. In the class of things that are $|P|$ are Bertrand Russell and Cleopatra but not the Empire State Building. Henceforth I shall call a class defined by an absolute predicate an *ontological* class or *category*. If we use the terminology introduced above, α-types are *categories*.

Apparently, anything whatever belongs to the category of things that are |thought about|, |interesting|, or |discussed at the Aristotelian society|. Also in a most general sense of the term (the sense preferred by Quine) anything whatsoever belongs to the category of things that |exists|.

To say of something that it |exists| or that it is |interesting| is to give no information whatsoever about the nature of the thing. For this reason, some philosophers have chosen to consider such categories trivial. On the other hand, to say of something that it is a |philosopher| does tell us something; we know at least that it is the sort of thing which is |angry| or a |citizen of the United States| and that it is not |prime| and not |valid|, and the like. It is evident that many absolute predicates define the same categories. Thus |interesting| and |discussed| define a single category, and so do |angry| and |sad|. This fact corresponds to our A-types since an A-type consists of a set of predicates

which span the same things. By absolutizing the predicates of any given A-type, we merely cut the number of predicates in that type by half.

Indeed, just as we can reduce the two predicates "philosopher" and "nonphilosopher" to one predicate $|P|$, so can we reduce *all* of the predicates of a given A-type to one single absolute predicate, since they are all "synonymous." To say that a thing is |angry| is to say no more but also no less than that it is |sad| or |alert|. The language of ontology is a bare skeleton of ordinary language, and for its purposes we require only *one* absolute predicate from each A-type; we can ignore all the synonyms. Each A-type defines a category (or α-type) and a single absolute predicate from the A-type defines the same category; for ontological purposes we could make do with that single one.

If now we take any ordinary language and absolutize all of its predicates so that instead of being able to say that a thing is P we could say only that it is $|P|$ we could then give only *ontological information*. Imagine a "Twenty Questions" game in which the player has something in mind for us to guess (it could be a valid argument or a bumblebee). And imagine that in asking the questions, we are permitted to use only absolute predicates. It is evident that we could never get enough information to specify the individual thing he has in mind. All we could do is determine the *sort* of thing it is. We might ask whether the thing is |interesting| but that would be a wasted question. We might ask whether it is |red| and if the answer were yes, we would know that he has nothing like a valid argument in mind, but something physical. Following that it would be a waste to ask further whether the thing is |green|. We might then ask whether it is |kind| and an affirmative answer to that would inform us that it is not a pebble or a tree or an inanimate object but that it is the sort of thing which is either kind or not, and so on. We could not get to distinguish the thing but we could get its ontological type in this way (more precisely, we could get its β-type). The category language is imbedded in every natural language. To expose it, all we need to do is absolutize the predicates. A language of absolute predicates is a purely ontological language. And every natural language has its ontological skeleton, its "ontology."

The *ontologist* is interested in categories; he is, *qua* ontologist, not interested in whether a thing is red or whether it is green but in whether it is colored. Even this is not altogether accurate: he is interested in its character of being colored or colorless. For the ontologist "colored" means |red| which is the same thing as colored or colorless. A toothache is neither, but water can be either red or not red or colored or colorless.

We speak as ontologists when, for example, we say that points belong to the category of extension even though they belong to the *class* of extensionless things. The category of extension is defined by the predicate |extended| and points belong to it.[15] Concepts do not belong to it since they are neither extended nor extensionless. Space (spatial) is another category word since it has no complement which is not categorial. And if the word "color" is taken to include that "color" we call "colorless," it too is a category word. There are quite a few words which can be taken *either* in their absolute sense as category words or in their class sense. Thus "exists," if taken as a category word, has no opposite. "Exists" then is the same as |exists|. The confusions from the discussion in Plato's *Sophist* to this day over the use of "exists" as a category or a class word are dispelled once we take care to keep the absolute or categorial meaning of "exists" separate from its ordinary predicate meaning. The *class* of things which do not exist belong to the *category* of existence. Flute-playing centaurs belong to the former by virtue of the fact that they belong to the latter. I could call a horse a flute-playing centaur and I would be mistaken since there are no flute-playing centaurs, but in this respect I am at least mistaken, something I would not be if I called the horse a prime number. The class of things that do not exist is limited to what we can mistakenly say does exist. A horse which is a prime number neither exists nor does not exist. But in saying that I predicate nothing of horses, I merely say that the category of existence is the ontology of the language as given by the absolute predicates of the language. "A horse which is a prime number" is not in the language, and neither is "round anger." Predicates that are not in the language cannot be used to say anything and we must perforce "be silent." The absolute predicate |is spoken of| defines the category of things that can be spoken of, a category which is coextensive with that of existence. But "cannot be spoken of," like "inexistent," is an illegitimate complement to an *absolute* predicate. Ramsey's remark that you can't whistle it either is the satirical remark of a discerning ontologist.

An absolute predicate defines a class of things but, like any ordinary predicate, it does so by singling out what the members of the class have

in common. I shall use the word "property" to refer to what the members of a class defined by a predicate have in common. What the members of an *ontological* class, or category, defined by an absolute predicate have in common I shall call a *feature*. Thus the predicate "red" defines a category which has a certain feature. There is no word to locate this feature unless we take color to locate the attribute of either having some color or being colorless. A paraphrase is "the red-or-nonredness" of a thing. Whether one interprets absolute predicates as locating categories or whether one interprets them as locating category features is a matter of indifference to the ontologist and should be a matter of indifference to the logician. Any logical laws which apply to absolute predicates will take either interpretation.

Are any features or categories of greater interest to the ontologist than others? One suspects, for example, that the category of existence is of greater ontological interest than the category of color. There are two sorts of categories which are of major importance to ontologists. There are the categories which are all inclusive, containing all others as subcategories, and those that are completely exclusive, containing no subcategories at all. Thus when Russell chose the predicate "philosopher," he was choosing one of the latter categories since no absolute predicate in the language defines a category of things included in the one defined by "philosopher."

We have as yet no right to assume that there must be categories of these two types. The existence of categories which include all others may be denied and is denied by those who say, for example, that "exists" does not span things of different types univocally. To be sure, they have "no evidence" for this since the transitivity rule is, as we saw, linguistically impossible. On the other hand, so long as we have no rule to enforce ambiguity, we have no assurance that "exists" and other terms such as "is thought about" are of the highest level. Such terms, if they *are* univocal, are *U*-related to all other terms and we need a proof for their existence in the language.

Nor do we have formal assurance of the existence of lowest-level categories, categories which include no others. For it could even be that categories merely overlap in membership and that no categories include others, though some perhaps are coextensive.

The existence of dominating categories and categories of the lowest level is however assured by a fundamental law which governs all categories. This law can be derived from a "syntactical" rule governing the distribution of category correct statements in a natural language. Equally, the rule can be derived from the law. Indeed the law of categories and the law governing the distribution of category mistakes are two expressions of a structural isomorphism which holds between "language" and "ontology." In its categorial form, the structural principle may be thus expressed:

> If C_1 and C_2 are any two categories, then either C_1 and C_2 have no members in common or C_1 is included in C_2 or C_2 is included in C_1.

Given this law and the already noted fact that the categories (α-types) defined by the predicates of any natural language are finite in number, it will follow that there must be one category that includes all others and several that include no others.

I shall call this the law of categorial inclusion since it states that whenever two categories have some common membership, one of the two is included in the other. In terms of "features" the law of categorial inclusion asserts that for any features F_1 and F_2 which characterize some given object, it is either the case that all objects possessing F_1 also possess F_2 or vice versa. In what follows, the symbol $|P|$ will be used for the absolute predicate *or* for the category which it defines. No serious harm is done by this double use; it is analogously traditional to use the same symbol for a class term and for the class it defines. The law of categorial inclusion may, accordingly, be formulated in three equivalent ways:

$$(T.1) \quad U(P\,Q) \equiv [(|P| \subset |Q| \vee (|Q| \subset |P|))]$$
$$U(P\,Q) \equiv (x)(|P|_x \supset |Q|_x) \vee (|Q|_x \supset |P|_x))$$
$$U(P\,Q) \equiv (x)[(x\varepsilon|P|) \supset (x\varepsilon|Q|)] \vee (x) [(x\varepsilon|Q|) \supset (x\varepsilon|P|)]$$

The proof of this law is given in an appendix to this chapter. An important theorem that is derivable from T.1 holds for any three terms P, Q, and R:

$$(T.2) \quad U(P,Q)\,U(Q,R)\,\mathcal{N}(P,R)$$
$$\equiv (|P| \subset |Q|)(|R| \subset |Q|)$$
$$\overline{(|Q| \subset |P|)}\,\overline{(|Q| \subset |R|)}$$
$$\overline{(|P| \subset |R|)}\,\overline{(|R| \subset |P|)}$$

The importance of T.2 lies in its clear statement of an equivalence between syntactical and categorial relations, between sense and non-sense gotten by conjoining terms, and the inclusions among the sets of things they span. From another side, T.2 states a simple criterion which validates the subject-predicate distinction. To see this clearly, let us substitute the symbol "$\rightarrow$" wherever we have the inclusion symbol "$\subset$" and let us interpret "$Q \leftarrow P$" to mean: "of (what is) P it is significant to say that it is Q." Or – what is the same thing – "that it is Q" is *predicable* of (what is) P. We how have

$$U(X, \Upsilon)\,U(X, z)\,\mathcal{N}(\Upsilon, z)$$
$$\equiv (X \leftarrow \Upsilon)(X \leftarrow z)$$
$$\overline{(\Upsilon \leftarrow X)}\,\overline{(z \leftarrow X)}\,\overline{(\Upsilon \leftarrow z)}\,\overline{(z \leftarrow \Upsilon)}$$

This tells us that the middle term X of two significant pairs (sentences) is always the predicate with respect to the two $\mathcal{N}$-related terms Υ and Z of a triad, $U(X, \Upsilon)\,U(X, z)\,\mathcal{N}(\Upsilon, Z)$. The relational expression "is predicable of" is thus seen to be isomorphic with the relational expression "contains." Both the relations of predication and of containment are *transitive* and *nonsymmetrical*. In this respect *the predicative tie between terms differs from the tie of significance or* U-*relatedness since the* U-*relation is, as we have seen, nontransitive and symmetrical.*

Aristotle always insisted on the metaphor of inclusion for "predication"; a paradigm for predication was saying of a species that it was included in a genus. The metaphor fails, if taken literally, in most cases. Thus Aristotle also insisted that being a man could not be predicated of what was white, but because he failed to make a clear distinction between class and category he could not rightly see why this was so. The criterion of inclusion works for categories but not for classes. For such cases Aristotle used a special theory of substance and attribute to ground the subject-predicate distinction. But "being human" is no less an attribute of a thing than being white, and most recent philosophers have rightly deplored the use of a special ontological doctrine to account for the subject-predicate distinction. It is nevertheless illegitimate to proceed from a repudiation of the substance-attribute distinction to a repudiation of the subject-predicate distinction. We do not, in fact, need the "substantival"-"adjectival" dichotomy with its metaphysical trappings for the subject-predicate distinction. We can just as easily show that in the pair (white, human) "human" is the subject term and "white" is the predicate term, as we could show that "man" is the subject term in the pair (man, white). All we need is the $UU\mathcal{N}$ triad and a third term such that U (white, x) and $\mathcal{N}$ (human, x). The term "sky" will do. Thus the view set forth in this essay supports the Aristotelian insistence on the nonsymmetry of predication[16] and does so for much the same reasons – the inclusion of *categories*. In having insisted on the substance-attribute theory for the nonsymmetry of predication, Aristotle was wrong. But he is less wrong than those who – in fear of metaphysical interference in pure logic – have abandoned the subject-predicate distinction altogether.[17]

A third theorem that follows from the law of categorial inclusion is purely syntactical. I have elsewhere called this theorem "the tree rule" since it distributes the monadic predicate terms of a language on the "nodes" of a hierarchical tree for purposes of allowing for conjoining them significantly and exhibiting which pairs of them are copredicable. T.3 can also be used to enforce distinctions of sense for certain expressions whose relations of cosignificance and lack of cosignificance is assumed to be known. T.3 is easily derivable from T.2. It holds for any four terms P, Q, R and S.

$$(T.3) \quad \sim [U(P\ Q)U(QR)U(PS)\mathcal{N}(PR)$$
$$\mathcal{N}(QS)]$$

Proof : $\quad U(P\ Q)U(QR)\mathcal{N}(PR) \supset$
$$(|P| \subset |Q|) \text{ by } T.2$$

$$U(P\ Q)U(PS)\mathcal{N}(QS) \supset (\overline{|Q| \subset |P|}) \text{ by } T.2$$
$$\therefore \sim [U(P\ Q)U(QR)U(PS)\mathcal{N}(PR)$$
$$\mathcal{N}(QS)] \quad Q.E.D.$$

If (A, B) is some significant subject-predicate sentence of the sort, say, that normally occurs in syllogistic argument, then the tree rule states that whatever makes sense with A makes sense with B, *or* whatever makes sense with B makes sense with A. Thus we cannot have $U(AB)\ U(AC)\ \mathcal{N}(BC)$ and *also* $U(AB)\ U(BD)\ \mathcal{N}(AD)$.

If we keep the arrow notation we can conveniently represent how the tree rule distributes the terms of the natural language into (a) relative positions for category correct predication and (b) B-types and A-types.

For an illustration we may use a "model natural language." There are five "roots" to the tree for that "language," corresponding to the number of its B-types (see figure 8.1). A B-type consists of a set of terms along a permitted path. Thus

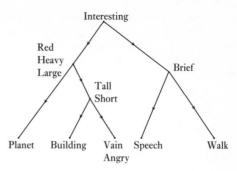

Figure 8.1

"interesting," "brief," "walk" is a B-type. There are eight nodes or locations. This corresponds to the number of A-types. And an A-type is a set of terms at the same location. Thus "planet" is one A-type and "heavy," "large," "red" is another.

The tree represents the permissible *way* of conjoining terms for significant sentences. If X and Υ are terms at different locations on the tree, then $U(X, \Upsilon)$ if and only if either $X \leftarrow \Upsilon$ or $\Upsilon \leftarrow X$ If X and Υ are at the same location, then $U(X, \Upsilon)$. On the other hand, if you cannot get from X to Υ or from Υ to X by a permitted path, then $\mathcal{N}(X, \Upsilon)$. Since the "paths" represent predicability, an $\mathcal{N}$-pair or category mistake may be defined as a statement formed by conjoining two terms, *neither* of which is predicable of the other.

The tree structure is only a graphical representation of the tree rule. It illustrates graphically the fact that any natural language must have at least one term at the apex, a term defining a category which includes all other categories. Also, such a term is univocal; if it were not we would have to give it different locations. (It would be different "terms" that have the same "token.") The tree structure makes clear that certain terms must be exclusive, defining categories which include no others.

Quine is therefore correct in his assertion that there can be "no evidence" against anyone who wishes to place existence at the apex. Furthermore, if there can be no evidence, then existence *is* univocal, since we accept a judgment of ambiguity only where it is logically enforceable. On the other hand, Quine is wrong in believing that we cannot *in general* get evidence for enforcing a judgment of ambiguity against a predicate that is predicated of things of different types. Thus he is wrong in saying that we can have no evidence for the ambiguity of "hard" in the pairs (hard, chair) and (hard, question). The following values which violate the tree rule constitute logical evidence for the ambiguity of either "hard" or "expensive." Figure 8.2 represents values inconsistent with the tree rule:

$$U(Q,H)U(H,E)\mathcal{N}(Q,E)U(E,D)\mathcal{N}(D,H).$$

These values cannot be placed on the tree structure. On the other hand, if we *split* the meaning of "hard," giving that "token" two type locations, we *can* dispose them on the tree (see figure 8.3). Thus the tree rule is a "clarification rule," a "univocity condition."

Quine is wrong about "hard" and right about "exists." Most other recent philosophers have been wrong about "exists" and right about "hard." Neither Quine nor Black seems to have realized that there is a logical structure distributing the terms of a language for significant pairing,[18] and that unless a group of term pairs satisfies the structural condition, some of the terms are equivocal. Russell, in his *Reply*, hoped for such a structure, and he rightly believed that it would turn out to be hierarchical. He did not himself discover it because he was bound by the seductive transitivity rule for the U-relation. But transitivity, as we saw, leads to an impossible structure which ends by locating all the terms of a language at one "node" and eliminating nonsensical pairs of terms altogether. Black, too, accepted the transitivity rule as the only possible one, and he concluded that the search for a type structure adequate for natural language was doomed, since too much ambiguity would then be generated. But the tree structure has the virtue of generating ambiguity where we want it and refraining from generating ambiguity where judgment of ambiguity would be counterintuitive. Black's argument against the Russell program is therefore voided as soon as we obtain a theory of types which provides a clarification rule that is not counterintuitive.

I should like, in concluding, to list some of the advantages gained from recognizing the tree structure as a governing condition for natural languages:

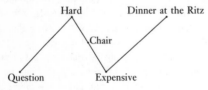

Figure 8.2

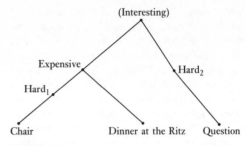

Figure 8.3

We obtain a satisfactory criterion for distinguishing the "natural" subject of a proposition.

We obtain a satisfactory clarification procedure for enforcing ambiguity at the type level.

We obtain a clear algorithm for the isomorphism which holds between the distribution of sense and nonsense in a language and the distribution of categorial features in the world.

We obtain a powerful technique for doing "logical geography," what Ryle and others have sometimes identified with "doing philosophy," though that is an overestimation of the importance of categorial analysis.

We obtain a satisfactory explanation for the high incidence of grammatical nonsense in any natural language. A glance at the tree structure makes it clear that most pairs of terms must be $\mathcal{N}$ in sense value.

The structure has the merit of tying together two aspects of philosophy which for most philosophers have been sundered in recent years: the theory of predication and the theory of types. Thus the theory and the technique it gives us is essentially an Aristotelian development.

And, finally, it is clear that all languages have the same ontological structures in an important sense. Whatever "sorts of things" a language discriminates, the notion of a sort remains the same and the sorting process is the same. At least this is so for any language containing expressions that we legitimately call "predicates."

Appendix: Proof of the Law of Categorial Inclusion

A sentence like "Some philosophers are quaint" is said – in one sense of "about" – to be about philosophers. In a second (categorial) sense, (P, Q) is about$_2$ whatever is either a philosopher or a nonphilosopher. Thus (philosophers, quaint) is not about$_2$ Hopi rituals even though Hopi rituals are among things that are either quaint or not quaint. On the other hand, Hopi *Indians* are among the things that (P, Q) is about$_2$. We may formulate this as a definition for any P and Q.

$$D.1 \quad U(P\,Q) \equiv (P\,Q) \text{ is about}_2 \ |P| \vee (P\,Q)$$
$$\text{is about}_2 \ |Q|$$

Axiom: (A.1) Whatever $(P\,Q)$ is about$_2$ is in the universe of discourse of $(P\,Q)$.

Let "$V(P\,Q)$ stand for the universe of discourse of a sentence conjoining the terms P and Q, then

$$(x)[(x \varepsilon V(P\,Q)) \equiv (x \varepsilon |P| \cdot |Q|)]$$

where $|P| \cdot |Q|$ is the same as $(P \vee \bar{P})(Q \vee \bar{Q})$ which is the same as the familiar expression for the universe of discourse of (PQ), namely:

$$P \cdot Q \vee P \cdot \bar{Q} \vee \bar{P} \cdot Q \vee \bar{P} \cdot \bar{Q}$$

T.1. (The law of categorial inclusion)

$$U(P\,Q) \equiv (|P| \subset |Q|) \vee (|Q| \subset |P|)$$

Proof:
By A.1 and D.1 we have

$$U(P\,Q) \equiv (|P| \subset V(P\,Q)) \vee (|Q| \subset V(P\,Q))$$
$$\equiv (|P| \subset |P| \cdot |Q|) \vee (|Q| \subset |P| \cdot |Q|)$$
$$\equiv (|P| \subset |Q|) \vee (|Q| \subset |P|)$$

Q.E.D.

Notes

1   There are four sections to the paper. Section I isolates the problem of types for natural language and develops four type concepts appropriate to it. Section II reformulates these concepts syntactically and reconsiders Black's general criticism of a formal theory of types for natural language. In Section III the relation of types to ambiguity, and a problem raised by Black, is examined in detail. Section IV is constructive; the type-structural principle is stated and proved. The ontological meaning of the principle is discussed and the principle is illustratively applied.

2   For an explicit statement of a view of ontology that does *not* logically distinguish it as a special discipline, see Quine's *Word and Object* (Cambridge, Mass., 1960), p. 275.

3   *Contemporary British Philosophy* (London and New York, 1924), I, 371.

4   Max Black, "Russell's Philosophy of Language," in *The Philosophy of Bertrand Russell* (ed. by P. A. Schilpp; Evanston and Chicago, 1944), p. 238.

5   For a formulation of a similar notion see A. Pap's last paper, "Types and Meaninglessness," *Mind*, LXIX, (1960), 48.

6   The U-relation is defined more elaborately in my paper "The Ordinary Language Tree," *Mind*, LXVIII (1959).

7   Black, *op. cit.*, p. 238.

8   *Ibid.*

9   *Ibid.*

10   *Ibid.*, p. 691.

11   Black, *op. cit.*, p. 239.

12   *Ibid.*, p. 240.

13   Ryle, *Concept of Mind* (New York, 1949), p. 23.

14   Quine, *op. cit.*, pp. 130–1.

15   Not all ontologists are alive to this. Thus Whitehead considers it a *problem* that points – being extensionless – are in the category of extension, and he develops a method for defining them in terms of extended things. Descartes is properly unworried about this.

16   For the view that predication is symmetrical see F. P. Ramsey's "Universals," *The Foundations of Mathematics* (London and New York, 1931), pp. 116 ff.

17   P. F. Strawson in *Individuals* (London, 1959), pp. 167 ff., uses a "category" criterion to defend the traditional distinction of subject and predicate. But his notion of "category" is not mine.

18   Indeed, Quine wishes to avoid a theory of types by classifying category mistakes as false "and false by meaning, if one likes." He believes this will "spare us . . . both the settling of categories and the respecting of them." But this also spares us all the benefits of a theory of types. And what can Quine mean by "false by meaning"? Cf. *Word and Object*, p. 229. Quine's avoidance of type theory probably stems from the use of the transitivity rule together with the assumption that "exists" is univocal. This gives the result that any two things are of the same type.

9

Propositions

George Bealer

Recent work in philosophy of language has raised significant problems for the traditional theory of propositions, engendering serious skepticism about its general workability. These problems are, I believe, tied to fundamental misconceptions about how the theory should be developed. The goal of this paper is to show how to develop the traditional theory in a way which solves the problems and puts this skepticism to rest. The problems fall into two groups. The first has to do with reductionism, specifically, attempts to reduce propositions to extensional entities – either extensional functions or sets. The second group concerns problems of fine-grained content – both traditional "Cicero"/"Tully" puzzles and recent variations on them which confront scientific essentialism. After characterizing the problems, I outline a non-reductionist approach – the algebraic approach – which avoids the problems associated with reductionism. I then go on to show how the theory can incorporate non-Platonic (as well as Platonic) modes of presentation. When these are implemented nondescriptively, they yield the sort of fine-grained distinctions which have been eluding us. The chapter closes by applying the theory to a cluster of remaining puzzles, including a pair of new puzzles facing scientific essentialism.

1. Introduction

This chapter begins in the middle of a long tale. To tell my part of the story, I will need to assume the

George Bealer, Propositions. *Mind*, 107, 425 (1998): 1–32.

central tenets of the traditional theory of propositions (for arguments in support of these tenets, see Bealer 1993a). These tenets include the following: (1) propositions are the primary bearers of such properties as necessity, possibility, impossibility, truth, and falsity; (2) they are mind-independent extra-linguistic abstract objects; (3) a belief state consists in a subject standing in the relation of believing to a proposition, and that proposition is the content of the belief (likewise for other intentional states – desire, decision, memory, etc.); (4) propositions are typically public: people commonly believe one and the same proposition and doing so is a prerequisite for successful communication; (5) propositions are what (literal utterances of declarative) sentences express or mean. Of course, some philosophers have been skeptical about abstract objects in general and for that reason alone have been skeptical about the traditional theory of propositions. But with the rise of modal logic, the resurgence of modal metaphysics, and the revolution in cognitive psychology and its realism about intentional states, this general skepticism strikes most philosophers as idle. Today, the traditional theory of propositions is the dominant view. All is not well with the theory, however. In the course of positive work on the theory, significant "internal" problems have emerged, and these problems have engendered a far more serious skepticism about the general workability of the traditional theory. In my view, these problems are tied to fundamental misconceptions of how the theory should be developed. The goal of this paper is to show how to develop the theory in a way which solves the problems and which puts this more serious form of skepticism to rest.

The problems I have in mind may be divided into two groups. The first has to do with reductionism. When people have tried to systematize the informal theory, they have found it difficult to avoid incorporating some form of reductionism. I have in mind the doctrine that propositions are really extensional functions from possible worlds to truth values; the doctrine that propositions are nothing but ordered sets (sequences, abstract trees, etc.) consisting of properties, relations, and perhaps particulars; the doctrine that properties (or concepts) are nothing but extensional functions from individuals to propositions; and so forth. While historically significant and formally elegant, these extensional reductions are simply not plausible: most of us have difficulty honestly believing that the very propositions we believe and assert are really functions or ordered sets, or that the very properties we see and feel are really functions. These reductions also have several problematic implications concerning existence and identity, implications which the informal theory, taken on its own, does not have. For example, these reductions suppress various distinctions which intuitively exist, or they proliferate distinctions which intuitively do not exist. Since these various shortcomings are mere artifacts of reductionism, it seems appropriate to adopt a non-reductionistic point of view from which propositions are seen as *sui generis* entities. But then another approach to systematizing the theory of propositions is needed.

The second group of problems concerns fine-grained content. Sentences containing co-referential names provide the most familiar illustration.[1] "Cicero is emulated more often than Tully" and "Tully is emulated more often than Cicero" prima facie do not mean *exactly* the same thing. So the proposition that Cicero is emulated more often than Tully and the proposition that Tully is emulated more often than Cicero would seem to differ somehow. But how can they? After all, proper names are rigid designators which are not synonymous with definite descriptions. Nor are ordinary proper-name sentences synonymous with metalinguistic sentences. Nor is it acceptable to resort to primitive mystery senses (Cicerocity, Tullyicity, etc.). These considerations have driven some philosophers to hold that such propositions are actually one and the same *singular* proposition – namely, that x is emulated more often than y (where $x = y =$ Cicero = Tully). But most

philosophers are unable to accept this singular-proposition theory with any conviction; it is simply too implausible. What is more, this theory implies that certain associated propositions cannot be simultaneously necessary and a posteriori: for example, the proposition that Cicero is *not* emulated more often than Tully. This problem also arises in more familiar examples: that Cicero is Tully; that Hesperus is Phosphorus; etc.[2] The singular-proposition theory thus clashes with the Kripke-Putnam doctrine of scientific essentialism, which has nearly universal acceptance. The intractability of these problems of fine-grained content has led Saul Kripke to declare, "I am unsure that the apparatus of 'propositions' does not break down in this area" (Kripke 1980, p. 21).

The two groups of problems – reductionism and fine-grained content – are related. For, as we shall see, the problematic implications of reductionism actually stand in the way of an acceptable treatment of fine-grained content. As I indicated, I believe that what is needed is a non-reductionistic theory of propositions. Showing how to develop one is the first goal of this paper. The second goal will be to show how this theory provides a framework for a new style of solution to problems of fine-grained content. Among the problems of content which this framework may be used to solve are those confronting scientific essentialism – the above problem of providing for propositions which can be both necessary and a posteriori, and additional problems which have not been discussed before.

Before beginning, I should say something about how I think of this paper. I do not conceive of it as an argumentative piece organized around a single line of argument but rather as belonging to another genre whose primary purpose is to give an overview of a *theory*, in this case, a non-reductionistic theory of propositions. Although in the course of the paper competing theories will be discussed critically, my remarks are not intended as refutations but rather as foils to help bring out the intuitive motivation of the theory I will be presenting or to isolate desiderata which the theory is designed to satisfy. I hope that readers – especially advocates of competing theories – will bear this in mind.

2. Discussion of the Reductionistic Theories

I begin with two preliminary remarks. First, in connection with the issue of reductionism, the primary question with which we are concerned is what propositions *are*. Are they identical to extensional functions, ordered sets, sequences, etc.; or are they *sui generis* entities, belonging to an altogether new category? This ontological question differs from the model-theoretic question of whether extensional entities might be used merely to *represent* propositions. While I am prepared to agree that the answer to the latter question is affirmative, this does not answer the ontological question. (For more on merely representing propositions, see note 11.) Second, I will take it as a desideratum that a theory of propositions should be formulated in such a way as to be compatible with *actualism* – the doctrine that everything there is actually exists. There are, I believe, compelling arguments for actualism and against possibilism – the doctrine that there truly are individuals that do not actually exist – but this is not the place to give them.[3] In any case, surely it is desirable that a theory should be compatible with actualism. I should say also that I do not deem Meinongian theories – and related theories of "nonconcrete substances" – to be actualist; "the golden mountain" does not denote any *actual object* in the ordinary sense of the term.

These two points have immediate implications for the possible-worlds reduction. The first has to do with actualism. According to the possible-worlds reduction, properties, relations, and propositions are reducible to set-theoretical constructs ultimately built up from possible (often nonactual) particulars – possible people, possible stones, possible worlds, etc. Propositions, for example, are supposed to be identical to functions from possible worlds to truth values (specifically, the truth value the proposition would have in that world). And properties are identical to functions from possible worlds to sets of things (specifically the set of possible things which would have the property in that world). For example, the proposition that I dream = the function that maps possible worlds in which I dream to the true and other possible worlds to the false. And a sensible property such as the aroma of coffee = the function that maps possible worlds to the set of things which have the aroma of coffee in that world. Clearly, these reductions are wedded to possibilism and so fail to meet the above desideratum. The second implication has to do with intuitive plausibility. When I believe (doubt, justify, assert) some proposition, do I believe (doubt, justify, assert) a function? On the face of it, this is not plausible.

Advocates of this reduction seem to have lost "the naive eye". The possible-worlds reductionist might try to reply that this objection is an instance of the so-called "fallacy of incomplete analysis": the prima facie implausible consequence results from wrongly mixing analyzed and unanalyzed notions; when the analysis is completed, the problem vanishes.[4] But this reply does not work in the context of the traditional theory of propositions, which we are assuming here. According to this theory, when we believe a proposition, we are straightforwardly related to it by the relation of believing, the familiar two-place relation. In this setting, given that the possible-worlds reduction tells us what propositions *are* (as opposed to how they might be represented model-theoretically), it follows that, when I believe that I am dreaming, I am related by the familiar relation of believing to a function. And this is surely implausible.

Another concern with the possible-worlds reduction is that it implies that all necessarily equivalent propositions are identical – a plainly unacceptable consequence. Many possible-worlds reductionists have responded to this problem by holding that propositions are really ordered sets (sequences, abstract trees) whose elements are possible-worlds constructs built up ultimately from possible particulars. For example, on this theory, the proposition that you dream is the ordered set <dreaming, you >, where the property of dreaming is treated, as before, as a function from possible worlds to sets of possible dreamers. Although this revisionary view avoids the present concern, it does not avoid the previous two. Moreover, since the revisionary view is a possibilist variation on the propositional-complex reduction, it is faced in addition with the issue of arbitrariness (see below) which confronts that view.[5]

A final concern with the revisionary possible-worlds reduction is whether it can really be reductionistic.[6] Intuitively, it is necessary *that some proposition is necessary*.[7] Let us apply the possible-worlds reduction of properties to the property of being a necessary proposition. This property would be the function (set of ordered pairs) from possible worlds to the set of necessary propositions. But the set of necessary propositions includes the proposition that some proposition is necessary (because, as just indicated, this proposition is itself necessary). Thus, this proposition belongs to a set belonging to an ordered pair belonging to the property of being necessary. But, according to the revisionary theory, this proposition is itself an ordered set, one of whose elements is the property of being necessary. Hence, the property of being necessary belongs to an ordered set which belongs to a set which belongs to an ordered pair which belongs to the property of being necessary. That is, being necessary $\in \ldots \in$ being necessary. Hence, the property of being necessary cannot be a set-theoretical construct built up entirely from possible *particulars* (possible people, possible stones, and the like). But the goal of possible-worlds reductionists is to reduce everything either to a particular or to a set ultimately built up entirely from particulars. The upshot is that the possible-worlds reduction fails for the property of being necessary. And, in general, it fails for every iterable property (this includes pretty much every philosophically interesting property). There is no choice but to acknowledge that these properties are irreducible *sui generis* entities. But if these are irreducible *sui generis* entities, uniformity supports the thesis that all other properties are as well.

We come next to the propositional-complex reduction. According to it, propositions are identical to ordered sets (sequences, abstract trees) whose elements are properties and relations (and perhaps particulars), where properties and relations are taken to be primitive entities. For example, the proposition that you dream is the ordered set <dreaming, you>, where the property of dreaming is taken to be a primitive entity. Similarly, the proposition that you dream and I think is the ordered set <conjunction, <dreaming, you>, <thinking, me >>; the proposition that someone dreams is the ordered set <existential generalization, dreaming >; and so forth. The first concern with this reduction is that, on the face of it, it is not intuitively plausible. When I believe (doubt, justify, assert) the proposition that you are dreaming, do I stand in the familiar relation of believing (doubting, asserting) to an ordered set? Moreover, as before, in the context of the traditional theory of propositions, it does no good to raise the point about the fallacy of incomplete analysis. The second concern with the propositional-complex theory is that there is no way to determine which ordered set is the alleged item I believe. Is it <dreaming, you>? Or is it <you, dreaming>? The choice is utterly arbitrary. Admitting this kind of wholesale arbitrariness into a theory would be unwarranted if there were

an otherwise acceptable alternative which is free of it.

Another concern about the propositional-complex theory is associated with the phenomenon of "transmodal quantification".[8] (This problem arises only for propositional-complex theories which are intended to be compatible with actualism. It does not arise for the above possible-worlds version of the theory, which is explicitly possibilist. A special reason for discussing the phenomenon of transmodal quantification here is that it provides a particularly difficult problem for any anti-existentialist version of actualism. But, as we shall see, an anti-existentialist version of actualism is required for an acceptable solution to the problem of fine-grained content.) The following intuitively true sentence is a simple illustration of transmodal quantification:

> Every x is such that, necessarily, for every y, the proposition that $x = y$ is either possible or impossible.[9]

We may symbolize this sentence thus:

(i) $(\forall x)\Box(\forall y)(\text{Possible}[x = y] \vee$
$$\text{Impossible}[x = y]).$$

On the propositional-complex theory, (i) is equivalent to:

(ii) $(\forall x)\Box(\forall y)(\text{Possible} < x, \text{identity}, y > \vee$
$$\text{Impossible} < x, \text{identity}, y >).$$

(A propositional-complex theorist might try to block this step by holding that it is an instance of the "fallacy of incomplete analysis". But, as before, this sort of reply does not work in the context of the traditional theory of propositions. On that theory, propositions are the primary bearers of the properties of possibility and impossibility, so given that the propositional-complex theory tells us what propositions *are*, explicitly identifying them with ordered-sets, the indicated step must be accepted.) There are two readings of (ii) depending on the scope of the singular term "$< x, \text{identity}, y >$". The narrow scope reading entails:

$$(\forall x)\Box(\forall y)(\exists v)v = < x, \text{identity}, y > .$$

Yet, necessarily, a set exists only if its elements exist. So the narrow scope reading of (ii) entails:

$$(\forall x)\Box(\exists v)v = x.$$

That is, everything necessarily exists. A false conclusion. (At least according to actualism, which we are assuming here. Possibilists, of course, would accept this conclusion. What is not the case on their view is that everything is necessarily actual.) On the other hand, consider the wide scope reading. On it, (ii) entails that every x is such that, necessarily, for all y, there exists an actual set $< x$, identity, $y >$. In symbols,

$$(\forall x)\Box(\forall y)(\exists_{\text{actual}}v)v =< x, \text{identity}, y > .$$

But here we have a similar difficulty. Necessarily, a set is actual only if its elements are actual. Thus, the wide scope reading of (ii) entails:

$$\Box(\forall y) \; y \text{ is actual.}$$

That is, necessarily, everything (including everything that might have existed) is among the things that actually exist. Again, a false conclusion: clearly it is possible that there should have existed something which is not among the things that actually exist. So, on both of its readings, (ii) entails falsehoods. But, according to the propositional-complex thesis, (ii) is equivalent to a true sentence, namely, (i). Thus, the propositional-complex theory fails to handle this example of transmodal quantification. And the problem generalizes. Of course, in this and the earlier problems, the underlying error is to think that propositions literally have *members* or *parts*, that things are literally *in* them. (Notice that the above argument is entirely consistent with actualism: I am not supposing that there are things which are not actual; I am only supposing that it is *possible* that there should have existed things which are not among the things that actually exist. Nowhere in the argument am I committed to the existence of non-actual possibilia, for the relevant quantifiers always occur within *intensional* contexts, viz. "it is possible that", "necessarily", etc. As such, these quantifiers have *no* range of values. That it is possible that there should have been more planets than there actually are does not entail that there are possible but non-actual planets.)

Consider next the propositional-function reduction. According to it, a property (or relation) is nothing but an extensional function from objects to propositions, where propositions are taken to be primitive entities. For example, the property being

in pain $= (\lambda x)$ (the proposition that x is in pain). For any given object x, the proposition that x is in pain $= (\lambda x)$ (the proposition that x is in pain) (x) = the result of applying the function (λx) (the proposition that x is in pain) to the argument x.[10] But is being in pain really a *function*? It is hard to see why one would accept this counterintuitive thesis given that there are straightforward, intuitive theories which take properties at face value and given that intuitions form the evidential basis for the theory of properties, relations, and propositions in the first place. Identifying being in pain with a function would seem to be a symptom of over-mathematizing philosophy.

Furthermore, the propositional-function reduction seems unable to accommodate a certain kind of fine-grained content. Take, for instance, the following case involving properties of integers. Being even $=$ being an x such that x is divisible by two, and being self-divisible $=$ being an x such that x is divisible by x. (The same point could be made using some other identities, stipulatively defined if necessary.) The following identities are then derivable on the propositional-function reduction:

> That two is even $= (\lambda x)$ (that x is even) (two) $= (\lambda x)$ (that x is divisible by two) (two) $=$ that two is divisible by two $= (\lambda x)$ (that x is divisible by x) (two) $= (\lambda x)$ (that x is self-divisible) (two) $=$ that two is self-divisible.

Thus, the proposition that two is even is identical to the proposition that two is self-divisible. But surely this is not so: someone could be consciously and explicitly thinking the former while not consciously and explicitly thinking the latter. Indeed, someone who is thinking the former might never have employed the concept of self-divisibility. Because the non-reductionist theory which we will be considering takes properties at face-value, not as functions, but as *sui generis* entities, this sort of problem never arises.

A final problem facing all three reductionistic theories (possible-worlds, propositional-complex, propositional-function) has to do with "degrees of granularity". As standardly formulated, each reductionistic theory is committed to the view that there is only one type of proposition; each theory excludes the idea that there might be several distinct types of propositions, ranging from coarse-grained to fine-grained. (Illustration: because $<$ conjunction, A, B $>\neq<$ conjunction, B, A $>$, the propositional-complex theory *entails* that the conjunction of A and $B \neq$ the conjunction of B and A; this rules out the possibility of another type of conjunctive proposition whose identity conditions are blind to the order of the conjuncts). Yet it can be argued that there are not only contexts calling for highly fine-grained propositions but also contexts calling for highly coarse-grained propositions, as well as contexts calling for propositions of intermediate granularity. An example of a type of proposition of intermediate granularity (which will be of use in §7) is a type which, while sensitive to individual contents, is insensitive to the various ways in which those contents might be combined as long as the same content inputs always yield necessarily equivalent outputs. Of course, to accommodate a multiplicity of types of propositions, the reductionistic theories might try to reduce the remaining types of propositions to equivalence classes or to sequences or whatever. But how artificial. On the non-reductionistic theory we will be considering, it is straightforward to treat a spectrum of distinct granularities concurrently without resorting to counterintuitive steps like these. This approach thus allows us to avoid a false dilemma that is common in recent discussions in philosophy of mind. "Are mental contents fine-grained or coarse-grained?" Answer: "Both, and often they are of intermediate granularity." (For ease of presentation, I will confine myself to a fine-grained setting except in §7.)

All the preceding problems result from the fact that each of the surveyed theories attempts to *reduce* intensional entities of one kind or another to extensional entities – either extensional functions or sets. I believe that this extensional reductionism has obscured basic facts about properties, relations, and propositions which hold the key to solving our other main problem – the problem of fine-grained content.[11] For all these reasons, it would seem that a non-reductionistic approach is appropriate.

3. A Non-Reductionistic Approach

Consider some truisms. The proposition that A & B is the conjunction of the proposition that A and the proposition that B. The proposition that not A is the negation of the proposition that A. The proposition that Fx is the predication of the property F of x. The proposition that there exists an F is the existential generalization of the property F. And so on. These truisms tell us what these propositions are essentially: they are by nature conjunctions, negations, singular predications, existential generalizations, etc. These are rudimental facts which require no further explanation and for which no further explanation is possible. Until the advent of extensionalism, this was the dominant point of view. It is what Plato and Aristotle gesture toward in their metaphor of truths arising from a "weaving together" of universals. I propose returning to this non-reductionist point of view.

The key to doing this is, ironically, to mimic a certain approach to extensional logic – the algebraic approach – but now in an intensional setting. To do this, one assumes that examples like those just given isolate fundamental logical operations – conjunction, negation, singular predication, existential generalization, and so forth – and one takes properties, relations, and propositions as *sui generis* entities. The primary aim is then to analyze their behavior with respect to the fundamental logical operations. This may be done by studying intensional model structures (intensional structures, for short).

An intensional structure consists of a domain, a set of logical operations, and a set of possible extensionalization functions. The domain partitions into subdomains: particulars, propositions, properties, binary relations, ternary relations, etc., taken as primitive entities. The set of logical operations includes those listed above plus certain auxiliary operations. The possible extensionalization functions assign an extension to each of the items in the domain: each proposition is assigned a truth value; each property is assigned a set of items in the domain; each binary relation is assigned a set of ordered pairs of items in the domain; etc. One extensionalization function is singled out as the actual extensionalization function: the propositions which are true relative to it are the propositions which are actually true; etc.[12]

To illustrate how this approach works, consider the operation of negation, neg. Let H be an extensionalization function. Then, neg must satisfy the following: for all propositions p in the domain, $H(\text{neg}(p)) = $ true iff $H(p) = $ false. Similarly, if conj is the operation of conjunction, then for all propositions p and q in the domain, $H(\text{conj}(p, q)) = $ true iff $H(p) = $ true and $H(q) = $ true. Likewise, for singular predication pred_s, which takes properties F and arbitrary items y in the domain to propositions in the domain. Then we have: $H(\text{pred}_s(F, y)) = $ true iff y is in the extension $H(F)$.

To deal with contingent existents, we single out a distinguished property in the domain, namely, existence (which we hereafter indicate with E).

For each possible existensionalization function H, $H(\mathcal{E})$ is the set of items in the domain which exist relative to H. The treatment of the quantificational operations is then straightforward. Consider the operation of existential generalization, exist. For properties F in the domain, exist(F) is the proposition that there exists an F. Then H(exist(F)) = true iff, for some y in $H(\mathcal{E})$, y is in $H(F)$. That is, the proposition that there exists an F is true relative to H iff, for some y that exists relative to H, y is in the extension of F.

This completes my sketch of the non-reductionist approach. Before I am able to present my solution to the problem of fine-grained content, however, I will have to develop three preliminary ideas which will serve as essential components of that solution. The first concerns existentialism and the problem of transmodal quantification (discussed in §2). The second concerns the kind of predication involved in descriptive propositions. The third concerns the distinction between Platonic and non-Platonic modes of presentation. In each case I will only be able to highlight the main points, but that should suffice for the larger purpose of clarifying how I propose to deal with the problem of fine-grained content.

4. Existentialism and Transmodal Quantification

Existentialists believe (roughly) that, necessarily, a proposition exists only if its "constituents" exist; anti-existentialists believe (roughly) the contrary.[13] Existentialists would be right if propositions were reducible to sets, sequences, or some other kind of extensional complex, for in that case propositions would literally have members or parts, things would be literally in them. But we saw above that such extensional reductionism is the wrong way to think of propositions. One sort of problem arose in connection with transmodal quantification, which is exhibited in sentences such as "Every x is such that, necessarily, for every y, either it is possible or impossible that $x = y$".[14] To illustrate how the non-reductionist approach can accommodate anti-existentialism, consider a somewhat simpler case: for all x, necessarily, it is possible that $x = x$.[15] In symbols, $(\forall x)$ Possible $[x = x]$. Anti-existentialists would hold: for all x, necessarily, there exists something – namely, the proposition that $x = x$ – which is possible. In symbols, $(\forall x)$ $(\exists u)$ (Possible $uu = [x = x]$). The non-reduction-

ist approach provides a framework for showing how the proposition $[x = x]$ could exist even when the contingent particular x did not. The proposition that $x = x$, like all propositions, is an irreducible intensional entity. Although the operation of singular predication maps self-identity and x to this proposition, one is free to hold that the existence of this proposition does not *entail* the existence of x. Consider an analogy. The author-of function maps this article to me. However, the existence of me does not *entail* the existence of this article; I could have refrained from writing it.

Diagrams can be helpful here. Figure 9.1 represents the actual relationship between the proposition $[x = x]$, the property self-identity, and x. G is the actual extensionalization function, and $G(\mathcal{E})$ the set of actually existing things. In this situation, all three items actually exist

Now consider the possible situation represented in figure 9.2. Here we have a possible but non-actual relationship between $[x = x]$, self-identity, and x. In this situation, $[x = x]$ and self-identity exist, but x does not. This account allows one to hold that, for all x, necessarily, the proposition that $x = x$ exists. That is, $(\forall x)$ $(\exists u)u = [x = x]$. This is what anti-existentialists hold.

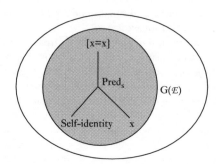

Figure 9.1

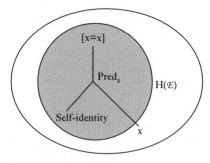

Figure 9.2

Traditional "logical atomism" is not quite right on the picture that emerges. Traditional atomism requires that, necessarily, existing propositions have complete analyses exclusively in terms of basic properties, basic relations, and existing particulars. But according to anti-existentialism, it is possible for a proposition to exist even if there did not exist relevant particulars ("constituents") that would be needed for such an analysis. Nevertheless, a *modal* logical atomism is feasible. The proposition that $x = x$, for example, would not have the indicated sort of analysis in the event that x did not exist; nevertheless, this proposition is such that it is *possible* for it have the indicated sort of analysis – specifically, this would be possible if x were to exist. Ever more complex cases (such as the transmodal case above) can be handled by iterating the same idea.[16] This treatment of propositions does not require mysterious primitive Haecceities for their analysis: a complete structural understanding can be had, as atomists thought, although it will be modal in some cases. I believe that this idea can be exploited to accommodate all the usual phenomena that lead some philosophers to adopt possibilism (vs. actualism) and eternalism (vs. presentism).[17]

5. Descriptions

I come now to the second preliminary topic – definite descriptions. There are four leading theories: Frege's, Russell's, Evans's, and Prior's. Each of these theories can easily be incorporated into our non-reductionist approach. I will illustrate this in the case of Frege's theory, which to many is the most intuitive of the four. The following sketch should suffice for our purposes.

Frege holds that ⌐ the F ⌐ is an ordinary singular term having a sense and often a reference. Such terms have the form ⌐ $(\iota x)(Fx)$ ⌐, where ⌐ (ιx) ⌐ is an unary operator which combines with a formula to yield a singular term. The singular term ⌐ the F ⌐ refers to the unique item satisfying the predicate ⌐ F ⌐ if there is one; if there is not, ⌐ the F ⌐ has no reference. The truth conditions are: (i) if ⌐ the F ⌐ has a reference, ⌐ The F Gs ⌐ is true (false) iff ⌐ $(\forall x)(Fx \to Gx)$ ⌐ is true (false); (ii) otherwise, ⌐ The F Gs ⌐ is neither true nor false. The truth-value gap in clause (ii) is not essential; gaps can be eliminated by the following revision of clause (ii): if ⌐ the F ⌐ has no reference, ⌐ The F Gs ⌐ is false. (I will adopt this simplifying convention.)

To incorporate Frege's theory, consider intensional structures in which the set of logical operations contains the logical operation *the* (akin to the Frege-Church operation ι). One may think of the values of *the* as "individual concepts": *the*(F) would then be the individual concept of being the F. (For each possible extensionalization function H, $H(the(F)) = H(F)$ if the latter has exactly one element; otherwise, it is the null set.) Consider now the property of being G and the individual concept of being the F. What is their relation to the proposition that the F Gs? Not singular predication: when the operation of singular predication is applied to the property of being G and the concept of being the F – that is, pred$_s$ $(G, the(F))$ – the value is the proposition that the concept of being the F Gs. This is a *very* different proposition! The relation of singular predication is, thus, not the relation holding between the property of being G, the concept of being the F, and the proposition that the F Gs. Rather, the relation holding between them is a quite distinct kind of predication, which may be called *descriptive predication* – pred$_d$, for short. Descriptive predication is implicit in the informal theory of Fregean senses: it is the relation holding between the sense of a predicate ⌐ G ⌐, the sense of a definite description ⌐ the F ⌐, and the sense of a sentence ⌐ The F Gs ⌐.[18] In order to capture the informal Fregean theory of definite descriptions in our non-reductionist approach, one thus considers intensional structures containing both *the* and pred$_d$ the proposition that the F Gs = pred$_d$ $(G, the(F))$. This proposition is true relative to an extensionalization function H iff, relative to H, the extension of being F has exactly one element and that element belongs to the extension of being G.

The operation of descriptive predication is also used for other sorts of descriptive propositions. For example, consider one of Stephen Neale's number-neutral descriptive propositions: the proposition that whoever shot Kennedy is crazy.[19] This proposition would be pred$_d$ $(C, whe(S))$, where *whe* is Neale's number-neutral description operation. This operation takes the property of shooting Kennedy (that is, S) as argument and gives as value the number-neutral descriptive property of being whoever shot Kennedy, that is, *whe*(S). Relative to a possible extensionalization function H, the proposition pred$_d$ $(C, whe(S))$ is true iff the extension of *whe*(S) is a non-empty subset of the extension of C. The point is that, in addition to various description operations – *the*, *whe*, etc. – there is an operation of descriptive predication which takes predicative intensions and subject intensions as arguments and gives associated propositions as values.

These remarks on descriptions illustrate a larger point: namely, the non-reductionist approach provides a framework for a *general semantics*. It does so without having to reduce properties, relations and propositions to possible-worlds constructs and without having to resort to the rigid type theory implicit in the usual possible-worlds categorial syntax. Davidson's truth-conditional approach also provides a general semantics; but, unlike the proposed approach, it does not identify the *propositions* meant by sentences and so does not conform to one of the central tenets of the traditional theory of propositions listed at the outset. Our approach, by contrast, does this in a straightforward fashion. At the same time, it preserves the valuable insights which have been uncovered by possible-worlds semantics and truth-conditional semantics. Indeed, once relevant syntactic structures are uncovered and once the accompanying truth conditions are found, the rest is virtually automatic: one need only restrict oneself to intensional structures which contain corresponding logical operations whose behavior matches those truth conditions.

6. Non-Platonic Modes of Presentation

The domain of an intensional structure is the union of relevant subdomains, where one of these subdomains is thought of as consisting of properties (or concepts).[20] But we could instead think of this subdomain as consisting of modes of access or modes of presentation (*Arten des Gegebenseins*). Properties (which are purely Platonic entities) are one kind of mode of presentation. But certain *constructed* entities also present things to us. For example, pictures do. Certain *socially* constructed entities also function in this capacity; the most prominent are linguistic entities. Indeed, linguistic entities provide the only access most of us have to various historical figures (e.g. Cicero). These linguistic entities have the important feature of being *public*, shared by whole communities.

Names are one kind of linguistic entity which provide us with access to objects. Think of all the people you know by name only. (In what follows names will be understood, not as mere phonological or orthographic types, but as fine-grained entities whose existence is an empirical fact and for which it is essential that they name what they do.[21] For example, Cicero the Illinois town and Cicero the famous orator share a name in the phonological or orthographic sense but not in the fine-grained sense. In the latter sense, but not the former, the existence of the two names is an empirical matter: the name of the town is fairly new; the name of the orator is very old. Given that the name of the town exists, it is essential to it that it name the town; likewise, given that the name of the orator exists, it is essential to it that it name the orator. This conception meshes perfectly with Kripke's rigid-designator conception of names. Names of this kind are "living names".) Naming practices are another kind of linguistic entity which provide us with access to objects. For example, the practice of using "Cicero" to refer to Cicero provides us with a kind of access to the orator. (On the Kripke picture, a naming practice consists of an initial act of baptism together with an ongoing convention for using the name with the intention of referring to whatever it was that was referred to by previous uses of the name. The practice thus provides those who follow it with a kind of access to the originally baptized object.) In much the same way, historical naming trees provide us with access to their termini; indeed, a naming tree may be thought of as a naming practice "spread out in history". In so far as these linguistic entities (names, practices, trees) provide us with access to objects, they qualify as modes of presentation. There is much to say about the metaphysics of these kinds of entities, but the foregoing should suffice for the purpose at hand.

My goal is to show how, in a non-reductionist setting, non-Platonic modes of presentation contribute to a new style of solution to puzzles about fine-grained content. For the purpose of illustration, it does not matter just which kind of non-Platonic mode we use: there is a natural one-one mapping from living names onto naming practices and a natural one-one mapping from naming practices onto naming trees. I will therefore use a neutral notation which finesses the question of just which of these types of non-Platonic modes is best; specifically, I will use expressions surrounded by straight double-quotes ("Cicero", "Tully", etc.) to denote the most promising one. Accordingly, "Cicero" might be our practice of using "Cicero" to refer to Cicero; or "Cicero" might be the historical naming tree associated with this practice; or "Cicero" might be the living name itself.[22]

In so far as "Cicero", "Tully", etc. present objects to us, there are natural intensional structures in which they are elements of the subdomain of modes of presentation. Since "Cicero" and "Tully" both present Cicero (= Tully), the extensionalization functions H in such intensional structures would behave accordingly: $H(\text{"Cicero"}) = \{\text{Cicero}\} = \{\text{Tully}\} = H(\text{"Tully"})$. This is so despite the fact that these two non-Platonic modes are distinct (i.e. "Cicero" $\neq$ "Tully"). In these intensional structures, relevant logical operations are defined for all modes of presentation – non-Platonic as well as Platonic. So, for example, the operation of descriptive predication $pred_d$ may take as arguments, say, the property of being a person and "Cicero". The result $pred_d$ (being a person, "Cicero") would be a proposition. Likewise, for $pred_d$ (being a person, "Tully"). These non-Platonic modes of presentation (as opposed to descriptive properties obtained from them by means of *the*, *whe*, or some other description operation) are themselves arguments in these descriptive predications.

Let us examine some of the features which these two propositions would have. Given that "Cicero" and "Tully" are distinct, $pred_d$ (being a person, "Cicero") and $pred_d$ (being a person, "Tully") would be distinct. Moreover, since the intensional structures under consideration are anti-existentialist in character, there could be circumstances in which these two propositions would exist even though the contingent, socially constructed modes of presentation "Cicero" and "Tully" would not exist. This is the very same point made in our discussion of anti-existentialism, except that here descriptive predication is playing the role played there by singular predication. Next, let us agree with essentialists like Kripke that every person is necessarily a person.[23] Given that $H(\text{"Cicero"}) = \{\text{Cicero}\} = \{\text{Tully}\} = H(\text{"Tully"})$, we know that $H(pred_d$ (being a person, "Cicero")) = true and $H(pred_d$ (being a person, "Tully")) = true. Since this holds for all possible extensionalization functions H,[24] our two propositions $pred_d$ (being a person, "Cicero") and $pred_d$ (being a person, "Tully") would be necessarily true. This is in agreement with Kripke and others who maintain that the proposition that Cicero is a person and the proposition that Tully is a person are necessarily true.[25]

Furthermore, our two propositions – $pred_d$ (being a person, "Cicero") and $pred_d$ (being a person, "Tully") – are distinct from all propositions expressible with the use of definite descriptions (with or without actuality operators). The proposition $pred_d$ (being a person, "Cicero"), for example, is distinct from each of the following: the proposition that the thing presented by "Cicero" is a person; the proposition that the thing presented by *this* non-Platonic mode of presentation is a person; the proposition that the thing actually named "Cicero" is a person; and so forth. Finally, these propositions – $pred_d$ (being a person, "Cicero") and $pred_d$ (being a person, "Tully") – are not metalinguistic in any of the following standard senses. First, given that our theory is anti-existentialist, the two propositions are ontologically independent of "Cicero" and "Tully" in the sense that it would be possible for the propositions to exist even if those socially constructed linguistic entities were not to exist.[26] Those entities are certainly not literally *in* or *parts of* the propositions. Second, the propositions are distinct from all propositions expressible by sentences containing metalinguistic vocabulary. Third, when a person – perhaps a child – is thinking of one of these propositions, the person need not be employing – and, indeed, might not even possess – any relevant concepts from linguistic theory (the concept of a name or the concept of a naming practice). These propositions are seamless; only in their logical analyses do the linguistic modes of presentation appear. (For more on this point, see §8.1–2.)

Let me sum up. Our goal is a theory of propositions in which, for example, the proposition that Cicero is a person and the proposition that Tully is a person have the following features. They should be distinct. They should be ontologically independent of contingently existing things in so far as they should be able to exist in situations in which relevant contingent things do not; the latter should not be literally *in* them. They should have the right modal value, namely, necessity. They should not be the sort of proposition expressible by sentences containing definite descriptions. Finally, they should not be metalinguistic in any of the standard senses mentioned above. Propositions such as $pred_d$ (being a person, "Cicero") and $pred_d$ (being a person, "Tully") have all these features and should therefore be considered promising candidates for the sort of propositions that have been eluding us.[27]

George Bealer

7. Names with Partial Content

The proposal just sketched relies on non-Platonic modes of presentation – "Cicero", "Tully", etc. – which are identified with living names, naming practices, or historical naming trees. There are other proposals which would feature other kinds of non-Platonic modes of presentation (e.g. clusters of recognitional routines causally involving Cicero in an essential way; percepts which are essentially individuated by their objects; expressions in the "language of thought"; etc.). In the present context, there is no need to declare any one of these proposals to be most promising. The point is that within the non-reductionist framework one is able to have finely distinguished propositions which are neither descriptive nor metalinguistic in the standard senses and which have all the other desired features.

On each of the above proposals, when we assert a sentence containing a name, our use of the name contributes absolutely no descriptive content to the asserted proposition. According to many philosophers, this is exactly the right outcome. Other philosophers, however, think that although a name does not have the sort of descriptive content which fixes a unique referent, a name nevertheless has *some* descriptive content (a "sortal content") – namely, a content which fixes the *sort* (or category) to which the referent must belong. (I will call this the "partial-content view" in contrast to the above no-content view.) For example, according to a single partial-content view, being a person might be the "partial content" of an ordinary personal name; being a building might be the partial content of an ordinary building name; being a country might be the partial content of an ordinary country name; and so forth.[28]

The above general framework allows one to systematize this kind of view. To get an idea of how to do this, consider an oversimplified version. On the no-content view, the proposition that Cicero is eloquent would be identified with the proposition $pred_d$ (eloquence, C) and C would be just the purely non-Platonic mode of presentation "Cicero". The partial-content view is exactly the same except that C might instead be the result of conjoining a purely non-Platonic mode ("Cicero") and a purely Platonic mode (being a person). That is, $C = conj$ ("Cicero", being a person). The idea is that, just as a purely non-Platonic mode can be

an argument in a descriptive predication – e.g. $pred_d$ (eloquence, "Cicero") – it can be an argument in a conjunction: $conj$("Cicero", being a person). C behaves as expected: x is in the extension of C iff "Cicero" presents x and x is a person.[29] Propositions expressed using names from other categories could be treated analogously. For example, the proposition that Liechtenstein is tiny might be identified with $pred_d$ (being tiny, L), where L is $conj$ ("Liechtenstein", being a country).

As it stands, this illustration of the partial content theory might not seem plausible. It is oversimplified on (at least) two counts. The first has to do with the topic of granularity mentioned at the close of §2. We indicated that there are good reasons to entertain a spectrum of distinct types of granularity ranging from coarse-grained to fine-grained. Suppose the proposition that Cicero is eloquent $= pred_d$(eloquence, C). I do not find it plausible that C is a hyper-fine-grained concept of the sort that has a logical form. In particular, if $C = conj$("Cicero", being a person), the kind of conjunction involved is not the same as that which is associated with propositions having logical form. On the contrary, C ought to have the sort of intermediate granularity described at the close of §2.[30] Starting with the contents "Cicero" and being a person and applying logical operations of the sort associated with this intermediate granularity, we can arrive at C in a variety of different ways (e.g. by conjoining the two contents in any order). We should not proliferate distinctions where, intuitively, there are none. As I have indicated, on the non-reductionist approach one can accommodate this intermediate type of granularity as well as more fine-grained types; not so on the reductionistic approaches.

The second count on which the above proposal is oversimplified is this. The above illustration associated a determinate sortal content with the name "Cicero", namely, being a person. But advocates of the partial-content theory need not hold that names have a *determinate* sortal content; they can hold that names have a content which serves merely to restrict the *range* of permissible sortals. For example, the proposition that Venus is bright might be something like $pred_d$ (brightness, V), where V is $conj$("Venus", v) and v is equivalent to a conjunction of default conditionals which restrict the range of permissible sorts to which Venus may belong. Although v does not entail that Venus be a planet, v rules out a great many possibilities, e.g. the possibility that Venus is a symphony. This revised proposal would thus accommodate the fact that certain ancient astronomers believed, without being irrational, that Venus and other heavenly bodies were holes in the heavens. Of course, if v is equivalent to a conjunction of default conditionals, this does not mean that v is identical to a fine-grained conjunction of such conditionals. Quite the contrary, the most plausible proposal is that v is a standard coarse-grained intension. (In §9.5 we will return to the idea that the sortal content of a name merely restricts the range of permissible sortals.)

I take no stand on which of these alternative treatments of names is best. Rather, my intention has been to show only that the proposed non-reductionist framework systematizes a full spectrum of theories, ranging from no-content theories to various partial-content theories and way over to traditional descriptivist theories. This spectrum provides distinctions in content which are cut any way one would want. If this is right, an adequate solution to the problem of fine-grained content ought to be feasible within the proposed framework. It may be a question which of the spectrum of alternatives is best, but systematizing it should not be a problem.

In what follows (except §9.5) I will suppose for simplicity that the no-content theory is correct; my remarks would also hold mutatis mutandis for partial-content theories.

8. Discussion

(1) I began the chapter by noting that on the traditional theory propositions are extra-linguistic entities. As I have indicated, our analysis conforms to this tenet. Consider our example of the proposition that Cicero is a person. Given our anti-existentialism, this proposition is ontologically independent of "Cicero" in the sense that it is possible for it to exist in situation in which "Cicero" does not exist; "Cicero" is not *in* or *part of* the proposition. Moreover, when one is thinking that Cicero is a person, one need not be employing – and might not even possess – any relevant concepts from linguistic theory. Finally, this proposition is not expressible by any sentence containing metalinguistic vocabulary (e.g. it is not expressed by a sentence such as "The thing presented by 'Cicero' is a person"). This point deserves some elaboration. There is an important distinction between the kind of analysis which gives a synonym of a sentence and the kind which gives a necessarily correct description of the logical form and content of the proposition expressed by the sentence. I have ventured the latter, not the former. It would be an elementary error to think that the existence of this kind of partly metalinguistic logical analysis implies the existence of a metalinguistic synonym. Indeed, there are many important points in philosophy and logic where synonyms are not available but analyses of the other kind are. The non-reductionist approach presents a general framework for studying this kind of analysis. Indeed, my opinion is that this approach is needed ultimately to clarify the relationship between natural languages and logicians' artificial languages.

(2) I have noted that, when a person – perhaps a child – believes the proposition $pred_d$ (being a person, "Cicero"), the person need not be employing – and might not even possess – any relevant concepts from linguistic theory (the concept of a living name or the concept of a naming practice). This proposition is seamless; only in its logical analysis does the linguistic mode of presentation "Cicero" appear. The point generalizes. Believing a proposition does not in general require having command of its logical analysis or the modes of presentation that show up in that analysis. Indeed, anti-individualist examples show that the identity of some modes of presentation is determined, not by the individual, but by a whole speech community. The individual might be deeply ignorant about the identity of the mode of presentation.[31]

This point meshes neatly with interpretive liberalism.[32] (The proposed theory of propositions is strictly speaking neutral on this view, however.) According to it, what is required for a belief ascription to be appropriate (at least in many cases) is simply a relevant sort of interpretive rationale regarding the subject's cognitive commitments. In some cases, those commitments might well be determined in part by other people. Indeed, the ascribed proposition might even involve modes of presentation which are introduced by the ascriber, or the ascriber's community. For example, an advocate of interpretive liberalism might hold that it would be appropriate to ascribe to Aristotle a belief that the Morning Star = the Evening Star, where the logical analysis of this proposition is in terms of descriptive predication, identity, and *our* modes of presentation "the Morning Star" and "the Evening Star".[33] In such cases, of course, the believers would not be acquainted with the propositions which are correctly ascribed to them as beliefs; acquaintance is an altogether different matter. Likewise, the beliefs that figure in a science of behavior might form a smaller class; science is also a different matter. The goal of this paper, of course, is not to give a systematic theory of belief ascription. Rather, the hope is to provide a theory of propositions rich enough to provide all the relevant contents needed to underwrite our belief-ascription practices. One can succeed at the latter goal without attempting the former. For that matter, one may even hold that a systematic theory of belief ascription is not possible. I need not take a stand on this question.

(3) I have been invoking both Platonic and non-Platonic modes of presentation. For something to be a Platonic mode of presentation, it is necessary and sufficient that it be a property or relation (or concept). But what does it take for something to be a non-Platonic mode of presentation? Three points are called for. First, though theoretically attractive, a general analysis (jointly necessary and sufficient conditions) for the notion of a mode of presentation is not *required*; it is enough to have a (relatively clear) grasp of what does and does not count as a mode of presentation in the intended sense. And this we have. Second, the non-reductionist approach (if correct) does make it possible to give a general analysis; a mode of presentation is any item for which relevant fundamental logical operations (e.g. predd) are well-defined.[34] We then have the following: something is a non-Platonic mode of presentation iff it is a mode of presentation and it is not Platonic. As long as the non-reductionist theory is correct, this analysis is free of counterexamples. Third, there remains a further question even if the analysis is correct: by virtue of what do particular kinds of non-Platonic modes of presentation present things? Here, too, answers would be theoretically attractive, but none are *required*. Nevertheless, I believe that there are answers. Because we have an analysis of the general notion of non-Platonic mode presentation, we are free to tackle the present question piecemeal. For example, by virtue of what do pictures present objects? By virtue of what do living names present objects? etc. To answer these questions, we should turn to the rich philosophical literature that deals with them. We find there a variety of promising approaches: causal, intentional (e.g. Gricean), historical, teleological, etc. Let the experts decide.[35]

(4) I have called upon non-Platonic modes of presentation in my explanation of various differences in fine-grained content; I have not taken a stand on how to integrate this explanation into our theory of language. One (to me, implausible) approach would be to identify non-Platonic modes of presentation as *senses* of proper names. More plausibly, the theory of propositions sketched here could be integrated into a semantics for whole sentences without holding that constituent proper names literally have any senses. What would be required is some regular connection between proper names and associated non-Platonic modes of presentation, and there is indeed such a connection for our standard kinds of proper names. Alternatively, the theory of propositions isolated here could be utilized in pragmatics alone. My goal has been to sketch a more satisfactory theory of propositions, not to take a stand on how it should be incorporated into a finished theory of language.

(5) In §2 I took it as a desideratum that a formulation of the theory of propositions should be consistent with actualism – the doctrine that everything there is actually exists. In the sort of intensional structures I have described, there are extensionalization functions H such that $H(E)$ contains something not contained in $G(E)$. If intensional structures are understood as I informally described them, the domain D would need to contain things that do not actually exist. Accordingly, they would not be actualist in character. In the present setting, the easiest way to make them fully actualist is to treat the domain D as consisting of actually existing particulars, modes of presentation, and propositions plus actually existing ersatz entities which play the role of "non-actuals".[36] In the end, however, it is preferable to adopt a more thoroughgoing intensionalism. The main idea is to build the theory around singular identity properties, that is, properties x for which it is possible for there to exist something y such that $x =$ the property of being identical to y. (In symbols, x is a singular identity property iff $\Diamond (\exists y) x = [v: v = y]$.) What makes this work is anti-existentialism – specifically, the fact that all properties (including singular identity properties) are anti-existentialist in character. In particular, each singular identity property x exists necessarily and does so even if there exists no object y in terms of which x may be analyzed. Because they exist necessarily, singular identity properties may play a role somewhat analogous to that which possible

individuals play in possibilist constructions, but without jeopardizing the actualist character of the theory.

In our original construction, existensionalization functions H tell us the possible extensions of a property (or relation) – that is, the set of things that actually have the property or that would have the property if things were different. In the thoroughgoing intensionalist construction, the main work is done instead by intensionalization functions. These functions tell us the "intension" of a property, namely, a relevant set of singular identity properties. In the case of the actual intensionalization functions, this is the set of singular identity properties which would pick out the items actually that would have the property if things were other than they actually are. Using intensinalization functions, we can then characterize, much as before, the behavior of the fundamental logical operations with respect to items in the domain. For example, relative to intensionalization function I, exist (F) = true iff, for some x in $I(\mathcal{E})$, x is in $I(F)$. That is, relative to I, the proposition that there exists an F is true iff, for some singular identity property x that is in the intension of the property existence, x is also in the intension of F. In this manner, we achieve a way of making our construction fully consistent with actualism.[37]

Applications

I will close by suggesting candidate solutions to some further puzzles about content.

(1) Kripke's (1979) puzzle about Pierre's beliefs.[38] Upon seeing a picture of a pretty-looking city labeled "Londres", Pierre states "Londres est jolie". Later, after living in an unattractive section of London, he states "London is not pretty". Let us agree that Pierre does not have explicitly contradictory beliefs. But what, then, does he believe? A promising answer is that the proposition he believes on the first occasion is predd (being pretty, "Londres") whereas the proposition he believes on the second occasion is neg(predd(being pretty, "London")).[39] These two propositions are not in contradiction, for predd(being pretty, "London")$\neq$ predd (being pretty, "Londres"). This is so because "London" $\neq$ "Londres".[40] This account satisfies Kripke's demand that Pierre's beliefs not be metalinguistic in any of the standard senses.

(2) The traditional problem of negative existentials. How can a sentence like "Pegasus does not exist" express a true proposition given that "Pegasus" lacks both a reference and a descriptive sense? The proposed solution is that the sentence expresses (something like) the true proposition neg(predd(existence, "Pegasus")).

In a similar vein, recall Geach's puzzle of intentional identity (see note 33). Suppose Geach's reporter says, "Hob believes that a witch blighted the sheep and Nob believes that she killed the cow. But, of course, there are no witches. So she does not exist". Suppose the reporter's negative existential utterance of "So she does not exist" expresses a true proposition. This proposition might be (something like): neg(predd(existence, "she")). Here "she" would be a non-Platonic mode of presentation, perhaps even the very token of the pronoun in the reporter's utterance.[41] We need not endorse exactly this hypothesis; but, if it is on the right track, our theory of propositions should, by similar means, be able to accommodate a variety of kindred phenomena (fiction, dreams, etc.) which have often led people to Meinongianism.

(3) A substitutivity failure involving synonymous predicates rather than co-referential names. How can the proposition that whatever chews masticates differ from the proposition that whatever masticates chews, given that chewing is the same property as masticating? A promising proposal is to explain the difference between these two propositions in terms of distinct non-Platonic modes of presentation of this property (e.g. "chew" and "masticate"). The two propositions are alike in all respects except that the *order* in which "chew" and "masticate" occur in their logical analyses is reversed.[42]

(4) A puzzle for scientific essentialism. Consider an English speaker who is familiar with the name "Phosphorus" but not "Hesperus". Suppose that by pure chance this person announces, "I hereby stipulate that 'Hesperus' is to be another name for Phosphorus". In this case, a line of reasoning akin to that used in the meter-stick example would commit Kripke to holding that there is something the person would thereby come to know a priori. Would it be the oft discussed necessity that Hesperus = Phosphorus? An answer in the affirmative would result in the downfall of the scientific essentialist doctrine that such necessities are essentially a posteriori. The proposed approach to fine-grained content yields

a natural solution to this problem. The new non-Platonic mode of presentation associated with the just introduced name differs from the long-standing non-Platonic mode of presentation associated with the old name. The proposition which our speaker comes to know a priori is a descriptive predication obtained from the new non-Platonic mode is the familiar proposition which is essentially a posteriori. In my opinion, some such solution is needed for harmonizing Kripke's scientific essentialism and the sort of a priori knowledge which results from stipulative definitions.

(5) A second puzzle for scientific essentialism. You and I have a vivid twin-earth intuition for water: if all and only water here on earth is composed of H_2O, then on a twin earth a stuff which has all the macroscopic properties of water (drinkable, thirst-quenching, etc.) but which is composed of XYZ ($\neq H_2O$) would *not* qualify as water. But you and I lack the corresponding twin-earth intuition for drink; indeed, we have the contrary intuition: even if all and only drink on earth is composed of H_2O, on a twin earth a stuff which has all the macroscopic properties of drink (drinkable, thirst-quenching, etc.) but which is composed of XYZ *would* nonetheless qualify as drink. What accounts for the difference? No doubt the answer begins with the fact that water is a compositional stuff whereas drink is a functional stuff (drink is *for* drinking and quenching thirst). (For more on this puzzle and the compositional-stuff/functional-stuff distinction, see Bealer 1987.) But how does the compositional/functional distinction help to explain the curious asymmetry in our intuitions?

An answer (though perhaps not the only answer) may be formulated within the partial-content theory sketched in §7. According to it, the Platonic concepts of being a compositional stuff and being a functional stuff figure somehow in the sortal content of respective propositions about water and food The simplest way this could happen would be that the sortal content of the former would just *be* the concept of being a compositional stuff, and the sortal content of the latter would just *be* the concept of being a functional stuff.[43] But this would be too hasty.

We have a wealth of other twin-earth intuitions which go against this simple proposal. Here are three illustrative examples concerning water. (i) If, like jade, all and only water here on earth falls into two distinct kinds whose instances, respectively, are samples of UVW and XYZ, then on a twin

earth a stuff all of whose instances are composed of XYZ *would* qualify as a *kind* of water, (ii) If, like live coral or caviar, all and only water here on earth is composed entirely of certain micro-organisms, then on a twin earth a stuff which contains no micro-organisms whatsoever but which nevertheless contains the same chemicals as those found in samples of water on earth would *not* qualify as water.[44] (iii) If every disjoint pair of samples of water here on earth have different microstructural compositions but nevertheless uniform macroscopic properties, then on a twin earth a stuff which has those same macroscopic properties would qualify as water.

In the case of drink, on the other hand, twin-earth intuitions have a pattern of their own which is distinctively different from that of the various twin-earth intuitions concerning water.

Considerations like these suggest that the simplified partial-content view suggested above needs to be replaced with a subtler view. It is here that the idea suggested in connection with the Venus example in §7 comes into play. There we saw that names need not have a *determinate* sortal content; rather, they can have a content which serves merely to restrict the range of permissible sortals. For example, in the case of "water", the sortal content would be an intension which encodes the information contained in the twin-earth intuitions. As in the Venus example, this sortal content would be a coarse-grained Platonic property equivalent to a conjunction of default conditionals. Of course, in the case of "drink" the sortal content would be different, as is reflected in the differing pattern in the twin-earth intuitions. In each case, however, the respective Platonic sortal content is what drives our intuitions. Those intuitions provide us with a limited amount of a priori knowledge about water and food (e.g. the a priori knowledge associated, pro and con, with the respective twin-earth examples themselves). By contrast, the non-Platonic components ("water" and "food") are largely opaque to intuition; our knowledge of relevant modal truths concerning them requires empirical investigation.

We have here the makings of an explanation of the a priori evidence (twin-earth intuitions, etc.) needed to justify the philosophical doctrine of scientific essentialism and, at the same time, an explanation of why various modal propositions about specific natural kinds (and their microstructure) require empirical investigation, making them essentially a posteriori. *Summary*. My overall purpose here has been twofold. First, I have tried to show how the traditional theory of propositions can be developed without resorting to reductionism. Second, I have tried to show how the resulting non-reductionist framework provides a promising style of solution to the problem of fine-grained content. I would not claim that these proposals are entirely correct; surely some adjustment will be needed. But I hope they make it plausible that the two problems – the problem of reductionism and the problem of fine-grained content – do not, as some of our contemporaries fear, undermine the traditional theory of propositions itself.[45]

Notes

1 I will focus on proper names, but there are analogous problems – and solutions (see §9.3) – involving predicates. For example, "Whatever chews masticates" and "Whatever masticates chews" prima facie do not mean *exactly* the same thing, but how is this possible given that "chew" and "masticate" are predicates for one and the same property? The solutions to these various problems can, I believe, be adapted to handle the problems Stephen Schiffer presents in "Belief Ascription" (1992) and other papers and, if desired, to systematize his resulting view that propositions are "shadows of sentences". See note 42 below.

2 Some singular-proposition theorists hope to use conversational pragmatics to explain the evident difference between, say, the proposition that Cicero is Tully and the proposition that Cicero is Cicero. But this does nothing to explain how the proposition that Cicero is Tully can be both necessary and a posteriori; according to scientific essentialism, however, *that very proposition* (not *other* propositions supplied by conversational pragmatics) must have both features.

3 See, for example, Adams (1974), Jubien (1988), Bealer and Mönnich (1989), and many others.

4 The fallacy of incomplete analysis is of a piece with the doctrine that a whole sentence (proposition) is the smallest unit of analysis. It has been invoked in defending Frege's analysis of number against the objection that it has the implausible consequence that numbers have elements, e.g. that $\{1\}$ is an element of the number 1. I need not take a stand on whether this defense of Frege succeeds. The point in the text is that possible-worlds theorists are in a different situation once they accept the basic tenets of the traditional theory of propositions.

5 In Bealer (1998b) I show that the transmodal problem which confronts the propositional-complex reduction also undermines possible-worlds reductions, and I further argue that the standard possible-worlds treatment of modal language is unsatisfactory.

6 This difficulty is not a Cantor-style worry about cardinality. (See, for example, Davies 1981, p. 262.) I am willing to assume that the latter worry can be avoided with some new kind of set theory.

Incidentally, there are variants of the present problem that beset the original possible-worlds reduction.

7 Possible-worlds theorists might deny this by appealing to a *Russell*-style theory of types, but there are persuasive arguments that a type-theoretic treatment of modal language is unacceptable. They might also respond by holding that there is no property of being a necessary proposition, but in the context this would be absurd.

8 In Bealer (1993a) I explain this problem of transmodal quantification in greater detail. In that discussion, the worry about the "fallacy of incomplete analysis" is avoided without having to assume the traditional theory of propositions, as I do here.

9 One could replace "$x = y$" with "if x and y exist, $x = y$".

10 On a closely related propositional-function theory (suggested by Alonzo Church and others), the sense of a predicate of individuals is a function from individual concepts (e.g. senses of proper names of individuals) to propositions. This theory runs into problems analogous to those discussed in the text. For further discussion of these and kindred points, see Bealer (1989).

11 In what follows I will indicate how to construct non-reductionist models (what I call "intensional structures") for the theory of properties, relations, and propositions. One could instead try to construct models based upon possible-worlds functions, propositional complexes, or propositional functions. Such models, however, would be mere representational devices: in them the entities playing the role of properties, relations, and propositions would not be the real thing but only artificial surrogates (extensional functions, ordered sets). By contrast, in the intensional structures described below, the entities playing that role are those very properties, relations, and propositions. Surely, if reductionism is mistaken, one ought to be able to construct models which are non-reductionist in this sense.

12 Thus, an intensional structure is a triple $< D, \tau, K >$. The domain D partitions into subdomains: $D_{-1}, D_0, D_1, D_2, \ldots$ Subdomain D_{-1} consists of particulars; D_0, propositions; D_1, properties; D_2, binary relations; etc. τ is a set of

logical operations on D. K is a set of extensionalization functions. G is a distinguished function in K which is the actual extensionalization function.

13 See Plantinga (1983). The special contribution of the non-reductionist approach is that it provides a way to develop anti-existentialism without having to posit necessarily unanalyzable individual essences (i.e. primitive "Haecceities").

14 In Bealer (1993a) I argue that no form of existentialism can accommodate transmodal sentences like these. I should emphasize, however, that the general non-reductionist approach given in the present paper is strictly neutral on the existentialism/anti-existentialism debate.

15 One could replace "$x = x$" with "if x exists, $x = x$".

16 The following intuitively true sentence can be treated in this way: "Possibly, there exists an x such that, possibly, there exists a y such that the proposition that x and y do not coexist is necessarily true".

17 For a qualification on the question of actualism, see §8.5.

18 If, instead, one were to systematize the informal theory by identifying the sense of a predicate of individuals with a function whose arguments are individual concepts and whose values are propositions, the relation of descriptive predication would collapse into a special case of the relation of application of function to argument. This approach, however, exposes the informal theory of senses to the flaws noted earlier in connection with the propositional-function reduction. When the informal theory is divorced from the propositional-function reduction, one arrives at the picture presented in the text.

19 See Neale (1990). Neale's elegant treatment provides truth conditions but does not identify the *propositions* expressed by such sentences. This remaining task is what is accomplished by the ideas being described in the text.

20 That is, the domain D is the union of disjoint subdomains $D_{-1}, D_0, D_1, D_2, \ldots$, where D_1 is thought of as consisting of properties (or concepts).

21 As Kit Fine says, "Under this alternative conception, what would be an empirical fact is that the word, or token of it, existed. But given the word, it would be essential that it meant what it did" (Fine 1994, p. 13).

22 If some other kind of non-Platonic mode of presentation (besides names, practices, trees) proved to be more promising, "Cicero" would be a mode of presentation of that kind.

23 For all $x \in D$, if $x \in G$ (being a person), then for all possible extensionalization functions H, $x \in H$ (being a person). (As before, G is the actual extensionalization function.) Some essentialists deny that each person is necessarily a person; instead, they hold that each person is such that, necessarily, *if he exists*, he is a person. If this is right, we would

require: if $x \in G$ (being a person), then, for all H, if $x \in H(E)$, $x \in H$ (being a person).

24 I am taking it for granted that "Cicero" and "Tully" are rigid. In the case of living names, it is essential to them that they name what they do. In any case, Kripke's doctrine is that names are rigid, whether or not they are living names. In the case of naming practices, if there were a practice of using "Cicero" to refer to someone other than Cicero, it would not be *our* practice (i.e. *this* very practice of using "Cicero" to refer to *him*). The same thing holds for historical naming trees, for the origin of an historical naming tree is an essential part of it. (This is not to say that every part of an historical naming tree is an essential part of it, any more than every part of an oak tree is an essential part of it.)

25 Likewise, pred_d (pred_d (identity, "Tully"), "Cicero") has the same modal value (i.e. necessity) that Kripke and others attribute to the proposition that Cicero = Tully. Because pred_d (pred_d (identity, "Tully"), "Cicero") is a posteriori, we are thus able to explain how the proposition that Cicero = Tully can be both necessary and a posteriori, as scientific essentialism requires. This generalizes to solve the problem (discussed at the outset of the paper and in note 2) which confronts singular-proposition and hidden-indexical theories. In §9.5 I will indicate how, at the same time, we are able to know a priori that, *if* Cicero = Tully, the proposition that Cicero = Tully is both necessary and a posteriori.

26 That is, there are possible extensionalization functions H such that pred_d(being a person, "Cicero") $\in H(E)$ and "Cicero" $\notin H(E)$.

27 The propositional-complex theory could be extended to incorporate non-Platonic modes of presentation. Predictably, our previous arguments would then apply against this extended theory. But there would be another problem as well. On the extended theory the proposition that Tully is a person would be identical to the ordered set <being a person, "Tully">. Intuitively, however, it would be possible for Tully to exist even if this ordered set did not, for it would be possible for Tully to exist and the non-Platonic mode "Tully" not to exist (for example, when Tully has no name at all). The extended propositional-complex theory therefore has the implausible consequence that there are possible circumstances in which the person Tully exists but the proposition that Tully is a person does not!

28 In Bealer (1998a) I develop this idea informally under the rubric of the "categorial parts" of a concept.

29 That is, for all extensionalization functions H, $x \in H(C)$ iff $x \in H$ ("Cicero") and $x \in H$ (being a person).

30 Why not identify C with a standard coarse-grained intension? The reason is that it would then be indis-

tinguishable from conj("Tully", being a person), and our solution to Frege's puzzle would fail.

31 These points, together with §9.3 and note 42, show why Stephen Schiffer's skepticism (1992) about a propositional treatment of mental content is not justified. To begin with, most of Schiffer's arguments are aimed against hidden-indexical theories; since the present theory is not of that type, those arguments do not apply. Schiffer's main arguments against the present theory would evidently be an adaptation of his arguments against Fregean theories. For that style of argument to work against our theory, evidently Schiffer would need to assume something like the following: if our analysis of the proposition that Cicero is a person were correct, then whoever believed this proposition would need to believe – or be disposed to believe – that "Cicero" is a mode of presentation of the object of his belief. (Likewise, Schiffer would evidently need to suppose that, if two people believe this proposition, they would have to "think of" Cicero in the same way, namely, as falling under the mode of presentation "Cicero".) But this requirement is implausible: to someone who believes this proposition, the proposition is seamless; no auxiliary beliefs about – or dispositions to have beliefs about – the indicated mode of presentation are required (and there is no one "way" in which the person must "think of" the object). If there is doubt about this, I suspect it results from a lingering commitment to a reductionist view of propositions, specifically, to some kind of propositional-complex theory. Indeed, Schiffer explicitly attributes such a view to contemporary Fregeans. True, if to believe a proposition is to believe an ordered set, say, $<$ mode$_1$, mode$_2$ $>$, there would be a temptation to think that the modes of presentation making up this ordered set are transparent to the believer. But genuine propositions are seamless, and the believer is typically in the dark about how they should be analyzed and, in particular, about what modes of presentation would be involved in the analysis.

32 A range of philosophers have advocated this view. For a development of an externalist version, see Bilgrami (1992).

33 Likewise, an advocate of interpretive liberalism might, as in P. T. Geach's example, hold that it would be appropriate for a reporter to say that Hob believes that a witch blighted the sheep and Nob believes that she killed the cow (Geach 1967). The logical analysis of Nob's proposition might involve the non-Platonic mode of presentation "she", where "she" might be the very token produced by the reporter. See §9.2 below.

34 For example, u is a mode of presentation iff pred$_d(v, u)$ has a value for some argument v.

35 Suppose that propositional-attitude states must be invoked in answering the indicated questions.

Someone might worry that the answers must then be circular. But it can be shown, I believe, that this is not so.

36 Here is one way in which this may be done. Singleton sets consisting of anti-existentialist singular identity properties are to be the indicated ersatz entities: a singleton set $\{x\}$ plays the role of a "non-actual" iff it is *possible* that there exist an entity y such that $x =$ the property of being identical to y but that there does not *actually* exist anything y such that $x =$ the property of being identical to y.

37 In this setting, all the elements of D are actually existing particulars and genuine properties, relations, and propositions.

38 Katz (1994) proposes an elegant descriptivist solution to Kripke's puzzle which is metalinguistic in a standard sense. Unlike Katz's solution, the proposal in the text is designed to be neither descriptivist nor metalinguistic in any standard sense.

39 Or he might also believe the singular proposition neg(pred$_s$(being pretty, London)). This proposition does not contradict the one he believed originally, for pred$_s$(being pretty, London) $\neq$ pred$_d$(being pretty, "Londres")).

If the interpretative liberalism described in §8.2 is correct, there might be an interpretative context in which it would be correct to report that Pierre believes both the proposition that London is pretty and its negation and, hence, that he has contradictory beliefs. Suppose so. Then the puzzle in the text would concern *other* interpretative contexts in which it would not be correct to report this. In such contexts, what propositions would we hold to be the objects of Pierre's beliefs when he sincerely asserts the indicated sentences? The proposal in the text is designed to answer that question.

40 Kripke (1979) poses a second puzzle. In one conversation Peter sincerely and literally states "Paderewski has musical talent". But not knowing that the prime minister is the famous pianist, Peter in a subsequent conversation sincerely and literally states "Paderewski does *not* have musical talent". On the most straightforward interpretation, I believe it would be appropriate to say that Peter asserts and believes contradictory propositions, for example, pred$_d$(having musical talent, "Paderewski") and neg(pred$_d$(having musical talent, "Paderewski")). One reason is this. Suppose that someone else, Paul, states the same two sentences except that Paul knows that the prime minister is the pianist. Although Paul speaks literally, he does not speak sincerely when he states the second sentence; on the contrary, he is telling a lie. Plainly, Paul asserts contradictory propositions. But surely he asserted the same things Peter asserted. To deny this, one would have to hold that Paul's mere intention to lie prevents Peter and Paul from

communicating! Now Peter believed what he asserted, for he spoke sincerely. Since he asserted the same contradictory propositions asserted by Paul, it follows that Peter's beliefs are contradictory. This, of course, does not show that Peter was irrational. Rationality is determined, not by *all* of a person's beliefs, but only by a more privileged subset of them. Such propositions may be straightforwardly characterized within the proposed theory of propositions. Note that this theory is not itself committed to Peter's having contradictory beliefs; alternative interpretations are plainly feasible within the theory.

41 Alternatively, "she" could be what Hans Kamp calls a discourse object (Kamp and Reyle 1993). Kamp's theory could be integrated into the theory of propositions presented here. This would fill a gap: as it stands his theory provides truth conditions for relevant sentences, but it does not tell us what *propositions* are expressed by such sentences.

42 Of course, it is also natural to use "Whatever masticates chews" to express a "mixed" proposition whose logical analysis involves both a non-Platonic mode of presentation ("masticate") and a Platonic mode (the property of chewing). Likewise for "Whatever chews masticates". The difference between these two mixed propositions resides solely in the *order* in which these modes of presentation appear in the analyses.

By generalizing the ideas in the text all the way, one can get a family of propositions whose logical analysis involves exclusively non-Platonic modes of presentation (living names, living predicates, etc.) – and, of course, logical operations. The resulting propositions may be thought of as mere "shadows of sentences", as in Schiffer's recent view (Schiffer 1994). Unlike Schiffer, however, one would not be forced to give up compositionality and the various highly plausible explanations it provides.

A related idea is that a non-Platonic mode of presentation "arthritis" might well be involved in the logical analysis of the oblique object-level use of "arthritis" discussed by Tyler Burge (1979).

43 The proposition that water is plentiful would be $\text{pred}_d(\text{plentiful}, W)$, where W is conj("water", being a compositional stuff). And the proposition that drink is plentiful would be $\text{pred}_d(\text{plentiful}, D)$, where D is conj("drink", being a functional stuff). There are, of course, associated *de re* propositions in whose analysis W would instead be conj(being identical to x, being a compositional stuff), where x is water itself, and D would be conj(being identical to y, being a functional stuff), where y is drink itself. But the moral would be much the same: if someone were to intuit *de re* propositions concerning water and drink, it would be the Platonic sortal contents, not the objects x and y themselves, that would drive the intuitions.

44 Analogy: Suppose that you kill the live coral, crush the result, and reconfigure the remaining powder into rock-like "reefs". Now synthesize a chemically equivalent rock-like material and configure it into "reefs" on twin earth. Is it really coral?

45 I gave earlier versions of this paper at the 1990 European Summer School in Logic, Linguistics, and Information at the University of Leuven, the 1992 American Philosophical Association Pacific Division Meeting, the University of Padua, École Polytechnique, Stanford University, UCLA, and University of Alberta. I am grateful for the very helpful comments made by members of the audiences during those sessions. I give a technical development of many of the ideas here in Bealer (1993b).

I presented the algebraic approach to the theory of propositions in "Theories of Properties, Relations, and Propositions" (1979), *Quality and Concept* (1982), and "Completeness in the Theory of Properties, Relations, and Propositions" (1983). The main ideas of this approach were developed in my dissertation, University of California at Berkeley, 1973.

References

Adams, Robert M. 1974: "Theories of Actuality". *Nous*, 8, pp. 211–31.

Bealer, George 1979: "Theories of Properties, Relations, and Propositions". *The Journal of Philosophy*, 76, pp. 634–48.

—— 1982: *Quality and Concept*. Oxford: Clarendon Press.

—— 1983: "Completeness in the Theory of Properties, Relations, and Propositions". *The Journal of Symbolic Logic*, 48, pp. 415–26.

—— 1987: "Philosophical Limits of Scientific Essentialism". *Philosophical Perspectives*, 1, pp. 289–365.

—— 1989: "On the Identification of Properties and Propositional Functions". *Linguistics and Philosophy*, 12, pp. 1–14.

—— 1993a: "Universals". *The Journal of Philosophy*, 90, pp. 5–32.

—— 1993b: "A Solution to Frege's Puzzle". *Philosophical Perspectives*, 7.

—— 1998a: "A Theory of Concepts and Concept Possession". *Philosophical Issues*, 8.

—— 1998b: "Universals and Properties", in S. Laurence and C. Macdonald (eds.) *Contemporary Readings in the Foundations of Metaphysics*, Oxford: Blackwell.

Bealer, G. and Mönnich U. 1989: "Property Theories". *Handbook of Philosophical Logic*, 4, pp. 133–251.

Bilgrami, Akeel 1992: *Belief and Meaning*. Oxford: Blackwell.

Burge, Tyler 1979: "Individualism and the Mental". *Midwest Studies in Philosophy*, 4, pp. 73–122.

Davies, Martin 1981: *Meaning, Quantification, Necessity: Themes in Philosophical Logic*. London: Routledge and Kegan Paul.

Fine, Kit 1994: "Essence and Modality". *Philosophical Perspectives*, 8, pp. 1–16.

Geach, P.T. 1967: "Intentional Identity". *The Journal of Philosophy*, 64, pp. 627–32.

Jubien, Michael 1988: "Problems with Possible Worlds", in D.F. Austin (ed.) *Philosophical Analysis*, Dordrecht: Kluwer, pp. 299–322.

Kamp, H. and Reyle, U. 1993: *From Discourse to Logic: Introduction to Model Theoretic Semantics of Natural Language, Formal Logic and Discourse Representation Theory*. Dordrecht: Kluwer.

Katz, Jerrold J. 1994: "Names without Bearers". *The Philosophical Review*, 103, pp. 1–40.

Kripke, Saul 1979: "A Puzzle about Belief", in A. Margalit (ed.) *Meaning and Use, Papers Presented at the Second Jerusalem Philosophical Encounter*, Dordrecht: D. Reidel, pp. 239–83.

——1980: *Naming and Necessity*. Cambridge, Mass.: Harvard University Press.

Neale, Stephen 1990: "Descriptive Pronouns and Donkey Anaphora". *The Journal of Philosophy*, 87, pp. 113–50.

Plantinga, Alvin 1983: "On Existentialism". *Philosophical Studies*, 44, pp. 1–20.

Schiffer, Stephen 1992: "Belief Ascription". *The Journal of Philosophy*, 89, pp. 499–521.

——1994: "A Paradox of Meaning". *Nous*, 28, pp. 279–324.

PART III

Quantifiers and Quantificational Theory

Introduction to Part III

The theory of quantifiers has been a major focus of interest and controversy in the philosophy of logic. Classical predicate logic interprets quantifiers existence-presuppositionally, quantifying only over existent objects in a semantic domain.

Yet even within classical predicate logic, a choice quickly emerged between two ways of understanding the nature of quantification. Quantifiers can be regarded objectually as involving a set of objects, all or some of which are said to belong to the extension of a predicate in a quantified logical expression. But quantifiers can also be interpreted substitutionally. A universal quantification is true just in case it remains true for all substitutions of terms of the same type as that of the universally bound variable. An existential quantification is true just in case it remains true for at least one substitution of any term of the same type as the existentially bound variable. By considering terms rather than objects, some substitutional quantificationalists in logic hope to avoid philosophical entanglements about the metaphysics of objects, and work out the truth conditions for quantified expressions in logic in a more self-contained way limited to the logic's immediate syntax and semantics.

Quantifiers have sometimes been understood as reducible and hence dispensable in logical theory, where a universal quantification of the form "For all x, x has property F", or $(\forall x)\ Fx$, is true if and only if Fa is true and Fb is true and Fc is true, and so on, for all the objects in the logic's semantic domain, Fa & Fb & Fc & ...& ... The trouble lies in the necessary clause, "for *all* the objects in the

logic's semantic domain," which entails an evident circularity in the attempt to explicate the concept "all" in universal quantifications and the use in predicate symbolic logic of the universal quantifier. An exactly parallel problem affects the proposal to reduce the existential quantifier in quantifications of the form, "There is some or exists at least one object x such that x has property F," "$(\exists x)\ Fx$," by means of disjunctions rather than conjunctions, in $Fa \lor Fb \lor Fc \lor ... \lor ...$ The problem here as before with the effort to reduce the universal quantifier is that a quantifier must be surreptitiously introduced into the analysis in order for the reduction to work.

In the case of the universal quantifier, we will not have effected a reduction of the quantifier when we try to replace it with the conjunction Fa & Fb & Fc & ...& ..., unless we know that these are *all* the objects, and that they *all* have property F. This immediately takes us back to the universal quantifier rather than providing a way of doing without it; similarly for the reduction of the existential quantifier by means of a string of disjunctions. The analysis of the universal and existential quantifiers in light of this objection is doomed either to inadequacy or circularity. The only solution to the problem that has been seriously considered in the philosophical literature is that of Ludwig Wittgenstein's *Tractatus Logico-Philosophicus*, in which the so-called picture theory of meaning prevents the set of all objects from being spoken of in a correct logical symbolism. Wittgenstein reduces the universal quantifier to conjunctions of singular predications and the existential quantifier to disjunctions of singular predications. The reduction appears to work only because the *Tractatus* distinction between what can be said and what can only be pictured or shown implies that the completeness of a conjunction or disjunction of singular predications in a reduction of the meaning of the conventional quantifiers in predicate logic is shown by these being all of the objects, which strictly speaking cannot be said. Equally, however, since it is shown or exhibited in the logic under complete analysis into its simplest elements, it does not need to be said. Unfortunately, to understate things, Wittgenstein's picture theory of meaning is no longer widely accepted, and was rejected even by Wittgenstein later in his career, as he turned from the logic of the *Tractatus* to the methods and analogies of his later philosophy. The effort to reduce quantifiers to propositional connectives like the conjunction and disjunction is generally understood as a failed effort in the early philosophy of logic, even for easily surveyable domains of finitely many objects serving as the values of quantifiers and quantifier-bound variables.

The essays in this section reflect a variety of philosophical problems about the logical status of quantifiers and quantification. Czeslaw Lejewski in "Logic and Existence," considers inferences that appear to contradict the classical quantifier rules of universal instantiation and existential generalization. He accordingly defines two interpretations of quantifiers, unrestricted and restricted, according to which quantification, respectively, either is or is not separated from the concept of existence. Lejewski concludes that inferences are correct under the unrestricted interpretation, but not under the restricted concept. Whereas in restricted quantification to write $(\exists x)Fx$ is (objectually interpreted) to say that some real existent object has property F, on Lejewski's preferred unrestricted interpretation, it is only to say that an object existent or nonexistent has the property. The difference is almost but not quite satisfactorily captured in ordinary English in the distinction between saying "There *exists* an x such that Fx" versus "There *is* an x such that Fx," the latter of which requires for its full expression a more explicit qualification as to the ontic neutrality of the quantifier.

Charles Parsons opens the controversy concerning objectual as opposed to substitutional interpretations of the quantifiers in his essay, "A Plea for Substitutional Quantification." Parsons

investigates the ontological implications of the substitutional interpretation, and the extent to which adopting a substitutional as opposed to objectual interpretation may make it possible to avoid certain types of ontological commitments, in particular, to abstract entities. Ruth Barcan Marcus, an early advocate of the substitutional interpretation of quantifiers, in her essay, "Nominalism and the Substitutional Quantifier," similarly looks into the question of whether the substitutional interpretation is a potential philosophical ally of nominalism. Nominalism is the metaphysical view that there are no abstract entities, but that we language users merely give the same name (Latin: *nomen*) to a multiplicity of things having similar characteristics. The difference is seen in the fact that on an objectual interpretation of the existential quantifier, to say that $(\exists x)PrimeNumber\text{-}x$ seems to be committed to the existence of prime numbers as real existent abstract objects, whereas on a substitutional interpretation, the sentence is made true provided that there is at least one substitution of a term (say, "3") for the existentially bound variable "x" for which the sentence is true, with no further need to inquire about the ontological status of 3 as an object, let alone as an abstract object. Marcus concludes that nominalists can indeed find aid and comfort in the substitutional interpretation, which she defends against several types of objections.

Thomas Baldwin, in "Interpretations of Quantifiers," takes as his task the clarification of alternative ways of understanding the semantics of quantifiers, with special emphasis on the relation between objectual, which he attributes to Tarski, and substitutional interpretations. In addition to providing a useful survey of the controversy, Baldwin considers the philosophical issue of whether alternative interpretations of the quantifiers are ultimately reducible to the objectual. By means of a formally elaborate development of counterexamples, Baldwin argues against the thesis that all quantification is or is finally reducible to Tarskian objectual quantification. Baldwin's argument, unlike Parsons's, does not constitute a recommendation for substitutional quantification, but proves if correct that at least substitutional quantification is not logically equivalent to the standard objectual interpretation.

A later Wittgenstein approach to problems of quantifiers is taken by Jaakko Hintikka in "Language Games for Quantifiers." Hintikka applies Wittgenstein's notion of a language game to the meaning of quantifications in logic and ordinary language. Like Wittgenstein, Hintikka examines a large variety of expressions in which quantifiers appear, and he pursues the games analogy to some depth, trying to identify the rules and purposes of such linguistic activities as a clue to their logically correct interpretation, ultimately in support of substitutional quantification. He describes an ingenious game in which quantifiers are used to mark moves in the game by which quantifiers are alternately iterated by a game player and an opponent, in which the player's object is to make a substitution instance for the quantifiers in a sentence by which the sentence comes out true, and the opponent's object is to try to do the same to make the sentence false. Variations on the game are further elaborated in an interesting series of complications, in which Hintikka emphasizes an analogy between gamesmanship in the language game for quantifiers and the ordinary activity of searching and trying to find something, notably a true or false substitution instance for a quantifier bound variable. Hintikka argues that insofar as the analogy holds, it implies that efforts to interpret quantifiers without taking into account this common feature of seeking and finding revealed by the family of language games he introduces are unlikely to succeed.

Further Reading

Davies, M. K. 1981: *Meaning, Quantification, Necessity*. London: Routledge.

Benthem, Johan van. 1986: *Essays in Logical Semantics*. Dordrecht: D. Reidel.

Fine, Kit. 1985: *Reasoning with Arbitrary Objects*. Oxford: Blackwell.

Gottlieb, Dale. 1980: *Ontological Economy: Substitutional Quantification and Mathematics*. Oxford: Oxford University Press.

Grover, Dorothy. 1992: *A Prosentential Theory of Truth*. Princeton: Princeton University Press.

Kripke, Saul A. 1976: "Is there a Problem about Substitutional Quantification?" in Gareth Evans and John McDowell (eds), *Truth and Meaning*: 325–419. Oxford: Oxford University Press.

Krynicki, Michal, et al. 1995: *Quantifiers: Logic, Models and Computation*. Vol. 1. Dordrecht: Kluwer Academic Publishers.

Lindström, Per. 1966: "First-Order Predicate Logic with Generalized Quantifiers." *Theoria*, 32: 186–95.

Quine, Willard Van Orman. 1953: *From a Logical Point of View*. Cambridge: Harvard University Press.

Richard, Mark. 1995: *Logic and Reality: Essays in Pure and Applied Logic*. Oxford: Oxford University Press.

10

Logic and Existence

Czeslaw Lejewski

I have given my essay this title because it roughly indicates the boundaries of the topic to be discussed and at the same time hints at the method that will be adopted in my analysis. The problem of existence will interest me only to the extent to which it enters the province of logical enquiry and I shall try to disentangle it a little by departing from the generally accepted interpretation of the quantifiers and by bringing in other concepts related to that of existence.

When we have to commit ourselves to asserting or rejecting propositions like

$$\text{electrons exist} \qquad (1)$$

$$\text{minds exist} \qquad (2)$$

$$\text{Pegasus exists,} \qquad (3)$$

our hesitation can be traced to two fold causes. In the first place we may not be willing to give our judgment because we are not quite certain what we mean by 'electrons' or 'minds', or we may not understand the word 'Pegasus'. In the second place we may be confused as regards the meaning of the term 'exist(s)'. It is the latter cause of our embarrassment that calls for closer attention. Let the physicist, the psychologist, and the mythologist deal with the meaning of the words 'electrons', 'minds', and 'Pegasus' respectively. The logician's task, as I understand it, will be to establish the meaning of

Czeslaw Lejewski, Logic and Existence. *The British Journal for the Philosophy of Science*, 5, 18 (1954): 104–19.

the constant term 'exist(s)' as it occurs in the function 'x exist(s)' where 'x' is a variable for which any noun–expression can be substituted.

I hope that it will be a permissible simplification to say that in recent times the discussion over the logical side of the problem of existence centres around what Professor Quine has written on the subject.[1] In presenting the views of this author I shall have to use a little more quotation than is customary as the whole matter is of exceptional subtlety.

On page 150 of Quine's *Mathematical Logic* we read:

> To say that *something* does not *exist*, or that there *is* something which *is not*, is clearly a contradiction in terms; hence '(x) (x exists)' must be true.

Let us translate this argument into a symbolic language so that its logical structure may become more perceptible. I think that the following translation stands a fair chance of being acceptable to Quine:

$$(\exists x)(x \text{ does not exist}) \equiv$$
$$(\exists x)(x \text{ exists}. \sim (x \text{ exists})) \qquad (4)$$

If instead of 'x does not exist' in the antecedent of (4) we write '$\sim (x$ exists)' then from (4) and from the circumstance that the consequent of (4), being a contradiction, is false, we get immediately

$$\sim (\exists x) \sim (x \text{ exists}), \qquad (5)$$

which in accordance with the law relating the existential quantifier to its universal counterpart is equivalent to

$$(x)(x \text{ exists}). \qquad (6)$$

This result seems to confirm our interpretation of the passage, which is in complete harmony with the opening paragraph of 'On What There Is' as this paragraph runs as follows:

> A curious thing about the ontological problem is its simplicity. It can be put into three Anglo-Saxon monosyllables: 'What is there?' It can be answered moreover in a word – 'Everything' – and everyone will accept this answer as true.[2]

But let us revert to page 150 of *Mathematical Logic*. The passage which we began to analyse just now continues thus:

> Moreover we should certainly expect leave to put any primitive name of our language for the 'x' of any matrix '$\ldots x \ldots$', and to infer the resulting singular statement from '(x) $(\ldots x \ldots)$'; it is difficult to contemplate any alternative logical rule for reasoning with names.

This logical rule, which in *Methods of Logic* is referred to by Quine as the rule of universal instantiation, owes its validity to a certain logical law which with the aid of symbols can be expressed in the following way:

$$(x)(Fx) \supset Fy. \qquad (7)$$

Now difficulties begin to appear and Quine sets them out as follows: But this rule of inference leads from the truth '(x) (x exists)' not only to the true conclusion 'Europe exists' but also to the controversial conclusion 'God exists' and the false conclusion 'Pegasus exists' if we accept 'Europe', 'God', and 'Pegasus' as primitive names in our language.[3]

From the whole passage quoted from page 150 of *Mathematical Logic* we seem to be entitled to conclude that for Quine (6), i.e. '(x) (x exists)', is a truth while (3), i.e. 'Pegasus exists', is a falsehood. Regarding the rule which allows us to infer 'Fy' from '(x) (Fx)', Quine cautiously remarks that

> it is difficult to contemplate any alternative logical rule for reasoning with names.

He is more outspoken in his 'Notes on Existence and Necessity', to which we now turn.

In that paper Quine discusses inferences which could be exemplified by the one whereby from

$$\text{Pegasus does not exist} \qquad (8)$$

we infer

$$(\exists x)(x \text{ does not exist}) \qquad (9)$$

in virtue of the rule which allows us to infer '$(\exists x)$ (Fx)' from 'Fy'.[4] In 'Notes on Existence and Necessity' and in *Methods of Logic* this rule is described as the rule of existential generalisation, and we may add at once that it derives its validity from the following logical law:

$$Fy \supset (\exists x)(Fx). \qquad (10)$$

According to Quine (8) would be true but (9) would be false. Regarding the rule he observes the following:

> The idea behind such inference is that whatever is true of the object designated by a given substantive is true of something; and clearly the inference loses its justification when the substantive in question does not happen to designate.[5]

I think that we have come to a point where a brief summary of Quine's argument may not appear to be superfluous. We have two inferences:

Inference 1

From

$$(x) \ (x \text{ exists})$$

we infer

$$\text{Pegasus exists}$$

by universal instantiation.

Inference 2

From

$$\text{Pegasus does not exist}$$

we infer

$$(\exists x) \ (x \text{ does not exist})$$

by existential generalisation.

According to Quine both these inferences are objectionable to our intuitions. In his opinion they lead from truths, '$(x)(x \text{ exists})$' and 'Pegasus does not exist', to falsehoods, 'Pegasus exists' and '$(\exists x)$ (x does not exist)'. In other words the logical laws (7) and (10), which we thought to be behind the rule of universal instantiation and the rule of existential generalisation, do not hold for every interpretation of 'F' and every substitution for the free variable. If we interpret 'F' as 'exists' and substitute 'Pegasus' for 'y', (7) turns out to be false. Similarly, (10) turns out to be false for the same substitution if we interpret 'F' as 'does not exist'. But no difficulty arises if the noun-expressions substituted for 'y' in (7) and (10) are non-empty:

$$(x)(x \text{ exists}) \supset \text{Socrates exists} \qquad (11)$$

$$\begin{array}{r} \text{Socrates does not exist} \supset \\ (\exists x)(x \text{ does not exist}) \end{array} \qquad (12)$$

are true propositions.

A remedy that might suggest itself to an unscrupulous mind would be to ban the use of empty noun-expressions and consider them as meaningless. Quine is right in not following this course. One may disagree as to the truth-value of the proposition 'Pegasus exists' but one would have to have attained an exceptionally high degree of sophistication to contend that the expression was meaningless. Quine does not think that empty noun-expressions are meaningless just because they do not designate anything. He allows for the use of such words as 'Pegasus', 'Cerberus', 'centaur', etc. under certain restrictions and tries to distinguish between logical laws which prove to be true for any noun-expressions, empty or non-empty, and those which hold for non-empty noun-expressions only. It follows from his remarks that before we can safely use certain laws established by logic, we have to find out whether the noun-expressions we may like to employ, are empty or not. This, however, seems to be a purely empirical question. Furthermore, all the restrictions which according to Quine must be observed whenever we reason with empty noun-expressions, will have to be observed also in the case of noun-expressions of which we do not know whether they are empty or not.

This state of affairs does not seem to be very satisfactory. The idea that some of our rules of inference should depend on empirical information, which may or may not be forthcoming, is so foreign to the character of logical enquiry that a thorough re-examination of the two inferences may prove to be worth our while. Let us then try to find out on what grounds (6) is asserted as true while (9) is rejected as false, and let us find out also on what grounds the rules of universal instantiation and existential generalisation are regarded as inapplicable to reasoning with empty names. In seeking answers to the above questions we shall have to turn to the interpretation of the quantifiers.

Regarding Quine's interpretation of the quantifiers, which is the one accepted by the majority of modern logicians, we have a very useful passage in the *Methods of Logic*. It reads as follows:

> If we think of the universe as limited to a finite set of objects $a, b, \ldots, h$, we can expand existential quantifications into alternations and universal quantifications into conjunctions; '$(\exists x) Fx$' and '$(x) Fx$' become respectively:
>
> $$Fa \lor Fb \lor \ldots \lor Fh, \quad Fa \cdot Fb \ldots \ldots Fh \text{[6]}$$

To have a still simpler though fictitious example let us think of the universe as limited to two objects **a** and **b**. Then the corresponding expansions would be:

$$Fa \lor F\mathbf{b} \text{ and } Fa \cdot F\mathbf{b}$$

Our language, which for reasons of simplicity needs not synonyms, may leave room for noun-expressions other than the singular names '**a**' and '**b**'. We may wish to have a noun-expression '**c**' which would designate neither of the two objects, in other words which would be empty, and also a noun-expression '**d**' which would designate either. Introducing noun-expressions is a linguistic matter. It does not affect our assumed universe, which continues to consist of **a** and **b** only. The new noun-expressions can now be put to use. For instance we can form the following true proposition; '**c** does not exist', and on turning '**d**' into a predicate-expression '**D**' we can further assert that '$(x) (\mathbf{D} \ x)$' is true. To say that something exists means the same as to say that it belongs to the universe. Thus '**a** exists' and '**b** exists' are true propositions. From the expansion of the existential quantification we see that either of these two propositions implies '$(\exists x)$ (x exists)'. But we have no ground to contend that '**c** does not exist' implies '$(\exists x)$ (x does not exist)'. Again since '**a** does not exist or **b** does not exist' is false, we conclude from the expansion that '$(\exists x)$ (x does not exist)' is also false. Hence '(x) (x exists)' is true. This is confirmed by the expansion of the universal quantification and in view of the circumstance that '**a** exists and **b** exists' is true. We also learn from this expansion that '(x) (x exists)' does not imply '**c** exists'. Within our fictitious universe the rule of universal instantiation and the rule of existential generalisation fail if applied to '**c**' or '**d**'. They are valid rules of inference if their application is restricted to reasoning with '**a**' and '**b**'.

But this is not the only possible interpretation of the quantifiers. With the aid of the same fictitious example I shall now present an interpretation which as far as I can judge, is in harmony with the one adopted for instance by Les'niewski of the Warsaw School.

Our universe consisting of **a** and **b** remains the same but the quantifiers read differently. Under the present interpretation '$(\exists x)$ (Fx)' becomes:

$$Fa \lor Fb \lor Fc \lor Fd$$

Correspondingly, '(x) (Fx)' is to mean:

$$Fa \,.\, Fb \,.\, Fc \,.\, Fd$$

Thus one can argue that '$(\exists x)$ (x does not exist)' is true because '**c** does not exist', which under the new interpretation is one of the components of the existential expansion, is true. Hence '(x) (x exists)' is false. This is confirmed by the corresponding universal expansion, which contains a false component, namely '**c** exists'. Under this interpretation the rule of universal instantiation and the rule of existential generalisation are valid without any restrictions. They can be safely applied in reasoning with any noun-expressions: singular non-empty like '**a**' and '**b**', empty like '**c**', or general non-empty like '**d**'. The noun-expression '**d**' need not be changed into the corresponding predicate-expression '**D**'.

These two different interpretations of the quantifiers, which in what follows, will be referred to as the *restricted* interpretation and the *unrestricted*

interpretation respectively, can now be generalised to apply to a universe with any number of objects. In the case of a finite universe we have finite expansions which are equivalent to their respective quantifications. If, however, we think of the universe as consisting of an infinite or unknown number of objects then we cannot have equivalences for the simple reason that we can never form complete expansion of our quantifications. Consequently we abandon equivalences in favour of implications. We say that an existential quantification is implied by any component of its infinite or unknown expansion and that a universal quantification implies any component of its infinite or unknown expansion. Now the expansions will vary depending on how we choose to interpret the quantifiers. Under the restricted interpretation every component of an expansion contains a noun-expression which designates only one of the objects belonging to the universe. Under the unrestricted interpretation every component of an expansion contains an expression of which we can only say that it is a meaningful noun-expression. It may designate only one of the objects belonging to the universe, it may designate more than one, or it may designate nothing at all.

The two interpretations of the quantifiers give rise to two different theories of quantification and we may well be expected to say a few words on the relation in which one theory stands to the other. In this respect the most important point is that whatever is said with the aid of the theory of restricted quantification, can be easily expressed in terms of the unrestricted quantification provided we are allowed to use the notion of existence. A few examples set out below in the form of two lists will suffice to illustrate the procedure:

I

Expressions to be understood in the light of the restricted interpretation:

$$(x)(Fx) \supset Fy \tag{7}$$

$$Fy \supset (\exists x)(Fx) \tag{10}$$

$$(x)(Fx) \equiv\, \sim (\exists x)(\sim Fx) \tag{13}$$

II

Corresponding translations to be understood in the light of the unrestricted interpretation:

$$(x)(x \text{ exists} \supset Fx) \supset Fy \qquad (7a)$$

$$Fy \supset (\exists x)(x \text{ exists} . Fx) \qquad (10a)$$

$$(x)(x \text{ exists} \supset Fx) \equiv \sim (\exists x)(x \text{ exists} \sim Fx) \quad (13a)$$

It is not difficult to check that under their respective interpretations the corresponding expressions in the two lists yield the same truth value for the same substitutions performed on the free variables regardless of how we choose to interpret the predicate letters. The general rule for translating expressions is simple: expressions of type '(x) (Fx)' and '$(\exists x)$ (Fx)' become expressions of type '(x) $(x \text{ exists} \supset Fx)$' and '$(\exists x)$ $(x \text{ exists} . Fx)$' respectively; other expressions remain unchanged.

Thus, for instance, (6) and (9) translated for the purpose of the unrestricted interpretation become

$$(x)(x \text{ exists} \supset x \text{ exists}) \qquad (14)$$

and

$$(\exists x)(x \text{ exists} . x \text{ does not exist}) \qquad (15)$$

respectively. These translations fully account for the assertion of (6) and the rejection of (9) under the restricted interpretation of the quantifiers. Similarly (7a) and (10a) make it clear why (7) and (10) do not turn out true for all interpretations of 'F' and for all substitutions for the free variable. For if we interpret 'F' as 'does not exist' and substitute 'Pegasus' for 'y' then the antecedent of (7a) becomes a tautology but at the same time the consequent turns out to be false. And again, if we interpret 'F' as 'does not exist' and substitute 'Pegasus' for 'y' then the antecedent of (10a) comes out true but the consequent must be rejected as a contradiction. Thus for certain interpretations of 'F' (7) and (10) turn out to be false if we substitute an empty noun-expression for the free variable. Consequently the rules of universal instantiation and existential generalisation, which derive their validity from (7) and (10), can no longer be applied without restrictions.

The position is different if we choose to understand the quantifiers in the light of the unrestricted interpretation. (3), which is 'Pegasus exists', and (8), which is 'Pegasus does not exist', are meaningful propositions either of which contains a noun-expression, viz. 'Pegasus'. Thus (3) and (8) may be regarded as components of quantificational expansions. Now, (3) being false, the corresponding universal quantification, i.e. '(x)

$(x$ (exists)', which ought to imply any component of its expansion, must also be false. On the other hand, (8) being a true proposition the corresponding existential quantification, i.e. '$(\exists x)$ (x does not exist)', which is implied by any component of its expansion, must also be true. Thus under the unrestricted interpretation of the quantifiers the two inferences on p. 148 cannot be used as counter examples to disprove the validity of the rules of universal instantiation and existential generalisation in application to reasoning with empty noun-expressions. In Inference I both the premiss and the conclusion are false, while in Inference II both the premiss and the conclusion are true. There is nothing wrong with the inferences provided we adopt the unrestricted interpretation of the quantifiers. Furthermore, under the unrestricted interpretation the logical laws (7) and (10) turn out to be universally true. For every proposition of type 'Fa' where 'a' stands for any noun-expression, empty or non-empty, is now regarded as a component of the quantificational expansions and consequently is implied by the corresponding proposition of type '(x) (Fx)' and implies, in turn, the corresponding proposition of type '$(\exists x)$ (Fx)' (7) and (10) being universally true, the rule of universal instantiation and the rule of existential generalisation are universally valid as the principles that are behind them are no longer principles by courtesy.[7]

The unrestricted interpretation of the quantifiers seems to remove yet another difficulty from quantification theory. It has been argued by several authors that

$$(\exists x)(Fx \vee \sim Fx) \qquad (16)$$

and

$$(x)(Fx) \supset (\exists x)(Fx), \qquad (17)$$

which are valid if the universe is not empty, fail for the empty universe as their truth depends on their being something. When discussing these laws Quine tries to dismiss the case of the empty universe as relatively pointless and reminds us that in arguments worthy of quantification theory the universe is known or confidently believed to be non-empty. This contention, however, does not quite remove our uneasiness particularly as (16) and (17), not unlike (7) and (10), are demonstrable in quantification theory.

On considering (16) and (17) we readily admit that these two formulae fail for the empty universe if we understand the quantifiers in accordance with the restricted interpretation. This becomes evident from

$$(\exists x)(x \text{ exists} \cdot (Fx \vee \sim Fx)) \qquad (16a)$$

and

$$(x)(x \text{ exists} \supset Fx) \supset (\exists x)(x \text{ exists} \cdot Fx), \quad (17a)$$

which are the corresponding translations of (16) and (17) to be understood in the light of the unrestricted interpretation. If there exists nothing then (16a) and the consequent of (17a) are obviously false while the antecedent of (17a) is obviously true. Under the unrestricted interpretation, however, (16) and (17) come out to be true irrespective of whether the universe is empty or non-empty. For (16) is implied by any component of type '$Fav \sim Fa$' where 'a' stands for a noun-expression. In particular it is implied by a component '$Fav \sim Fa$' in which 'a' stands for an empty noun-expression. Such a component is true for all choices of universe and so is (16). In the case of (17) we argue as follows: if we assume that the antecedent of (17) is true then a proposition of type 'Fa' where 'a' stands for an empty noun-expression must also be true in harmony with the unrestricted interpretation of the universal quantifier. Now any such proposition implies the proposition of type '$(\exists x) (Fx)$', which again must be true. Thus in the establishing of the truth value of (16) and (17) the problem of whether the universe is empty or non-empty is altogether irrelevant on condition, of course, that we adopt the unrestricted interpretation of the quantifiers.

It ought to be evident from what has already been said that under the unrestricted interpretation existential quantifications have no existential import. In fact it would be misleading to read '$(\exists x)(Fx)$' as 'there exists an x such that Fx'. The non-committal 'for some x, Fx' seems to be more appropriate. Similarly the terms 'existential quantification' and 'existential quantifier' no longer apply and could be conveniently replaced by such expressions as 'particular quantification' and 'particular quantifier'. The rule of existential generalisation could perhaps be referred to as the rule of 'particular generalisation'.

Finally, the unrestricted interpretation in comparison with the restricted one appears to me to be a nearer approximation to ordinary usage. Somehow we do not believe that *everything exists* and we do not see a contradiction in saying that *something does not exist*. It is only from logicians who favour the restricted interpretation that we learn that things are the other way round. We may further add that the unrestricted interpretation of the quantifiers is in complete harmony with the formal quantification theory. I do not know of any formulae which are demonstrable in the formal quantification theory and which, under the unrestricted interpretation, are not applicable to reasoning with empty noun-expressions or do not hold for universes of some specific size.

When we consider (7), (10), (13), (16), and (17) as understood in the light of the restricted interpretation and compare them with their corresponding translations for the purpose of the unrestricted interpretation, i.e. with (7a), (10a), (13a), (16a), and (17a), we cannot fail to notice that the idea of the restricted quantification is not a simple one. The translations reveal that it can be analysed into two separate constituents: the idea of the unrestricted quantification on the one hand and the notion of existence on the other. In my opinion the most serious disadvantage of the theory of the restricted quantification is that by merging the idea of quantification with the notion of existence it has put logicians and philosophers on a wrong track in their endeavours to elucidate the problem of existence in logic. In what follows we shall adhere to the theory of unrestricted quantification and we shall attack the problem of existence in logic by determining the meaning of the constant term 'exist(s)' as used in the function 'x exist(s)'.

From the logical point of view there are two satisfactory methods of determining the meaning of a constant term. The one consists in setting forth a set of axioms for the term in question. The other is adopted whenever we give a definition of the term in question with the aid of other terms whose meaning has already been determined axiomatically.[10] We may add at once that we shall employ the latter method.

The meaning of 'exist(s)' can best be determined on the basis of the logic of noun-expressions constructed as a deductive system by Leśniewski in Warsaw in 1920 and called by him 'Ontology'.[11] The original system of Leśniewski's Ontology is based on singular inclusion (*a is b* or in symbols $a \, \varepsilon \, b$) as the only primitive function. For various reasons, however, I prefer to continue my analysis of 'exist(s)' with reference to a system of Ontology based on ordinary inclusion, which I shall write in the following manner:

$$a \subset b \qquad (18)$$

I shall read it 'all a is b' or 'all a's are b's'. I prefer doing this because ordinary inclusion seems to be more intuitive to an English speaking reader than Leśniewski's singular inclusion. Thus for instance ordinary inclusion has recently been used by Woodger in his 'Science without Properties'[12] for the purpose of constructing a language whose general tendency approximates the tendencies embodied in Ontology.

The functor of ordinary inclusion is a proposition forming functor for two arguments either of which is a noun-expression. If in (18) we substitute constant noun-expressions for the variables 'a' and 'b' then the result of the substitution will be true if and only if everything named, or designated, by the noun-expression substituted for 'a' is also named by the noun-expression substituted for 'b'. It may be of some historical interest to mention that the above semantic characterisation of inclusion can be traced back to Hobbes who used it in order to determine the meaning of the copula 'est' in propositions such as 'homo est animal'.[13]

From the semantic characterisation of inclusion[14] it is evident that the following propositions are true:

> man $\subset$ animal
> man $\subset$ man
> Socrates $\subset$ man
> Socrates $\subset$ Socrates
> Pegasus $\subset$ animal
> Pegasus $\subset$ Socrates
> Pegasus $\subset$ Pegasus

The last three propositions are true because nothing is designated by 'Pegasus'. Thus whatever is designated by 'Pegasus', is designated by anything you like. The corresponding proposition can be formulated in symbols as follows:

$$(a)(\text{Pegasus} \subset a) \qquad (19)$$

If instead of 'Pegasus' in (19) we write the constant noun-expression 'Λ', which designates nothing, then we shall get the following ontological thesis:

$$(a)(\Lambda \subset a) \qquad (20)$$

'Λ' can be defined in terms of inclusion but for the sake of simplicity I prefer to introduce it as an undefined term with the aid of (20).

In order to determine the meaning of 'exist(s)' we shall need three definitions, which I write below in the form of equivalences:

$$(a)(\text{ex}(a) \equiv (\exists b)(\sim (a \subset b))) \qquad (21)$$

$$(a)(\text{sol}(a) \equiv (b, c, d)(\sim (c \subset d) \cdot (b \subset a) \cdot$$
$$(c \subset a) \supset (b \subset c))) \qquad (22)$$

$$(a)(\text{ob}(a) \equiv \text{ex}(a) \cdot \text{sol}(a))^{[15]} \qquad (23)$$

For the present we need not trouble ourselves with the question how to read the newly defined functors. We can proceed straight on to the consequences which can be deduced from (20) and the three definitions.

Thus from (21) we immediately get

$$\text{ex}(\Lambda) \equiv (\exists a)(\sim (\Lambda \subset a) \qquad (24)$$

Since from (20) we know that

$$\sim (\exists a)(\sim (\Lambda \subset a) \qquad (25)$$

we use (25) and (24) to show that

$$\sim (\text{ex}(\Lambda)) \qquad (26)$$

From (26) we obtain, by particular generalisation,

$$(\exists a)(\sim (\text{ex}(a))) \qquad (27)$$

which is equivalent to

$$\sim (a)(\text{ex}(a)) \qquad (28)$$

From (23) and (26) we conclude that

$$\sim (\text{ob}(\Lambda)) \qquad (29)$$

From (29) we get

$$(\exists a)(\sim (\text{ob}(a))) \qquad (30)$$

which is equivalent to

$$\sim (a)(\text{ob}(a)) \qquad (31)$$

We can now draw Pegasus into our deductions. From (19) we immediately obtain

$$\sim (\exists a)(\sim (\text{Pegasus} \subset a)) \qquad (32)$$

and use it together with (21) to show that

$$\sim (\text{ex}(\text{Pegasus})) \qquad (33)$$

From (23) and (33) we derive

$$\sim (\text{ob}(\text{Pegasus})) \qquad (34)$$

Now (27), (28), (30), (31), (33), and (34) show that the functors 'ex' and 'ob' are very close approximations of 'exist(s)'. We remember that under the unrestricted interpretation of the quantifiers '(x) (x exists)' is false and so is '(a) (ex (a))' and '(a) (ob (a))' as is evident from (28) and (31). Under the same interpretation '$(\exists x)$ (x does not exist)'-comes out true and so does '$(\exists a)(\sim (\text{ex}(a))$' and '$(\exists a)$ (($\sim$ (ob(a))$)$' as is evident from (27) and (30).

Further evidence is supplied by (33) and (34) from which it follows that 'ex(Pegasus)' and 'ob (Pegasus)' are false just as 'Pegasus exists' is admittedly false. It remains then to be explained what is the difference in the meaning of 'ex' and 'ob'. We can find the required explanation if we consider the meaning of (22), which is a definition of 'sol'. The right hand side of this definition turns out to be true in two cases: if there is no such a thing as a or if there is only one a. Thus 'sol(a)' can be read as 'there is at most one a'. Now if we agree to read 'ex(a)' as 'a exists' or as 'a's exist' then in accordance with (23) 'ob (a)' will have to be read as 'there exists exactly one a', which is equivalent to 'a is an object' or to 'a is an individual'. Thus the distinction between 'ex' and 'ob' roughly corresponds to the one made by Quine in his 'Designation and Existence', where he talks about *general* existence statements and *singular* existence statements.[16]

We have already remarked that under the restricted interpretation every component of quantificational expansions contains a noun-expression which designates only one of the objects belonging to the universe. It therefore follows that the function 'x exists' as used by us when we discussed the two interpretations of the quantifiers, means in fact the same as 'there exists exactly one x' which is the rendering of the symbolic 'ob(x)'. The functor 'ex', on the other hand, appears to be a very close approximation of the 'exist(s)' as used in ordinary language as it forms true propositions with noun-expressions which may designate more objects than one.

I wish to conclude with a brief summary of the results. The aim of the paper was to analyse rather than criticise. I started by examining two inferences which appeared to disprove the validity of the rules of universal instantiation and existential generalisation in application to reasoning with empty noun-expressions. Then I distinguished two different interpretations of the quantifiers and argued that under what I called the unrestricted interpretation the two inferences were correct. Further arguments in favour of the unrestricted interpretation of the quantifiers were brought in, and in particular it was found that by adopting the unrestricted interpretation it was possible to separate the notion of existence from the idea of quantification. With the aid of the functor of inclusion two functors were defined of which one expressed the notion of existence as underlying the theory of restricted quantification while the other approximated the term 'exist(s)' as used in ordinary language.

It may be useful to supplement this summary by indicating some aspects of the problem of existence which have not been included in the discussion. I analysed the theory of quantification so far as it was applied in connection with variables for which noun-expressions could be substituted and my enquiry into the meaning of 'exist(s)' was limited to cases where this functor was used with noun-expressions designating concrete objects or with noun-expressions that were empty. It remains to explore, among other things, in what sense the quantifiers can be used to bind predicate variables and what we mean when we say that colours exist or that numbers exist. These are far more difficult problems, which may call for a separate paper or rather for a number of separate papers.

Notes

The first draft of this paper was presented to a post-graduate seminar at the London School of Economics on 12 November 1953, and was also read and criticised by Professors J. Łukasiewicz, K. R. Popper, W. V. Quine, and J. H. Woodger, from whose generous comments I have benefited much.

1 Quine's most important contributions in this connection are the following: 'A Logical Approach to

the Ontological Problem', *Journal of Unified Science*, Chicago, 1940, 9. This paper was read at the Fifth International Congress for the Unity of Science, Cambridge (Mass.), 1939; 'Designation and Existence', *The Journal of Philosophy*, New York, 1939, 36, also in *Readings in Philosophical Analysis*, edited by H. Feigl and W. Sellars, New York, 1949; 'Notes on Existence and Necessity', *The Journal of Philosophy*, New York, 1943, 40; 'On What There Is', *The Review of Metaphysics*, New Haven, 1948, 2, also reprinted in *Proceedings of the Aristotelian Society, Supplementary Volume XXV*, London, 1951.

This list would have to be supplemented with the titles of several, more technical papers, published by Quine in *The Journal of Symbolic Logic*, and also with some passages from his *Mathematical Logic*, Cambridge (Mass.), 1947 (second printing), and *Methods of Logic*, London, 1952.

2 See W. V. Quine, 'On What There Is', *The Review of Metaphysics*, New Haven, 1948, 2, 21.

3 See W. V. Quine, *Mathematical Logic*, Cambridge (Mass.), 1947, 150

4 See W. V. Quine, 'Notes on Existence and Necessity', *The Journal of Philosophy*, New York, 1943, 40. The inference has been rephrased so that it may conform with the example taken from *Mathematical Logic*. The original propositions are 'There is no such thing as Pegasus' and '$\exists x$ (there is no such thing as x)', respectively. See op. cit. 116.

5 See W. V. Quine, op. cit. 116

6 See W. V. Quine, *Methods of Logic*, London, 1952, 88

7 See W. V. Quine, 'Notes on Existence and Necessity', *The Journal of Philosophy*, New Haven, 1943, 40, 118

8 For details see W. V. Quine, *From a Logical Point of View*, Cambridge (Mass.), 1953, 160 sq.

9 See W. V. Quine, *Methods of Logic*, London, 1952, 96

10 See J. Łukasiewicz 'The Principle of Individuation', *Proceedings of the Aristotelian Society*, Sup. Vol. 27, London, 1953, 77 sq.

11 See S. Leśniewski, 'Über die Grundlagen der Ontologie', *Comptes rendus des séances de la Société des Sciences et des Lettres de Varsovie*, Classe III, 1930, 23. For a brief account of Ontology see K. Ajdukiewicz, 'On the Notion of Existence', *Studia Philosophica*, Posnaniae, 1951, 8 sq., or J. ukasiewicz, 'The Principle of Individuation', *Proceedings of the Aristotelian Society*, Supplementary Volume XXVII, London, 1953, 77 sq.

12 See this *Journal*, 1951, 2

13 Hobbes wrote: 'Ut qui dicit *homo est animal* intellegi ita vult ac si dixisset "si quem recte *hominem* dicimus eundem etiam *animal* recte dicimus".' See 'Leviathan', *Opera Philosophica*, iii, 497 (Molesworth); see also 'De Corpore', *Opera Philosophica* i, 27 (Molesworth).

14 Strictly speaking the meaning of inclusion ought to have been determined axiomatically. I understand from Dr B. Sobociński that Leśniewski had an axiom for inclusion. It has never been published and I never saw it when I was studying with Leśniewski in Warsaw before the war. But I found some time ago that a system of Ontology can be built up on the basis of the following single axiom:
$$(a,b)((a \subset b) \equiv (c,d)(\sim (c \subset d) \cdot (c \subset a) \supset$$
$$(\exists e,f)(\sim (e \subset f) \cdot (e \subset c) \cdot (e \subset b) \cdot (g,h,i)$$
$$(\sim (h \subset i) \cdot (g \subset e) \cdot (h \subset e) \supset (g \subset h))))).$$

15 In Leśniewski's original system of Ontology the three functors are defined as follows:
$$(a)(\mathrm{ex}(a) \equiv (\exists b)(b\ \varepsilon\ a))$$
$$(a)(\mathrm{sol}(a) \equiv (b,c)(b\ \varepsilon\ a) \cdot (c\ \varepsilon\ a) \supset (b\ \varepsilon\ c)))$$
$$(a)(\mathrm{ob}(a) \equiv (\exists b)(a\ \varepsilon\ b))$$

See T. Kotarbński, *Elementy teorji poznania, logiki formalnej i metodologji nauk* (Elements of Epistemology, Formal Logic, and Methodology), Lwów, 1929, 235 sq.; see also K. Ajdukiewicz, 'On the Notion of Existence', *Studia Philosophica*, Posnaniae, 1951, 4, 8, and J. Łukasiewicz, 'The Principle of Individuation', *Proceedings of the Aristotelian Society*, Supplementary Volume XXVII, London, 1953, 79 sq.

16 See W. V. Quine, 'Designation and Existence', in *Readings in Philosophical Analysis*, edited by H. Feigl and W. Sellars, New York, 1949, 44 sq.

11

A Plea for Substitutional Quantification

Charles Parsons

In this note I shall discuss the relevance to ontology of what is called the *substitutional* interpretation of quantifiers. According to this interpretation, a sentence of the form '$(\exists x)\ Fx$' is true if and only if there is some closed term 't' of the language such that 'Ft' is true. This is opposed to the *objectual* interpretation according to which '$(\exists x)\ Fx$' is true if and only if there is some object x in the universe of discourse such that 'F' is *true of* that object.[1]

Ontology is not the only connection in which substitutional quantification has been discussed in recent years. It has been advocated as a justification for restrictions on the substitutivity of identity in intensional languages[2] or has been found necessary to make sense of restrictions adopted in certain systems.[3] With this matter I shall not be concerned.

It might seem that in discussions of ontology the substitutional interpretation of quantifiers would be advocated in order to make acceptable otherwise questionable ontological commitments. In fact this has not been done widely, although it does seem to be an important part of Wilfrid Sellars' account of abstract entities.[4] The issue of the ontological relevance of substitutional quantification has been raised most explicitly by Quine, essentially to debunk it. He argues that only an interpretation of a theory in terms of *objectual* quantification attributes an ontology to it.

Classical first-order quantification theory on the objectual interpretation, according to Quine,

embodies the fundamental concept of existence. He acknowledges the existence of other possible concepts of existence. But he holds that substitutional quantification does not embody a genuine concept of existence at all.

I should like to argue that the existential quantifier substitutionally interpreted has a genuine claim to express a concept of existence which has its own interest and which may offer the best explication of the sense in which "linguistic" abstract entities – propositions, attributes, classes in the sense of extensions of predicates[5] – may be said to exist. I shall then raise a difficulty for the view (which Sellars may hold) that all quantification over abstract entities can be taken to be substitutional.

Quine argues as follows for the view that substitutional quantification does not correspond to a genuine concept of existence:

> Substitutional quantification makes good sense, explicable in terms of truth and substitution, no matter what substitution class we take – even that whose sole member is the left-hand parenthesis. To conclude that entities are being assumed that trivially, and that far out, is simply to drop ontological questions. Nor can we introduce any control by saying that only substitutional quantification in the substitution class of singular terms is to count as a version of existence. We just now saw one reason for this, and there is another: the very notion of singular terms appeals implicitly to classical or objectual quantification.[6]

Charles Parsons, A Plea for Substitutional Quantification. *The Journal of Philosophy*, 68, 8 (1971): 231–7.

In answer to the first objection, we should point out two formal features of the category of singular terms that mark substitutional quantification with respect to it as far less trivial than with respect to, say, the left parenthesis. First, it admits identity with the property of substitutivity *salva veritate*. Second, it has infinitely many members that are distinguishable by the identity relation. This has the consequence that '$(\forall x)\ Fx$' is stronger than any conjunction that can be formed of sentences of the form 'Ft', while '$(\exists x)\ Fx$' is weaker than any disjunction of such sentences.

With respect to the claim that the very notion of singular terms appeals implicitly to classical or objectual quantification, we might hope for a purely syntactical characterization of singular terms. However, that would not yet yield the distinction between singular terms that genuinely refer and those which do not; in a language in which the latter possibility arises, the substitutional quantifier for singular terms would express not existence but something closer to Meinong's "being an object."

However, we can concede Quine's point here for a certain central core class of singular terms, which we might suppose to denote objects whose existence we do not expect to explicate by substitutional quantification. We might then make certain analogical extensions of the class of singular terms in such a way that they are related to quantifications construed as substitutional. The criterion for "genuine reference" is given in other terms.

For example, the following is a natural way to introduce a predicative theory of classes (extensions of predicates). Let 'F' stand for a one-place predicate of some first-order language. We first rewrite 'Ft' as '$t\varepsilon\{x\colon Fx\}$' and (taking '$\alpha$', '$\beta$', ... as schematic letters for expressions of the form '$\{x\colon Fx\}$') define '$\alpha = \beta$' as '$(\forall x)(x\varepsilon\alpha \equiv x\varepsilon\beta)$'. So far we have just made the contextual definitions involved in the theory of virtual classes.[7] We then allow the abstracts to be replaced by quantifiable variables of a new sort. The substitution interpretation gives truth conditions for formulas in the enlarged notation. The process can be repeated to introduce classes of higher levels.[8]

The advantage of substitutional quantification in this particular case is that it fits the idea that the classes involved are not "real" independently of the expressions for them. More precisely, we know the condition for a predicate to "have an extension" (that it be true or false of each object in the universe) and for two predicates to "have the same

extension" without independently identifying the extension. The fact that the substitution interpretation yields truth conditions for quantified sentences means that everything necessary for speaking of these classes as entities is present, and the request for some more absolute verification of their existence seems senseless.

The obstacle to the introduction of attributes in the same way is, of course, the problem of the criterion of identity. But the procedure goes through, given a suitable intensional equivalence relation. For example, we might introduce "virtual attributes" by rewriting 'Ft' as '$t\delta[x\colon Fx]$', introducing 'ξ', 'η' ... as schematic letters, defining '$\xi = \eta$' as '$\Box(\forall x)(x\delta\xi \equiv x\delta\eta)$', and then introducing attribute variables and substitutional quantification. Then two predicates express the same attribute provided they are necessarily coextensive.

The same procedure could be followed for other intensional equivalences, provided that they can be expressed in the object language.

Consideration of examples such as these leads to the conclusion that in the case where the terms involved have a nontrivial equivalence relation with infinitely many equivalence classes, substitutional quantification gives rise to a genuine "doctrine of being" to be set alongside Quine's and others. It parallels certain idealistic theories of the existence of physical things, such as the account of perception in Husserl's *Ideen*.

It might be thought preferable in our case and perhaps in all cases where the substitution interpretation is workable, to formulate the theory by quantifying over expressions themselves or over Gödel numbers that represent them. If one is talking of expressions or numbers already, this has the advantage of ontological economy, and in some cases, such as when one begins with elementary number theory, it makes more explicit the mathematical strength of the theory.[9] The substitutional approach avoids the artificiality involved in introducing an apparatus (be it Gödel numbering or some other) for talking *about* expressions, and it avoids the unnatural feature that identity of expressions does not correspond to identity of extensions or attributes.

In the case of attributes, however, some proposed criteria of identity, such as synonymy, are metalinguistic. Then the above substitutional introduction of attributes does not apply. Here some form of quantification over linguistic types gives the most natural formulation. An example is

Sellars' construal of attributes as synonymity-types of expression-tokens.

The manner in which we have introduced classes suggests a rather arbitrary limitation in the case where the universe for the first-order variables contains unnamed objects. For consider a two-place predicate 'F'. In a theory of virtual classes, we would admit the abstract '$\{x:Fxy\}$' with the free variable 'y', but substitutional quantification as we have explained it encompasses only closed terms. If we wish to say that for every y the class $\{x:Fxy\}$ exists, then the notion of substitutional quantification must be generalized. Suppose a language has variables of two sorts, 'X', 'Y', ... which are substitutionally interpreted, and 'x', 'y' ... which are objectually interpreted over a universe U. Then the fundamental notion (see fn 1) is satisfaction of a formula by a sequence of elements of U. A sequence s satisfies '$(\exists X)FX$' if and only if for some term 'T' of the upper-case sort, with free variables only of the lower-case sort, some extension of s satisfies 'FT'.[10]

In this case we can no longer say that classes are not real independently of expressions for them, but each class is a projection of a relation of which this *can* be said. We can say that classes are not real independently of expressions for them and individuals of the universe.

The instances of substitutional quantification we have discussed would suggest that in the process of analogical extension of the category of singular terms, the syntactic characteristics of this category are not all essential. Thus in an extensional language the role of identity can be taken over for one-place predicates by the truth of '$(\forall x)(Fx \equiv Gx)$', and the introduction of 'ramified second-order' substitutional quantifiers seems to differ only notationally from the above introduction of classes.[11] However, such a notational step as the introduction of 'ε' and abstracts is necessary if one is to take the further step of reducing the two-sorted theory to a one-sorted one. (The resulting quantifiers would have an interpretation which mixes the substitutional and the objectual.)

In connection with attributes one might be inclined to retreat another step from singular terms and forsake identity. In other words, one might regard quantification over attributes as substitutional quantification of predicates, with no equivalence relation with properties corresponding to those of identity. Here I would agree with Quine

that these "attributes" would be at best second-class entities. The ability to get at "the same object" from different points of view – different individual minds, different places and times, different characterizations by language – is one of the essentials of objective knowledge. If this is lacking, then the entities involved should be denied objective existence.

Can all quantification over abstract entities be construed as substitutional? Evidently not if sets as intended by the usual (impredicative) set theories are included. Otherwise we could certainly set up a theory that talked of numbers, of classes in a ramified hierarchy, and even (again in a ramified hierarchy) of propositions and attributes, where the quantifiers over these entities admitted a substitutional interpretation.[12]

Nonetheless there is an obstacle to taking this as implying that nonsubstitutional quantification over abstract entities is avoidable, short of set theory. The difficulty is that the truth conditions for substitutionally quantified sentences themselves involve quantification over expression-types:

'$(\exists x) Fx$' is true if for some *closed term* 't', 'Ft' is true.

Thus the question arises whether the language in which we give this explanation quantifies substitutionally or objectually over expressions. If we give the latter answer, we have of course given up the claim to rely only on substitutional quantification of abstract entities.

In the former case, the same question arises again about the semantics of the metalanguage. We are embarked on a regress that we shall have to end at some point. Then we shall be using a quantifier over expressions that we shall have to either accept as objectual or show in some other way to be substitutional. One might hope to interpret it so that it does not range over abstract entities at all, for example so that there is quantification only over tokens. The ways of doing this that seem to me at all promising involve introducing modality either explicitly or in the interpretation of the quantifier, so that one does not get an ontology of tokens in a Quinean sense.[13]

The only way I can see of showing the quantifier to be substitutional would be to show that the *given* sense of quantification over expression-types in a natural language, say English, is substitutional. This seems to me very implausible.

However, the most this argument would show is that we could not know or prove that the only quantification over abstract entities that we relied on was substitutional. It could still be that an outside observer could interpret our talk in this way. To refute the view that abstract entities (short of set theory) exist only in the substitutional sense, one needs to give a more convincing analysis of such entities as expression-types and numbers, as I have attempted to do elsewhere.[14]

Notes

I owe to Sidney Morgenbesser and W. V. Quine the stimulus to write this paper. I am also indebted to Hao Wang for a valuable discussion, and to Quine for illuminating comments on an earlier version.

1 It is noteworthy that the substitutional interpretation allows truth of, say, first-order quantified sentences to be given a direct inductive definition, while in the objectual interpretation the fundamental notion is truth *of* (satisfaction), and truth is defined in terms of it. Davidson's version of the correspondence theory of truth would not be applicable to a substitutional language. See "True to the Facts," *Journal of Philosophy*, LXVI, 21 (Nov. 6, 1969): 748–64.

Quine has pointed out to me that in a language with infinitely many singular terms, a problem arises about defining truth for *atomic* formulas. Objectual quantification can be nontrivial for a language with no singular terms at all, but, if there are such, the problem can be resolved by an auxiliary definition which assigns them denotations, relative to a sequence that codes an assignment to the free variables. In the substitutional case, we need to define the truth of an atomic formula $Pt_1 \ldots t_m$ directly for closed terms $t_1 \ldots t_m$, for example, inductively by reducing the case for more complex terms to that for less complex terms. In the usual language of elementary number theory, closed terms are constructed from '0' by applications of various function symbols which (except for the successor symbol, say 'S') have associated with them defining equations that can be regarded as rules for reducing closed terms to canonical form, namely, as numerals (a numeral is 'S' applied finitely many times to '0'), so that an atomic formula $Pt_1 \ldots t_m$ is true if and only if $Pn_1 \ldots n_m$ is true, where n_i is the numeral corresponding to t_i. The truth of predicates applied to numerals is defined either trivially (as in the case of '=') or in a similar recursive manner.

Quine discusses this issue in §6 of an unpublished paper, "Truth and Disquotation."

2 Ruth Barcan Marcus, "Modalities and Intensional Languages," *Synthese*, XIII, 4 (December 1961): 303–22. Reprinted in I. M. Copi and J. A. Gould, eds., *Contemporary Readings in Logical Theory* (New York: Macmillan, 1967), pp. 278–93. Cf. W. V. Quine, "Reply to Professor Marcus," *Synthese, loc. cit.*: 323–30; reprinted in Copi and Gould, pp. 293–9; also in *The Ways of Paradox* (New York: Random House, 1966), pp. 175–82.

3 Particularly Hintikka's. See Dagfinn Føllesdal, "Interpretation of Quantifiers," in B. van Rootselaar and J. F. Staal, eds., *Logic, Methodology, and Philosophy of Science* III (Amsterdam: North Holland, 1968), pp. 271–81, and papers by Hintikka and Føllesdal referred to there.

4 "Abstract Entities," *Review of Metaphysics*, XVI, 4 (June 1963): 627–71, reprinted in *Philosophical Perspectives* (Springfield, Ill.: Charles C. Thomas, 1967), pp. 229–69. Sellars' general strategy is to treat attributes and classes as analogous to linguistic types and then to quantify substitutionally over them. This seems to be open to the objection presented below. Sellars' account of classes seems to yield a predicative theory of classes and thus would not justify set theory. See "Classes as Abstract Entities and the Russell Paradox," *Review of Metaphysics*, XVII, 1 (September 1963): 67–90; also *Philosophical Perspectives*, pp. 270–90. In studying these two papers I have relied heavily on Gilbert Harman's lucid review of *Philosophical Perspectives*, this *Journal of Philosophy*, LXVI, 5 (March 13, 1969): 133–44.

5 This account of classes would suggest distinguishing *classes* in this sense from *sets* as the objects of set theory. One can, I believe, motivate the requirement of predicativity for the former. It is they which are paralleled to attributes. It is noteworthy that there is no reason to make impredicative assumptions about the existence of attributes, unless (as in Quine's interpretation of Russell's no-class theory) one seeks to reduce sets to attributes.

6 *Ontological Relativity and Other Essays* (New York: Columbia, 1969), p. 106. Cf. pp. 63–4.

7 Quine, *Set Theory and Its Logic* (Cambridge, Mass.: Harvard, 2nd ed. 1969), p. 15.

8 Quine carries out the first stage of this substitutional introduction of classes in *Philosophy of Logic* (Englewood Cliffs, N.J.: Prentice-Hall, 1970), pp. 93–4. If classes are introduced in this way in a language that is not extensional, such as modal logic, then the restrictions on substitutivity of identity associated with a substitutional semantics have point.

9 See for example the last section of my "Ontology and Mathematics," *The Philosophical Review*, LXXX, 2 (April 1971): 151–76.

10 The direct construal of classes as expressions fails in this case, and if the universe is of larger cardinality than the set of expressions of the language, classes

159

cannot be so construed even artificially. But of course classes *can* be construed as pairs consisting of an expression and a sequence of substituends for the free variables.

11 Montgomery Furth in "Two Types of Denotation," *Studies in Logical Theory*, American Philosophical Quarterly Monograph Series no. 2 (Oxford, Blackwell, 1968), pp. 9–45, reconstructs along these lines Frege's idea of predicates as "denoting" concepts rather than objects. He does not remark that on this reconstruction Frege is unjustified in using full (impredicative) second-order logic for quantifying over concepts (more generally, functions). But replacing it by a ramified second-order logic would require him to abandon his Cantorian conception of cardinal number.

Frege's principle that words have meaning (Bedeutung) only in the context of proposition, and his use of it to defend his thesis that numbers are objects, suggests a substitutional account of quantification over "logical objects" such as (on his view) numbers and extensions. Cf. my "Frege's Theory of Number," in Max Black, ed., *Philosophy in America* (London: Allen & Unwin, 1965), pp. 180–203.

12 Whether in the original sense or in the generalized sense of two paragraphs back would depend on whether the universe of concrete individuals contained unnamed objects. One would suppose the projections referred to above would be needed for some applications.

13 See section III of "Ontology and Mathematics," cited in note 9 above.

14 *Ibid.*

12

Nominalism and the Substitutional Quantifier

Ruth Barcan Marcus

It has been suggested that a substitutional semantics for quantification theory lends itself to nominalistic aims. I should like in this paper to explore that claim.

Debates about nominalism and realism can be seen in relief against background theories about the relation of a language to the objects which the language purports to be about. Confining ourselves to those parts of a language which are vehicles for truth claims, complete sentences, or statements if you like, the supposition of nominalists and realists alike is that there are, in any meaningful statement, links between some or all of the words in the statement, taken singly or in concatenation, and objects which the statements are about. Statements contrive somehow to mention or refer, directly or obliquely, to objects. Plato,[1] in arguing against the Sophists' claim that erroneous beliefs are not about anything, says, "Whenever there is a statement it must be about something," and that, he claimed, holds for true statements as well as false ones.

Statements, true or false, speak of objects. In this, nominalists and realists are generally in agreement. The disagreement on the metaphysical side is about which objects; what exactly is being mentioned, directly or indirectly by a statement. The disagreement on the linguistic side is about which words are doing the mentioning. Which words in the statement are bearing the burden of reference; all of them, some of them, and if not all of them,

what work is being done by the others. The question echoes the distinction between categorematic (referring) and syncategorematic (nonreferring) terms. Historically, the focus of the debate has been the claim of realists that predicate expressions (often broadly conceived to include common nouns and the like as well as verbs) can with a bit of pushing and shoving, be seen as designating objects; the universals. Among the universals are properties, attributes, relations, or the less abstract, but abstract nevertheless, classes or sets. The realist further claims that those objects are of a categorically different kind, or at least a different species from the particulars. Particulars are the concrete individuals which are the nominalists' preferred ontology. The relation between particulars and the purported designata of predicates is called misleadingly, since it seems a grammatical term, that of "predication." Historically, as we know, there is considerable variation as to what counts as concrete individuals. Nominalists have made varying claims, some of them reductionist, as to whether there are basic particulars such as events, physical atoms, sense data, time slices of physical objects, out of which other particulars are constructed. But in all its vicissitudes, the primary motivation of nominalism in virtually all of its manifestations has not merely been an insistence on the one category of individuatable objects. There is the empirical thrust. The nominalist's individuals are of a kind which can be confronted or in the least, make up such confrontable or encounterable individuals. They can, so to speak, put in an appearance. Encounterability by the

Ruth Barcan Marcus, Nominalism and the Substitutional Quantifier. *The Monist* **61, 3 (1978): 351–62.**

mind's eye is not generally counted in the spirit of nominalism.

The empirical momentum of nominalism carries it beyond the disclaimer about universals. The nominalist sets himself the task of arguing that abstract "entities" such as numbers, minds, propositions, even where categorically construable as individuals, are in the least otiose, or alternatively, not the abstract objects they are claimed to be. Numbers, for example, may be seen as constructable out of inscriptions; propositions may be seen as an outcome of confusion of material and formal mode and the like. In summary, nominalism has traditionally moved along two tracks. First, there are not two sorts of things, universals and particulars which bear an irreducible relation to one another. Second, the empirical thrust, individuals are in one way or another held to be encounterable objects. A philosopher who moves along either track designates himself as nominalistically inclined.

We noted above that nominalist-realist debates will be reflected in accounts of which expressions in a statement bear the burden of reference. A philosopher whose ontology includes universals, as well as propositions, numbers and other abstract objects must articulate which components of a statement mention such objects. The philosopher who eschews such putative objects must explain how those components, if they do not refer, are to be understood. How do they work? What do they contribute to the meaning, the content, or more modestly, the truth conditions of the statement? Displaying the referential apparatus of a statement often takes the form of providing an "analysis;" e.g., replacing it by one which is arguably equivalent but which is said better to display or articulate the locus of reference. Russell's theory of descriptions and Quine's conversion of proper names into predicates are two related examples.

If it is names which are the vehicles of reference, then nominalist-realist disagreements will be reflected in what is to be counted as a name. The tendency has been to call any expression a name, however distant from the familiar grammatical category of nouns, provided it is seen as referring. Similarly, genuine name status is denied to terms which are relieved of the burden of reference however they may have been classified grammatically. Quine,[2] for example, denies that any nouns need to be construed as names, proper or otherwise.

Setting aside questions of origin; whether it is someone's convictions about ontology, meager or ample, which leads him to view some words or concatenations of words as referring names, or whether it is the surface grammar which compels the ontology, or the interplay between them, it is surely the case that there are few words or word sequences about which there has been uniform agreement as to whether they refer; whether "logical grammar" reveals them as names. There are those who have claimed that a sentence names a proposition, or it names a possible state of affairs. For Frege a sentence is contextually ambiguous naming the true or the false in *oratio recta* and a thought or a proposition in *oratio obliqua*. Quantifiers such as 'nothing' have been interpreted as naming nothingness (*vide* Husserl) or the set of nonexistent objects. The more traditionally syncategorematic expressions such as 'or', 'not', 'and' have not always been spared reference. 'Not' is seen as naming the falsity property or, more constrained, the set of false propositions. 'Or' names alternativeness of or the set of pairs of propositions at least one of which has the truth property and so on. Being itself has been viewed as referent of the verb 'to be'.

There has been more general agreement about the role of proper names, names of individuals, as reference bearers but here too, there are demurrers. It has been claimed that to be a genuine proper name, the name *must* refer for otherwise it is without meaning and any sentence of which it is a part would not be sufficiently definite to warrant its having a truth value. Russell, noting that there are meaningful statements with vacuous proper names, argues that it is not ordinary, but rather "logically" proper names which refer and those proper names defy incorporation into any common tongue. Quine, in one of his philosophical stances, assimilates proper names into predicates altogether. The words which do the referring in 'Socrates is a philosopher' do not even occur in the surface structure of that sentence. They are implicit, to be made explicit by the use of quantifiers and variables as in 'There is something that Socratizes and is a philosopher.' Nevertheless, for the nominalist with an ontology of empirically distinguishable objects, proper names are seen as a primary vehicle for reference. Those objects are of the kind which at least theoretically, can be properly named by an act of ostension.

Let us suppose that the realists we are juxtaposing against the nominalists are not of the most lavish kind. Both agree that there are concrete individuals which are not predicated of anything.

The realist also admits referents of predicates; universals, (or more modestly sets) which are of a different category in that the relationship between an individual and a universal is not eliminable or reducible to a relation among individuals. The realist generally holds the relation of predication to be irreflexive and asymmetric. If the realist claims, as he usually does, that properties and relations may themselves have the properties and enter into relationships, then if the relation of predication is taken as univocal, it is generally held to be intransitive: a hierarchical ordering with individuals at the base – the zero level objects.

A major task of nominalists is then to explain how predicates work. In recent years, attempts to give a formal account of nominalism have gone in two directions. The first is to reconstruct the prediction relation as one which holds between individuals. The second is to deny altogether the referential function of predicates. Predication ceases to be understood as a relation between objects.

The first kind of reconstruction may take different forms.[3] One is to conceive of a predicate as having divided reference. Let 'S' name some individual and let 'P' be a monadic predicate, then 'S is P' is interpreted as saying that S is identical with one of the referents of P. 'P' does not name a set here. The relation of predication is that of identity with one of the referents of the predicate. There is no new object for the predicate to name. Another reconstruction which reduces predication to a relation among zero level individuals is to view it as inclusion between parts and wholes all of which are individuals and where the whole is generated by its ultimate parts. The part whole analysis can take two forms. In 'S is P', S may count as the part of P the whole analogous to some interpretations of mass nouns where for example, 'water' is viewed as the name of an individual made up of dispersed individual parts. An alternative is to count P as the part and S the whole. The case where, for example, individuals are seen as bundles of qualities and it is the qualities which are the ultimate individual parts.

A further reductive alternative is to take the relation of predication as similarity and 'P' as naming some selected individual which serves as a standard. Predication is then likeness with respect to some feature of S and some feature of P.

In the foregoing proposals, the predicate 'P' is claimed to refer, whether singly or multiply. The relation of predication is one between individuals

of the same type level whether it be similarity, identity or part-whole. Contrasted with such reductive theories is the other direction a nominalist reconstruction can take. Predication is not seen as a relation between objects. It is viewed as a grammatical construction which generates open sentences from predicates and variables when arranged in proper order as in 'x flies' or 'x fears y'. Those constructions can be understood by an English speaker without there being something to be named by 'fears' or 'flies'. The open sentences generated by predication are satisfied or not satisfied by individuals or sequences of individuals. They are, speaking elliptically, true of the objects which satisfy them.

It is not my purpose to evaluate the success of the various nominalistic enterprises. Indeed, I do not see the proposals as necessarily competitive since there is no reason to suppose that predication demands a uniform analysis. In the present paper, I will be concerned primarily with the last mentioned alternative, or weakly realist modifications of it: I will be considering either the no-name theory of predication which views predicates as akin to the syncategorematics or weakly realist extensions which views predicates as naming sets of individuals, and predication as a relation of membership.

In contrast to the non-referential role which nominalism has traditionally tried to assign to expressions which do not name individuals, names of individuals have traditionally been assigned an important referential role. Proper names were viewed as linguistic "signs" for concrete, particular, encounterable objects. Hobbes saw proper names as linguistic conventions devised to function like natural, non-linguistic signs of actual objects. With the development of formal logic and its standard semantics, proper names have been taken on a more subsidiary role even for those with nominalist inclinations. It is important for the subsequent discussion of the relation between the substitutional quantifier and nominalism to consider the grounds for the shift in the role assigned to proper names. There is the obvious fact that of the nominalists' nameable objects, very few are actually named. Meaningful sentences, true or false, which are about such objects, may contain no names at all such as 'Something is green'. However, implicit in even medieval nominalism[4] is the suggestion that the absence of actual names is accidental. The nominalist's objects are in principle nameable and (the meaning of) sentences like 'Something is green' were taken as abbreviating a finite disjunction of singular sentences where expressions in subject position are proper names. (Also, implicit here is that names, given that they are conventional signs, are theoretically always available). Similarly, the universal quantifier was interpreted as abbreviating a conjunction of singular sentences. In modern quantification theory, it was not the absence of actual names, but rather the possibility of an infinity of objects which was the catalyst for introducing quantifier as primitive logical operators. An adequate language for referring to infinitely many objects would seem to require variables and quantifiers in addition to names. But Quine and others have pressed even further. Do we need proper names of individuals at all? Can variables and quantifiers be made to bear the entire burden of reference? The suggestion is already manifest in Russell's theory of descriptions. Russell noted that singular descriptions function grammatically (in surface grammar) like ordinary proper names. But there are vacuous descriptions such as 'the present king of France' and, since for Russell, *genuine* names must refer, singular descriptions are not genuine names. Yet, statements in which vacuous descriptions occur are not incomplete; they have a truth value. So, there must be a way of unpacking statements with singular descriptions to preserve their "content" and in which singular descriptions are seen not to be genuine names. The theory of descriptions provides the mode of translation. 'The present king of France is bald' becomes roughly "There is something and just one, such that it is a present king of France and bald". Unpacked the statement contains quantifiers and other logical operators, variables and predicates. Russell, without abandoning proper names as a vehicle for reference altogether (he retained the elusive "logically" proper names) does go on to say that what prompts the analysis for singular descriptions seems also to prompt it for ordinary proper names. If it makes sense, as it seems to, to ask whether Homer exists, then there are vacuous ordinary proper names. Ordinary proper names must therefore also fail to be genuine proper names and Russell sees them as classifiable along with the singular descriptions. He called them "truncated descriptions." Whether Russell is claiming that we can select out some particular descriptive characterization of which the ordinary proper name is an abbreviation is not of concern to us here. Once the similarity is noted, the analysis

can be pressed. On the theory of descriptions, descriptive phrases work like predicates and the most straightforward recognition of that logical role for ordinary proper names is to convert names directly into predicates. Hence Quine's unabashed proposal that we transform ordinary proper names into verbs in our formal or "regimented" language. 'Pegasus is a winged horse' goes into 'There is something and only one such that it Pegasizes, is winged, and is a horse'. As in the case of vacuous descriptions, the latter turns out to be false. Pursuing this analysis Quine[5] calls proper names, even where they name individuals which are in a domain of genuine objects, "a frill." They are he says, "a mere convenience and strictly redundant."

It should be noted that whereas the no-name theory of *predicates* is consistent with nominalist aims, the redundancy theory of proper names *does*, in my view, represent a departure from traditional nominalism. It is true that the redundancy theory of proper names does not claim that proper names do not refer but only that the work can better be done by quantifiers and variables. Still, the redundancy theory does claim a *priority* for quantifiers and variables as the machinery for reference. In this there is a considerable departure from traditional nominalism where the role of names as conventional signs for objects has been central to the theory of reference. I want to claim that one of the connections which holds between substitutional quantification and nominalism is that in substitutional theory, names are not frills. They are not redundant and eliminable. The juncture at which substitutional theory and the referential theory of quantifiers overlap is where the substitution class consists of genuine proper names: where the names link up with objects.

Consider a standard first order language without identity. It has a denumerable stock of variables, individual constants, and predicate letters for n'adic predicates. It contains sentential connectives and quantifiers. Formulae are defined inductively. Closed formulae are sentences. Individual constants correspond to proper *names*. A standard interpretation of such a language is given roughly as follows. A domain of individuals is specified over which variables and quantifiers are said to "range." Individual constants do not range but name specific objects. On the no-name theory of predication, predicates name nothing. On the more standard interpretations, sets of objects are assigned to predicates; just those sets of n'tuples which satisfy the open atomic formula containing the predicate. Truth is defined for sentences of the language *via* the semantical notion of satisfaction of formula by a sequence of objects. The procedure is familiar and we need not spell it out.[6] Given the inductive definition of truth is derivative. It is a property of quence of objects, the definition of truth is derivative. It is a property of sentences. A sentence is true just in case it is satisfied by some sequence. What should be noted is that variables do not function as mere place markers. They take objects as values relative to a sequence of objects. Since satisfaction of quantifies formulae is defined relative to objects in the domain they can be read with existential import: "There is something such that. . . ." "Everything is such that. . . ."

On a substitutional semantics of the same first order language, a domain of objects is not specified. Variables do not range over objects. They are place markers for substituends. Satisfaction relative to objects is not defined. Atomic sentences are assigned truth values. Truth for sentences built up out of the sentential connectives are defined in the usual way. The quantifier clauses in the truth definition say that

> *(x)Ax* is true just in case *A(t)* is true for all names *t*
> *(∃x)Ax* is true just in case *A(t)* is true for at least one name *t*.

In the above summary characterization of a substitutional semantics the substitution class is taken as the class of proper names; just those expressions which on the referential interpretation refer univocally to objects. However, given the detachment of the substitutional quantifier from reference, and given the truth definition in terms of replacement of variables by expressions, substitution classes (and associated quantifiers) can be expanded. Predicates and sentences can, *inter alia*, also compose substitution classes. If sentences are to be included, inductive requirements constrain permissable substitutions to those which reduce complexity.[7] The same would hold had individual descriptions been included in the substitution class of names.

Before proceeding to the question of the relevance of substitutional semantics to nominalistic aims, a word about further comparisons between the alternative interpretations. Saul Kripke,[8] in a recent important paper, has given the most definitive and detailed account of the substitutional quantifier to date. He sees the substitutional quantifier as appended to a base language, all of whose sentences are taken as atomic relative to that extension. His generalization allows as a base language, a first order language with referential quantifier. The substitutional first order language presented in the present paper may be viewed as a minimal extension allowed by Kripke's more general characterization, the base language being one which contains no quantifiers.[9] What Kripke proposes is that the substitutional quantifier is not a replacement for, or in competition with, the standard interpretation. If notational differences are preserved which distinguish both kinds of quantifiers and variables, the two kinds can occur concurrently and coherently in the extended language. I have a different view of the matter. I see the substitutional account as the most general. Of the many substitution classes for which the quantifier may be defined, one contains expressions which are vehicles for immediate reference; the grammatically proper names. That names may have such a special role with respect to encounterable objects seemed to me apparent.[10] *How* they come to such a role has been illuminated by the causal theory of names elaborated by Kripke[11] and others. Proper names, unlike definite descriptions, can be used by speakers to refer to objects without mediation of "concepts" or descriptive clusters. They may be used to capture and institutionalize an act of ostension.

Now it is perfectly clear that we have no such stock of actual names nor must we have. A substitutional first order language is after all formal, regimented and theoretical. It supposes initially a denumerably infinite set of names, and we have the expressive wherewithal for generating them. Now suppose our denumerably infinite stock of names *do* refer to objects. Let those objects make up our reference class; a domain. Kripke has shown that under those conditions, we can introduce a substitutional analogue of satisfaction of a formula relative to that domain. If all of the contexts of the interpreted language are transparent then the substitutional analogue of satisfaction converges with the referential definition of satisfaction. Under those conditions the quantifiers can be read with existential import. I see the referential quantifier as a limiting case. Substitutional quantification together with a substitution class of names which defines a reference class of objects, yields a referential quantifier. If our substitutional language allows wider substitution classes beyond the set of referring names then of course it is important to distinguish with an alternative notation quantification where substituends are referring names. For it is *those* latter quantifiers which can be read back into English as 'There is something such that' and 'Everything is such that'. They have existential import.[12]

I should like now to discuss the ways in which a substitutional interpretation of the quantifier lends itself to nominalistic aims. That it does so lend itself is apparent but that aspect has perhaps been misconstrued. Quine,[13] who originally regarded the substitutional interpretation of the quantifier as incoherent, and one behind which there lurked use-mention confusions, has over the years, given his nominalistic dispositions, come to notice its appeal. In the recent *Roots of Reference* he sees it as reflecting early language acquisition in his speculative theory of language learning and he goes on to attempt a substitutional interpretation of sets the "existence" of which he describes as a major concession to realism. He believes it fails for sets and is disappointed. Others have viewed substitutional theory with alarm because, given the shibboleths "To be is to be the value of a bound variable" or "Existence is what existential quantification expresses" it would seem that, upon translation into a substitutional language, ordinary English sentences like 'There are philosophers' are divested of their existential import. But that of course supposes that the quantifiers are always the primary locus of reference. There are alternative analyses for locating reference in an interpreted language. Names and their relation to *nameable* objects is one such alternative. The burden of reference is shifted back unequivocally to name relation. As I argued in an earlier paper[14] "Where the subject matter is well defined, i.e., where we are *already* ontologically committed ... then alright; to be is to be the value of a variable. If we already believe in the existence of physical objects ... then if in our interpretation (in a first order language) they turn up as objects over which variables range, it squares with the status (ontological) they have already been granted." But if the standard semantics of first order logic is taken as paradigmatic, it also *inflates* ontology, or alternatively places rigid constraints on the formal languages available for paraphrase. Consider first opaque contexts. 'Hesperus is Phosphorus' and 'John believes that Hesperus is Hesperus' can be

true while 'John believes that Hesperus is Phosphorus' might be false. Given that substitutivity of identity holds in referential first order languages with identity, such direct translation would require as in Frege, that in opaque contexts, names refer to something other than their ordinary referents such as the *senses* of the names. On the substitutional view, there is nothing incoherent about such failures of substitutivity even where the names 'Hesperus' and 'Phosphorus' refer to the same physical object. We need not inflate ontology with elusive abstract objects such as senses.

The nominalist finds that standard semantics shackles him to first order languages if, as nominalists are wont, he is to make do without abstract higher order objects. Substitutional semantics permits quantifiers with predicates as substituends without a *prima facie* presumption of reference to universals. Of course in those instances the quantifier paraphrases cannot be 'There exist....' or 'Everything is such that....' and kindred locutions. There are, even in ordinary use, quantifier phrases which seem to be ontologically more neutral as in 'It is sometimes the case that species and kinds are in the course of evolution, extinguished'. It does not seem to me that the presence there of a quantifier *forces* an ontology of kinds or species. If the case is to be made for reference of kind terms, it would, as in the case of proper names, have to be made independently. Translation into a substitutional language does not force the ontology. It remains, literally, and until the case for reference can be made, *à façon de parler*. That is the way the nominalist would like to keep it.[15]

Particularly illuminating is the case of higher order quantification where variables take sentences as substituends. On a referential theory, that commits us to designata of sentences. Are they propositions, thoughts, states of affairs, facts? Problems associated with each of those alternatives have afflicted philosophy. What are the identity conditions for such objects, how are they individuated? If the objects are thoughts aren't we back to psychologism? If the objects are facts or states of affairs there is the nagging business of negative facts, negative states of affairs and so on. Not so for the substitutional semantics. On such a view, to have quantified sentences with sentences as substituends is very natural. '(p) (p∨-p)' need not be paraphrased as 'Any proposition bears the excluded middle relation to its negation'.

Indeed on the substitutional view we can in a natural way quantify in and out of quotation contexts. Expressions, unlike non-linguistic objects, lend themselves to being named by a simple function like a quotation function which at the same time displays the object named. Indeed on the substitutional view we can introduce a truth predicate into our object language without generating a liar paradox. As I showed elsewhere[16] general inductive constraints which are required of any definition, when applied to the definition of the quantifiers, thwarts the antinomy. All this without introducing propositions or other elusive referents for sentences – a great comfort to the nominalist.

Also consistent with nominalist aims is that it articulates a distinction between truth and reference, with the burden of reference to be born by just those expressions which do in fact refer – the names of individuals. If nominalism is linked to empiricism, as it usually is, individuals are in principle confrontable, encounterable, dubbable by an act of ostension or, in the least, are made up of or make up such encounterable objects. Since we encounter so few objects and name even fewer, it seems there is a gap to be filled. How any name can have this ostensive role has been, as we noted above, illuminated by the causal theory of names. What the nominalist further requires is that individuals be a kind which are theoretically, properly nameable. For domains so defined, the substitutional quantifier can be read referentially.

It is important to notice again that the relation of identity, holding as it does between individuals, cannot sensibly be introduced into the substitutional language except where the expressions flanking the identity sign are genuine proper names of individuals. Nor will substitutivity always hold for identity. Conversely, substitutivity

salve veritate cannot define identity since two expressions may be everywhere intersubstitutable and not refer at all. Identity and substitutivity converge where there is reference and transparency of context.[17]

Critics of substitutional semantics have pointed out that if there are nondenumerably many objects, there might, on the substitutional view be true universal sentences which are falsified by an unnamed object and there must always be some such, for names are denumerable. But the fact that every *referential* first order language which has a nondenumberable model must have a denumerable one gives little advantage to the referential view. There are however other reasons which leave the nominalist unperturbed. The nominalist has always been diffident about non-denumerable collections and he looks to alternative accounts of, for example, the real numbers. He is even suspicious of denumerable infinities but sees them as a more natural extension in much the same way that the substitutional quantifier is a natural extension of conjunction and disjunction for a denumerably infinite substitution class.

What the nominalist might look for in the way of an ideal formal language is[18] type meretic with a denumerable stock of proper names at level zero. All or some denumerably infinite subset of those names may be taken as referring to nominalistically acceptable objects. At level zero, where substituends are referring names, the quantifiers may be read existentially. Beyond level zero, the variables and quantifiers are read substitutionally. There need be no new objects of reference for higher order expressions like predicates, sentences, sentential connectives. Now it is not at all clear that such a program is wholly feasible, but it is surely a nominalistic program.

Notes

1 Plato, *The Sophist*, 262E, in F.M. Cornford, *Plato's Theory of Knowledge* (London: K. Paul, Trench, Trubner, 1935).

2 W.V. Quine, *Philosophy of Logic* (Englewood Cliffs, N.J.: Prentice-Hall, 1970), pp. 22–30.

3 For an excellent account of such reductionist nominalistic programs, see R.A. Eberle, *Nominalistic Systems* (Dordrecht, Holland: D. Reidel, 1970).

4 See Ernest A. Moody, "Medieval Logic," *Encyclopedia of Philosophy* (New York: Macmillan, 1967) edited by P. Edwards, Vol. 4, pp. 530–1.

5 W.V. Quine, *Philosophy of Logic* (Englewood Cliffs, N.J.: Prentice-Hall, 1970), p. 25.

6 See for example W.V. Quine, *Philosophy of Logic*, pp. 35–46. Also, Saul Kripke, "Is There a Problem about Substitutional Quantification?" in *Truth and Meaning* (Oxford: Clarendon Press, 1976), ed. G. Evans and J. McDowell, p. 328.

7 See my "Quantification and Ontology," *Noûs* 4 (1972): 246–8 and 250.

8 Saul Kripke, "Is There a Problem about Substitutional Quantification?" in *Truth and Meaning*, ed.

G. Evans and J. McDowell (Oxford: Clarendon Press, 1976).

9 For a more complete account of a minimal substitutional semantics, see J.M. Dunn and N.D. Belnap, "The Substitution Interpretation of the Quantifiers," *Noûs* 2 (1968): 177–85.

10 See my "Modalities and Intensional Languages," in *Boston Studies in Philosophy of Science*, ed. M. Wartofsky (Dordrecht, Holland: D. Reidel, 1963), pp. 77–96. Reprinted in *Contemporary Readings in Logical Theory*, ed. I. Copi and J. Gould (New York: Macmillan, 1967).

11 See Saul Kripke, "Identity and Necessity," in *Identity and Individuation*, ed. M. Munitz (New York: New York University Press, 1971) and "Naming and Necessity," in *Semantics of Natural Language*, ed. D. Davidson and G. Harmon (Dordrecht, Holland: D. Reidel, 1972). Also K. Donnellan, "Proper Names and Identifying Descriptions," in *Semantics of Natural Languages*.

12 If our substitution class of names is extended to include nonreferring names as well, then it is for the denumerable subset of referring names that the quantifiers are read with existential import.

13 W.V. Quine, "Reply to Professor Marcus," in *Ways of Paradox* (New York: Random House, 1966). The shift in Quine's view of substitutional quantification can be traced through "Ontological Relativity," *Ontological Relativity and Other Essays* (New York: Columbia University Press, 1969), and *Roots of Reference* (La Salle, Ill.: Open Court Publishing Co., 1973).

14 "Quantification and Ontology," cited in note 7 above.

15 Kripke has suggested in "Naming and Necessity" that species names and kind names are proper names of abstract objects, i.e., essences. This is a case where a nominalistic reduction with predication taken as similarity with respect to structure seems to me more appropriate with some initial sample taken as standard. Not because such a reduction is a desideratum in all cases of predication but because it fits the common sense picture for species and kind terms. Structural features of things count as essential properties. Such properties can be characterized without at the same time requiring that there be essences. See my "Essential Attribution," *Journal of Philosophy*, 67 (1971) 7.

16 "Quantification and Ontology," *Noûs*, 4 (1972).

17 See Kripke, "Is There a Problem about Substitutional Quantification?" sections 3 and 6. Cited in note 8 above.

18 See Kripke, ibid., p. 368.

13

Interpretations of Quantifiers

Thomas Baldwin

Contemporary theories of truth use a variety of interpretations of quantifiers. Some theories base their interpretations on Tarski's famous paper (1936); others use a substitutional interpretation; while others use yet further interpretations. Although it seems unlikely that the proliferation of interpretations reveals an equal range of substantively different options, there also seems no *a priori* reason to suppose that, in the end, all interpretations are one. The present paper is an attempt to make clear the relations between some of these interpretations, particularly those between substitutional and Tarskian interpretations. This enterprise is not novel: in a famous paper (1970), Wallace argued that all interpretations of quantifiers are, in the end, variants of that proposed by Tarski. Wallace's paper has attracted many critics, most of whom have focused on the argument by which Wallace purports to show that a substitutional interpretation is a variant of the Tarskian approach, and a careful examination of the controversy surrounding this argument provides an excellent route into the general issue of the relations between interpretations of quantifiers.

I

Wallace's argument can be approached by considering a single case of the application of a substitu-

tional interpretation to an existentially quantified sentence, as in

(1) $\overline{(\exists x)(x \text{ smokes})}$ is true $\leftrightarrow (\exists \alpha)$
       $(\text{Sub}(\alpha, \bar{x}, \overline{x \text{ smokes}})$ is true)

(where, following Wallace, the result of placing a horizontal bar over an object-language expression is to be regarded as forming a structural descriptive name of the expression, 'α' is a sorted variable which takes as values the members of some subclass of object-language singular terms, the substitution class of singular terms, and 'Sub (a, b, c)' means 'the result of substituting a for all occurrences of b in c').

Wallace argued, in effect, that (1) does not by itself present all that is necessary if one is to be able to assess the substitutional approach to quantifiers; for, he claimed, such an assessment can be made only when it has been shown how, starting from (1), one can derive the T-sentence '$\overline{(\exists x)(x \text{ smokes})}$ is true $\leftrightarrow (\exists x)(x \text{ smokes})$' (I shall call this sentence the 'EQ T-sentence'). And, he further argued, the way to construct such a proof within a finitely axiomatised semantic theory is to take a theory which includes among its theorems the propositions:

(2) $(\forall \alpha)(\text{Sub}(\alpha, \bar{x}, \overline{x \text{ smokes}})$ is true $\leftrightarrow$
       $\text{den}(\alpha) \text{ smokes})$

(3) $(\forall \alpha)(\exists x)(\text{den}(\alpha) = x)$

(4) $(\forall x)(\exists \alpha)(\text{den}(\alpha) = x)$

Thomas Baldwin, Interpretations of Quantifiers.
Mind, 88, 350 (1979): 215–40.

(actually Wallace claimed (1970, p. 130) that (3) does not require explicit statement, given the functional notation for denotation; but this claim assumes that denotation is not a partial function when applied to the substitution class, an assumption which certainly merits explicit statement). Finally, Wallace claimed, propositions (2)–(4) suffice to ensure that one can find within the resulting semantic theory the characteristic features of a theory with a referential interpretation, where, by his talk of a 'referential interpretation', Wallace meant one which follows Tarski's approach.

That final claim will be examined critically in the second part of this paper; in this part I shall consider the views of Wallace's critics who have sought to fault his argument at two earlier stages: at the point where Wallace claims that in giving a substitutional interpretation by itself, as in (1), one does not complete the task of an adequate semantic theory, and at the point where Wallace claims that a proof of the EQ T-sentence that starts from (1) requires also (2)–(4).

Both Camp (1975, pp. 179–88) and Kripke (1976, pp. 333–49) have queried Wallace's demand that an adequate semantic theory should generate T-sentences as theorems, and thus his insistence that (1) does not supply by itself all that is required. For, they argue, (1) fixes absolutely clearly and definitively the truth-conditions of $\overline{(\exists x)(x \text{ smokes})}$; so what more does Wallace want with his demand for T-sentences? It seems to me that the ground for Wallace's demand lies in his conception of the goal of semantic theory. Wallace writes, in his response to Camp (1975, p. 190):

> Camp writes: 'Remember that we are concerned with truth theories as interpretations of initially uninterpreted artificial languages' (Camp 1975, p. 175). This was not my concern. I use formalization merely as a device for clarifying an explanatory job which arises in ordinary language for ordinary language.

Wallace's concern, I suggest, was to assess rival explanations of why certain sentences have the truth-conditions they do have. These explanations perform the 'explanatory job' of which he speaks, and for him they are the goal of any adequate semantic theory. Such a goal requires that one present as *explanandum* an account of the truth-conditions of these sentences, but nothing could fulfil this requirement better than the relevant homophonic T-sentences. Thus, to take my

example, Wallace's conception of an adequate semantic theory was not one which fixes the truth-conditions of $\overline{(\exists x)(x \text{ smokes})}$, but one which explains the EQ T-sentence. Where explanation is taken in a hypothetico–deductive manner, this goal becomes that of the deduction of the EQ T-sentence from the hypotheses of the theory. So the derivation of the EQ T-sentence from (1)–(4) fulfils Wallace's conception of the goal of an adequate semantic theory, whereas (1) by itself does not.

My only criticism of Wallace in this matter (if I have correctly understood him) is a verbal one: his use of the phrase 'adequate semantic theory' is unfortunate, in that it wrongly implies that a semantic theory which does not generate proofs of homophonic T-sentences is inadequate and therefore faulty. Perhaps the phrase 'explanatory semantic theory' would have been a happier choice. But this is only a verbal point, and once Wallace's basic concern is made explicit, his insistence on the derivability of T-sentences emerges as entirely reasonable.

The second point on which Wallace has been criticised is his claim that a proof of the EQ T-sentence from (1) requires propositions (2)–(4), and his critics have presented alternative proofs which, they claim, do not require these propositions. One such critic is Gottlieb (1974) who argues (in effect) that in place of (2)–(4) one can make do with the T-sentences for all the atomic sentences of the form 'a smokes', that is, with equivalences such as $\overline{\text{'Harry smokes}}$ is true $\leftrightarrow$ Harry smokes'. For with such equivalences one can argue as follows:

$\overline{(\exists x)(x \text{ smokes})}$ is true $\leftrightarrow (\exists x)(\text{Sub}(\alpha, \bar{x}, \overline{x \text{ smokes}})$ is true)

i.e. $\leftrightarrow \overline{\text{Harry smokes}}$ is true or John smokes is true or . .

i.e. $\leftrightarrow$ Harry smokes or John smokes or . .

i.e. $\leftrightarrow (\exists x) (x \text{ smokes})$.

Wallace, I think, was aware of the possibility of such an argument, but he rejected it (1970, p. 129) on the ground that the inferences from the first line to the second and from the third line to the fourth are invalid. Gottlieb, however, counters this objection by arguing that under a substitutional interpretation of the quantifiers in the metalanguage, these inferences are valid, and thus that if Wallace refuses to accept them he is begging the point at issue.

Gottlieb's point is that Wallace overlooked a feature of logical consequence which holds under a substitutional interpretation but not under a referential one, namely that $(\exists x)$ (Fx) Fa_1 or .. or Fa_1 or .. (where 'a_1', .., 'a_i', .. are all the members of the substitution class), and that, as a result, Wallace wrongly dismissed in advance the derivation which Gottlieb offers. Now, that there is the difference between the two interpretations which Gottlieb alleges is indisputable; but its significance in the present context seems to me disputable. As I stressed in the previous discussion of Wallace's insistence on the derivability of T-sentences, Wallace was not concerned with constraints on some previously uninterpreted quantifier notation; his concern was to explicate the semantic role of essentially familiar quantifier idioms. Hence for Wallace it is important that if one demarcates the substitution class of singular terms at all strictly, it is easy to provide counter-examples to the proposition that if for some x, Fx then Fa_1 or .. or Fa_i or ... Such counter-examples will then bring the response that the substitution class has been demarcated too strictly; but this response is tantamount to the assumption that everything in the domain is to be deemed to be denoted by a member of the substitution class, i.e. that Wallace's proposition (4) is to be assumed to hold. So, although a substitutional interpretation does validate Gottlieb's proposition, his argument as a whole does not establish the dispensability of Wallace's proposition (4); for unless that proposition is assumed to hold, there will be reason not to take Gottlieb's object-language quantifiers as regimented versions of our familiar idioms.

But what of Wallace's other propositions (2) and (3)? Doesn't Gottlieb at least show that these are dispensable? His argument requires that one have as theorems the T-sentences for all atomic sentences. Clearly, if one had as theorems (2) and particular propositions giving the denotation for each member of the substitution class, one could derive the required T-sentences. But such an approach, introducing (2) explicitly and (3) implicitly, seeks to close the argument too briefly. The question is whether one could not derive the T-sentences in some other way. One way would be to take the atomic T-sentences themselves as axioms. Given, not unreasonably, a finite stock of basic singular terms and predicates, this proposal would not violate Wallace's finite axiomatisability requirement; but it would, I think, violate the motive behind this requirement – namely that an

adequate (i.e. explanatory) semantic theory should represent the essential semantic roles of the different parts of our language. We obviously do not treat atomic subject–predicate sentences as unanalysed semantic units; knowing the truth-conditions of many sentences in which 'smokes' occurs and of many sentences in which 'Harry' occurs, we can grasp the truth-conditions of 'Harry smokes' without having to learn them afresh. In brief, our grasp of the truth-conditions of atomic sentences has a recursive structure. Nor is this just a contingent fact about us and our language. Without a recursive structure, the ability to introduce reference to new items, or to call attention to fresh properties of familiar items, would be crippled, and that ability seems essential to a being which finds its place in the world, a feature of our lives which I take to be no accident. Hence it is not just through a preference for theoretical simplicity that one can require that an explanatory semantic theory should have a recursive structure even in its account of the truth-conditions of atomic subject–predicate sentences, and the problem with which Gottlieb's argument leaves one is whether this requirement can be met without introducing into the theory propositions which entail Wallace's (2) and (3).

This problem will be best treated whilst considering the argument advanced by Camp, who has proposed a derivation of the EQ T-sentence from (1) without recourse either to Wallace's (2)–(4) or to Gottlieb's T-sentences for atomic sentences.[1] The essential trick is the introduction of a functor 'trans " "', where 'trans "a" = b' can be understood as 'the object-language translation of "a" is b'; thus if one assumes, as I shall, that object- and metalanguage share the same class of singular terms, it will be true that trans "Harry" = $\overline{\text{Harry}}$ etc. With this new functor, all one needs to derive the EQ T-sentence from (1) are the propositions:

(2)′ $(\forall y)$ (Sub (trans "y", $\bar{x}$, $\overline{\text{x smokes}}$) is true $\leftrightarrow$ y smokes)

(3)′ $(\forall \alpha)(\exists x)(\alpha = \text{trans "x"})$

(4)′ $(\forall x(\exists \alpha)(\alpha = \text{trans "x"})$

And these propositions, it is said, are clearly distinct from Wallace's (2)–(4); for there is nothing in (2)′–(4)′ which implies that the members of the substitution class have denotations at all.

At this point the discussion of Gottlieb's argument can be briefly recalled. I left it with the problem as to whether one could give a recursive account of the truth-conditions of atomic subject–predicate sentences without introducing (2) and (3). If Camp is correct, this is clearly possible; for all one needs is (2)′ and particular principles such as 'trans "Harry" = $\overline{\text{Harry}}$'. Since this solution to the question raised by Gottlieb's argument presupposes Camp's approach, however, it is on the latter approach that I shall concentrate.

Wallace has attempted to show in his response to Camp (Wallace 1975) that (2)′–(4)′ do, after all, entail his own propositions (2)–(4). But, for reasons which need not detain us here, that attempt is unsuccessful (Kripke (1976, p. 417) identifies one flaw in Wallace's response). Nonetheless, Wallace's position can still be defended. As a glance at (2)′–(4)′ will indicate, Camp's argument makes essential use of quantification into quotes; furthermore, his argument entails that the quantifier which is used in the EQ T-sentence admits of quantification into quotes, and it is this feature which turns his derivation of the EQ T-sentence into a Pyrrhic victory. For quantification into quotes is a nonsense if one thinks of the natural language idioms whose truth-conditions the EQ T-sentence is supposed to capture. There is no way in which pronouns within quotes can be sensibly regarded as having antecedents outside the quotes. Hence it cannot be right to formalise these natural language idioms with quantifiers for which quantification into quotes is legitimate.

It may be objected that any theory which uses a substitutional interpretation of quantifiers must license quantification into quoted contexts. For, it may be said, this is licensed by the very principles of the interpretation itself. But this depends upon whether or not the presence within quotes of a letter typographically similar to a free variable must count as an occurrence of that variable for which a substitution by a singular term should be made in suitable circumstances; and there is certainly nothing which compels one to count such a letter in this way. Indeed, there is nothing mandatory here either way, and one can introduce a quantifier notation for which quantification into quoted contexts is legitimate. But that use of quantifiers and variables must be radically distinct from their ordinary use, which is Wallace's concern.

In order to forestall misunderstanding, I should add that I am not here arguing that quantification into quotes is to be rejected because it leads to paradoxes. Kripke argues persuasively that, with careful handling, it will not do so (1976, p. 368). Nor am I arguing that Camp's derivation of the

EQ T-sentence is to be rejected merely because it employs quantification into quotes. My point is only that the theory behind his derivation rules itself out of court as an appropriate semantics for natural language quantifiers by its commitment to legitimating quantification into quotes for such quantifiers. Wallace's theory, by contrast, carries no such commitment; so my defence of Wallace rests on the claim that the only way to derive the EQ T-sentence from the substitutional interpretation (1) without legitimating quantification into quotes for natural language quantifiers is to use a theory which has Wallace's propositions (2)–(4) as theorems.

II

So far I have defended Wallace against his critics; I shall now argue against him myself through a critical examination of his claim that once one locates a substitutional interpretation within an explanatory semantic theory, one can find within the resulting theory the characteristic features of a Tarskian theory. To this end some features of a Tarskian theory must be presented: the application of a Tarskian interpretation to $\overline{(\exists x_1)(x_1 \text{smokes})}$ yields

(5) $(\forall s)((\exists x_i)(\overline{x_i \text{smokes}}$ is true of s $\leftrightarrow$
     $(\exists s')(s' \underset{i}{\approx} s \,\&\, \overline{x_1 \text{smokes}}$ *is true of s′*$))$

(where I adopt the idiom '. . is true of s′ instead of the more usual 's satisfies . .', it is assumed that all variables in the object-language have been assigned numerical indices, for which 'i' is schematic, and 's' $\underset{1}{\approx}$s' means 's′ differs from s in at most the ith place'). In addition to (5) and the standard definition of absolute truth as truth of all sequences, further propositions, analogous to (2)–(4), are required for the proof of the EQ T-sentence from (5), and these can be formulated as follows:

(6) $(\forall s)(\overline{x_1 \text{smokes}}$ is true of s $\leftrightarrow$ Val(i, s) smokes)

(7) $(\forall s)(\exists x)(x = \text{Val}(i, s))$

(8) $(\forall s)(\forall x)(\exists s')(s' \underset{i}{\approx} s \,\&\, x = \text{Val}(i, s'))$

(where 'Val(i,s)' means 'the ith member of s'). Wallace's thesis that one can find within an explanatory substitutional theory the characteristics of a Tarskian theory leads one, therefore, to expect that he will show how (6)–(8) are derivable from (2)–(4). And Wallace does, in effect, undertake this task although he discusses only the derivation of (6). What Wallace does (1970, p. 131) is to show that if one suitably redefines all the key non-logical expressions in (6), one can make (6) say just what (2) says. In detail: suppose one takes sequences to be sequences of members of the substitution class, and takes '$\overline{x_i \text{ smokes}}$ is true of s' to mean 'Sub(i^{th} member of s, $\overline{x_i}$, $\overline{x_i \text{ smokes}}$) is true)', and 'Val(n, s)' to mean 'Den(n^{th} member of s)': then (6) will say just what (2) says. The same definitions have the consequence that (7) can be made to say what (3) says, but the first clause of (8) – '$s' \underset{i}{\approx} s'$ – presents a problem since nothing similar is to be found in (4). This last problem can be neglected, however, since it is less important than the fact that this derivation of (6) is a charade. Wallace has not shown that (6), in its intended sense, is derivable from (2); all he has shown is that by suitable redefinitions (6) can be made to say what (2) says.

It is hard to know what Wallace thought he was doing here. What he says is that if a substitutionalist explains T-sentences such as the EQ T-sentence he 'uses resources that define satisfaction' (1970, p. 145) and he cannot prevent 'having his theory collapse into R's [sc. Tarski's theory]' (1975, p. 191). But how does showing that the Tarskian proposition (6) can be made to say what the substitutional interpretation (2) says count as defining satisfaction in substitutional terms or even collapsing a substitutional theory into a Tarskian theory? These descriptions seem at best more appropriate to what would be the opposite of Wallace's procedure – some manner of redefining the substitutional (2) so that it says no more than the Tarskian (6). Further, with no constraints on admissible redefinitions, anything can be made to follow from anything; so one must ask whether Wallace's procedure satisfies some constraint which makes it less than wholly vacuous.

On the first of these points, it is not difficult to cook up suitable redefinitions which will make (2) say just what (6) says. Suppose one takes the 'singular terms' of the substitution class to be ordered pairs whose first member is a sequence and whose second member is a numeral, and that '$\alpha(I)$' means 'the first member of α' and '$\alpha(2)$' is similarly defined; suppose, further, that 'Sub(α, $\overline{x}$, $\overline{x \text{ smokes}}$) is true' means '$\overline{x^{\cap}_{\alpha(2)}\text{smokes}}$ is true of $\alpha(I)$' (where the symbol '$\cap$' expresses concatenation), and 'Den(α)' means 'Val(the denotation of $\alpha(2)$, $\alpha(1)$)': then (2) will say just what (6) says, and similarly, (3) will

say just what (7) says, and in this case what (4) will have been made to say does follow from (8).

The ease with which the opposite of Wallace's procedure can be concocted shows the relevance of the second point about the need for constraints on admissible redefinitions in order to prevent Humpty Dumpty's kind of vacuity. But the trouble is that one constraint on definitions which must be met if they are to figure in genuine derivations, namely that they should express truths where the words employed are understood in their normal sense, is just not met by Wallace's procedure. For example, a member of a sequence is not in general the same as its own denotation (even where it has a denotation), so why should one pay any attention to the consequences of supposing that 'Val(n, s)' means 'Den(n^{th} member of s)'? The only way I can see in which Wallace's procedure points to anything non-vacuous is that because it uses only correspondence rules which link non-logical expressions, it demonstrates (what was obvious anyway) that there is a close formal similarity between the Tarskian theory and the substitutional one, although the differences between (1) and (5), (and similarly between (4) and (8)), and the fact that the substitutional theory needs nothing analogous to the Tarskian theory's definition of absolute truth, show that the two theories do not have quite the same logical form. This formal similarity, however, certainly does not imply that in any substantive fashion the theories are the same, or that one can find the characteristic features of a Tarskian theory within a substitutional theory.

III

The conclusion of the last section was that there seems to be no more than a formal similarity between Tarskian and substitutional interpretations. Yet this is not the whole story; for there are other connections of a more substantive nature between the two interpretations. But the elucidation of these connections is a more complex matter than Wallace envisaged, and requires further examination of both interpretations. I shall postpone further discussion of the Tarskian one until the next section; here I shall develop a variant of the substitutional one through discussion of a familiar objection to substitutional theories, and explore how this variant relates to further non-Tarskian interpretations which have had little attention in recent discussions.

In the first section I argued that the use of a substitutional interpretation in an explanatory semantic theory commits one to accepting that everything in the domain is denoted by some member of the substitution class, or, in brief,

(4) $(\forall x)(\exists \alpha)(x = \text{den}(\alpha))$.

This proposition has often been felt to be objectionable, so much so, indeed, that some substitutionalists have despaired of giving a necessary condition for the truth of existentially quantified sentences. In a similar vein, others, worried about indenumerable domains, have appealed to the Löwenheim–Skolem theorem to dissipate such domains (e.g. Haack 1974, pp. 145–6). It seems in fact that the Löwenheim–Skolem theorem cannot be properly used in this way (cf. Quine 1973, pp. 114–15, Weston 1974), but the main objection to (4) must surely come, not from indenumerable domains, but from the absurdity of the supposition that everything has a name. Here, as elsewhere in logic, we need to preserve 'that feeling for reality which ought to be preserved even in the most abstract and general studies' (Russell 1919, p. 169). It may be said that we could coherently add names whenever required (Geach 1962, p. 160); and, leaving aside the problem of indenumerable domains, this may be true. But it does not alter the absurdity of thinking that the truth of general claims about grains of sand requires one to assume that the substitution class includes a name for each grain of sand.

My initial aim, therefore, is to formulate a modification of the substitutional interpretation (1) which enables one to dispense with (4) and its problems. In order to specify this modification in terms which make it both plausible and comprehensible, however, it is necessary to make a brief detour into the business of handling context-dependent phrases within semantic theory. There are many ways in which context-dependence can be handled, but I shall here simply use features of one way without discussing its merits. The basic feature of this approach is that concepts of truth and denotation are relativized to contexts of utterance, enabling one to formulate biconditionals such as

(9) $\overline{\text{He smokes}}$ is true in c $\leftrightarrow$ den($\overline{\text{He}}$, c) smokes.

I hasten to add that, as a paradigm for an account of context-dependence, (9) is obviously oversim-

ple. It gives no indication of the treatment to be provided for demonstrative phrases such as $\overline{\text{This man}}$, where the role of the common noun needs to be elucidated, and there is the further problem of passing from (9) to something more like a T-sentence without introducing context-dependence into the metalanguage. However, by the use of restricted quantifiers and other devices, it is possible to propose more complex paradigms than (9) which look plausible. But since these developments do not materially affect the argument to be proposed here, I shall not pursue them. I shall invoke only simple context-dependent singular terms and I shall assume that the specification of a context of utterance of a sentence is sufficient to provide an account of the unique denotation in that context of each singular term in the sentence. Indeed a context may be viewed simply as a function from singular terms to objects, and, as a result, quantification over contexts need not be restricted to actual ones, since possible contexts will only be further sets of ordered pairs. This view of contexts makes the concept of denotation redundant, but I shall retain it for expository purposes, simply as the function which assigns to a singular term its value for a given context.

Once the concepts of truth and denotation have been relativized to contexts, they must apply as such throughout one's semantic theory. However, since one also wants to be able to talk of 'absolute truth', this can be defined as truth in all contexts, and although the application of this definition raises difficult issues, I shall adopt it here. By and large, context-dependence features merely as an idle parameter in the elucidation of the truth-conditions of complex sentences in terms of those of simpler ones, and a straightforward modification of the simple substitutional interpretation (1) yields:

(10) $(\forall c)(\overline{(\exists x)(x \text{ smokes})}$ is true in c $\leftrightarrow$ $(\exists \alpha)(\text{Sub}(\alpha, \bar{x}, \overline{x \text{ smokes}})$ is true in c))

But (10) does not help with the problem of unnamed objects raised by (4). Proof of the EQ T-sentence from (10) requires (in addition to the definition of absolute truth as truth in all contexts, a proposition required throughout the following discussion which I won't always state explicitly):

(11) $(\forall c)(\forall \alpha)(\text{Sub}(\alpha, \bar{x}, \overline{x \text{ smokes}})$ in true in c $\leftrightarrow$ den(α, c) smokes)

$$(12) \quad (\forall c)(\forall \alpha)(\exists x)(x = den(\alpha, c))$$

$$(13) \quad (\forall c)(\forall x)(\exists \alpha)(x = den(\alpha, c))$$

and (13) raises the problem raised by (4). (12), it might seem, raises a further problem, in that it requires that contexts be, in effect, total functions, defined for all the members of the substitution class. But this is not a real problem: for (12) does not rule out the existence of contexts which one could regard as partial functions; it only requires one to exclude them from the theory.

In place of (10) I want to propose a more complex modification of (1) which makes further use of reference to contexts –

$$(14) \quad (\forall c)\overline{((\exists x)(x \text{ smokes}) \text{ is true in } c \leftrightarrow} \\ (\exists c')(\exists \alpha)(c' \text{ differs from } c \text{ at} \\ \underline{\text{most in}} \text{ assignment to } \alpha \text{ } Sub(\alpha, \bar{x}, \\ \overline{x \text{ smokes}}) \text{ is true in } c')).$$

What is important about (14) is the introduction of a fresh context c' to which the denotation of the context-dependent singular term that is introduced as substitute is to be relative. The other novelty of (14), the clause 'c' differs from c at most in assignment to α', is added only to handle cases of multiple quantification for reasons similar to those which require the familiar clause 's' differs from s at most in the ith place' in the Tarskian interpretation; I shall henceforth abbreviate the former clause as '$c' \underset{\alpha}{\approx} c$'. (14) requires no special alterations in the basic interpretative clauses of a substitutional theory beyond those required by (10). But it differs crucially from (10) in the propositions required for the proof of the EQ T-sentence: in this case they are (11), (12) and

$$(15) \quad (\forall c)(\forall x)(\exists \alpha)(\exists c')(c' \underset{\alpha}{\approx} c \text{ \& } x = den(\alpha, c'))$$

which plays the role played before by (13) or (4). Given (15) there is no need to cast about for singular terms of the substitution class with which to exhaust the domain. Instead, one has only to produce pairs of singular term plus context with which to exhaust the domain; and since there is no limit to possible contexts of utterance, the problems to which (4) gives rise do not arise here. Thus instead of assuming that each grain of sand is individually denoted by a member of the substitution class, one has only to assume that that class contains singular terms which, in a suitably

defined context, can be used to denote any grain of sand. It is obvious that if the substitution class contains demonstratives, this assumption is unproblematic.

A complex substitutional interpretation, such as is applied in (14), provides, therefore, a solution to the difficulty about unnamed objects, a difficulty which has seemed to many to indicate a fundamental inadequacy in substitutional theories. The ideas which lie behind (14) are not original, although perhaps the terminology is. Both Mates (1965, pp. 54–57) and Jeffrey (Boolos and Jeffrey 1973, pp. 104–5), for example, propound interpretations which are in some respects similar to (14) although, among other differences, where I talk of contexts they talk of interpretations, by which they mean assignments of values in the model-theoretic sense. Three reasons motivate may change of terminology: first, it seems desirable to keep model theory and the characterisation of validity separate from a theory about truth-conditions, despite the obvious connections between the two. Secondly, although the extension of a predicate varies from assignment to assignment, that variation is irrelevant to a discussion of quantifiers and variables; hence, for me, the extension of a simple predicate is not context-dependent. Thirdly, I hope by my talk of contexts to acknowledge a striking feature of our ordinary use of pronouns – that the same phrases, barring minor transformations, occur, now as pronouns with antecedents, now as context-dependent demonstratives. This seems unlikely to be an accident, and it suggests that at least where a pronoun occurs within a subordinate clause with its antecedent outside that clause, its use may be understood by reference to the use of the same word or phrase as a demonstrative, taking the pronoun's antecedent to be an implicit specification of a context for the utterance of the demonstrative. Thus one might say that 'it is true of some man that he smokes' is true if and only if 'he smokes' is true in a context in which some man is referred to. And this thought is, to some extent, captured in (14) by the introduction of the fresh context c' on the right side.

The logical relations between (1), (10), and (14) are of some interest. Consider first (10) and (1): one might expect that, given the definition of absolute truth as truth in all contexts, (10) would imply (1), though not *vice versa*, since the analogous implication does hold where sentential connectives are concerned

Thomas Baldwin

(compare (10) with '($\forall$ c) ($\overline{\text{Not}}^{\cap}$ σ is true in c) $\leftrightarrow$ σ is not true in c)'

and (1) with '($\forall$c)($\overline{\text{Not}}^{\cap}$ σ is true in c) $\leftrightarrow$ ($\forall$ c) (σ is not true in c)'). But the quantifier '($\exists\alpha$)' on the right side of (1) prevents this implication, for, given only the definition of absolute truth, the right side of (1) is equivalent to, not '($\forall$c($\exists\alpha$)(Sub(α, $\overline{\text{x}}$, $\overline{\text{x smokes}}$) is true in c)', but to '($\exists\alpha$)($\forall$c)(Sub(α, x, $\overline{\text{x smokes}}$) is true in c)'. What is needed, I think, to restore the implication is the assumption that the singular terms invoked by (10) have the same denotation in all contexts (i.e., in effect, that there is just one context). Given this assumption, the definition of absolute truth, and (11), (10) implies (1), although the converse does not hold.

Relations between (10) and (14) are considerably closer than those between (1) and (10), as their common use of (11) and (12) to derive the EQ T-sentence leads one to expect. The right side of (10) is equivalent to

($\exists\alpha$)($\exists c'$)(c' = c & Sub(α, $\overline{\text{x}}$, $\overline{\text{x smokes}}$) is true in c')

hence, since if c' = c then $c' \underset{\alpha}{\approx}$ c, this implies by itself the right side of (14). Conversely, since the assumption that a singular term has the same denotation in all contexts implies that if $c' \underset{\alpha}{\approx}$ c

then c' = c, given just that assumption the right side of (14)
implies that of (10): so (10) and (14) are equivalent on that assumption. Since (10) implies (1) given this same assumption, (11) and the definition of absolute truth, it follows that (10) offers only a very limited resting place between (14) and (1).

Although the ideas which lie behind (14) are to be found in Mates' theory, his theory actually differs from (14) in more than terminology. For in place of (14) Mates has (in my terminology):

(16) ($\forall$c)(($\overline{\text{($\exists$x)(x smokes)}}$)
($\exists c'$)($c' \underset{\bar{a}}{\approx}$ c & $\overline{\text{a smokes}}$ is true in c'))

where $\bar{a}$ is the first singular term not in $\overline{\text{($\exists$x)(x smokes)}}$. Mates is here assuming some enumeration of singular terms which enables the selection of $\bar{a}$ to be definite. This isn't strictly necessary, for $\bar{a}$ could be any singular term not in $\overline{\text{($\exists$x)(x smokes)}}$, but it is convenient. The require-

ment that $\bar{a}$ should not be in $\overline{\text{($\exists$x)(x smokes)}}$ is itself needed for more complex cases, e.g. to stop any chance of inferring $\overline{\text{a loves a}}$ from $\overline{\text{($\exists$x)(x loves a)}}$. The relations between (16) and (14) are, as usual, best examined in the light of the full theory required for the derivation of the EQ T-sentence from (16) –

(17) ($\forall$c)($\overline{\text{a smokes}}$ is true in
c $\leftrightarrow$ den($\bar{a}$, c)smokes)
(18) ($\forall$c)($\exists$x)(x = den($\bar{a}$, c))
(19) ($\forall$c)($\forall$x)($\exists c'$)($c' \underset{\bar{a}}{\approx}$ c & x = den($\bar{a}$, c')).

Since (11) and (12) are just generalized versions of (17) and (18), it is the difference between (15) and (19) that reveals the difference between (14) and (16): (19) implies (15), but the converse does not hold, since (19) requires that $\bar{a}$ denote anything in the domain, given a suitable context, whereas (15) makes no such demand of any one singular term. This difference arises from the fact that in (16) Mates requires that the substitution of the specific singular term $\bar{a}$ should yield truth, whereas the relatively straight substitutional approach of (14) demands only that some substitution should yield truth. More formally, by reversing the derivations of the EQ T-sentence from (14) and (16), one can show that (14) and (16) are equivalent given all of (11), (12), (15), (17)–(19). Hence, given the logical relations among all these premises, one can infer that (14) and (16) are equivalent given only (11), (12), and (19), and the role of (12) and (19) here can be taken by a single proposition which shows precisely how Mates requires for $\bar{a}$ what the substitutional approach of (14) requires of singular terms in general, namely

($\forall$c)($\forall\alpha$)($\forall c'$($\exists c''$)($c'' \underset{\bar{a}}{\approx}$ c & den($\bar{a}$, c'') = den(α, c'))

Mates' theory is a minimally substitutional theory. I want now to compare it with a theory which is not substitutional at all, but which nonetheless stands very close to Mates' theory. This theory can be approached by reconsidering a point I mentioned when discussing (14), that much the same phrases occur, now as pronouns with antecedents, now as context-dependent demonstratives. For this observation suggests that one should formulate an interpretation of quantifiers in which one assigns context-dependent denotations to variables themselves, thereby obviating the need for any substitution of singular terms for them. An interpretation of this kind would be –

(20) $(\forall d)\overline{((\exists x)(x \text{ smokes})}$ is true in $d \leftrightarrow$
$(\exists d')(d' \underset{\bar{x}}{\approx} d \ \& \ \overline{x \text{ smokes}}$ is true in $d'))$

(where 'd' and 'd'' take as values contexts for variables, i.e. functions from variables to members of the domain). Although the idioms of (20) are novel, it expresses an interpretation of quantifiers which harks at least back to Church (1956, p. 175), and I shall call it 'Church's interpretation'. Proof of the EQ T-sentence from (20) requires –

(21) $(\forall d)\overline{(x \text{ smokes}}$ is true in $d \leftrightarrow$ den
   $(\bar{x}, d)$ smokes)

(22) $(\forall d)(\exists x)(x = \text{den}(\bar{x}, d))$

(23) $(\forall d)(\forall x)(\exists d')(d' \underset{\bar{x}}{\approx} d \ \& \ x = \text{den}(\bar{x}, d'))$

and it is obvious at a glance that Church's (20)–(23) are very similar to Mates' (16)–(19).

In comparing these theories one should bear in mind that they apply to different classes of expressions: truth in c is not defined for expressions with free variables, and truth in d is not defined for expressions with singular terms. Nonetheless, it seems clear that much the same work is being done by the singular terms which Mates introduces and by the free variables which Church uses. So, to show how the conditions under which Mates holds a proposition with no free variables to be true are equivalent to the conditions under which Church holds an analogous proposition with no singular terms to be true, one needs to suppose that there is a function, call it *equ*, which establishes a 1–1 correspondence between singular terms and variables. As (18), (19), (22), and (23) indicate, contexts for singular terms, c, and contexts for variables, d, are total functions with the same range; so the function *equ* also establishes a 1–1 correspondence between them: for any c, there is a unique d such that $d = \text{equ}^{-1} \ o \ c$ and *vice versa*.[2] Hence $\text{den}(\bar{a}, c) = \text{den} (\bar{x}, d)$ where $\text{equ}(\bar{a}) = \bar{x}$ and $d = \text{equ}^{-1} \ o \ c$, and $c' \approx \bar{a} \ c$ if and only if $d' \underset{\bar{x}}{\approx} d$ where, in addition, d' $= \text{equ}^{-1} \ o \ c'$. So, given that $\text{equ}(\bar{a}) = (\bar{x})$, (18) and (19) are equivalent to (22) and (23); it also follows that the right-hand sides of (17) and (21) are equivalent, and thus that the truth in c of $\overline{a \text{ smokes}}$ is the same as the truth in d of $\overline{x \text{ smokes}}$. The right-hand sides of (16) and (20), however, present a problem: although they are equivalent if one assumes that $\text{equ}(\bar{a}) = \bar{x}$, there is no guarantee that the condition under which $\bar{a}$ is selected in (16) will always lead to the selection of a singular term that is paired by *equ* with the variable

selected by the condition used in (20), and precisely this undesired situation will arise if one considers the analogues of (16) and (20) when the object-language sentence is $\overline{(\exists y)(y \text{ smokes})}$ (call these analogues (16y) and (20y)).

This lack of fit reflects an arbitrariness in the conditions which lead to the choice of $\bar{a}$ and $\bar{y}$ on the right-hand sides of (16y) and (20y). (16y) is just one instance of a general schema, call it (16y)', in which any singular term not in $\overline{(\exists y)(y \text{ smokes})}$ is allowed to be substituted for $\bar{y}$ in y smokes, and, similarly, (20y) is just one instance of a general schema, call it (20y)', in which any variable is allowed to be substituted for $\bar{y}$ in $\overline{y \text{ smokes})}$ as long as it is free for $\bar{y}$ in $\overline{(\exists y)(y \text{ smokes})}$. Whatever particular 1–1 correspondence between singular terms and variables is assumed to hold, it is clear that there will be choices of singular term for (16y)' and variable for (20y)' such that the singular term and variable thus chosen are paired in the assumed correspondence. So there must be instances of (16y)' and (20y)' whose right-hand sides are equivalent given the assumed 1–1 correspondence. Since it is easy to show, given the other assumptions of the two theories, that all instances of (16y)' are equivalent, and, similarly, that all instances of (20y)' are equivalent, the required equivalence between the right-hand sides of (16y) and (20y) is thereby established. Hence the theories of Mates and Church are equivalent in the sense that the truth in c of a proposition with no free variables and the truth in d of an analogous proposition with no singular terms coincide at every stage.

I shall discuss in the next section how all these interpretations relate to the Tarskian interpretation (5), but I want to raise here the different question of whether they are, in some sense, 'referential'. I have already discussed Wallace's claim that the simple substitutional interpretation (1) is referential, in the sense that (1) is reducible to the Tarskian interpretation (5). But the falsity of this claim does not entail that a substitutional interpretation is not referential if one understands the word 'referential' in some other way. One common view (cf. Quine 1973, pp. 98–9), which I shall here follow, is that existential, or ontological, commitment is central to the question of whether an interpretation is referential: an interpretation is referential if and only if under that interpretation an existentially quantified sentence carries existential implications (the need to raise this question makes one wish that the existential quantifier was called the 'singular quantifier', but I will stick to the usual name). It might be thought that it follows from the explanatory approach to semantic theory which I have here adopted that an interpretation must be referential if it is to be in any way adequate: that unless it is referential, in this sense, it cannot correctly capture our natural idioms. But this depends upon whether one thinks that sentences such as 'Some things don't exist' are inherently nonsense, and I am going to assume that this is not the case, and, therefore, that the question of the existential import of the existential quantifier can be seriously raised.

The resolution of this question is not as straightforward as some have thought. Consider the simple substitutional interpretation (1): it may seem that the possibility of singular terms with nonexistent denotations in the object-language entails that this interpretation is not referential. But, on the other hand, it may also seem that Wallace's proposition (3) entails that such singular terms are irrelevant to the truth of existentially quantified sentences, and thus that (1) is, after all, referential. The truth of the matter in this case seems to me to depend upon one's attitude to the metalanguage: if it is assumed that existential quantifiers in the metalanguage have existential import, then the existential quantifier in (3) has this import and (1) must be regarded as a referential interpretation. Indeed, unless this were so, the EQ T-sentence would be false. But since the question at issue is precisely whether existential quantifiers can be coherently handled without assigning them existential commitments, it seems presumptuous to beg this question for the metalanguage. Once this assumption is dropped, there is no reason for thinking that the existential quantifier in (3) has existential commitments, and thus no reason for thinking that even when the substitutional interpretation (1) is combined with (2)–(4), the resulting account of the existential quantifier must be referential.

The same considerations about not presuming in advance that metalanguage quantifiers have existential commitments apply to other interpretations, and it may seem therefore that none of them will prove referential. However, there is a difference between the simple substitutional interpretation (1) and the others discussed in this section which is relevant to the point at issue. They all make the truth of an existentially quantified sentence depend on the truth of a corresponding sentence in which a demonstrative or something similar occurs; and, it

may be said, demonstratives can only be used to denote in a given context what does in fact exist. That is, although we can use names which have a definite, though nonexistent, denotation, the use of context-dependent demonstratives to denote what does not exist is problematic. For how can what does not exist figure in the context of an utterance in such a way as to fix the denotation in that context of a demonstrative? Now it may be that the appearance of a difficulty here for demonstrative denotation of the nonexistent is illusory, but to pursue this matter further it would be necessary to discuss context-dependence in more detail than is appropriate here. I have only sought to indicate a line of thought which will yield the conclusion that some interpretations of quantifiers are referential. If this line of thought is not convincing, then, I think, no interpretation, not even a Tarskian one, can be shown to be referential.

This possibility, or lack of it, of denoting the non-existent affects the relations between 'absolute' denotation and denotation in all contexts, and thus casts doubt on the definition of absolute truth as truth in all contexts. For if 'den $(\alpha, c) = a$' entails 'a exists' whereas 'den$(\alpha) = a$' does not, then the latter cannot be equivalent to '$(\forall c)$ (den$(\alpha, c) = a)$'. In which case there will be no easy way of moving from (10) to (1). But I shall not pursue this matter here.

IV

It is obvious at a glance that the Tarskian interpretation (5) is much more similar to the interpretations (14), (16), and (20) which I have just discussed than it is to the simple substitutional interpretation (1). But in at least one respect the Tarskian interpretation still differs from these other interpretations, in that it requires that object-language variables be indexed. For these indices do not merely provide a notational variant for the more familiar convention of using a different letter for variables bound by a different quantifier. $\overline{x_2 \text{ loves } x_1}$ is true of $\langle \text{Mary}, \text{John}, .. \rangle$ if and only if John loves Mary, and not *vice versa*, whereas x loves y provides no similar clue to the conditions of its satisfaction by the same sequence. The indices, therefore, have a semantic role which is operative when the variables they index occur free, and to give a full picture of the relations between Tarskian and other interpretations this role must be elucidated.

This second role of the indices is to provide for an enumeration of object-language variables. This can be understood in two ways: one can either suppose that the indices simply belong to the metalanguage itself, so that they are just representative of an enumeration of the variables, with 'x_i' short for 'the ith variable' and a harmless confusion of use and mention in descriptions such as '$(\exists x_i)(x_i \text{ smokes})$'. Or, more naturally, one can suppose that the indices belong to the object-language, and that there is a 1–1 function *denn* from the indexed variables to natural numbers such that denn $(\overline{x_i}) = i$ etc. The introduction of this function *denn* requires nothing that is not implicit in a Tarskian theory itself. Some such function is implicit in (5) in the move from the object-language $\overline{(\exists x_i)(x_i \text{ smokes})}$ to the metalanguage's '$(\exists s')(s' \approx is)$', and the function thus presupposed is required by the theory to be 1–1, for otherwise inferences such as that from $\overline{(\exists x_i)(\exists x_j)(x_i \text{ loves } x_j)}$ to $\overline{(\exists x_i)(x_i \text{ loves } x_i)}$ would be validated where denn$(\overline{x_i}) = $ denn $(\overline{x_j})$. I shall take this second, more natural, approach, and assume, therefore, that the object-language variables are enumerated by *denn*$^{-1}$.

It is now easy to provide the framework for a comparison of Tarskian and non-Tarskian theories. Sequences are functions from natural numbers, and contexts for variables, d, are functions from variables with the same range; so *denn* provides the link between them. For any sequence a there is a unique context d such that d = denn o s, and *vice versa*; hence, there are analogues here for the identities which I set up when discussing the conditions under which Church's and Mates' theories are equivalent: e.g. den $(\overline{x_i}, d) = $ Val(denn $(\overline{x_i})$, s) where d = denn o s, and, where, in addition, d' = denn o s', $s'\underset{\text{denn}(\overline{x_i})}{\approx} s$ if and only if $'\underset{\overline{x_i}}{\approx} d$. In the light of these identities, one should look again at the characteristic Tarskian propositions (5) and (6), or, rather, the propositions obtained from them by substituting 'denn$(\overline{x_i})$' for 'i' throughout:

(24) $(\forall s)\overline{((\exists x_i)(x_i \text{ smokes})} \text{ is true of s} \leftrightarrow$

   $(\exists s')(s'\underset{\text{denn}(\overline{x_i})}{\approx} s \,\&\, \overline{x_i \text{ smokes}}$

   is true of s'))

(25) $(\forall s)\overline{(x_i \text{ smokes}} \text{ is true of s} \leftrightarrow$ Val(denn $(\overline{x_i}), s)$ smokes).

Application of the identities to these propositions shows their right-hand sides to be equivalent to

the right-hand sides of Church's (20) and (21) (with, of course, indexed variables in the object-language). Hence truth of s and truth in d coincide and Tarski's theory is, to all intents, the same as Church's. Apparent differences between them arise primarily from a difference in strategy: Church has contexts to assign denotations directly to variables, where Tarski has indices to provide an enumeration of variables, and it is then by means of this enumeration that variables are indirectly assigned denotations (or 'values') *via* sequences. Church's approach, I am bound to say, seems simpler, but there is no harm in Tarski's as long as one does not attempt to suppress the need for *denn*, and thereby to foster the illusion that Tarskian theories proceed without assigning denotations to anything.

It is now obvious how Tarski's theory relates to the overtly substitutional theories based on (1), (10), (14), and (16). Its relationship will be just an extension of the relationship between Church's theory and these theories, and by building up the assumptions used at each stage to show how these theories are connected, it would be possible to show in detail how to derive (1) from (5). But to spell this out in detail would only be to repeat the argument of the previous section and it is of more interest to observe that one can formulate Tarskian versions of the overtly substitutional theories discussed before.

Church's theory used contexts for variables, d; most of the other theories discussed in the previous section used contexts for singular terms, c. Hence to establish a 1–1 correspondence between these latter contexts and sequences, an enumeration of singular terms is needed. This will be provided by compounding *equ* and *denn*: for if equ$(\bar{a}) = \overline{x_i}$ then denn(equ$(\bar{a})) = i$. I shall abbreviate 'equ o denn' as 'dequ'. It is clear that one can now use *dequ* to do all the work done before by *denn*: e.g. given a sequence s, there is a unique context c such that c = dequ o s. Hence, Mates' (20) is equivalent to

(26) $(\forall s)\overline{((\exists x_i)(x_i \text{ smokes})} \text{ is true of s} \leftrightarrow$

   $(\exists s')(s'\underset{\text{dequ'}a}{\approx} s \,\&\, \overline{a \text{ smokes}}$

   is true of s'))

where $\bar{a}$ is the first singular term not in $\overline{(\exists x_i)(x_i \text{ smokes})}$. It is easy to see that the relationship between (26) and (24) is exactly the same as that between (16) and (20). By means of *dequ* one can also formulate an interpretation equivalent to the complex substitutional interpretation (14) –

$$(27) \quad (\forall s)(\overline{(\exists x_i)(x_i \text{ smokes})} \text{ is true of } s \leftrightarrow$$
$$(\exists \alpha)(\exists s')(s' \underset{\text{dequ}'a(\alpha)}{\approx} s \ \& \ Sub(\alpha, \overline{x_i},$$
$$\overline{x_i \text{ smokes}}) \text{ is true of } s'))$$

and this will be the basis of a viable theory of a mixed Tarskian and substitutional nature.

One can now proceed to formulate a Tarskian version of the manifestly substitutional (10); what is of more interest is the Tarskian version of the simple substitutional (1). It is simply (1) itself. The Tarskian version of (2) is, however,

$$(28) \quad (\forall \alpha)(Sub(\alpha, \overline{x_i}, \overline{x_i \text{ smokes}}) \text{ is true} \leftrightarrow$$
$$Val(dequ(\alpha)) \text{ smokes})$$

where *Val* is a function from numbers to objects in the domain. And just as (1) is more or less derivable from (14) given the assumption that the denotation of each singular term in the substitution class is the same in all contexts, (1) is in a similar way derivable from (27) on the assumption that the 'value' of a number is the same in all sequences, i.e. that the theory invokes just one sequence.

V

The burden of my argument in the last section was that although the simple substitutional interpretation (1) and the standard Tarskian interpretation (5) occupy the opposite ends of a spectrum of interpretations of the existential quantifier, once one spells out the intermediate interpretations ((10), (14), (16), and (20)) one can find a substantive link between them. However, I have so far discussed only interpretations of the existential quantifier, and what now needs examination is whether the situation is essentially the same for interpretations of other quantifiers. Take first the universal quantifier: the analogues here of (1) and (5) are familiar, but the analogues of the intermediate interpretations need to be stated. They are (with '$\overline{Sx}$' from now on for '$\overline{x \text{ smokes}}$'):

$$(10\forall) \quad (\forall c)(\overline{(\forall x(Sx)} \text{ is true in } c \leftrightarrow$$
$$(\forall \alpha)\overset{-\cap}{S} \alpha \text{ is true in } c)$$

$$(14\forall) \quad (\forall c)(\overline{(\forall x)(Sx)} \text{ is true in } c \leftrightarrow$$
$$(\forall c')(\forall \alpha)(c' \underset{\alpha}{\approx} c \rightarrow$$
$$\overset{-\cap}{S} \alpha \text{ is true in } c'))$$

$$(16\forall) \quad (\forall c)(\overline{(\forall x)(Sx)} \text{ is true in } c$$
$$\leftrightarrow (\forall c')(c' \underset{\bar{\alpha}}{\approx} c \rightarrow \overline{Sa} \text{ is true in } c'))$$

$$(20\forall) \quad (\forall d)(\overline{(\forall x)(Sx)} \text{ is true in } d$$
$$\leftrightarrow (\forall d')(d' \underset{\bar{x}}{\approx} d \rightarrow \overline{Sx} \text{ is in } d')).$$

There is no problem about the choice of (10$\forall$), (16$\forall$), and (20$\forall$); but the choice of (14$\forall$) needs justification. For it might be thought that it should run

$$(14\forall)' \quad (\forall c)(\overline{(\forall x)(Sx)} \text{ is true in } c \leftrightarrow$$
$$(\forall c')(\exists \alpha)(c' \underset{\alpha}{\approx} c \rightarrow$$
$$\overset{-\cap}{S} \alpha \text{ is true in } c'))$$

and, if this latter proposal were correct my general story would not hold. For (14$\forall$)' is not intermediate between (10$\forall$) and (16$\forall$) in the way that (14$\forall$) is. Nonetheless, the choice of (14$\forall$) can be justified. The propositions which in each case sufficed to derive the EQ T-sentence from (10), (16) and (20) also suffice in each case to derive the analogous universally quantified T-sentence from (10$\forall$), (16$\forall$), and (20$\forall$), and unless this were so these would not be the correct analogues of (10), (16), and (20). Hence the fact that the same universally quantified T-sentence is derivable from (14$\forall$) given (11), (12), and (15), but not from (14$\forall$)' on the same premises, shows that (14$\forall$) is the correct analogue of (14).

It seems, therefore, that my argument can be straightforwardly generalised to interpretations of other quantifiers. Yet the truth is not so simple. For consider the quantifier 'For no x, . . x . .' (I shall write this as '(No x) (. . x . .)': extrapolating from (14) and (14$\forall$), one is led to suggest the interpretation:

$$(14N) \quad (\forall c)(\overline{(No \ x)(Sx)} \text{ is true in } c \leftrightarrow$$
$$(No \ \alpha)(No \ c')(c' \approx c \overset{-\cap}{S} \alpha \text{ is true in } c'))$$
$$\underset{\alpha}{}$$

Yet (14N) is false. This can be seen by observing that since '(No x)(Sx)' is equivalent to '($\forall$ x) (Not (Sx))', (14N) is equivalent to the manifestly incorrect

$(\forall c)(\overline{(\forall x)(\text{Not}(Sx))}$ is true in $c \leftrightarrow$

$$(\forall \alpha)(\exists c')(c' \approx c \ \& \ \overset{-\cap}{\underset{\alpha}{S}} \alpha \text{ is true in } c'))$$

The way round this problem is to recognize that (14) and (14 $\forall$) are not correctly formulated for the purposes of extrapolation, and the device that is needed is an unordered pair quantifier such as '$(\exists \alpha, c')(\ldots \alpha \ldots c' \ldots)$'. The intuitive sense of such quantifiers is clear, and their semantics are not essentially different from those of familiar quantifiers (though I shall only be using them in the metalanguage). (14) and (14 $\forall$) are equivalent to, respectively,

$(14)^*$ $\quad (\forall c)(\overline{(\exists x)(Sx)}$ is true in $c \leftrightarrow$

$$(\exists \alpha, c'(c' \approx c \ \& \ \overset{-\cap}{\underset{\alpha}{S}} \alpha \text{ is true in } c'))$$

$(14\forall)^*$ $\quad (\forall c)(\overline{(\forall x)(Sx)}$ is true in $c \leftrightarrow$

$$(\forall \alpha, c'(c' \approx c \rightarrow \overset{-\cap}{\underset{\alpha}{S}} \alpha \text{ is true in } c'))$$

which do now provide the basis for a suitable extrapolation to $\overline{(\text{No } x)(Sx)}$

$(14N)^*$ $\quad (\forall c)(\overline{(\text{No } x)(Sx)}$ is true in $c \leftrightarrow$

$$(\text{No } \alpha, c')(c' \approx c \ \& \ \overset{-\cap}{\underset{\alpha}{S}} \alpha \text{ is true in } c'))$$

$(14N)^*$ is not equivalent to (14N), and one can see that it is correct by applying to it the general equivalence between

'(No x, y) $(\ldots x \ldots y \ldots)$' and '($\forall$ x, y) (Not $(\ldots x \ldots y \ldots)$)' to infer:

$(\forall c)(\overline{(\forall x)(\text{Not}(Sx))}$ is true in $c \leftrightarrow$

$$(\forall \alpha, c')(c' \approx c \rightarrow \text{Not} \ \overset{-\cap}{\underset{\alpha}{S}} \alpha \text{ is true in } c'))$$

which is precisely what $(14\forall)^*$ leads one to expect. In order to vindicate $(14N)^*$ fully, one should show both that the appropriate T-sentence is derivable from $(14N)^*$ and (11), (12), and (15), and that $(14N)^*$ is suitably intermediate between the analogues of (16) and (10) for $\overline{(\text{No } x)(Sx)}$. But the truth of both these claims follows from the truth of the similar claims about $(14\forall)^*$, and I shall not fill in the details.

So it does now look as if my argument can be generalised to other quantifiers. However, the full story is more complex. Once one looks beyond the familiar Aristotelian quantifiers ('All', 'Some', etc.) to less familiar plurality quantifiers ('Many', 'Several', etc.) and the numerical quantifiers, the form of the substitutional interpretations I have discussed turns out to be inadequate. Just how this inadequacy should be met, and the general argument of this paper extended, I shall not here discuss.

Notes

I am enormously indebted to Dr. T. J. Smiley for repeated criticisms of earlier drafts of this paper.

1   Camp's argument is in some ways similar to that propounded by Kripke (1976, pp. 355–68). But the relationship between Wallace and Kripke is a complex matter which I discuss in another paper in *Analysis*, 1978.

2   I write composition of functions in the order appropriate to the relative product of a pair of relations, which is the opposite of that employed in the ordinary 'f (g (x))' notation.

References

Boolos, G. and Jeffrey, R. 1973. *Computability and Logic*, London: Cambridge University Press.

Camp, J. 1975. 'Truth and Substitution Quantifiers', *Nous*, 9.

Church, A. 1956. *Introduction to Mathematical Logic, Vol. I*, Princeton: Princeton University Press.

Geach, P. 1962. *Reference and Generality*, Ithaca: Cornell University Press.

Gottlieb, D. 1974. 'Reference and Ontology', *Journal of Philosophy* 71.

Haack, S. 1974. *Deviant Logic*, Cambridge: Cambridge University Press.

Kripke, S. 1976. 'Is there a Problem about Substitutional Quantification?' in *Truth and Meaning* (eds. Evans, G. and McDowell, J.), Oxford: Oxford University Press.

Mates, B. 1965. *Elementary Logic*, New York: Oxford University Press.

Quine, W. 1973. *Roots of Reference*, La Salle: Open Court.

Thomas Baldwin

Russell, B. 1919. *Introduction to Mathematical Philosophy*, London: Allen and Unwin.

Tarski, A. 1936. 'Der Wahrheitsbegriff in den formalisierten Sprachen', *Studia Philosophica* I, translated as 'The Concept of Truth in Formalised Languages' in A. Tarski: *Logic, Semantics, Metamathematics*, Oxford, 1956: Oxford University Press.

Wallace, J. 1970. 'On the Frame of Reference', *Synthese*, 22.

Wallace, J. 1975. 'Response to Camp', *Nous*, 9.

Weston, T. 1974. 'Theories whose Quantification cannot be Substitutional', *Nous*, 8.

Williams, C. 1976. *What is Truth,?* Cambridge: Cambridge University Press.

14

Language-Games for Quantifiers

Jaakko Hintikka

Logical Expressions

One way of looking at logic is to view it as a study of certain words and phrases which we may label *logical expressions*. Whether or not one can thus obtain a general definition of the province of logic, this point of view is useful for many purposes.[1] For instance, quantification theory may be characterized from this point of view as the study of the phrases "there is," and "for every" over and above the study of the words "not," "and," and "or," which are already studied in propositional logic, plus whatever terms are required to express predication. I shall call these phrases and other expressions with similar meanings *quantifying expressions*.[2]

In books and papers on logic, some aspects of the behavior of these expressions are studied. However, they are usually studied mainly as they appear in more or less strictly regimented systems of formal logic. The meaning they have in unregimented discourse is not often discussed directly, nor is the relevance of these formal studies to the more ordinary uses of the quantifying expressions "there is," and "for every." In this paper I shall deal with these questions, questions on whose importance I scarcely need to enlarge.

Meaning as Use

Plenty of advice is in fact available to tell me how to straighten the defect just mentioned. Much of

Jaakko Hintikka, Language-Games for Quantifiers. *Studies in Logical Theory.* Ed. Nicholas Rescher. Oxford: Blackwell Publishers, 1968. 46–73

this advice is summed up in the famous remark of Wittgenstein's: "The meaning of a word is its use in the language."[3] This dictum is not unequivocal, however, not even if we recall that it was only supposed by Wittgenstein to cover a large class of words, not the meanings of all possible words that there are. Here I am not interested in bringing out all the different aspects of Wittgenstein's advice. For my present purposes it suffices to confine our attention to one of the most important things Wittgenstein apparently meant by his dictum. This aspect of his remark has not always been brought out as clearly as it ought to have been.

It is perhaps easier to say what in Wittgenstein's *dictum* I am *not* interested in (for the purposes of this paper). Sometimes distinction is made between the use of words and the use of language.[4] Under the former title philosophers have considered the use of words for the purpose of forming sentences or for referring. Under the latter title, they have usually considered the different language acts or speech acts which one can perform by uttering or by writing a sentence. The uses of language are then those uses which one can make by uttering or writing something.

It seems to me that this distinction is not an exhaustive one, and that the uses of words which I am primarily interested in here are largely forgotten if the situation is described in these terms. It is obvious that Wittgenstein did not have in mind only the uses of words for the purpose of constructing sentences out of them when he coined his slogan. Furthermore, he certainly did not have in mind only the acts one can perform by saying something or in saying something. It is not for nothing that Wittgenstein often speaks of the uses of *Wörter*, that is to say, of individual words, and not only of the uses of *Worte*, that is to say, of words articulated into sentences.[5] The study of the different types of speech-acts does not exhaust the import of Wittgenstein's advice. The uses we are invited to consider do not always take the form of locutionary or illocutionary acts. Wittgenstein is not asking what we do or can do by uttering a sentence. He is also asking what we must be able to do or what people must generally do in order for us to understand a word.[6] He is calling our attention to a certain environment of types of action or activities which a word often has and outside which it loses its meaning (or its use, if you prefer).

These activities may be activities one performs by uttering a sentence, but they need not be. The verb "thank" loses its use (or meaning) in the absence of the custom of thanking. This custom happens to be such that one can thank by saying "thank you." However, the fact that one can do this is largely inessential to the connection which there is between the custom (or institution) of thanking and the meaning of the verb "to thank." For we could use this verb meaningfully even if it were not our custom to thank by saying anything but (for instance) merely by means of certain gestures. As our actual customs go, it is certainly possible to thank someone without using the verb "to thank." In the case of certain other words, for instance, of the verb "to score" (in a game), the activities we must be able to master, if only from the point of view of a spectator, are such that they are never performed merely by saying something. Thus, for one who is primarily interested in the activities which constitute the natural environment of a word and from which it gets its meaning, the things one can do by means of words are not of a central importance. What is important is the connection between words and the activities which typically surround it. The aspect of Wittgenstein's advice which I want to take up here is therefore closely related to his notion of a language-game. "I shall also call the whole, consisting of language and the activities into which it is woven, the 'language-game'"; "Here the term language-game is meant to bring into prominence the fact that the speaking of language is part of an activity, or a form of life."[7] The emphasis is here as much and more on the actions in the framework of which the use of words occurs as on the actions

which one can perform by using certain words. The activities which typically surround a word and from which it gets its meaning might be called the language-game in which the word in question is at home.

Relation to Operationalism

An extreme, and exaggerated, form of this dependence of certain words on non-linguistic activities for their meaning is claimed to obtain by the group of doctrines known as operationalism.[8] In spite of the vagueness and crudity of operationalistic doctrines some aspects of these views merit a comparison with those aspects of Wittgenstein's ideas we are interested in here. It is important to realize, however, that the interpretation I am putting on Wittgenstein's words does not commit me to anything like operationalism. On a typical operationalistic view, to make a statement containing operationally defined words is to make a prediction, as it were, concerning the outcome of the operations which are associated with these words. What is more, it is normally required that these operations can be performed once and for all. It is required, moreover, that they can be performed in only one way. It is also required that to each operationally defined word there is but one defining activity or "operation" associated with it.

These three requirements (together with other similar requirements which strict operationalism imposes on the activities from which our words receive their meaning) seem to me exceedingly narrow-minded. There does not seem to be any reason to deny that a word may be connected with an activity or mode of action which does not necessarily terminate or whose termination point is at least unpredictable. There also seems to be no reason whatsoever to deny that the activities in question can be performed in many alternative ways. Furthermore, one has to realize that a word may be connected with reality not through a single operation, but rather through a network of subtle interrelations which involve a good many theoretical assumptions.

In spite of all these shortcomings, there are some purposes which an operationalistic view of language may serve. It serves to bring out, albeit in a distorted form, one aspect of the notion of "the use of language" which is sometimes forgotten. If its exaggerations are removed, it offers a simplified model with which we may compare some of the things which actually happen when a language is being used. In any case, this is the assumption I shall be working on in this paper.

Verbs and Activities

It can be given a somewhat more linguistic turn. Actions and activities are in our language typically represented by verbs. As a consequence, an answer to the question: "What activities constitute the natural environment of a word?" may sometimes be reformulated as an answer to the question: "What verbs are there to which the word in question has an especially intimate logical relation?"[9] Of course, it cannot be assumed that this reformulation is viable in all cases nor assumed that for every word there is but one verb to which it is related logically. For instance, the word which has probably been studied more than any other philosophically interesting word, the word "good," has several different verbs associated with it in this manner. They include the verbs "to evaluate," "to grade," "to praise," "to commend," "to recommend," and "to appreciate."[10] On a given occasion, a statement which contains the word "good" can perhaps be paraphrased in terms of one of these verbs, but no single one of them enables us to reformulate (in context) all the sentences containing the word "good." It is also obvious that if the activities which are expressed by the verbs just listed would cease, the word "good" would lose much of its use and in a sense therefore much of its meaning. There is thus a logical connection between the word "good" and the verbs listed, a connection which is the more interesting the more clearly the paraphrases we can obtain in terms of these verbs bring out the logical conditions of the use of the word "good."

Verbs for Quantifiers

it seems to me that there is an even more interesting instance of this in the philosophy of logic. There are verbs which are not merely logical relatives of the quantifiers "there is," and "for all," but which are veritable next of kin of theirs. These verbs are not to be found among the verbs a philosopher is apt to think in connection with logic, for instance, not among the verbs "to infer," "to follow," "to deduce," "to contradict," and "to refute."[11] In no important case can a quantifier be paraphrased in terms of them, although interesting attempts have been made to connect the most important rules for operating with quantifiers with the notions of inference and deduction.[12]

There are much better candidates for the role, namely, such verbs as "to search," "to look for," "to seek," and "to find." In more than one natural language, existence is in fact expressed by speaking of what "can be found" (cf. e.g., the Swedish phrase "det finns" which literally taken means just this). E. Gilson writes that according to Averroës, "the Arabic word meaning 'to exist' came from a root originally meaning 'found', because it seems to have been a common notion that, for any given thing, to exist meant approximately 'to be found there'."[13] In the everyday parlance of mathematicians, existence is typically expressed in this way. It is also obvious enough that instead of "there are black swans" we can in many contexts say "one can find black swans," and, instead of "all swans are white," one can sometimes say "no swans can be found which are not white." One "language-game" in which quantifiers can naturally occur is what I shall call the language-game of seeking and finding; and it seems to me that this is by far the most important kind of language-game in which they can occur. In this respect, the case of quantifiers is different from that of the word "good" which can occur in the context of many different types of activity none of which seems much more interesting logically than the others.

Caveats

There are of course, circumstances in which quantified sentences cannot naturally be rewritten in terms of seeking and finding. "There are mountains on the Moon" is more naturally paraphrased as "One can see mountains on the Moon" than as "One can find mountains on the Moon." In this case, coming to know the existence of the objects in question is a matter of direct observation and therefore ill-suited to the verbs "to seek" or "to search" which normally suggest that some amount of effort and of shifting one's point of view is needed. It is important to realize, however, that ascertaining the existence of individual objects by direct observation is a very special case of coming to know the existence of individuals. What is apt to mislead one is that in the most typical cases a search terminates in a situation in which one is confronted by a directly observable object. However, this does not make it true to say that the existence of the object in question was discovered by direct observation, for that would entirely overlook what seems to be the most important element in the situation, viz. the activities of seeking or trying to find.[14] Saying that we always come to know the existence of individual objects by sensible perception is like saying that one comes to London from New York by bus when what one means is that one flies over and then takes a bus to London from the airport.

It can also be pointed out that when the situations are described more closely in which we allegedly become aware of the existence of certain objects merely by witnessing them, we very often find ourselves using words that are closely similar logically to words for searching and seeking. In order to see an object which is at hand, it does not always suffice to open one's eyes; we very often have to scan our visual field even though we do not have to move ourselves from place to place bodily. Words like "scan" are obviously related to words for seeking and searching. (Scanning as *visual* searching.)[15]

There is also an opposite type of case in which a paraphrase of a quantified sentence in terms of searching and finding does not sit quite happily. It may be illustrated by the sentence "there are transuranium elements" which it would be a little awkward to paraphrase as "one can find transuranic elements." What misfires here is the fact that to speak simply of seeking and finding often suggests that no highly technical methods are required to get at the entities in question. It is more natural to say e.g., that one can produce transuranium elements. It is of some interest to note that paraphrases in terms of seeking and finding become perceptibly less awkward if the methods used are specified, thus eliminating the source of awkwardness. It is perfectly natural to say, for instance, that transuranium elements were found by such-and-such methods.

In general, the words "to seek" and "to find" apply most aptly to the middle range of cases in which an effort has to be made to become aware of the existence (or non-existence) in question but in which no greatly sophisticated procedures are needed. We may of course imagine circumstances in which this middle range of cases becomes increasingly less important. Then verbs other than "to seek" and "to find" might become more

important for the meaning of the quantifying expressions of the language in question.

These qualifications nevertheless do not seriously reflect on the importance of the two verbs for appreciating the logic of quantifying expressions. It may be that quantifiers are sometimes better served by the verb "to produce" than by "to find," but many of the relevant logical features of these two verbs are closely similar. Nor do our qualifications sever the discussion from what we find in ordinary discourse. In natural language existence and universality are often expressed by speaking of the outcomes of different courses of action. A case in point is the German idiom "es gibt" whose origin is betrayed by such sentences as "Wenn du hingehst, so gibt es Unglück" (meaning literally: "if you go there, "it gives" misfortune" – an example listed in Hermann Paul's *Wörterbuch*). In the informal jargon of mathematicians, universality is often expressed by such phrases as "no matter which number you take..." The exceptional cases in which "to seek" and "to find" do not give us very natural paraphrases of the quantifiers may even be considered, for our limited purposes, as special cases of seeking and finding in an extended sense. Direct observation is a "trivial case" of finding, and the discovery of an object by a complicated technical procedure may perhaps be considered as the issue of a search conducted by very special means. In this extended sense, it may thus be said that all our knowledge of the existence of external objects is obtained by means of the activities of seeking and finding.

Quantifiers Not Operationalistically Interpretable

In a sense, the meaning of quantifiers is thus their role ("use") in the language games of seeking and finding, with all the qualifications which I have indicated. On this view, a statement containing quantifiers is comparable with a prediction concerning the outcome of certain processes of searching. These processes are the processes of seeking which we would have to carry out in order to verify the sentence in question. Of course, nothing is said of how these procedures should be conducted. One is also abstracting from all the contingent limitations of our actual capacity of search. Thus the processes of seeking and finding are not "operations" of the kind an operationalistic theory of meaning envisages. One can almost say that, on the contrary, the notions of existence and universality receive their importance from the fact that all the individuals that are known to exist cannot be produced by "operations" whose course is determined in advance. In so far as there is an effective method of verifying or falsifying existential sentences, there is little point in using these sentences. If there were such a method, existential sentences could be replaced by sentences which speak of the particular instances of the claimed existence which are *per hypothesis* obtainable.

How deeply this uncertainty about the outcome of seeking and finding really cuts is indicated by the undecidability of quantification theory. What this undecidability means may be roughly explained by saying that one cannot always predict how far one would have to go in an attempted model set construction in order to bring out the possible inconsistency which may lurk in the set which we are trying to imbed in a model set. In another paper I shall argue that there is a certain analogy between the processes of model set construction and the activities of seeking and finding which one has to perform in verifying or falsifying sentences.[16] In view of this analogy, we may perhaps say that the processes of seeking and finding are as unpredictable as model set constructions.

Furthermore, there usually are many alternative ways of trying to construct a model set for a given set of sentences. Correspondingly, there usually are many alternative ways of trying to verify a sentence by looking for suitable individuals. It is impossible to give general rules as to which alternative will yield a model set, if such there be. Likewise, there does not seem to be much hope of telling which one of many alternative ways of looking for individuals, which would verify a given sentence, is the likeliest one to produce results. In some sense, the activities of seeking and finding therefore present irreducible alternatives. All this shows how far a cry the activities of seeking and looking for are from the operations which an operationalist is willing to countenance.

Language-Games as Games Proper

One way of explaining my theory of what it means to understand quantifiers is to say that according to it one can understand quantifiers if one knows how to play certain kinds of *games*. Whatever there is to be said of the use of the Wittgensteinian term "language-game" in general, here the word "game" at any rate sits especially happily. This happiness is not only due to whatever informal similarities there are between games proper and those activities which Gilbert Ryle has called "the game of exploring the world."[17] It is primarily due to the fact that in the case of quantifiers, the relevant "language-games" can also be formulated as games in the precise game-theoretical sense of the word.

In these games, one's opponent can be thought of in different ways: he may be simply nature, but he may also be some recalcitrant *malin genie* making the most of his chances of frustrating us. The game is most easily explained in the case of sentences in the prenex normal form (initial string of quantifiers followed by a "matrix" which does not contain any quantifiers). Since all quantificational sentences (classically interpreted) can be converted into this form, the explanation of the "game" that goes together with such a sentence will be in effect rather general.

My end in the game is to make a substitution-instance of the matrix true. My opponent's ("nature's") aim is to make the outcome of the game to be a false substitution-instance of the matrix. Each existential quantifier marks my move: I choose (produce, find) an individual whose name is to be substituted for the corresponding bound variable.[18] Each universal quantifier marks a move by my opponent: he is free to produce an individual whose name is to be substituted for the variables bound to the universal quantifier. The order of the moves corresponds to the order of the quantifiers.

It is readily seen that quite a few things which are ordinarily expressed by speaking of quantified sentences can be expressed by speaking of the correlated games. For instance, for a sentence to be true it is necessary and sufficient that I have (as a matter of fact) a winning strategy in the correlated game, in the sense of game theory.[19]

On the other hand, it is quite clear that the games which this interpretation associates with quantificational sentences are to all intents and purposes tantamount to the games ("language-games") of looking for and finding. The imaginary opponent merely serves to highlight our own attempts to make sure that certain kinds of counter-examples cannot be found (that the opponent "cannot defeat us"). Hence our interpretation does in a sense bring out all there is to be brought out in the logic of quantification.

The naturalness of the game-theoretic point of view is illustrated by the fact that this interpretation is sometimes resorted to spontaneously by writers who are explaining the meaning of quantifiers in non-systematic contexts. Developed more systematically, it has been employed by Leon Henkin, not only to explain the meaning of the usual kind of quantification, but to extend it further in one direction.[20]

Notice that the question as to what the individual moves are to be *called* is left open by the game-theoretic interpretation which I have sketched. The applicability of whatever term we want to use will depend on the details of the situation. In one of them, seeking and finding may be the most apt words; in another, producing might be a better one. In this respect, the game-theoretic interpretation is neutral with respect to the choice between these different descriptive expressions. It also brings out the fact that this choice is largely immaterial for my purposes, for clearly the games in question have the same character (same structure) no matter what the procedures are *called* that lead me to choose one individual rather than another. Hence many of the language-games which I have called games of seeking and finding might be as well (and better) called something else. All this is closely related to what I said earlier of the applicability of the various words of the natural language to the language-games in question.

The games just described are in many ways closely related to the systematic theory of quantification, and might even open possibilities of generalizing it. Some possibilities and some results that have already been reached in this direction are indicated in the appendix. Here I shall only explain how the game-theoretic interpretation can be extended to sentences which are not in the prenex form. Again the game proceeds from the whole sentence to substitution-instances of its sub-sentences. My aim is to end up with a true atomic sentence. The rules for quantifiers remain the same. Disjunction now marks my move: I have to choose a disjunct with reference to which the game is continued. Conjunction marks a move by my opponent: he chooses a conjunct with reference to which the game is continued. Negation $\sim F$ has the effect of changing the roles of the players, after which the game continues by reference to F. This serves to define the game correlated with any quantificational sentence, assuming that a domain of individuals is given with the appropriate predicates defined on this domain.

The games which are thus correlated with quantificational sentences are closely connected with

the activities by means of which one can try to verify these sentences. As far as my own moves are concerned, precisely the same things are involved in the verification of quantificational sentences and in the games we have correlated with them. In the case of my opponent's moves, I have to make sure that I cannot be defeated by any of his strategies. This can be thought of as involving a temporary switch of roles: I have to play the role of the devil's (or the nature's) advocate – that is, the role of my opponent – for a while in order to see what possibilities he has of defeating me. This is neatly reflected by the possibility of replacing the universal quantifier $(\forall x)$ by $\sim (\exists x) \sim$, which eliminates my opponent's move but involves a temporary exchange of roles.

With this proviso, the games I have described are in effect the activities by means of which one can try to verify quantificational sentences. By describing these games in some detail one can thus see what the activities are of whose outcomes we are making, as it were, a prediction when we assert a quantificational sentence. All this illustrated the close logical connection which (I am arguing) there is between quantifiers and the "games" of looking for and finding.

Presuppositions of the Language-Games of Seeking and Finding

The justification for this connection must lie to a considerable extent in the light which this connection throws on the logical behavior of the quantifying expressions of ordinary language and of formal logic. Does it throw any such light?

If quantifiers go together with the verbs "to seek," "to look for," and "to find," the conditions for the significant (or, as some students of language would like us to say, non-deviant) use of quantifiers must be approximately the same as the conditions for the use of these verbs. Now what is required for the notions of seeking and looking for to make sense? Two main requirements obviously have to be met. First, the field of search must somehow be defined, however partially. Second, there must be ways of ascertaining when one has found the individual or the kind of individual one has been looking for. These are obviously also requirements that have to be satisfied in order for the games properly described above to be playable.

I shall call these requirements the first and the second requirement. Both of them are relevant to the logical behavior of quantifying expressions in ordinary language and in the formal systems of logic. We shall examine them in the order in which they were mentioned.

The first requirement helps us to understand, *inter alia*, why unqualified statements of existence are apt to strike one as odd (deviant). We are likely to find any number of perfectly natural utterances of the form "there are chairs upstairs," or "there is an infinity of prime numbers," but it is doubtful whether we can find many non-deviant utterances of the form "there are numbers" or "there are chairs" outside the philosophers' discussions.

It is now easy to see what is wrong with these unqualified statements. Part of the function of the missing qualification is to indicate what this field of search is: hence the meaning of these statements is incomplete, and can only be gathered from the context at best.

It is interesting to note that a very small change alters the situation radically. The statement "there are black swans" is perfectly in order, as might indeed be expected from our point of view. In this statement the class of swans constitutes the relevant field of search, or part of it, which is taken to be given clearly enough for the operations of seeking and finding to make sense. Attention is concentrated, so to speak, on the additional question whether within this well-defined universe of discourse one can find swans of a particular color.

There is an interesting asymmetry here between positive and negative statements. Although sentences like "there are swans" are very often awkward to utter, similar negative statements like "there are no dodos" are perfectly in order. Again an explanation is forthcoming. In an unqualified negative statement the field of search does not matter (if it does, the statement is dangerously vague), and hence the need for specifying it is much smaller than is the corresponding positive statement. These, in turn, can lose their awkwardness when contrasted to a real or imagined effort to deny the existence of the individuals in question. As Peter Geach has urged on me,[21] there is nothing wrong with a sentence like "there *are* swans, and they really are ugly in their first year, just as Hans Andersen says."

The same point emerges also from the observation of other quantifying expressions of ordinary language. Such words as "some," "any," and "all" are, in Austin's phrase, substantive-hungry. No matter whether the statement "there are swans" makes sense or not, it cannot be paraphrased in terms of "some" without bringing in new words which serve to indicate the relevant field of search, for instance, "Some extant birds are swans." The words "some" and "any" occur in such constructions as "some X" or "some X's" and "any X," where X is a general noun. Part of the function of this general noun, and a reason why it is needed, is to indicate the field of search which is being presupposed. Where such a field of search or part of it is available, these words can be used. Thus "There are black swans," becomes "Some swans are black." A statement like "All ravens are black" is therefore not quite accurately translated into the language of formal logic by "$(\forall x)$ (x is a raven $\supset x$ is black)," for in this translation some definitely given large universe of discourse is being presupposed while in the original the extent of the underlying field of search was left largely unspecified, the only relevant assumption being that it must include all ravens.[22]

Often the exact boundaries of the field of search are not clearly defined; there is a similar vagueness in the meaning of the corresponding quantified sentences. Austin once posed the question (it was one of the problems which have been published in *Analysis*) whether the statement "All swans are white" refers to whatever swans there may be on the canals of Mars.[23] As emerged from the answers, there is a complication here in that the inductive evidence on which we may think of the statement to be based may tacitly restrict its scope to terrestial swans. Apart from this complication, however, the statement serves to illustrate the vagueness I have in mind.

Formal logicians usually assume that all the different fields of search can be happily pooled together into one big "universe of discourse." There may be reasons for this complacency, but the situation would merit a closer look. The difficulty of pooling different fields of search together does not lie primarily in the dissimilarity of the entities which thus have to be treated as equal. A more important problem is due to the fact that there may be interdependencies between individuals in the different fields of search. One may look for rivers of different kinds, and one may look for waters of different kinds. However, there cannot exist rivers without there also existing waters.[24]

In the applications of logic the frequent indeterminacy of the pertinent field of search is shown especially clearly by the odd results of the process of contraposition. It seems rather odd to paraphrase "every man is selfish" by "no unselfish thing is a man." These two sentences will be logically equivalent as soon as the relevant field of search has been fixed. But the sentences themselves do not specify this field, and they presuppose different things concerning it. "Every man is selfish" presupposes that the class of all men is part of the field of search. "No unselfish thing is a man" presupposes that the totality of unselfish things has been defined clearly enough to be amenable to our activities of seeking and finding. Hence these two sentences do not have the same logical powers in ordinary discourse.

These odd results of contraposition cannot be explained away in the way in which some philosophers have sought to explain away some of the paradoxes of confirmation, that is to say, by reference to the relative sizes of the classes involved. In the case at hand such an attempt would presumably consist of pointing out that there are many more things (and things of many different sorts) which cannot be said to be selfish than there are human beings, and of arguing that this makes it more natural to use the former class as an antecedent of a general implication than the latter. However, this maneuver does not help at all. "No indivisible entity is a material body" is markedly more deviant than "every material body is divisible," all the more so in the mouth of a materialist.

In the same way, the statements "some swans are black" and "some black objects are swans" are not equivalent in ordinary discourse. The former presupposes that the relevant field of search includes all swans, the latter that it includes all black objects.

In relation to the requirement that the field of search is to be delineated, the verb "to produce" behaves somewhat differently from the verb "to look for." The methods of producing an object of a certain kind both with respect to their scope and with respect to the nature of the procedures involved are restricted somewhat less narrowly than the methods of finding one. In this sense, the "field of search" connected with production is wider and more flexible than those connected with searching and finding. This may be part of the reason why it is more natural to say, for instance, "we can produce transuranium elements" or "we can produce neutrinos" than to say, "we can find transuranium elements" or, "we can find neutrinos." Sometimes this difference is connected with doubts about whether the

objects produced exist objectively apart from our methods of production. However, even where this is not at issue, the difference between the verbs "to produce" and "to find" is marked enough, as it seems to be in the examples I just gave. All this tends to make the verb "to produce" somewhat more amenable to the purposes of a formal logician, who needs a large, all-comprehensive field of search for his "universe of discourse," than the verb "to find."

End-Points of Search

The second requirement is likewise of considerable interest. In order for the notions of seeking and finding to make sense, and hence for the quantifiers to make sense, we must have some idea of the circumstances in which we can stop and claim to have found what we have been looking for. In brief, the conditions of having found the thing we are looking for must be determined. These may often be defined with reference to the results of further search; i.e., quantifiers may occur within the scope of other quantifiers; but ultimately our conditions will normally specify absolute stopping-points for our search. Of course, the conditions of "really having found" something are not always without a certain vagueness. The paradigmatic case is that of being able to point to a physical object or to a man and to say: "There is one!" But how the other cases shade into this one is not always very clear. However, this vagueness does not sever the logic of seeking and finding from that of existence. The difficulties which there often are in deciding whether entities which we cannot immediately confront (such as a neutrino, a field, or a gene) "really exist" or not are largely difficulties in deciding what is to count as finding or producing one of these entities.[25] As Stephen Toulmin puts it, certain things are generally taken to be sufficient for the purpose of showing the "real existence" of physical entities, "for instance, cloud-chamber pictures of α-rays, electron microscope photographs, or, as a second best, audible clicks from a Geiger counter."[26] The reason why these count as demonstrations of actual existence is that they are, again in Toulmin's words, "sufficiently like being shown a living dodo on the lawn" or, in my terms, sufficiently like the paradigmatic cases of finding an object by directly confronting it. Thus for a working physicist "the question, 'Do neutrinos exist?' acts as an invitation to 'produce a neutrino,' preferably by making it visible' – or, as we may equally well say, to find a neutrino for us to witness.

The second requirement also seems to me to be relevant to the evaluation of a famous "argument" of G. E. Moore. Norman Malcolm has suggested that what looks like arguments in Moore should often be construed as reminders that certain concepts have a logically correct use in our language.[27] On this view, Moore did not have to produce *true* or *paradigmatic* examples of the use of these concepts in order to accomplish his end, although he certainly did try to do so himself. What happens now to this view if it is applied to Moore's famous "proof of the external world"?[28] The crucial concept here is that of existence. What do we have to be reminded of in order to bring it home to us that we can use it impeccably as applied to what Moore calls "external objects" or "objects which are to be met with in space"? It follows from what I have said that there are two main things one has to ascertain in order to make sure that a concept of existence applies to objects of a certain sort; they are incorporated in my first and second requirement. The first is not crucial here, partly because we are dealing with the question whether there are any "external objects" at all. This being so, we are in effect facing a potential denial of the existence of any "external objects" at all, which makes the precise specification of the field of search less crucial in the same way it did in our dodo example earlier.

Hence the main burden falls on the requirement that we must have criteria of having found whatever we are looking for. This requirement in effect says that it must make sense to say, "Now I have found an X" in order for the concept of existence to be applicable to X's. How could one hope to bring home to an audience that we do in fact have such criteria for deciding when we have found "an external object" or have met "an object to be met with in space"? Clearly by staging as paradigmatic an instance of a confrontation with an "external object" as one could imagine. One displays an "external object" and says, "Here is one"; one displays another and says, "Here is another." And this is precisely what Moore does in his "proof of the external world": he waves a hand and says, "Here is a hand."

What Moore does thus receives a perfectly reasonable and indeed predictable sense when seen in the light in which Malcolm wants to view Moore's philosophical activity in general. By enacting his little scene, Moore reminds us that we know perfectly well what it means to be confronted with an "external object" so as to be able to say, "Here is one!" and that one of the main presuppositions of our use of the concept of existence is therefore satisfied. In Moore there is, of course, also the implication that in the ensuing sense of existence, it is indeed obvious that there are "external objects." I would agree with Malcolm, however, that for this purpose Moore's skit is both unnecessary and perhaps even insufficient. It matters little whether on the actual occasion before the British Academy Moore actually succeeded in pointing to his hand or to any other external object.[29] What matters is only the fact that we can in principle do this and that we also often succeed in doing so. Moore is not as much proving the existence of the external world as pointing out that we have in fact an impeccable concept of existence as applied to hands, chairs, houses and other commonplace "external objects."

I am not quite sure whether our concept of existence as applied to commonplace external objects is quite as unproblematic as Moore's argument presupposes (on the construction I have put on it). However, even if it is not, there is a point Moore's argument makes: In so far as we do have a satisfactory idea of what it means for external objects to exist, it must make sense to speak of finding them and confronting them. If we want to criticize the former idea, we have to examine the latter idea more closely.

It may be argued that the interest of Moore's "proof" is difficult to bring out in other ways. For instance, it does not help to ask what Moore was doing when he said, "Here is one hand, and here is another." He certainly was not informing his audience of something they did not know before. Nor is there any other natural purpose in view which his statement could serve. The whole question of the *use* of his statement seems oddly out of place.

Moore's argument cannot be construed as a formal inference, either. We may admit that hands are external objects, but this does not carry us very far. The crucial statement "this is a hand" or "here is a hand" should presumably be taken as a subject-predicate of the form $P(a)$. I have pointed out elsewhere that from this we can only infer $(\exists x)P(x)$ (i.e., "hands exist") if we have an additional premiss of the form $(\exists x)(x = a)$ which ensures that the object referred to by the term a ("this object") exists.[30] However, this is just what we cannot assume here. To assume that the hand

Moore is waving really exists is to beg the very question he is asking. Hence his argument does not have any validity as a formal proof. We can draw existential conclusions without explicit or hidden existential premisses as little as we can derive as "ought" from an "is." Whatever persuasiveness Moore's famous "proof" has derives from its being the kind of paradigmatic confrontation with an external object which we must have in order for the notion of existence to be applicable.

Marking the Different Moves

In order to bring out more fully the connection between quantifying expressions and the activities of seeking and finding and to perceive some of the consequences of this connection it is advisable to consider somewhat more complicated cases. Consider as an example the sentence "Some Englishman has seen all the countries of the world." In order to verify this sentence, we therefore have to fix upon one individual at a time and investigate whether he perhaps satisfies this double requirement. This means that we have to distinguish him, for the time being at least, from the other individuals whom we also have to keep an eye on. If we know his name, we may use it. If not, we may assign some conventional designation to him, like the John Does and Richard Roes of legal parlance. If the context allows, we may also speak simply of *this* man or *that* man. The necessity of distinguishing him from others in some way or another is closely related to our second requirement for the meaningfulness of quantifying expressions. We must have ways of marking the different moves in our game; we must be able to distinguish not only the end-points but also the branching-points of the different possible courses which our interconnected processes of seeking and finding may take. Even if we have already come across an Englishman such as we are looking for, we still have to distinguish him from others while we make sure that he is related to each of the countries of the world in the required way.

This new requirement is closely related to recent disputes concerning the dispensability of free singular terms in favor of mere variables of quantification. (Certain aspects of the controversy cannot be touched here; for instance, the question whether it is possible to teach and to learn a language without free singular terms – a subject of which we all seem to know very little.) The

requirement just mentioned is probably part of the truth which there seems to be in the contention of those who think of singular terms as being indispensable. It is e.g., closely related to the point which Mr. P. F. Strawson has expressed by saying "there could not be a form of words having the meaning 'There is something or other which has attribute A' unless there were also a form of words having the meaning '*This* thing has attribute A'."[31] We must, in fact, have, it seems, some ways of referring to one particular individual rather than to others for a while at least, in order for the language-games of seeking and finding to be practicable and hence for quantifying expressions to make sense.

This much is certainly true. However, certain other contentions of the defenders of free singular terms do not follow from it. For instance, it does not follow that there is something in the actual body of our knowledge which we cannot express in terms of quantifiers and bound variables although we can express it by means of free singular terms.

It does not follow, either, that there must be a category of proper names, demonstratives, or other free singular terms in one's language. We must require that there are ways of marking the end-points and other crucial junctures of our interlocking processes of search, processes which are (*inter alia*) required for the verification of sentences with more than one layer of quantifiers. Consider the simplest case as an example. This is what was called the second requirement. It says that the end-points of search must be somehow recognizable. This recognition must of course be marked in the language-game in question. It may be the case that we can simply say: "*This* is the kind of object we have been looking for" (say one with the attribute A). It does not follow, however, that we must be able to mark the endpoints by *saying* of the particular object we have reached that it has the attribute A. Instead of saying anything about this particular individual we might say in general terms "Now we know that there is an object with the attribute A." Of course, in order for such utterances to serve to mark the end-points of search we must have some nonverbal means of making it known that we assert the existence of at least one individual of the appropriate kind on the basis of witnessing that particular individual we actually witnessed. From the necessity of employing such nonverbal devices of communication it does not follow, however, that there must be an expression in the language which can serve this purpose. Turning Strawson's formulation around, we might say that there need not be any *form of words* having the meaning "This thing has attribute *A*" in a language although the language in question contains a form of words having the meaning "there is something with the attribute *A*." However, there must be some alternative way of indicating the same thing, that is to say, of bringing out what the former expresses over and above the latter. There must be nonverbal means to call one's attention to particular individuals even though there need not be verbal means for doing so.[32]

General Morals

There is also a general moral or two to be drawn from our observations. If there really obtains the close relationship between quantifiers and the activities of searching and trying to find, we have a stronger reason than ever to be suspicious of the Carnapian methods which have been criticized in some of my earlier papers.[33] The use of these methods sometimes presupposes, it was argued, that all the individuals in the universe of discourse are known. In any case, not very much attention is paid in these methods to the discovery and introduction of new individuals. If the use of quantifiers is essentially connected with the activities of seeking and finding new individuals, we cannot hope that any methods which make no provision for such activities will throw much light on the logic of quantification. It seems to me significant that some of the main theoretical difficulties to which the application of Carnapian methods lead arise in connection with quantified sentences.

To conclude with another general point: We can perhaps now see one partial reason for the interest of the formal logic of quantification. If it is true that the processes of seeking and finding are the most important processes by means of which we become aware of the existence of individuals, and if it is also true that the language-games of seeking and finding are the natural context of quantifiers, then the study of the logical behavior of quantifiers is largely a study of the structure of some of the most important processes by means of which we obtain our knowledge. It is perhaps worth noting that the formal logic of quantification can have this interest independently of how closely it reproduces the ways in which we in the natural language refer

to the activities of seeking and finding. As a brief *dictum* we might perhaps say this: Quantification theory is a regimented way of speaking of the activities of seeking and finding. It is not a regimentation of the ways in which we speak of these activities in *ordinary language*. If quantification theory helps us to carry out the processes of seeking and finding or at the very least helps us to clear up our ideas concerning them, it has an interesting application even if it should turn out not to apply very well to a direct study and regimentation of ordinary language. In a sequel to this paper I shall try to bring out at least one way in which the formal logic of quantification helps us with our language-games of seeking and finding. The "thought" we carry out in formal logic will turn out to be relevant to the non-linguistic "action" in a clear-cut fashion.

Appendix: Language-Games and Systematic Logical Theory

Although the game-theoretic point of view on first-order logic which was sketched in the body of this paper apparently has never been discussed in its full generality before, it is obviously closely related to a number of issues and approaches in systematic logical theory. Here only a few relatively informal remarks will be made to illustrate the naturalness and importance of the connection between the logic of quantification and the games of searching and looking for.

The game-theoretic approach is closely related to the idea of eliminating quantifiers in favor of functions and functionals, and to the basic idea of the so-called "no counter-example interpretation."[34] For instance, there is obviously a very close connection between the truth of a statement of the form

$$(I) \quad (\exists x)(\forall y)(\exists z)F(x, y, z)$$

where the variables are assumed to range over natural numbers, and the statement

$$(II) \quad (\exists x)(\exists f)(\forall y)F(x, y, f(x))$$

with a function variable f. This function and a number x are precisely what determines "my" strategy in the game correlated with (I). Hence the force of (II) is in effect to say that there is a winning strategy in the game correlated with (I). If a suitable x and f can in fact be given, the existential quantifiers in (II) can be dropped, leaving us with a quantifier-free statement.[35]

I shall not discuss how simple observations of this sort are utilized in the "no counter-example interpretation" or in other developments in logical theory. I have merely tried to illustrate the main idea, which seems clear enough: We take a sentence or formula (e.g., a number-theoretic one), correlate with it a game along the lines indicated, and then express by an explicit statement the fact that there is a winning strategy in this game. This new statement will then serve as an interpretation of the original sentence or formula.

This general technique admits of many variations. One may try to consider, not the game correlated with a statement, but rather the game correlated with its negation. If games of infinite length are used, we may require that they have to be won in a finite number of moves, and so on. Perhaps the most important variation is the possibility of choosing the strategy set in different ways.

If f is allowed to range over *arbitrary* (number-theoretical) functions in our example, (II) is true if and only if (I) is true in the classical arithmetic. It lies very close at hand, however, to suggest that the class of pure strategies we "really" have available is narrower than that. This means restricting the range of the function quantifier in (II). For instance, it might appear natural to let f range over recursive functions only. (How could anyone actually use a strategy given by a non-recursive function?) This will correspond to some nonclassical sense of truth and falsity for (I).[36] In this way, we can perhaps see with some clarity what it could mean actually to employ a nonclassical logic in one's "games of exploring the world": it could mean to use a restricted pure strategy set in the game correlated with (I). Alternatively, or in addition to this, the use of a nonclassical conception of logic could also mean defining the moves of the game which are connected with the different connectives and quantifiers in a way different from the characterizations of these moves given earlier.

It seems to me that a number of approaches and arguments in the foundational studies might become more accessible to a philosophical scrutiny when looked upon from this game-theoretic point of view, although their precise connections with the game-theoretical concepts and ideas often remain to be worked out.

The following observation has struck me as being especially suggestive: There is a very close connection between the concept of a truth-value of a sentence and the game-theoretical concept of the value of the correlated game. If I have a winning strategy, the value of the game is the payoff of winning, i.e., the "value" of winning the game. This is also precisely the case in which the sentence is true. Hence the payoff of winning as a value of the game can be identified with the truth-value "true" of the sentence, and correspondingly for falsity.

It follows that the fact that classical logic is two-valued is virtually tantamount to the fact that the games correlated with classically interpreted statements like (I) admit of pure optimal strategies. That this should be the case is not quite immediate, for in the case of an infinite domain the games have infinite (pure) strategy sets. The existence of pure optimal strategies nevertheless follows from well-known general results which rely essentially on the fact that we are dealing with games with perfect information.

However, if suitable changes are made in our assumptions, optimal strategies (if any) might turn out to be mixed. The weights of the different pure strategies involved in this mixture could then perhaps serve as models of nonclassical truth-values.

This idea remains to be explored, as far as I know. However, it is obvious that there are extant theories which could be, and perhaps have been, conceived of in a game-theoretic spirit. One example among many is Gödel's suggested extension of the finitistic point of view.[37] Here each arithmetical statement is interpreted in terms of another one which can be taken to be essentially a statement to the effect that a certain game correlated with the first statement has a winning strategy. The pure strategy sets are assumed to be restricted to those than can be defined by means of recursive functions and functionals.

Furthermore, a not insubstantial amount of important systematic work in the model theory of first-order logic either has been or can readily be described in game-theoretic terms. Here I shall give only a few indications of some of the results that have been reached. In the application of game theoretic ideas just outlined, a game is connected with each statement, interpreted so as to speak of a certain piece of world or of a "model." Two such models are said to be elementarily equivalent if and only if they are equivalent with respect to all the different games we have described. Now Ehrenfeucht and Fraïssé have in effect shown how for the purpose of describing elementary equivalence this variety of games can be replaced by a single game of comparing the two models.[38] In this game, a move by my opponent (who has the first move) consists in picking out an individual a from one of the two models, say M (of his own choosing). My next move consists in trying to choose from the other model M' an individual a' whose relations to those members of M' which have been picked out earlier match the relations of a to the corresponding members of M and whose attributes match the attributes of a. If I cannot do this, I lose; if I do not lose after any finite number of moves, I win. Then M and M' are elementarily equivalent if and only if I have a winning strategy in the game so defined.

It turns out that this game, and all the truncated versions one obtains by restricting both players to a finite number of moves, are connected very closely with what I have called distributive normal forms and discussed elsewhere in some detail.[39] For instance, I have a winning strategy in the truncated game with precisely d moves for each player if and only if the same constituent with depth d is true both in M and in M'. Then (and only then) the two models M and M' are also equivalent for the purposes of all games correlated with statements of depth d or less. (Depth is roughly speaking characterized as the number of layers of quantifiers in a sentence.) In certain other respects, too, a consideration of constituents helps us to appreciate the close connection which there obtains between the games of comparing two different models and the games correlated with statements.

These examples perhaps suffice to illustrate my suggestion that the logic of quantification is essentially the logic of certain kinds of games of seeking and finding (or whatever you want to call them).

The most systematic earlier use of game-theoretical ideas in quantification theory is due to Paul Lorenzen and developed further by Wolfgang Stegmüller and K. Lorenz (*inter alia*).[40] Some connections between their approach and the above remarks are obvious. However, there is also a difference which from a philosophical point of view is very important. The games I have described are related to the uses of logical symbols in finding out something about the world. They are not "indoor games"; they are "played" in the wide world among whatever objects our statements speak about. An essential part of all these games consists in trying to find individuals which satisfy certain requirements.

In contrast to our games of seeking and finding, the games of Lorenzen and Stegmüller are "dialogical games" which are played so to speak "indoors" by means of verbal "challenges" and "responses." These may be made, e.g., by writing down suitable sequences of symbols.

As was already pointed out, there are of course very close connections between the formal games of Lorenzen and Stegmüller and the games which I have described and which have been called language-games. If one is merely interested in suitable technical problems in logic, there may not be much to choose between the two types of games. However, from a philosophical point of view, the difference seems to be absolutely crucial. Only considerations which pertain to "games of exploring the world" can be hoped to throw any light on the role of our logical concepts in the meaningful use of language.

In fact, it seems to me that a sharp distinction has to be made between such "outdoor" games of exploring the world in order to verify or falsify certain (interpreted) statements by producing suitable individuals and such "indoor" games as, e.g., proving that certain uninterpreted formulae are logical truths by manipulating sequences of symbols in a suitable way. Unless this distinction is made, the relevance of games of the latter type cannot be satisfactorily described. In another paper, I shall try to show in what way the formal language-game of proving or disproving quantificational formulae can help us in the "field games" of trying to verify or falsify quantificational statements.

If there is anything to be learned from the possibility of applying game-theoretic concepts to the systematic theory of first-order logic, it is that the study of the *use* of a language (or a part of a language) can be as purely logical and philosophical an enterprise as the study of logical syntax or the study of the referential relations between language and the world. It seems to me that the familiar Carnapian trichotomy syntax-semantics-pragmatics is often misunderstood to imply that all the study of language in use (as distinguished from its formal aspects and from its referential relations to the world) belongs to the psychology and sociology of language or to some such non-philosophical and nonlogical discipline.[41] Without wanting to detract from the interest and importance of these studies, it ought to be clear that the use of language can be studied in abstraction from the psychological and sociological conditions of the people using it quite as well as syntax can be studied in abstraction from the psychological make-up and social context of the people who write or utter the sentences whose syntax we are studying. (Of course, this is not to say that import-ant factual connections might be found in both cases.) The study of the games correlated with quantificational sentences perhaps serves to illustrate the possibility and interest of such purely logical pragmatics.

Notes

1 On the subject of logical vocabulary, see P. F. Strawson, *Introduction to Logical Theory* (London, 1952), pp. 47–9, 57; W. V. Quine, "Mr. Strawson on Logical Theory," *Mind*, vol. 62 (1953), pp. 433–51, especially p. 437.

2 In this paper, only those quantifying expressions are studied which are roughly synonymous with the usual existential and universal quantifiers. Non-standard quantifiers, such as "at least two," "at most three," "many," "most," etc. are illuminated only in so far as they behave in the same way as standard quantifiers or are definable in terms of these. Furthermore, all differences between the different ordinary-language equivalents to standard quantifiers are disregarded, although some of them are of considerable interest. In particular, I shall disregard the close relation which there is between some of these idioms (e.g., "some," "all," etc.) and the "quantitative" relation of a whole to a part. Interesting as this relationship is in many respects, not just as a reason for some of the differences between different quantifying expressions, it is in my view less important than the problem of inter-preting quantifying expressions when they are con-ceived of in the usual terms of "ranging over" a domain of discrete individuals. Of the quantifying expressions of ordinary language, "there is" (or "exists"), and "for every" perhaps come closest to this type of quantifying expression and are therefore considered here in the first place.

3 Ludwig Wittgenstein, *Philosophische Untersuchungen – Philosophical Investigations* (Oxford, 1953), Pt. I, sect. 43: "For a *large* class of cases – though not for all – in which we employ the word 'meaning' it can be defined thus: the meaning of a word is its use in the language."

4 Cf. e.g., Gilbert Ryle, "Ordinary Language," *The Philosophical Review*, vol. 62 (1953), pp. 167–186.

5 *Philosophical Investigations*, Pt. I, sects. 6, 9, 10, and 11.

6 Ryle, *op. cit.*, warns us not to mistake *use* (in speaking of the use of language) to mean *utilization*. But surely Wittgenstein constantly assimilates these ideas to each other. His favorite term *Gebrauch* is ambiguous in the same way as the English word *use*, and could often be taken in the sense of usage; but on other occasions the presence of the ideas of application and utilization are unmistakable. These ideas are often still more obvious when Wittgenstein uses words like *Verwendung* or *Anwendung*, which he also frequently does. (See *Philosophical Investigations*, Pt. I, sects. 11, 20, 21, 23, 41, 42, 54, 68, and 84.)

7 *Philosophical Investigations*, Pt. I, sects. 7 and 23.

8 For operationalism, cf. e.g., the symposium on "The Present State of Operationalism" in *The Validation of Scientific Theories*, ed. by Philip G. Frank (Boston, 1955).

9 The multiplicity and variety of the different language-games which are involved in the use of language partly explains the Protean character of the grammatical category of verbs. The variety in the logical functions of different verbs is in fact much greater than one would gather from most logical and philosophical discussions of the different grammatical categories.

10 Cf. R. M. Hare, *The Language of Morals* (Oxford, 1952), and Paul Ziff, *Semantic Analysis* (Ithaca, 1960), last chapter.

11 Cf. P. F. Strawson, *op. cit.*, pp. 1–4, 15–25.

12 Notice that one cannot teach the meanings of quantifiers as a radically new idea by listing e.g., semantical truth conditions. The learner must know the metalanguage in which these truth-conditions are formulated. These formulations will themselves turn on the use of the quantifiers of the metalanguage. Hence the most that one can accomplish in this way is to teach the meaning of quantifiers in one language in terms of the quantifiers of another language. From our point of view, to convey the meaning of quantifiers to someone as a radically new idea is to teach him to play the language-games that go together with quantifiers, and to teach him the relation of the different quantifying expressions to these games.

13 Etienne Gilson, *The Christian Philosophy of St. Thomas Aquinas* (London, 1957), p. 39.

14 For the conceptual situation, the crucial question is perhaps not whether one's mind is a "ghost in a machine" which can only receive messages from the external world through the receptive mechanisms of the "machine," but whether the mind can actually move the machine around so as to have a choice of what it can or cannot perceive. The possibility of active operations on one's environment at will seems to be deeply imbedded in our conceptual structure,

although in some curious way it gets eliminated in our conscious experience. On this point, cf. Eino Kaila, "Die konzeptuellen und perzeptuellen Komponenten der Alltagserfahrung," *Acta Philosophica Fennica*, vol. 13 (1962), especially pp. 71–3.

15 I find that Kurt Baier makes use of this very word in his discussion of the concept of existence. See "Existence," *Proceedings of the Aristotelian Society*, vol. 61 (1960–1), pp. 19–40, especially p. 24.

16 For the concept of a model set, see e.g., Jaakko Hintikka, "A Program and a Set of Concepts for Philosophical Logic," *The Monist*, vol. 51 (1967), pp. 69–92 and "Form and Content in Quantification Theory," *Acta Philosophica Fennica*, vol. 8 (1955), pp. 5–55. Model sets may be thought of as partial descriptions of possible states of affairs; they are consistent, and any consistent set of first-order sentences can be imbedded in at least one of them. A suitable complete proof procedure for first-order logic can be thought of as a method of trying to construct such a description for $\sim F$. If this attempt comes to a dead end, we have proved F. To decide whether F is provable, we thus have to know how far an attempted counter-example construction has to proceed in order to bring out whatever inconsistency there may lurk in $\sim F$. Because a decision procedure is impossible, we know that this cannot be recursively predicted. This unpredictability of model set constructions illustrates vividly the tremendous difference between them and the predictable operations of the operationalists.

17 Gilbert Ryle, "Sensations" in *Contemporary British Philosophy*, Third Series, ed. by H. D. Lewis (London, 1956), p. 442.

18 Notice that this individual need not have a name prior to a move of this kind.

19 See R. Duncan Luce and Howard Raiffa, *Games and Decisions* (New York, 1957) or Anatol Rapoport, *Two-Person Game Theory: The Essential Ideas* (Ann Arbor, 1966).

20 See Leon Henkin, "Some Remarks on Infinitely Long Formulas" in *Infinitistic Methods*, Proceedings of a Symposium on Foundations of Mathematics (Warsaw, 1961), pp. 176–83. For a further development of Henkin's observations, see J. H. Keisler, "Finite Approximations of Infinitely Long Formulas" in *The Theory of Models, Proceedings of the 1963 International Symposium at Berkeley*, ed. by J. W. Addison, Leon Henkin and Alfred Tarski (Amsterdam, 1965), pp. 158–69 especially pp. 160–1.

21 Private communication.

22 For a detailed discussion of a number of problems in this area (from a somewhat different point of view), see Ernest W. Adams, "Probability and the Logic of Conditionals" in *Aspects of Inductive Logic*, ed. by Jaakko Hintikka and Patrick Suppes (Amsterdam, 1966), pp. 265–316.

23 See J. L. Austin, "Report on Analysis 'Problem' No. 12," *Analysis*, vol. 18 (1957–8), pp. 97–101 (with two "solutions" to the problem).

24 Cf. Peter Geach, *Reference and Generality* (Ithaca, 1962), and W. V. Quine, "Unification of Universes in Set Theory," *The Journal of Symbolic Logic*, vol. 21 (1956), pp. 267–9.

25 According to some reports, Ernst Mach's standard reply to those who claimed that atoms exist was "Have you seen one?" (I derive this item of information from Stephen Brush, "Mach and Atomism," *Synthese*, vol. 18 (1968).)

26 Stephen Toulmin, *Philosophy of Science* (London, 1953), pp. 135–7.

27 Norman Malcolm, "George Edward Moore" in his *Knowledge and Certainty: Essays and Lectures* (Englewood Cliffs, 1963), pp. 163–83.

28 G. E. Moore, "Proof of an External World," *Proceedings of the British Academy*, vol. 25 (1939); reprinted in G. E. Moore, *Philosophical Papers* (London, 1959), ch. 7.

29 If you have inverting goggles on (of the kind now used in some psychological experiments), then it may actually be difficult for you to point to your hand. Does this make it more difficult for you to "prove the existence of an external world" in Moore's sense?

30 See Jaakko Hintikka, "On the Logic of Existence and Necessity," *The Monist*, vol. 50 (1966), pp. 55–76.

31 Cf. W. V. Quine, *Methods of Logic* (New York, 1950), pp. 220–4; W. V. Quine, *From a Logical Point of View* (Cambridge, Mass., 1953), pp. 7–8, 13, 146 and 166–7; W. V. Quine, *World and Object* (Cambridge, Mass., 1960), pp. 179–186; P. F. Strawson, "Singular Terms and Predication," *The Journal of Philosophy*, vol. 58 (1961), pp. 393–412; P. F. Strawson, *Individuals* (London, 1959), pp. 199–203; P. F. Strawson, "Singular Terms, Ontology, and Identity," *Mind*, vol. 65 (1956), pp. 433–54.

32 It may also be the case that it is in many cases *practically* impossible to get along with nonverbal means only. I do not see, however, any general logical argument for not being able to do so in some cases.

33 Jaakko Hintikka, "Are Logical Truths Tautologies?" in *Deskription, Analytizität und Existenz*, ed. by P. Weingartner (Munich and Salzburg, 1966), pp. 215–33. (See especially pp. 221–3.)

34 See William Tait, "The Substitution Method," *The Journal of Symbolic Logic*, vol. 30 (1965), pp. 175–92.

35 For a brief survey of a number of developments in this direction, see Andrzej Mostowski, "Thirty Years of Foundational Studies," *Acta Philosophica Fennica*, vol. 17 (1966), lecture IV.

36 Of course, the interpretation of the sentential connectives is also important here.

37 Kurt Gödel, "Über eine bisher noch nicht benutzte Erweiterung des finiten Standpunktes," *Dialectica*, vol. 12 (1958), pp. 76–83.

38 A. Ehrenfeucht, "An Application of Games to the Completeness Problem for Formalized Theories," *Fundamenta Mathematicae*, vol. 49 (1960–1), pp. 129–41; R. Fraïssé, "Sur quelques classifications des relations basées sur des isomorphismes restraintes," *Publications Scientifiques de l'Université d'Alger*, Serie A, vol. 2 (1955), pp. 15–60 and pp. 273–95.

39 Jaakko Hintikka, "Distributive Normal Forms in First-Order Logic" in *Formal Systems and Recursive Functions*, ed. by J. N. Crossley and M. A. E. Dummett (Amsterdam, 1965), pp. 47–90; Jaakko Hintikka, "Distributive Normal Forms and Deductive Interpolation," *Zeitschrift für mathematische Logik und Grundlagen der Mathematik*, vol. 10 (1964), pp. 185–91. The truncated versions of the comparison-game are also very closely related to the games which were correlated with distributive normal forms in the first place.

40 See Paul Lorenzen, "Ein dialogisches Konstruktivi-tätskriterium" in *Infinitistic Methods*, Proceedings of a Symposium on Foundations of Mathematics (Warsaw, 1961); Paul Lorenzen, *Metamathematik* (Mannheim, 1962); K. Lorenz, *Arithmetik und Logik als Spiele* (Doctoral Dissertation, Kiel, 1961); K. Lorenz, "Dialogspiele als semantische Grundlage von Logikkalkülen," *Archiv für mathematische Logik und Grundlagenforschung* (forthcoming); Wolfgang Stegmüller, "Remarks on the Completeness of Logical Systems Relative to the Validity-Concepts of P. Lorenzen and K. Lorenz," *Notre Dame Journal of Formal Logic*, vol. 5 (1964), pp. 81–112.

41 Clear examples of this line of thought are found in Colin Cherry, *On Human Communication* (second edition Cambridge, Mass., 1966), p. 223; and in A. Pap, *Semantics, and Necessary Truth* (New Haven, 1958), p. 434. See also Charles Morris, "Pragmatism and Logical Empiricism" in *The Philosophy of Rudolf Carnap*, ed. by P. A. Schilpp (La Salle, 1963) pp. 87–98, especially pp. 88–9. Carnap's reply in the same volume (p. 861) shows that the confusion I am criticizing cannot be attributed to his present position, whatever effects his earlier statements on the subject may have had.

PART IV

Validity, Inference, and Entailment

Introduction to Part IV

Logic as the study and theory of deductively valid reasoning is essentially connected with the analysis of inference and entailment. The standard definition of deductive validity is that an argument is deductively valid just in case if its assumptions are true, then its conclusions must also be true, or such that it is logically impossible for its assumptions to be true and its conclusions false. The concept in similar form can be traced at least implicitly throughout the history of logic, all the way back to Aristotle and his predecessors.

An important theory of logical consequence is attributed to Bernard Bolzano and later adapted by Tarski. The idea of the theory is that an inference is deductively valid, or a proposition is a deductively valid logical consequence of an assumption set of propositions, if and only if, holding fixed all of the logical terms, and allowing all the nonlogical terms to be freely uniformly exchanged for any others, there is no assignment of truth values to the propositions in the assumption set and the conclusions of the inference such that for any assumption the propositions in the assumption set are true and the conclusions false.

Consider as an example the deductively valid argument, 'If snow is white, then grass is green; snow is white; therefore, grass is green.' Now substitute for the word 'snow' wherever it appears the word 'bread,' for 'white' the word 'comatose,' for 'grass' the word 'yesterday,' and for 'green' the word 'powerful,' leaving all the specifically logical connectives, 'if-then,' 'is' and 'therefore' in place and unchanged, and imagine this being done for all such possible substitutions of terms. Then for the

proposed substitution we obtain the equally deductively valid argument 'If bread is comatose, then yesterday is powerful; bread is comatose; therefore, yesterday is powerful.' The fact that the resulting predications are nonsensical only serves to reinforce the main point of Bolzano's analysis, as a way of implementing the idea that logical validity is a property of the general logical form rather than the specific content of the propositions in an inference. The substitutions already tried out are sufficiently random and arbitrary to suggest that no other substitution would result in an inference where the assumptions are true or the conclusion false, confirming the assumption that this argument is a formally deductively valid inference in *modus ponendo ponens*.

Bolzano's concept in any event is not intended as a practical method to be used as a kind of decision procedure to test an argument for deductively valid consequence. It is rather a condition to be satisfied in the abstract by any valid inference. Of course, if there is an identifiable counterexample in which we locate a substitution that does not preserve the truth of the conclusion for an assignment of truth to the assumptions, if in that sense we discover that it is possible for the assumptions of the argument to be true and the conclusion false, then we have the definite result that the inference is deductively invalid. But Bolzano's definition of logical consequence does not tell us how to search for suitable counterexamples. Here is an application in which the assumptions and conclusions of the original inference are all true, but where the assumptions become true and the conclusion false under an appropriate substitution. Consider the argument: 'If grass is green, then snow is white; snow is white; therefore, grass is green.' The assumptions and conclusion are all true. But there exists a substitution instance which reveals the inference to be deductively invalid, when we perform the necessary uniform replacements of terms in order to obtain: 'If fire is ice-cold, then bread is nourishing; bread is nourishing; therefore, fire is ice-cold.' The assumptions on this substitution of terms in the argument are true, because a condition 'if–then' statement with a false antecedent or 'if' clause, like this one, is true by truth table definition, and because it happens to be true that bread is nourishing. But the conclusion that fire is ice-cold is obviously false. Hence, the argument is seen by Bolzano's concept to be deductively invalid.

The basic idea of Bolzano's and Tarski's concept of logical consequence is that by means of a model set theoretical analysis, the concept of logical truth is ordinary (nonlogical) truth or satisfaction-preservation under substitution of all nonlogical terms in a sentence. Somewhat more formally, we can say that if S is a sentence to be evaluated for logical truth in language L, then S' is a sentence function obtained from S by replacing all nonlogical terms in S by corresponding variable terms for objects, properties, connections, and operations. The logical terms if any in S are held fixed in S', but all other terms are permitted to vary. Then S is said to be logically true if and only if S' is satisfaction-preserving on all sequences of objects in appropriate satisfaction domains for the variables in S'. This in turn means that S is logically true if and only if all the sentences obtained from sentence function S' by resubstituting names, predicates, connectives, and operators for corresponding variables in S' from the entire available satisfaction domains in each category produces only sentences true in L. The logical truth of S in this way is equated with the ordinary truth of the universal closure of S' in $\forall v_1 \ldots \forall v_n[S']$. The chief difficulty encountered by this analysis of logical consequence, as Tarski acknowledged in several of his writings on the topic, is that of distinguishing unambiguously and philosophically unproblematically between logical and nonlogical terms, without which the criterion cannot effectively be applied. To be able in some sense to distinguish correctly between logical and nonlogical terms presupposes a prior ability to distinguish

between logical consequences and deductively invalid inferences.

Although the ordinary concept of deductive validity has been serviceable for most analytic purposes in the philosophy of logic, and in logical theory and its applications, there are also difficulties in the definition that have given rise to a number of critical innovations in the theory of valid inference and logical entailment. The paradoxes of strict implication have suggested to some commentators that the classical definition of deductive validity might be defective. The paradoxes concern inferences in which the assumptions are logically impossible or conclusions are logically necessary, which, according to the standard definition, are deductively valid, even if trivially so, so to speak, by default. An inference whose assumptions cannot be true is an inference whose assumptions cannot be true and its conclusions false, regardless of what its conclusions state. The same holds for an inference whose conclusions cannot be false, regardless of the content of its assumptions. Although generations of logicians have lived peacefully with the paradoxes of strict implication, others have found it intolerable that in some inferences it should be possible for a deductively valid inference to take place where there is no conceptual connection whatsoever between the assumptions and conclusions of a valid deduction. The dissatisfaction with classical implication in light especially of the paradoxes of strict implication has been a source of philosophical inspiration for relevance and paraconsistent logics.

These themes are explored in essays by Rolf George, who, in "Bolzano's Concept of Consequence," explains Bolzano's 'substitution' theory of logical consequence, and indicates how it can be used to account for the logic of enthymemes, or arguments with suppressed assumptions or conclusions. The model is carried forward in more formal terms by Alfred Tarski, in his seminal essay, "On the Concept of Logical Consequence," where he outlines his more formalized variation of Bolzano's concept and points toward difficulties centering on the distinction between logical and extralogical terms. It should be obvious enough that in any of the above illustrations we would not obtain accurate evaluations of the deductive validity or invalidity of the inferences in question if we permitted substitutions to be made for what we otherwise recognize as logical terms like 'if–then,' 'and,' 'or,' 'not,' 'therefore,' and others. But how do we know in advance, and how can we decide in the case of gray areas precisely which terms are logical and which are extralogical? The problem has haunted this standard way of thinking about logical consequence since its inception.

A classic contribution to the development of relevance logic and the theory of relevant entailment is found in Alan Ross Anderson and Nuel D. Belnap's essay, "The Pure Calculus of Entailment." Anderson and Belnap explain the 'implicational paradoxes' in which deductively valid inference seems to be trivialized, especially where the assumptions of an argument cannot possibly be jointly true or the conclusions cannot possibly be false. The paradoxes are interpreted as establishing a motivation for a new theory of relevant entailment, arguing that the weakness of the standard concept of logical implication is evident in the fact that it gives rise to the paradoxes. In place of the classical model, Anderson and Belnap propose to take seriously the idea that in logical proofs a conclusion is supposed to follow *from* the assumptions, in the sense that their content must be involved in the conclusion. With a variety of syntactical devices and modified axioms, the authors sketch a new theory of logical implication that satisfies a relevance principle, illustrating its advantages in a natural deduction framework.

Stephen Read distinguishes between formal and material models of logical consequence in his instructive essay, "Formal and Material Consequence." Read observes that a deductively invalid argument with true assumptions and a true conclusion does not immediately lend itself to criticism as being such that it is possible for its assumptions to be true and its conclusion false, unless we maintain that the argument is of such a logical form that another instance of the same form has true assumptions and a false conclusion. This is a variation of the method we deployed above in explaining Bolzano's concept of logical consequence. The trouble is, as Read also rightly remarks, that *every* inference, even if it is deductively valid, and even if it has a deductively valid form, also has a deductively invalid form. In the case of *modus ponens*, for example, we need only ascribe such form to the argument that we represent each of the assumptions and the conclusion in their entirety by means of a distinct propositional symbol, and the resulting logical form is sure to be deductively invalid in the sense of having at least one substitution instance in which the assumptions are true and the conclusion false. Read argues that problematic cases make it necessary to look beyond issues of logical form to the material or substantive content of the propositions in some deductive inferences, by appealing to science, mathematics, or metaphysics, in order to decide in a particular instance whether or not it is possible for an argument's assumptions to be true and its conclusions false. He proposes strategies for working with the logical evaluation of inferences that are materially valid for reasons that are not purely formally logical.

Finally, John Etchemendy, who has raised interesting and controversial criticisms of Tarski's concept of logical consequence, in this precursor essay to his booklength study, *The Concept of Logical Consequence*, discusses "Tarski on Truth and Logical Consequence." Etchemendy explains Tarski's theory of truth and clarifies what he regards as misunderstandings about Tarski's project and its relation to the formal theory of semantics. Etchemendy argues that although Tarski happens to have provided foundations for formal semantics by means of his theory of truth, work in that area actually conflicts with Etchemendy's interpretation of Tarski's philosophical purpose. This element of Etchemendy's discussion touches base with several of the important issues raised about Tarski's theory of truth in formal languages discussed above in Part II, in connection with essays by Davidson, Tarski, Field, and Kripke.

Trading again on the fact that Tarski admittedly offers no hard and fast basis for the distinction between logical and extralogical terms, Etchemendy argues that Tarski's definition of logical consequence is defective, and diagnoses the difficulty as a weakness in the concept whereby any inference can be understood as deductively valid or deductively invalid according to Tarski's account when a suitable choice of logical constants is made to hold fixed under substitution of all extralogical terms. The most extreme case, and for that reason the philosophically least interesting from the standpoint of criticizing Tarski's theory in historical context, is that in which a deductively valid inference is interpreted as invalid by holding no terms fixed and permitting all substitutions, or in which the terms in a deductively invalid argument that happens to have true assumptions and conclusions are all fixed as logical and none set aside as extralogical, so that no substitutions are authorized. Etchemendy argues that the provisions needed to prevent such abuses of Tarski's criterion counterintuitively extend the original consequence relation.

Further Reading

Anderson, Alan R. and Belnap, Nuel D. 1975: *Entailment: The Logic of Relevance and Necessity.* 2 vols. Princeton: Princeton University Press.

Berg, Jan. 1962: *Bolzano's Logic.* Stockholm: Almqvist & Wiskell.

Beth, E. W. 1961: *Semantic Entailment and Formal Derivability.* Amsterdam: North Holland.

Bolzano, Bernard. 1972: *Theory of Science.* Rolf George (trans. and ed.). Oxford: Blackwell.

Diaz, M. R. 1981: *Topics in the Logic of Relevance.* Munich: Philosophia Verlag.

Dummett, Michael. 1978: *Truth and Other Enigmas.* Cambridge: Harvard University Press.

Etchemendy, John. 1990: *The Concept of Logical Consequence.* Cambridge: Harvard University Press.

Read, Stephen. 1988: *Relevant Logic: A Philosophical Examination of Inference.* Oxford: Blackwell.

Tarski, Alfred. 1956: *Logic, Semantics, Metamathematics: Papers from 1923 to 1938.* Oxford: Clarendon Press.

Wójcicki, Ryszard. 1988: *Theory of Logical Calculi: Basic Theory of Consequence.* Dordrecht: Kluwer Academic Publishers.

15

Bolzano's Concept of Consequence

Rolf George

Plainly, to identify a speech as an argument and to understand its premises and conclusion is not the same as knowing what argument is intended. What is missing?

Bernard Bolzano defines the concept of consequence thus:

> Propositions $M, N, O, \ldots$ *follow* from propositions $A, B, C, D, \ldots$ with respect to variable parts $i, j, \ldots$ if every class of ideas whose substitution for $i, j, \ldots$ makes each of $A, B, C, D, \ldots$ true also makes all of $M, N, O, \ldots$ true.[1]

The $i, j \ldots$ are constants tagged for substitution; I shall call them *variands*. We do not often state them explicitly, but resort to hints like "It follows by modus ponens..." or "He found himself on the horns of a dilemma...." Usually we rely on convention and context. But this leaves many arguments irremediably opaque. Bolzano gives the following example:

> Since all humans have an irresistible yearning for enduring existence, and since even the most virtuous must be miserable in the thought that some day they will cease to exist, we justly expect from God's infinite benevolence that he will not annihilate us in death (WL § 164, No. 2).

If this is intended as an argument, then, following Bolzano, some of its constants must be meant as

Rolf George, Bolzano's Concept of Consequence.
The Journal of Philosophy, 83, 10 (1986): 558–64.

variands; but it is wholly unclear which. If no variands were intended, then this would merely be a string of assertions.

It is tempting to think that if a putative argument is not so muddled as to resist all analysis, then a transcription into modern symbolic notation, the textbook exercise "Put this argument in symbolic form," would identify the variands. Bolzano would deny this. He holds, rather, that to state a consequence unambiguously requires an explicit listing of variands. Since this is not done even in rigorously formal contexts, ambiguities can occur even there.

Consider $A \supset B, B \supset A \models A \supset A$. Is this meant to turn on the conclusion's being a previously established theorem, or is it a syllogism? The ambiguity is removed if variands are appointed, e.g., by drawing boxes around them, thus:

(1) $\boxed{A \supset B}, \boxed{B \supset A} \models \boxed{A} \supset \boxed{A}$

(2) $\boxed{A} \supset \boxed{B}, \boxed{B} \supset \boxed{A} \models \boxed{A} \supset \boxed{A}$

In this dispensation, these are distinct arguments, both valid. (1) shows that the premises do not matter, since boxed items, even if complex, may be (uniformly) replaced by arbitrary sentences, even atoms. (2), on the other hand, is a syllogism. For the classical logician, the distinction does not matter. He can think of the argument(s) as derived from the schema $p, q \models r \supset r$, which yields only valid arguments. But Bolzano's concept of form is different. Here the word, and not the variable, stands at the beginning, and the form is identified with the set of arguments generated from a given argument by variation, i.e., substitution on variands.[2] A form, then, is not a schema. Arguments are not "obtained" from forms by the substitution of constants for variables, and it is not, strictly speaking, correct to say that forms are valid or invalid, though we may say, by extension, that forms are valid if they contain only valid arguments, and invalid if this is not so.

The conception of consequence here adumbrated has two features that should recommend it to logicians who are concerned not with the development of formal systems, but with the analysis of informally stated arguments and the identification of fallacies.

The first of these is that arguments of invalid form are invalid. In the classical view, this is not the case, as Gerald Massey has pointed out with clarity and vigor.[3] For example, the schema "Affirming the Consequent" has as instances certain valid arguments, e.g., $A \supset A$, $A \models A$. More importantly, every classical syllogism is an instance of the invalid form $p, q \models r$. Since this sort of thing sometimes occurs, one is never justified, so the argument goes, in judging an argument fallacious just because it is an instance of an invalid form, particularly given the apparently unfinished state of logic.

In Bolzano's view, the evaluation of any argument must begin with the identification of variands. If their variation generates an invalid form, the argument is invalid; if not, not. It is of course possible to make mistakes in this, just as sentences can be misunderstood. It is a cultural, and perhaps even a human, failing that we do not usually indicate the variands explicitly. But these are problems of communication. Plainly, it is often possible, and sometimes important, to identify formal fallacies. It therefore seems that in this respect Bolzano's account of consequence is superior to the classical.

A second positive feature of Bolzano's conception is that it gives a promising account of enthymemes. Although he concentrates on arguments in which all indexical elements are variands (this being the proper province of logic, cf. WL §223), his definition does not exclude cases in which only some of them are. We readily identify 'Socrates' as the variand in 'Socrates was a man, therefore Socrates was mortal'. That is, we understand this argument as implicitly claiming that every substitution on 'Socrates' that makes the premise true also makes the conclusion true. If we had to con-

struct a device for computing the "missing premise" (which we intuitively take to be 'All men are mortal'), we would have it state that fact. It would, that is, form the universal closure on the variand, over the conditional consisting of premise and conclusion, and *voilà*, the missing premise results. This procedure works for all syllogistic enthymemes, and is only slightly more complex when no singular terms are involved. No principle of charity or other proviso is needed. I venture the guess that some such computation is going on even in our own minds when, with a speed that must compel wonder, we determine what all the world takes to be the missing premise in such a case.

I must correct a point I made in earlier papers,[4] to the effect that the variands in an enthymeme are the items shared by premise and conclusion. It is an accident that this works for syllogisms. More complex enthymemes require a different treatment. Consider "If I buy cheap tickets, my girl friend will be angry. I buy either cheap or expensive tickets. Therefore either my girl friend will be angry, or I will be broke." In a flash we see that a suitable missing premise is 'If I buy expensive tickets, then I will be broke'. This dictates that the variands be 'I buy cheap tickets' and 'My girl friend will be angry'. But to determine the variands in this way is to put the cart before the horse. There must be a procedure that finds them first and computes the missing premise from that information. But I do not know, at this time, what it is. And matters would be even more complex if unneeded premises were present.

Bolzano's construal of consequence also sheds some light on the "deductivism" controversy. If deductivism means that only deductive arguments are good arguments, then Bolzano assuredly is an anti-deductivist. It is just wrong, in his view, to cast enthymemes, which are often good arguments, into the same darkness as the grossest *non sequiturs*, and a principled formal treatment of them is here suggested. On the other hand, he could conceivably be called a deductivist because he does not allow purely material arguments, that is, arguments without variands. I myself find the notion of such an argument unintelligible, and will not pursue the matter.

Let me now state some formal features of Bolzano consequence, and some other matters, without proof. Since these consequences are triads, some of the points could not be stated in the conventional rendition of arguments.

Bolzano defines the concepts of compatibility and analyticity as follows: a set of sentences Γ is *analytic* with respect to a set of variands v if every substitution on the elements of v makes all its elements true, and *compatible* with respect to *itupsilon* if some substitution on v makes all of them true. Allow the list of variands to contain items that do not occur in the argument, or the set of sentences; that is, allow this list to contain "idle" elements. This makes it possible to specify, for example, that the list should contain all and only atomic sentences. (In this case the consequence will be said to be *classical*.)

Indicating the set of variands above the turnstile, abbreviating 'Γ is compatible (analytic) with respect to v' as Comp $(\Gamma; v)$ and Anal $(\Gamma; v)$, and writing 'v, A' for '$v \cup \{A\}$', the following hold:[5]

I.   If A is a sentence idle in v, A, then $\Gamma \models^{v} \Delta$ iff $\Gamma \models^{v,A} \Delta$, Comp $(\Gamma; v)$ iff Comp $(\Gamma; v, A)$, and Anal $(\Gamma; v)$ iff Anal $(\Gamma; v, A)$.

II. If $\Gamma \models \Delta$ and $\Delta \models \Theta$, then $\Gamma \models \Theta$ (WL §155, No. 24).

III. If $\Gamma \models^{v, \omega} \Delta$ with ω idle, and $\Delta \models^{v, \omega} \Theta$ with v idle, then $\Gamma \models^{v, \omega} \Theta$ (WL §155, No. 23).

IV. If $\Gamma \models \Delta$ and $\Gamma \models \Theta$, then $\Gamma \models \Delta, \Theta$ (WL §155, No. 22.).

With this in hand, let us next look at C. I. Lewis's "Independent Proof" for *ex absurdo quodlibet*. From the viewpoint of Bolzano consequence it appears as a sophism, at least in the form in which it is usually presented.

Lewis's argument can be rendered thus:

(1) $A \& -A$ Premise
(2) A from 1 by simplification
(3) $-A$ from 1 by simplification
(4) $A \vee B$ from 2 by weakening
(5) B from 3 and 4 by disjunctive syllogism

A rigorous rendition in Bolzano style invokes the theorems I, II, and IV above. This is left as an exercise.

The first and second steps are said to be based on the law that from any conjunction either conjunct may be inferred. From our point of view, this can only mean that the variands in the premise are 'A' and '$-A$'. Only then (i.e., if 'A' and '$-A$' are varied independently of each other: $\boxed{A}, \boxed{-A} \models \boxed{A}$) can the form (i.e., the set generated from the

premise) contain *all* conjunctions. And, presumably, *this* set is envisaged in the talk about 'any conjunction.' But, if this is so, then the disjunctive syllogism cannot be executed, for '$-A$' does not now function as the negation of 'A'. The variands that allow the argument to go through are 'A' and 'B'. But, if *they* are chosen, then the law that sanctions the first two steps is not "From a conjunction infer either conjunct" but, rather, "From the conjunction of a sentence and its denial infer either" – hardly a law of much dignity, and one that we shall presently dispute.

The sophism, from our point of view, lies in a peculiar kind of equivocation. We have seen that arguments, like sentences, can be ambiguous. Now Lewis's "Independent Proof" must be read one way (with variands 'A', 'B') to make it go through, and another way (with variands 'A', '$-A$', 'B') to make good on the claim that the laws in question are, as Lewis put it, "unavoidable consequences of indispensable laws of inference."[6] But on this construal the argument fails.

Bolzano imposed a further condition. He required that the premises of any consequence by *compatible* with respect to the set of variands v of the consequence. He did not forbid the conclusion(s) of a consequence to be analytic with respect to v (cf., e.g., WL §155 No. 12). This asymmetry is awkward and leads, e.g., to the rejection of transposition. I shall deviate here from Bolzano and explore a consequence relation that requires the premises to be compatible and the conclusion(s) to be nonanalytic with respect to the variands. Let us call the consequence relation so defined "Bolzano Consequence in the Narrow sense" (BCN), symbolized by 'N='.

BCN comes close to an entailment relation suggested by T. J. Smiley, who takes it that a true entailment is "a substitution instance of a tautological implication whose components are neither contradictory nor tautological."[7] Alan Ross Anderson and Nuel Belnap have proved that if an entailment relation satisfies this condition, then it is *relevant* in the sense of sharing a subsentence.[8] The same holds for BCN:

V.   If $\Gamma \, N\overset{v}{=} \Delta$, then v contains a variand common to both Γ and Δ.

Suppose that it does not. Then v can be represented as the disjoint set v', v'', where v' contains only variands in Γ, and v'' only variands in Δ. But Comp$(\Gamma; v)$, and, since v'' is here idle in v, it follows by (I) that Comp(Γ;v'). Analogously, since not Anal(Γ;v), and v' is here idle, it follows that not Anal(Δ;v''). There are then substitutions on v, i.e., on v' in Γ and on v'' in Δ, which make the former true and the latter false. Hence, contrary to our assumption, $\Gamma N \underset{=}{\overset{v}{}} \Delta$ fails. So premises and conclusion share a subsentence.

It is plain that Lewis's "Independent Proof" fails in BCN, for the first two steps must now be construed with 'A' and '$-A$' as variands. It is thus not the disjunctive syllogism that fails, but the chain: we are constrained (so as to be able to begin) to construe the argument in this way, and when we come to the disjunctive syllogism we are stopped. Deductive explosions are thus made impossible.

The following can be said in support of BCN: we must expect a reasoner to know what his argument is. That is, he must know his variands. If he does not, he is in fact not reasoning, but asserting strings of sentences. Is it then too much to ask that the premises be compatible, and the conclusions not analytic, with respect to these same variands? Are we not simply asking that he should not *consciously* employ inconsistent premises? Indeed, by requesting this we are not asking even that he should assure that his premises are taken from a consistent subregion of a possibly inconsistent set of propositions. We merely require that his premises may be deemed consistent by someone who does not fully understand them, but knows the variands. BCN allows inconsistencies in a body of beliefs, which may creep into premises of arguments, and yet allows the logician the cherished freedom of saying important things about matters he does not understand and of which he does not know whether they are true.

Good things come at a price. In this case the price is *case argument*. In discrediting the disjunctive syllogism, Anderson and Belnap point (by implicaiton) to the following: the premise of $(A \lor B)$ & $-A \models B$ is equivalent to $(A$ & $-A) \lor (A$ & $B)$. By case argument we obtain $A - A \models B$. Thus it seems that the acceptance of the disjunctive syllogism leads at once to *ex absurdo quodlibet*, a result to be avoided. But case argument does not hold in BCN. Instead we have the rule:

$$\frac{\Gamma \lor \Delta \; N \underset{=}{\overset{v}{}} \Theta}{\Gamma \; N \underset{=}{\overset{v}{}} \Theta \text{ and } \Theta \; N \underset{=}{\overset{v}{}} \Theta}$$ provided that comp $(\Gamma;v)$ and comp$(\Delta;v)$

In other words, reasoner must recheck the compatibility of his premises with respect to variands after each application of case argument, and remove those which don't satisfy the compatibility requirement. For, plainly, if A & $-A N \underset{=}{\overset{\Delta}{}}$? cannot be the first step of an argument, it can also not be the nth step.

The classical notion of consequence relies on the principle, always unstated, that arguments are derived from schemata, as if a reasoner, like the demiurge, always gazed upon forms while creating his product. We can now see that, in BCN, this can be framed as an antitheorem. Suppose a consequence had a molecular variand. Replace it by its immediate subsentence(s). Call the new argument "a more fine-grained associate" of the first. The anti-theorem then is "If an argument is valid, then all its more fine-grained associates also are." If this is preferred to the compatibility requirement, then Bolzano consequence collapses into classical. But, conceivably, BCN is a workable alternative, though further exploration may disclose monstrous complications that diminish its initial attractiveness.

Notes

Presented in an APA symposium on Concepts of Entailment, December 28, 1986. Christopher J. Martin was co-symposiast, and John E. Nolt commented.

I thank the Center for Philosophy of Science, Pittsburgh, where I was a Fellow when I wrote this, and friends and critics Nicholas Rescher, Gerald Massey, and Nuel Belnap.

1 *Wissenschaftslehre* (Sulzbach, 1837), §155, no. 2, vol. II, pp. 199 ff. Translated as *Theory of Science*, R. George, ed. (Oxford: Blackwell, 1972), p. 209. Henceforth WL.

2 The use of the term 'form' as synonym for 'species' or 'set' is justified by a whimsical reference to Cicero: "*Quod enim utroque verbo* [i.e., '*forma*' and '*species*'] *idem significatur.*" Cicero, *Topica* 30. Bolzano held that logic is a formal science in *this* sense. Cf. WL §81, note 1.

3 "The Fallacy behind Fallacies," in P. A. French, T. E. Vehling, Jr., and H. K. Wettstein, eds., *The Foundations of Analytic Philosophy* (Minneapolis: Minnesota UP, 1981), pp. 499 ff.

4 "Enthymematic Consequence," *American Philosophical Quarterly*, ix, 1 (January 1972): 113–16, and

"Bolzano's Consequence, Relevance, and Enthymemes," *Journal of Philosophical Logic*, XII, 3 (August 1983): 299–318, p. 315.

5 Bolzano has many more theorems than are here given, and he gives slightly different versions than we have here. Also, to do propositional logic in this system, one needs a rule of precedence: the longest elements of v should be "boxed" first, then the next longest, down to the atoms, if any.

6 C. I. Lewis and C. H. Langford, *Symbolic Logic* (New York: Dover, 1959), p. 512.

7 "Entailment and Deducibility," *Proceedings of the Aristotelian Society*, LIX, (1959): 233–254.

8 *Entailment* (Princeton, N.J.: University Press, 1975), pp. 215–20.

16

On the Concept of Logical Consequence

Alfred Tarski

THE concept of *logical consequence* is one of those whose introduction into the field of strict formal investigation was not a matter of arbitrary decision on the part of this or that investigator; in defining this concept, efforts were made to adhere to the common usage of the language of everyday life. But these efforts have been confronted with the difficulties which usually present themselves in such cases. With respect to the clarity of its content the common concept of consequence is in no way superior to other concepts of everyday language. Its extension is not sharply bounded and its usage fluctuates. Any attempt to bring into harmony all possible vague, sometimes contradictory, tendencies which are connected with the use of this concept, is certainly doomed to failure. We must reconcile ourselves from the start to the fact that every precise definition of this concept will show arbitrary features to a greater or less degree.

Even until recently many logicians believed that they had succeeded, by means of a relatively meagre stock of concepts, in grasping almost exactly the content of the common concept of consequence, or rather in defining a new concept which coincided in extent with the common one. Such a belief could easily arise amidst the new achievements of the methodology of deductive science. Thanks to the progress of mathematical logic we have learnt, during the course of recent

Alfred Tarski, On the Concept of Logical Consequence. *Logic, Semantics, Metamathematics: Papers from 1923 to 1938.* Trans. J. H. Woodger. Oxford: Clarendon Press, 1956. 409–20.

decades, how to present mathematical disciplines in the shape of formalized deductive theories. In these theories, as is well known, the proof of every theorem reduces to single or repeated application of some simple rules of inference – such as the rules of substitution and detachment. These rules tell us what transformations of a purely structural kind (i.e. transformations in which only the external structure of sentences is involved) are to be performed upon the axioms or theorems already proved in the theory, in order that the sentences obtained as a result of such transformations may themselves be regarded as proved. Logicians thought that these few rules of inference exhausted the content of the concept of consequence. Whenever a sentence follows from others, it can be obtained from them – so it was thought – in more or less complicated ways by means of the transformations prescribed by the rules. In order to defend this view against sceptics who doubted whether the concept of consequence when formalized in this way really coincided in extent with the common one, the logicians were able to bring forward a weighty argument: the fact that they had actually succeeded in reproducing in the shape of formalized proofs all the exact reasonings which had ever been carried out in mathematics.

Nevertheless we know today that the scepticism was quite justified and that the view sketched above cannot be maintained. Some years ago I gave a quite elementary example of a theory which shows the following peculiarity: among its theorems there occur such sentences as:

A_0. 0 *possesses the given property P,*
A_1. 1 *possesses the given property P,*

and, in general, all particular sentences of the form

A_n. *n possesses the given property P,*

where '*n*' represents any symbol which denotes a natural number in a given (e.g. decimal) number system. On the other hand the universal sentence:

A. *Every natural number possesses the given property P,*

cannot be proved on the basis of the theory in question by means of the normal rules of inference. This fact seems to me to speak for itself. It shows that the formalized concept of consequence, as it is generally used by mathematical logicians, by no means coincides with the common concept. Yet intuitively it seems certain that the universal sentence *A* follows in the usual sense from the totality of particular sentences $A_0, A_1, \ldots, A_n, \ldots$ .Provided all these sentences are true, the sentence *A* must also be true.

In connexion with situations of the kind just described it has proved to be possible to formulate new rules of inference which do not differ from the old ones in their logical structure, are intuitively equally infallible, i.e. always lead from true sentences to true sentences, but cannot be reduced to the old rules. An example of such a rule is the so-called rule of infinite induction according to which the sentence *A* can be regarded as proved provided all the sentences $A_0, A_1, \ldots, A_n, \ldots$ have been proved (the symbols 'A_0', 'A_1', etc., being used in the same sense as previously). But this rule, on account of its infinitistic nature, is in essential respects different from the old rules. It can only be applied in the construction of a theory if we have first succeeded in proving infinitely many sentences of this theory – a state of affairs which is never realized in practice. But this defect can easily be overcome by means of a certain modification of the new rule. For this purpose we consider the sentence *B* which asserts that all the sentences $A_0, A_1, \ldots, A_n, \ldots$ are *provable* on the basis of the rules of inference hitherto used (not that they have actually been proved). We then set up the following rule: if the sentence *B* is proved, then the corresponding sentence *A* can be accepted as proved. But here it might still be objected that the sentence *B* is not at all a sentence of the theory

under construction, but belongs to the so-called metatheory (i.e. the theory of the theory discussed) and that in consequence a practical application of the rule in question will always require a transition from the theory to the metatheory. In order to avoid this objection we shall restrict consideration to those deductive theories in which the arithmetic of natural numbers can be developed, and observe that in every such theory all the concepts and sentences of the corresponding metatheory can be interpreted (since a one-one correspondence can be established between expressions of a language and natural numbers). We can replace in the rule discussed the sentence *B* by the sentence *B'*, which is the arithmetical interpretation of *B*. In this way we reach a rule which does not deviate essentially from the rules of inference, either in the conditions of its applicability or in the nature of the concepts involved in its formulation or, finally, in its intuitive infallibility (although it is considerably more complicated).

Now it is possible to state other rules of like nature, and even as many of them as we please. Actually it suffices in fact to notice that the rule last formulated is essentially dependent upon the extension of the concept 'sentence provable on the basis of the rules hitherto used'. But when we adopt this rule we thereby widen the extension of this concept. Then, for the widened extension we can set up a new, analogous rule, and so on *ad infinitum*. It would be interesting to investigate whether there are any objective reasons for assigning a special position to the rules ordinarily used.

The conjecture now suggests itself that we can finally succeed in grasping the full intuitive content of the concept of consequence by the method sketched above, i.e. by supplementing the rules of inference used in the construction of deductive theories. By making use of the results of K. Gödel we can show that this conjecture is untenable. In every deductive theory (apart from certain theories of a particularly elementary nature), however much we supplement the ordinary rules of inference by new purely structural rules, it is possible to construct sentences which follow, in the usual sense, from the theorems of this theory, but which nevertheless cannot be proved in this theory on the basis of the accepted rules of inference.[1] In order to obtain the proper concept of consequence, which is close in essentials to the common concept, we must resort to quite different methods and apply quite different conceptual apparatus in defining it. It is perhaps not superfluous to point out in advance that – in comparison with the new – the old concept of consequence as commonly used by mathematical logicians in no way loses its importance. This concept will probably always have a decisive significance for the practical construction of deductive theories, as an instrument which allows us to prove or disprove particular sentences of these theories. It seems, however, that in considerations of a general theoretical nature the proper concept of consequence must be placed in the foreground.

The first attempt to formulate a precise definition of the proper concept of consequence was that of R. Carnap. But this attempt is connected rather closely with the particular properties of the formalized language which was chosen as the subject of investigation. The definition proposed by Carnap can be formulated as follows:

> The sentence X follows logically from the sentences of the class K if and only if the class consisting of all the sentences of K and of the negation of X is contradictory.

The decisive element of the above definition obviously is the concept 'contradictory'. Carnap's definition of this concept is too complicated and special to be reproduced here without long and troublesome explanations.

I should like to sketch here a general method which, it seems to me, enables us to construct an adequate definition of the concept of consequence for a comprehensive class of formalized languages. I emphasize, however, that the proposed treatment of the concept of consequence makes no very high claim to complete originality. The ideas involved in this treatment will certainly seem to be something well known, or even something of his own, to many a logician who has given close attention to the concept of consequence and has tried to characterize it more precisely. Nevertheless it seems to me that only the methods which have been developed in recent years for the establishment of scientific semantics, and the concepts defined with their aid, allow us to present these ideas in an exact form.

Certain considerations of an intuitive nature will form our starting-point. Consider any class K of sentences and a sentence X which follows from the sentences of this class. From an intuitive standpoint it can never happen that both the class K consists only of true sentences and the sentence X is false. Moreover, since we are concerned here with the concept of logical, i.e. *formal*, conse-

quence, and thus with a relation which is to be uniquely determined by the form of the sentences between which it holds, this relation cannot be influenced in any way by empirical knowledge, and in particular by knowledge of the objects to which the sentence X or the sentences of the class K refer. The consequence relation cannot be affected by replacing the designations of the objects referred to in these sentences by the designations of any other objects. The two circumstances just indicated, which seem to be very characteristic and essential for the proper concept of consequence, may be jointly expressed in the following statement:

> (F) If, in the sentences of the class K and in the sentence X, the constants – apart from purely logical constants – are replaced by any other constants (like signs being everywhere replaced by like signs), and if we denote the class of sentences thus obtained from K by 'K'', and the sentence obtained from X by 'X'', then the sentence X' must be true provided only that all sentences of the class K' are true.

[For the sake of simplifying the discussion certain incidental complications are disregarded, both here and in what follows. They are connected partly with the theory of logical types, and partly with the necessity of eliminating any defined signs which may possibly occur in the sentences concerned, i.e. of replacing them by primitive signs.]

In the statement (F) we have obtained a necessary condition for the sentence X to be a consequence of the class K. The question now arises whether this condition is also sufficient. If this question were to be answered in the affirmative, the problem of formulating an adequate definition of the concept of consequence would be solved affirmatively. The only difficulty would be connected with the term 'true' which occurs in the condition (F). But this term can be exactly and adequately defined in semantics.

Unfortunately the situation is not so favourable. It may, and it does, happen – it is not difficult to show this by considering special formalized languages – that the sentence X does not follow in the ordinary sense from the sentences of the class K although the condition (F) is satisfied. This condition may in fact be satisfied only because the language with which we are dealing does not possess a sufficient stock of extra-logical constants. The condition (F) could be regarded as sufficient for the sentence X to follow from the class K only if the designations of all possible objects occurred in the language in question. This assumption, however, is fictitious and can never be realized. We must therefore look for some means of expressing the intentions of the condition (F) which will be completely independent of that fictitious assumption.

Such a means is provided by semantics. Among the fundamental concepts of semantics we have the concept of the *satisfaction of a sentential function* by single objects or by a sequence of objects. It would be superfluous to give here a precise explanation of the content of this concept. The intuitive meaning of such phrases as: *John and Peter satisfy the condition 'X and Y are brothers'*, or *the triple of numbers 2, 3, and 5 satisfies the equation 'x + y = z'*, can give rise to no doubts. The concept of satisfaction – like other semantical concepts – must always be relativized to some particular language. The details of its precise definition depend on the structure of this language. Nevertheless, a general method can be developed which enables us to construct such definitions for a comprehensive class of formalized languages. Unfortunately, for technical reasons, it would be impossible to sketch this method here even in its general outlines.

One of the concepts which can be defined in terms of the concept of satisfaction is the concept of *model*. Let us assume that in the language we are considering certain variables correspond to every extra-logical constant, and in such a way that every sentence becomes a sentential function if the constants in it are replaced by the corresponding variables. Let L be any class of sentences. We replace all extra-logical constants which occur in the sentences belonging to L by corresponding variables, like constants being replaced by like variables, and unlike by unlike. In this way we obtain a class L' of sentential functions. An arbitrary sequence of objects which satisfies every sentential function of the class L' will be called a *model* or *realization of the class L of sentences* (in just this sense one usually speaks of models of an axiom system of a deductive theory). If, in particular, the class L consists of a single sentence X, we shall also call the model of the class L the *model of the sentence X*.

In terms of these concepts we can define the concept of logical consequence as follows:

> The sentence X follows logically from the sentences of the class K if and only if every model of the class K is also a model of the sentence X.[2]

It seems to me that everyone who understands the content of the above definition must admit that it agrees quite well with common usage. This becomes still clearer from its various consequences. In particular, it can be proved, on the basis of this definition, that every consequence of true sentences must be true, and also that the consequence relation which holds between given sentences is completely independent of the sense of the extra-logical constants which occur in these sentences. In brief, it can be shown that the condition (F) formulated above is necessary if the sentence X is to follow from the sentences of the class K. On the other hand, this condition is in general not sufficient, since the concept of consequence here defined (in agreement with the standpoint we have taken) is independent of the richness in concepts of the language being investigated.

Finally, it is not difficult to reconcile the proposed definition with that of Carnap. For we can agree to call a class of sentences *contradictory* if it possesses no model. Analogously, a class of sentences can be called *analytical* if every sequence of objects is a model of it. Both of these concepts can be related not only to classes of sentences but also to single sentences. Let us assume further that, in the language with which we are dealing, for every sentence X there exists a negation of this sentence, i.e. a sentence Y which has as a model those and only those sequences of objects which are not models of the sentence X (this assumption is rather essential for Carnap's construction). On the basis of all these conventions and assumptions it is easy to prove the *equivalence of the two definitions*. We can also show – just as does Carnap – that those and only those sentences are analytical which follow from every class of sentences (in particular from the empty class), and those and only those are contradictory from which every sentence follows.

I am not at all of the opinion that in the result of the above discussion the problem of a materially adequate definition of the concept of consequence has been completely solved. On the contrary, I still see several open questions, only one of which – perhaps the most important – I shall point out here.

Underlying our whole construction is the division of all terms of the language discussed into logical and extra-logical. This division is certainly not quite arbitrary. If, for example, we were to include among the extra-logical signs the implication sign, or the universal quantifier, then our definition of the concept of consequence would lead to results which obviously contradict ordinary usage. On the other hand, no objective grounds are known to me which permit us to draw a sharp boundary between the two groups of terms. It seems to be possible to include among logical terms some which are usually regarded by logicians as extra-logical without running into consequences which stand in sharp contrast to ordinary usage. In the extreme case we could regard all terms of the language as logical. The concept of *formal* consequence would then coincide with that of *material* consequence. The sentence X would in this case follow from the class K of sentences if either X were true or at least one sentence of the class K were false.[3]

In order to see the importance of this problem for certain general philosophical views it suffices to note that the division of terms into logical and extra-logical also plays an essential part in clarifying the concept 'analytical'. But according to many logicians this last concept is to be regarded

as the exact formal correlate of the concept of *tautology* (i.e. of a statement which 'says nothing about reality'), a concept which to me personally seems rather vague, but which has been of fundamental importance for the philosophical discussions of L. Wittgenstein and the whole Vienna Circle.

Further research will doubtless greatly clarify the problem which interests us. Perhaps it will be possible to find important objective arguments which will enable us to justify the traditional boundary between logical and extra-logical expressions. But I also consider it to be quite possible that investigations will bring no positive results in this direction, so that we shall be compelled to regard such concepts as 'logical consequence', 'analytical statement', 'and 'tautology' as relative concepts which must, on each occasion, be related to a definite, although in greater or less degree arbitrary, division of terms into logical and extra-logical. The fluctuation in the common usage of the concept of consequence would – in part at least – be quite naturally reflected in such a compulsory situation.

Notes

This is a summary of an address given at the International Congress of Scientific Philosophy in Paris, 1935. The article first appeared in print in Polish under the title 'O pojciu wynikania logieznego' in *Przegla Filozoficzny*, vol. 39 (1936), pp. 58–68, and then in German under the title 'Über den Begriff der logischen Folgerung', *Actes du Congrès International de Philosophie Scientifique*, vol. 7 (Actualités Scientifiques et Industrielles, vol. 394), Paris, 1936, pp. 1–11.

1 In order to anticipate possible objections the range of application of the result just formulated should be determined more exactly and the logical nature of the rules of inference exhibited more clearly; in particular it should be exactly explained what is meant by the structural character of these rules.

2 After the original of this paper had appeared in print, H. Scholz in his article 'Die Wissenschaftslehre Bolzanos, Eine Jahrhundert-Betrachtung', *Abhandlungen der Fries'schen Schule*, new series, vol. 6, pp. 399–472 (see in particular p. 472, footnote 58) pointed out a far-reaching analogy between this definition of consequence and the one suggested by B. Bolzano about a hundred years earlier.

3 It will perhaps be instructive to juxtapose the three concepts: 'derivability', 'formal consequence', and 'material consequence', for the special case when the class K, from which the given sentence X follows, consists of only a finite number of sentences: $Y_1, Y_2, \ldots, Y_n$. Let us denote by the symbol 'Z' the conditional sentence (the implication) whose antecedent is the conjunction of the sentences $Y_1, Y_2, \ldots, Y_n$ and whose consequent is the sentence X. The following equivalences can then be established:

the sentence X is (logically) derivable from the sentences of the class K if and only if the sentence Z is logically provable (i.e. derivable from the axioms of logic);
the sentence X follows formally from the sentences of the class K if and only if the sentence Z is analytical;
the sentence X follows materially from the sentences of the class K if and only if the sentence Z is true.

In view of the analogy indicated between the several variants of the concept of consequence, the question presents itself whether it would not be useful to introduce, in addition to the special concepts, a general concept of a relative character, and indeed the concept of *consequence with respect to a class L of sentences*. If we make use again of the previous notation (limiting ourselves to the case when the class K is finite), we can define this concept as follows:

the sentence X follows from the sentences of the class K with respect to the class L of sentences if and only if the sentence Z belongs to the class L.

On the basis of this definition, derivability would coincide with consequences with respect to the class of all logically provable sentences, formal consequences would be consequences with respect to the class of all analytical sentences, and material consequences those with respect to the class of all true sentences.

17

The Pure Calculus of Entailment[1]

Alan Ross Anderson and Nuel D. Belnap, Jr.

The "implicational paradoxes" are treated by most contemporary logicians somewhat as follows:

"The two-valued propositional calculus sanctions as valid many of the obvious and satisfactory inferences which we recognize intuitively as valid, such as

$$(A \rightarrow . B \rightarrow C) \rightarrow . A \rightarrow B \rightarrow . A \rightarrow C,[2]$$

and

$$A \rightarrow B \rightarrow . B \rightarrow C \rightarrow . A \rightarrow C;$$

it consequently suggests itself as a candidate for a formal analysis of implication. To be sure, there are certain odd theorems such as

$$A \rightarrow . B \rightarrow A$$

and

$$A \rightarrow . B \rightarrow B$$

which might offend the naive, and indeed these have been referred to in the literature as 'paradoxes of implication.' But this terminology reflects a misunderstanding. 'If A, then if B then A' really

Alan Ross Anderson and Nuel D. Belnap. Jr., The Pure Calculus of Entailment, *The Journal of Philosophical Logic*, 27 (1962), pp. 19–52, reprinted by permission of Association for Symbolic Logic, Vassar College, New York. All rights reserved. The reproduction is by special permission for this publication only.

means no more than 'Either not-A, or else not-B or A,' and the latter is clearly a logical truth; hence so is the former. Properly understood, there are no 'paradoxes' of implication.

"Of course this is a rather weak sense of 'implication,' and one may for certain purposes be interested in a stronger sense of the word. We find a formalization of a stronger sense in modal logics, where we consider strict implication, taking 'if A then B' to mean 'It is impossible that (A and not-B).' And, *mutatis mutandis*, some rather odd formulas are provable here too. But again nothing 'paradoxical' is going on; the matter just needs to be understood properly – that's all.

"And the weak sense of 'if... then –' can be given formal clothing, after Tarski-Bernays as in Łukasiewicz 1929,[3] as follows.

$$A \rightarrow . B \rightarrow A$$
$$A \rightarrow B \rightarrow . B \rightarrow C \rightarrow . A \rightarrow C$$
$$A \rightarrow B \rightarrow A \rightarrow A$$

with a rule of *modus ponens*."

The position just outlined will be found stated in many places and by many people; we shall refer to it as the Official view. We agree with the Official view that there are no paradoxes of implication, but for reasons which are quite different from those ordinarily given. To be sure there is a misunderstanding involved, but it does not consist in the fact that the strict and material "implication" relations are "odd kinds" of implication, but rather in the claim that material and strict "implication" are "kinds" of implication at all. We will defend the view that material "implication" is *not* an implication relation in detail in the course of this paper, but it might help at the outset to give an example which will indicate the sort of criticism we plan to lodge.

Let us imagine a logician who offers the following formalization as an explication or reconstruction of implication in formal terms. In addition to the rule of *modus ponens* he takes as primitive the following three axioms:

$$A \rightarrow A$$
$$A \rightarrow B \rightarrow . B \rightarrow C \rightarrow . A \rightarrow C$$
$$A \rightarrow B \rightarrow . B \rightarrow A$$

One might find those who would object that "if...then −" doesn't seem to be symmetrical, and that the third axiom is objectionable. But our logician has an answer to that. "There is nothing paradoxical about the third axiom; it is just a matter of understanding the formalism properly. 'If A then B' means simply 'Either A and B are both true, or else they are both false,' and if we understand the arrow in that way, then our rule will never allow us to infer a false proposition from a true one, and moreover all the axioms are evidently logical truths. The implication relations of this system may not *exactly* coincide with the intuitions of naive, untutored folk, but it is quite adequate for my needs, and for the rest of us who are reasonably sophisticated. And it has the important property, common to all kinds of implication, of *never leading from truth to falsehood*."

There are of course some differences between the situation just sketched and the Official view outlined above, but in point of perversity, muddle-headedness, and downright error, they seem to us entirely on a par. Of course proponents of the view that material and strict "implication" have something to do with implication have frequently apologized by saying that the name "material implication" is "somewhat misleading," since it suggests a closer relation with implication than actually obtains. But we can think of lots of no more "misleading" names for the relation: "material conjunction," for example, or "material disjunction," or "immaterial negation." "Material implication" is *not* a "kind" of implication, or so we hold; it is no more a kind of implication than a blunderbuss is a kind of buss.

This brief polemical blast will serve to set the tone for our subsequent investigations, which will concern the matter of trying to give a formal analysis of the notion of logical implication,[4] variously referred to also as "entailment", or "the converse of deducibility" (Moore 1920), expressed in such logical locutions as "if...then −," "implies," "entails," etc., and answering to such conclusion-signalling logical phrases as "therefore," "it follows that," "hence," "consequently," and the like. There have been numerous previous attempts to capture the notion, but we do not take it as our task here to survey the literature.[5] The exposition will rather be analytic, and we draw only on such material as is directly relevant to a point under discussion.

We shall proceed as follows. In section I we consider the implicational part H_I of the intuitionist propositional calculus, especially from the point of view of Fitch 1952. In sections II and III we argue that H_I is unsatisfactory as a formalization of entailment on two distinct counts, and in section IV we offer a system E_I (derived from Ackermann 1956) intended to capture the notion of implication or deducibility. Section V is devoted to showing that E_I is free of features which embarrass the other formal theories considered.

I

Since we wish to interpret "A → B"[6] as "A entails B," or "B is deducible from A," we clearly want to be able to *assert* A → B whenever there exists a deduction of B from A; i.e., we will want a rule of "Entailment Introduction" (hereafter "→ I") having the property that if

A	hypothesis (hereafter "hyp")
⋮	
B	[conclusion]

is a valid deduction of B from A, then A → B shall follow from that deduction.

Moreover, the fact that such a deduction exists, or correspondingly that an entailment A → B holds, warrants the *inference* of B from A. That is, we expect also that an Elimination Rule (henceforth "→ E") will obtain for →, in the sense that whenever A → B is asserted, we shall be entitled to infer B from A.

So much is simple and obvious, and presumably not open to question. Problems arise, however, when we ask what constitutes a "valid deduction" of B from A. How may we fill in the dots in the proof scheme above?

At least one rule seems as simple and obvious as the foregoing. Certainly the supposition A warrants the (trivial) inference that A; and if B has been deduced from A, we are entitled to infer B on the supposition A. That is, we may *repeat* ourselves:

1	A	hyp
	⋮	
i	B	?
	⋮	
i	B	i, repetition (henceforth "rep")
	⋮	

This rule leads immediately to the following theorem, the *law of identity*:[7]

1	A	hyp
2	A	1, rep
3	A→A	1–2, → I

But obviously more is required if a theory of entailment is to be developed, and we therefore consider initially a device contained in the variant of natural deduction due to Fitch 1952, which allows us to construct *within* proofs of entailment, further proofs of entailment called "subordinate proofs," or "subproofs." In the course of a deduction, under the supposition that A (say), we may begin a new deduction, with a new hypothesis:

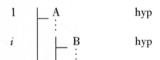

1	A	hyp
	⋮	
i	B	hyp
	⋮	

The new subproof is to be conceived of as an "item" of the proof of which A is the hypothesis, entirely on a par with A and any other propositions occurring in that proof. And the subproof of which B is hypothesis might itself have a consequence (by → I) occurring in the proof of which A is the hypothesis.

We next ask whether or not the hypothesis A holds also under the assumption B. In the system of Fitch 1952, the rules are so arranged that (for example) the hypothesis A may also be repeated under the assumption that B, such a

repetition being called a "reiteration" to distinguish it from repetitions within the same proof or subproof:

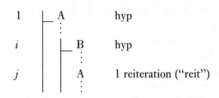

1	A	hyp
	⋮	
i	B	hyp
	⋮	
j	A	1 reiteration ("reit")
	⋮	

We designate as H_I* the system defined by the five rules, → I, → E, hyp, rep, and reit. A proof is *categorical* if all hypotheses in the proof have been discharged by use of → I; and A is a *theorem* if A is the last step of a categorical proof. These rules lead naturally and easily to proofs of intuitively satisfactory theorems about entailment, such as the following *law of transitivity*:[8]

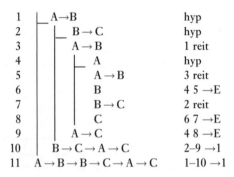

1	A→B	hyp
2	B → C	hyp
3	A → B	1 reit
4	A	hyp
5	A → B	3 reit
6	B	4 5 →E
7	B → C	2 reit
8	C	6 7 →E
9	A → C	4 8 →E
10	B → C → A → C	2–9 →1
11	A → B → B → C → A → C	1–10 →1

The proof method also has the advantage, in common with other systems of natural deduction, of motivating proofs: in order to prove A → B, (perhaps under some hypothesis or hypotheses) we follow the simple and obvious strategy of playing both ends against the middle: breaking up the conclusion to be proved, and setting up subproofs by hyp until we find one with a variable as last step. Only then do we begin applying reit, rep, and → E.

Our description of H_I* has been somewhat informal, and for the purpose of checking proofs it would be desirable to have a more rigorous formulation. We think of the following as designed primarily for *testing* rather than *constructing* proofs (though of course the distinction is heuristic rather than logical), and we therefore call this the *Test Formulation* of Fitch's system.

In order to motivate the Test Formulation, we notice that with each i-th step A_i in the proofs above there is associated first a number of vertical lines to the left of A_i (which we shall call the *rank* of A_i), secondly a class of formulas (including A_i) which are candidates for application of the rule of repetition to yield a next step for the proof, thirdly a class of candidates for application of the rule of reiteration, to yield the next step, and fourthly a hypothesis (if the proof has one) which may together with the final step of the deduction furnish an entailment as next step, as a consequence of the deduction. Accordingly we define a *proof* as consisting of a sequence $A_1, \ldots, A_n$ of wffs, not necessarily distinct, for each A_i of which is defined a *rank* $R(A_i)$, a class of *repeatable wffs* Rep(A_i), a class of *reiteratable wffs* Reit(A_i), and (if $R(A_i) > 0$) an *immediate hypothesis* $H(A_i)$. These are all defined by simultaneous induction as follows:

Basis: (a) A_1 is any wff.
  (b) $R(A_1) = 1$.
  (c) Rep $(A_1) = \{A_1\}$.
  (d) Reit $(A_1) = \wedge$.
  (e) $H(A_1) = A_1$.

Now suppose we have A_j, $R(A_j)$, Reit(A_j), and $H(A_j)$, for every $j < k$. Then $A_1, \ldots, A_k$ is a proof provided $A_1, \ldots, A_{k-1}$ is a proof and A_k statisfies one of the following five conditions:

(1) (hyp) (a) A_k is any wff.
  (b) $R(A_k) = R(A_{k-1}) + 1$
  (c) Rep $(A_k) = \{A_k\}$
  (d) Reit $(A_k) = Rep(A_{k-1})$
  (e) $H(A_k) = A_k$
(2) (rep) If A_j is in Rep (A_{k-1}), then
  (a) $A_k = A_j$
  (b) $R(A_k) = R(A_{k-1})$
  (c) Rep $(A_k) = Rep(A_{k-1}) \cup \{A_k\}$
  (d) Reit $(A_k) = $Reit$(A_{k-1})$
  (e) $H(A_k) = H(A_{k-1})$ (if $H(A_{k-1})$ is defined; otherwise $H(A_k)$ is undefined)
(3) (reit) If A_j is in Reit (A_{k-1}), then
  (a) $A_k = A_j$
  (b)–(e) as in (2)
(4) ($\to$ E) If A_j is in Rep (A_{k-1}) and $A_j \to B(= A_i)$ is in Rep(A_{k-1}), then
  (a) $A_k = B$
  (b)–(e) as in (2)
(5) ($\to$ I) (a) $A_k = H(A_{k-1}) \to A_{k-1}$
  (b) $R(A_k) = R(A_{k-1}) - 1$

(c) Rep $(A_k) = $Reit$(A_{k-1}) \cup \{A_k\}$
(d) If $R(A_k) > 0$, then Reit(A_k) = Reit(A_j), where $H(A_{k-1}) = A_{j+1}$; and if $R(A_k) = 0$, Reit$(A_k) = \wedge$.
(e) If $R(A_k) > 0$, then $H(A_k)$ = $H(A_j)$. where $H(A_{k-1}) = A_{j+1}$; and if $R(A_k) = 0$, $H(A_k)$ is undefined.

Then A is a *theorem* if there is a proof in which A has rank zero.

The basis clause and rule (1) enable us to begin new deductions, and (2)–(5) correspond to rep, reit, $\to$ E and $\to$I respectively. If we use a sequence of n vertical strokes to represent a rank of n, we may arrange proofs as follows:

	$R(A_i)$ Step	rule	Rep (A_i)	Reit (A_i)	$H(A_i)$
A_1:	$\vert$ $A \to B$	hyp	$\{A_1\}$	$\wedge$	A_1
A_2:	$\Vert$ $B \to C$	hyp	$\{A_2\}$	$\{A_1\}$	A_2
A_3:	$\Vert$ $A \to B$	A_1 reit	$\{A_{2-3}\}$	$\{A_1\}$	A_2
A_4:	$\Vert\vert$ A	hyp	$\{A_4\}$	$\{A_{2-3}\}$	A_4
A_5:	$\Vert\vert$ $A \to B$	A_3 reit	$\{A_{4-5}\}$	$\{A_{2-3}\}$	A_4
A_6:	$\Vert\vert$ B	$A_{4-5} \to$ E	$\{A_{4-6}\}$	$\{A_{2-3}\}$	A_4
A_7:	$\Vert\vert$ $B \to C$	A_2 reit	$\{A_{4-7}\}$	$\{A_{2-3}\}$	A_4
A_8:	$\Vert\vert$ C	$A_{6-7} \to$ E	$\{A_{4-8}\}$	$\{A_{2-3}\}$	A_4
A_9:	$\Vert$ $A \to C$	$A_{4-8} \to$ I	$\{A_{2-3}, A_9\}$	$\{A_1\}$	A_2
A_{10}:	$\vert$ $B \to C \to$				
	$.A \to C$	$A_{2-9} \to$ I	$\{A_1, A_{10}\}$	$\wedge$	A_1
A_{11}:	$A \to B \to$				
	$.B \to C \to$				
	$.A \to C$	$A_{1-10} \to$ I	$\{A_{11}\}$	$\wedge$	–

Then if we connect the lines indicating rank, we have a format that looks much like the proof of the law of transitivity given earlier.

The foregoing formulation makes explicit the techniques involved in constructing subproofs, and similar formulations may be found for other systems to be considered subsequently. But making the procedure explicit leads to some loss as regards intuitive naturalness and obviousness, and we shall in the sequel continue to use the rather less formal approach with which we began, relying on the reader to see that the whole matter could be discussed more rigorously, along the lines just indicated.

As a further simplification we allow reiterations directly into subsubproofs, etc., with the understanding that a complete proof requires that reiterations be performed always from one proof into another proof immediately subordinate to it. As an example (step 6 below), we prove the *self-distributive law* ($H_1 2$, below):

1	$A \to . B \to C$	hyp
2	$A \to B$	hyp
3	A	hyp
4	$A \to B$	2 reit
5	B	34 $\to$E
6	$A \to . B \to C$	1 reit
7	$B \to C$	3 6 $\to$E
8	C	5 7 $\to$E
9	$A \to C$	3–8 $\to$I
10	$A \to B \to . A \to C$	2–9 $\to$I
11	$(A \to . B \to C) \to . A \to B \to . A$	1–10 $\to$1

Fitch 1952 shows (essentially) that the set of theorems of H_I* stemming from these rules is identical with the pure implicational fragment H_I of the intuitionist propositional calculus of Heyting 1930, which consists of the following two axioms, with $\to$ E as the sole rule:

$H_I 1.$ $A \to . B \to A$

$H_I 2.$ $(A \to . B \to C) \to . A \to B \to . A \to C$

In order to introduce terminology and to exemplify a pattern of argument which we shall have further occasion to use, we shall reproduce Fitch's proof that the two formulations are equivalent.

To see that the subproof formulation H_I* contains the axiomatic formulation H_I, we deduce the axioms of H_I in H_I* ($H_I 2$ was just proved and $H_I 1$ is proved below) and then observe that the only rule of H_I is also a rule of H_I*. It follows that H_I* contains H_I.

To see that the axiomatic system H_I contains the subproof formulation H_I*, we first introduce the notion of a *quasi-proof* in H_I*; a quasi-proof differs from a proof only in that we may introduce axioms or theorems of H_I as steps (and of course use these, and steps derived from them, as premisses for rep, reit, or $\to$ E). Clearly this does not increase the stock of theorems of H_I*, since we may think of a step A, inserted under this rule, as coming by reiteration from a previous proof of A in H_I* (which we know exists since H_I* contains H_I).

Our object then is to show how subproofs in a quasi-proof in H_I* may be systematically eliminated in favor of theorems of H_I and uses of $\to$ E, in such a way that we are ultimately left with a sequence of formulas all of which are theorems of H_I. This reduction procedure always begins with an *innermost subproof*, by which we mean a subproof Q which has no proofs subordinate to it. Let

Q be an innermost subproof of a quasi-proof P of H_I*, where the steps of Q are $A_1, \ldots, A_n$, let Q' be the sequence $A_1 \to A_1$, $A_1 \to A_2, \ldots,$ $A_1 \to A_n$, and let P' be the result of replacing the subproof Q of P by the sequence Q' of wffs. Our task is now to show that P' is a quasi-proof, by showing how to insert theorems of H_I among the wffs of Q', in such a way that each step of Q' may be justified by reit, rep, or $\to$ E. First we need a theorem of H_I:

1.	$(A \to . B \to A \to A) \to . (A \to . B \to A)$	
	$\to . A \to A$	$H_I 2$
2.	$A \to . B \to A \to A$	$H_I 1$
3.	$A \to . B \to A$	$H_I 1$
4.	$A \to A$	1 2 3 $\to$ E (twice)

Then an inductive argument shows that we may justify steps in Q' as follows:

$A_1 \to A_1$ is justified by the theorem above.

If A_i was by rep in Q, then $A_1 \to A_i$ is by rep in Q'.

If A_i was by reit in Q, then in Q' insert $A_i \to . A_1 \to A_i$ ($H_I 1$) and use $\to$ E to get $A_1 \to A_i$ (the minor premiss being an item of the quasi-proof in P to which Q is subordinate, hence also preceding Q' in P').

If A_i was by $\to$E in Q, with premisses A_j and $A_j \to A_i$, then in Q' we have $A_1 \to A_j$ and $A_1 \to . A_j \to A_i$. Then insert $H_I 2$ and use $\to$ E twice to get $A_1 \to A_i$ as required.[9]

Finally, the step $A_1 \to A_n$, treated as a consequence of Q in P, may be treated in Q' as a consequence by rep of the immediately preceding step $A_1 \to A_n$.

Repeated application of this reduction then converts any proof in H_I* into a sequence of formulas all of which are theorems of H_I; hence the latter system contains the former, and the two are equivalent. Notice incidentally that the choice of axioms for H_I may be thought of as motivated by a wish to prove H_I and H_I* equivalent: they are *exactly* what is required to carry out the inductive argument above.

(We retain the terminology *quasi-proof* and *innermost subproof* for use in later arguments which are closely similar to the foregoing.)

The axioms of H_I also enable us to prove a slightly different form of the result above. We consider proofs with no subproofs, but with multiple hypotheses, and we define a *proof of B from hypotheses* $A_1, \ldots, A_n$ (in the Official way) as a sequence $S_1, \ldots, S_m$, B of wffs, each of which is either an axiom, or one of the hypotheses A_i, or a consequence of predecessors by $\rightarrow$ E. Then we arrive by very similar methods at the Official form of the *Deduction Theorem*: if there exists a proof of B from the hypotheses $A_1, \ldots, A_n$, then there exists a proof of $A_n \rightarrow B$ on the hypotheses $A_1, \ldots, A_{n-1}$; and conversely.

We return now to consideration of $H_I 1$, which is proved in H_I* as follows:

1	A	hyp
2	B	hyp
3	A	1 reit
4	B→A	2–3 →1
5	A→B→C	1–4 →I

Thus far the theorems proved by the subordinate proof method have all seemed natural and obvious truths about our intuitive idea of *entailment*. But here we come upon a theorem which shocks our intuitions (at least our untutored intuitions), for the theorem seems to say that anything whatever has A as a logical consequence, provided only that A is true. To be sure, there is an interpretation[10] we could place on the arrow which would make $A \rightarrow .B \rightarrow A$ true, but if the formal machinery is offered as an analysis or reconstruction of the notion of entailment, or formal deducibility, the principle seems outrageous, – such at least is almost certain to be the initial reaction to the theorem, as anyone who has taught elementary logic very well knows. Such theorems as $A \rightarrow .B \rightarrow A$ and $A \rightarrow .B \rightarrow B$ are of course familiar, and much discussed under the heading of "implicational paradoxes." The commonest attitude among logicians (as was remarked at the outset) is simply to accept the paradoxes as in some sense true, and at the same time to recognize that the formalism doesn't *quite* capture our intuitive use of "if...then –" (such in fact being our own attitude until the late fall of 1958). In what follows we will try to analyze the sources of the discomfort occasioned by such "implicational" paradoxes, and in the course of the argument offer reasons for believing that H_I simply doesn't capture a notion of implication or entailment at all, or at least no more than (say) an equivalence relation captures the notion of "if...then –." True, equivalence relations and entailment are both transitive and reflexive, but this similarity is not sufficient to

enable us to *identify* entailment with any equivalence relation, since entailment is not symmetrical, and to say so is to make a false statement. Likewise, entailment and the connective of H_I are both transitive and reflexive, but again this similarity is not sufficient to enable us to identify implication or entailment with the arrow of H_I, since in H_I one can prove $A \rightarrow .B \rightarrow A$, which is false of entailment and its converse, formal deducibility. Such a view is of course heterodox in logical circles, and will be rejected by many. Curry 1959, for example, has argued (in four closely-reasoned pages) that $A \rightarrow .B \rightarrow A$, "far from being paradoxical," is, for any *proper* implication, "a platitude." A "proper" implication is defined by Curry as any implication which has the following properties: there is a proof of B from the hypotheses $A_1, \ldots, A_{n-1}, A_n$ (in the Official sense of "proof from hypotheses") if and only if there is a proof of $A_n \rightarrow B$ from the hypotheses $A_1, \ldots, A_{n-1}$. On these grounds $A \rightarrow .B \rightarrow A$ is indeed a platitude: there is surely a proof of A from the hypotheses A, B; and hence for any "proper" implication, a proof of $B \rightarrow A$ from the hypothesis A; and hence a proof without hypotheses of $A \rightarrow .B \rightarrow A$.[11]

Curry goes on to dub the implicational relation of H_I "absolute implication" on the grounds that H_I is the minimal system having this property. But we notice at once that H_I is "absolute" only relatively, i.e., relatively to the Official definition of "proof from hypotheses." From this point of view, our remarks to follow may be construed as arguing the impropriety of accepting the Official definition of "proof from hypotheses," as a basis for defining a "proper implication"; as we shall claim, the Official view captures neither "proof" (a matter involving logical necessity), nor "from" (a matter requiring relevance). But even those with intuitions so sophisticated that $A \rightarrow .B \rightarrow A$ seems tolerable might still find some interest in an attempt to analyze our initial feelings of repugnance in its presence.

Why does $A \rightarrow .B \rightarrow A$ seem so queer? We believe that its oddness is due to two isolable features of the principle, which we consider forthwith.

II

Necessity

For more than two millennia logicians have taught that logic is a *formal* matter, and that the validity of an inference depends not on material considerations, but on formal considerations alone. The companion view that the validity of a valid inference is no accident of nature, but rather a property a valid inference has necessarily, has had an equally illustrious history. But both of these conditions are violated if we take the arrow of H_I to express implication. For if A is contingent, then $A \rightarrow .B \rightarrow A$ says that an entailment $B \rightarrow A$ follows from or is deducible from a contingent proposition – in defiance of the condition that formal considerations *alone* validate valid inferences. And if A should be a true contingent proposition, then $B \rightarrow A$ is also contingently true, and an entailment is established as holding because of an accident of nature.

It has been said in defence of $A \rightarrow .B \rightarrow A$ as an entailment that at least it is "safe," in the sense that if A is true, then it is always safe to infer A from an arbitrary B, since we run no risk of uttering a falsehood in doing so; this thought ("Safety First") seems to be behind attempts, in a number of elementary logic texts, to justify the claim that $A \rightarrow .B \rightarrow A$ has something to do with implication. In reply we of course admit that if A is true then it is "safe" to say so (i.e., $A \rightarrow A$). But saying that A is true on the irrelevant assumption that B, is *not* to deduce A from B, nor to establish that B implies A, in *any* sensible sense of "implies." Of course we *can* say "Assume that snow is puce. Seven is a prime number." But if we say "Assume that snow is puce. *It follows that* (or *consequently*, or *therefore*, or *it may validly be inferred that*) seven is a prime number," then we have simply spoken falsely. A man who assumes the continuum hypothesis, and then remarks that it is a nice day, is not inferring the latter from the former, – even if he keeps his supposition fixed firmly in mind while noting the weather. And since a (true) A does not follow from an (arbitrary) B, we reject $A \rightarrow .B \rightarrow A$ as expressing a truth of entailment or implication, a rejection which is in line with the view (often expressed even by those who hold that $A \rightarrow .B \rightarrow A$ expresses a fact about implication or entailment or "if...then –") that entailments, if true at all, are necessarily true.

How can we modify the formulation of H_I in such a way as to guarantee that the logical truths expressible in it shall be necessary, rather than contingent? As a start, we might reflect that in our usual mathematical or logical proofs, we demand that all the conditions required for the conclusion be stated in the hypothesis of a theo-

rem. After the word "*Proof:*" in a mathematical treatise, mathematical writers seem to feel that no more hypotheses may be introduced – and it is regarded as a criticism of a proof if not all the required hypotheses are stated explicitly at the outset. Of course additional machinery *may* be invoked in the proof, but this must be of a logical character, i.e., in addition to the hypotheses, we may use only logically necessary propositions in the argument. These considerations suggest that we should be allowed to import into a deduction (i.e., into a subproof by reit) only propositions which, if true at all, are necessarily true: i.e., we should reiterate only entailments. And indeed such a restriction on reiteration would immediately rule out $A \rightarrow .B \rightarrow A$ as a theorem, while countenancing all the other theorems we have proved thus far. We call the system with reiteration so restricted $S4_I*$, and proceed to prove it equivalent to the following axiomatic formulation, which we call $S4_I$, since it is the pure strict "implicational" fragment of Lewis's S4.[12]

$S4_I1.$ $A \rightarrow A$
$S4_I2.$ $(A \rightarrow .B \rightarrow C) \rightarrow$
$\qquad\qquad\qquad .A \rightarrow B \rightarrow .A \rightarrow C$
$S4_I3.$ $A \rightarrow B.C \rightarrow .A \rightarrow B$

It is a trivial matter to prove the axioms of $S4_I$ in $S4_I*$, and the only rule of $S4_I(\rightarrow E)$ is also a rule of $S4_I^*$; hence $S4_I^*$ contains $S4_I$. To establish the converse, we show how to convert any quasi-proof of a theorem A in $S4_I^*$ into a proof of A in $S4_I$.

Theorem

Let $A_1, \ldots, A_n$ be the propositional items of an innermost subproof Q of a quasi-proof P, and let Q' be the sequence $A_1 \rightarrow A_1, \ldots, A_1 \rightarrow A_n$, and finally let P' be the result of replacing the subproof Q in P by the sequence of propositions Q'. Then P' is a quasi-proof.

Proof. By induction on n. For $n = 1$ we note that $A_1 \rightarrow A_1$ is an instance of $S4_I1$. Then assuming the theorem for all $i < n$, consider $A_1 \rightarrow A_n$.

Case 1. A_n is by repetition in Q of A_i. Then treat $A_1 \rightarrow A_n$ in Q' as a repetition of $A_1 \rightarrow A_i$.

Case 2. A_n is a reiteration in Q of B. Then B has the form $C \rightarrow D$, by the restriction on reiteration. Then insert $C \rightarrow D. A_1 \rightarrow .C \rightarrow D$ in Q' by $S4_I$ 3, and treat $A_1 \rightarrow .C \rightarrow D$ (i.e., $A_1 \rightarrow A_n$) as a consequence of $C \rightarrow D$ (i.e., B), and $S4_I3$ by $\rightarrow E$.

Case 3. A_n follows in Q from A_i and $A_i \rightarrow A_n$ by $\rightarrow$ E. Then by the inductive hypothesis we have $A_1 \rightarrow A_i$ and $A_1 \rightarrow . A_i \rightarrow A_n$ in Q'. Then $A_1 \rightarrow A_n$ is a consequence of the latter and S4₁2, with two uses of $\rightarrow$ E.

Finally, the step $A_1 \rightarrow A_n$, regarded as a consequence of Q in P, may now be regarded as a repetition of the final step $A_1 \rightarrow A_n$ of Q' in P'.

Hence P' is a quasi-proof. And repeated application of this technique to P' eventually leads to a sequence P'' of wffs, each of which is a theorem of S4₁. Hence S4₁ includes S4₁*, and the two are equivalent.

Theorem

If there is a proof of B on hypotheses $A_1, \ldots, A_n$, (in the Official sense), where each A_i, $1 \overset{\leq}{=} i \overset{\leq}{=} n$, has the form $C \rightarrow D$, then there is a proof of $A_n \rightarrow B$ on hypotheses $A_1, \ldots, A_{n-1}$. (Barcan Marcus 1946.)

(We remark that a Test Formulation of S4₁ arises if we add to the "if" clause of (3) the requirement that A_j be of the form $B \rightarrow C$. Notice again that the choice of S4₁1 $-$ 3 may be thought of as motivated exactly by the wish to prove an appropriate deduction theorem.)

The restriction on reiteration then suffices to remove one objectionable feature of H₁, since it is now no longer possible to establish an entailment $B \rightarrow A$ on the (perhaps contingent) ground that A is simply true. But of course it is well known that the "implication" relation of S4 is also paradoxical, since we can easily establish that an arbitrary irrelevant proposition B "implies" A, provided A is a necessary truth. $A \rightarrow A$ is necessarily true, and from it and S4₁3 follows $B \rightarrow . A \rightarrow A$, where B may be totally irrelevant to $A \rightarrow A$. This defect leads us to consider an alternative restriction on H₁, designed to exclude such fallacies of relevance.

III

Relevance

For more than two millennia logicians have taught that a necessary condition for the validity of an inference from A to B is that A be relevant to B. Virtually every logic book up to the present century has a chapter on fallacies of relevance, and many contemporary elementary texts have fol-

lowed the same plan. (Notice that contemporary writers, in the later and more formal chapters of their books, seem explicitly to contradict the earlier chapters, when they try desperately to con the students into accepting material or strict "implication" as a "kind" of implication relation, in spite of the fact that these relations countenance fallacies of relevance.) But the denial that relevance is essential to a valid argument (a denial which is implicit in the view that strict "implication" is an implication relation) seems to us flatly in error.

Imagine, if you can, a situation as follows. A mathematician writes a paper on Banach spaces, and after proving a couple of theorems he concludes with a conjecture. As a footnote to the conjecture, he writes: "In addition to its intrinsic interest, this conjecture has connections with other parts of mathematics which might not immediately occur to the reader. For example, if the conjecture is true, then the first order functional calculus is complete; whereas if it is false, then it implies that Fermat's last conjecture is correct." The editor replies that the paper is obviously acceptable, but he finds the final footnote perplexing; he can see no connection whatever between the conjecture and the "other parts of mathematics," and none is indicated in the footnote. So the mathematician replies, "Well, I was using 'if . . . then $-$' and 'implies' in the way that logicians have claimed I was: the first order functional calculus *is* complete, and necessarily so, so anything implies that fact $-$ and if the conjecture is false it is presumably impossible, and hence implies anything. And if you object to this usage, it is simply because you have not understood the technical sense of 'if . . . then $-$' worked out so nicely for us by logicians." And to this the editor counters: 'I *understand* the technical bit all right, but it is simply not correct. In spite of what most logicians say about us, the standards maintained by this journal require that the antecedent of an "if . . . then $-$' statement must be *relevant* to the conclusion drawn. And you have given no evidence that your conjecture about Banach spaces is relevant either to the completeness theorem or to Fermat's conjecture."

The editor's point is of course that though the technical meaning is clear, it is simply not the same as the meaning ascribed to "if . . . then $-$" in the pages of his journal. Furthermore, he has put his finger precisely on the difficulty: to argue from the necessary truth of *A* to *if B then A* is simply to commit a fallacy of relevance. The fancy that relevance is irrelevant to validity strikes us as ludicruous, and we therefore make an attempt to explicate the notion of relevance of A to B.

For this we return to the notion of proof from hypotheses, the leading idea being that we want to infer $A \rightarrow B$ from "a proof of B from the hypothesis A." As we pointed out before, in the usual axiomatic formulations of propositional calculi the matter is handled as follows. We say that $A_1, \ldots, A_n$ is a proof of B from the hypothesis A, if $A = A_1, B = A_n$, and each $A_i (i > 1)$ is either an axiom or else a consequence of predecessors among $A_1, \ldots, A_n$ by one of the rules. But in the presence of a deduction theorem of the form: from a proof of B on the hypothesis A, to infer $A \rightarrow B$, this definition leads immediately to fallacies of relevance; for if B is a theorem independently of A, then we have $A \rightarrow B$ where A may be irrelevant to B. For example, in a system with $A \rightarrow A$ as an axiom, we have

1	⊢ B	hyp
2	⌐ A→A	axiom
3	B→A→A	1–2, → I

In this example we indeed proved $A \rightarrow A$, but it is crashingly obvious that we did not prove it *from* the hypothesis B: the defect lies in the definition, which fails to take seriously the word "from" in "proof *from* hypotheses." And this fact suggests a solution to the problem: we should devise a technique for keeping track of the steps used, and then allow application of the introduction rule only when A is relevant to B in the sense that A is *used* in arriving at B.

As a start in this direction, we suggest prefixing a start (say) to the hypothesis of a deduction, and also to the conclusion of an application of $\rightarrow$ E just in case at least one premiss has a star, steps introduced as axioms being unstarred. Restriction of $\rightarrow$ I to cases where in accordance with these rules both A and B are starred would then exclude theorems of the form $A \rightarrow B$, where B is proved independently of A.

In other words, what is wanted is a system for which there is provable a deduction theorem, to the effect that there exists a proof of B *from* the hypothesis A if and only if $A \rightarrow B$ is provable. And we now consider the question of choosing axioms in such a way as to guarantee this result. In view of the rule $\rightarrow$ E, the implication in one direction is trivial; we consider the converse.

Suppose we have a proof

*	A_1	hyp
	⋮	
	A_i	
	⋮	
*	A_n	

of A_n from the hypothesis A_1, and we wish to convert this into an axiomatic proof of $A_1 \rightarrow A_n$. A natural and obvious suggestion would be to consider replacing each starred A_i by $A_1 \rightarrow A_i$ (since the starred steps are the ones to which A_1 is relevant), and try to show that the result is a proof without hypotheses. What axioms would be required to carry the induction through?

For the basis case we obviously require as an axiom $A \rightarrow A$. And in the inductive step, where we consider steps A_i and $A_i \rightarrow A_j$ of the original proof, four cases may arise.

(1) Neither premiss is starred. Then in the axiomatic proof, A_i, $A_i \rightarrow A_j$, and A_j all remain unaltered, so $\rightarrow$ E may be used as before.

(2) The minor premiss is starred and the major one is not. Then in the axiomatic proof we have $A_1 \rightarrow A_i$ and $A_i \rightarrow A_j$; so we need to be able to infer $A_1 \rightarrow A_j$ from these (since the star on A_i guarantees a star on A_j in the original proof).

(3) The major premiss is starred and the minor one is not. Then in the axiomatic proof we have $A_1 \rightarrow . A_i \rightarrow A_j$ and A_i, so we need to be able to infer $A_1 \rightarrow A_j$ from these.

(4) And finally both may be starred, in which case we have $A_1 \rightarrow . A_i \rightarrow A_j$ and $A_1 \rightarrow A_i$ in the axiomatic proof, from which again we need to infer $A_1 \rightarrow A_j$.

Summarizing: the proof of an appropriate deduction theorem where relevance is demanded would require the axiom $A \rightarrow A$ together with the validity of the following inferences:

From $A \rightarrow B$ and $B \rightarrow C$ to infer $A \rightarrow C$;
From $A \rightarrow .B \rightarrow C$ and B to infer $A \rightarrow C$;
From $A \rightarrow .B \rightarrow C$ and $A \rightarrow B$ to infer $A \rightarrow C$.

It then seems plausible to consider the following axiomatic system as capturing the notion of relevance:

$A \rightarrow A$ (*identity*)
$A \rightarrow B \rightarrow . B \rightarrow C \rightarrow . A \rightarrow C$ (*transitivity*)
$(A \rightarrow . B \rightarrow C) \rightarrow . B \rightarrow . A \rightarrow C$
         (*permutation*)
$(A \rightarrow . B \rightarrow C) \rightarrow . A \rightarrow B \rightarrow . A \rightarrow C$
         (*self-distribution*)

And without further proof we state that for this system W_I' we have the following.

Theorem

$A \rightarrow B$ is a theorem of W_I' just in case there is a proof of B *from* the hypothesis A (in the starred sense).

Equivalent systems have been investigated by Moh Shaw-Kwei 1950 and Church 1951. Church calls his system the "weak positive implicational propositional calculus," (W_I), and uses the following axioms:

W_I1. $A \rightarrow A$ (*identity*)

W_I2. $A \rightarrow B \rightarrow . C \rightarrow A \rightarrow . C \rightarrow B$
                         (*transitivity*)

W_I3. $(A \rightarrow . B \rightarrow C) \rightarrow . B \rightarrow . A \rightarrow C$
                         (*Permutation*)

W_I4. $(A \rightarrow . A \rightarrow B) \rightarrow . A \rightarrow B$
                         (*contraction*)

The proof that W_I' and W_I are equivalent is left to the reader.

A generalization of the deduction theorem above was proved by both Moh Shaw-Kwei and Church; modified to suit present purposes, it may be stated as follows:

Theorem

If there exists a proof of B on the hypotheses $A_1, \ldots, A_n$, in which all of $A_1, \ldots, A_n$ are used in arriving at B, then there is a proof of $A_n \rightarrow B$ from $A_1, \ldots, A_{n-1}$ satisfying the same condition.

So put, the result acquires a rather peculiar appearance: it seems odd that we should have to use *all* the hypotheses. One would have thought that for a group of hypotheses to be relevant to a conclusion, it would suffice if *some* of the hypotheses were used – at least if we think of the hypotheses as taken conjointly. (Cf. the "entailment" theorem of Belnap 1960.) The peculiarity arises because of a tendency (thus far not commented on) to confound $(A_1 \wedge \ldots \wedge A_n) \rightarrow B$ with $A_1 \rightarrow . A_2 \rightarrow . \ldots . A_n \rightarrow B$.[13] But in the former case, we would not expect to require that *all* the A_i be relevant to B. We shall give reasons presently, deriving from another formulation of W_I, for thinking it sensible to require each of the A_i in the nested implication to be relevant to B; a feature of the situation which will lead us to make a sharp distinction between $(A_1 \wedge \ldots \wedge A_n) \rightarrow B$ and

$A_1 \rightarrow . \ldots . A_n \rightarrow B$. (It is presumably the failure to make this distinction which leads Curry 1959 to say of the relation considered in Church's theorem that it is one "which is not ordinarily considered in deductive methodology at all.")

We feel that the star formulation of the deduction theorem makes clearer what is at stake in Church's calculus. On the other hand Church's own deduction theorem has the merit of allowing for proof of nested entailments in a more perspicuous way than is available in the star formulation. Our next task therefore is to try to combine these approaches so as to obtain the advantages of both.

Returning now to a consideration of subordinate proofs, it seems natural to try to extend the star treatment, using some other symbol for deductions carried out in a subproof, but retaining the same rules for carrying this symbol along. We might consider a proof of contraction in which the inner hypothesis is distinguished by a dagger rather than a star:

1	$A \rightarrow . A \rightarrow B$	$*$	hyp
2	A	$\dagger$	hyp

(the different relevance marks reflecting the initial assumption that the two formulas, as hypotheses, are irrelevant to each other). Then generalizing the starring rules, we might require that in applications of $\rightarrow$ E, the conclusion B must carry all the relevance marks of both premises A and $A \rightarrow B$, thus:

1	$A \rightarrow . A \rightarrow B$	$*$		hyp
2	A		$\dagger$	hyp
3	$A \rightarrow A \rightarrow B$	$*$		1 reit
4	$A \rightarrow B$	$*$	$\dagger$	2 3 $\rightarrow$E
5	B	$*$	$\dagger$	2 4 $\rightarrow$E

To motivate the restriction on $\rightarrow$ I, we recall that in proofs involving only stars, it was required that both A and B have stars, and that the star was discharged on $A \rightarrow B$ in the conclusion of a deduction. This suggests the following generalization: that in drawing the conclusion $A \rightarrow B$ by $\rightarrow$ I, we require that the relevance symbol on A also be present among those of B, and that in the conclusion $A \rightarrow B$ the relevance symbol of A (like the hypothesis A itself) be discharged. Two applications of this rule then lead from the proof above to

$$6 \mid \quad A \rightarrow B \; * \qquad\qquad 2\text{-}5 \rightarrow I$$
$$7 \quad (A \rightarrow . A \rightarrow B) \rightarrow . A \rightarrow B \qquad 1\; 6 \rightarrow I$$

But of course the easiest way of handling the matter is to use classes of numerals to mark the relevance conditions, since then we may have as many nested subproofs as we wish, each with a distinct numeral (which we shall write as a subscript) for its hypothesis. More precisely we allow that: (1) one may introduce a new hypothesis $A_{\{k\}}$, where k should be different from all subscripts on hypotheses of proofs to which the new proof is subordinate – it suffices to take k as the rank of A (see Test Formulations); (2) from A_a and $A \rightarrow B_b$ we may infer $B_{a \cup b}$; (3) from a proof of B_a from the hypothesis $A_{\{k\}}$, where k is in a, we may infer $A \rightarrow B_{a-\{k\}}$; and reit and rep retain subscripts (where a, b, c, range over classes of numerals).

As an example we prove the *law of assertion*.

$$
\begin{array}{lll}
1 & \quad\; A_{\{1\}} & \text{hyp} \\
2 & \qquad A \rightarrow B_{(2)} & \text{hyp} \\
3 & \qquad A_{\{1\}} & 1 \text{ reit} \\
4 & \quad\; A_{\{1,2\}} & 2\;3 \rightarrow 1 \\
5 & A \rightarrow A \rightarrow B & 2\text{-}4 \rightarrow 1 \\
6 & A \rightarrow . A \rightarrow B \rightarrow B & 1\text{-}5 \rightarrow 1 \\
\end{array}
$$

To see that this generalization W_I* is also equivalent to W_I, observe first that the axioms of W_I are easily proved in W_I*; hence W_I* contains W_I. The proof of the converse involves little more than repeated application, beginning with innermost subproofs, of the techniques used in proving the deduction theorem for W_I; it will be left to the reader.

(We remark that a Test Formulation of W_I arises if to the formulation for H_I we add the following clauses defining a set of "relevance indices" $\text{Rel}(A_i)$ for each i-th step

Basis: (f) $\text{Rel}(A_1) = \{1\}$
(1) (f) $\text{Rel}(A_k) = \{R(A_k)\}$
(2) (f) $\text{Rel}(A_k) = \text{Rel}(A_j)$
(3) (f) $\text{Rel}(A_k) = \text{Rel}(A_j)$
(4) (f) $\text{Rel}(A_k) = \text{Rel}(A_j) \cup \text{Rel}(A_j)$
(5) If $\text{Rel}(H(A_{k-1})) \subset \text{Rel}(A_{k-1})$, then
(a)–(e) as before, and
(f) $\text{Rel}(A_k) = \text{Rel}(A_{k-1}) - -\text{Rel}(H(A_{k-1}).)$

If the subscripting device is taken as an explication of relevance, then it is seen that Church's W_I does secure relevance, since $A \rightarrow B$ is provable in W_I only if A is relevant to B.

But if W_I is taken as an explication of entailment, then the requirement of necessity for a valid inference is lost. Consider the following special case of the law of assertion, just proved:

$$A \rightarrow . A \rightarrow A \rightarrow A.$$

This says that if A is true, then it follows from A $\rightarrow$ A. But it seems reasonable to suppose that any logical consequence of A $\rightarrow$ A should be necessarily true. (Note that in the familiar systems of modal logic, consequences of necessary truths are necessary.) We certainly do in practice recognize that there are truths which do not follow from a law of logic – but W_I obliterates this distinction. It seems evident, therefore, that a satisfactory theory of implication will require both relevance (like W_I) *and* necessity (like $S4_I$).

IV

Necessity and relevance

We therefore consider the system E_I^{14} which arises when we recognize that valid inferences require both necessity and relevance. Since the restrictions are most transparent as applied to the subproof format, we begin by considering the system E_I* which results from imposing the restriction on reiteration (of $S4_I*$) together with the subscript requirements (of W_I*).[15] We summarize the rules of E_I* as follows:

(1) Hyp. A step may be introduced as the hypothesis of a new subproof, and each new hypothesis receives a unit class $\{k\}$ of numerical subscripts, where k is the rank of A.

(2) Rep. A_a may be repeated, retaining the relevance indices a.

(3) Reit. $(A \rightarrow B)_a$ may be reiterated, retaining a.

(4) $\rightarrow$ E. From A_a and $(A \rightarrow B)_b$ to infer $B_{a \cup b}$.

(5) $\rightarrow$ I. From a proof of B_a on hypothesis $A_{\{k\}}$ to infer $(A \rightarrow B)'_{a-\{k\}}$ provided k is in a.

(For a Test Formulation of E_I* we simply combine the restriction on reiteration for $S4_I*$ with the subscript requirements for W_I*.)

It develops that an axiomatic counterpart of E_I* has also been considered in the literature, E_I* in fact being equivalent to the pure implicational fragment E_I' of Ackermann 1956,[16] defined by the following axioms and rules:

$E_I1.$ $A \rightarrow A$

$E_I2.$ $A \rightarrow B \rightarrow .B \rightarrow C \rightarrow .A \rightarrow C$

$E_I3.$ $A \rightarrow B \rightarrow .C \rightarrow A \rightarrow .C \rightarrow B$

$E_I4.$ $(A \rightarrow .A \rightarrow B) \rightarrow .A \rightarrow B$

Rules: $\rightarrow E$

(δ) From A and $B \rightarrow .A \rightarrow C$ to infer $B \rightarrow C$.

(δ) is essentially a rule of permutation, giving the *effect* of the formula $(B \rightarrow .A \rightarrow C) \rightarrow .A \rightarrow .B \rightarrow C$. The latter, however, is not provable in Ackermann's calculus, and addition of such a law of permutation would reduce Ackermann's system to Church's. Moreover, rule (δ) requires the restriction (as Ackermann 1956 points out) that the minor premiss A be a theorem, else one could pass from a contingently true A, by way of $A \rightarrow A \rightarrow .A \rightarrow A$, to $A \rightarrow A \rightarrow A$, thus again obliterating the distinction between necessary and contingent truth. (δ) is therefore non-normal, in the sense that no corresponding entailment is provable.

This situation may be remedied, however, if we replace (δ) by the following axiom

$E_I5.$ $A \rightarrow A \rightarrow B \rightarrow B$,

which yields an equivalent set of theorems, as we now see. Let E_I' be E_I1–4, $\rightarrow E$ and (δ), and let E_I'' be E_I1–5 and $\rightarrow E$. E_I5 is immediate in E_I', from E_I' and $A \rightarrow A \rightarrow B \rightarrow .A \rightarrow A \rightarrow B$ by (δ); hence E_I' contains E_I''. To prove (δ) in E_I'' we assume the first two steps below obtained, and proceed as indicated (after noting that in the pure implicational calculus the minor premiss of (δ) must be an entailment):

1. $A \rightarrow B$
2. $C \rightarrow .A \rightarrow B \rightarrow D$
3. $B \rightarrow B \rightarrow .A \rightarrow B$ $1\ E_I2 \rightarrow E$
4. $A \rightarrow B \rightarrow D \rightarrow .B \rightarrow B \rightarrow D$
                     $3\ E_I2 \rightarrow E$
5. $C \rightarrow .B \rightarrow B \rightarrow D$ $2\ 4$ transitivity
6. $C \rightarrow D$ $5\ E_I5$ transitivity

Hence E_I' and E_I'' are equivalent.

Proof of equivalence of E_I* with E_I' proceeds most easily by way of E_I''. That E_I* contains E_I'' is trivial; the construction of proofs of the axioms by the subproof technique is left to the reader. To reduce proofs in E_I* to proofs in E_I'', we require the following

Lemma

If A_a is a step of a subproof Q (of a quasi-proof in E_I*) with hypothesis $H_{\{k\}}$, where k is not in a, then we may also obtain $A \rightarrow B \rightarrow B_a$ in Q (for arbitrary B), with the help of theorems of E_I'' and $\rightarrow E$.

Proof. We first require a theorem of E_I''.

$E_I6.$ $A \rightarrow B \rightarrow .A \rightarrow B \rightarrow C \rightarrow C$
1. $A \rightarrow B \rightarrow .A \rightarrow A \rightarrow .A \rightarrow B$
                          E_I3
2. $(A \rightarrow A \rightarrow .A \rightarrow B) \rightarrow .A \rightarrow B$
     $\rightarrow C \rightarrow .A \rightarrow A \rightarrow C$ E_I2
3. $A \rightarrow B \rightarrow .A \rightarrow B \rightarrow C \rightarrow .A$
     $\rightarrow A \rightarrow C$ $1\ 2$ transitivity
4. $(A \rightarrow B \rightarrow C \rightarrow .A \rightarrow A \rightarrow C)$
     $\rightarrow .A \rightarrow B \rightarrow C \rightarrow C$
                    $E_I5 E_I3 \rightarrow E$
5. $A \rightarrow B \rightarrow .A \rightarrow B \rightarrow C \rightarrow C$
                    $3\ 4$ transitivity

The proof of the lemma is by induction. The *first* A_a in the proof, with k not in a, must be obtained by reiteration, hence has the form $C \rightarrow D$. Then insert $C \rightarrow D \rightarrow .C \rightarrow D \rightarrow B \rightarrow B(E_I6)$ and use $\rightarrow E$ to obtain $C \rightarrow D \rightarrow B \rightarrow B_a$, i.e., $A \rightarrow B \rightarrow B_a$. Any other A_a with k not in a, must either be obtained from reit (in which case we argue as before) or else from C_c and $C \rightarrow A_b$ by $\rightarrow E$, where $a = b \cup c$ and k is in neither b nor c. Then by the inductive hypotheses, we may obtain $C \rightarrow A \rightarrow A_c$ and $C \rightarrow A \rightarrow B \rightarrow B_b$. Then insert

$$C \rightarrow A \rightarrow A \rightarrow .A \rightarrow B \rightarrow .C \rightarrow A \rightarrow B \ (E_I2)$$

and use $\rightarrow E$ to get $A \rightarrow B \rightarrow .C \rightarrow A \rightarrow B_c$; and insertion of

$$(A \rightarrow B \rightarrow .C \rightarrow A \rightarrow B) \rightarrow .C \rightarrow A \rightarrow B \rightarrow B \rightarrow .A \rightarrow B \rightarrow B \ (E_I2)$$

and two uses of $\rightarrow E$ then leads to the desired result $A \rightarrow B \rightarrow B_{b \cup c}$, i.e., $A \rightarrow B \rightarrow B_a$. Notice that only theorems of E_I'' and $\to E$ were used in obtaining the lemma.

To prove that E_I* is contained in E_I'', we again consider an innermost subproof Q of a proof P in E_I*, with steps $A_{1\{k\}}, \ldots, A_{ia_i}, \ldots, A_{na_n}$ and we let A_{ia_i}' be $(A_1 \to A_i)_{a_i-\{k\}}$ or A_{ia_i} according as k is or is not in a_i. Then we replace Q by the sequence Q' of A_{ia_i}', obtaining P', and the theorem may be stated as follows:

Theorem

Under these conditions theorems of E_I'' may be inserted in Q' in such a way as to make P' a quasi-proof. (Anderson 1959).

Proof. Basis. $A_{1\{k\}}'$ is $A_1 \to A_1$, and may be treated as an insertion of E_I1.

If any A_a in Q is a consequence of a preceding step by rep or reit, then A_a' may be treated in Q' as a repetition.

If any A_a is a consequence of B_b' and $(B \to A)_c$ in Q, where $a = b \cup c$, then we distinguish four cases:

(i) k is in neither b nor c. Then B_b' is B_b, $(B \to A)_c'$ is $(B \to A)_c$, and $A_{b \cup c}$, i.e., A_a', follows by $\to E$ in Q'.

(ii) k is in neither b nor c. Then B_b' is $(A_1 \to B)_{b-\{k\}}$, and $(B \to A)_c'$ is $(B \to A)_c$. Then insert E_I2, and use $\to E$ twice to get $(A_1 \to A)_{(b \cup c)-\{k\}}$, i.e., A_a'.

(iii) k is in c but not b. Then B_b' is B_b, and $(B \to A)_c'$ is $(A_1 \to .B \to A)_{c-\{k\}}$. Since k is not in b, we have by the lemma $(B \to A \to A)_b$. Then insertion of

$$(A_1 \to .B \to A) \to .B \to A \to A \to .A_1 \to A \quad (E_I2)$$

yields $(A_1 \to A)_{(b \cup c)-\{k\}}$, i.e., A_a', by two uses of $\to E$.

(iv) k is in both c and b. Then we have $(A_1 \to B)_{b-\{k\}}$ and $(A_1 \to .B \to A)_{c-\{k\}}$. Inserting E_I2 we have $A_1 \to B \to .B \to A \to .A_1 \to A$, whence $(B \to A \to .A_1 \to A)_{b-\{k\}}$ by $\to E$, and $(A_1 \to .A_1 \to A)_{(b \cup c)-\{k\}}$ by transitivity. Then insert E_I4 and use $\to E$ to get $(A_1 \to A)_{a-\{k\}}$, i.e., A_a', as required.

To complete the proof we observe that the restriction on the introduction rule guarantees that k is in a_n, hence the final step A_{na_n}' of Q' is $(A_1 \to A_n)_{a_n-\{k\}}$. But then the conclusion $(A_1 \to A_n)_{a_n-\{k\}}$ from Q by $\to I$ in P can be regarded in P' as a repetition of the last wff of Q'.

Hence P' is a quasi-proof.

Repeated application of these techniques then leads ultimately to a sequence of wffs each of which is either an axiom of E_I'', or else a consequence of predecessors by $\to E$, and hence a theorem of E_I''. And since E_I'' is equivalent with E_I', this establishes the equivalence of E_I* with Ackermann's implicational calculus.

The equivalence of E_I* with E_I' gives us an easy proof technique for E_I', and we now state a summary list of laws of entailment, proofs of which will be left to the reader.

Identity: $A \to A$
Transitivity: (Suffixing) $A \to B \to .B \to C \to .A \to C$
(Prefixing) $A \to B \to .C \to A \to .C \to B$
Contraction: $(A \to .A \to B) \to .A \to B$
Self-distribution:
$(A \to .B \to C) \to .A \to B \to .A \to C$
Restricted permutation: $(A \to .B \to C \to D) \to .B \to C \to .A \to D$
Restricted conditioned modus ponens: $B \to C \to .(A \to .B \to C \to D) \to .A \to D$
Restricted assertion: $A \to B \to .A \to B \to C \to C$
Specialized assertion: $A \to A \to B \to B$
Replacement of the middle: $D \to B \to .(A \to .B \to C) \to (A \to .D \to C)$
Replacement of the third: $C \to D \to .(A \to .B \to C) \to (A \to .B \to D)$
Prefixing in the consequent: $(A \to .B \to C) \to .A \to .D \to B \to .D \to C$
Suffixing in the consequent: $(A \to .B \to C) \to .A \to .C \to D \to .B \to D$

The foregoing seems to us to be a strong and natural list of valid entailments, all of which are *necessarily* true, and in each of which the antecedent is *relevant* to the consequent. And of course each is provable in all of the systems H_I, $S4_I$, and W_I considered previously. But the latter all contain in addition "paradoxical" assertions, which we now discuss under two headings; fallacies of modality, and fallacies of relevance.

V

Fallacies of modality

We have in earlier discussions remarked that entailments, if true at all, are necessarily true, and that if A follows from a law of logic, then A is necessarily true. We begin consideration of modal fallacies by showing that a theory of necessity is contained in E_I*, and that it has the expected properties. We define "it is necessary that A" as follows (Anderson and Belnap 1959):

$$NA = \text{df } A \to A \to A.^{17}$$

The motivation for this choice of a definition of NA lies in the belief that A is necessary if and only if A follows from a logical truth. The choice of $A \to A$ as *the* logical truth from which a necessary A must follow is justified by the fact that if A follows from any true entailment $B \to C$, then it follows from $A \to A$, a fact expressed in the following theorem.

1	$B \to C_{\{1\}}$	hyp
2	$B \to C \to A_{\{2\}}$	hyp
3	$A \to A_{\{3\}}$	hyp
4	$B \to C_{\{1\}}$	1 reit
5	$B \to C \to A_{\{2\}}$	2 reit
6	$A_{\{2\}}$	1 reit
7	$A_{\{1,2,3\}}$	4 5 →E
8	$A \to A \to A_{\{1,2\}}$	3 7 →E
9	$B \to C \to A \to NA_{\{1\}}$	2–8 →I
10	$B \to C \to B \to C \to A \to NA$	1–9 →1

We find support for this proposal in the fact that in such systems as M (Feys 1937; von Wright 1951), S4, and S5, NA (either taken as primitive, or defined as not-possible-not A) is strictly equivalent to (hence intersubstitutable with) $A \to A \to A$. (This observation for S4 and S5 was made by Lemmon *et al.* 1956.)

We give as examples some further proofs of theorems involving necessity.

1	$A \to A \to A_{\{1\}}$	hyp
2	$A_{\{2\}}$	hyp
3	$A_{\{3\}}$	2 rep
4	$A \to A$	2–3 → I
5	$A_{\{2\}}$	1–4 → E
6	$NA \to A$	1–5 → I

1	$A \to A \to B_{\{1\}}$	hyp
2	$B \to B_{\{2\}}$	hyp
3	$A_{\{3\}}$	hyp
4	$A_{\{3\}}$	3 reit
5	$A \to A$	3–4 →I
6	$A \to A \to B_{(1)}$	1 reit
7	$B_{\{3\}}$	5 6 →E
8	$B_{\{1,2\}}$	2 7 →E
9	$B \to B \to B_{\{1\}}$	2–8 →I
10	$A \to A \to B \to NB$	1–9 →I

The first says that necessity implies truth (a special case of the *specialized law of assertion*), and the second that if B follows the *law of identity*, then B is necessarily true (which accords with previous informal observations). We add some other easily provable theorems.

$$A \to B \to . NA \to NB$$
$$A \to B \to N(A \to B)$$
$$A \to B \to C \to . A \to B \to NC$$
$$NB \to . (A \to . B \to C) \to . A \to C$$
$$NA \to NNA$$

The first expresses distributivity of necessity over entailment. The second (a special case of *restricted assertion*) says that entailments, if true at all, are necessarily true. The third that if C follows from an entailment, then the necessity of C also follows from that entailment (which we may also express by saying that if C follows from an entailment, then if the entailment is true, then C is necessary). The next corresponds to Ackermann's rule (δ), expressing his requirement that, for application of (δ), B must be a *logische Identität*: where B is necessary, we may infer $A \to C$ from $A \to . B \to C$. And the last says that necessity implies necessary necessity (so to speak): a corollary of $A \to B \to N(A \to B)$ together with the fact that necessity is defined in terms of entailment.

Modal fallacies arise when it is claimed that entailments follow from, or are entailed by, *contingent* propositions. In the pure theory of entailment, contingency can be carried only by propositional variables (in view of $A \to B \to N(A \to B)$), and the following guarantees that E_I* is free of modal fallacies.

Theorem

If A is a propositional variable, then for no B and C is $A \to . B \to C$ provable in E_I*. (Ackermann 1956.)

Proof. Consider the following matrix (adapted from Ackermann):

	0	1	2
0	2	2	2
1	0	2	0
*2	0	0	2

The axioms of E_I'' all take the value 2 for all assignments of values under this matrix. Moreover, $\rightarrow$E preserves this property. But for any $A \rightarrow . B \rightarrow C$, where A is a propositional variable, we can assign A the value 1, giving $A \rightarrow . B \rightarrow C$ the value 0 regardless of the value of B and C. Hence no such $A \rightarrow . B \rightarrow C$ is provable.

The theorem serves to rule out such formulas as $A \rightarrow . A \rightarrow A$ and $A \rightarrow . B \rightarrow B$, which are standard "implicational paradoxes" embodying modal fallacies, and this fact clearly accords with (untutored) intuitions. Consider $A \rightarrow . A \rightarrow A$. Though "snow is white" and "that snow is white entails that snow is white" are both true – the latter necessarily so – it seems implausible that "snow is white" should *entail* that it entails itself. It does entail itself, of course, but the color of snow seems irrelevant to that fact of logic. We would think someone arguing rather badly if he tried to convince us that snow is white entails itself by showing us some snow.

Also ruled out as involving fallacies of modality are such formulas as the unrestricted "law" of assertion:

$$A \rightarrow . A \rightarrow B \rightarrow B,$$

and the "law" of permutation

$$(A \rightarrow . B \rightarrow C) \rightarrow . B \rightarrow . A \rightarrow C,$$

which would lead from $A \rightarrow B \rightarrow . A \rightarrow B$ to the "law" of assertion.

$A \rightarrow . B \rightarrow A$ also involves a modal fallacy, as we have argued before. Of the systems considered previously $A \rightarrow . B \rightarrow A$ is provable only in H_I, but corresponding fallacies are to be found in both $S4_I$:

$$A \rightarrow B \rightarrow . C \rightarrow . A \rightarrow B, \text{ and}$$
$$B \rightarrow . A \rightarrow A,$$

and in W_I:

$$A \rightarrow . A \rightarrow A \rightarrow A, \text{ (i.e., } A \rightarrow NA\text{)}.$$

The latter is of special interest in connection with our proposed definition of necessity. There are six fairly well known pure "implicational" calculi in the literature, three of which make modal distinctions (E_I, $S4_I$, and $S5_I$), and three of which do not (W_I, H_I, and P_I, the "implicational" fragment of the two-valued calculus). Consider the following set of schemata.

(1) $A \rightarrow A \rightarrow B \rightarrow B$
(2) $A \rightarrow B \rightarrow . B \rightarrow C \rightarrow . A \rightarrow C$
(3) $(A \rightarrow . A \rightarrow B) \rightarrow . A \rightarrow B$
(4) $A \rightarrow B \rightarrow . C \rightarrow . A \rightarrow B$
(5) $(A \rightarrow B \rightarrow C \rightarrow . A \rightarrow B) \rightarrow . A \rightarrow B$
(6) $A \rightarrow . A \rightarrow A \rightarrow A$

Then for the systems maintaining modal distinctions we have

$$E_I = \{(1), (2), (3)\},$$
$$S4_I = \{(1), (2), (3), (4)\}, \text{ and}$$
$$S5_I = \{(1), (2), (3), (4), (5)\}.$$

And each of the significant systems which collapse modal distinctions can be got by adding (6) to the appropriate modal system:

$$E_I + (6) = W_I,$$
$$S4_I + (6) = H_I, \text{ and}$$
$$S5_I + (6) = P_I.[18]$$

So (6), which may be written $A \rightarrow NA$, is precisely the thesis which destroys modality. We take this as indirect evidence for the appropriateness of the definition $NA =_{df} A \rightarrow A \rightarrow A$. And if we accept this definition as appropriate, then these results provide strong grounds for rejecting W_I, H_I, and P_I, as analyses of implication or entailment.

Fallacies of relevance

Many of the foregoing modal fallacies also embody fallacies of relevance, sanctioning the inference from A to B even though A and B may be totally disparate in meaning. The archetype of fallacies of relevance is $A \rightarrow . B \rightarrow A$, which would enable us to infer that Bach wrote the Coffee Cantata from the premiss that the Van Allen belt is doughnut-shaped – or indeed from any premiss you like.

In arguing that E_I satisfies a principle of relevance, we venture, somewhat gingerly, on new ground. We offer two conditions, the first as necessary and sufficient, the second as necessary only.

1. The subscripting technique as applied in W_I and E_I may be construed as a formal analysis of the intuitive idea that for A to be relevant to B it must be possible to *use* A in a deduction of B from A. It need not be *necessary* to use A in the deduction of B from A – and indeed this is a familiar situation in mathematics and logic. It not infrequently happens that the hypotheses of a theorem,

though all relevant to a conclusion, are subsequently found to be unnecessarily strong. An example is provided by Gödel's original incompleteness theorem, which required the assumption of ω-consistency. Rosser subsequently showed that this condition was not required for the proof of incompleteness – but surely no one would hold that ω-consistency was *irrelevant* to Gödel's result. Similarly in the following example (due to Smiley 1959), effort is wasted, since the antecedent is used in the proof of the consequent, though it need not be.

1	$A \rightarrow B_{\{1\}}$	hyp
2	$B \rightarrow A_{\{2\}}$	hyp
3	$B_{\{3\}}$	hyp
4	$B \rightarrow A_{\{2\}}$	2 reit
5	$A_{\{2,3\}}$	3 4 $\rightarrow$E
6	$A \rightarrow B_{\{1\}}$	1 reit
7	$B_{\{1,2,3\}}$	5 6 $\rightarrow$E
8	$A_{\{1,2,3\}}$	4 7 $\rightarrow$E
9	$B \rightarrow A_{\{1,2\}}$	3–8 $\rightarrow$I
10	$B \rightarrow A \rightarrow B \rightarrow A_{\{1\}}$	2–9 $\rightarrow$1
11	$A \rightarrow B \rightarrow B \rightarrow A \rightarrow B \rightarrow A_{\{1\}}$	1–10 $\rightarrow$1

A similar proof yields

$$B \rightarrow A \rightarrow . A \rightarrow B \rightarrow . B \rightarrow A.$$

(The point in both cases is that the antecedent and the antecedent of the consequent can be made to "cycle," producing one or the other as consequent of the consequent.)

The law $A \rightarrow B \rightarrow . B \rightarrow A \rightarrow . B \rightarrow A$ requires special justification, because it violates a plausible condition due to Smiley 1959: he demands that every true entailment be a "substitution instance of a tautological implication whose components are neither contradictory nor tautological." Thus Smiley's criterion allows $A \rightarrow A \rightarrow . A \rightarrow A$ (with the consequent necessary) on the grounds that it is a substitution instance of $B \rightarrow B$ (with consequent possibly contingent). But it would exclude $A \rightarrow B \rightarrow .$ $B \rightarrow A \rightarrow . B \rightarrow A$ on the ground that the latter is *not* a substitution instance of a tautology with a possibly contingent consequent.

From the point of view we have been urging, Smiley's criterion is misguided. The validity of an entailment has nothing to do with whether or not the components are true, false, necessary, or impossible; it has to do solely with whether or not there is a necessary connection between antecedent and consequent. Hence it is a mistake (we feel) to try to build a sieve which will "strain out" entailments from the set of material or strict "implications" present in some system of truth-functions, or of truth-functions with modality. Even so, however, it is of interest to note that if A and B are truth-functions, then the entailments $A \rightarrow B$ provable in E (Anderson and Belnap 1958) are all substitution-instances of provable entailments with both A and B contingent. (This follows from Belnap 1959b; note that $A \supset B \rightarrow . B \supset A \supset . B \supset A$, where $A \supset B = \bar{A} \vee B$, is not a true entailment.) One might indeed think of Belnap 1959b as a modification of the criterion of von Wright 1957: "A entails B, if and only if, by means of logic, it is possible to come to know the truth of $A \rightarrow B$ without coming to know the falsehood of A or the truth of B," (again of course where A and B are purely truth-functional).

But where A or B involves entailment, this sort of approach fails; and in particular, though of course $A \rightarrow B$ should be a sufficient condition for the material "implication" from A to B, there seems no good reason to suppose that the result of substituting the horseshoe for the arrow throughout an arbitrary truth concerning entailments would be a truth-functional tautology. We seem to be unable to give criteria involving only extensional considerations for detecting the fundamentally intensional notion of entailment.

Though the entailment $B \rightarrow A \rightarrow . A \rightarrow B \rightarrow .$ $A \rightarrow B$ violates Smiley's condition, we can quote Smiley himself in support of it (and of its proof): "...inferences may be justified on more grounds than one, and the present theory requires not that there should be *no* cogent way of reaching the conclusion *without* using all the premisses, but only that there should be *some* cogent way of reaching it *with* all the premisses used."[19]

On the latter grounds we can justify $A \rightarrow B \rightarrow . B \rightarrow A \rightarrow . B \rightarrow A$; but we notice that

$$A \rightarrow B \rightarrow . A \rightarrow B \rightarrow . A \rightarrow B,$$

is ruled out by a matrix which we discuss in connection with the second formal condition for relevance in the pure calculus of entailment.

2. Informal discussions of implication or entailment have frequently demanded "relevance" of A to B as a necessary condition for the truth of $A \rightarrow B$, where relevance is construed as involving

some "meaning content" common to both A and B.[20] A formal condition for "common meaning content" becomes almost obvious once we note that commonality of meaning in propositional logic is carried by commonality of propositional variables. So we propose as a *necessary* (but not sufficient) condition for the relevance of A to B in the pure theory of entailment, that A and B must share a variable. If this property fails, then the variables in A and B may be assigned propositional values, in such a way that the resulting A' and B' have no meaning content in common, and are totally irrelevant to each other. E_I avoids such fallacies of relevance, as is shown by the following

Theorem

If $A \rightarrow B$ is provable in E_I, then A and B share a variable. (Belnap 1959.)

Proof. Consider the following matrix (a finite adaptation of a matrix due to Sugihara 1955):

	0	1	2	3
0	3	3	3	3
1	0	2	2	3
*2	0	1	2	3
*3	0	0	0	3

The axioms of E take values 2 or 3 for all assignments of values to the variables, and the rule $\rightarrow$ E preserves this property. But if A and B share no variables, then we may assign the value 3 to all the variables of A (yielding $A = 3$), and 2 to all the variables of B (yielding $B = 2$), and $3 \rightarrow 2$ takes the undesignated value 0. Hence if A and B fail to share a variable, $A \rightarrow B$ is unprovable.

We remark that the first of the two conditions has to do with entailment in its guise as the converse of deducibility, and in this sense is a purely syntactical completeness theorem: A is *relevant* to B, when $A \rightarrow B$, just if there exists a proof (satisfying certain conditions) of B *from* the hypothesis A. The second condition, however, concerns entailment conceived of as a relation of logical consequence, and is semantical in character, since it has to do with possible assignments of values to the propositional variables. The problem of finding suitable necessary and sufficient semantical conditions for relevance has proved refractory, and we leave it open.

The matrix given in the second condition above also satisfies $(A \rightarrow . B \rightarrow C) \rightarrow . B \rightarrow . A \rightarrow C$; it follows that W_I is also free of fallacies of relevance

(in the sense of satisfying the necessary condition of sharing variables), as we would expect from the previous discussion. Among fallacies of relevance which are *not* modal fallacies we mention

$$A \rightarrow A \rightarrow . B \rightarrow B.$$

It is interesting to note also that the same matrix can be used to rule out expressions involving fallacies of relevance even when antecedent and consequent *do* share a variable. We define *antecedent part of* A and *consequent part of* A inductively as follows: A is a consequent part of A, and if $B \rightarrow C$ is a consequent {antecedent} part of A, then B is an antecedent {consequent} part of A, and C is a consequent {antecedent} part of A.

Theorem

If A is a theorem of E_I (or, indeed, of W_I), then every variable occurring in A occurs at least once as an antecedent part and at least once as a consequent part of A. (Compare Smiley 1959, note 21.)

Proof. If a variable p occurs only as an antecedent {consequent} part of A, assign p the value 3 {0}; and assign all other variables in A the value 2. This assignment of values to the variables of A gives A the value 0. The proof is left to the reader.

The designation "antecedent" and "consequent" parts derives from a Gentzen formulation of E_I (Belnap 1959a). The ultimate premisses of a *sequenzen-kalkül* proof of B are primes $p \vdash p$, where, roughly speaking, the left p appears in B as an antecedent part, and the right p as a consequent part. For this reason, the theorem may be regarded as saying that the "tight" relevance condition satisfied by the primes is preserved in passing down the proof-tree to B.

As an immediate corollary, we see that no variable may occur just once in a theorem of E_I, which suggests that each variable-occurrence is essential to the theorem; theorems have no loose pieces, so to speak, which can be jiggled about while the rest of the theorem stays put. Hence

$$A \rightarrow B \rightarrow . B \rightarrow B,$$
$$A \rightarrow B \rightarrow . A \rightarrow A,$$

and Peirce's "law"

$$A \rightarrow B \rightarrow A \rightarrow A,$$

all fail in E_I. The intuitive sense of Pierce's formula is usually expressed in this way: one says "Well, if A follows simply from the fact that A entails something, then A must be true – since obviously A must entail something, itself for example." But this reading, designed to make the formula sound plausible, seems also designed to pull the wool over our eyes, since an essential premiss is suppressed. It is of course true that if A follows from the fact that it entails *something it does entail* (an assumption hidden in the word "fact" above), *then* A must be true, and a theorem to this effect is provable in E_I:

$$A \to B \to . A \to B \to A \to A$$

(a special case of *restricted assertion*). But if A follows from the (quite possibly false) assumption that A entails B, this would hardly guarantee the truth of A.

We have argued that valid inferences are necessarily valid, and that the antecedent in a valid inference must be relevant to the consequent. In view of the long history of logic as a topic for investigation, and the near unanimity on these two points among logicians, it is surprising, indeed startling, that these issues should require re-arguing. That they do need arguing is a consequence of the almost equally unanimous contradictorily opposed feeling on the part of contemporary logicians that material and strict "implication" are implication relations, and that therefore necessity and relevance are not required for true implications. But, if we may be permitted to apply a result of the ingenious Bishop of Halberstadt,[21] if *both* of these views are correct, it follows that Man is a donkey.[22]

Notes

1   This research was supported in part by the Office of Naval Research, Group Psychology Branch, Contract No. SAR/Nonr-609(16). Permission is granted for reproduction, translation, publication, and disposal in whole or in part by or for the U. S. Government.

2   Throughout we use the following notation. The sole primitive constants are $\to$, (,), and we assume that propositional variables are specified. A, B, C, D,...A_i... are metalinguistic variables ranging over wffs, which are specified in the usual way. Parentheses are omitted under the conventions of Church, *Introduction to Mathematical Logic*: outermost parentheses are omitted; a dot may replace a left-hand parenthesis, the mate of which is to be restored at the end of the parenthetical part in which the dot occurs (otherwise at the end of the formula); otherwise parentheses are to be restored by association to the left. Example: $(A \to . B \to C) \to . A \to B \to . A \to C$ abbreviates $((A \to (B \to C)) \to ((A \to B) \to (A \to C)))$. We use axiom schemata, throughout, instead of a rule of substitution (even when discussing systems, e.g. Church 1951, which are formulated with a substitution rule); and we translate the notation of cited authors into our own.

3   See the list of references at the end of this paper.

4   We should add, in a soberer tone, that though we would prefer to follow Kneale 1946 in substituting "Philonian junction" for "material implication," we are nevertheless prepared to award the word "implication" to the modern logical tradition. Indeed we are not in a position to do much else; the literature has a claim on the word stemming from Squatter's Rights. But for the purposes of this study we use it as a synonym for what has more recently been called "entailment," pointing out in justification that some authors *have* urged that "material implication" and "strict implication" have a close connection with the notion of a logically valid inference.

5   Such surveys are essayed in Belnap 1960 and Bennett 1954.

6   We are taking entailment to be a relation between propositions, rather than sentences or statements, and with this understanding we will in the future observe a distinction between use and mention only where it seems essential.

7   $A \to A$ represents the archetypal form of inference, the trivial foundation of all reasoning, in spite of those who would call it "merely a case of stuttering." Strawson (1952, p. 15) says that

> a man who repeats himself does not reason. But it is inconsistent to assert and deny the same thing. So a logician will say that a statement has to itself the relationship [entailment] he is interested in.

Strawson has got the cart before the horse: we hold that the reason A and $\bar{A}$ are inconsistent is precisely because A follows from itself, rather than conversely. Note that in the system E of Anderson and Belnap 1958, we have $A \to A \to \overline{A \wedge A}$ but not $\overline{A \wedge A} \to . A \to A$, just as we have $A \to B \to \overline{A \wedge B}$ but not $\overline{A \wedge B} \to . A \to B$.

8   Lewis (Lewis and Langford 1932, p. 496) doubts whether this proposition should be regarded as a

valid principle of deduction: it would never lead to any inference $A \rightarrow C$ which would be questionable when $A \rightarrow B$ and $B \rightarrow C$ are given premisses; but it gives the inference $B \rightarrow C \rightarrow . A \rightarrow C$ whenever $A \rightarrow B$ is a premiss. Except as an elliptical statement for "$(A \rightarrow B) \wedge (B \rightarrow C) \rightarrow .. A \rightarrow C$ and $A \rightarrow B$ is true," this inference is dubious. On the contrary, Ackermann 1956 is surely right that "unter der Voraussetzung $A \rightarrow B$ ist der Schluss von $B \rightarrow C$ auf $A \rightarrow C$ logisch zwingend." The mathematician is involved in no ellipsis in arguing that "if the lemma is deducible from the axioms, then this entails that the deducibility of the theorem from the axioms is entailed by the deducibility of the theorem from the lemma."

9   And of course at some stage of the reduction A_i may be a theorem of H_I inserted at a previous stage of the reduction, in which case we simply regard it as an insertion in P'. Here and elsewhere we assume this step tacitly.

10   Myhill 1953 has shown that in $H_I A \rightarrow B$ is interdeducible with $(\exists r)(r \wedge ((r \wedge A)\ 3\ B))$, under plausible assumptions about strict implication. In a forthcoming paper, Belnap proves that in the system E of Anderson and Belnap 1958, with propositional quantifiers added, intuitionistic implication $A \supset B$ may be defined as $(\exists r)(r \wedge ((r \wedge A) \rightarrow B))$, and intuitionistic negation $\neg A$ as $A \supset (p)p$. Some may therefore wish to regard intuitionistic implication as a kind of enthymematic implication, as when we say that it "follows" from the assertion that Socrates is a man, that he is also mortal. But this is *not* a relation of deducibility or entailment; the latter holds only when all required premises are stated explicitly in the antecedent. We agree (in spirit) with the classical position regarding enthymemes, as stated e.g. by Joseph 1925:

> An enthymeme indeed is not a particular form of argument, but a particular way of stating an argument. The name is given to a syllogism with one premiss – or, it may be, the conclusion – suppressed. Nearly all syllogisms are, as a matter of fact, stated as enthymemes, except in the examples of a logical treatise, or the conduct of a formal disputation. It must not be supposed, however, that we are the less arguing in syllogism, because we use one member of the argument without its being explicitly stated.

We note in passing that the principle of exportation has the effect of confusing valid arguments with enthymemes.

11   Curry calls this a proof of $A \rightarrow . B \rightarrow A$ "from nothing." We remark that this expression invites the interpretation "there is nothing from which $A \rightarrow . B \rightarrow A$ is deducible," in which case we would seem to have done little toward showing that it is true. But of course Curry is not confused on this point; he means that $A \rightarrow . B \rightarrow A$ is deducible "from" the null set of premises – in the reason-shattering, Official sense of "from."

12   This was conjectured by Lemmon *et al.* 1956, and is verifiable by a *sequenzen-kalkül* formulation of S4 got by adding standard Gentzen rules for negation and disjunction to the formulation of $S4_1$ of Kripke. Formulations of this kind are also available for the system E_1 discussed below; see Belnap 1960 and Kripke. Kripke's formulation is simpler, and alone leads to a decision procedure for E_1, while Belnap's formulation allows a more direct interpretation with respect to E_I.

13   The tendency is not universal; see for example Lewis and Langford 1932, p. 165, and Barcan Marcus 1953.

14   We reserve this designation for the formulation of Anderson, Belnap, and Wallace, 1960. Axioms: $A \rightarrow A \rightarrow B \rightarrow B$, $A \rightarrow B \rightarrow .B \rightarrow C \rightarrow .A \rightarrow C$, and $(A \rightarrow . A \rightarrow B) \rightarrow . A \rightarrow B$; rule: $\rightarrow$ E.

15   E_I* is not, however, the intersection of $S4_I*$ and W_I*. We are indebted to Saul Kripke for a counterexample: $A \rightarrow . (A \rightarrow . A \rightarrow B) \rightarrow . A \rightarrow B$ is provable in both the latter systems, but not in E_I*.

16   The present order of exposition was adopted for reasons connected with the philosophical points to be made, but it should not be allowed to obscure the extent of our considerable indebtedness to this paper of Ackermann.

17   Of course we do not mean to suggest that in saying that A is necessary we *mean* that A follows from $A \rightarrow A$; the definition indicates rather that if one *did* mean this by "A is necessary," or "NA", then it would turn out that N had all the right properties as we see below. We are indebted to A. N. Prior for pointing out to us in correspondence that, conversely, with plausible assumptions $(NA \rightarrow A, A \rightarrow B \rightarrow N(A \rightarrow B),$ and $NA \rightarrow . A \rightarrow B \rightarrow NB)$ about N (taken as primitive), NA and $A \rightarrow A \rightarrow A$ entail each other.

18   These six postulates are not independent as they stand. Independence can be secured, though not elegantly, by substituting $(4')A \rightarrow B \rightarrow . C \rightarrow . C \rightarrow . A \rightarrow B$ for (4), and $(5')(A \rightarrow B \rightarrow . A \rightarrow B \rightarrow . C \rightarrow . A \rightarrow B) \rightarrow . A \rightarrow B$ for (5). We sketch the proof of independence: for (1), with elements 0, 1, and 2 (2 designated), let $0 \rightarrow A = A \rightarrow 2 = 2$, and otherwise $A \rightarrow B = 0$; by a result of Jaskowski 1948, (2) is independent in the system got by replacing $A \rightarrow B$ by D throughout $(4')$ and $(5')$, and hence independent in P_I; (3) alone is not satisfied when the arrow is interpreted as material equivalence; for $(4')$, with elements 0, 1, and 2 (2 designated), let $0 \rightarrow A = A \rightarrow A = 2, 2 \rightarrow 1 = 1$, and otherwise $A \rightarrow B = 0$; $(5')$ is not in H_I; (6) is not in $S5_I$.

19 Actually, this condition won't do either, as is easily seen by examples. Proof of the uniqueness of the identity element in an Abelian group does not invoke the fact that the group operation is commutative; it nevertheless *follows* from the axioms for an Abelian group that the identity element is unique – or at any rate everyone says so. What is required is that there be *some* cogent way of reaching the conclusion with *some* of the (conjoined) premisses used. But this point will have to await discussion of truth-functions in connection with entailment.

20 This call for common "meaning content" comes from a variety of quarters. Nelson (1930, p. 445) says that implication "is a necessary connection between meanings"; that A implies B only when B "arises out of the meaning of" A; Baylis (1931, p. 397) that if A implies B then "the intensional meaning of B is identical with a part of the intensional meaning of A"; and Blanshard (1939, vol. 2, p. 390) that "what lies at the root of the common man's objection [to strict implication] is the stubborn feeling that implication has something to do with the *meaning* of propositions, and that any mode of connecting them which disregards this meaning and ties them together despite of it is too artificial to satisfy the demand of thought."

21 Ca. 1316–90.

22 The results of this paper have been extended to entailment with truth-functions. With plausible axioms for negation, conjunction, and disjunction (due largely to Ackermann) we obtain a system E (Anderson and Belnap 1958) in which (1) all truth-functional tautologies are provable, (2) relevance, in the sense of variable-sharing, is retained (Belnap 1959), and (3) a syntactical completeness theorem, relatively to a subproof formulation, is provable (Anderson 1959). These results extend also to a pure functional calculus of first order.

Bibliography

Wilhelm Ackermann, *Begründung einer strengen Implikation*, *Journal of Symbolic Logic*, vol. 21 (1956), pp. 113–18.

Alan Ross Anderson, *Completeness theorems for the systems E of entailment and EQ of entailment with quantification*, Technical report no. 6, Office of Naval Research Contract no. SAR/Nonr-609(16), New Haven, 1959. (Also forthcoming in the *Zeitschrift für mathematische Logik und Grundlagen der Mathematik.*)

Alan Ross Anderson and Nuel D. Belnap, Jr., *A modification of Ackermann's "rigorous implication,"* [abstract], *Journal of Symbolic Logic*, vol. 23 (1958), pp. 457–8.

Alan Ross Anderson and Nuel D. Belnap, Jr., *Modalities in Ackermann's "rigorous implication,"* *Journal of Symbolic Logic*, vol. 24 (1959), pp. 107–1.

Alan Ross Anderson, Nuel D. Belnap, Jr., and John R. Wallace, *Independent axiom schemata for the pure theory of entailment*, *Zeitschrift für mathematische Logik und Grundlagen der Mathematik*, vol. 6 (1960), pp. 93–5.

Ruth Barcan Marcus, *The deduction theorem in a functional calculus of first order based on strict implication*, *Journal of Symbolic Logic*, vol. 11 (1946), pp. 115–18.

Ruth Barcan Marcus, *Strict implication, deducibility, and the deduction theorem, Journal of Symbolic Logic*, vol. 18 (1953), pp. 234–6.

Charles A. Baylis, *Implication and subsumption, Monist*, vol. 41 (1931), pp. 392–9.

Nuel D. Belnap, Jr., *Entailment and relevance, Journal of Symbolic Logic* (1959).

Nuel D. Belnap, Jr., *Pure rigorous implication as a sequenzen-kalkül* [abstract], *Journal of Symbolic Logic*, vol. 24 (1959a), pp. 282–3.

Nuel D. Belnap, Jr., *Tautological entailments*, [abstract] *Journal of Symbolic Logic* (1959b).

Nuel D. Belnap, Jr., *A formal analysis of entailment*, Technical report no. 7, Office of Naval Research Contract no. SAR/Nonr-609(16), New Haven, 1960.

Jonathan F. Bennett, *Meaning and implication, Mind*, n.s. vol. 63 (1954), pp. 451–63.

Brand Blanshard, *The nature of thought*, London, 1939.

Philotheus Boehner, *Medieval logic*, Manchester, 1952.

Alonzo Church, *The weak theory of implication, Kontroliertes Denken* (Festgabe zum 60 Geburtstag von Prof. W. Britzelmayr), Munich, 1951.

Haskell B. Curry, *The interpretation of formalized implication, Theoria*, vol. 25 (1959), pp. 1–26.

Austin E. Duncan-Jones, *Is strict implication the same as entailment? Analysis*, vol. 2 (1935), pp. 70–8.

Robert Feys, *Les logiques nouvelles des modalités, Revue néoscolastique de philosophie*, vol. 40 (1937), pp. 517–53, and vol. 41 (1938), pp. 217–52.

Frederic B. Fitch, *Symbolic logic*, New York, 1952.

Arend Heyting, *Die formalen Regeln der intuitionistischen Logik, Sitzungsberichte der Preussischen Akademie der Wissenschaften*, Physikalisch-mathematische Klasse (1930), pp. 42–56, 57–71, 158–69.

Stanislaw Jaśkowski, *Trois contributions au calcul des propositions bivalent, Studia Societatis Scientiarum Torunensis*, section A, vol. 1 no. 1 (1948), pp. 1–15.

H. W. B. Joseph, *An introduction to logic*, London, 1925.

William Kneale, *Truths of logic, Proceedings of the Aristotelian Society*, vol. 64 (1946), pp. 207–34.

Saul A. Kripke, *The problem of entailment*, [abstract], *Journal of Symbolic Logic*

E. J. Lemmon, C. A. Meredith, D. Meredith, A. N. Prior, and I. Thomas, *Calculi of pure strict implication* (mimeographed), 1956.

Alan Ross Anderson and Nuel D. Belnap, Jr.

C. I. Lewis and C. H. Langford, *Symbolic logic*, New York, 1932.

Jan Łukasiewicz, *Elementy logiki matematycznej*, mimeographed Warsaw 1929, printed Warsaw 1958.

G. E. Moore, *External and internal relations*, *Proceedings of the Aristotelian Society*, n.s. vol. 20 (1920), pp. 40–62.

Moh Shaw-Kwei, *The deduction theorems and two new logical systems*, *Methodos*, vol. 2 (1950), pp. 56–75.

John Myhill, *On the interpretation of the sign "⊃"*, *Journal of Symbolic Logic*, vol. 18 (1953), pp. 60–2.

E. J. Nelson, *Intensional relations*, *Mind*, n.s. vol. 39 (1930), pp. 440–53.

T. J. Smiley, *Entailment and deducibility*, *Proceedings of the Aristotelian Society*, vol. 59 (1959), pp. 233–254.

P. F. Strawson, *Introduction to logical theory*, London, 1952.

Takeo Sugihara, *Strict implication free from implicational paradoxes*, *Memoirs of the Faculty of Liberal Arts, Fukui University*, Series I (1955), pp. 55–9.

Georg H. von Wright, *An essay in modal logic*, Amsterdam, 1951.

Georg H. von Wright, *Logical studies*, London, 1957.

18

Formal and Material Consequence

Stephen Read

Invalidity

How do we show that an argument is invalid? Consider this example:

(1) All cats are animals
     Some animals have tails
     So some cats have tails.

The premises are true and so is the conclusion. Yet there is an obvious sense in which the truth of the premises does not guarantee that of the conclusion. The argument is invalid. But how can we show that invalidity?

One thought is, that arguments of the same sort, or form, actually lead from truth to falsity. Although their premises are true, their conclusions are false. The same could have been true of (1), though in fact it isn't. What we might try, therefore, is to formalise the argument, and show that the form is invalid. Using the above example, we obtain

(2) $(\forall x)(Fx \rightarrow Gx), (\exists x)(Gx \,\&\, Hx) \vdash (\exists x)(Fx \,\&\, Hx),$

where Fx reads 'x is a cat', Gx is 'x is an animal' and Hx is 'x has a tail'. To show this form is invalid, we find another instance of it, with a different key, but in which, though the premises are still true, the conclusion is false. For example, we might let Fx and Gx read as before, but let Hx read 'x is a dog':

Stephen Read, Formal and Material Consequence. *Journal of Philosophical Logic*, 23 (1994): 247–65.

(3) All cats are animals
     Some animals are dogs
     So some cats are dogs.

The premises are true and the conclusion false. So this argument really is invalid. Since every instance of a valid form is valid, (2) is an invalid form.

Does this show that (1) is invalid? Not immediately; for every valid argument is in instance of some invalid form. For example, every two premise argument is an instance of the form

(4) $P, Q, \vdash R,$

which is patently invalid. But that does not show that every two-premise argument is invalid.

The trouble with (4), of course, is that it does not reveal sufficient structure. What we try to do when we formalise an argument like (1) is to articulate its structure so that if there is a dependency of the conclusion on the premises it will be revealed. Such a technique is ideal when we find a form which is valid and of which the argument is an instance. But what if we cannot – as with (1)?

What we may be tempted to say is that (2) reveals as much structure in (1) as can be revealed. Since (2) is invalid, this means that (1) has failed its best possible chance to be shown valid, and so must be invalid.

It does show that (1) is not valid in virtue of its form. But does that show it is not valid? How else might it be valid? In a valid argument, the truth of the premises must somehow rule out the falsity of the conclusion. So it must be impossible for the premises to be true and the conclusion false. Could the premises of (1) be true and the conclusion false?

Suppose the world were much as it is now, but cats evolved to become tailless – Manx cats take over, say. In such a world, all cats are animals, some animals have tails (cats no longer do, but dogs are unchanged), but now no cats have tails. We have represented to ourselves a situation in which the premises are true and the conclusion false. So the truth of the premises does not guarantee that of the conclusion. (1) is invalid.

John Etchemendy (1990) contrasts "interpretational" with "representational semantics". In representational semantics we describe a situation, perhaps different from how things actually are, in which the propositions take various values. In interpretational semantics, we interpret certain expressions differently from their actual interpretation to much the same effect. When we formalised (1) as (2) and then interpreted the predicate letters in (2) to obtain (3), we varied the interpretation – we effectively interpreted 'have tails' to mean 'are dogs'. Under this interpretation (retaining the standard interpretation of 'cat' and 'animal' but varying that of 'have tails') the premises come out true and the conclusion false. Similarly, representing a situation in which no cat has a tail, we describe one in which the premises of (1) are true and the conclusion false. Either way, whether interpretationally or representationally, we seek to show that (1) is invalid.

The terminology of 'interpretation' versus 'representation' is not altogether a felicitous one. Talk of representations suggests unwanted mental models, representing things to ourselves; and in both cases, interpretations are what is at stake, on the one hand, keeping interpretations fixed but considering varying situations, on the other, keeping the situation fixed by allowing the interpretation to vary. A more perspicuous terminology might be to speak of substitutional semantics on the one hand, where we substitute different expressions within a substitution-class for certain expressions, to see if truth results;[1] and of modal semantics on the other, evaluating the statements in different possible situations. This is what we did with (1) – first we substituted 'are dogs' for 'have tails', so that the conclusion of (3) came out false while its premises were true; then we interpreted (1) in a world of Manx cats, whereby the conclu-sion of (1) itself came out false while its premises remained true.

Nonetheless, provided it is properly under-stood, the term 'representational' does signifi-cantly demarcate a semantic approach in which the interpretation of the language is fixed while the situations represented vary, different from one where one varies the interpretation within a fixed world. Moreover, the purely substitutional approach found (as Etchemendy notes, 1990: 28 ff.) in Bolzano has been extended by Tarski and later exponents to exclude limitations caused by lack of expressiveness in the language or by exi-gencies of the actual situation. So I will retain Etchemendy's terminology.

The crucial fact, however, is that the interpret-ational approach is limited – and limited in prin-ciple – in a way the representational one is not. Consider the argument:

(5)   Iain is a bachelor
       So Iain is unmarried.

If we substitute other expressions for 'Iain', 'unmarried' and 'bachelor', we can easily obtain an argument with true premises and false con-clusion. So according to the interpretational criterion, (5) is invalid. Does it follow that (5) is really invalid? No. For there is no situation, however different from how things are, of which the premise of (5) is true and its conclusion false.

The representational account of validity says that

(R)   an argument is valid if there is no possible situation where the premises are true and the conclusion false.

The interpretational account says that

(I)   an argument is valid if there is no (pos-sible) interpretation of the expressions (other than a reserved class of "logical" expressions) in the argument under which the premises come out true and the con-clusion false.

So on a representational account, (5) is valid, whereas on the interpretational one the result is different; and it seems clear that the representa-tional account is the correct one. (5) is indeed valid. The truth of the premises guarantees that of the conclusion – it is impossible for the premises to be true and the conclusion false.

We can mark the distinction here. (5) is materially, but not formally valid. Its validity depends not on any form it exhibits, but on the content of certain expressions in it. (5) is valid on account of the meanings of the expressions 'unmarried' and 'bachelor'. If we let their interpretation vary arbitrarily, we can make the premises true and the conclusion false. But that overlooks the fact that the interpretation of these two expressions is linked – their interpretation is not independent.

One might try to capture this connection formally, by insisting that the proper formalisation of (5) is something like

(6) $Fa \ \& \ Ga \vdash Ga,$

where Fa reads 'Iain is male' and Ga reads 'Iain is unmarried'. But that strategy will work only if there are logically independent semantic primitives. The famous colour exclusion problem showed that particular idea to be mistaken. Nothing red is green and vice versa, but neither is obviously more primitive than the other, and the problem recurs for any term to which each might be reduced.

Moreover, interpretational semantics cannot account for the transivity of certain relations:

(7)   Iain is taller than Bill and Bill is taller than Mary
       So Iain is taller than Mary.

If we are allowed to substitute other expressions for 'taller than', this valid inference will be declared invalid. But if we keep the interpretation of 'taller than' fixed then we cannot make the conclusion of

(8)   No one is taller than everyone
       So someone is taller than someone else,

false, and so cannot give an interpretation exhibiting true premises and false conclusion. For (8) is invalid; and its conclusion is only contingently true; we might all have been the same height. But unless we are allowed to replace some expression in it, we cannot make the conclusion false – on the interpretational account. The interpretational account, therefore, fails to capture the correct account of validity. Either we may vary the interpretation of 'taller than' freely – in which case, we

give the wrong answer about (7) – or we may not vary it at all – in which case, we give the wrong answer about (8). Either way, the interpretational account gets it wrong.[2]

We may sum up our first thoughts as follows. Our reflections suggest:

(i)   that not all valid arguments are valid in virtue of form, but are materially valid;

and

(ii)   that validity is ultimately a matter of the impossibility of having true premises and a false conclusion, that is, ultimately a representational matter, not an interpretational one.

Reductionism

But this conclusion is not universally accepted. Indeed, the logical community seems roughly evenly divided – not to say, split asunder – on the question. The reason is the modality contained in (ii). What is this 'impossibility' which is referred to there? How is it to be understood – in particular, how is it to be understood if it means any more than, 'however the constituent expressions are interpreted'?

What the advocates of interpretational semantics are urging here is a reductionism about necessity. Representational semantics requires reference to various possible situations other than the actual one. If we are worried about the reality of these different possibilities – in particular, if we are worried about their epistemology, how we could know how they were constituted and what would be the case in them – we may seek to reduce their possibility to something we feel is within our grasp, namely, various different interpretations. These different *possible* interpretations can be made actual, by considering substitution-classes, and so do not suffer the remoteness of non-actual situations. We replace talk of whether a proposition might be true in a different world or situation, with how the expressions in it might be replaced by others or differently interpreted. This seems harmless enough, for there seems little to choose between, for example, conceiving of a situation in which snow is not white, but say, red, and considering the replacement of 'white' by 'red', that is, effectively conceiving an interpretation in which 'white' means not white, but say, red.

There is all the difference in the world, however. For, as Etchemendy (1988: 64) points out in his survey article on Tarski, if 'snow' comes to mean grass, 'Snow is white' will not then be true – but snow will still be white. In other words, changing the interpretation of the words changes the truth-values of the sentences, but it does not change the facts. Indeed, that is the very point of the manoeuvre, to keep the facts the same, for fear of trespassing on the unknowable, other worlds beyond our compass.

Yet that shift to interpretations loses an essential element in the analysis of validity. If Iain gets married, he ceases to be a bachelor, whereas changing the meaning of 'unmarried' has no such effect – not even that which is of course the important point here, changing the truth-value of 'Iain is a bachelor'. What is lost in interpretational semantics is the analytical linkage between expressions. For interpretational semantics properly to replace representational semantics we would need a theory which took account of these connections. But for that to be possible would require that all such connections be open to structural, or formal, articulation. The point of examples (7) and (8) was to question whether this is possible.

How can interpretational semantics – and the reductionist position on necessity – retain such an attraction if it fails so readily to provide an adequate account of validity? For it is certainly widely accepted as providing the orthodox account of the notion. There are at least two reasons. One is the numbing effect that the horror of real necessity produces – an ability to overlook the defects of reductionism if the alternative is thought to be worse. (This is a familiar aspect of any reductionism.) Another is that the counter-examples can be dismissed as not really a matter of logic: for example, the analytical connections in (5) and (7) can be seen as really a matter of meaning – it is part of the meaning of 'taller than' that is transitive, but not of logic; others, for example, the rule of infinite induction, can be set aside as again not really logic, but essentially mathematical. Logic is now seen – now redefined – as the study of *formal* consequence, those validities resulting not from the matter and content of the constituent expressions, but from the formal structure.

Etchemendy identifies a third reason for overlooking the counter-examples, an argument whose analysis will show us more about the important distinction between representation and interpretation. He calls it 'Tarski's Fallacy' (1990: chapter 6).[3] Of course, it is not a fallacy explicitly committed by Tarski. But Etchemendy does make it a plausible explanation of what lay beneath Tarski's advocacy of the interpretational approach.

The idea of the interpretational approach is this. Let us say that an argument is Tarski-valid if no variation in the interpretations of expressions other than the fixed (logical) terms makes the premises true and the conclusion (for the same interpretation) false. This much can then be deduced: it is impossible that no variation have this effect and at the same time the premises be true and the conclusion false. Tarski-validity is clearly incompatible with true premises and false conclusion. It is tempting to conclude that Tarski-validity must guarantee real validity. If Tarski-validity rules out true premises and false conclusion, does this not mean that it entails the impossibility of such a combination – that is, the impossibility of true premises and false conclusion, so that the argument really is valid?

The move is a modal fallacy, for *necessitas consequentis* (the necessity of the consequent) does not follow from *necessitas consequentiae* (the necessity of the consequence itself). Let V represent Tarski-validity and U the combination of true premises and false conclusion. Then what is true is

$$\sim \Diamond(V \mathbin{\&} U);$$

but what is needed for Tarski-validity to ensure real validity is

$$V \rightarrow \sim \Diamond U.$$

An *ad hominem* demonstration of the illegitimacy of this inference might come from letting V stand for some contingent truth and U for its contradictory, $\sim V$. Then $V \mathbin{\&} \sim V$ is certainly impossible, while *ex hypothesi* V is true and $\sim \Diamond \sim V$ false.

What this refutation ignores, of course, is the possibility of some analytical connection between Tarski-validity and real validity. Perhaps it is the case that the possibilities for reinterpretation are limited by the possibilities for real change, so that interpretational semantics is not completely independent of representational semantics. What we must turn to now is the general question of their relation.

The Suppressed Premise Strategy

In fact, Etchemendy claims to prove that, in the first order case, Tarski-validity does ensure real validity – that is, the interpretational account does not overgenerate. His argument draws on an observation of Kreisel's about informal rigour. For whereas Tarski-validity is a formal notion, precisely expressed in terms of available interpretations of expressions over an appropriate domain, real validity is an informal notion relying on an intuitive notion of impossibility.

The proof is, however, very simple. Concentrate first, says Etchemendy, on some favoured deductive system for first order logic: let $D(\alpha)$ represent '(the sequent) α is derivable in this deductive system', and let Val(α) represent 'α is (really) valid'. Finally, let $V(\alpha)$ represent 'α is Tarski-valid'. The proof starts from the observation that the deductive system is intuitively sound – that practice has shown us that the deductive system (abstracting from its relationship to Tarski-validity) does not overgenerate:

$$(\forall\alpha)(D\alpha \rightarrow \text{Val}\alpha).$$

We now appeal to a formal result, the completeness of first order logic (with respect to interpretational semantics):

$$(\forall\alpha)(V\alpha \rightarrow D\alpha).$$

We immediately obtain, by transivity,

$$(\forall\alpha)(V\alpha \rightarrow \text{Val}\alpha),$$

assuring us that Tarski-validity (V) does not exceed real validity (Val).

This is a quite extraordinary argument. What is it supposed to show? Etchemendy has led us to consider Tarski's account of validity, and has given reasons for us to be sceptical about its extensional correctness – *via* attacks on its intensional formulation. He then invites us to take some deductive consequence relation, provably equivalent to that suspect account of validity, and concludes from its intuitive soundness that it really is sound.

Nonetheless, the following tempting objection is mistaken. Etchemendy's proof purports to show that every argument valid in first order (classical) logic is really valid. But there are many counter-examples to this claim – or at least, even if they are not accepted as counter-examples, Etchemendy's argument is far too quick with what is a matter of deep contention. Take, for example, the principle *ex falso quodlibet*, from A and $\sim A$ to B, or the principle of double negation, from $\sim\sim A$ to A. Surely the best that Etchemendy's argument can do is to focus our attention back on his premise, namely, that D is intuitively sound – that $D\alpha$ entails Valα. The proof seems to add nothing to that claim.

But this is not so. What Etchemendy's (and Kreisel's) point shows is that Tarski-validity is extensionally safe for any provably complete deductive system which one believes is intuitively sound. That is, whatever your scruples, let $D(\alpha)$ represent 'α is provable in my preferred first order logic' – whether classical, intuitionistic, relevant or whatever. Then, if you have a completeness proof for this logic relative to its Tarski semantics, its intuitive soundness (for you) will carry over to its Tarski soundness, that is, Tarski-validity, suitably defined – i.e. the use of interpretational semantics – will not proclaim any really invalid arguments to be valid. Tarski-validity will be safe in the sense that it will not overgenerate.

It is not, however, a result with which to get carried away. It assumes we already have a Tarski-complete proof procedure – so that demonstrating validity is not a particular problem. The purpose of the semantics is to show invalidity. But what guarantee have we that Tarski-invalidity entails real invalidity? We saw in §1 that there is no guarantee at all, that it does not.

Nonetheless, Etchemendy sets out to adapt Kreisel's remark to show that, again for first order logic, we do not have undergeneration either – that real validity entails Tarski-validity. However, he himself points out that his result has limited significance, applying only to the common logical truths of a class of languages, that is, where we have already abstracted from logical truth particular to a certain language, in other words, where the logical truth in question does not depend on the particular meanings of any of the terms involved which are not common to all the languages.

We saw in §1 that this overlooks vital features of validity. Arguments (5) and (7) are valid, yet their validity depends on the particular interpretation of 'married', 'bachelor' and 'taller than'. Allowing their interpretation to vary arbitrarily loses sight of this dependency; fixing it prohibits consideration of other ways in which validity can fail.

Interpretational semantics cannot do justice to the possibilities of representation and the facts of validity. An argument is valid if and only if there is no possible situation where the premises are true and the conclusion false.

The reductionist, or formalist, has another strategy open to him, however. Somehow this obscurantist reference to real possibilities must be removed. Perhaps the way to do it is to demand that these analytical connections which defy formalisation and undermine interpretational semantics be explicitly stated. That is, if arguments such as (5) and (7) are valid, they are only really valid when the suppressed premise, revealing the underlying connections, is made explicit. In the case of (5), what is needed is an extra premise stating that all bachelors are unmarried; in the case of (7), a premise to the effect that 'taller than' is transitive.

The suppressed premise strategy appears in Etchemendy (1990, p. 68) in the guise of 'cross-term restrictions'. This is a somewhat misleading name in general. In the case of (5), we require that the terms 'bachelor' and 'unmarried' be linked, so that the interpretation of 'bachelor' be restricted to a subset of that of 'unmarried'. That is clearly a 'cross-term' restriction – the restriction on the interpretation of 'bachelor' is relative to that of 'unmarried'. However, the restriction needed on 'taller than' in (7) (that it be interpreted only by transitive relations) is 'cross-term' only in a degenerate sense – it simply and absolutely restricts the interpretation of 'taller than' with no reference to any other term.

There is something very puzzling about the suppressed premise strategy, however. What exactly is added to the argument by making the hidden premise explicit? It may well have psychological value, in clarifying the reason for the argument's validity. But it cannot turn an unsound argument into a sound one.

For suppose (5) were in fact invalid. Then, at least for Iain, that he is a bachelor would not entail that he was unmarried (so not all bachelors would be unmarried). The added premise would, therefore, be false. Hence the expanded argument:

(9)   Iain is a bachelor
      All bachelors are unmarried
      So Iain is unmarried,

would have a false premise.

Of course, the point of the suppressed premise move is that the added premise should be true, as

in the case of (5) it is. Indeed, it must be logically true. This is not brought out clearly by (5), for if its added premise, 'All bachelors are unmarried', were not logically true it would be false. Contrast:

(10) All bachelors are unmarried
      So Iain is unmarried.

If we add the extra premise that Iain is a bachelor, we obtain a valid argument. But (10) is not valid, for the premise can be true and the conclusion false. So it does not suffice simply to add true premises to an argument to show that it is really valid. The added premises must be logically true.

This may recall the notion of enthymeme, which is used in this broad way to refer to any argument, such as (10), which can be converted to a valid argument (9) by the addition of a true premise. But that is not the current strategy, which is to add premises which are logically necessary. Our focus is on arguments whose premises cannot be true and conclusion false, and yet which do not instantiate a valid form. For them, the added premise will be logically true. Another worry arises, nevertheless – or rather, the original worry in a new guise. For the modality which the reductionist sought to remove by the suppressed premise strategy has now shifted to the added premise. Which added premises are acceptable and which not – which are the logical truths?

The interpretational approach is often coupled with the idea that logic is topic-neutral – what is purely logical abstracts away from the specific content and presents a formal schema. But will the supposed divide between the specific and the general – between content and form – support the weight put on it?

It will not. Interpretational semantics has to mark off a class of expressions (logical constants) which are immune to variation. For if all expressions could vary their interpretation, only the most trivial examples would be accounted valid. But examples (5) and (7) above show that the class cannot in fact bail out the interpretational approach.

In fact, one can see dissatisfaction with this problem lying behind Quine's attack on the notion of analyticity. Hart (1991) recalls the debate between Tarski and Quine (believers in 'plain truth') and Carnap (a believer, as Hart puts it, in 'fancy') over the nature of logical consequence. As long as one recognises analytical, and so logical, connections between expressions, interpretational semantics will be guaranteed to undergenerate. The only solution available to an advocate of 'plain truth' is to disparage such connections, suggesting they are open to revision, and so not logically compelling after all.

Yet this strategy must fail – on pain of dismissing logic altogether. For logic requires a separation between simple truth – whether the constituent statements of an argument are true or false – and modality – whether the (possible) truth of the premises guarantees that of the conclusion. The reductionist strategy transfers this distinction from the statements themselves (are the connections analytic or synthetic?) to that of form and content (separating the logical constants – whose interpretation may not vary – from the substantive content, which is removed). But if we refuse to recognise a set of inferential connections between substantive expressions as analytical, neither can we recognise a set of expressions as logical constants, as resistant to reinterpretation with everything else.

'Fancy,' or logical necessity, lies at the heart of logical consequence. Valid arguments are those whose premises cannot, logically, be true when their conclusions are false. This requires that we remain prepared to study the inferential connections in (5) and (7), as much as those in (1) and (3).

Representations triumphant

To return to the suppressed premise strategy, however: the puzzle remains. The extra premise is strictly redundant. For if the original argument were invalid, the added premise would not be logically true. Given that it is logically true, it follows that the unexpanded argument was already valid. Hence it was (logically) unnecessary to add the extra premise.

The point is reminiscent of a familiar puzzle about *Modus Ponens*, that the major premise is either false or unnecessary:

A, if A then B/so B.

If the major premise is true, then B follows from A, and so the major premise is redundant. So either the major premise is false, or not needed at all. Either way, it contributes nothing to the argument.

Of course, what we are looking at in the suppressed premise strategy is not whether B simply follows (perhaps contingently on other assumptions) from A, but whether the conclusion is entailed by the premises – whether the argument from A to B is valid. So our problem concerns the logical, and not merely contingent, truth of the major premise. Nonetheless, the problems have a striking structural similarity. If the added premise is available (i.e. is logically true) then it is not needed (the argument is valid without it); so if the argument is invalid without it, the additional premise is not logically true, and so not available to be added.

There is another, and more instructive, way of seeing the point about *Modus Ponens*, however. A conditional records the fact that we may correctly proceed from its antecedent to its consequent. That is all there is to the meaning of conditionals. We might call it a redundancy theory of conditionals, on analogy with the redundancy theory of truth. Not that the correctness of this view of conditionals depends on that for truth. Indeed, as we saw in §2, the truth-predicate is not always redundant, as in 'If "white" comes to mean red, "Snow is white" will not be true', where ' "Snow is white" will not be true' cannot be replaced without loss of truth by 'snow will not be white'. Nonetheless, the idea is the same: conditionals do not make reference to some strange species of conditional fact, but simply record successful passage from one fact (the antecedent) to another. Indeed, just as the redundancy theory of truth does not claim that all talk of truth can be eliminated, neither does the redundancy theory of conditionals. The redundancy theory of truth claims that ' "All cats are animals" is true' says no more and no less than 'All cats are animals', and here talk of truth is eliminable; but in 'What Iain said is true' it is not. So too with conditionals.

This is the burden of normalisation. Any proof in which an application of Conditional Proof follows one of *Modus Ponens* (with the same formula as conclusion of one and major premise of the other) is more complex than is necessary. A reduction step is possible:

$$
\begin{array}{ccc}
 & [A] & \\
 & \Pi_2 & \Pi_1 \\
\Pi_1 & \underline{\quad B \quad} & A \\
\underline{A \quad \text{If } A \text{ then } B} & \Rightarrow \text{ (reduces to)} & \Pi_2 \\
B & & B \\
\Pi_3 & & \Pi_3
\end{array} \qquad (1)
$$

Here the statement of 'If A then B' is redundant. Π_2 not only shows that B is derivable from A, but actually derives it.

Where conditionals come in useful is where we don't actually have Π_2, the crucial derivation, only a report of its existence. The case parallels that for truth. Truth enables us to carry various reports around under certain descriptions (e.g. 'what Iain said') without all the bothersome detail. Similarly, conditionals enable us to transmit a record of proof without its detail. If B does indeed follow from A, then in some sense we need neither the proof, nor the record, validly to move from A to B. But in order to be *assured* that the step is valid, we can rely either on the proof, or, if we simply have a reliable report – 'if A then B' – that the step is valid, we can use *Modus Ponens* to articulate it.

The *Modus Ponens* puzzle is dramatic. But the puzzle also affects the other connectives. The introduction rule for a connective states the ground on which statements containing that connective can be made. The Cut principle (or normalisation) then links the introduction rule to an elimination rule in such a way as to guarantee conservativeness – that is, adding a connective via its introduction rules does not affect the provability of statements lacking that connective. So & E, $\vee E$ and so on are equally redundant – when tied to the grounds for assertion of the major premise a reduction procedure eliminates the inference and the major premise. But this redundancy is theoretical, not real. The logical connectives are useful in bundling information – that B follows from A in the case of conditionals, that one of A or B is true in the case of disjunction, and so on. We may no longer have access to the derivation of B from A, or to the information about which of A or B is true, respectively, but 'If A then B' and 'A or B' carry that assurance forward so that if in the first case, we come to find out that A is true, we can infer B, or if in the second, we should find out that C follows from A and from B equally, that C. The logical connectives import no information of their own, but serve to record combinations of other facts.

Does this response to the puzzle about *Modus Ponens* help us with the puzzle about the suppressed premise strategy? It tells us two things: first, that the added premise adds psychological perspicuity, in spelling out why the argument is valid. In that sense, it is not redundant, any more than the conditional is in *Modus Ponens*. But at the same time, it is not essential. It would be wrong to say that an argument is valid in an extended sense if an expanded argument, containing an extra, logically true premise, is really valid, if that should imply

that arguments valid in the extended sense are not really valid. If the major premise of an application of *Modus Ponens* is true, then its conclusion does indeed follow from its minor premise, and the major premise is redundant – except for assuring us of that consequence. Similarly, if the extra premise added to an argument is logically true, then the conclusion does follow from the remaining premises – so arguments valid with added premises really are valid. What the extra premise does is to assure us of – and perhaps explain to us – the validity of the unexpanded argument.

Our puzzle about the suppressed premise strategy should now be solved. The extra premise adds clarification, but it does not serve to turn an invalid argument into a valid one. The strategy cannot, therefore, be used as a defence of interpretational semantics. Recall that the problem we are faced with is that interpretational semantics cannot be controlled so as to match, and serve as a replacement for, representational semantics. Allowing certain expressions to vary their interpretation undergenerates; fixing their interpretation overgenerates. The suppressed premise strategy tries to close this gap by restricting the variation so that it varies no further than the validity of the argument (if it is valid) may permit.

In this it may succeed – indeed, as stated, it must succeed. For if the argument is valid, then there must be some fact about the interpretation of premises and conclusion which rules out the possibility that the premises are true and the conclusion false. Explicating the fact which rules out the possibility of true premises and false conclusion will result in a logically true statement whose truth will serve to restrict the permissible interpretations of premise and conclusion, so that the truth of the conclusion cannot drift away from that of the other premises without falsifying the premise which has been added. In other words, representational semantics guarantees that the suppressed premise (or "cross-term") extension of interpretational semantics will succeed.[4]

Logic

What the believer in the suppressed premise approach to material validity must convince us of, is that the restriction on possible interpretations can be formulated and stated as a separate (in itself insufficient, but jointly sufficient) logically true added premise. It may be that, provided there is no limit on the richness of the resources available, this can always be done. The important point, however, is that the added premise does not turn an invalid argument into a valid one. It turns a materially valid argument into a formally valid one, by suitably restricting the range of formal counter-examples. For validity is at root a matter of what can be represented. It is representability which makes the (original) argument valid, and which makes the added premise logically true. There are arguments which are valid and not formally valid. To show invalidity we must, in the end, turn to representations in which the premises are true and the conclusion false.

Logic is the study of valid inference. Sometimes that validity is purely a matter of form – elaborating the way the logical connectives bundle information together, and drawing conclusions from it. But that does not exhaust the study of validity.

Commensurate with this wider brief for the logician, taking him out of the closet of the study of pure form into the wider world of material consequence, is a serious limitation on what can be expected of the logician. What is logic for? Logic can tell us what counts as a valid argument, what the criterion for validity is – what is needed for an argument to be valid. But only rarely can it tell us which arguments actually are valid. Indeed, where it can tell us this, is precisely in the study of pure form. Beyond that, we are faced with a need to discover whether the premises can be true and the conclusion false. To decide this may be a complex issue in metaphysics, for example, or in

mathematics. Since 2^{127} is even, we may ask whether it follows that it is the sum of two primes. If Goldbach's Conjecture is true, it does. But the logician cannot answer that question. The logician's task is to observe that Goldbach's Conjecture will serve to entail the conclusion – for if every even number[5] is, as a matter of mathematical necessity, the sum of two primes, then it is impossible that 2^{127} be even and that 2^{127} not be the sum of two primes. Similarly, if determinism is incompatible with free will, one may validly infer the falsity of determinism from the presence of free will (or contrariwise). This may seem to invite the metaphysician dangerously into the logical arena. Should logic not be topic-neutral, and insulated from such intrusion? But that is not so. The topic-neutrality of logic need not mean there is a pure subject matter for logic; rather, that the logician may need to go everywhere, into mathematics and even into metaphysics. Nor need we deny that making the suppressed premises explicit is not a useful task. Where possible, exhibiting a pure form of argument can yield clarification, and can show validity by abstracting a valid form.

What must be acknowledged is that belief that every valid argument is valid in virtue of form is a myth, and exclusive concentration on the study of pure forms of argument does a disservice both to logic and to those who can be helped by it. Validity is a question of the impossibility of true premises and false conclusion for whatever reason, and there are arguments which are materially valid and where that reason is not purely logical.

Notes

1 Indeed, Etchemendy (1983: 326 ff.) called it the "substitutional/interpretational theory".

2 One strategy for the formalist here is to reduce the preordering on people to a partial ordering on heights, so reducing the transitivity of 'taller than' to that of 'greater than'. But the same problem now arises for 'greater than': if it is not a logical term, interpretational semantics will allow its interpretation to vary so that the analogue of (7) is deemed invalid; while if its interpretation is kept fixed, the analogue of (8) comes out valid – but it is not, for everything might have been the same size.

3 In his (1983: 330) he called it 'Bolzano's Fallacy'.

4 Does adoption of the representational account of validity, asks the referee, commit me to the belief that a necessarily true conclusion follows from any set of premises whatever? For if an argument is valid

if and only if it is impossible for the premises to be true and conclusion false, then surely if the conclusion cannot be false, it cannot be false in conjunction with any set of premises, and so follows validly from them. I have deliberately kept the body of this paper neutral, as I see it, between the classicist, the intuitionist, the relevantist and others. I do not, however, believe that the modal – that is, the representational – account of validity has this consequence. I have discussed the matter at some length elsewhere (Read 1988: especially chapter 3). In brief, Tarski's generic conditions on consequence, Weakening (or Monotonicity) and Cut (with its special case, Suppression) are correct only if properly controlled. That control requires that premises can be augmented only in a weak way, by a loose kind of extensional binding; but necessary truths can be suppressed only when bound in a strong way, by a tight and intensional binding. So the tempting move to irrelevance turns on an equivocation and lack of care over the interpretation of conjunction in the formula "impossible for the premises to be true and conclusion false". See also Read 1981.

5 Greater than 2.

References

Etchemendy, J. 1983: "The Doctrine of Logic as Form", *Linguistics and Philosophy*, 6, pp. 319–34.

Etchemendy, J. 1988: "Tarski on Truth and Logical Consequence", *Journal of Symbolic Logic*, 53, pp. 51–79.

Etchemendy, J. 1990: *The Concept of Logical Consequence*, Cambridge, Mass.: Harvard University Press.

Hart, W. D. 1991: "Critical notice of Etchemendy (1990)", *The Philosophical Quarterly*, 41, pp. 500–5.

Read, S. L. 1981: "Validity and the intensional sense of 'and'", *Australasian Journal of Philosophy*, 59, pp. 301–7.

Read, S. L. 1988: *Relevant Logic*, Oxford: Blackwell.

19

Tarski on Truth and Logical Consequence

John Etchemendy

Tarski's writings on the concepts of truth and logical consequence rank among the most influential works in both logic and philosophy of the twentieth century. Because of this, it would be impossible to give a careful and accurate account of how far that influence reaches and of the complex route by which it spread. In logic, Tarski's methods of defining satisfaction and truth, as well as his work pioneering general model-theoretic techniques, have been entirely absorbed into the way the subject is presently done; they have become part of the fabric of contemporary logic, material presented in the initial pages of every modern textbook on the subject. In philosophy, the influence has been equally pervasive, extending not only to work in semantics and the philosophies of logic and language, but to less obviously allied areas such as epistemology and the philosophy of science as well.

Rather than try to chart the wide-ranging influence of these writings or catalog the important research they have inspired, I will concentrate on various confusions and misunderstandings that continue to surround this work. For in spite of the extensive attention the work has received in the past fifty years, especially in the philosophical literature, misunderstandings of both conceptual

John Etchemendy, "Tarski on Truth and Logical Consequence," *The Journal of Symbolic Logic*, 53 (1988), pp. 51–79, reprinted by permission of Association for Symbolic Logic, Vassar College, New York. All rights reserved. The reproduction is by special permission for this publication only.

and historical sorts are still remarkably widespread. Indeed in the philosophical community, recent reactions to Tarski's work on truth range from Karl Popper's "intense joy and relief" at Tarski's "legitimation" of the notion [1974, p. 399], to Hilary Putnam's assessment that "as a philosophical account of truth, Tarski's theory fails as badly as it is possible for an account to fail" [1985, p. 64]. Opinions have not exactly converged.

This paper has two parts, which can be read independently. In the first part, I discuss Tarski's definition of truth, paying particular attention to the project Tarski saw himself engaged in, and to the relation of that project to the field of semantics. For the obscurity of this relation is the main source of confusion and dispute about the philosophical significance of the work. As I point out, the relation is little more than a fortuitous accident: although Tarski indeed laid the groundwork for formal semantics, there is an important sense in which his own goal conflicts directly with that of the other project. In the second part of the paper, I turn to Tarski's account of logical truth and logical consequence. Here my emphasis is more historical than conceptual. In particular, it is commonly thought that the modern, model-theoretic analysis of logical truth and logical consequence derive from Tarski's early work on these notions. But this piece of lore is incorrect. Tarski made substantial and far-reaching contributions to our understanding of these concepts, but they are different from those he is ordinarily thought to have made.

John Etchemendy

Truth

Tarski's main work on truth appeared in the Polish monograph [33^m], which was then translated into German and an important postscript added in [35b]. The results contained in the monograph, with the exception of Tarski's theorem on the undefinability of arithmetical truth, were reported at various lectures during 1930 and 1931, as well as in the abstract [30/31ª] and a short article [32]. The undefinability theorem was added to the Polish monograph, with acknowledgment to Gödel, after it had gone to press. Informal presentations of the work on truth, with discussions of some of its philosophical implications, later appeared in [36] (and its German translation, [36f]), [44a], and [69].

Two remarkably divergent areas of philosophical research have grown out of this work, both of which are pursued even more actively today than in the twenty-five years immediately following the monograph's publication. These areas are, first, the analysis of truth and semantic paradox, and second, what has come to be known as "formal" semantics.[1] Recent work in the former field, especially since the publication of Kripke [1975], has been largely directed toward an account of semantic paradox in natural language. The latter field, formal semantics, itself divides into two competing approaches: truth-conditional semantics, with the work of Davidson and his followers, and model-theoretic semantics, a diverse field that includes, for example, the work on natural language by Montague and his followers.

How did Tarski's monograph give rise to these two independent lines of research? As is clear from the introductory sections of the monograph, Tarski's own concern was the former project, the analysis of truth. But it happens that the form his solution takes appears, at least at first glance, to serve equally as a characterization of the semantic properties of the language whose truth predicate is defined. This appearance is what ultimately gave rise to the important field of formal semantics. However the appearance is actually quite misleading, for reasons I will point out. In particular, it would be a mistake to construe Tarski as taking part in this latter, semantic project, since the two goals turn out to be in quite direct opposition to one another. Tarski's aim was to provide an eliminative definition of truth, in effect to "absorb" the concept into a metatheory containing no semantic

concepts; formal semantics, in contrast, must presuppose a fixed, metatheoretic notion of truth, which it then employs in characterizing the semantic properties of the language. Tarski was not doing semantics, at least in the commonly accepted sense of the term, but there is more to the divergence than just that. For without setting aside Tarski's principal goal, there is a sense in which semantics simply cannot be done.

Truth and paradox

It is important, first of all, to appreciate the broader context Tarski saw his project fitting into. We all know that Tarski's aim was to provide a definition of truth, or more accurately, to develop general techniques for defining truth predicates for a wide range of formalized languages. Yet this characterization of his goal leaves out an extremely significant feature of the project. For providing an explicit definition of truth was itself seen by Tarski as a solution to an important problem, a problem other than simply the question of whether and when truth is definable. Put simply, Tarski's overriding motivation was the question of whether the very notion of truth is a coherent one. Among logicians, this motivation tends to be obscured by Tarski's well-known negative result about arithmetical truth, the theorem for which the monograph is principally remembered. Among philosophers, the motivation also tends to be overlooked, though here due to the conflation of the two projects described above.

The problem Tarski addressed was this. Our ordinary concept of truth is, on the one hand, an extremely important one; it occurs frequently, not only in everyday discourse, but in mathematical and scientific discourse as well. Further, it is clear that many uses of this concept cannot easily be avoided, perhaps cannot be avoided at all. This is especially apparent for uses involving quantification. When we talk, say, about all statements of a given form being true, or about the truth of all the premises of some unspecified argument, it is hard to see how we might express similar thoughts without employing the notion of truth. On the other hand, the very same concept is known to give rise to paradox, to allow the derivation of an explicit contradiction from what seem perfectly obvious principles. This is an intolerable situation: the concept seems essential, essential even to the pursuit of science and mathematics, yet it threatens to introduce inconsistency into any discipline in which it is employed. What is needed is a concept of truth that will at least serve the scientific and mathematical purposes to which the everyday notion is put, but which can be guaranteed free of inconsistency. Providing such a concept was Tarski's first and foremost goal.

Now achieving this goal does not *demand* an explicit definition of truth. Indeed in the course of the monograph Tarski entertains various other approaches to the problem, such as treating the notion of truth as primitive and giving it an axiomatic characterization.[2] Introducing the concept of truth into a theory by means of an explicit, eliminative definition is just one way to meet the challenge described above. But it has one very important advantage over other ways, such as the axiomatic treatment: by giving such a definition, we are assured of the consistency of the resulting theory, relative of course to the consistency of our initial theory, in virtue of the very eliminability of the defined expression.

This last point deserves emphasis. Tarski's concern about the consistency of the concept of truth, his principal motivation for the enterprise, places a premium on the eliminability of our definition of truth. For it is this feature that provides our guarantee that the introduction of truth has not brought with it any contradiction, indeed, that the new theory is a conservative extension of the old. Without this feature, our introduction of a truth predicate would be in need of an explicit consistency proof; with it, the consistency is automatically assured by the very procedure we use to introduce the concept.

Of course eliminability alone, though it guarantees consistency, does not guarantee that the concept defined will serve the purposes of a truth predicate. To use Tarski's terminology, the definition must not only be "formally correct," it must be "materially adequate" as well. The predicate we introduce must, in other words, apply to all and only the true sentences of our original language. Thus Tarski introduces what he calls *Convention T*: In order for a definition of the truth predicate for a language to be judged adequate, we require that it have among its consequences all sentences of the form

$$(T) \qquad x \text{ is true if and only if } p,$$

where "p" is replaced by a sentence of the object language, the language whose truth predicate we are defining, and "x" is replaced by a structural

description, say a quotation name, of that very sentence. Or, if the metalanguage does not contain the object language as a proper part, we allow "p" to be replaced by a translation of the sentence referred to by the structural description. To use Tarski's example, one instance of this schema might be the following:

$$(1) \qquad \text{'It is snowing' is true if and only} \\ \text{if it is snowing.}$$

Or, with translation required:

$$(2) \qquad \text{'Es schneit' is true if and only} \\ \text{if it is snowing.}$$

Convention T embodies a striking insight, though one that is easily overlooked. Recall that during the late twenties, while Tarski was working on these problems, it would have been natural to expect a definition of truth, at least for mathematical languages, to take proof-theoretic form. The expectation was for a definition of the following sort: "All and only sentences derivable from such and such axioms by repeated application of such and such rules are true." Of course we now know, thanks to Gödel's incompleteness results, that such definitions are by and large impossible. But quite independent of these results, Tarski rejected this approach, arguing that there is no reason a definition of truth should also provide what he called a "criterion" of truth. As we would now put it, a definition of truth need not give us any effective procedure for deciding or enumerating the set of truths.[3]

Requiring that all instances of schema T follow from our definition guarantees that the newly introduced predicate will have exactly the right extension, that it will apply to all and only the true sentences of the language. The same assurance could come, of course, from a proof-theoretic definition employing a sound and complete axiomatization for the language in question. The difference is that Convention T provides the assurance while still permitting a completely noneffective specification of the desired set. Tarski saw quite clearly the desirability of this more "permissive" approach to defining truth, even before it was found to be, very often, the only avenue available.

Tarski called sentences like (1) and (2) "partial definitions of truth," and frequently described his project as providing a definition equivalent to the conjunction of all such instances of T for the language in question. Indeed, he points out that if the language had only a finite number of sentences, say 'S_1', 'S_2', 'S_3', ..., 'S_n', then the following would be a perfectly acceptable definition of truth:

(3) x is true if and only if $(x = 'S_1'$ and $S_1)$ or

$\qquad (x = 'S_2'$ and $S_2)$ or

$\qquad (x = 'S_3'$ and $S_3)$ or

$$\vdots$$

$\qquad (x = 'S_n'$ and $S_n)$

This definition in effect employs a simple list of the sentences of the object language, each sentence appearing first in quotes – named or structurally described – and then subsequently used, without quotes, in its ordinary sense. But Convention T is clearly satisfied by this definition: all instances of our schema follow easily from (3) plus certain simple syntactic facts (i.e., that 'S_i' $\neq$ 'S_j', when $i \neq j$) which Tarski assumes already provable in the metatheory.

We normally think of Tarski's detour through satisfaction and his use of recursive techniques as the two most distinctive features of his definition of truth. But notice that both of these features are only forced upon him in virtue of, first, the infinity of sentences of the standard object language, and second, the finite length of individual sentences in his metalanguage. Tarski himself suggests the above, list-like definition for finite languages, and had he allowed infinite disjunctions in the metalanguage, the same technique could have been carried over to standard languages as well.[4] Both recursion and satisfaction would then have been avoided.

The point I want to emphasize here is that, as Tarski saw his project, there was no reason in principle to prefer the usual recursive definition of truth to a list-like definition of the sort given in (3), though at the time, he considered the latter option unavailable for all but finite languages. This fact should not surprise us, at least if we keep in mind the motivation described earlier: both definitions clearly avoid the inconsistencies that plague the ordinary notion of truth; both are extensionally correct, and provably so. But if we think of Tarski as doing something more, in particular, if we imagine him engaged in the project of formal semantics, then this same fact should strike us as quite puzzling. For a list-like definition of truth seems

to provide little information, if any, about the semantic properties of the object language. Such definitions appear, at least intuitively, far less illuminating than their recursive counterparts. To understand exactly what this intuitive difference comes to, we need to consider the relation between a definition of truth and a semantic theory of the language in question.

Truth and semantics

Three related points need to be made about the relation between Tarski's project and formal semantics. The first concerns the question of whether a Tarskian definition of truth in itself illuminates the semantic properties of the object language. The second concerns the question of how a Tarskian definition of truth must be supplemented in order to arrive at a full-fledged semantic theory of the language. Finally, the third concerns the question of whether Tarski's definition can be construed as an analysis of the notion of truth as it appears in semantic theories.

The answer to the first question is *no*: there is a clear sense in which the theory that results from a Tarskian definition of truth, whether we give a list-like definition or the more familiar recursive definition, cannot possibly illuminate the semantic properties of the object language. To appreciate this, we need only take seriously the eliminative nature of these definitions. Both definitions reduce the concept of truth to various logical, syntactic and set-theoretic notions; in this respect, the recursive definition differs from the list definition only in the set-theoretic machinery it employs. But it follows from this that any consequence of either definition must already be a truth of logic, syntax or set theory, that is, a truth already provable in a metatheory that makes no mention whatsoever of semantic notions.

Consider a trivial example, just to drive the point home. Suppose we are dealing with a finite language, say one that contains just the two sentences 'S' and 'R', meaning, respectively, that it is snowing and that it is raining. Before we give a Tarskian definition of truth, it is natural to think of the two instances of schema T,

(4) 'S' is true if and only if it is snowing,

(5) 'R' is true if and only if it is raining,

as expressing important semantic facts about the language. In particular, it is natural to think of these as describing the truth-conditions of our two sentences. Intuitively, (4) and (5) hold because of the meanings of '*S*' and '*R*'; a semantic fact, if ever there was one. But when we give a Tarskian definition of "is true," these become the following truths of logic and syntax:

(4′) [('*S*' = '*S*' and it is snowing) or
      ('*S*' = '*R*' and it is raining)]
      iff it is snowing;

(5′) [('*R*' = '*S*' and it is snowing) or
      ('*R*' = '*R*' and it is raining)]
      iff it is raining.

These latter sentences clearly carry no information about the semantic properties of our language, *not even about the truth-conditions of its sentences*. There are various ways to emphasize this; we might note, for example, that a person could know what is expressed by (4′) and (5′) without knowing anything whatsoever about the meanings of the sentences '*S*' and '*R*', or that (4′) and (5′) would remain true even if all the semantic properties of this language were to change. But however we emphasize it, the point remains the same: the semantic facts about a language, those we aim to characterize in formal semantics, are not simply facts of logic, syntax and set theory. Yet these facts are the only kind that can possibly follow from a Tarskian definition of truth.[5]

To make this point as clear as possible, I have used a finite language and a "list-like" definition of truth. But the same sort of reduction underlies Tarski's recursive definition of truth for standard languages, as a bit of reflection will confirm. The point is in no way dependent on whether the definition takes the trivial form of a list, or whether it employs more interesting, recursive techniques; nor does it matter whether truth is defined directly, or whether we proceed through the ancillary concept of satisfaction. When we are out to characterize the semantic properties of a language, say the meanings or truth conditions of its sentences, our aim is simply orthogonal to Tarski's. For Tarski's aim was to eliminate the semantic notions, notions whose consistency seemed questionable, in favor of syntactic and set-theoretic notions.

This brings me to the second point, which concerns how a definition of truth can be converted into an account of the semantic properties of the object language. Interestingly, the answer to this question will also make clear the reason the first point is so frequently overlooked. That reason has to do with the ease with which we read substantive content into what is intended as a stipulative definition, the ease with which we replace the "if and only if" of definition with the "if and only if" of axioms or theorems. Consider an analogy. If I define a set, call it *EVEN*, as the set containing all sums of two odd primes, it would be a confusion to object that my definition presupposed Goldbach's conjecture. Definitions presuppose nothing, at least nothing relevant here; where Goldbach's conjecture comes in is with the claim that every even number greater than 2 is a member of *EVEN*, of the set just defined. To be sure, the name I chose for the set may be misleading, but the definition itself does not thereby become a substantive claim.

Now certain important semantic properties of a language can be described by taking the notion of truth as primitive and charting the ways in which the truth values of various sentences in the language depend on the truth values of others. When we do this, the claims we make will sometimes look strikingly like clauses in a recursive definition of truth. For example, we might offer the following claims about the semantic functioning of the expressions '¬' and '∧' in a simple language:

(6) $\forall p$ ('¬' $\ulcorner p$ is true iff p is not true),

(7) $\forall p, q$ ($p \ulcorner$ '∧' $\ulcorner q$ is true iff both p and q are true).

These are substantive claims about the language – witness the fact that, for example, (7) would be false if '∧' meant *or*. But of course in making these claims we must take our pretheoretic notion of truth as fixed; we must not, in other words, confuse the "iff" with the connective of definition. Though they may look like clauses in a definition of truth, to construe them as such would be a confusion: *definitions* make no claims, provide no information; (6) and (7), in contrast, yield genuine information about the semantic properties of the language.[6]

We can now see what underlies our intuition that a "list-like" definition of truth, such as (3), is somehow less illuminating than the more familiar recursive definition. Tarski himself, as we have noted, saw no reason to prefer the one style of definition over the other. From the Tarskian perspective, recursive techniques simply allow us to define the set of truths for standard languages without employing an infinitary metalanguage. To be sure, we may harbor objections to the use of an infinitary language, or perhaps not countenance such languages at all; in either case this would militate in favor of the recursive approach. But these reasons have nothing to do with the intuitive difference between the two styles of definition.

The difference only shows up when we construe these, not as definitions of the set of true sentences, but as substantive claims about the semantic properties of the language, claims that employ a primitive, undefined notion of truth. There is a marked difference between a semantic theory that includes the claims (6) and (7), and a theory that only includes a – perhaps infinitary – version of (3). The latter theory makes no direct claim about the semantic functioning of any subsentential expressions in the language, expressions like '¬' and '∧'; the former, on the other hand, does. Given this obvious difference between the two imagined semantic theories, it becomes easy to isolate the perceived difference between the two styles of definition. We might put it this way: if we define a set *TRUE* using the standard recursive definition, *then the claim that all and only the true sentences of the language are members of TRUE is logically equivalent to the more illuminating of the above semantic theories*. On the other hand, if we define that very same set using the list-like definition, our subsequent claim is equivalent to that made by the *less* informative theory. Of course, both of these claims again employ our fixed, pretheoretic understanding of "true"; neither is a consequence of the definition, neither is a mere truth of logic, syntax and set theory.[7]

It is not surprising that two definitions which in fact specify the same set should display such different characteristics. Indeed, assuming Goldbach's conjecture, we can construct a parallel case with *EVEN*: We can then define the very same set either as the set containing 2 plus all sums of two odd primes, or as the set containing every natural number evenly divisible by 2. But depending on which definition we choose, the subsequent claim that all even numbers are in *EVEN* will have strikingly different import, being in the one case a significant number-theoretic fact, in the other a mere triviality.

The answer to our second question, then, is this. Getting from a Tarskian definition of truth to a substantive account of the semantic properties of the object language may involve as little as the reintroduction of a primitive notion of truth. For

the subsequent claim that all and only the true sentences are members of the set defined may then provide genuine information about the semantic properties of the language, may indeed be logically equivalent to an illuminating semantic theory of the language. Of course, the content of this claim will depend on the details of the definition itself, just as our claim that all and only the even numbers are members of *EVEN* fluctuates with our characterization of *EVEN*. Here is where Tarski's work, though directed at a quite different goal, contributed so much to the project of formal semantics. For in giving his explicit definition of truth, Tarski introduced precisely the mathematical techniques needed for an illuminating account of the semantic properties of certain simple languages. A list-like definition, though it would have served Tarski's own purposes equally well, would have made no comparable contribution to semantics.

This brings me to my final point. So far I have emphasized that Tarski's aim was not to give a semantic theory of the object language, but to define a predicate which, in virtue of its satisfying Convention T, could safely be used to express what would otherwise require the use of a concept whose consistency seemed questionable. What makes it hard to keep this difference firmly in view is the fact that, thanks to the techniques Tarski uses in his definition, the claim that all and only the true sentences of the language are members of the defined set takes on genuine semantic import. Yet such claims are most emphatically not part of Tarski's project, but in an obvious sense conflict with it, involving as they do the uneliminated use of a notion of truth.

Notice, though, that the very fact that such a claim provides genuine information about the language tells us something important about Tarski's definition. When we defined *EVEN* as the set of numbers divisible by two, the claim that the even numbers were members of *EVEN* was trivial, for the simple reason that our definition directly captured the sense ordinarily given this expression. But the claim that the true sentences of the object language are members of *TRUE*, where this latter is given a Tarskian definition, is far from trivial, being equivalent to a semantic theory containing substantive claims such as (6) and (7). This shows that the sense of the expression "true" occurring in this claim is by no means captured by the definition given *TRUE*. Or, to put it another way, a Tarskian definition does not provide an analysis of the concept of truth as it appears in semantic claims such as (6) and (7).[8] If it did, the assertion that the true sentences were members of *TRUE* would be devoid of content, certainly not a substantive claim about the language in question.

We have actually seen one upshot of this fact already. Recall our observation that (4) seemed to express a significant semantic fact:

(4)　'*S*' is true if and only if it is snowing,

while the sentence that resulted from replacing "is true" by a Tarskian definition was, in contrast, a truth of logic, syntax and set theory. While (4) is a contingent, perhaps empirical truth, the following is a necessary truth, assuming a Tarskian definition of *TRUE*:

(4)　'*S*' ∈ *TRUE* if and only if it is snowing.

This striking change from (4″) to (4) would not occur if the definition of *TRUE* simply provided an analysis of the corresponding concept employed in (4).[9]

Let us call the conception of truth that figures into claims such as (4) the "semantical conception," it being the sense of truth presupposed in contemporary semantics. I choose "semantical" since Tarski himself appropriates the more euphonious "semantic conception of truth" for the conception embodied in his own definition. According to the semantical conception, truth is a property of sentences or perhaps, of utterances of sentences. In this initial respect, Tarski's account agrees with this conception of truth. However, the crucial feature of the semantical conception is that there is a substantive difference between the propositions expressed for example, by the following two sentences:

(8)　Snow is white.
(9)　'Snow is white' is true.

The first of these makes a claim that depends only on the color of snow; the second claim, on the other hand, depends both on the color of snow and the meaning of the sentence 'Snow is white.' For this reason the states of affairs described can vary independently: 'Snow is white' might have been false, though snow was still white; if, for instance, 'snow' had meant *grass*. And conversely, snow might not have been white, though 'Snow is white' was still true; say if 'snow' had meant

vanilla ice cream. On the semantical conception of truth, (8) and (9) say quite different things, things linked to one another only in virtue of the meaning that the subject of (9), the sentence 'Snow is white,' happens to have. It is precisely because of this difference that the biconditional:

(10)　'Snow is white' is true if and only if snow is white

carries information about the meaning of the sentence 'Snow is white.'[10]

My third point, then, just comes to this: Tarski's definition does not provide an analysis of the semantical conception of truth, the conception presupposed in contemporary semantics. Notice in passing, though, that there is a certain irony in the way we have arrived at this observation. For the main reason this has not been widely recognized is the fact that a Tarskian definition seems to provide such striking illumination about the semantic properties of the language. And indeed, as we have acknowledged, the claim that the true sentences are members of *TRUE* does give us genuine semantic information about the object language, the same information provided by a semantic theory of that language. But the very fact that this claim is illuminating, that it provides information about contingent properties of the language, is conclusive proof that the Tarskian definition is *not* an analysis of the semantical conception of truth. For if it were just an analysis, that claim would be, if not trivial, at any rate a conceptual, not a contingent truth.

The analysis of truth

We have seen that Tarski was not himself doing formal semantics, though the techniques he introduced made the step to semantics, in effect, a straightforward matter of reintroducing an undefined notion of truth. Recognizing this relationship in turn makes it clear that Tarski's definition does not provide an analysis of the semantical conception of truth. I will conclude this section with a brief discussion of two questions this last observation gives rise to. The first is whether there is some other common conception of truth more closely captured by Tarski's definition. For it is clear that the semantical conception of truth is not the only one; indeed, it is not even the conception underlying the most common uses of the truth predicate in ordinary language. The second question, and perhaps the more important one, is whether Tarski's original goal is in any way affected by the adequacy of the resulting definition *as an analysis*. We know, after all, that its extensional adequacy is guaranteed by adherence to Convention T.

The answer to the first of these questions is probably *no*; construed as an analysis, Tarski's definition seems a hybrid of different pretheoretic conceptions of truth. It is useful to think about it this way. The point at which we diverged from the semantical conception of truth was back with Convention T. There, we did not just require that all instances of schema T should *hold* given our definition, that they should all *as a matter of fact* come out true; rather, we required that those instances be *provable from* the definition. This strong requirement would indeed be appropriate if instances of the schema were analytic: if they held, as we might say, "by definition." But on the semantical conception of truth, they are simply not; instances of schema T come out true thanks to facts about the object language, not just in virtue of the meaning of the truth predicate contained in them.

Still, there *are* common uses of the truth predicate according to which sentences very much like instances of T seem analytic, specifically, uses in which truth is attributed to propositions or statements rather than sentences. Consider, for example, the following claim:

(11)   The proposition that snow is white is true if and only if snow is white.

Now we could replace "proposition" here with various other terms, say "assertion," "claim," "statement," or "allegation," without affecting the intuitive analyticity of the result. But what is important to note is that the conception of truth employed in (11) is not the semantical conception, indeed, that truth is not here attributed to sentences at all. What we have is a *propositional* conception of truth, one in which truth is taken to be a property of extralinguistic entities of some sort. On such a conception it seems reasonable to require, not simply that sentences like (11) hold, but that they hold in virtue of the meaning of "true," and so should be consequences of our definition.

If we construe Tarski's definition as an analysis, it seems clear that the concept analyzed is some combination of the semantical conception and the propositional conception. It shares with the

semantical conception the view that truth is a property of sentences. But it shares with the propositional conception the view that truth applies to its objects independently of linguistic or semantic facts about any particular language. No ordinary use of the expression "true" combines these two aspects of Tarski's definition. The definition captures features of both conceptions, but is an analysis of neither.[11]

Let us turn then to the second question. At the beginning of this section, I emphasized that Tarski's original goal was to provide a concept of truth that could serve the scientific and mathematical purposes to which the ordinary notion is put, but which can be guaranteed free of inconsistency. In the end, what Tarski shows is that for any of a wide variety of languages, we can define a predicate that provably applies to all and only the true sentences of the language, and further, that we can define this predicate using relatively innocuous syntactic and set-theoretic notions. What we end up with, though, is not an *analysis* of any pretheoretic notion of truth, even when restricted to the language in question. But do these deviations from the ordinary concepts make any difference?

The answer is that they can, but usually will not. Generally, when we employ a truth predicate we are engaging in what is known in the philosophical literature as *semantic ascent*. Roughly speaking, semantic ascent simply enables us to recover or reassert a proposition, but to do so indirectly, without actually using a sentence that would, in the more usual fashion, express that same proposition. There are various reasons such a device comes in handy, reasons I will not go into here. The important point, though, is that the purpose of semantic ascent, despite its misleading name, is *not* the introduction of semantic topics into otherwise nonsemantic claims, but rather the indirect access that it gives us to the original, nonsemantic claims.

The point is a simple one. In most cases in which we use an ordinary truth predicate, specifically, those where the predicate functions as a device for semantic ascent, a Tarskian truth predicate will serve equally well. Where such a predicate will fail is precisely when peculiarly semantic claims are at issue, for example in giving a semantic theory of a language. Thus, if I remark that, had (8) not been true, winter would have been a much more colorful season, my claim would be equally well expressed with a Tarskian truth predicate. For here my intent is simply to assert, albeit indirectly, that *had snow not been white*, winter would have been more colorful. In such uses, the very strong equivalence between (8) and (9) is precisely what we would want; any introduction of semantic issues would be irrelevant and misleading. On the other hand, a Tarskian truth predicate will not allow us to make claims where the intent is distinctively semantic, say: Had 'snow' meant *grass*, (8) would not have been true. A Tarskian reformulation of this would turn it into nonsense; the meaning of 'snow' is, after all, completely irrelevant to the color of snow.

We have seen that to do semantics we must reintroduce a primitive notion of truth: a Tarskian truth predicate does not allow us to make the substantive semantic claims, like (4)–(7), that constitute, in part, the goal of semantics. Now there is a certain irony here that should not go unmentioned. For although Tarski provides a solution to the semantic paradoxes usable in a wide range of situations, that solution is specifically not available to those doing semantics. Tarski's eliminable concept of truth is fine for semantic ascent, but not for semantics.

If we keep in mind Tarski's original project, most of the philosophical confusions about his definition can easily be sorted out. Tarski was not doing formal semantics, nor did he give us an analysis of the semantical conception of truth, the conception employed in that discipline. Tarski's goal was to provide a predicate that would avoid the inconsistencies of truth predicates in ordinary language, but nonetheless allow us to express important claims in which those pretheoretic notions play a crucial role. For most purposes, a Tarskian truth predicate will indeed allow such expression, and allow it while handily avoiding the specter of semantic paradox. Clearly, Tarski carried out this project with striking success.

Logical Consequence

In his early writings on the consequence relation, including [28ᵃb], [30c] and [30e], Tarski makes no attempt to define or analyze the concept of logical consequence. In these articles he introduces the concept as a primitive, in the form of the operation Cn that takes a set X to the set $Cn(X)$ of its consequences. He then offers a minimal, axiomatic characterization of this notion, one that guarantees little more than that Cn is a closure operation on the set of sentences. Using the concept so charac-

terized, he then defines such allied notions as logical truth, consistency, deductive closure, and finite axiomatizability. His stated aim in these papers is to clarify various relationships among these central concepts of logic and metamathematics, and to establish some of their elementary properties.[12] For our purposes what is most striking about these early papers, especially against their historical backdrop, is the extraordinary generality and abstractness of the perspective adopted. They contain the first explicitly formal treatment of the *metatheoretic* concept of consequence, in contrast to the common practice of giving formal specifications of the consequence relation itself.

Throughout these early discussions, though, Tarski assumes a purely syntactic or proof-theoretic view of the underlying intuitive meaning of $Cn(X)$ by saying that this is to contain all those sentences which "can be obtained [from X] by means of certain operations called *rules of inference*."[13] In this respect, Tarski's perspective conformed to the syntactic view of the consequence relation prevalent at the time, the view that for one sentence to be a logical consequence of others is simply for that sentence to be derivable from the others by means of some standard system of deduction. In 1933 Tarski began to express reservations about this conception of the consequence relation, first in some rather elliptical remarks in the monograph on truth,[14] and later quite explicitly in [33]. But it was not until 1936, in a well-known article devoted to the subject of logical consequence, that he proposed a semantic analysis of the relation. This article appeared both in Polish [36a] and in German translation [36g]; it is translated into English in [56ᵐ].

It is now completely standard to treat the notions of logical truth and logical consequence semantically, using the familiar model-theoretic definitions of these notions. According to these definitions, a sentence is logically true if it is true in all interpretations (or models) of the language; similarly, a sentence is a consequence of a set of sentences if it is true in all interpretations in which every member of the given set is true. An interpretation or model consists of the specification of a domain of quantification and, from within that domain, appropriate extensions for the predicates, function symbols and individual constants of the language.

These definitions are frequently credited to Tarski, either to the monograph on truth, or to the 1936 article on logical consequence. These attributions are, however, incorrect. In neither place did Tarski give accounts of logical truth and logical consequence equivalent to the modern definitions. In the monograph on truth, Tarski still presupposed proof-theoretic definitions, though as I have indicated he already had reservations about the adequacy of the syntactic approach. On the other hand, in the 1936 article he gave a semantic account of the logical notions, but one that is *not* equivalent to the standard, model-theoretic definitions. It was not until [53m] that the standard definitions appeared in a work by Tarski, but by then the treatment was familiar from such works as Kemeny [1948] and Henkin [1949].

The model-theoretic account of logical truth and logical consequence cannot accurately be attributed to Tarski; indeed the history of this analysis is probably too complex to support the attribution to any single author. In this section, I will describe the semantic account Tarski actually offered in 1936, and explain why he did not come up with, and indeed seems to have consciously avoided, the standard definitions. In spite of that, Tarski's views about logical truth and logical consequence have had an important effect on our conception of logic, which I will describe at the end of this section. The effect is somewhat more subtle than is commonly supposed, but not for that reason any less profound.

The model-theoretic account

Before turning to Tarski's 1936 account, it will be useful to make some preliminary observations about the familiar, model-theoretic definitions of logical truth and logical consequence. The observations do not concern the technical details of the account, which I assume are well known, but rather some philosophical issues that are rarely explicitly discussed. The points are fairly simple, but it would be impossible to explain exactly how Tarski's 1936 paper connects up with the standard tradition without at least making them explicit.

The first point is just that the standard model-theoretic account is widely assumed, whether rightly or wrongly, to provide genuine analyses of the notions of logical truth and logical consequence. I do not mean by this that logicians or philosophers often discuss this point, or for that matter even feel the need to mention it. But the assumption is implicit in our treatment of the account, and specifically, in the difference between our treatment of these definitions and syntactic

accounts which, at least with first-order languages, yield coextensive results.

Let me explain. Obviously, from a purely mathematical point of view, the only criterion of adequacy we need impose on a definition is that it have the right extension, that it genuinely determine the set of objects to which the intuitive concept applies. But as far as extensional adequacy goes, there are a multitude of equally correct (or equally incorrect) definitions of first-order consequence: when we specify any one of the many equivalent proof procedures for first-order languages, we have defined the consequence relation as adequately as when we define the relation model-theoretically. But from among these coextensive definitions, the model-theoretic account is typically afforded a special status, a status most clearly reflected in soundness and completeness theorems.

Whenever we give a mathematical characterization of an intuitive notion, the question of the extensional adequacy of the definition immediately arises. In some instances the adequacy is just obvious, when the definition simply spells out our intuitive notion, replacing it with a clearer and more precise analysis. In other cases, though, for example with Church's or Turing's characterization of the class of computable functions, the extensional adequacy is not immediately apparent. Here, we all recognize the difficulty of the question of extensional adequacy, and also that the question does not admit of a directly mathematical answer: we can only compare the intuitive notion with its precise counterparts in, so to speak, a piecemeal way, say by looking at individual functions to see where they fall, and perhaps supplementing these considerations by noting the coincidence of the many formal definitions. But sometimes the adequacy question is thought to be more amenable to mathematical treatment. A case in point concerns syntactic or proof-theoretic definitions of first-order consequence.

With syntactic characterizations of consequence, the issue of extensional adequacy is posed in the form of two separate questions: is the proof theory *complete*, that is, can we prove everything we *should* be able to prove, and is it *sound*, can we prove anything we *shouldn't*? These questions naturally come up as soon as a formal system of deduction is put forward; indeed, they have been raised about specific deductive systems since the very beginning of formal logic, since Aristotle proposed his syllogistic. But until quite recently, logicians were in precisely the same position with respect to these questions as we now are with formal characterizations of computability. It seemed that settling these issues could not admit of mathematical proof, and in particular, that our only evidence for the *completeness* of a deductive system came from our repeated success in formalizing specific instances of intuitively valid reasoning. As Hilbert once put it, the evidence accrued "through experiment". What changed this was the emergence of precise semantic accounts of logical truth and logical consequence. With the model-theoretic definition of consequence available, questions of soundness and completeness of deductive systems could be raised in mathematically tractable form.

The model-theoretic definition is now used to prove the extensional adequacy, the soundness and completeness, of the various proof-theoretic characterizations of consequence. What is revealing is that its own adequacy is thought to need no such demonstration. We do not prove the "soundness" and "completeness" of the model-theoretic account of consequence; indeed the very idea would strike most of us as deeply confused. Our attitude here is characteristic of our attitude toward an analysis: extensional adequacy is guaranteed on a *conceptual* level, by our close adherence to the intuitive notion we aim to characterize. It is in this sense that the model-theoretic account is treated as a genuine analysis of the intuitive notions of logical truth and logical consequence.

This brings me to my second point. Notice that a good deal of the above discussion did not deal directly with the intuitive notion of logical consequence, but rather with the more technical notion of *first-order* consequence. This raises the question of how this technical concept fits into the picture. The standard view, I think, is this. The model-theoretic account provides an analysis of consequence applicable to various sorts of languages: first-order, second-order, infinitary, and so forth. When we apply it specifically to, say, a first-order language, it gives us a definition of the logical consequence relation – restricted, of course, to that first-order language. Thus, although the notion of a first-order *language* may be a technical one, the notion of first-order *consequence* is just meant to be the restriction of the intuitive concept of logical consequence to these languages. This concept is what is thought to be captured by the model-theoretic account.

The last point I want to make before turning to Tarski's account is historical. I emphasized above

that the key breakthrough that allows us to address the issue of completeness mathematically is the semantic analysis of logical truth and logical consequence. This is clearly relevant to our current concern, since Tarski himself did not propose a semantic account of these notions until 1936, while the completeness theorem for first-order logic was proven in 1929. Indeed, the basic idea underlying the model-theoretic account was relatively common in clear articulation of the idea seems to have been in a review by Bernays [1922], though it no doubt reached the widest audience in Hilbert and Ackermann's introductory text [1928]. Of course it is central to Gödel's proof of the completeness theorem in [1929] and [1930].

In light of this, it may seem surprising that the model-theoretic definitions are often attributed to Tarski. Still, it would be a mistake to think the attribution rests on a simple, historical error. For there are various weaknesses in these early versions of the model-theoretic account not found in Tarski's own account. First of all, the model-theoretic definitions presuppose the notion of the truth of a sentence in a model or on an interpretation, and this notion was not rigorously defined by any of the earlier authors.[15] Second, these authors either ignore the notion of consequence entirely, or else reduce it to the logical truth of the corresponding conditional statement; this is a significant point which I will return to later. Finally, and perhaps most important, there is no indication that these earlier authors saw clearly that the account they gave really presupposes a significant piece of philosophical analysis, one in need of some justification.

The model-theoretic definitions are so deeply ingrained that it is easy to overlook this last point ourselves. Yet if we compare the initial explanations of logical consequence that we give to introductory students, explanations which refer essentially to modal or epistemic notions, with the model-theoretic definition of the same concept, we see immediately that there is a significant difference between the two. What Tarski saw clearly, and emphatically expressed in the 1936 article, was first, the need to provide an explicit analysis of our intuitive concepts of logical truth and logical consequence, and second, the possibility of applying his semantic techniques to the rigorous definition of these notions. In addition, he gave an independent definition of consequence rather than trying to reduce this notion to that of logical truth. What Tarski did not give, contrary to the received opinion, is an account equivalent to the usual model-theoretic definitions.

Tarski's account

Let me describe the definitions Tarski gives in the 1936 paper, in order to highlight the feature of the standard definitions missing from the account. Tarski assumes, first of all, that we are interested in a fully interpreted language; this is important to keep in mind. He then assumes that we have, perhaps arbitrarily, divided the primitive constants of the language into two classes, the logical signs and the nonlogical signs. For purposes of example, assume we have a monadic, first-order language with identity and individual constants, and that we are treating all and only the monadic predicates and individual constants as nonlogical. Tarski's next step is to introduce, for each category of nonlogical constant, an infinite collection of variables of the same category, and to define satisfaction for the formulas of the expanded language. For us, this would involve introducing a set of monadic predicate variables and a set of individual variables (which can, but need not, be distinct from the individual variables already in the language), and defining always free, the latter either free or bound.

Suppose now that we have a sentence of our original language which we want to test for logical truth. To fix ideas, imagine the sentence is the following:

$$(12) \qquad (\forall x)ODD(x) \rightarrow ODD(2).$$

According to the procedure set out by Tarski, we start by uniformly replacing the nonlogical constants in the sentence with new variables. Given our choice of logical constants, this will result in the following open sentence of the expanded language:

$$(13) \qquad (\forall x)Y(x) \rightarrow Y(z).$$

The original sentence is logically true, according to Tarski's definition, just in case the corresponding formula is satisfied by all sequences. In our example, this will indeed be the case, for any assignment of a set to 'Y' and an individual to 'z' will either satisfy '$Y(z)$' or else fail to satisfy '$(\forall x)Y(x)$'. This is just to say, of course, that the second-order sentence,

$$(14) \qquad (\forall Y)(\forall z)[(\forall x)Y(x) \rightarrow Y(z)]$$

happens to be true. This will hold quite generally: if the universal closure of the formula is true, then the original sentence will, by Tarski's definition, be logically true.

Tarski's account of logical consequence is the obvious analogue of the above. To check whether a sentence φ is a logical consequence of a set Σ of sentences, we first substitute variables for nonlogical constants, guaranteeing uniformity throughout, and then see whether every sequence that satisfies each formula in the resulting set Σ' also satisfies the formula φ' resulting from φ. If so, φ is a consequence of Σ; if not, not.

Before getting to the principal point of divergence, let me remark first on an inessential difference between Tarski's account and the standard model-theoretic definitions. In the procedure described here, there is no mention of providing new interpretations of any expressions in the language. Throughout, all constants have fixed interpretations, and all variables act as ordinary variables. We did not reinterpret the predicate 'ODD', assigning it various extensions, but rather bodily replaced it with the variable 'Y', which was then assigned different values by different sequences. Yet obviously, the effect of reinterpreting 'ODD' on the truth of (12) will precisely parallel the effect of assigning values to 'Y' on the satisfaction of (13). Indeed, we might see the technique of assigning alternative extensions to predicate constants as a simple shortcut for Tarski's replacement of these with variables, the constants merely acting as variables of convenience. Personally, I prefer Tarski's more cumbersome procedure, since it is less likely to be misunderstood; but for now, I just point out that this particular difference is not substantive.

It does not matter whether we talk about the truth of (12) under various interpretations of the nonlogical constants, or the satisfaction of (13) by various sequences. Nevertheless, there remains a significant difference between Tarski's definitions and the standard ones. For the standard account, besides requiring that we canvass all reinterpretations of the nonlogical constants, also requires that we vary the domain of quantification. However, as long as the quantifiers are treated as logical constants, Tarski's analysis always leaves the domain of quantification fixed. Because of this, sentences like (15) will come out logically true on Tarski's account:

$$(15) \qquad (\exists x)(\exists y)(x \neq y).$$

This simply because on the present selection of logical constants, there are no nonlogical constants in the sentence to replace with variables. Thus, such sentences are logically true just in case they happen to be true; true, of course, on the intended interpretation.

Now nothing in Tarski's account precludes our treating the quantifiers as nonlogical constants. But this move will not make his definitions agree with the standard ones, either. Basically, the problem is that the Tarskian analysis only allows for independent variations in our interpretation of the chosen nonlogical constants, while the model-theoretic account introduces a crucial dependence between the domain of quantification and the interpretation of the other parameters: the interpretation of the latter must always be drawn from within the chosen domain. This may seem a perfectly natural requirement, but from the Tarskian perspective the restriction is as unmotivated as imposing joint constraints on the interpretations of, say, two different predicates, or perhaps a predicate and an individual constant. Yet without this dependence, Tarski's definitions will never yield standard results, even when the quantifiers are treated as nonlogical constants.[16]

Now it may well strike us as puzzling that, in 1936, Tarski should suggest definitions of logical truth and logical consequence at odds with the standard conception. For one thing, he could hardly have overlooked the fact that if we accept his definitions, Gödel's completeness theorem can no longer be thought of as demonstrating "completeness." That is, if Tarski's account of the logical notions is correct, what Gödel showed is not that the derivability relation coincides with the genuine consequence relation, or that every logical truth is provable in the standard calculus. Indeed, according to Tarski's account, the semantic and syntactic notions are simply not coextensive; witness the fact that (15) and its ilk are not derivable in any standard calculus. Further, the failure of coincidence is not dependent on our choice of logical constants; no choice will produce a consequence relation extensionally equivalent to the syntactically defined relation.

To add further to the puzzle, we need only look back at Tarski's monograph on truth. We have seen that what appears to be missing from the 1936 account is variation in the domain of quantification. Yet in the monograph on truth, Tarski explicitly defines, for the language of class theory, the notion of a "true sentence in the individual domain a" for variable a – a concept he describes as important to "the Göttingen school grouped around Hilbert." He then embarks on an extended discussion of results that can be proven about sentences of class theory that come out true in every individual domain. Here, Tarski is concerned with the effect of changing one parameter of an interpreted language: the domain of individuals. But throughout this treatment, the interpretation of the predicates of the language remains fixed; Tarski does not reinterpret the nonlogical constants as he moves from domain to domain.

We can think of the standard, model-theoretic analysis of the logical notions as involving two features, variation in the domain of quantification and reinterpretation of the nonlogical constants. In various places, Tarski gave explicit treatments of both of these notions: the first he treated extensively in the monograph on truth; the second is, in effect, the technique used to define the logical notions in his 1936 article. The standard account results from putting these two featurs together in a particular way, and that is precisely what Tarski did not do. This in spite of the fact that he could not have failed to notice the divergence of his analysis from that presupposed by Bernays, Hilbert, Gödel and others.

Tarski's motivation

To understand why Tarski did not come up with definitions equivalent to the standard ones, it is important to appreciate the motivation that led to his 1936 account. Tarski emphasizes that his goal is to give a definition of logical consequence that captures, as far as possible, the "essentials" of our ordinary concept. His goal is, in other words, analysis. But his statement of dissatisfaction with earlier definitions is revealing. As is clear from the following passage, he begins addressing his objections to the common syntactic characterizations of the consequence relation:

[U]ntil recently many logicians believed that they had succeeded, by means of a relatively meagre stock of concepts, in grasping almost exactly the content of the common concept of consequence, or rather in defining a new concept which coincided in extent with the common one. [According to these logicians] the proof of every theorem reduces to single or repeated application of some simple rules of inference – such as the rules of substitution and detachment.... Whenever a sentence follows from others, it can be obtained from them – so it was thought – in more or less complicated ways by means of the transformations prescribed by the rules. In order to defend this view against sceptics who doubted whether the concept of consequence when formalized in this way really coincided in extent with the common one, the logicians were able to bring forward a weighty argument: the fact that they had actually succeeded in reproducing in the shape of formalized proofs all the exact reasonings which had ever been carried out in mathematics. [56^m, p. 409]

Note that Tarski specifically raises the issue of justifying the extensional adequacy of proof-theoretic characterizations of logical consequence. But note the striking omission of any mention of Gödel's completeness theorem, by most lights the "experimental" evidence for completeness. The reason for the omission, though, soon becomes clear. For Tarski goes on to say that we now know the standard syntactic characterizations of consequence *do not* coincide in extent with the "proper" concept of logical consequence. He gives two reasons for this claim. First he cites the existence of ω-incomplete theories; as he puts it, theories that contain, for each numeral n, the sentence,

(A_n) n possesses the given property P,

but which do not contain the universal sentence,

(A)   Every natural number possesses the given property P.

Tarski concludes:

This fact seems to me to speak for itself. It shows that the formalized concept of consequence, as it is generally used by mathematical logicians, by no means coincides with the common concept. Yet intuitively it seems certain that the universal sentence A follows in the usual sense from the totality of particular sentences $A_0, A_1, \ldots, A_n, \ldots$. Provided all these sentences are true, the sentence A must also be true. [56^m, pp. 410–11]

Tarski's second reason is meant to block the suggestion that the syntactic definition of consequence simply be supplemented with a formalized version of the ω-rule, a rule that would allow derivations of A from sentences asserting the provability of the A_n. Although such a rule "would not deviate essentially" from more familiar rules, the addition would be futile, Tarski says, thanks to Gödel's incompleteness results:

In every deductive theory (apart from certain theories of a particularly elementary nature), however much we supplement the ordinary rules of inference by new purely structural rules, it is possible to construct sentences which follow, in the usual sense, from the theorems of this theory, but which nevertheless cannot be proved in this theory on the basis of the accepted rules of inference. [56^m, p. 412]

Tarski's point is that the Gödel sentence for a given theory should be judged a logical consequence of that theory: after all, it cannot be false if the sentences of the theory are all true. Yet there can be no fixed, proof-theoretic characterization of consequence that will, for every first-order theory, allow derivations of the corresponding Gödel sentence.[17]

Whether or not we agree with his interpretation of the incompleteness results, it should be abundantly clear from these examples that Tarski did not think the existing syntactic accounts of consequence were even correct *in extension*. That is, in Tarski's view, standard deductive systems *do not*, and natural extensions of them *cannot*, capture the logical consequence relation *even restricted to first-order languages*. In this case Gödel's completeness theorem, by demonstrating the equivalence of the syntactic and model-theoretic accounts, does not show that the syntactic accounts are extensionally adequate. Rather it shows that the standard model-theoretic definition is equally *inadequate*. In particular, on Tarski's view the standard account cannot possibly capture our intuitive concept of logical consequence; it cannot possibly be an acceptable analysis of that notion.

Not only is Tarski's 1936 account of logical consequence not equivalent to the model-theoretic definition, he clearly avoided such an account with open eyes. I will not here try to assess the analysis he actually gave, or for that matter the competing model-theoretic analysis; elsewhere, I have argued that neither is adequate.[18] But two questions should surely be addressed, if only briefly. The first concerns the 1936 account directly: How did Tarski see his own definition of consequence avoiding the very same objections he leveled against the competing definitions? Why shouldn't ω-incompleteness, or the Gödel sentences, also present problems for *his* analysis? The second question has to do with the apparent change in Tarski's viewpoint between 1936 and 1953. As I indicated earlier, in [53^m] Tarski employs the standard, model-theoretic definition of logical consequence. What led him to give up the earlier analysis in favor of definitions subject to the very same objections raised in his earlier paper?

The answer to the first question lies in the flexibility Tarski allows in our choice of "logical" constants. Clearly, if we choose to treat the numerals '0', '1', '2', ..., as logical constants, as well as the quantifier 'every natural number', then sentence A will come out a consequence of the infinite sentences $A_0, A_1, A_2, \ldots$; after all, any set that contains each natural number contains every natural number. Gödel sentences are a bit trickier, due to their potential variety: all we can really say is that they will indeed come out as consequences of their corresponding theories if we treat all expressions in the language as logical constants. Unfortunately, this involves a certain trivialization of Tarski's analysis. For with this choice of logical constants, a true sentence is a logical consequence of *any* set of sentences whatsoever.

This in fact points up a serious weakness in Tarski's account. It is clear that any given instance of the intuitive consequence relation can be made out to be a "Tarskian" consequence, at least on some selection of logical constants. But as soon as we extend this selection beyond the standard constants we also introduce many Tarskian consequences that are *not* instances of the intuitive relation.[19] Thus although we can avoid, in a piecemeal way, any specific objection that the definition is too restrictive – by just adding more expressions to the list of logical constants – the effect of doing so is invariably a relation far more extensive than the intuitive consequence relation. There seems to be no *single* choice of logical constants that is neither too restrictive nor too permissive.

How about our second question? Tarski was surely aware of the above flaw in his 1936 definitions, and it was no doubt partly responsible for his later giving them up. But this in itself does not explain why he subsequently came to *endorse* the standard account, in spite of the considerations

raised in the earlier article. Unfortunately there is very little to go on here, since Tarski never again addressed the philosophical issues raised in the 1936 article. Indeed in his introductory logic text [41^m], although he discusses similar issues in some detail, there is no mention at all of analyzing logical truth or logical consequence semantically. Instead he seems to offer a syntactic gloss of the consequence relation (pp. 118–19), perhaps a sign of his dissatisfaction with the 1936 definitions. Then later, when he gives the standard model-theoretic definitions in [53^m], he says nothing about the divergence of these definitions from the earlier account.

One relevant factor here may have been his frequent meetings with Carnap and Quine, during the 1940–1 academic year, to discuss logical truth, analyticity, and related topics. Both Carnap and Quine report that in these discussions Tarski joined Quine in attacking Carnap's reliance on the analytic/synthetic distinction.[20] It may well be that Tarski also joined Quine in drawing a sharp distinction between the notions of logical consequence and analytic entailment, where the former is given something like the model-theoretic analysis, while the latter is thought to inherit the alleged obscurity involved in the notion of analyticity. If so, the objections Tarski raised in his 1936 article could be set aside as involving analytic entailment, not logical consequence at all. This would have cleared the way for Tarski's subsequent endorsement of the standard account. But this is only speculation.

Logical consequence vs. logical truth

Tarski was a proponent of a semantic analysis of the concepts of logical truth and logical consequence. He was also one of the most influential forces in establishing model theory as an independent discipline. But it is inaccurate to attribute to him the model-theoretic definitions of the logical notions, both for historical reasons and to do justice to the philosophical concerns he addressed in the 1936 article, concerns that count against the standard semantic analysis as well as its syntactic counterparts. Personally, I think these concerns have never been dealt with adequately, but to discuss them further would lead us beyond Tarski's own contribution to the subject. There is, though, an important way in which Tarski's views about logical truth and logical consequence have had a substantial effect on the modern view of logic, and our discussion would not be complete if it were left unmentioned. The effect is somewhat more subtle, and concerns a change in emphasis between the notions of logical truth and logical consequence, but it carries with it an attendant change in our conception of what logic is all about.

Throughout much of this century, the predominant conception of logic was one inherited from Frege and Russell, a conception according to which the primary subject of logic, like the primary subject of arithmetic or geometry, was a particular body of truths: logical truths in the former case, arithmetical or geometric in the latter. This conception grew naturally out of the syntactic, and specifically *axiomatic*, treatment of logic adopted by these authors. From the axiomatic perspective all deductive disciplines proceed in exactly the same way: we begin by assuming, without proof, various truths of the given sort, and then derive other truths as consequences of these initial assumptions. Because of this, it it natural to think of the derived truths as logically dependent on the axioms that allow their derivation, and to see the goal of formalization, whether of logic or of some other mathematical discipline, as the discovery of axioms sufficient to yield the entirety of the body of truths in question.

This conception of logic now strikes us as rather odd, indeed as something of an anomaly in the history of logic. We no longer view logic as having a body of truths, the logical truths, as its principal concern; we do not, in this respect, think of it as parallel to other mathematical disciplines. If anything, we think of the consequence relation itself as the primary subject of logic, and view logical truth as simply the degenerate instance of this relation: logical truths are those that follow from *any* set of assumptions whatsoever, or alternatively, from no assumptions at all. In particular, they are not dependent on a set of peculiarly logical axioms. This distinction between logic, as concerned with consequence or deduction in general, and other deductive disciplines, concerned with specific truths, is difficult to draw from the axiomatic perspective. It also conflicts with the logicist's philosophical doctrine that mathematics and logic are one and the same, though the main features of this earlier conception extended far beyond the logicist camp.

There are several distinctive features that set our current view apart from the Frege-Russell conception, all closely related. First, and most obvious, is the emphasis on the consequence rela-

tion, and corresponding de-emphasis of the notion of logical truth. Second, there is the particular view of the relation between logical truth and logical consequence, according to which the former is simply a degenerate instance of the latter. Finally, there is the view that logic is not just another theory on a par with arithmetic or geometry, one dealing with its own distinctive body of truths, but rather a metadiscipline concerned with deductive theories in general. All of these are consistent and recurring themes in Tarski's work.

Consider, for example, the emphasis on logical consequence over logical truth. We find this emphasis in virtually all of Tarski's treatments of these notions, from the earliest syntactic accounts to the later semantic analyses. I remarked earlier that in [30c] and [30e], Tarski employs the single primitive Cn, which takes a set of sentences to the set of its logical consequences, and that he defines logical truth in terms of this notion. I did not, however, mention the content of this definition, which is quite striking. For even in these early papers he defines the logical truths as the members of $Cn(\emptyset)$, as the limiting case of the consequence relation. This definition may seem perfectly obvious from our present perspective, but recall that in these papers Tarski presupposes a traditional syntactic account of the consequence relation, describing $Cn(X)$ as the set of sentences that can be derived from X by means of rules of inference. Thus this characterization of logical truth involves a subtle, and distinctly non-Russellian, contrast between the status of logical and nonlogical axioms: the former must themselves be construed as *rules of inference*, as part of the mechanism of deduction itself, while the latter are seen as genuine premises or assumptions on which their consequences depend. This distinction is now easily motivated by the semantic account of the logical notions, as well as the various non-axiomatically-based deductive systems later devised by Jaśkowski, Gentzen and others. But at the time of these papers the distinction was unusual.[21]

Tarski continues to emphasize logical consequence over logical truth in his later, semantic account, and to define the latter as a degenerate version of the former: indeed the emphasis is already apparent from the title of the 1936 paper, *Über den Begriff der logischen Folgerung*. Of course we might well assume that taking logical truth as the limiting case of consequence became completely natural once the semantic perspective was adopted, but in fact Tarski's approach here is in marked contrast to other authors who gave semantic accounts during that period. Without exception, these authors adopt precisely the opposite approach: they first define logical truth and then, if they offer an explicit account of consequence at all, they do so by reducing it to the logical truth of the corresponding conditional.[22] The modern, Tarskian approach did not become common practice until well into the fifties, a quarter century after the emergence of the semantic viewpoint.

It would be hard to canvass all the various ways in which Tarski's work led to this realignment of the modern conception of logic, and certainly there were many other influences that contributed to the ultimate rejection of the Frege-Russell perspective. But let me conclude by discussing one thing that seems quite revealing of this change in viewpoint: the evolution of our intuitive understanding of Gödel's completeness theorem. It is now common to present the completeness theorem along the lines described in §2.1, according to which its main intuitive content concerns the coincidence of syntactic and semantic characterizations of the consequence relation. On this reading, the natural way to state the theorem is the following, where Σ is an arbitrary, possibly infinite set of sentences:

(16)   If $\Sigma \models \varphi$ then $\Sigma \vdash \varphi$.

What is not widely recognized is that this is a relatively late construal of Gödel's results, indeed one that seems, not surprisingly, to have originated with Tarski in [53^m, pp. 8–9]. Prior to this, the results were presented in one of two forms. The first derived its interest directly from the Frege-Russell conception of logic, and the question of whether the chosen logical axioms had as consequences the entire body of truths in question. Gödel's own descriptions of his first result take this form:

> When one provides an axiomatic foundation for logic, as, for example, is done in *Principia mathematica*, the question arises whether the axioms initially adopted are "complete," that is, whether they actually suffice for the formal deduction of every correct proposition of logic.[23]

What Gödel is describing here is sometimes called the "weak" completeness theorem, which we would now state as a reduced version of (16):

(17)   If $\models \varphi$ then $\vdash \varphi$.

In a sense, though, (17) obscures the intuitive reading Gödel gives the result, a reading that would be more faithfully captured by the following, where 'PM' denotes the logical axioms of the *Principia*:

(17′) If φ is a logical truth, then PM $\vdash \varphi$.

What this statement emphasizes is that from Gödel's point of view the result addresses precisely the same question as his later incompleteness theorem, though of course about a different "body of truths" and a different set of axioms. (17′) guarantees that all first-order *logical* truths can indeed be derived from the *Principia* axioms, while the incompleteness result shows that, in contrast, there are first-order *arithmetical* truths that are not derivable from the Peano axioms.

The weak completeness theorem is not equivalent to (16), since Σ may contain an infinite number of sentences. But Gödel did prove a version of the theorem equivalent to (16) for countable languages. However neither he, nor anyone else at the time, stated that theorem in the form later suggested by Tarski, as a justification of the extensional adequacy of the syntactic characterization of consequence. Instead, the following formulation was used:

(18)   If Σ is (syntactically) consistent, then Σ has a model.

Though this is equivalent to (16), the early interest in this formulation had nothing to do with its relation to the notion of semantic consequence. Rather it was seen as a partial response to a criticism of Hilbert made first by Frege and later by Brouwer. The criticism had to do with whether the syntactic consistency of an uninterpreted theory was sufficient to guarantee that the theory was realizable, and hence could, as Hilbert suggested, be a substitute for truth in the mathematical domain. From that perspective, the result is more aptly described as a *model existence* theorem, rather than a *completeness* theorem, and its intuitive interest is strikingly different from that of (16).

What delayed the reformulation of (18) into (16) for so long? There are two reasons, both of which should by now be apparent. On the one hand, Tarski had given a semantic account of consequence that was independent of logical truth, but as we have seen his account was not equivalent to the model-theoretic definition required to get from (18) to (16). But on the other hand, all other authors who analyzed consequence semantically did so *through* the notion of logical truth, which from the Frege-Russell perspective took priority. Because of this, even when the intuitive question addressed by (16) was raised, it could only be approached indirectly. Indeed in the second edition of Hilbert and Ackermann's text, the authors specifically ask whether every intuitive consequence of an arbitrary set of first-order sentences is derivable – exactly the question that (16), or (18), is thought to answer:

> We will examine...the question of whether every statement which would intuitively be regarded as a consequence of [an arbitrary system of axioms] can be obtained from them by means of the formal method of derivation. [1950, p. 107]

Ultimately Hilbert and Ackermann conclude that Gödel's completeness theorem does indeed yield a positive answer to this question:

> We can [thus] say that any consequence of an axiom system of the first order can also be derived from it by means of the formal method of derivation set forth at the beginning of this section. [ibid., p. 112]

What is revealing here is the way they arrive at this conclusion. First they assume that the "axiom system" in question is *finite*, and hence that for any intuitive consequence β of the axioms $\alpha_1, \ldots, \alpha_n$, the following will be a logical truth:

$$\alpha_1 \wedge \ldots \wedge \alpha_n \to \beta.$$

They then appeal to (17') – not (18)! – to conclude that this conditional is derivable in the system, and hence that its consequent will be as well, by detachment. Thus even when the right question was asked – the question of the *general* adequacy of our deductive technique – the answer proceeded in the wrong way, through weak completeness and the derivability of a specific logical truth. This of course could never give the full justification offered by (16). For that, we needed Tarski's emphasis on the priority and independence of the consequence relation, combined with the standard model-theoretic definitions of the logical notions.

This is just one example of how Tarski's understanding of the relation between logical consequence and logical truth, and his perspective on the scope and concerns of the discipline of logic, have become part and parcel of our present conception of the subject. As we have seen, his contribution to that conception is perhaps more subtle, but also more global in nature, than is frequently supposed. Indeed, it would be hard to overestimate the importance of Tarski's influence on our current perspective, an influence marked throughout by extraordinary foresight, conceptual clarity, and sensitivity to philosophical and foundational issues.

Notes

My work on this paper was made possible in part by a grant from the System Development Foundation; it was completed at the Center for the Study of Language and Information on computer equipment provided by the Xerox Corporation. My understanding of Tarski's work on truth has benefitted from discussions with many people, in particular, Jon Barwise and Scott Soames; helpful comments on an earlier draft of this paper were received from Jon Barwise, Ned Block, Wilfrid Hodges, David Israel, Julius Moravscik, Patrick Suppes, Anthony Ungar and the referee. I would like to thank both the institutions and the colleagues.

1 The expression "formal semantics" is a rather unfortunate one, for a couple of reasons: first, the semantic theories so called are rarely, if ever, presented in anything approximating axiomatic form, and second, the Hilbertian connotations of the adjective give the expression an anomalous air. Presumably, the term is meant to contrast with "informal" or "nonmathematical" treatments of semantics.

2 Tarski actually gives just such a treatment for what he calls "languages of infinite order", and proves the consistency of the resulting theory (interestingly, using a "compactness" style argument). He resorts to such a treatment because at the time of publication of the Polish monograph he was unwilling to countenance languages of transfinite order, and so was convinced that truth was *absolutely* undefinable for languages of order ω. In the postscript added to the German edition, he remarks that this unwillingness was mistaken, and endorses what is now con-

sidered the proper understanding of the undefinability result.

3 In a footnote to §1 of his monograph, where schema T first appears, Tarski remarks that most of the discussion in that section derives from unpublished lectures given by Leśniewski. Perhaps because of this remark – Leśniewski's lecture notes were destroyed in 1944 – it has been suggested that Leśniewski, rather than Tarski, was the originator of the criterion of adequacy expressed in Convention T. (This suggestion has been made, for example, by Luschei [1962, p. 33].) But elsewhere, Tarski explicitly denies this:

> Leśniewski did not anticipate the possibility of a rigorous development of the theory of truth, and still less of a definition of this notion; hence, while indicating equivalences of the form (T) as premisses in the antinomy of the liar, he did not conceive them as any sufficient conditions for an adequate usage (or definition) of the notion of truth. [44a, p. 371, n. 7]

Tarski's debt to Leśniewski in §1 of the monograph seems to have been primarily in the account of the liar paradox (though he credits Łukasiewicz for the specific formulation of the paradox) and in the discussion of quotation.

4 Tarski did not entertain the possibility of infinitary languages at all in the monograph on truth; much later, he studied the properties of such languages, though not in connection with defining truth. See, for example, [58], [58^a], [58a] and [61^aa].

5 In the early years of truth-conditional (or "Davidsonian") semantics, the stated goal was to provide a Tarskian definition of truth for the language whose semantic properties were to be studied. (See Davidson [1967].) An argument frequently used by Davidson and others to justify this as the proper goal of a semantic theory was that the instances of schema T which followed from the definition can be thought of as characterizing the fluent speaker's semantic knowledge: the idea was that to know the meaning of 'S' is just to know what is expressed by (4). But this argument involved a confusion, for as we have seen, we can know what is expressed by (4') – which is, after all, the relevant instance of the schema – without knowing anything about the meaning of 'S'. Most proponents of truth-conditional semantics now see their goal somewhat differently, partly due to this realization.

6 When dealing with a formal language, it may seem more natural to think of (6), (7) and the like as *conventionally specifying* the meanings of the respective symbols, rather than as claims about pre-existing meanings. Thus logicians frequently speak of a definition of truth (or a definition of truth in a model) as *giving* the semantics of the language. I will continue to speak of them as *claims*, though all my remarks will apply equally on the alternative construal. Defining a set of sentences, or a relation between sentences and models, in itself does absolutely nothing toward fixing the meanings of expressions in the language.

7 The difference between these two styles of definition has frequently been misdiagnosed. For example in [1972], Hartry Field takes Tarski's aim to be the reduction of the semantic concept of truth to concepts acceptable to a physicalist, and argues that he is only partially successful in achieving this goal. According to Field, Tarski successfully reduces truth to the notion of "primitive denotation", the relationship that holds between names and their denotation, predicates and their extensions, and function symbols and their graphs. Field considers Tarski's treatment of primitive denotation inadequate, however, since the treatment is simply to give a list-like definition of the relationship; on Field's view, an adequate account of primitive denotation would have to bring in those facts about the linguistic community in virtue of which this denotation relation holds. The problem with Field's view, as Scott Soames points out in [1984], is that if we apply this criterion, the reduction of truth to primitive denotation is equally inadequate, since it offers no illumination concerning the facts in virtue of which, say, 'and' means *and*.

Where Field was misled, it seems, is in thinking that the source of the perceived difference between recursive and list-like definitions has to do with a reduction of semantic facts to facts in virtue of which those semantic facts hold. But the perceived difference has nothing to do with such a reduction, and indeed arises only in claims involving the unreduced notion of truth.

8 Hilary Putnam makes this point in [1985], and it is on this basis that he concludes that Tarski's account "fails as badly as it is possible for an account to fail." This is, to say the least, an overreaction to an otherwise sound observation: Tarski's definition does not provide an analysis of one important conception of truth. If we assume that this was his goal, and further that this is the only such project of philosophical interest, then we would be justified in concluding both that he had failed and that the definition was only of technical interest. But both assumptions are obviously incorrect.

9 In [1984], Soames suggests that the fact that instances of schema T such as (4'') are not contingent might seem less objectionable if we construe languages as abstract objects "bearing their semantic properties essentially." The idea is that on this construal of a language, had 'S' not meant that it is snowing, it would not have been a sentence in the language whose truth predicate we have just defined. Thus (4'') is indeed a necessary truth, but

on the suggested conception of a language, so is (4), at least if we read "is true" as "is a true sentence of *L*." Still, (4″) is true simply due to facts of logic, syntax and set theory, and these are presumably quite different from the semantic facts underlying (4), even on this conception of a language. Soames, I think, would agree, since he recognizes that (4″) is independent of the meaning of '*S*'.

10 There is, of course, something odd about (10), in that we would not be in a position to extract this information if we did not already understand the very sentence in question, it appearing on the right-hand side of the biconditional as well as the left. But this does not affect the substantive claim made by (10); it merely explains why instances of scheme T appear more illuminating when the object language is not identical with, and so must be translated into, the metalanguage. In this regard it is helpful to recall that the translation of (10) into, say, German would be "Die Aussage 'Snow is white' ist wahr dann und nur dann, wenn Schnee weiß ist." (10) is a claim *about* an English sentence which happens also to be made *in* English.

11 Tarski may have been aware of these deviations. For instance, in [44a] we find several disclaimers in the following vein:

> I clearly realize ... that the common meaning of the word "*true*" – as that of any other word of everyday language – is to some extent vague, and that its usage more or less fluctuates. Hence the problem of assigning to this word a fixed and exact meaning is relatively unspecified, and every solution of this problem implies necessarily

a certain deviation from the practice of everyday language. [44a, p. 360]

12 See Vaught [1986] for a discussion of the results presented in these papers.

13 The translation is from [56ᵐ, p. 30]. See also [56ᵐ, p. 63].

14 See, for example, [56ᵐ, p. 252n, and pp. 259ff.].

15 See Feferman [1984] for a discussion of pre-Tarskian appeals to the notion of truth.

16 For a more detailed discussion of this problem, see my [1982].

17 Of course, to make good on this claim we would have to be more precise about what constitutes an acceptable "proof-theoretic" characterization of consequence, that is, what kind of rule is "purely structural," as Tarski puts it. Presumably, Tarski had in mind some requirement of effectiveness, or perhaps arithmetical definability.

18 See my [1982] and [1983].

19 This problem actually comes up even with the standard selection of logical constants. Note, for instance, that on Tarski's account (15) is a logical consequence of any set of sentences, as long as '∃', '¬' and '=' are treated as logical constants.

20 See Carnap's autobiographical essay in Schilpp [1963, pp. 63 ff.], and Quine [1985, pp. 149 ff.].

21 It is possible that Tarski was influenced here by the early, unpublished work of Jaśkowski. See Prawitz [1965, p. 98], for a discussion of the history of natural deduction.

22 See, for example, the second edition of Hilbert and Ackermann [1928], in particular Chapter III, §11.

23 [1930a], translated in [1986, p. 125]. See also [1929] and [1930] for similar characterizations.

References

For publications by Tarski, see the *Bibliography of Alfred Tarski*, *Journal of Symbolic Logic*, vol. 51 (1986), pp. 913–41. Publications of other authors are listed below.

Paul Bernays [1922] Review of a paper by Behmann, *Jahrbuch über die Fortschritte der Mathematik*, vol. 48, pp. 1119–20.

Donald Davidson [1967] Truth and meaning, *Synthese*, vol. 17, pp. 304–23.

John Etchemendy [1982] *Tarski, model theory and logical truth*, University Microfilms, Ann Arbor, Michigan.

——[1983] The doctrine of logic as form, *Linguistics and Philosophy*, vol. 6, pp. 319–34.

Solomon Feferman [1984] Kurt Gödel: conviction and caution, *Philosophia Naturalis*, vol. 21, pp. 546–62.

Hartry Field [1972] Tarski's theory of truth, *Journal of Philosophy*, vol. 69, pp. 347–75.

Kurt Gödel [1929] Über die Vollständigkeit des Logik-kalküls, Doctoral dissertation, University of Vienna; reprinted, with translation, in Gödel [1986].

——[1930] Die Vollständigkeit der Axiome des logischen Funktionenkalküts, *Monatshefte für Mathematik und Physik*, vol. 37, pp. 349–60; reprinted, with translation, in Gödel [1986].

——[1930a] Über die Vollständigkeit des Logikkalküls (Abstract), *Die Naturwissenschaften*, vol. 18, p. 1068; reprinted, with translation, in Gödel [1986].

——[1986] *Collected works*. Vol. I, Clarendon Press, Oxford, 1986.

Leon Henkin [1949] The completeness of the first-order functional calculus, *Journal of Symbolic Logic*, vol. 14, pp. 159–66.

David Hilbert [1929] Probleme der Grundlegung der Mathematik, *Mathematische Annalen*, vol. 102, pp. 1–9.

David Hilbert and Wilhelm Ackermann [1928] *Grundzüge der theoretischen Logik*, Springer-Verlag, Berlin, 1928 (2nd ed., 1938; translated in [1950]).

——[1950] *Principles of mathematical logic*, Chelsea, New York.

John Kemeny [1948] Models of logical systems, *Journal of Symbolic Logic*, vol. 13, pp. 16–30.

Saul Kripke [1975] Outline of a theory of truth, *Journal of Philosophy*, vol. 72, pp. 690–716.

Eugene Luschei [1962] *The logical systems of Leśniewski*, North-Holland, Amsterdam.

Karl Popper [1974] Some philosophical comments on Tarski's theory of truth, *Proceedings of the Tarski symposium*, Proceedings of Symposia in Pure Mathematics, vol. 25, American Mathematical Society, Providence, Rhode Island, pp. 397–409.

Dag Prawitz [1965] *Natural deduction: a proof-theoretical study*, Almqvist & Wiksell, Stockholm.

Hilary Putnam [1985] A comparison of something with something else, *New Literary History*, vol. 17, pp. 61–79.

Willard van Orman Quine [1985] *The time of my life*, MIT Press, Cambridge, Massachusetts.

Paul Schilpp (editor) [1963] *The philosophy of Rudolf Carnap*, Open Court Press, La Salle, Illinois.

Scott Soames [1984] What is a theory of truth? *Journal of Philosophy*, vol. 81, pp. 411–29.

Patrick Suppes [1988] Philosophical implications of Tarski's work, *Journal of Symbolic Logic*, vol. 53, pp. 80–91.

Robert Vaught [1986] Alfred Tarski's work in model theory, *Journal of Symbolic Logic*, vol. 51, pp. 869–82.

PART V

Modality, Intensionality, and Propositional Attitude

Introduction to Part V

The concept of a mode of a proposition was recognized already in medieval logic. Modal logic is a formalization of the ways in which the truth value of a proposition can be qualified. The proposition, 'It is raining,' may be true or false. Whatever its truth value, we can say, for example, 'It is possible that it is raining,' 'It is necessary that it is raining,' 'It is possible but not necessary that it is raining,' 'It is impossible that it is raining,' and so on. These qualifications are made in alethic modal logic, concerning the logical modalities of necessity and possibility. It is also possible to qualify the truth value of such a sentence by many other kinds of modalities, including deontic modalities of moral obligation and permission, doxastic modalities of belief and doubt, epistemic modalities concerning concepts of knowledge and ignorance, and temporal modalities in the logic of time.

Although formal systems of alethic modality were developed relatively early in the twentieth century, they were not given an exact formal interpretation until the 1950s, when Jaakko Hintikka and Saul A. Kripke independently presented model set theoretical semantics for modal logic. The idea of this powerful semantic method is to specify a set of complete and consistent sets of propositions, complete in the sense that for every proposition either the proposition or its negation is included in the set, and consistent in the sense that no set contains both a proposition and its negation. Each complete and consistent set of propositions is said either to be or less controversially to describe a distinct logically possible world, or a way in which the world might have been, including the actual world as the realiza-

tion of one possibility. A logically necessary proposition is interpreted as one that holds true in every logically possible world, and a logically possible proposition is interpreted as one that holds true in at least one logically possible world.

Logical necessity and logical possibility are interpreted as interderivable in a duality relation. A proposition is logically necessarily true if and only if it is not logically possible that the proposition is not true. From this it also follows that a proposition is logically possibly true if and only if it is not logically necessary that the proposition is not true. Predicate and quantified modal logic is interpreted in a more complicated fashion by considering the objects that exist in different logically possible worlds, and formally specifying different types of accessibility relations between the propositions about such objects that hold true in each world. Weak accessibility relations limit accessibility to reflexivity, where each world is accessible only to itself; adventurous systems extend accessibility to other worlds for the interpretation of iterated modalities and quantified modalities by means of symmetric, transitive, and more specialized kinds of relations. Other, nonalethic, modal logics are similarly defined and interpreted for special modal operators symbolizing deontic, doxastic, epistemic, temporal, and even more exotic modalities.

Modal logics have been widely used in a variety of analytic contexts, representing philosophical relations and clarifying and solving philosophical problems. They have also been responsible for raising philosophical difficulties of their own. The very idea of a modal logic has been seen as problematic. Some philosophers have not wanted to deny the fact that the truth values of certain propositions can be modally qualified, but they have questioned whether modal qualifications can be formalized in a system that deserves to be called a logic in the true sense of the word. The problem is that modal logics are said to be intensional, in that they involve logical and linguistic contexts that do not support the intersubstitution of coreferential terms and logically equivalent subpropositions *salva veritate*, preserving the truth values of the propositions in which the substitutions are made. A famous example that has had a significant influence in philosophical discussions especially of quantified modal logic is Willard Van Orman Quine's argument that: 'Necessarily, 9 is greater than 6; the number of planets is 9; therefore, necessarily, the number of planets is greater than 6.' The assumptions are true, but the conclusion, which results from substituting 'the number of planets' in the second assumption for '9' in the first assumption, happens to be false. The implication is supposed to be that modal contexts are referentially opaque or intensional. For logicians like Quine who regard logic as essentially extensional, and who have advocated a 'flight from intension,' the intensionality of modal contexts disqualifies them as unformalizable in a genuine logic. Quine has recently modified his opposition to modal logics and quantified modal logics, but for many other logicians there remains an air of suspicion about whether or not modal formalisms are really logics on a par with classical logical systems.

The fact that a virtually unlimited variety of distinct axioms and corresponding accessibility relations in model set theoretical semantics results in a huge plurality of modal logics is another source of philosophical doubts about the legitimacy of modal logic. The ontological status of logically possible worlds, even when these are interpreted only as maximally complete and consistent sets of propositions, also call the philosophical status of modal logic into question. There are also philosophical concerns about the requirements of transworld identity, of the sameness of objects from one logically possible world to another. If it is possible for objects to be different than they happen to be in the actual world, or in any chosen world, then the same objects could presumably be so different in some worlds that they would be practically impossible to recognize, not only in the sense of defying our ability to determine their identity if we were to encounter them by surveying the individuals that inhabit particular logically possible worlds, but even considered more abstractly in terms of their identity conditions as specified by the properties they have in any particular world. These issues are addressed in essays by John E. Nolt, in asking "What Are Logically Possible Worlds?" and more critically by Quine in "Quantifiers and Propositional Attitudes."

Saul A. Kripke, in his landmark lectures on *Naming and Necessity*, sought to mitigate these difficulties by proposing a different model of modalities. For Kripke, the issue is not how the same object could be recognized in different logically possible worlds as a matter of discovery, but that transworld identity is instead the result of decision or stipulation. We simply stipulate, for example, that in some logically possible world Aristotle never studied with Plato, since, although it is true that Aristotle studied with Plato, it is logically possible that he did not, in the sense that it is logically possible for him to have chosen not to study or was never offered the opportunity of studying with Plato. Kripke's alternative conception of transworld identity is helpful, but not entirely satisfactory. Stipulating that the same object has different properties in some different logically possible worlds goes only so far in accounting for transworld identity, because it does not explain the transworld identity of objects for which no specific stipulation has been made. If we think realistically about there being logical possibilities that no one has ever thought of, then Kripke's modal conceptualist idea of stipulating rather than discovering preexistent transworld identities will not account for all identities of objects across logically possible worlds.

Another solution to the problem with philosophical drawbacks of its own is found in the modal semantics of David Lewis's counterpart theory. Lewis's position here is represented in his chapter, "Counterpart Theory and Quantified Modal Logic," which is intended in part as a reply to Quine. Lewis follows G. W. Leibniz in arguing that strictly speaking different logically possible worlds do not contain identical objects, but only objects that are similar to as counterparts of one another to varying degrees with respect to particular categories of properties. The range of variations is limited by Lewis so as to fall within constraints that can accommodate the intuitive Aristotelian distinction between essential and accidental properties. Lewis's approach to modal logic neatly avoids the dilemmas of transworld identity, but it has impressed some critics as failing to do justice to the intuitive assumption that when we say, for example, that Aristotle might not have studied with Plato we mean that the very same person, Aristotle in the actual world, might not have studied with Plato, in the sense that in some other logically possible world or worlds the very individual who in our world actually studied with Plato in that world did not study with Plato.

Thus, many philosophical difficulties continue to animate ongoing discussion of the advantages and disadvantages of alternative modal logics and semantic and philosophical interpretations of modal logic. The chapters by Dagfinn Føllesdal, on "Interpretation of Quantifiers" and by Ruth Barcan Marcus, offering "A Backward Look at Quine's Animadversions on Modalities," each address the skepticism with which Quine has greeted modal logic and especially quantified modal logic. Føllesdal and Marcus in different ways focus attention on the objection according to which modal contexts do not support intersubstitution of coreferential terms or logically equivalent expressions *salva veritate*. Føllesdal criticizes Hintikka's efforts to formulate a modal logic that avoids the traditional substitutivity axiom of identity, sometimes expressed in the form of Leibniz's law. But Føllesdal also believes that the formulas of quantified modal logic can be formally interpreted as compatible with Quine's thesis that any adequate theory of logical quantifiers must entail Leibniz's intersubstitutivity axiom of identity. He develops the theory formally, and argues that Hintikka's system, although logically consistent, depends on a nonstandard substitutional interpretation of the quantifiers – a conclusion of which Hintikka was no doubt aware, as an advocate of the substitutional interpretation, and which he surely would have seen as vital to a correct theory of quantified modal logic rather than an embarrassment. Føllesdal's point, however, is that such a consequence tends to support Quine's thesis about the relation between quantification and the substitutivity of identity in modal contexts, as opposed to Hintikka's argument that the two are logically independent, as manifested in the details of his quantified modal logic.

Marcus reflects on Quine's quarrels with quantified modal logic. She finds that the discussion Quine generated in his series of attacks on modalities has on the whole been productive. But she takes issue with all of Quine's major conclusions, arguing that some of Quine's objections involving intersubstitution of proper names in modal con-

texts can be avoided by linguistic distinctions between definite descriptions and genuine proper names with fixed reference but lacking lexical meaning, further affirmations of which approach Marcus cites in later theories of direct reference. Marcus notes that as Quine's concerns about intersubtitutivity were dispelled they gave place to his more serious concerns about the essentialism that seemed to be implied by modal logics. The complaint is that essentialism as in Aristotle requires a sorting of properties into two classes, those that are necessary to an object and those that are accidental, which Quine throughout his battle with modalities found inherently problematic. Marcus concludes that the participation of Quine and his targets and critics has had a salutary effect on the evolution of modal logic and its philosophy, but she does not regard Quine as having successfully refuted the formal or philosophical assumptions of modal logic.

Quine's criticisms again set the stage for lively philosophical interaction about modality, the logic of quantifiers, and the problems of quantifying into intensional propositional attitude contexts. Just as intersubstitution of coreferential terms or logically equivalent expressions in some modal contexts are not truth-preserving, so similar intersubstitutions in propositional attitude contexts are intensional or not truth-preserving. If I believe that Mark Twain wrote *Tom Sawyer*, and if Mark Twain is identical to Samuel Clemens, it does not validly follow, upon substituting the name 'Samuel Clemens' for the name 'Mark Twain' in the true statement of my belief, that a true sentence will result of the form, 'I believe that Samuel Clemens wrote *Tom Sawyer*.' I might not believe that this is true, even if in fact it is true that Samuel Clemens wrote this book, because I might not believe that Mark Twain is Samuel Clemens, and I might never have even heard of Samuel Clemens. The problems of quantifying into propositional attitude contexts were first systematically remarked by Quine. Since then, many logicians and philosophers of language and mind have been preoccupied with the analysis of such contexts. The thesis of the intentionality of mind or its 'aboutness' in being directed toward certain objects, is indirectly related to the intensionality of propositional attitude contexts that describe certain states of mind, notably belief and doubt, desire and repulsion, hope and fear, love and hate, and many others. This makes the logic of intensional propositional attitude contexts of major interest to philosophers working in the philosophy of mind, who are curious to know what can and cannot be logically inferred about a subject's psychological states as formulated in intensional statements of intentional propositional attitudes.

David Kaplan's chapter "Quantifying In" is the classic treatment of these themes, taking Quine's original essay on "Quantifiers and Propositional Attitudes" as his point of departure. Kaplan distinguishes a wide variety of cases in ordinary language, which he clarifies and categorizes by means of logical devices with explicit variations of scope. He interprets these contexts in a Fregean fashion in terms of the distinction between sense and reference, and Frege's method of exporting terms from opaque indirect to direct referential positions, in order to avoid Quinean problems of substitutivity failure.

Graeme Forbes's chapter, "Substitutivity and the Coherence of Quantifying In," takes up some of the same issues in offering a different sort of reply to Quine. Forbes rejects the Fregean approach to quantifying in on grounds of inadequacy in cases involving attitude ascriptions. He offers instead what he takes to be a deeper analysis of why substitution fails in objectual and propositional attitude contexts. Finally, through a perceptive consideration of individual cases he recommends a three- rather than two–place analysis of such contexts, in which an attitude applies as a function whose arguments are the subject, the object, and the mode of presentation in which the object is presented to the subject. By appealing in particular to the third of these three factors, Forbes is able to leverage reference to a subject's ways of thinking about a situation-type in order to capitalize on differences in attitude toward identical states of affairs in order to explain substitution failure in cases that are problematic for Frege, Quine, and Kaplan.

Michael Jubien's chapter, "The Intensionality of Ontological Commitment," which closes this selection on modality, intensionality, and propositional attitudes, takes issue with extensional criteria of ontological commitment. Jubien considers ostensible reference to nonexistent objects by two intuitively distinct but equally false scientific theories. If we are to make sense of the fact that the theories are different, then their difference, Jubien argues, cannot be explained extensionally in terms of their making distinct ontological commitments. The reason is that on an extensional interpretation, following similar arguments previously offered by Noam Chomsky and Israel Scheffler, and Richard Cartwright, the theories in question are either ontically committed to the null set in declaring their beliefs, respectively, say, in phlogiston and the aether, neither of which exist, so that the extensions of their predicates in the actual world are both perfectly empty; or they are ontically committed to the universal set, on the grounds that in classical logic by truth table definition every proposition is material implied by a false proposition; or they are ontically committed to an arbitrary existent object. Jubien rejects all three possibilities and concludes that ontological commitment is intensional rather than extensional, that extensional models of ontological commitment are inadequate in such cases. He recommends a solution to the problem in which the theories in question are distinguished on the basis of a Quinean linguistic ascent, holding that the theories in question are distinct by virtue of being ontically committed to the form of the name by which the theories' nonexistent objects are ostensibly designated. Finally, he discusses substitution failure for such applications on his theory that names so interpreted are nonreferential.

Further Reading

Carnap, Rudolf. 1947: *Meaning and Necessity: A Study in Modal Logic.* Chicago: University of Chicago Press.

Chellas, Brian F. 1980: *Modal Logic: An Introduction.* Cambridge: Cambridge University Press.

Forbes, Graeme. 1985: *The Metaphysics of Modality.* Oxford: Oxford University Press.

Hughes, G. E. and Creswell, M. J. 1996: *A New Introduction to Modal Logic.* London: Routledge.

Kripke, Saul A. 1980: *Naming and Necessity.* Cambridge: Harvard University Press.

Lewis, David K. 1973: *Counterfactuals.* Cambridge: Harvard University Press.

Linsky, Leonard. 1971: *Reference and Modality.* Oxford: Oxford University Press.

Marcus, Ruth Barcan. 1993: *Modalities.* New York: Oxford University Press.

Plantinga, Alvin. 1974: *The Nature of Necessity.* Oxford: Oxford University Press.

Richard, Mark. 1990: *Propositional Attitudes: An Essay on Thoughts and How We Ascribe Them.* Cambridge: Cambridge University Press.

20

What are Possible Worlds?

John E. Nolt

My question concerns possible worlds. By 'possible worlds' I mean, quite literally, worlds. Worlds are universes. The most interesting of them are spatiotemporal manifolds in which people live, time passes, and events unfold. Of these one, the actual world, is especially important to us.

What I do not mean by 'possible worlds' are maximal consistent sets of propositions, maximal states of affairs construed as actual but abstract objects, set-theoretic models, or similar mathematical or Platonic structures.[1] Frankly, I don't believe in such things. But whether they exist or not, they do not concern me here.

What do concern me here, however, are possible *worlds*. I don't believe in possible worlds, either – except of course for the actual one. That is, I don't believe they exist. But I do contend that they are possible and that understanding their possibility is a way of understanding what they are. Such is the thesis of this paper.

I hold the same to be true *mutatis mutandis* if for 'world' we substitute such terms as 'situation', 'scenario' or 'state of affairs'. (All of these suggest entities "smaller than" worlds.) Merely possible situations, scenarios, and states of affairs do not exist, but they are possible, and understanding their possibility is a way of understanding what they are. These "smaller" entities, however, will be mentioned only briefly and incidentally in the course of this paper.

John E. Nolt, What are Possible Worlds? *Mind*, 95, 380 (1986): 432–45.

Crucial to the thesis just stated is a distinction between existence and possibility. Consider the statement

(1) It is possible for spacetime to be Newtonian

and its equivalent

(2) A world in which spacetime is Newtonian is possible.

Both are true, provided that the term 'possible' is read in a logical or conceptual sense. (This is the only sense in which 'possible' will be used in this paper.) But many of us have serious reservations about the truth of

(3) A world in which spacetime is Newtonian exists.

(3) says more than either (1) or (2). A sufficient condition for the truth of (1) and (2) is that we can assert without self-contradiction that spacetime is Newtonian. But this is hardly sufficient for (3). (3) says that a Newtonian world exists, and we are reading 'world' literally. The mere consistency of an assertion does not guarantee the existence of a universe in which that assertion is true. Consequently, the mere possibility of a world is something quite distinct from its existence.

It might be objected that since consistency is simply existence of a model, the consistency of a statement *does* entail the existence of a "world" in which it is true.[2] But this objection confuses models with worlds. Newtonian spacetime can be modelled in set theory and perhaps even in some physical systems, but such models are not literally Newtonian universes. Nor does their existence entail the existence of any Newtonian universe. Yet the consistency of a statement does entail the logical possibility of a world in which the statement is true. Hence the conclusion stands: the mere possibility of a world is not the same thing as its existence.

But what does it mean to say that something exists? In plain English 'exists' and 'is actual' are synonymous. Hobbits, for example, do not exist, because they are not actual. Only confusion can result from the rejoinder that they exist as possible hobbits, as if 'possible' were a predicate satisfied simply by some subset of the domain of existing things. On the contrary, the totality of what is possible vastly exceeds the totality of what exists in the ordinary sense of the term. Thus, if we treat 'exists' as a quantifier in the usual way and regard 'is possible' as a predicate, the domain of the quantifier is too narrow to accommodate the full extension of the predicate. If we now expand the domain of quantification to include merely possible objects, we can no longer consistently interpret the quantifier as 'exists', for not all the objects in that domain exist. Rather, the existential quantifier now means 'there is possible' or 'there could be'. Similarly, the universal quantifier does not mean 'for all', where 'all' means 'all that exists'; it means 'for all possible'. Thus, 'is possible' functions not as a predicate, to be applied within the domain of existing things, but as a quantifier whose domain subsumes the domain of existing things.[3]

We are right, then, to have reservations about (3); for either it is straightforwardly false (if 'exists' means 'exists') or it is just a misleading formulation of (2), in which case it would be better to stick with (2) itself.

Nevertheless, some philosophers hold statements like (3) to be true.[4] The reason is simple. There are occasions on which it is both useful and natural to quantify over possible worlds. This is so, for example, when we give truth conditions for the operator '◇':

(4)   ◇p is true iff $\exists x$ (x is a (possible) world & p is true in x).

Now these philosophers, for various reasons, do not want to abandon such quantification. And they assume that quantification entails commitment to the existence of the values of the quantified variables. Hence they conclude that they are committed to the existence of possible worlds.

I agree that quantification of this form should not be abandoned. But I do not think it commits us to the values of the variables. Just writing the backwards 'E', of course, does not commit one to the existence of anything, since it is simply a syntactic form. Only if it is interpreted to mean 'there exists' does it bear an ontological burden. But I have argued that when used to quantify over possibilia, it should be read not as 'there exists', but as 'there is possible' or 'there could be'. Thus the appropriate English rendering of (4) is

(5)   ◇p is true iff there could be x such that x is a world and p is true in x,

not

(6)   ◇p is true iff there exists x such that x is a possible world and p is true in x.

Likewise, the appropriate English rendering of

(7) $\exists x$ (x is a (possible) world & spacetime is Newtonian in x)

is (2), not (3).

This is not to say that when '$\exists$' is used to quantify over possible worlds it should be read as '◇$\exists$'. The '$\exists$' in '◇$\exists$' ranges not over worlds, but over the domains associated with them, and '◇' is in effect an existential quantifier over worlds. But on the interpretation of '$\exists$' that interests me here, '$\exists$' ranges straightforwardly and objectually over worlds themselves; yet it asserts only possibility, not existence, and hence carries no existential commitment. Such an interpretation can be seen to be perfectly intelligible, provided that we can make sense of a simple game of make-believe.

To describe this game, we must make some distinctions. We shall need to consider both those quantifiers that assert existence and those quantifiers that do not. Let us call the existential quantifier that asserts existence, together with its universal dual, *standard quantifiers*. Standard quantifiers are interpreted objectually over domains of existing objects. And let us call the "existential" quantifier over worlds, together with its universal dual, *possibilistic quantifiers*. Possibilistic quantifiers are to be interpreted objectually over a domain of worlds, not all of which exist.

Let us further distinguish two languages, which for our purposes need be characterized only roughly. The first is the language of possibilistic quantification, or *possibilistic language*, whose predicates are predicates of worlds. The second is a standardly quantified language, which we may take to be the set of declarative statements of English, except for those that contain modal operators, possibilistic quantifiers, and other modal locutions. To avoid irrelevancies involving semantic paradox, we shall also omit statements containing such expressions as 'true' and 'satisfies'. For the sake of clarity, we shall sometimes write the sentences of this language semiformally, using regimented notation for quantifiers and connectives. The predicates of this standardly quantified language are typically predicates of individuals, not of worlds. We shall call this language the *descriptive language*.

Now, the only thing that matters in determining whether a world of a certain description is (logically) possible is whether the description itself is consistent. More precisely, what counts as a logically possible world is governed in part by the following rules:

(i) The actual world counts as a possible world.

(ii) If A is a consistent statement (or consistent set of statements) of the descriptive language, then there counts as possible at least one world in which (each member of) A is true.

(iii) If A is an inconsistent statement (or set of statements) of the descriptive language, then no world in which A is true counts as possible.

It is evident that talk about logically possible worlds presupposes these rules. I have used the locution 'counts as possible' to emphasize that rules (i)–(iii) are prescriptive, not descriptive. They are to be read, not as a definition that picks out from among already given worlds those that are possible, but as instructions for playing a game of "make-believe". It is this game that we must understand in order to see what possible worlds are.

An immediate consequence of (iii) is:

(iii') If A and B are consistent statements (or consistent sets of statements) of the descriptive language whose conjunction (union) is inconsistent, then any world in which (each member of) A is true is distinct from any world in which (each member of) B is true.

The effect of rules (i)–(iii) is to "set up" the domain of quantification for the possibilistic language. To some extent we can tell what is included in this domain and what is excluded from it by determining which statements of the descriptive language are consistent.

Of course, rules (i)–(iii) are not the only principles governing the (logical) possibility of worlds. Certainly, if we are talking about worlds (as opposed to "smaller" entities like situations, scenarios, or states of affairs) we will need a maximality condition – something like this: for every possible world w and every statement A of the descriptive language, either A or its negation is true in w.

Yet even with the addition of this condition, the totality of possible worlds is not fully defined, for there is nothing to prevent many worlds from corresponding to the same maximal consistent set of statements of the descriptive language.[5] That, I will argue later, is as it should be.

There is, however, another respect in which rules (i)–(iii) fail to provide a completely rigorous characterization of the domain of possible worlds, and that is their use of the term 'consistent'. The descriptive language, we have said, is a fragment of English. But the notion of consistency is well-defined only for certain formalized languages. Therefore, the notion of consistency used in rules (i)–(iii) must be to some degree vague and informal.

Where we draw its boundaries is largely a matter of convenience, not of logic or of fact. Minimally, it will exclude formal contradictions (i.e. those statements which cannot be true in virtue of the semantic rules governing the standard logical operators). But we may also want it to exclude more.

We may want it, for example, to exclude arithmetical falsehoods. Consistency, then, will also be a function of the semantics of such terms as '$+$' and '$\times$'. Such terms will have for us a fixed interpretation (their standard interpretation over the natural numbers), just as the usual logical operators do, and any statement false on this interpretation will thereby be regarded as inconsistent.[6] Our concept of consistency will now be *essentially* informal, since the set of arithmetical falsehoods cannot be formally (i.e. recursively) specified.

We may also want our concept of consistency to exclude statements like

(8) $\exists x$ (x is round & x is square),

or

(9) $\exists x$ (x is taller than x),

which, though not formally contradictory, are nevertheless false on any interpretation in which their predicates have their usual senses. Their inconsistency, in other words, is a function of the semantics of both logical operators and predicates.

We may even wish to exclude statements whose falsehood is not a function of semantics alone. Consider, for example, the statement made by the sentence

(10)   This substance does not have atomic number 79,

uttered with reference to a lump of gold (whose atomic number is 79). Since having atomic number 79 is arguably essential to the substance ostended, we may wish to regard this statement as inconsistent in an informal sense.[7] Not, however, that the same sentence uttered with reference to a hunk of lead is not only consistent, but true. The semantic contribution of the sentence is the same in each case; what differs is the context. Thus, if we regard (10) as inconsistent, we will conclude that context, too, may play a role in consistency.

The context dependence of the truth of (10) has its source in the demonstrative 'this substance'. The semantic principle governing this phrase fixes its reference to whatever substance is indicated by the context. But it does not stipulate which substance this is, nor what properties are definitive of (i.e. essential to) this substance. These things can only be known empirically. If the substance ostended is gold, one of the essential properties (given current scientific doctrine) is the property of having atomic number 79. It is only by "completing" the interpretation of the phrase with these context-dependent considerations that we can recognize the inconsistency of the statement in question. Thus, if we admit inconsistency in this sense, then inconsistency is not always detectable a priori. Where semantic interpretation

is context-dependent, it may depend on aspects of context which can only be known empirically.

It does not follow, of course, that statements that are actually consistent might not have been consistent if the empirical facts had been different. We have seen that when (10) is uttered in one context (with reference to a hunk of lead) we get consistency and when it is uttered in another (with reference to a lump of gold) we get inconsistency. But this does not mean that the consistency of a statement is subject to the whim of empirical fact. Rather, it shows that statement identity may depend on empirical fact. What we have here is not a single statement that is consistent in one context and inconsistent in another, but rather two statements that are distinguished by context. Changing the context replaces one statement by another. It does not make a formerly consistent statement inconsistent.[8]

My aim in discussing the various notions of consistency has been merely to sketch the range of options available to us in interpreting rules (i)–(iii). For the purposes of this paper we need not choose among these options. In practice, the choice may be made differently for different purposes.[9] No matter which choice is made, however, consistency is determined at least in part by semantic rules, and perhaps also in part by those aspects of context needed to fix an interpretation. If these factors do not rule out the truth of a statement, then that statement is consistent. If they do, it is inconsistent.

Since we lack a general account of semantic rules, this account of consistency may seem unconscionably vague. But in specific instances in which the relevant rules are thoroughly understood, it is self-evidently correct. Consider, for example, the inconsistency of statements of the form 'p & $\neg p$'. This inconsistency is a product of the semantic rules governing the operators '$\neg$' and '&'. The rules are: '$\neg$' reverses truth value; '&' forms compounds that are true only if both components are true. Thus, it is perfectly evident that these rules prohibit the truth of any statement of the form 'p & $\neg p$'. Because the semantic rules governing '$\neg$' and '&' are thoroughly understood, the nature of the inconsistency is utterly transparent.

It may be objected, however, that with respect to the more informal notions of consistency this sort of explanation is ultimately circular. I set out to explain what possible worlds are in terms of consistency. Consistency is a function of semantic rules and (perhaps) context. But how are these rules to be spelled out, if not with reference to possible worlds? The inconsistency of (8), for example, is a result of the senses of 'is round' and 'is square'. But the most obvious way to represent the semantic rules that constitute these senses is as functions from possible worlds to extensions. Hence the explanation runs in a circle.

There *is* a circle here, but it is not vicious. Of all the elements of this circle, the semantic rules which constitute senses are the most familiar. The rules governing expressions like 'is round' and 'is square', however, are familiar, not in the sense that we can formulate them fully and precisely, but in the sense that we know how to use them. That is how we detect consistency and inconsistency in practice.

Since explanation should proceed from the more familiar to the less familiar, these practically and intuitively understood rules are the appropriate starting point. The question 'Why can't there be worlds in which statements of the form 'p & $\neg p$' are true?' is correctly and enlighteningly answered by explaining the semantics of '$\neg$' and '&'. Similarly, the question 'Why can't there be worlds containing round squares?' is correctly and enlighteningly answered by appealing to our pretheoretical understanding of the way 'is round' and 'is square' work. The latter explanation may utilize imprecise intuitions, but it does not involve possible worlds. If we reverse the direction of explanation, however, the explanation falls flat. The question 'Why do the semantic rules governing '$\neg$' and '&' work the way they do?' is not enlighteningly answered by appeal to the fact that there can be no worlds in which 'p & $\neg p$' is true. Nor do we enhance our understanding of how the senses of 'is round' and 'is square' make (8) inconsistent by pointing out that there can be no worlds containing round squares. The semantic rules constituting senses are thus conceptually prior to possible worlds. (It is not wholly irrelevant in this regard that consistency and inconsistency were recognized and understood to a considerable degree at least two millennia before Leibniz popularized the notion of a possible world.)

It is by appeal to our practical and intuitive understanding of semantic rules that I hope to shed light on the question of what possible worlds are. Perhaps on other occasions we will find it useful to represent these rules as functions from worlds to extensions. Still, that will not alter the fact that they were initially understood independently of the worlds concept. The movement, then, will have been from a working understanding of semantic rules, to a working understanding of possible worlds, back to a theoretical representation of the rules with which we started. If this theoretical representation were the only way of understanding semantic rules, then the circle would be vicious. But since our initial understanding is independent of this theoretical understanding, the circle is not vicious, but hermeneutic.

Having laid the groundwork, let us now return to the question 'What are possible worlds?' Two answers suggest themselves immediately: (1) possible worlds are possible states of affairs that are maximal in some sense, and (2) possible worlds are maximal consistent sets of statements of the descriptive language.

The first answer I take to be true but unilluminating. It needs to be augmented by an account of possible states of affairs. This account will either regard possible states of affairs as genuine possibilia, components of worlds (universes) that are possible but (except in one case) do not exist, or it will not. If not, then it will take them to be actual abstract entities of some sort. In that case it is not an answer to my question. For no worlds other than our own are actual; hence these actual abstract entities are not worlds. But my question was about worlds.

On the other hand, if possible states of affairs are regarded as genuine possibilia, then I accept (1). But I do not think it is particularly useful to analyse possible worlds in terms of possible states of affairs. Rather, I want to elucidate both concepts from a totally different perspective.

Answer (2) proposes an ontological reduction of worlds to sets of statements. But, as I have already indicated, this sort of answer will not do. For sets of statements, like other sorts of actual abstract entities, are not worlds.

At this point, those who favour (2) or some other sort of ontological reduction are likely to reply that I have missed the point. Reduction establishes identity; possible worlds are just these sets, and hence they are the very things that interest me.

That, however, is not true. The things that interest me have properties (being a universe in which people live and breathe, for example) that sets of statements and similar abstract entities lack. There is no identity here.

Other proponents of reduction might reply that reduction means elimination. The (alleged) fact that we can replace possible worlds talk with talk of sets of statements (or similar abstract entities) shows, they may hold, that the non-actual worlds that interest me do not exist.

But I have already granted that; we are in agreement.

This odd twist of the dialectic points to a deeper *dis*agreement. The reductivist sees the non-existence of merely possible worlds as an *objection* to possibilistic discourse. This is because the reductivist's paradigm of language use is theory or description of what actually exists. Thus, when a form of discourse concerns itself with nonexistent things, it strikes him as pointless and illegitimate.

I, on the other hand, am suggesting that the paradigm by which possibilistic discourse is understood should be games of make-believe. From this perspective, the non-existence of merely possible worlds is not an objection, but precisely what one would expect. Possibilistic quantification is quantification over a mostly make-believe domain. But that does not make it pointless. Since the domain is structured by rules (i)–(iii), possibilistic discourse conveys quite definite information. This information has two aspects; it concerns both statements and worlds. Consider, for example, the assertion

(11) There could be a world in which human civilization is destroyed by nuclear war.

This assertion conveys the information that the statement

(12) Human civilization is destroyed by nuclear war.

is consistent. But that is not all it conveys – nor, perhaps, what is most important. For the possibilistic language game is played by taking (11) to be referring, not to (12), but to a world in which (12) is true. Of course that world may be make-believe. But then again it may not. What endows possibilistic discourse with utility (and sometimes poignancy) is that one world in its domain is not make-believe – and (since we lack a complete description of the actual world) in a sense we do not know which one. It is, therefore, of more than just semantic concern that there could be a world in which human civilization is destroyed by nuclear war.

Yet those for whom theory or description are the paradigms of language use are likely to remain sceptical of the legitimacy of possibilistic discourse. Someone might argue as follows. Let the peculiarities of this sort of discourse be granted. Still, *something* must make possibilistically quantified statements true or false, and the theory of this something is their semantic metatheory. Now this metatheory *is* a theory, and as such it must live up to its ontological commitments; it must therefore provide truth conditions for possibilistically quantified statements solely in terms of existing things. Without such a metatheory, possibilistic quantification is unintelligible.

This appears to be a forceful objection. Indeed, I am unable to provide the semantic metatheory that it demands. (One could, of course, give truth conditions in terms of maximal consistent sets of statements. But not only would this be the wrong semantics for talk about *worlds*; it would also be inadequate, since the number of worlds may exceed the number of maximal consistent sets of statements – a consideration to which I will return shortly.) This does not mean that possibilistic quantifiers lack truth conditions. In fact, their truth conditions are trivial. In the simplest case, where ϕ is an open sentence with only x free, they are just this:

$\exists x \phi$ is true iff there could be a world satisfying ϕ,

$\forall x \phi$ is true iff every possible world satisfies ϕ.

The problem is that possibilistic quantifiers reappear in the metalanguage. The metalanguage requires us to engage in the same sort of make-believe that the object language employs.

The objection claims that this is not enough. It demands that truth conditions be formulated solely in terms of actually existing things. Now, a purely actualistic metatheory may well be desirable. But if we cannot have it, must we really concede, as the objection demands, that possibilistic quantification is unintelligible? What is the argument?

One might suspect a vicious circle here. To understand the possibilistic language, we must first understand its truth conditions. Hence, if its truth conditions can only be given in possibilistic language, we cannot come to understand it without first having understood it. Therefore we cannot come to understand it at all; it is unintelligible.

But this reasoning rests on a false assumption. It is not true that to understand a language we must first understand its truth conditions. Long before anyone had explained the truth conditions of standard quantification to us, we understood standard quantification and used it correctly. Indeed, we could not have understood its truth conditions until we had first learned to use it, since those truth conditions employ standard quantification in precisely the way in which the truth conditions for possibilistic quantifiers employ possibilistic quantification. We first understood standard quantification, not by being given its truth conditions, but by observing it in use.

In the preceding pages I have explained and exemplified the use of possibilistic quantifiers. In particular, I have tried to show how, in accordance with rules (i)–(iii), patterns of consistency in the descriptive language are taken to guarantee the possibility of corresponding worlds and hence to "set up" the domain of possibilistic quantification. To understand these functions of language simply *is* to understand what possible worlds are, for the possibility of worlds (note that I do not say 'their existence') is constituted solely by the absence of inconsistency from the corresponding descriptions. (The actual world is no exception, since its inclusion in the domain via rule (i) makes sense only on the presupposition that it is consistently describable.) Non-actual worlds do not "exist out there" as structured wholes independent of our linguistic inventions. That way of thinking about them confuses them with actual things and misconstrues talk about them as theory or description. Rather, their identity and structure as a domain of objects is the product of a game of "make-believe" played with statements of the descriptive language.

This is not to say that possible worlds are nothing more than language. They are worlds, as I have argued all along. But in saying that they are worlds, I am already using the possibilistic language. That is, I am already engaged in the sort of "make-believe" that we are trying to understand.

An analogy may be helpful here. Anyone who has read the works of J. R. R. Tolkien and who understands their use (story-telling) knows what a hobbit is. To such a person it is evident that hobbits do not somehow "exist out there" as fully defined structured wholes. Their "existence", such as it is, is nothing more than a make-believe projection of Tolkien's language. Yet this is not to say that hobbits are nothing more than language. On the contrary, they are small rational animals with woolly toes. But in saying this, I am already using the fictive language, i.e. engaging in the "make-believe", that we are trying to understand. (I am certainly not describing or theorizing

in a way that involves ontological commitment; to think that I am is to misunderstand me completely.)

Possibilistic language is the apparatus of a game in which we speak of possible worlds as objects, even though (apart from the actual world) no such objects exist. Rules (i)–(iii) provide specific directions for play. As we noted, however, these rules, even together with a maximality condition, do not completely define the domain of possible worlds. Though they do imply that to each maximal consistent set of statements of the descriptive language there corresponds *at least* one possible world, they do not imply that for each there is *only* one. They leave that question open. This, I contend, is not a deficiency of the rules, but a virtue. For the domain of possible worlds is indefinite in just the way that these rules are. In other words, rules (i)–(iii), plus a maximality condition, define this domain as completely as it can be defined without imposing arbitrary constraints. To see this, note that the descriptive language may grow. Tomorrow it may contain more expressions than it does today. These expressions will enable us to formulate new pairs of consistent statements whose conjunction is inconsistent and hence (by rule (iii')) to discriminate a multiplicity of worlds for each of those that we can discern today.

To illustrate this process of discrimination, let us consider a simplified example. Suppose our descriptive language contains only one name (say 'the Earth') and one predicate (say 'is spherical'), plus the logical operator for negation. In this language we can make only two non-equivalent statements: 'The Earth is spherical' and 'The Earth is not spherical'. These are mutually inconsistent, and so by rules (ii) and (iii') *at least* two worlds are possible – one in which the Earth is spherical and one in which it is not. Now, suppose we add the predicate 'is cubical' to our language. The set containing the statements 'The Earth is spherical' and 'The Earth is cubical' is inconsistent; so by rule (iii) no world corresponding to this set is possible. But by rules (ii) and (iii') at least three worlds are possible, one corresponding to each of the following three pairs of statements:

(A) 'The Earth is spherical', 'The Earth is not cubical'

(B) 'The Earth is not spherical', 'The Earth is cubical'

(C) 'The Earth is not spherical', 'The Earth is not cubical'.

The possible world(s) associated in our original language with the statement 'The Earth is spherical' is (are) clearly the same as the world(s) now associated with (A). But the world(s) originally associated with the statement 'The Earth is not spherical' has (have) been further articulated into at least two worlds, those associated with (B) and (C). Note, however, that these are not "new" possibilities. They are already implicit among the possibilities originally associated with the statement 'The Earth is not spherical'. Thus expansion of our language does not create new possibilities. It merely subdivides and articulates the old ones.

Now, there is no reason to think that language growth ever comes to an end. That is, there is no reason to believe in some ultimate descriptive language so rich that it could not be richer. (We could always, it seems, add one more predicate or one more name, just as we can always increase any ordinal number by one. Thus, the idea of an all-inclusive language seems no more credible than the idea of a greatest ordinal number.) If an all-inclusive descriptive language were possible, then each maximal consistent set of its statements would correspond to exactly one ultimate possible world. But if, as seems likely, there can be no such language, then possible worlds are in a sense infinitely divisible. At every given point in history we can distinguish as many of them as there are maximal consistent sets of statements in our descriptive language. But later each of these may be resolved into many more. Any attempt to bound the domain of possible worlds by adding further conditions to rules (i)–(iii) and the maximality condition would arbitrarily limit this process of resolution. There is thus no generally applicable justification for adding such conditions.

The infinite divisibility of possible worlds may be abhorrent to classically tempered minds, but it does not matter much in practice. If we want the effect of a well-defined domain of worlds, we can always specify some precise descriptive language and then ignore differences among worlds that are not expressible in this language. As a result we will recognize only one world corresponding to each maximal consistent set of statements of this language. Technically, this result can be achieved by the device of identifying indiscernibles.[10]

But all this raises a final objection. Since non-actual worlds, on my view, derive whatever structure they have from patterns of coherence in the descriptive language, what would happen if there were no descriptive language at all? It would seem to follow that no non-actual world would be possible, which is surely absurd.

This objection, however, is mistaken. It invites us to consider a counter-factual situation in which there is no descriptive language and assumes that in doing so we are prevented from using the descriptive language we now possess. But that is not the way counterfactual discourse works. We always apply our current linguistic and conceptual resources to any possible situation we consider, and as a result counterfactual changes in languages have no effect on the structure of possible worlds *as determined by these linguistic and conceptual resources*. This practice implies that each world is accessible from all worlds, since the descriptive language and rules (i)–(iii) are held constant as we shift our viewpoint from world to world. Hence even in worlds where there is no language, all the worlds possible for us are still possible. Thus it is not true that if there were no descriptive language, no non-actual worlds would be possible.

Now, this answer may seem evasive. What the objection really wants us to do (and what I refused to do in the previous paragraph) is to imagine what happens to possible worlds from the point of view of a person who has no descriptive language. We are to consider this possible situation, not as outsiders looking in through the spectacles of our own language (which is the usual procedure), but empathetically, from the viewpoint of the languageless person himself. Now it ought to be clear that whatever we discover about this person's conception of possible worlds is irrelevant to the structure of possible worlds *from our point of view*. The possible worlds that matter to us are structured by our language games, not by his. Nevertheless, it might be illuminating to imagine how things seem to him.

To make this thought experiment easier, let us imagine that this person speaks our descriptive language initially, but then slowly loses it. His language, that is, can express fewer and fewer statements, until at last it can express none. The result with respect to his conception of possible worlds will be just the reverse of the progressive articulation that occurs with language growth. Worlds will seem to "merge", rather than to "fission". Previously distinguished worlds will become indistinguishable. Finally, no descriptive statements will be left. At this point, rules (i)–(iii), which "set up" the domain of possible worlds, imply neither the possibility nor the impossibility of any non-actual world. The only thing they still imply categorically is that the actual world is possible. The question of the possibility of other worlds is not decided in the negative; it is simply undecided. Thus it is in no sense true (even from this person's point of view) that nothing non-actual is possible. Rather, a precondition for distinguishing the possible from the actual is lacking. All previously distinguishable worlds (including the actual one) have from his viewpoint merged into undifferentiation.

Thus we can see that by enriching or impoverishing the descriptive language we can vary the degree of articulation of the domain of possible worlds. But in this process nothing becomes possible that was not possible before, and nothing ceases to be possible. Possible worlds or situations previously distinguished may cease to be distinguished. But possibility itself is neither created nor destroyed.

In this paper I have tried to explain what merely possible worlds (and also merely possible situations, scenarios, and states of affairs) are by offering an account of their possibility. I have not tried to do more than that. Thus my explanation leaves many questions unanswered. I have not, for example, addressed the question of how this game of make-believe is useful in decision-making and other practical activities. Obviously, part of the answer lies in our ignorance. Often we do not know which possibilities are actual and which are not; our decisions must therefore prepare us for non-actual as well as actual situations. But, of course, much more than this needs to be said. Nor have I discussed the problem of possibilistic quantification over individuals and the closely related problem of transworld identity. But these are issues for another context.[11]

Notes

1 For an example of a theory that takes possible worlds to be actual but abstract states of affairs, see Alvin Plantinga, 'Actualism and Possible Worlds', *Theoria*, 1976, 139–60; reprinted in Michael J. Loux, ed., *The Possible and the Actual: Readings in the Metaphysics of Modality*, Ithaca and London, Cornell University Press, 1979. According to Plantinga, all possible states of affairs exist, but most of them do not obtain. I criticized this view in 'Sets and Possible Worlds', *Philosophical Studies*, 1983, 21–35.

2 Actually, on my view, consistency is not the existence of a model but the possibility of a model. The set-theoretic structures we invoke to prove consistency are in general merely possible, not actual, objects. This view is elaborated in 'Sets and Possible Worlds', Nolt, op. cit.; 'Mathematical Intuition', *Philosophy and Phenomenological Research*, 1983, 189–211; and 'Abstraction and Modality', *Philosophical Studies*, 1980, 111–27.

3 Of course, once such quantifiers are introduced, there can be no objection to having a predicate meaning 'is possible'. But it is of little use, since it is true of every object in the domain of quantification.

4 Most notably, David Lewis in *Counterfactuals*, Cambridge, Mass., Harvard University Press, 1973, chapter 4, and *On the Plurality of Worlds*, Oxford, Basil Blackwell, 1986.

5 A maximal consistent set of statements for a language L is a consistent set of statements of L which contains for each statement A of L either A or its negation.

6 Numbers are generally regarded as abstract entities, and since I announced at the beginning of this paper that I do not believe in such things, I may seem to

have contradicted myself. For the resolution of this apparent conflict, see the works cited in n. 2. In short, the resolution is this: talk of numbers is really possibilistic talk about familiar, concrete things.

7 For an account of the essentialist intuitions on which this claim of inconsistency might be based, see Saul Kripke, *Naming and Necessity*, Cambridge, Mass., Harvard University Press, 1972, esp. pp. 123–5. Kripke himself, however, does not say that statements like (10) are inconsistent.

8 We might suspect, however, that contingent fact affects consistency in a more subtle way. Perhaps one day empirical discoveries will force us to revise our conception of a physical substance so that atomic number is no longer a criterion of substance identity. Then we might no longer see any inconsistency in asserting with reference to a lump of gold that *this substance* does not have atomic number 79. Some big questions lurk in the shadows of this suspicion – including a very big one about reidentification of statements, and ultimately of possible worlds, across differing conceptual schemes. But this is not the place to draw them out.

9 Since consistency is linked by rules (i)–(iii) to logical possibility (and thereby to related notions such as validity, necessary truth and logical equivalence), choosing any but the minimal notion of consistency will, in effect, broaden our conception of logic. If we treat (8) as inconsistent, for example, then we shall treat the inference

x is round
$\therefore$ x is not square

as deductively valid even without the additional premiss

$$\forall x(x \text{ is round} \rightarrow x \text{ is not square})$$

that would be needed to make it valid when transcribed into the predicate calculus. The result, if this idea is taken seriously, is an *informal* logic, which (I have argued elsewhere) is more useful for some purposes than standard formal logics. See my 'Possible Worlds and Imagination in Informal Logic', *Informal Logic*, 1984, 14–17 and *Informal Logic: Possible Worlds and Imagination*, New York, McGraw-Hill, 1984.

10 For an account of this device see W. V. Quine, 'Logic and the Reification of Universals', in *From a Logical Point of View*, New York, Harper & Row, 1961, 102–29.

11 I would like to thank Steve Humphrey for the raucous conversations that stimulated my interest in this topic. This paper was extensively revised in the light of perceptive comments by Graeme Forbes, who undoubtedly still disagrees with most of it. Simon Blackburn also provided some very helpful criticisms.

21

Quantifiers and Propositional Attitudes

W. V. Quine

I

The incorrectness of rendering 'Ctesias is hunting unicorns' in the fashion:

$(\exists x)$ (x is a unicorn · Ctesias is hunting x)

is conveniently attested by the non-existence of unicorns, but is not due simply to that zoological lacuna. It would be equally incorrect to render 'Ernest is hunting lions' as:

(1) $(\exists x)$ (x is a lion . Ernest is hunting x),

where Ernest is a sportsman in Africa. The force of (1) is rather that there is some individual lion (or several) which Ernest is hunting; stray circus property, for example.

The contrast recurs in 'I want a sloop.' The version:

(2) $(\exists x)$ (x is a . I want x)

is suitable insofar only as there may be said to be a certain sloop that I want. If what I seek is mere relief from slooplessness, then (2) conveys the wrong idea.

The contrast is that between what may be called the *relational* sense of lion-hunting or sloop-wanting, viz., (1)–(2), and the likelier or *notional* sense.

W. V. Quine, Quantifiers and Propositional Attitudes. *The Journal of Philosophy*, **53**, 5 (1956): 177–87.

Appreciation of the difference is evinced in Latin and Romance languages by a distinction of mood in subordinate clauses; thus 'Procuro un perro que habla' has the relational sense:

$(\exists x)$ x is a dog . x talks . I seek x)

as against the notional 'Procuro un perro que hable':

I strive that $(\exists x)$ (x is a dog . x talks . I find x).

Pending considerations to the contrary in later pages, we may represent the contrast strikingly in terms of permutations of components. Thus (1) and (2) may be expanded (with some premediated violence to both logic and grammer) thus:

(3) $(\exists x)$ (x is a lion . Ernest strives that Ernest finds x),

(4) $(\exists x)$ (x is a sloop . I wish that I have x),

whereas 'Ernest is hunting lions' and 'I want a sloop' in their notional senses may be rendered rather thus:

(5)   Ernest strives that $(\exists x)$ (x is a . Ernest finds x),

(6)   I wish that $(\exists x)$ (x is a sloop.I have x).

The contrasting versions (3)–(6) have been wrought by so paraphrasing 'hunt' and 'want' as to uncover the locutions 'strive that' and 'wish that,' expressive of what Russell has called *propositional attitudes*. Now of all examples of propositional attitudes, the first and foremost is *belief*; and, true to form, this example can be used to point up the contrast between relational and notional senses still better than (3)–(6) do. Consider the relational and notional senses of believing in spies:

(7) $(\exists x)$ (Ralph believes that x is a spy),

(8) Ralph believes that $(\exists x)$ (x is a spy).

Both may perhaps be ambiguously phrased as 'Ralph believes that someone is a spy,' but they may be unambiguously phrased respectively as 'There is someone whom Ralph believes to be a spy' and 'Ralph believes there are spies.' The difference is vast; indeed, if Ralph is like most of us, (8) is true and (7) false.

In moving over to propositional attitudes, as we did in (3)–(6), we gain not only the graphic structural contrast between (3)–(4) and (5)–(6) but also a certain generality. For, we can now multiply examples of striving and wishing, unrelated to hunting and wanting. Thus we get the relational and notional senses of wishing for a president:

(9) $(\exists x)$ (Witold wishes that x is president),

(10) Witold wishes that $(\exists x)$ (x is president).

According to (9), Witold has his candidate; according to (10) he merely wishes the appropriate form of government were in force. Also we open other propositional attitudes to similar consideration – as witness (7)–(8).

However, the suggested formulations of the relational senses – viz., (3), (4), (7), and (9) – all involve quantifying into a propositional-attitude idiom from outside. This is a dubious business, as may be seen from the following example.

There is a certain man in a brown hat whom Ralph has glimpsed several times under questionable circumstances on which we need not enter here; suffice it to say that Ralph suspects he is a spy. Also there is a gray-haired man, vaguely known to Ralph as rather a pillar of the community, whom Ralph is not aware of having seen except once at the beach. Now Ralph does not know it, but the men are one and the same. Can we say of this *man* (Bernard J. Ortcutt, to give him a name) that

Ralph believes him to be a spy? If so, we find ourselves accepting a conjunction of the type:

(11) w sincerely denies '...'
      . w believes that ...

as true, with one and the same sentence in both blanks. For, Ralph is ready enough to say, in all sincerity, 'Bernard J. Ortcutt is no spy.' If, on the other hand, with a view to disallowing situations of the type (11), we rule simultaneously that

(12) Ralph believes that the man in the brown hat is a spy,

(13) Ralph does not believe that the man seen at the beach is a spy,

then we cease to affirm any relationship between Ralph and any man at all. Both of the component 'that'-clauses are indeed about the man Ortcutt; but the 'that' must be viewed in (12) and (13) as sealing those clauses off, thereby rendering (12) and (13) compatible because not, as wholes, about Ortcutt at all. It then becomes improper to quantify as in (7); 'believes that' becomes, in a word, referentially opaque.[1]

No question arises over (8); it exhibits only a quantification *within* the 'believes that' context, not a quantification *into* it. What goes by the board, when we rule (12) and (13) both true, is just (7). Yet we are scarcely prepared to sacrifice the relational construction 'There is someone whom Ralph believes to be a spy,' which (7) as against (8) was supposed to reproduce.

The obvious next move is to try to make the best of our dilemma by distinguishing two senses of belief: $belief_1$, which disallows (11), and $belief_2$, which tolerates (11) but makes sense of (7). For $belief_1$, accordingly, we sustain (12)–(13) and ban (7) as nonsense. For $belief_2$, on the other hand, we sustain (7); and for *this* sense of belief we must reject (13) and acquiesce in the conclusion that Ralph $believes_2$ that the man at the beach is a spy even though he *also* $believes_2$ (and $believes_1$) that the man at the beach is not a spy.

II

But there is a more suggestive treatment. Beginning with a single sense of belief, viz., $belief_1$ above, let us think of this at first as a relation between the believer and a certain *intension*, named by the 'that'-clause. Intensions are creatures of darkness, and I shall rejoice with the reader when they are exorcised, but first I want to make certain points with help of them. Now intensions named thus by 'that'-clauses, without free variables, I shall speak of more specifically as intensions of degree 0, or propositions. In addition I shall (for the moment) recognize intensions of degree 1, or attributes. These are to be named by prefixing a variable to a sentence in which it occurs free; thus z (z is a spy) is spyhood. Similarly we may specify intensions of higher degrees by prefixing multiple variables.

Now just as we have recognized a dyadic relation of belief between a believer and a proposition, thus:

(14)   Ralph believes that Ortcutt is a spy,

so we may recognize also a triadic relation of belief among a believer, an object, and an attribute, thus:

(15)   Ralph believes z (z is a spy)
       of Ortcutt.

For reasons which will appear, this is to be viewed not as dyadic belief between Ralph and the proposition *that* Ortcutt has z (z is a spy), but rather as an irreducibly triadic relation among the three things Ralph, z (z is a spy), and Ortcutt. Similarly there is tetradic belief:

(16)   Tom believes yz (y denounced z)
       of Cicero and Catiline,

and so on.

Now we can clap on a hard and fast rule against quantifying into propositional-attitude idioms; but we give it the form now of a rule against quantifying into names of intensions. Thus, though (7) as it stands becomes unallowable, we can meet the needs which prompted (7) by quantifying rather into the triadic belief construction, thus:

(17) $(\exists x)$ [Ralph believes $z(z$ is a spy) of x].

Here then, in place of (7), is our new way of saying that there is someone whom Ralph believes to be a spy.

Belief$_1$ was belief so construed that a proposition might be believed when an object was specified in it in one way, and yet not believed when the same object was specified in another way; witness (12)–(13). Hereafter we can adhere uniformly to

this narrow sense of belief, both for the dyadic case and for triadic and higher; in each case the term which names the intension (whether proposition or attribute or intension of higher degree) is to be looked on as referentially opaque.

The situation (11) is thus excluded. At the same time the effect of belief$_2$ can be gained, simply by ascending from dyadic to triadic belief as in (15). For (15) does relate the men Ralph and Ortcutt precisely as belief$_2$ was intended to do. (15) does remain true of Ortcutt under any designation; and hence the legitimacy of (17).

Similarly, whereas from:

   Tom believes that Cicero denounced Catiline

we cannot conclude:

   Tom believes that Tully denounced Catiline,

on the other hand we can conclude from:

   Tom believes y (y denounced Catiline) of Cicero

that

   Tom believes y (y denounced Catiline) of Tully,

and also that

(18) $(\exists x)$ [Tom believes y
       (y denounced Catiline) of x].

From (16), similarly, we may infer that

(19) $(\exists w)(\exists x)$ [Tom believes yz
       (y denounced z) of w and x].

Such quantifications as:

   $(\exists x)$ (Tom believes that x denounced Catiline),
   $(\exists x)$ [Tom believes y (y denounced x) of Cicero]

still count as nonsense, along with (7); but such legitimate purposes as these might have served are served by (17)–(19) and the like. Our names of intensions, and these only, are what count as referentially opaque.

Let us sum up our findings concerning the seven numbered statements about Ralph. (7) is now counted as nonsense, (8) as true, (12)–(13) as true, (14) as false, and (15) and (17) as true. Another that is true is:

(20)   Ralph believes that the man seen
         at the beach is not a spy,

which of course must not be confused with (13).

The kind of exportation which leads from (14) to (15) should doubtless be viewed in general as implicative. Under the terms of our illustrative story, (14) happens to be false; but (20) is true, and it leads by exportation to:

(21)   Ralph believes z (z is not a spy) of
         the man seen at the beach.

The man at the beach, hence Ortcutt, does not receive reference in (20), because of referential opacity; but he does in (21), so we may conclude from (21) that

(22)   Ralph believes z (z is not a spy)
         of Ortcutt.

Thus (15) and (22) both count as true. This is not, however, to charge Ralph with contradictory beliefs. Such a charge might reasonably be read into:

(23)   Ralph believes z(z is a spy . z is
         not a spy) of Ortcutt,

but this merely goes to show that it is undesirable to look upon (15) and (22) as implying (23).

It hardly needs be said that the barbarous usage illustrated in (15)–(19) and (21)–(23) is not urged as a practical reform. It is put forward by way of straightening out a theoretical difficulty, which, summed up, was as follows: Belief contexts are referentially opaque; therefore it is *prima facie* meaningless to quantify into them (at least with respect to persons or other extensional objects[2]); how then to provide for those indispensable relational statements of belief, like 'There is someone whom Ralph believes to be a spy'?

Let it not be supposed that the theory which we have been examining is just a matter of allowing unbridled quantification into belief contexts after all, with a legalistic change of notation. On the contrary, the crucial choice recurs at each point:

quantify if you will, but pay the price of accepting situations of the type (11) with respect to each point at which you choose to quantify. In other words: distinguish as you please between referential and non-referential positions, but keep track, so as to treat each kind appropriately. The notation of intensions, of degree one and higher, is in effect a device for inking in a boundary between referential and non-referential occurrences of terms.

III

Striving and wishing, like believing, are propositional attitudes and referentially opaque. (3) and (4) are objectionable in the same way as (7), and our recent treatment of belief can be repeated for these propositional attitudes. Thus, just as (7) gave way to (17), so (3) and (4) give way to:

(24) $(\exists x)$ [x is a lion . Ernest strives z
         (Ernest finds z) of x],

(25) $(\exists x)$[x is a sloop . I wish z
         (I have z) of x],

a certain breach of idiom being allowed for the sake of analogy in the case of 'strives.'

These examples came from a study of hunting and wanting. Observing in (3)–(4) the quantification into opaque contexts, then, we might have retreated to (1)–(2) and foreborne to paraphrase them into terms of striving and wishing. For (1)–(2) were quite straightforward renderings of lion-hunting and sloop-wanting in their relational senses; it was only the notional senses that really needed the breakdown into terms of striving and wishing, (5)–(6).

Actually, though, it would be myopic to leave the relational senses of lion-hunting and sloop-wanting at the unanalyzed stage (1)–(2). For, whether or not we choose to put these over into terms of wishing and striving, there are other relational cases of wishing and striving which require our consideration anyway – as witness (9). The untenable formulations (3)–(4) may indeed be either corrected as (24)–(25) or condensed back into (1)–(2); on the other hand we have no choice but to correct the untenable (9) on the pattern of (24)–(25), viz., as:

$(\exists x)$ [Witold wishes y (y is president) of x].

The untenable versions (3)–(4) and (9) all had to do with wishing and striving in the relational sense. We see in contrast that (5)–(6) and (10), on the notional side of wishing and striving, are innocent of any illicit quantification into opaque contexts from outside. But now notice that exactly the same trouble begins also on the notional side, as soon as we try to say not just that Ernest hunts lions and I want a sloop, but that *someone* hunts lions or wants a sloop. This move carries us, ostensibly, from (5)–(6) to:

(26) $(\exists w)[w$ strives that $(\exists x)$
         $(x$ is a lion . w finds $x)]$,

(27) $(\exists w)[w$ wishes that $(\exists x)$
         $(x$ is a sloop . w has $x)]$,

and these do quantify unallowably into opaque contexts.

We know how, with help of the attribute apparatus, to put (26)–(27) in order; the pattern, indeed, is substantially before us in (24)–(25). Admissible versions are:

$(\exists w)[w$ strives $y(\exists x)x$ is a lion . y finds $x)$
of $w]$,

$(\exists w)[w$ wishes $y(\exists x)(x$ is a sloop . y has $x)$
of $w]$,

or briefly:

(28) $(\exists w)[w$ strives y (y finds a lion) of $w]$,

(29) $(\exists w)[w$ wishes y (y has a sloop) of $w]$.

Such quantification of the subject of the propositional attitude can of course occur in belief as well; and, if the subject is mentioned in the belief itself, the above pattern is the one to use. Thus 'Someone believes he is Napoleon' must be rendered:

$(\exists w)[w$ believes y ($y =$ Napoleon) of $w]$.

For concreteness I have been discussing belief primarily, and two other propositional attitudes secondarily: striving and wishing. The treatment is, we see, closely parallel for the three; and it will pretty evidently carry over to other propositional attitudes as well – e.g., hope, fear, surprise. In all cases my concern is, of course, with a special technical aspect of the propositional attitudes: the problem of quantifying in.

IV

There are good reasons for being discontent with an analysis that leaves us with propositions, attributes, and the rest of the intensions. Intensions are less economical than extensions (truth values, classes, relations), in that they are more narrowly individuated. The principle of their individuation, moreover, is obscure.

Commonly logical equivalence is adopted as the principle of individuation of intensions. More explicitly: if S and S' are any two sentences with n (≥ 0) free variables, the same in each, then the respective intensions which we name by putting the n variables (or 'that,' if $n = 0$) before S and S' shall be one and the same intension if and only if S and S' are logically equivalent. But the relevant concept of logical equivalence raises serious questions in turn.[3]

Worse, granted certain usual logical machinery (such as is available in *Principia Mathematica*), this principle of individuation can be shown to contradict itself. For I have proved elsewhere,[4] using machinery solely of *Principia*, that if logical equivalence is taken as a sufficient condition of identity of attributes then mere coextensiveness becomes a sufficient condition as well. But then it follows that logical equivalence is not a necessary condition; so the described principle of individuation contradicts itself.

The champion of intensions can be trusted, in the face of this result, to abandon either that principle of individuation of intensions or some one of the principles from *Principia* which was used in the proof. The fact remains that the intensions are at best a pretty obscure lot.

Yet it is evident enough that we cannot, in the foregoing treatment of propositional attitudes, drop the intensions in favor of the corresponding extensions. Thus, to take a trivial example, consider 'w is hunting unicorns.' On the analogy of (29), it becomes:

w strives y (y finds a unicorn) of w.

Correspondingly for the hunting of griffins. Hence, if anyone w is to hunt unicorns without hunting griffins, the attributes

y (y finds a unicorn),
y (y finds a griffin)

must be distinct. But the corresponding classes are identical, being empty. So it is indeed the attributes, and not the classes, that were needed in our formulation. The same moral could be drawn, though less briefly, without appeal to empty cases.

But there is a way of dodging the intensions which merits serious consideration. Instead of speaking of intensions we can speak of sentences, naming these by quotation. Instead of:

w believes that . . .

we may say:

w believes-true '. . . . .'.

Instead of:

(30) w believes y (. . . y . . .) of x

we may say:

(31) w believes '. . . y . . .' satisfied by x.

The words 'believes satisfied by' here, like 'believes of' before, would be viewed as an irreducibly triadic predicate. A similar shift can be made in the case of the other propositional attitudes, of course, and in the tetradic and higher cases.

This semantical reformulation is not, of course, intended to suggest that the subject of the propositional attitude speaks the language of the quotation, or any language. We may treat a mouse's fear of a cat as his fearing true a certain English sentence. This is unnatural without being therefore wrong. It is a little like describing a prehistoric ocean current as clockwise.

How, where, and on what grounds to draw a boundary between those who believe or wish or strive that p, and those who do not quite believe or wish or strive that p, is undeniably a vague and obscure affair. However, if anyone does approve of speaking of belief of a proposition at all and of speaking of a proposition in turn as meant by a sentence, then certainly he cannot object to our semantical reformulation 'w believes-true S' on any special grounds of obscurity; for, 'w believes-true S' is explicitly definable in *his* terms as 'w believes the proposition meant by S.' Similarly for the semantical reformulation (31) of (30); similarly for the tetradic and higher cases; and similarly for wishing, striving, and other propositional attitudes.

Our semantical versions do involve a relativity to language, however, which must be made explicit. When we say that w believes-true S, we need to be able to say what language the sentence S is thought of as belonging to; not because w needs to understand S, but because S might by coincidence exist (as a linguistic form) with very different meanings in two languages.[5] Strictly, therefore, we should think of the dyadic "believes-true S' as expanded to a triadic 'w believes-true S in L'; and correspondingly for (31) and its suite.

As noted two paragraphs back, the semantical form of expression:

(32) w believes – true '. . .' in L

can be explained in intensional terms, for persons who favor them, as:

(33) w believes the proposition meant by
       '. . .' in L,

thus leaving no cause for protest on the score of relative clarity. Protest may still be heard, however, on a different score: (32) and (33), though equivalent to each other, are not strictly equivalent to the 'w believes that. . . . .' which is our real concern. For, it is argued, in order to infer (33) we need not only the information about w which 'w believes that. . . . .' provides, but also some extraneous information about the language L. Church[6] brings the point out by appeal to translations, substantially as follows. The respective statements:

w believes that there are unicorns,
w believes the proposition meant by
'There are unicorns' in English

go into German as:

(34) w glaubt, dass es Einho gibt,
(35) w glaubt diejenige Aussage, die
       "There are unicorns" auf Englisch
       bedeutet,

and clearly (34) does not provide enough information to enable a German ignorant of English to infer (35).

The same reasoning can be used to show that 'There are unicorns' is not strictly or analytically equivalent to:

'There are unicorns' is true in English.

Nor, indeed, was Tarski's truth paradigm intended to assert analytic equivalence. Similarly, then, for (32) in relation to 'w believes that. . . . .'; a systematic agreement in truth value can be claimed, and no more. This limitation will prove of little moment to persons who share my skepticism about analyticity.

What I find more disturbing about the semantical versions, such as (32), is the need of dragging in the language concept at all. What is a language? What degree of fixity is supposed? When do we have one language and not two? The propositional attitudes are dim affairs to begin with, and it is a pity to have to add obscurity to obscurity by bringing in language variables too. Only let it not be supposed that any clarity is gained by restituting the intensions.

Notes

This paper sums up some points which I have set forth in various lectures at Harvard and Oxford from 1952 onward.

1 See *From a Logical Point of View* (Harvard University Press, 1953), pp. 142–59; also "Three Grades of Modal Involvement," *Proceedings of the Eleventh International Congress of Philosophy*, Vol. 14, pp. 65–81.

2 See *From a Logical Point of View*, pp. 150–4.

3 See "Two Dogmas of Empiricism," in *From a Logical Point of View*; also "Carnap and Logical Truth," in Paul Arthur Schilpp (editor), *The Philosophy of Rudolf Carnap*, Library of Living Philosophers.

4 At the end of "On Frege's Way Out," *Mind*, Vol. 64 (1955).

5 This point is made by Alonzo Church, "On Carnap's Analysis of Statements of Assertion and Belief," *Analysis*, Vol. 10 (1950), pp. 97–9.

6 Op. cit., with an acknowledgment to Langford.

22

Counterpart Theory and Quantified Modal Logic

David Lewis

I. Counterpart Theory

WE can conduct formalized discourse about most topics perfectly well by means of our all-purpose extensional logic, provided with predicates and a domain of quantification suited to the subject matter at hand. That is what we do when our topic is numbers, or sets, or wholes and parts, or strings of symbols. That is what we do when our topic is modality: what might be and what must be, essence and accident. Then we introduce modal operators to create a special-purpose, nonextensional logic. Why this departure from our custom? Is it a historical accident, or was it forced on us somehow by the very nature of the topic of modality?

It was not forced on us. We have an alternative. Instead of formalizing our modal discourse by means of modal operators, we could follow our usual practice. We could stick to our standard logic (quantification theory with identity and without ineliminable singular terms) and provide it with predicates and a domain of quantification suited to the topic of modality. That done, certain expressions are available which take the place of modal operators. The new predicates required, together with postulates on them, constitute the system I call *Counterpart Theory*.

The primitive predicates of counterpart theory are these four:

David Lewis, Counterpart Theory and Quantified Modal Logic. *The Journal of Philosophy*, 65, 5 (1968): 113–26.

Wx (x is a possible world)
Ixy (x is in possible world y)
Ax (x is actual)
Cxy (x is a counterpart of y).

The domain of quantification is to contain every possible world and everything in every world. The primitives are to be understood according to their English readings and the following postulates:

P1: $\forall x \forall y(Ixy \supset Wy)$
    (Nothing is in anything except a world)
P2: $\forall x \forall y \forall z(Ixy \ \& \ Ixz . \supset y = z)$
    (Nothing is in two worlds)
P3: $\forall x \forall y(Cxy \supset \exists z Ixz)$
    (Whatever is a counterpart is in a world)
P4: $\forall x \forall y(Cxy \supset \exists z Iyz)$
    (Whatever has a counterpart is in a world)
P5: $\forall x \forall y \forall z(Ixy \ \& \ Izy \ \& \ Cxz . \supset x = z)$
    (Nothing is a counterpart of anything else in its world)
P6: $\forall x \forall y(Ixy \supset Cxx)$
    (Anything in a world is a counterpart of itself)
P7: $\exists x(Wx \ \& \ \forall y(Iyx \equiv Ay))$
    (Some world contains all and only actual things)
P8: $\exists x Ax$
    (Something is actual)

The world mentioned in P7 is unique, by P2 and P8. Let us abbreviate its description:

$$@ = df \ {}^\imath x \forall y(Iyx \equiv Ay) \quad \text{(the actual world)}$$

Unactualized possibles, things in worlds other than the actual world, have often been deemed "entia non grata",[1] largely because it is not clear when they are or are not identical. But identity literally understood is no problem for us. Within any one world, things of every category are individuated just as they are in the actual world; things in different worlds are *never* identical, by P2. The counterpart relation is our substitute for identity between things in different worlds.[2] Where some would say that you are in several worlds, in which you have somewhat different properties and somewhat different properties and somewhat different things happen to you, I prefer to say that you are in the actual world and no other, but you have counterparts in several other worlds. Your counterparts resemble you closely in content and context in important respects. They resemble you more closely than do the other things in their worlds. But they are not really you. For each of them is in his own world, and only you are here in the actual world. Indeed we might say, speaking casually, that your counterparts are you in other worlds, that they and you are the same; but this sameness is no more a literal identity than the sameness between you today and you tomorrow. It would be better to say that your counterparts are men you *would have been*, had the world been otherwise.[3]

The counterpart relation is a relation of similarity. So it is problematic in the way all relations of similarity are: it is the resultant of similarities and dissimilarities in a multitude of respects, weighted by the importances of the various respects[4] and by the degrees of the similarities.[5]

Carnap,[6] Kanger,[7] Hintikka,[8] Kripke,[9] Montague,[10] and others have proposed interpretations of quantified modal logic on which one thing is allowed to be in several worlds. A reader of this persuasion might suspect that he and I differ only verbally: that what I call a thing in a world is just what he would call a ⟨thing, world⟩ pair, and that what he calls the same thing in several worlds is just what I would call a class of mutual counterparts. But beware. Our difference is not just verbal, for I enjoy a generality he cannot match. The counterpart relation will not, in general, be an equivalence relation. So it will not hold just between those of his ⟨thing, world⟩ pairs with the same first term, no matter how he may choose to identify things between worlds.

It would not have been plausible to postulate that the counterpart relation was transitive. Suppose x_1 in world w_1 resembles you closely in many respects, far more closely than anything else in w_1 does. And suppose x_2 in world w_2 resembles x_1 closely, far more closely than anything else in w_2 does. So x_2 is a counterpart of your counterpart x_1. Yet x_2 might not resemble you very closely, and something else in w_2 might resemble you more closely. If so, x_2 is not your counterpart.

It would not have been plausible to postulate that the counterpart relation was symmetric. Suppose x_3 in world w_3 is a sort of blend of you and your brother; x_3 resembles both of you closely, far more closely than anything else in w_3 resembles either one of you. So x_3 is your counterpart. But suppose also that the resemblance between x_3 and your brother is far closer than that between x_3 and you. If so, you are not a counterpart of x_3.

It would not have been plausible to postulate that nothing in any world had more than one counterpart in any other world. Suppose x_{4a} and x_{4b} in world w_4 are twins; both resemble you closely; both resemble you far more closely than anything else in w_4 does; both resemble you equally. If so, both are your counterparts.

It would not have been plausible to postulate that no two things in any world had a common counterpart in any other world. Suppose you resemble both the twins x_{4a} and x_{4b} far more closely than anything else in the actual world does. If so, you are a counterpart of both.

It would not have been plausible to postulate that, for any two worlds, anything in one was a counterpart of something in the other. Suppose there is something x_5 in world w_5 – say, Batman – which does not much resemble anything actual. If so, x_5 is not a counterpart of anything in the actual world.

It would not have been plausible to postulate that, for any two worlds, anything in one had some counterpart in the other. Suppose whatever thing x_6 in world w_6 it is that resembles you more closely than anything else in w_6 is nevertheless quite unlike you; nothing in w_6 resembles you at all closely. If so, you have no counterpart in w_6.

II. Translation

Counterpart theory and quantified modal logic seem to have the same subject matter; seem to provide two rival ways of formalizing our modal discourse. In that case they should be intertranslatable; indeed they are. Hence I need not give directions for formalizing modal discourse directly by means of counterpart theory; I can assume the reader is accustomed to formalizing modal discourse by means of modal operators, so I need only give directions for translating sentences of quantified modal logic into sentences of counterpart theory.

Counterpart theory has at least three advantages over quantified modal logic as a vehicle for formalized discourse about modality. (1) Counterpart theory is a theory, not a special-purpose intensional logic. (2) Whereas the obscurity of quantified modal logic has proved intractable, that of counterpart theory is at least divided, if not conquered. We can trace it to its two independent sources. There is our uncertainty about analyticity, and, hence, about whether certain descriptions describe possible worlds; and there is our uncertainty about the relative importance of different respects of similarity and dissimilarity, and, hence, about which things are counterparts of which. (3) If the translation scheme I am about to propose is correct, every sentence of quantified modal logic has the same meaning as a sentence of counterpart theory, its translation; but not every sentence of counterpart theory is, or is equivalent to, the translation of any sentence of quantified modal logic. Therefore, starting with a fixed stock of predicates other than those of counterpart theory, we can say more by adding counterpart theory than we can by adding modal operators.

Now let us examine my proposed translation scheme.[11] We begin with some important special cases, leading up to a general definition.

First consider a closed (0-place) sentence with a single, initial modal operator: $\Box\phi$ or $\Diamond\phi$. It is given the familiar translation: $\forall\beta(W\beta \supset \phi^\beta)$ (ϕ holds in any possible world β) or $\exists\beta(W\beta\phi^\beta)$ (ϕ holds in some possible world β). To form the sentence ϕ^β (ϕ holds in world β) from the given sentence ϕ, we need only restrict the range of each quantifier in ϕ to the domain of things in the world denoted by β; that is, we replace $\forall\alpha$ by $\forall\alpha(I\alpha\beta \supset \ldots)$ and $\exists\alpha$ by $\exists\alpha(I\alpha\beta \& \ldots)$ throughout ϕ.

Next consider a 1-place open sentence with a single, initial modal operator: $\Box\phi\alpha$ or $\Diamond\phi\alpha$. It is given the translation $\forall\beta\forall\gamma(W\beta \& I\gamma\beta \& C\gamma\alpha . \supset \phi^\beta\gamma)$ (ϕ holds of every counterpart γ of α in any world β) or $\exists\beta\exists\gamma(W\beta \& I\gamma\beta \& C\gamma\alpha \& \phi^\beta\gamma)$ (ϕ holds of some counterpart γ of α in some world β). Likewise for an open sentence with any number of places.

If the modal operator is not initial, we translate the subsentence it governs. And if there are quan-

tifiers that do not lie within the scope of any modal operator, we must restrict their range to the domain of things in the actual world; for that is their range in quantified modal logic, whereas an unrestricted quantifier in counterpart theory would range at least over all the worlds and everything in any of them. A sentence of quantified modal logic that contains *no* modal operator – a nonmodal sentence in a modal context – is therefore translated simply by restricting its quantifiers to things in the actual world.

Finally, consider a sentence in which there are modal operators within the scopes of other modal operators. Then we must work inward; to obtain ϕ^β from ϕ we must not only restrict quantifiers in ϕ but also translate any subsentences of ϕ with initial modal operators.

The general translation scheme can best be presented as a direct definition of the translation of a sentence ϕ of quantified modal logic:

T1: The translation of ϕ is $\phi^@$ (ϕ holds in the actual world); that is, in primitive notation, $\exists\beta(\forall\alpha(I\alpha\beta \equiv A\alpha) \& \phi^\beta)$

followed by a recursive definition of ϕ^β (ϕ holds in world β)

T2a: ϕ^β is ϕ, if ϕ is atomic
T2b: $(\sim\phi)^\beta$ is $\sim\phi^\beta$
T2c: $(\phi\psi)^\beta$ is $\phi^\beta\psi^\beta$
T2d: $(\phi\psi)^\beta$ is $\phi^\beta\psi^\beta$
T2e: $(\phi \supset \psi)^\beta$ is $\phi^\beta \supset \psi^\beta$
T2f: $(\phi \equiv \psi)^\beta$ is $\phi^\beta \equiv \psi^\beta$
T2g: $(\forall\alpha\phi)^\beta$ is $\forall\alpha(I\alpha\beta \supset \phi^\beta)$
T2h: $(\exists\alpha\phi)^\beta$ is $\exists\alpha(I\alpha\beta \& \phi^\beta)$
T2i: $(\Box\phi\alpha_1 \ldots \alpha_n)^\beta$ is $\forall\beta_1\forall\gamma_1 \ldots \forall\gamma_n)$
       $(W\beta_1 \& I\gamma_1\beta_1 \& C\gamma_1\alpha_1 \& \ldots \&$
       $\gamma_n\beta_1 \& C\gamma_n\alpha_n . \supset \phi^{\beta_1}\gamma_1 \ldots \gamma_n)$
T2j: $(\Diamond\phi\alpha_1 \ldots \alpha_n)^\beta$ is $\exists\beta_1\exists\gamma_1 \ldots \exists\gamma_n$
       $W\beta_1 \& I\gamma_1\beta_1 \& C\gamma_1\alpha_1 \& \ldots \& I\gamma_n$
       $\beta_1 \& C\gamma_n\alpha_n \& \phi^{\beta_1}\gamma_1 \ldots \gamma_n)$

Using these two definitions, we find, for example, that

$\forall xFx$
$\Diamond\exists xFx$
$\Box Fx$
$\forall x(Fx \supset \Box Fx)$
$\Box\Diamond Fx$

are translated, respectively, as

$\forall x(Ix@ \supset Fx)$

(Everything actual is an F)

$\exists y(Wy \,\&\, \exists x(Ixy \,\&\, Fx))$

(Some possible world contains an F)

$\forall y_1 \forall x_1 (Wy_1 \,\&\, Ix_1y_1 \,\&\, Cx_1x . \supset Fx_1)$

(Every counterpart of x, in any world, is an F)

$\forall x(Ix@ \supset . Fx \supset \forall y_1 \forall x_1 (Wy_1 \,\&\, Ix_1y_1 \,\&\, Cx_1x .$
$\supset Fx_1))$

(If anything is a counterpart of an actual F, then it is an F)

$\forall y_1 \forall x_1 (Wy_1 \,\&\, Ix_1y_1 \,\&\, Cx_1x . \supset \exists y_2 \exists x_2$
$(Wy_2 \,\&\, Ix_2y_2 \,\&\, Cx_2x_1 \,\&\, Fx_2))$

(Every counterpart of x has a counterpart which is an F)

The reverse translation, from sentences of counterpart theory to sentences of quantified modal logic, can be done by finite search whenever it can be done at all. For if a modal sentence ψ is the translation of a sentence ϕ of counterpart theory, then ψ must be shorter than ϕ and ϕ must contain no predicates or variables not in ϕ. But not every sentence of counterpart theory is the translation of a modal sentence, or even an equivalent of the translation of a modal sentence. For instance, our postulates P1–P7 are not.

It may disturb us that the translation of $\forall x \Box \exists y (x = y)$ (everything actual necessarily exists) comes out true even if something actual lacks a counterpart in some world. To avoid this, we might be tempted to adopt the alternative translation scheme, brought to my attention by David Kaplan, in which T2i and T2j are replaced by

T2i': $(\Box \phi \alpha_1 \ldots \alpha_n)^\beta$ is $\forall \beta_1 (W\beta_1 \supset \exists \gamma_1 \ldots$

$\exists \gamma_n (I\gamma_1\beta_1 \,\&\, C\gamma_1\alpha_1 \,\&\, \ldots \,\&\, I\gamma_n\beta_1 \,\&\,$
$C\gamma_n\alpha_n \,\&\, \phi_1^\beta \gamma_1 \ldots \gamma_n))$

T2j': $(\Diamond \phi \alpha_1 \ldots \alpha_n)^\beta$ is $\exists \beta_1 (W\beta_1 \,\&\, \forall \gamma_1 \ldots$

$\forall \gamma_n (I\gamma_1\beta_1 \,\&\, C\gamma_1\alpha_1 \,\&\, \ldots \,\&\, I\gamma_n\beta_1 \,\&\,$
$\gamma_n\alpha_n . \supset$

$\phi_1^\beta \gamma_1 \ldots \gamma_n))$

with heterogeneous rather than homogeneous quantifiers. Out of the frying pan, into the fire: with T2j', $\exists x \Diamond (x \neq x)$ (something actual is possibly non-self-identical) comes out true unless everything actual has a counterpart in every

world! We might compromise by taking T2i' and T2j, but at the price of sacrificing the ordinary duality of necessity and possibility.[12] So I chose to take T2i and T2j.

III. Essentialism

Quine has often warned us that by quantifying past modal operators we commit ourselves to the view that "an object, of itself and by whatever name or none, must be seen as having some of its traits necessarily and others contingently, despite the fact that the latter traits follow just as analytically from some ways of specifying the object as the former traits do from other ways of specifying it."[13] This so-called "Aristotelian essentialism" – the doctrine of essences not relative to specifications – "should be every bit as congenial to [the champion of quantified modal logic] as quantified modal logic itself."[14]

Agreed. Essentialism is congenial. We do have a way of saying that an attribute is an essential attribute of an object – essential regardless of how the object happens to have been specified and regardless of whether the attribute follows analytically from any or all specifications of the object.

Consider the attribute expressed by a 1-place sentence ϕ and the object denoted by a singular term[15] ζ. To say that this attribute is an essential attribute of this object is to assert the translation of $\Box \phi \zeta$.

But we have not yet considered how to translate a modal sentence containing a singular term. For we know that any singular term ζ may be treated as a description $\tau \alpha (\psi \alpha)$ (although often only by letting ψ contain some artificial predicate made from a proper name); and we know that any description may be eliminated by Russell's contextual definition. Our translation scheme did not take account of singular terms because they need never occur in the primitive notation of quantified modal logic. We must always eliminate singular terms before translating; afterwards, if we like, we can restore them.

There is just one hitch: before eliminating a description, we must assign it a scope. Different choices of scope will, in general, lead to nonequivalent translations. This is so even if the eliminated description denotes precisely one thing in the actual world and in every possible world.[16]

Taking ζ as a description $\tau \alpha (\psi \alpha)$ and assigning it narrow scope, our sentence $\Box \phi \zeta$ is interpreted as

$$\Box\exists\alpha(\forall\delta(\psi\delta \equiv \delta = \alpha) \ \& \ \phi\alpha)$$

Its translation under this interpretation is

$$\forall\beta(W\beta \supset \exists\alpha(I\alpha\beta \ \& \ \forall\delta(I\delta\beta \supset . \psi^{\beta}\delta \equiv \delta = \alpha) \\ \& \ \phi^{\beta}\alpha))$$

(Any possible world β contains a unique α such that $\psi^{\beta}\alpha$; and for any such α, $\phi^{\beta}\alpha$)

This is an interpretation *de dicto*: the modal operator attaches to the already closed sentence $\phi\zeta$. It is referentially opaque: the translation of an ostensible use of Leibniz's Law

$$\Box\phi\zeta$$
$$\therefore \frac{\eta = \zeta}{\Box\phi\eta}$$

or of an ostensible existential generalization

$$\frac{\Box\phi\zeta}{\therefore \exists\alpha\Box\phi\alpha}$$

is an invalid argument if the terms involved are taken as descriptions with narrow scope.

Taking ζ as a description with wide scope, $\Box\phi\zeta$ is interepreted as

$$\exists\alpha(\forall\delta(\psi\delta \equiv \delta = \alpha) \ \& \ \Box\phi\alpha)$$

and translated as

$$\exists\alpha(I\alpha@ \ \& \ \forall\delta(I\delta@ \supset . \psi^{@}\delta \equiv \delta = \alpha) \\ \& \ \forall\beta\forall\gamma(W\beta \ \& \ I\gamma\beta \ \& \ C\gamma\alpha . \supset \phi^{\beta}\gamma))$$

(The actual world contains a unique α such that $\psi^{@}\alpha$; and for any counterpart γ thereof, in any world β, $\phi^{\beta}\gamma$)

This is an interpretation *de re*: the modal operator attaches to the open sentence ϕ to form a new open modal sentence $\Box\phi$, and the attribute expressed by $\Box\phi$ is then predicated of the actual thing denoted by ζ. This interpretation is referentially transparent: the translation of an ostensible use of Leibniz's law or of an ostensible existential generalization is a valid argument if the terms involved are taken as descriptions with wide scope.

How are we to choose between the two interpretations of $\Box\phi\zeta$? Often we cannot, unless by fiat; there is a genuine ambiguity. But there are several conditions that tend to favor the wide-scope interpretation as the more natural: (1) whenever ζ is a description formed by turning a proper name into an artificial predicate; (2) whenever the description ζ has what Donellan calls its referential use;[17] (3) whenever we are prepared to accept

ζ is something α such that necessarily $\phi\alpha$

as one possible English reading of $\Box\phi\zeta$. (The force of the third condition is due to the fact that $\exists\alpha(\zeta = \alpha\Box\phi\alpha)$ is unambiguously equivalent to $\Box\phi\zeta$ with ζ given wide scope.[18])

The translations of $\Box\phi\zeta$ under its two interpretations are logically independent. Neither follows from the other just by itself. But with the aid of suitable auxiliary premises we can go in both directions. The inference from the narrow-scope translation to the wide-scope translation (exportation[19]) requires the further premise

$$\exists\alpha(I\alpha@ \ \& \ \forall\beta\forall\gamma(I\gamma\beta \ \& \ C\gamma\alpha . \supset \forall\delta(I\delta\beta \\ \supset . \psi^{\beta}\delta \equiv \delta = \gamma)))$$

(There is something α in the actual world, any counterpart γ of which is the only thing δ in its world β such that $\psi^{\beta}\delta$

which is a simplified equivalent of the translation of $\exists\alpha\Box(\zeta = \alpha)$ with ζ given narrow scope.[20] The inference from the wide-scope translation to the narrow-scope translation (importation) requires the same auxiliary premise, and another as well:

$$\exists\alpha(I\alpha@ \ \& \ \forall\delta(I\delta@ . \supset \psi^{@}\delta \equiv \delta = \alpha) \\ \& \ \forall\beta(W\beta \supset \exists\gamma(I\gamma\beta \ \& \ C\gamma\alpha)))$$

(The unique α in the actual world such that $\psi^{@}\alpha$, has at least one counterpart γ in any world β)

This second auxiliary premise is not equivalent to the translation of any modal sentence.[21]

In general, of course, there will be more than two ways to assign scopes. Consider $\Box\Diamond(\eta = \zeta)$. Each description may be given narrow, medium, or wide scope; so there are nine nonequivalent translations.

It is the wide-scope, *de re*, transparent translation of $\Box\phi\zeta$ which says that the attribute expressed by ϕ is an essential attribute of the thing denoted by ζ. In short, an essential attribute of something is an attribute it shares with all its counterparts. All your counterparts are probably human; if so, you are essentially human. All your counterparts are even more probably corporeal; if so, you are essentially corporeal.

An attribute that something shares with all its counterparts is an essential attribute of that thing, part of its essence. The whole of its essence is the intersection of its essential attributes, the attribute it shares with all and only its counterparts. (*The* attribute, because there is no need to distinguish attributes that are coextensive not only in the actual world but also in every possible world.) There may or may not be an open sentence that expresses the attribute that is the essence of something; to assert that the attribute expressed by ϕ is the essence of the thing denoted by ζ is to assert

$$\exists \alpha (I\alpha@ \ \& \ \forall \delta (I\delta@ \supset . \ \psi^@ \delta \equiv \delta = \alpha)$$
$$\& \ \forall \beta \forall \gamma (I\gamma \beta \supset . \ C\gamma \alpha \equiv \phi^\beta \gamma))$$

(The actual world contains a unique α such that $\psi^@ \alpha$; and for anything γ in any world β, γ is a counterpart of α if and only if $\phi^\beta \gamma$)

This sentence is not equivalent to the translation of any modal sentence.

Essence and counterpart are interdefinable. We have just defined the essence of something as the attribute it shares with all and only its counterparts; a counterpart of something is anything having the attribute which is its essence. (This is not to say that that attribute is the *counterpart's* essence, or even an essential attribute of the counterpart.)

Perhaps there are certain attributes that can only be essential attributes of things, never accidents. Perhaps every human must be essentially human; more likely, perhaps everything corporeal must be essentially corporeal. The attribute expressed by ϕ is of this sort, incapable of being an accident, just in case it is closed under the counterpart relation; that is, just in case

$$\forall \alpha \forall \gamma \forall \beta_1 (I\alpha \beta \ \& \ I\gamma \beta_1 \ \& \ C\gamma \alpha \ \& \ \phi^\beta \alpha . \supset \phi_1^\beta \gamma)$$

(For any counterpart γ in any world β_1 of anything α in any world β, if $\phi^\beta \alpha$ then $\phi_1^\beta \gamma$)

This is a simplified equivalent of the translation of

$$\Box \forall \alpha (\phi \alpha \supset \Box \phi \alpha)$$

We might wonder whether these attributes incapable of being accidents are what we call "natural kinds." But notice first that we must disregard the necessarily universal attribute, expressed, for instance, by the open sentence $\alpha = \alpha$, since it is an essential attribute of everything. And notice second that arbitrary unions of attributes incapable of being accidents are themselves attributes incapable of being accidents; so to exclude gerrymanders we must confine ourselves to *minimal* attributes incapable of being accidents. All of these may indeed be natural kinds; but these cannot be the only natural kinds, since some unions and all intersections of natural kinds are themselves natural kinds.

IV. Modal Principles

Translation into counterpart theory can settle disputed questions in quantified modal logic. We can test a suggested modal principle by seeing whether its translation is a theorem of counterpart theory; or, if not, whether the extra postulates that would make it a theorem are plausible. We shall consider eight principles and find only one that should be accepted.

$$\Box \phi \prec \Box \Box \phi \quad \text{(Becker's principle)}$$

The translation is not a theorem unless ϕ is a closed sentence, but would have been a theorem in general under the rejected postulate that the counterpart relation was transitive.

$$\phi \prec \Box \Diamond \phi \quad \text{(Brouwer's principle)}$$

The translation is not a theorem unless ϕ is a closed sentence, but would have been a theorem in general under the rejected postulate that the counterpart relation was symmetric.

$$\alpha_1 = \alpha_2 \prec \Box \alpha_1 = \alpha_2$$
(α_1 and α_2 not the same variable)

The translation is not a theorem, but would have been under the rejected postulate that nothing in any world had more than one counterpart in any other world.

$$\alpha_1 \neq \alpha_2 \prec \Box \alpha_1 \neq \alpha_2$$
(α_1 and α_2 not the same variable)

The translation is not a theorem, but would have been under the rejected postulate that no two things in any world had a common counterpart in any other world.

$$\forall\alpha\Box\phi\alpha \prec \Box\forall\alpha\phi\alpha \quad \text{(Barcan's principle)}$$

The translation is not a theorem, but would have been under the rejected postulate that, for any two worlds, anything in one was a counterpart of something in the other.

$$\exists\alpha\Box\phi\alpha \prec \Box\exists\alpha\phi\alpha$$

The translation is not a theorem, but would have been under the rejected postulate that, for any two worlds, anything in one had some counterpart in the other.

$$\Box\forall\alpha\phi\alpha \prec \forall\alpha\Box\phi\alpha$$

(Converse of Barcan's principle)

The translation is a theorem.

$$\Box\exists\alpha\phi\alpha \prec \exists\alpha\Box\phi\alpha$$

The translation is not a theorem, nor would it have been under any extra postulates with even the slightest plausibility.

V. Relative Modalities

Just as a sentence ϕ is necessary if it holds in all worlds, so ϕ is causally necessary if it holds in all worlds compatible with the laws of nature; obligatory for you if it holds in all worlds in which you act rightly; implicitly known, believed, hoped, asserted, or perceived by you if it holds in all worlds compatible with the content of your knowledge, beliefs, hopes, assertions, or perceptions. These, and many more, are *relative* modalities, expressible by quantifications over restricted ranges of worlds. We can write any dual pair of relative modalities as

$$\Box^i\delta_1\ldots\delta_m$$
$$\Diamond^i\delta_1\ldots\delta_m$$

where the index i indicates how the restriction of worlds is to be made and the m arguments $\delta_1, \ldots, \delta_m$, with $m \geq 0$, denote things to be considered in making the restriction (say, the person whose implicit knowledge we are talking about). To every dual pair of relative modalities there corresponds a characteristic relation

$$R^i xyz_1\ldots z_m \text{ (world } x \text{ is } i\text{-related to world } y$$
$$\text{and } z_1, \ldots, z_m \text{ therein)}$$

governed by the postulate

P9: $\forall x\forall y\forall z_1\ldots\forall z_m(R^i xyz_1\ldots z_m \supset .Wx$
& Wy & Iz_1y & $\ldots$ & $Iz_my)$

The characteristic relation gives the appropriate restriction: we are to consider only worlds i-related to whatever world we are in (and certain things in it). Necessity and possibility themselves are that pair of relative modalities whose characteristic relation is just the 2-place universal relation between worlds.[22]

We can easily extend our translation scheme to handle sentences containing miscellaneous modal operators. We will treat them just as we do necessity and possibility, except that quantifiers over worlds will range over only those worlds which bear the appropriate characteristic relation to some world and perhaps some things in it. The translation of ϕ remains $\phi^@$; we need only add two new clauses to the recursive definition of ϕ:

*T2i**: $(\Box^i\delta_1\ldots\delta_m\phi\alpha_1\ldots\alpha_n)^\beta \text{is} \forall\beta_1\forall\gamma_1\ldots$
$\forall\gamma_n(R^i\beta_1\beta\delta_1\ldots\delta_m$ & $I\gamma_1\beta_1$ & $C\gamma_1\alpha_1$
& $\ldots$ & $I\gamma_n\beta_1$ & $C\gamma_n\alpha_n . \supset \phi^{\beta_1}$
$\gamma_1\ldots\gamma_n)$

*T2j**: $(\Diamond^i\delta_1\ldots\delta_m\phi\alpha_1\ldots\alpha_n)^\beta \text{ is } \exists\beta_1\exists\gamma_1\ldots$
$\exists\gamma_n(R^i\beta_1\beta\delta_1\ldots\delta_m$ & $I\gamma_1\beta_1$ & $C\gamma_1\alpha_1$
& $\ldots$ & $I\gamma_n\beta_1$ & $C\gamma_n\alpha_n$ & $\phi_1^\beta\gamma_1\ldots\gamma_n)$

(since necessity and possibility are relative modalities, we no longer need T2i and T2j). For example our translations of

$$\Box^i\phi$$
$$\Box^j\delta\psi\alpha$$
$$\Box^i\Box^j\delta\phi$$

where ϕ is a 0-place sentence, ψ is a 1-place sentence, $\Box^i$ is a 1-place relative modality, and $\Box^j$ is a 1-place relative modality, are, respectively,

$$\forall\beta(R^i\beta@ \supset \phi^\beta)$$
(ϕ holds in any world i-related to the actual world)

$$\forall\beta\forall\gamma(R^j\beta@\delta \text{ & } I\gamma\beta \text{ & } C\gamma\alpha . \supset \psi^\beta\alpha)$$
(ψ holds of any counterpart γ of α in any world β j-related to the actual world and δ therein)

$\forall \beta_1 \forall \gamma (R^i \beta @ \& I\gamma\beta_1 \& C\gamma\delta . \supset \forall \beta_2$

$(R^j \beta_2 \beta_1 \gamma \supset \phi_2^\beta))$

(ϕ holds in any world β_2 such that, for some world β_1 that is i-related to the actual world and for some counterpart γ in β_1 of δ, β_2 is j-related to β_1 and γ)

The third example illustrates the fact that free variables occurring as arguments of relative modal operators may need to be handled by means of the counterpart relation.

Our previous discussion of singular terms as eliminable descriptions subject to ambiguity of scope carries over, with one change: in general, the auxiliary premise for exportation (and the first of two auxiliary premises for importation) must be the translation of $\Box^i \delta_1 \ldots \delta_m (\zeta = \zeta)$ with one occurrence of ζ given wide scope and the other given narrow scope. The translation of $\exists \alpha \Box^i \delta_1 \ldots \delta_m (\zeta = \alpha)$ will do only for those relative modalities, like necessity, for which $R^i @@\delta_1 \ldots \delta_m$ – and, hence, the translation of $\Box^i \delta_1 \ldots \delta_m \phi \supset \phi$ – are theorems under the appropriate postulates on the i-relation. More generally, the argument

$^i\delta_1 \ldots \delta_m \phi \eta$

$\underline{\Box^i \delta_1 \ldots \delta_m (\eta = \zeta)}$

$\therefore \Box^i \delta_1 \ldots \delta_m \phi \zeta$

where ϕ is a 1-place sentence, has a valid translation if ζ is given wide scope and η is given narrow scope throughout.

Principles corresponding to those discussed in section IV can be formulated for any relative modality (or, in the case of Becker's and Brouwer's principles, for any mixture of relative modalities). The acceptability of such principles will depend, in general, not just on the logical properties of the counterpart relation and the i-relations involved, but on the logical relations *between* the counterpart relation and the i-relations. For example, consider a relative necessity without arguments, so that its characteristic i-relation will be 2-place. (Such an i-relation is often called an *accessibility* relation between worlds.) And consider Becker's principle for this relative necessity (but with '$\prec$' still defined in terms of necessity itself): $\Box^i \phi \prec^i \Box^i \Box^i \phi$; that is, $\Box(\Box^i \phi \supset \Box^i \Box^i \phi)$. It is often said that Becker's principle holds just in case accessibility is transitive, which is correct if ϕ is a closed sentence. But for open ϕ, Becker's principle holds just in case

$\forall x_1 \forall y_1 \forall x_2 \forall y_2 \forall x_3 \forall y_3 (Ix_1 y_1 \&\} Ix_2 y_2 \&$

$Ix_3 y_3 \& Cx_2 x_1 \& Cx_3 x_2 \& R^i y_2 y_1 \& R^i y_3 y_2$

$. \supset . Cx_3 x_1 \& R^i y_3 y_1)$

even if neither accessibility nor the counterpart relation is transitive.

Notes

I am indebted to David Kaplan, whose criticisms have resulted in many important improvements. A. N. Prior has informed me that my theory resembles a treatment of *de re* modality communicated to him by P.T. Geach in 1964.

1   W. V. Quine, *Word and Object* (Cambridge, Mass.: MIT Press, 1960), p. 245.

2   Yet with this substitute in use, it would not matter if some things *were* identical with their counterparts after all! P2 serves only to rule out avoidable problems of individuation.

3   This way of describing counterparts is due to L. Sprague de Camp, "The Wheels of If," in *Unknown Fantasy Fiction*, October, 1940.

4   As discussed in Michael A. Slote, "The Theory of Important Criteria," *Journal of Philosophy*, LXIII, 8 (Apr. 14, 1966): 211–24.

5   The counterpart relation is very like the relation of intersubjective correspondence discussed in Rudolf Carnap, *Der Logische Aufbau der Welt* (Berlin-Schlactensee: Weltkreis-Verlag, 1928), sec. 146.

6   "Modalities and Quantification," *Journal of Symbolic Logic*, XI, 2 (June 1946): 33–64.

7   *Provability in Logic* (Stockholm: Almqvist and Wiksell, 1957).

8   "Modality as Referential Multiplicity," *Ajatus*, XX (1957): 49–64.

9   "A Completeness Theorem in Modal Logic," *Journal of Symbolic Logic*, XXIV, 1 (March 1959): 1–14; "Semantical Considerations on Modal Logic," *Acta Philosophica Fennica*, XVI (1963): 83–94.

10 "Logical Necessity, Physical Necessity, Ethics, and Quantifiers," *Inquiry*, III (1960): 259–69.

11 *Notation*: Sentences are mentioned by means of the Greek letters 'ϕ', 'ψ', . . .; variables by means of 'α', 'β', 'γ', 'δ', . . . If ϕ is any n-place sentence and $\alpha_1 \ldots \alpha_n$ are any n different variables, then $\phi \alpha_1 \ldots \alpha_n$ is the sentence obtained by substituting α_1 uniformly for the alphabetically first free variable in ϕ, α_2 for the second, and so on. Variables introduced in translation are to be chosen in some systematic way that prevents confusion of bound

variables. Symbolic expressions are used autonymously.

12 If we also postulate that the counterpart relation is an equivalence relation, we get an interpretation like that of Føllesdal in "Referential Opacity in Modal Logic" (unpublished Ph.D. dissertation, Harvard, 1961), sec. 20, and in "A Model-Theoretic Approach to Causal Logic," forthcoming in *Det Kongeliger Norske Videnskabers Selskabs Forhandlinger*.

13 "Reference and Modality," in *From a Logical Point of View*, 2d ed. (Cambridge, Mass.: Harvard, 1961), p. 155.

14 "Reply to Professor Marcus," in *The Ways of Paradox* (New York: Random House, 1966), p. 182.

15 *Notation*: Terms are mentioned by means of the Greek letters 'ζ', 'η',.... The sentence $\phi\zeta$ is that obtained by substituting the term ζ uniformly into the 1-place sentence ϕ.

16 I follow Arthur Smullyan's treatment of scope ambiguity in modal sentences, given in "Modality and Description," *Journal of Symbolic Logic*, XIII, 1 (March 1948): 31–7, as qualified by Wilson's objection, in *The Concept of Language* (Toronto: University Press, 1959), p. 43, that some ostensible uses of

Leibniz's law on modal sentences are invalid under *any* choice of scope in the conclusion.

17 "Reference and Definite Descriptions," *Philosophical Review*, LXXV, 3 (July 1966): 281–304.

18 Cf. Hintikka, *Knowledge and Belief* (Ithaca, N.Y.: Cornell, 1962), pp. 156–7.

19 I follow Quine's use of this term in "Quantifiers and Propositional Attitudes," in *The Ways of Paradox*, p. 188.

20 Cf. Hintikka, *op. cit.*, pp. 138–55.

21 But under any variant translation in which T2i is replaced by T2i′, it would be equivalent to the translation of $\square\exists\alpha(\zeta = \alpha)$ (ζ necessarily exists) with ζ given wide scope.

22 Cf. Hintikka, "Quantifiers in Deontic Logic," *Societas Scientiarum Fennica, Commentationes Humanarum Litterarum*, XXIII, 4; Kanger, *op. cit.*; Kripke, *op. cit.*; Montague, *op. cit.*; Prior, "Possible Worlds," *Philosophical Quarterly*, XII, 46 (January 1962): 36–43; Hintikka, *Knowledge and Belief*, pp. 42–49; Føllesdal, "Quantification into Causal Contexts," in *Boston Studies in the Philosophy of Science*, II (New York: Humanities Press, 1965), pp. 263–74; Hintikka, "The Logic of Perception," presented at the 1967 Oberlin Colloquium in Philosophy.

23

Interpretation of Quantifiers

Dagfin Føllesdal

1

Quantification theory might seem to be a well defined province of logic. Its syntactical and semantical features are quite well known to us, thanks to the work of Löwenheim, Skolem, Herbrand, Gödel, Church and numerous others.

One of the notable features of quantification, according to Quine [1943, pp. 123–127; 1953a, p. 150; 1953b, pp. 79–80; 1960, pp. 166–168] is its close connection with the substitutivity of identity: any interpretation of quantifiers requires the traditional substitutivity axioms of identity, that is statements of the form:

(1) $(x)(y)(x = y \supset \cdot Fx \supset Fy)$

to be true (*Quine's thesis*), cf. esp. Quine [1953b, p. 79, formula (51)]. Here 'F' stands for any predicate, simple or complex.

Note that it is the *interpretation* of the quantifiers that requires statements of form (1) to be true. Quine's thesis is therefore not refuted by merely exhibiting a system of quantification theory in which (1) is not a theorem. If Quine is right, such a system would be *semantically* incomplete, there would be formulas in the system, like (1),

Dagfin Føllesdal, Interpretation of Quantifiers. *Logic, Methodology and Philosophy of Science III*. Proceedings of the Third International Congress for Logic, Methodology and Philosophy of Science, Amsterdam, 1967. Amsterdam: North-Holland Publishing Company, 1968. 271–81.

which are valid, that is, true under every interpretation, but not provable.

Quine has pointed out that as a consequence of this, the prospects of a quantified modal logic seem dim (Quine [1943, p. 127; 1953a, pp. 150–156; 1953b, pp. 80–81; 1960, pp. 197–198]). However, one of the foremost proponents of quantified modal logic, Jaakko Hintikka, has rejected Quine's thesis and argued that there is no such connection between substitutivity and quantification. To quote the closing sentence of Hintikka [1961]: "...our considerations serve to show that the principle of substitutivity of identicals is normally unacceptable in modal logic."

Hintikka has not only rejected Quine's thesis. He has constructed a system of quantified modal logic in which (1) is not a theorem and, what is more important, he has developed a semantics for these systems which does not require (1) to be true.[1]

What better evidence could there be against Quine's thesis?

In view of all thus evidence it might seem foolhardy not to give up the thesis. Yet in a paper, "Quantification into causal contexts" which I read to the previous Congress for Logic, Methodology and Philosophy of Science, in Jerusalem 1964 (Føllesdal [1965]) I gave an argument in support of Quine's thesis, and I also indicated how one may get a semantics for quantified modal logic that is compatible with the thesis.

In that paper, I concentrated on arguing for the thesis and did not discuss how the seemingly so overwhelming evidence against it could be disposed of. The present paper is an attempt to do this. I shall first outline briefly a semantics for quantified modal logic that is compatible with Quine's thesis, and then go on to consider Hintikka's semantic proposal in order to see whether it does actually constitute counterevidence to Quine's thesis.

2

The formulas of quantified modal logic are constructed by help of a finite or denumerable set of primitive predicates. An n-place predicate with its variable places filled with variables or other singular terms that satisfy a condition that will be stated in section 3 is called an *atomic formula*. Atomic formulas are formulas and so are all and only those closed and open sentences which can be obtained from formulas by help of truth-functional connectives, quantifiers, and the symbols '$\Box$' and '$\Diamond$'.

Let us now see how these formulas can be given an interpretation that is compatible with Quine's thesis. There are several ways of giving such interpretations, the semantic proposals of Kripke [1959, 1963a, 1963b, 1965], Montague [1960, 1967a, 1967b] and Scott [1967] are examples. They all have in common that (1) comes out valid in them.

In non-modal quantification theory the formulas are usually interpreted by specifying a universe and assigning extensions to the general terms and references to the singular terms.

Modal quantification theory may be interpreted in a similar fashion, except that here more than mere extensions matter. One has to consider other possible situations, states of affairs, courses of events, points of view, worlds, etc. and determine what extensions the terms have in them.

Formally, what one may do, is to consider a set K of such situations, states, courses of events, points of view, or worlds H. With each H is associated a set Ψ (H), intuitively the set of individuals in H, and to each n-adic predicate π^n is assigned an extension $\Phi(\pi^n, H)$ in each H, where $\Phi(\pi^n, H)$ is a subset of $(\Psi(H))^n$ (the nth Cartesian product of $\Psi(H)$ with itself). To the identity predicate, I, in particular, Φ assigns in each H the set of ordered pairs of members of Ψ (H) whose first and second members are identical, thus $\Phi(I, H) = \{\langle x, y \rangle : x \in \Psi(H) \cdot y \in \Psi(H) \cdot x = y\}$. The function Φ is called a *model*.

A more or less complicated structure may be imposed upon the set K; in the following we shall assume that a dyadic relation R is defined on K, and that one particular member of K, which we shall call G, is given a preferred position; intuitively G is the actual situation, state, course of events, point of view, or world. An ordered triple $\langle$ G, K, $R \rangle$ will be called a *model system*.

The truthvalue $\Phi(\ulcorner \pi^n(\alpha_1, \ldots, \alpha_n) \urcorner, H)$ of an atomic formula $\ulcorner \pi^n(\alpha_1, \ldots, \alpha_n) \urcorner$ in H relative to an assignment of objects $a_1, \ldots, a_n$ of $\bigcup_{H \in K} \Psi$ (H) to $\alpha_1, \ldots, \alpha_n$ can now be defined as follows:

(i) $\Phi(\ulcorner \pi^n(\alpha_1, \ldots, \alpha_n) \urcorner, H) = T$ if the n-tuple $\langle a_1, \ldots, a_n \rangle \in \Phi(\pi^n, H)$.

(ii) $\Phi(\ulcorner \pi^n(\alpha_1, \ldots, \alpha_n) \urcorner, H) = F$ if $\langle a_1, \ldots, a_n \rangle \notin \Phi(\pi^n, H)$ and $\langle a_1, \ldots, a_n \rangle \in (\Psi(H))^n$.

(iii) If $\langle a_1, \ldots, a_n \rangle \notin (\Psi(H))^n$, then $\ulcorner \pi^n (\alpha_1, \ldots, \alpha_n) \urcorner$ is without a truth value in H.[2]

Given these assignments for atomic formulas, the assignments for complex formulas can be built up by induction as follows:

I. A compound is without a truth value in H if and only if it has a component which is without a truth value in H.

II. If all components of a compound have a truth value in H then the truth value of the compound is determined as follows:

$\Phi(\ulcorner \sim \varphi \urcorner, H) = T$ if and only if $\Phi(\varphi, H) = F$; otherwise $\Phi(\ulcorner \sim \varphi \urcorner, H) = F$,

$\Phi(\ulcorner \varphi \cdot \psi \urcorner, H) = T$ if and only if $\Phi(\varphi, H) = T$ and $\Phi(\psi, H) = T$; otherwise $\Phi(\ulcorner \varphi \cdot \Psi \urcorner, H) = F$ etc. for the other truth functional connectives,

$\Phi(\ulcorner \Box \varphi \urcorner, H) = T$ if and only if $\Phi(\varphi, H') = T$ for every H' $\in$ K such that HRH'; otherwise $\Phi(\ulcorner \Box \varphi \urcorner, H) = F$,

$\Phi(\ulcorner \Diamond \varphi \urcorner, H) = T$ if and only if $\Phi(\varphi, H') = T$ for at least one H' $\in$ K such that HRH', otherwise $\Phi(\ulcorner \Diamond \varphi \urcorner, H) = F$.

(Note that according to the general rule I, $\ulcorner \Box \varphi \urcorner$ and $\ulcorner \Diamond \varphi \urcorner$ are without truth values in H if and only if φ is without truth value in H.)

If $\alpha, \beta_1, \ldots, \beta_n$ are all the free variables in a formula φ, then $\Phi(\ulcorner (\alpha)\varphi \urcorner, H) = T$ relative to an assignment of $b_1, \ldots, b_n$ to $\beta_1, \ldots, \beta_n$ (where the b_i are members of $\Psi(H)$) if and only if $\Phi(\varphi, H) = T$ relative to every assignment of

$a, b_1, \ldots, b_n$ to $\alpha, \beta_1, \ldots, \beta_n$, where $a \in \Psi(\mathrm{H})$. Otherwise, $\Phi(\ulcorner(\alpha)\varphi\urcorner, \mathrm{H}) = \mathrm{F}$ relative to the given assignment. (The formula $\ulcorner(\alpha)\varphi\urcorner$ is without a truth value in H relative to an assignment of $b_1, \ldots, b_n$ to $\beta_1, \ldots, \beta_n$ if not all the b_i are members of $\Psi(\mathrm{H})$.)

We now define *validity* as follows: Let φ' be the universal closure of φ; then φ is valid if and only if $\Phi(\varphi', \mathrm{G}) = \mathrm{T}$ for every model Φ on every model system $\langle \mathrm{G}, \mathrm{K}, R \rangle$.

This completes the presentation of a semantics of quantified modal logic.

The notion of possible situations, states of affairs, courses of events, points of view, or worlds is of course at least as vague and problematic as the ideas of necessity and possibility themselves, and I want to emphasize that here I am concerned solely with certain formal, model theoretic structures. These show, I hope, how quantified modal logic can be made *formally* respectable, free from logical difficulties. They do not suffice to make it *philosophically* respectable. Their main relevance for philosophic discussion seems to be that they show that if one is to take exception to quantified modal logic, it has to be on philosophic grounds, and not on logical ones.

3

In this semantics, (1) is valid. One might wonder what then happens in the cases that have caused difficulties for modal logic, as for example in connection with '9 = the number of planets'. The answer is that this all depends upon what the singular terms of our modal theory are. Terms that behave like singular terms in ordinary extensional contexts often cease to do so in modal contexts. Thus for example 'the number of planets' behaves like a good singular term in extensional contexts, it has its fixed and unique reference. However, in modal contexts it attaches now to one object, now to another. Other terms, like 'the moon of the earth' presently attach to one definite object, in other possible worlds there might, conceivably, be several moons of the earth, or none. Russell, when he created his theory of descriptions, pointed out that in extensional contexts, a description '$(x)Fx$' can be treated as a definite singular term only when there is a unique object satisfying 'Fx', that is only when $(\exists y)(x)(Fx \equiv ..x = y)$, and that words like 'Pegasus' which cause difficulties in extensional logic, should be regarded as disguised descriptions, that can be eliminated by help of his theory. Similarly in modal logic, the descriptions that cause difficulties are those that fail to satisfy a condition stronger than but similar to Russell's, viz. '$(\exists y)\Box \ldots \Box(x)(Fx \equiv ..x = y)$', where the number of '$\Box$'s depends upon the number of layers of modal operators within whose scope the description occurs. If terms that cause difficulties are treated as disguised description occurs. If terms that cause difficulties are treated as disguised descriptions and eliminated (with due regard to the scopes of these descriptions) our difficulties vanish. (Cf. e.g. Church [1942] and Fitch [1949].)

The simplest, and also most satisfactory solution, for reasons having to do with tests for well-formedness, would be to eliminate all singular terms, as suggested by Russell and Quine, in favor of variables and general terms. These variables of quantification would then be our only singular terms; and this is the point I made in my above-mentioned paper: in order to get a satisfactory semantics for quantified modal logic these variables of quantification have to obey the universal substitutivity of identity, so that if 'x' and 'y' are quantifiable variables, and $x = y$, then 'x' can be substituted for 'y' in any context, salva veritate.

The terms that cause trouble, like 'the number of planets', can, if we want, be retained in our vocabulary, but we must treat them as a special category of terms that have the same position within modal logic as that which definite descriptions lacking a descriptum have within extensional logic: they do not obey the usual rules of inference for singular terms, like substitution, existential generalization and universal instantiation.

As is often done with descriptions in extensional logic, we may also, if we want, put the restricting conditions into the rules of inference, thereby restricting them rather than our vocabulary. This is to some extent a matter of taste. What is important is that whatever we do, our variables of quantification, our *bindable* variables, obey the universal substitutivity of identity.

The *expressive power* of our system is not affected by whether we put our restrictions upon the class of singular terms or into the rules of inference.

Thus, for example[3], the distinction between

> it is necessary that the next president of Brazil, whoever he may be, is an F

and

> it is necessary of the individual who as a matter of fact will be the next president of Brazil, that he is an F

is expressed in the following way if we retain in our vocabulary of singular terms "irregular" terms like 'the next president of Brazil', or for short 'b':

$$\Box Fb$$

and

$$(\exists x)(x = b . \Box Fx)$$

while the distinction will be expressed in the following way if we restrict our vocabulary of singular terms and write 'B' for 'is a next president of Brazil':

$$\Box(\exists y)[(x)(Bx \equiv .x = y).Fy]$$

$$(\exists y)[(x)(Bx \equiv .x = y).\Box Fy].$$

As we see, and might expect, the paraphrases become more complicated when we choose to restrict our vocabulary. On the other hand, these paraphrases make explicit what exactly is meant by our two original statements, so explicit indeed that we do not have to make any restriction on our rules of inference. When we choose to leave the vocabulary unrestricted, the paraphrases become, as we have seen, simpler, but on the other hand they do not carry on the face of them exactly what was meant by the original statements. Their meaning becomes fully explicit only when we start applying the rules of inference for singular terms and find that 'b' does not fulfill the restrictions that have been put into those rules.

4

Now, after we have seen one way of constructing a semantics for quantified modal logic, let us examine Hintikka's semantic proposal.

Hintikka's semantics is in many respects similar to the semantics that has been outlined in the preceding pages. In fact, the latter is modelled on the former and is nothing but an attempt to keep Hintikka's basic ideas and modify them so as to overcome the difficulties that will be discussed in this section.

One main difference between the two semantics is that Hintikka's models are sets of formulas, an extension of Carnap's state descriptions, and not algebraic structures of the kind considered here.

A *model set* μ of formulas may be thought of as a partial description of a possible state of affairs or a possible course of events, a description that is just large enough to show that the described state of affairs is logically possible: A set of (quantificational) formulas is satisfiable if and only if it is imbeddable in a model set, cf. e.g. Hintikka [1963, p. 66, 1966b, p. 58]. The conditions that a model set has to satisfy, are designed to insure this. Complete lists of conditions are given in several of Hintikka's works, for example in Hintikka [1957a, 1961, 1962 and 1963]. In this paper our concern is with the following conditions for identity:

(C. self =) μ does not contain any formula of the form $\sim (a = a)$;

(C. =)   If $F \in \mu$, $(a = b) \in \mu$, and if G is like F except for the interchange of a and b at some (or all) of their occurrences, then $G \in \mu$ provided that F and G are atomic formulas or identities,

and the conditions for the quantifiers, which in the first presentation of the semantics (Hintikka [1957a, p. 10]) had the following form:

(C.E)   If $(\exists x)F \in \mu$, then $F(a/x) \in \mu$ for some free variable a;

(C.U)   If $(x)F \in \mu$, then $F(b/x) \in \mu$ for every free variable b occurring in the formulas of μ.

The modal operators are interpreted in terms of *model systems*: A model system is a set Ω of model sets, ordered by a dyadic relation R and satisfying the following conditions:

(C.N)   If $F \in \mu\Omega$, then $F \in \mu$;

(C.M)   If $\Diamond F \in \mu \in \Omega$, then there is in Ω at least one $\mu*$ such that $\mu R\mu*$ and $F \in \mu*$;

(C.N$^+$)   If $F \in \mu \in \Omega$, then for every $\mu* \in \Omega$ such that $\mu R\mu *$, $F \in \mu*$.

A set of formulas is now satisfiable if and only if it is imbeddable in a member of a model system.

Condition (C. self =) expresses the reflexivity of identity. Condition (C. =) expresses the *restricted* substitutivity of identity, substitutivity restricted to atomic, i.e. non-modal contexts. The unrestricted substitutivity of identity, advocated by Quine, is of course compatible with this condition; (C. =) continues to hold if one adds a condition that requires identity to be universally substitutive. However, the two sets of conditions would lead to incompatible decisions concerning satisfiability. Thus, for example, the negation of (1) viz:

$$(2) \qquad (\exists x)(\exists y)(x = y \cdot Fx \cdot -Fy)$$

where 'F' may be non-atomic and e.g. contain modal operators, is satisfiable in Hintikka's semantics, but it is not satisfiable if the restriction in (C. =) to atomic contexts is removed.

Hintikka's semantics as it stands is therefore incompatible with Quine's thesis; it offers an interpretation of the quantifiers which does not require (1) to be valid.

Our problem now is: how is it possible for Hintikka to interpret the quantifiers so as to make (1) invalid, i.e. (2) satisfiable?

To get some insight into this, let us see how the following instance of (2) is interpreted in Hintikka's semantics:

$$(3) \qquad (\exists x)(\exists y)(x = y \cdot \Box Gx \cdot Gy).$$

This formula is imbeddable in the following model system:

$$\mu: (\exists x)(\exists y)(x = y \cdot \Box Gx \cdot -\Box Gy)$$
$$(\exists y)(a = y \cdot \Box Ga \cdot -\Box Gy)$$
$$a = b \cdot \Box Ga \cdot -\Box Gb$$
$$a = b \cdot \Box Ga \cdot -\Box Gb$$
$$Ga$$
$$Gb$$

$$\mu * \text{ (where } \mu \, R\mu*): \quad -Gb$$
$$Ga.$$

As explained in Hintikka [1957b], this means intuitively that the two terms 'a' and 'b', which happen to refer to the same object in our actual world μ, refer to distinct objects in some possible world $\mu*$, in which one of these objects is G, the other non-G.

The situation is clear as long as we consider only the terms. However, ordinarily a quantifier

is interpreted as saying something not about terms, but about objects referred to by terms, and one might wonder what happens to the object which in our actual world is the common reference of 'a' and 'b' when we pass into the possible world $\mu*$. Is this object G or is it non-G in $\mu*$?

Hintikka insists that his quantifiers range not over terms, but over objects referred to by such terms: "... the values of the variables have to be real, fullfledged individuals – which seems to me the only way of making satisfactory sense of quantification." Hintikka [1967a, p. 38, cp. also e.g. 1957b]. However, although this may be Hintikka's intention, his semantic conditions do not adequately reflect this. They are conditions on expressions, not on objects referred to by these expressions. And, as we have just observed, it is hard to see how Hintikka's "substitutional" conditions for the quantifiers can be regarded as conditions on the objects referred to. (Cf. also my argument on p. 269 of Føllesdal [1965].)

In Hintikka's later writings, the conditions for the quantifiers are changed to

(C.E')   If $(\exists x)F \in \mu$, then $F(a/x) \in \mu$ *and* $(\exists x)\Box(a = x) \in \mu$ for some free individual symbol a;

(C.U')   If $(x)F \in \mu$ and $(\exists y)\Box(b = y) \in \mu$, then $F(b/x) \in \mu$,

for the case where the variable 'x' occurs within the scope of just one modal operator in F, and to more complicated conditions where 'x' occurs within the scope of several modal operators, cf. Hintikka [1962, pp. 146–147] and later works.

After this change, formula (3) is still imbeddable in a model system, namely the same system as before, with the following formulas added:

$$\text{Additions to } \mu: (\exists x)\Box(a = x)$$
$$(\exists x)\Box(b = x)$$
$$\Box(a = c)$$
$$\Box(b = d)$$
$$a = c$$
$$b = d$$
$$Gc$$
$$Gd;$$

$$\text{Additions to } \mu*:a = c$$
$$b = d$$
$$- Gd$$
$$Gc$$

So this semantics, too, is incompatible with Quine's thesis. And, since the fate of the object referred to by 'a' and 'b' in μ remains in the dark, the same difficulties as before arise in connection with the interpretation of the quantifiers.

In addition, the revised rules introduce another anomaly in the interpretation of the quantifiers; the quantifiers now become *context dependent*: in order to see what a quantifier means one has to look at all the occurrences of the variable that is bound by it; the interpretation of the quantifier comes to depend on the number and kind of modal operators within whose scope the variable occurs.

Thus, for example, the formula '$(x)\,\square Fx$' does not read, as one might expect, 'every object is necessarily F', but rather something like 'every object *that is referred to by a free individual symbol that attaches to it in every possible world* is necessarily F'.

There are other difficulties in connection with Hintikka's interpretation of the quantifiers. For example, as in other "substitutional" approaches, the universe is assumed to have no more objects than there are expressions, i.e. it is apparently supposed to be finite or denumerable. No sense is given to the notion of interpretation in a non-denumerable domain. For this reason, deep semantical results, like the Löwenheim-Skolem theorem, become pointless trivialities on this approach. Thanks to this theorem, however, Hintikka's semantics supplies an interpretation, of

sorts, in a finite or denumerable domain for every formula that is satisfiable. But it does not provide us with a more general notion of interpretation. In my opinion, Hintikka's approach is therefore of interest and importance as a test for satisfiability, a proof procedure, but not as a general semantics for quantified modal logic.

The limitation to denumerable universes can be lifted if one uses a language with non-denumerably many constants. However, the other, more serious difficulties that have been discussed earlier, remain. So why then use a "substitutional" interpretation at all, why not use an interpretation in terms of models, for example of the kind outlined in part 2 of this paper.

I hope that it is clear from what I have said that my objection against Hintikka's semantics for quantified modal logic is not that it gives rise to inconsistencies, it does not; but that it is based on what I have called a *substitutional*, or *expressional* interpretation of the quantifier. The difference between this interpretation and the standard interpretation might seem insignificant, particularly when one confines one's attention to extensional contexts. But here, as in many other cases, consideration of what happens in non-extensional contexts brings out the differences. The differences, and the ensuing difficulties in Hintikka's interpretation of the quantifiers, seem to me to be so decisive as to make Hintikka's interpretation evidence for, rather than evidence against, Quine's thesis concerning the intimate connection between quantification and the substitutivity of identity.

Notes

1 See the articles and book by Hintikka listed in the references at the end of this paper.

2 This idea of letting some formulas be without a truth value in some possible worlds is reminiscent of Frege's and several others' treatment of names without a reference (cf. Frege's informal writings, especially "Über Sinn und Bedeutung"). As far as I know, the first to use it in modal logic was Prior

in his system Q in Prior [1957]; cf. also Prior [1967].

3 I choose this particular example, since Hintikka has argued, in [1967b, p. 143], that on this approach the distinction between the two sentences in this example cannot be made. (Cf. also Hintikka [1966a, p. 7, and 1967a, pp. 46 ff.].)

References

Church, Alonzo, 1942, Review of Quine, 'Whitehead and the rise of modern logic'. *Journal of Symbolic Logic* 7, pp. 100–1.

Fitch, Frederic B., 1949, The problem of the Morning Star and the Evening Star. *Philosophy of Science* 16, pp. 137–41.

Føllesdal, Dagfin, 1965, Quantification into causal contexts. *Boston Studies in the Philosophy of Science*, Vol. II (Humanities Press, New York, N.Y.) pp. 263–74.

Hintikka, Jaakko, 1957a, Quantifiers in deontic logic. *Societas Scientiarum Fennica, Commentationes Humanarum Litterarum* 23, no. 4.

—— 1957b, Modality as referential multiplicity. *Ajatus* 20, pp. 49–64.

—— 1961, Modality and quantification. *Theoria* 27, pp. 119–28.

—— 1962, *Knowledge and Belief. An Introduction to the Logic of the Two Notions* (Cornell University Press, Ithaca, N.Y.).

—— 1963, The modes of modality. *Acta Philosophica Fennica* 16, pp. 65–81.

—— 1966a, 'Knowing oneself' and other problems in epistemic logic. *Theoria* 32, pp. 1–13.

—— 1966b, Studies in the logic of existence and necessity. *The Monist* 50, pp. 55–76.

—— 1967a, Individuals, possible worlds, and epistemic logic. *Noûs* 1, pp. 33–62.

—— 1967b, Existence and identity in epistemic contexts: A comment on Føllesdal's paper. *Theoria* 33, pp. 138–47.

Kanger, Stig, 1957, *Provability in Logic*. Stockholm studies in philosophy, Vol. 1 (Almqvist & Wiksell, Stockholm).

Kripke, Saul, 1959, A completeness theorem in modal logic. *Journal of Symbolic Logic* 24, pp. 1–14.

—— 1963a Semantical analysis of modal logic, I. Normal modal propositional calculi. *Zeitschrift für mathematische Logik und Grundlagen der Mathematik* 9, pp. 67–96.

—— 1963b, Semantical considerations on modal logic. *Acta Philosophica Fennica* 16, pp. 83–94.

—— 1965 Semantical analysis of intuitionistic logic I, in: *Formal Systems and Recursive Functions*, eds. J. Crossley and M. Dummett (North-Holland, Amsterdam) pp. 92–130.

Montague, Richard, 1960, Logical necessity, physical necessity, ethics, and quantifiers. *Inquiry* 3, pp. 259–69.

—— 1967a, Pragmatics and intensional logic. Mimeographed, UCLA, forthcoming in *Dialectica*.

—— 1967b, Pragmatics, Mimeographed, UCLA.

Prior, A.N., 1957, *Time and Modality* (Clarendon Press, Oxford).

—— 1967, *Past, Present and Future* (Clarendon Press, Oxford).

Quine, W. V., 1943, Notes on existence and necessity. *Journal of Philosophy* 40, pp. 113–27.

—— 1953a, 1961, *From a Logical Point of View* (Harvard University Press, Cambridge, Mass.).

—— 1953b, Three grades of modal involvement. *Proceedings of XIth International Congress of Philosophy*, Brussels, Vol. 14, pp. 65–81.

—— 1956, Quantifiers and propositional attitudes. *Journal of Philosophy* 53, pp. 177–87.

—— 1960, *Word and Object* (Harvard University Press, Cambridge, Mass.).

Scott, Dana, 1967, An outline for quantified intensional logic. Mimeographed, Stanford, June 1967.

Thomason, Richmond H., 1967, Some completeness results for modal predicate calculi. Mimeographed, Yale University.

24

A Backward Look at Quine's Animadversions on Modalities

Ruth Barcan Marcus

In this chapter I will reflect on Quine's animadversions on modalities, the debates they provoked and some of the outcomes. My reflections will be loosely historical and personally reminiscent.[1]

Quine traces his disaffection with modal logic to what he saw as the primary motivation for C.I. Lewis in devising modal propositional logic; a motivation which Quine attributes to a central confusion about use and mention. What Lewis was seen as doing was appending to the familiar propositional calculus, operators, axioms and rules which were supposed to capture notions like validity, logical truth, consistency and most particularly, logical consequence. That project was perceived as undermining advances achieved by Tarski, Carnap and others when they took those semantical notions as metalogical and *about* the expressions of an interpreted formal calculus. In 1962 Quine says

> Professor Marcus struck the right note when she represented me as suggesting that modern modal logic was conceived in sin: the sin of confusing use and mention. She rightly did not represent me as holding that modal logic *requires* confusion of use and mention. My point was a historical one, having to do with Russell's confusion of 'if-then' with 'implies.'

Ruth Barcan Marcus, A Backward Look at Quine's Animadversions on Modalities. *Perspectives on Quine.* Ed. Robert B. Barrett and Roger F. Gibson. Oxford: Blackwell Publishers, 1990. 230–43

Lewis founded modern [propositional] modal logic, but Russell provoked him to it. For whereas there is much to be said for the material conditional as a version of 'if-then', there is nothing to be said for it as a version of 'implies'; and Russell called it implication, thus apparently leaving no place open for genuine deductive connections between sentences. Lewis moved to save the connections. But his way was not, as one could have wished, to sort out Russell's confusion of 'implies' with 'if-then.' Instead, preserving that confusion, he propounded a strict conditional and called *it* 'implication.'[2]

Quine ruefully concluded on that occasion that the use – mention confusion seems also to be 'a sustaining force, engendering an illusion of understanding'.[3]

But clearly the judgement is harsh. Carnap in 1934 made a similar point but with important differences. He says

> Russell's choice of the designation 'implication' for the sentential junction with the characteristic TFTT has turned out to be a very unfortunate one. The words 'to imply' in the English language mean the same as 'to contain' or 'to involve.' Whether the choice of the name was due to a confusion of implication with the consequence relation I do not know; but, in any case, this nomenclature has been the cause of much confusion in the minds of many, and it is

even possible that it is to blame for the fact that a number of people, though aware of the difference between implication and the consequence relation, still think that the symbol of implication ought really to express the consequence-relation and they count it as a failure on the part of this symbol that it does not do so.[4]

Carnap at the same time continues to use 'implication' for the material conditional and does not use it for 'consequence'.[5] He goes on to introduce a stronger conditional which he calls 'L-implication' into his sample object languages; a conditional which is supposed to have the feature, that 'A L-implies B' is valid just in case 'A implies B' is valid. On a special notion of equipollence 'A L-implies B' is supposed to be equipollent to the metalinguistic 'B' is a consequence of 'A'. Where an equipollence holds, he calls the object language correlates 'quasi-syntactic'. When Carnap moves from syntax to semantics he does not abandon those quasi-syntactic object language constants. He continues to urge that for sentences with non-extensional or modal expressions 'it will still be convenient to translate sentences of this kind not only into the metalanguage but *in addition or instead* into syntactical [object language] sentences with respect to a suitably constructed calculus.'[6] Indeed in sorting logical from non-logical signs of a formalized language he includes among the logical signs those for what he calls the 'logical modalities', among them a sign for Lewis's strict implication.[7] Also, in sorting out projects for future study as he was wont, he especially singles out formalized accounts of languages with signs for what he calls logical, physical and causal modalities.[8] Now Carnap was no use-mention confuser. Still, he granted that there were good grounds which justified formal treatments of modalities. What also remained was to arrive at a plausible semantical account of modal languages.

As we know, early intuitions about modal logic were too shaky even to ground a choice among some of the alternative Lewis systems to say nothing of the added complexities of extending such systems to include as I did,[9] quantification theory, identity, a theory of types and no presumption of extensionality for properties. But the absence of an adequate semantics was not a deterrent. It is well to keep in mind that *Principia Mathematica*, authored by notorious use-mention confusers, long preceded formalized semantics.

Quine's scoldings diminished but did not stem the interest in modal logic. It continued, for one reason or another, to engage the attention of some logicians and philosophers including exacting mathematical logicians.[10] Granted that for a long time and under Quine's influence it was considered by many philosophers to be misdirected and misconceived.

A footnote to Quine's historical point about historical origins. It is, I believe, inaccurate to claim that the preoccupation with the search for an object language surrogate for deducibility was Lewis's only motivation. Consider the following quotation. The author is discussing Leibnizian possible worlds and says

> This conception of possible worlds is not jejune: the actual world as far as anyone knows it, is merely one of many such which are possible. For example, I do not know at the moment how much money I have in my pocket, let us say it is thirty cents. The world which is just like this one except that I should have thirty-five cents in my pocket now is a consistently thinkable world.... an analytic proposition is one which would apply to or be true of every possible world.[11]

That is C. I. Lewis in 1943 speaking, not David Lewis.

By the 1950s Quine begins to give a millimeter. He now allows that 'there are three different degrees to which we may allow our logic, or semantics, to embrace the idea of necessity.'[12] As it turns out these embraces range from cool to stone cold. The first degree takes a modal term as a semantic predicate which attaches to sentence names, although it may not be exactly reducible to validity. The second more 'drastic' degree is to take necessity as operating on closed sentences suggesting *de dicto* use. The third most 'grave' degree is where, like the negation sign, it may operate on open sentences as in '$\square$ (x is a man)'. Although difficulties are noted for the first degree, it is the second and especially the third which in the late 1940s became the primary target and remain the target. However, over the years some criticisms are withdrawn or tempered, new criticisms emerge, and finally the whole thrust shifts from a concern with motivation, paradoxes, puzzles, senselessness of interpretations of modal logic to claims about model logic's repugnant essentialist commitments.

One can get a sense of the changing shape of the arguments as one moves from 'The problem of interpreting modal logic'[13] in 1947 through the 1953, 1961 and 1980 versions of the paper 'Reference and modality'.[14] It should be noted that Quine's more recent preoccupation was not so much with modal quantification theories like those of Church and Carnap grounded as they were in a Fregean structure which takes non-logical terms such as singular terms to be systematically ambiguous;[15] what they refer to and what they mean will alter with context.[16] In Frege's overworked (and unfortunate) example, 'The Evening Star' and 'the Morning Star' in

(1)   the Evening Star = the Morning Star

refer to one and the same thing but in

(2)   John believes that the Evening Star = the Morning Star

those terms shift reference to non-identical senses for Frege or something like non-identical senses or concepts or intensions in Church and Carnap. The swelling of ontology was for Quine a *prima facie* ground for rejection. For me the ground for rejection was the systematic ambiguity.

I am ignorant as to whether Frege also took modal operators as generating opaque contexts. Although there appear to be similarities with respect to *some* substitution failures as between modalized sentences and non-modalized sentences with verbs for propositional attitudes, the presence of an agent as subject in the attitudinal assertions marks an important difference. Modal sentences such as

(3)   □ (the Evening Star = the Evening Star)
(4)   □ (the Evening Star = the Morning Star)

are not related to an agent's beliefs or attitudes. Although the move from (1) and (3) to (4) is also claimed to be a move from truth to falsity as in analogous belief contexts, those differences will make a difference.

Quine suggests that quotation contexts are the paradigm for opacity as in

(5)   John says 'the Evening Star = the Morning Star'.

but here even a shift to intensions is precluded. The independent meaningfulness of any proper part of (5) in the scope of 'says' is erased by quotation.

There was a time for Carnap[17] and perhaps still for Davidson[18] when belief sentences like (2) [John believes that the Evening Star = the Morning Star.] were analyzed into a relation between a subject and a sentence. It seemed oddly prejudicial that Quine continued to press the quotation analogy as the least objectionable approach to modalities (degree one involvement) but does not press it for propositional attitude sentences with which it has far greater affinity.[19]

The more substantive arguments Quine mustered over the years were, as noted, directed against second and third degree modal involvement. The criticisms are interwoven but they can roughly be sorted into those which might be seen as internal difficulties which lead to puzzlement, bafflement, senselessness and the like when one tries to interpret sentences with modal operators and quantifiers and those which maintain that even if claims of puzzlement were set aside or resolved, modal logic commits us to some undesirable and unacceptable philosophical or ontological or semantical views. Of the latter kind are for example a purported forced shift to intensions or a commitment to 'essentialism'. The background assumption of my modal quantification theory and those which followed along the same lines was that there was no need to make a Fregean shift or to suppose systematic ambiguity. It was that non-Fregean context within which most of the debate fell. A forced Fregean shift relative to context would itself be a criticism and a sufficient deterrent. I took reference as univocal in and out of modal contexts.

Included in the second grade of modal involvement are sentences of modal propositional logic, as in the Lewis systems. Not much remains of Quine's criticisms of modal propositional logic beyond the dubious charge of misguided motivation. Occasionally Quine mentions the unsettled views about acceptable postulates for modal operators within the scope of other modal operators such as in '□□A' or '□(A ⊃ ◇ B)' and the like, but the unsettledness is regarded as a symptom and it is not explored independently.[20]

Still the latter is of interest given some historical analogies between the extension of non-modal sentential logic to include quantification theory and the extension of quantification theory to include modal operators. Close formal analogies hold between the universal and existential quantifiers and the operators for necessity and possibility.[21] There was in the early history of predicate logic also an occasional unsettledness about quantifiers in the scope of other quantifiers especially when the variables of quantification varied as in '(x) (Ax ⊃ (∃ y) Fy)'. It has been plausibly claimed that Wittgenstein was baffled by such iterations.[22] In addition to iteration puzzles it was sometimes argued that quantifiers are otiose since they can be defined in terms of conjunction and disjunction or, taking classes as primitive, in terms of relations between classes. An adequate semantics for resolving those occasional perplexities about quantifiers in standard logic came well after *Principia Mathematica* in the work of Tarski and Carnap. Formal systems of quantified modal logic were similarly developed in the late 1940s and preceded semantical accounts. Kanger's semantical strategy for modal logic was not published until 1957 and unfortunately was not known by the likes of me.[23] Kripke's[24] and Hintikka's[25] semantics for quantified alethic modal logic were not published until later. What the debate about iterated modalities might come to was articulated in those studies.

As noted above the fact of conflicting intuitions about iterated modalities was not enlisted by Quine as a substantive argument against propositional modal logic. In fact on the level of propositional calculus there remained no substantive criticism other than the spectre of use – mention confusions. The serious quarrel is with quantified modal logic. In his autobiographical remarks[26] he speaks of my early papers[27] as taking up the 'challenge' as did Carnap[28] and Church.[29] Since Carnap's and Church's background theory presupposed reference shifts to intensions and were unacceptable on that account, the primary target became modal quantification theory as given in my early papers. Quine graciously notes in his review of the first (1946) 'the absence of use mention confusions . . . a virtue rare in the modality literature.'[30] But alas I fell from grace on the matter of use and mention in 1962 in conjunction with a symposium paper to which he replied.[31]

Returning now to Quine's response to the challenge of quantified modal logic, I should like to touch on some features of my systems of quantified modal logic which were especially relevant to the debate. The modal propositional base was Lewis's S2 extended to S4 and S5. The latter

two include axioms for iterated modalities. The non-modal base is type-theoretic second order quantification theory with individual constants, an abstraction operator, no description operator and identity defined. The abstraction operator is seen as forming attributes not sets. The latter, i.e., sets, are viewed as collections of just those things which have the attribute. The axioms are given as schemata. A modal axiom is included about mixture of modal operators and quantifiers. Two metatheorems should be mentioned since I believe that an appreciation of them would have deflected some of Quine's subsequent criticisms about the perplexities engendered by modal quantification theory.

The first theorem is that for the material biconditional, substitution is restricted to non-modal contexts. Substitution is unrestricted for the strict biconditional in modal contexts for quantified S4 and S5.

The second is the theorem about the necessity of identity

$$\mathrm{NI}(\alpha)(\beta)((\alpha = \beta) \supset \Box(\alpha = \beta))$$

where 'α' and 'β' are syntactic notation for individual variables. NI also holds where '⊃' is replaced by '≺'.

A tangential remark. As I proceed with the review of Quine's arguments there is a sense of *déjà vu*, since I will be going over some of the same ground covered in the above mentioned 1962 symposium at Harvard where Quine commented. Present at the time were Kripke still an undergraduate and Føllesdal who had recently completed graduate study. Like the one whose namesake I am, I was in alien corn and I appreciated Kripke's support during the discussion of what he took, not always correctly, to be some of my views. I began with some general considerations which justify modal logic. In summary I urged that motivations went far beyond the search for an object language correlate of validity and consequence. Modalities including causal and physical modalities are firmly entrenched in common and scientific language. I also took it as non-controversial that our ordinary discourse as well as scientific discourse presupposes that there are things; fixed objects of reference. In formal semantics they are what is in the domain of the interpretation of a language as Quine used to remind us. I urged more generally that 'things' are what may properly enter into the identity relation.

If we are to talk about things in a public language, if we are to entertain the possibility that a thing might not have had properties which in actual fact uniquely describe it or if a thing remains what it is through many vicissitudes but ceases to exist altogether through others, then there is a semantical role for genuine proper names which is different from the semantical role of singular descriptions. I called this directly referring role 'tagging' beyond which those names have no meaning. Singular descriptions can as Russell explains in *Principia Mathematica* be surrogate for genuine proper names in suitably restricted extensional contexts – where taking them as flanking an identity sign instead of unpacking them in accordance with the theory of descriptions will not, on substitution, take us from truths to falsehoods.

I pointed out that

> it often happens, in a growing, changing language, that a descriptive phrase comes to be used as a proper name – an identifying tag – and the descriptive meaning is lost or ignored. Sometimes we use devices such as capitalization with or without dropping the definite article to indicate a change in use.[32]

Capitalization like the artifice of single quotes is commonly used to deny independent meaning to those parts of an expression ordinarily taken as contributing to the meaning of the whole.

Against those recollections consider Quine's arguments about the Evening Star and the Morning Star which is supposed to render modal logic incoherent. It is interesting to trace the arguments through 'The problem of interpreting modal logic' in 1947 and the 1953, 1961 and 1980 versions of Reference and modality.'[33] In the 1953 and 1961 versions he acknowledges Smullyan's proposed solution which purports to employ the theory of descriptions but Quine criticizes the employment as 'an alteration of Russell's familiar logic of descriptions' because 'Smullyan allows difference of scope to affect truth value even in cases where the description concerned succeeds in naming.'[34] But of course it was a mistake for Quine to claim that Smullyan had 'altered' Russell's logic of descriptions. It was in fact an exact employment as laid out in 'On denoting' and exemplified there by Russell in his analysis of apparent substitution failures in contexts of epistemological attitudes. It is a central point of Russell's theory that in such contexts even singular descriptions which succeed

in denoting one thing must be unpacked. Quine's claim in 1953 and 1961 that for Russell 'change in the scope of a description was indifferent to the truth value of any statement, however, unless the description failed to name' was false and missed what Russell regarded as an innovative feature of the theory. In the 1980 revision those passages about Smullyan's purported misemployment of the theory of descriptions are deleted and replaced. Now the solution of Smullyan is represented as 'taking a leaf from Russell', and it is seen that 'scope is indifferent to extensional contexts. But it can still matter in intensional ones.' In summary, by 1980 it is finally seen that by fully employing the theory of descriptions and allowing for fixed reference of ordinary proper names the substitution failure is dispelled. But now Quine points out that the successful analysis places a modal operator in the scope of a quantifier and in front of an open sentence which means 'adopting an invidious attitude toward certain ways of uniquely specifying [an object] x' and 'favoring other ways ... as somehow better revealing "the essence" of the object'.[35] So the issue is now the spectre of essentialism: a sorting of properties as essential or non-essential to objects which have them.

Some further comments on the arguments from substitution failure and essentialism. As Quine actually presented it, 'the Evening Star' and 'the Morning Star' are capitalized. If the descriptions have thereby been converted into proper names then there is in accordance with the necessity of identity (NI) no substitution failure. Substitutivity of proper names goes through in modal contexts *salva veritate*. So here Quine would have to question direct fixed reference for 'genuine proper names' or the plausibility of necessity of identity or both.

One of Quine's early criticisms *was* directed against the necessity of identity (NI). In 1953 he claims that NI *forces* a shift from extensions to intensions. What went unnoticed is that one of the powers of the theory of descriptions is that it unpacks so-called 'contingent' identities generally requiring at least one singular description into material equivalences which cannot be intersubstituted within the scope of the necessity operator. Indeed, the Smullyan solution to the substitution puzzle falls under the general substitution theorems for biconditionals mentioned above.

By 1961 the claim that modal contexts generally and NI in particular *force* a replacement of extensions by intensions has been abandoned. Instead he says that my preparedness 'to accept . . . essentialist presuppositions seems rather hinted at'[36] by NI. The spectre of essentialism again. By 1962 concerns about NI seem to vanish altogether so long as we stick to variables. Quine notices that the proof of NI requires only the necessity of self-identity and substitutivity for identity. What could be less controversial?

On the matter of proper names Quine sees more serious difficulties. He says

Prof Marcus developed a contrast between proper names and descriptions . . . I see trouble anyway in the contrast . . . as Prof Marcus draws it. Her paradigm of the assigning of proper names is tagging. We may tag the planet Venus some fine evening, with the proper name, 'Hesperus.' We may tag the same planet again some day before sunrise with the proper name 'Phosphorous'. When at last we discover that we have tagged the same planet twice our discovery is empirical. And not because the proper names were descriptions.[37]

Among considerations informing my view was the claim of linguists that proper names are not lexical items at all. They lack 'lexical meaning'.

Quine saw trouble. I did not. Empirical discoveries do not identities make. So even on the matter of supposing as I did that there were directly referring proper names – it appeared that for Quine the trouble also came down to essentialism since it suggested to him that objects have their proper names necessarily. Kripke during the discussion which ensued after Quine's comments reinforced Quine's view with his remark 'such an assumption of names is equivalent to essentialism.'[38] But that was not *my* claim. Socrates might have been named Euthyphro, he would not thereby be Euthyphro. My claims about the special semantic role of proper names re-emerged in the early 1970s in theories of direct reference.

So, as we trace Quine's arguments over time we notice that most of them are dispelled as originally proposed and are replaced by arguments about modal logic's commitments to essentialism. Since it does not require modal logic to note that for example, being self-identical and being married to Xantippe are different kinds of properties which Socrates has, one expects a more *direct* attack on what seems on the face of it a very plausible sorting of properties.

There are two arguments in which Quine directly attacks such a sorting of properties directly. The first in *Word and Object* (1960) has to do with the bewilderment that is supposed to be induced by the premisses (1) Mathematicians are necessarily rational and not necessarily two-legged and (2) Cyclists are necessarily two-legged and not necessarily rational and (3) Someone, call him John, is both a cyclist and a mathematician. Quine asks 'Is this individual necessarily rational and contingently two-legged or vice versa' and concludes 'there is no semblance of sense in rating some of his attributes as necessary and others as contingent.'[39]

Of course the premisses here are ambiguous as to where the modal operator is located in the conditional sentences. Are we saying that implicit in the first premiss is '$\Box$ (x) (Mx $\supset$ Rx)' or '(x) (Mx $\supset$ $\Box$ Rx)' (we assume for simplicity, the Barcan formula.) If the reading of the implicit conditional premisses is like the latter with the modal operator attached to the consequent, the premisses are inconsistent. If more plausibly the former then nothing baffling follows. That argument, addressed in 1962, does not surface again in Quine's later critiques of modal logic.

A second direct assault seems to be that extensionality for sets is threatened, for shouldn't the set of creatures with a kidney and creatures with a heart be identical although the equivalence between them is the set analogue of the material biconditional. The answer to this is 'yes', but it is also more complicated and is one which I presented elsewhere.[40] In summary, sets may be taken as collections of objects satisfying various descriptions. Being uniquely a first star of the evening and being uniquely a first star of the morning are weakly equivalent attributes but the objects which satisfy both are, if identical, necessarily so. The unit set Venus is self-identical however Venus is uniquely described. Identity for sets is an extrapolation of the identity of individuals and given NI if such collections are identical they are necessarily so. The attribute, as in the case of singular descriptions, may be seen using Kripke's phase, as 'fixing the reference'. What finally seems to remain of Quine's critique is again essentialism yet without any head-on account of what makes it invidious.

What then is invidious about what Quine calls 'Aristotelian essentialism'? Aristotle has complex theories about universals, particulars, substances, species, essence and accident. Furthermore it has been persuasively argued that Aristotle's modalities are temporalized, and relative to the actual.[41] Still there are features of his views which illuminate the debate and are related to what contemporary authors have called metaphysical modalities.

For Aristotle, particular objects which have independent existence are directly referred to as 'a this'. Particulars like Socrates or the Sun cannot be 'defined' by specification of a unique set of essential properties. Even with respects to the Sun which for Aristotle is unchanging and taken to be uniquely and eternally rotating around the earth he says, speculatively, that if the Sun were to stop moving it would still be the Sun, and if another body were to rotate in the same path around the earth it would not be the Sun.[42] One can only suppose here that Aristotle had some views of modalities beyond the temporal ones which are not made explicit.[43]

For Aristotle essential properties are sortal. Objects which have them, have them necessarily but there are objects which do not or might not have them. Being an entity is a non-sortal property as presumably would be being self-identical. Also seemingly excluded are properties which are uniquely sortal such as being identical to Socrates but which are parasitic on non-sortal necessary properties such as self-identity.

There are in Aristotle additional constraints on essential properties of particulars such as sorting things from their parts but we need not consider those elaborations. Now surely Quine can have no objection to such non-sortal necessary properties or those parasitic on the latter for they correspond to those predicates formed from logically valid sentences. Any device for forming predicates from sentences does not exclude valid sentences as sentences from which predicates can be formed.

Curiously, Quine's examples of repugnant essential properties are just such non-controversial necessary properties such as self-identity and he characterizes essential properties in such a way as to include them.[44] In a recurrent example he uses, the property of being self-identical is taken as necessary and the property of being self-identical while P where 'P' is some contingent truth, is taken as contingent. He says that A is an essential property and B is a contingent property where

$$QE \ (\exists x)(\Box Ax \cdot Bx \cdot -\Box Bx)$$

But that is not sufficient for troublesome essentialism.

In a paper on essential properties I mentioned three candidates for characterizing such properties.[45] The crucial one in the notation of my quantified modal logic says of an attribute ŷAy that it is essential where

$$ES \ (\hat{y}Ay(z))(\exists x)(\exists z)(\Box(\hat{y}Ay(x)) \cdot -\Box(\hat{y}Ay(z)))$$

I argued that on ES modal logic accommodated talk about such properties but there seemed to be no *commitment* to them in the sense that on interpretation an essentialist truth was a consequence of the axioms and rules.

T. Parsons extended ES to include n-adic predicates (excluding trivial parasitic ones) and proved that there were models of modal quantification theory consistent with taking as false all instances of ES extended to n-adic predicates.[46] But there are also models of modal logic consistent with the truth of non-trivial essentialist claims. Models with truths of the essentialist kind as in ES go beyond the purely logical necessities and this is perhaps the juncture at which one might say the metaphysical modalities begin. Indeed assumptions like the essentiality of being a tiger would seem to have to be imported.

Nor am I agreeing that metaphysical modalities are invidious. They have an important role in common as well as scientific discourse. A particular instance of a species such as tiger, or of a physical kind such as gold would seem to have non-purely logical necessary properties as was argued by Aristotle as well as contemporary philosophers.[47]

It may be that what concerns Quine has finally little to do with interpretations of modal logic or use – mention confusions or senselessness. It may be that what lies behind his concern is that it presents one of the challenges to his attack on *any* analytic/synthetic distinction where even logical truths are included among analytic truths. Recall that on Quine's characterization of essential truths, predicates formed from valid sentences like being green, or not green or being self-identical are also to be included among the predicates which he takes to be invidious. Indeed such predicates seem to be among his recurrent examples.

Even if Quine were correct in claiming that there are *no* sentences including those we call logically valid which justify sorting propositions or properties into necessary and non-necessary where the sorting remains fixed over the history of its use, that should not be confused with the fact that at any time in the history of the language there will be such a sorting. I believe that the whole debate about the analytic/synthetic distinction has been blurred by failing to distinguish language viewed synchronically and language viewed diachronically (i.e., historically). The logical necessities remain so stable over time as to present the most obvious challenge to Quine's claim, synchronically as well as diachronically.[48]

I have not discussed another notion related to essentialism, that of *individual* essences nor do I propose to go on about them except to remind you of Aristotle's claim that particular 'cannot be defined'. If we think of an essence, not as an intensional object but as a finite set of non-indexical general properties which uniquely sorts a particular object from all others in all possible circumstances or more metaphysically across worlds, then there are strong arguments questioning the plausibility of such transworld identification.[49] Kripke and others sought such properties in origins; I doubt that such a search can succeed. Aristotle seems to me correct when he says that the 'essence' (in the sense of essential properties) of a particular is what it shares with all of that species and does not serve to distinguish further among particulars of the species.

In conclusion a few tangential remarks. The debate has on the whole been productive. Quine's criticisms while discouraging some, had a way of stimulating interest in modal logic, modal semantics, theories of kinds and physical modalities. Theories of direct reference finally flourished in the 1970s. Many who had once shared Quine's views adopted new ones as the force of his arguments diminished. The work of Føllesdal is an interesting example. In 1966 he made available a monograph which was a revised version of his 1961 Harvard dissertation.[50] There he suggests three approaches to substitutivity failures of singular terms in modal contexts. The first, the Quinian solution, was to convert all singular terms to predicates as in 'Socratize'. The second places a restriction on *which* singular terms may be intersubstituted in modal contexts. The third is to use

Russellian description theory for all singular terms. The second solution seems to accommodate what Kripke later (1971) called rigid designators which include proper names as well as some descriptions. But it does not distinguish as I did the special semantical role of proper names as compared with rigid descriptions. Føllesdal discusses the advantages and disadvantages of each approach. The first is cumbersome. The second requires *inter alia* that what counts as a singular name varies as we move from extensional to modal logic. The third, Russellian descriptions, is seen to have as its 'main drawback' problems of substitutivity which he says 'could be avoided if we base our theory of descriptions on a set of contextual definitions different from that of Russell'. Had a special pre-formal role for proper names of direct reference been recognized at that time some of the difficulties with Føllesdal's solution two would have been dispelled. As for solution three he was, as was Quine, mistaken in the claim that Russell's theory would have to be revised. Føllesdal's preference is for the first Quinian solution; Socratize. But what Føllesdal's does not reject in 1966 is the importance of preserving modal distinctions and in this respect he has gone beyond Quine. He bends his efforts to 'make sense' of 'Aristotelian essentialism' (Quine's version) and says 'to make sense of Aristotelian essentialism and to make sense of open sentences with an "N" prefixed are one and the same problem.'

Føllesdal in his 1986 paper for the Quine volume of the Library of Living Philosophers now endorses the special role of proper names and theory of direct reference.[51] There is no longer a problem of 'making sense' of expressions with model operators attached to open sentences or modal operators in the scope of quantifiers. He points to results such as Parsons's and mine which are about the absence in some models of modal logic of commitment to non-trivial necessary properties and hence the absence of a *commitment* to essentialism (of the non-Quinian sortal version), without at the same time denying the 'meaningfulness' of essentialism. We have come a long way.

In all of the debates Quine has been a gadfly, but in that he is in good company.

Notes

1 For a sharply honed examination of Quine on the more inclusive subject of opacity, a study of David Kaplan's paper in The Library of Living Philosophers volume on Quine will repay the strenuous effort it demands. L. Hahn and P. Schilpp (eds), *The Philosophy of W. V. Quine* (Open Court, 1986).

2 'Reply to Professor Marcus', *Synthese*, 13 (1961), p. 323. Reprinted in Marx Wartofsky (ed.), *Boston Studies in Philosophy of Science* (Reidel, 1963) and in *The Ways of Paradox and Other Essays* (Random House, 1966). I have inserted quotes around the occurrences of 'implication'. Also inserted is '[propositional]'.

3 Ibid., p. 324.

4 *The Logical Syntax of Language* (Harcourt, Brace, 1937), p. 255. The earlier German edition was 1934. Italics mine.

5 Ibid. See esp. §§ 63–9. § 69 concerns the logic of modalities.

6 *Introduction to Semantics* (Harvard University Press, 1942), p. 249.

7 Ibid., § 13.

8 Ibid., p. 243.

9 R. C. Barcan, (later Marcus) 'A functional calculus of first order based on strict implication', *Journal of Symbolic Logic*, 11 (1946). 'The identity of individuals in a strict functional calculus of second order', *ibid.*, 12 (1947).

10 Among those who wrote on modal logic before 1960 were A. Bayart, R. Carnap, A. Church, H. B. Curry, M. Dummett, F. Fitch, A. Tarski, S. Kanger, E. J. Lemmon, J. Łukasiewicz, J. McKinsey, A. Prior, B. Sobociński, G. H. Von Wright.

11 'The modes of meaning', *Philosophy and Phenomenological Research*, IV, 2 (1943–4), p. 234.

12 'Three grades of modal involvement', *Proceedings of the XIth International Congress of Philosophy 1953*, vol. 14 (North-Holland). Reprinted in *The Ways of Paradox* (Harvard, 1966). Quotation is from the latter, p. 156. Quine, citing the interdefinability of the modal operators confines the discussion to the necessity operator.

13 *Journal of Symbolic Logic*, 12, no. 2 (1947).

14 *From a Logical Point of View* (Harvard University Press, 1953). Revised 1961 and again 1980.

15 A. Church, 'A formulation of the logic of sense and denotation', Abstract, *Journal of Symbolic Logic*, XI (1946) p. 31. Paper in P. Henle et al. (eds), *Structure, Method and Meaning* (Liberal Arts Press, 1951).

16 'Modalities and quantification', *Journal of Symbolic Logic*, 11 (1946). *Meaning and Necessity* (University of Chicago, 1947).

17 *Meaning and Necessity* (University of Chicago, 1947), § 13.

18 Cf. 'Thought and talk', in S. Guttenplan (ed.), (Oxford University Press, 1975).

19 A. Church in 'On Carnap's analysis of statements of assertion and belief', *Analysis*, 10, 5 (1950) (reprinted in L. Linsky (ed.), *Reference and Modality* (Oxford, 1971)) pointed to some serious difficulties with such an account. That sentential account has resurfaced in another form as in Fodor where belief relates an agent to a sentence in 'the language of thought'.

20 'There grades of modal involvement', pp. 168–71 of *The Ways of Paradox*.

21 Indeed David Lewis takes them as quantifiers of a kind. See *Counterfactuals* (Harvard, 1973).

22 Robert Fogelin, *Wittgenstein* (Routledge and Kegan Paul, 1987). See chapter 6, pp. 78–82. Fogelin's claims have been challenged but they are plausible.

23 *Provability in Logic* (Stockholm, 1957).

24 'Semantical considerations on modal logic', *Acta Philosophica Fennica* (1963). Reprinted elsewhere. A semantics restricted to quantified S5 appears in *The Journal of Symbolic Logic*, 24 (1959), pp. 1–15 and pp. 323–4.

25 'The modes of modality', *Acta Philosophica Fennica* (1963). Reprinted elsewhere. Hintikka had also proposed a semantics for quantified deontic logic in 'Quantifiers in deontic logic', *Societas Scientarum Fennica*, 4 (1957).

26 *The Philosophy of W. V. Quine, op. cit.*, p. 26.

27 See note 9. Those papers were reviewed by Quine in the *Journal of Symbolic Logic*, 11 (1946), p. 96 and 12 (1947): p. 95. A correction of the 1947 review in 23 (1958), p. 342.

28 See note 16.

29 See note 15.

30 See note 27.

31 That symposium was sponsored by the Boston Colloquium in the Philosophy of science and took place in February of 1962. In conjunction with that symposium 'Modalities and intensional languages' and Quine's comments were published in *Synthese* 1961 and in M. Wartofsky (ed.), *Boston Studies in the Philosophy of Science 1961/1962* (Reidel, 1963). Also included in the latter volume is a much edited 'Discussion' from a tape of the original discussion and lists Quine, Kripke, Føllesdal and McCarthy and myself as participants. My paper and Quine's comments are also reprinted elsewhere, Quine's under the title 'Reply to Professor Marcus'.

32 Ibid. See p. 83 of the *Boston Studies* reprinting. The special semantic role of proper names is also dis-

cussed in the paper 'Extensionality', *Mind*, ns 69 (1960).

33 See notes 13 and 14. In the 1953 version of 'Reference and modality' see p. 155 and note 9. In the 1980 version see p. 154 and note 9 in *From a Logical Point of View*.

34 'Modality and description', *Journal of Symbolic Logic*, 13 (1948). Reprinted elsewhere.

35 The 1980 version of 'Reference and modality' in *From a Logical Point of View*. See note 14 above.

36 *From a Logical Point of View*, the 1961 and 1980 revision, p. 156. See note 14 above.

37 W. V. Quine, 'Comments', *Boston Studies in the Philosophy of Science* (Reidel, 1963) p. 101. (Reprinted in *Ways of Paradox* p. 179.)

38 Ibid. R. B. Marcus, W. V. Quine, S. Kripke, J. McCarthy and D. Føllesdal, 'Discussion', p. 116.
   In response to the query about determining who or what was the reference of a proper name I said one might look in a dictionary. I had in mind something like a biographical dictionary or those parts of a dictionary so headed, or like *The Oxford Classical Dictionary* which consists mostly in providing information *about* the objects named.

39 *Word and Object* (Cambridge, Mass.: 1960), p. 199. On my quantified modal logic permutation holds for '□' and the universal quantifier which is relevant to the summary of the argument.

40 'Classes and attributes in extended modal systems', *Acta Philosophica Fennica* 16 (1963) 'Classes, collections and individuals', *American Philosophical Quarterly* (1974). The necessary identity of sets is also discussed in a review of Smullyan's 'Modality and description', *Journal of Symbolic Logic* 13 (1948).

41 See S. Waterlow (Broadie), *Passage and Possibility: A Study of Aristotle's Modal Concepts* (Oxford, 1982).

42 *Metaphysics*, VII. 15, W. D. Ross (trans.), in *Collected Works of Aristotle* (Random House, 1941).

43 I have been helped recently in threading my way through some of Aristotle's texts by J. Lear, *Aristotle: The Desire to Understand* (Cambridge, 1988).

44 'Three grades of modal involvement', in *Ways of Paradox*. See esp. p. 176.

45 'Essentialism in modal logic', *Nous* I (1967). These arguments were presented more informally in my 'Modalities and intensional languages', *Synthese* 1961 and elsewhere. See note 31.

46 T. Parsons, 'Essentialism and quantified modal logic', *Philosophical Review LXXVIII*, 1 (1969). An additional constraint excludes predicates like 'identical to Socrates'.

47 S. Kripke, 'Identity and necessity', M. Munitz (ed.), *Identity and Individuation* (New York, 1971) and 'Naming and necessity', D. Davidson et al. (eds), *Semantics of Natural Languages* (Holland, 1972). Both are reprinted elsewhere. Also H. Putnam, 'The meaning of meaning' in Keith Gunderson (ed.), *Language, Mind, and Knowledge* (Minnesota, 1975). Reprinted elsewhere. See also R. Barcan Marcus, 'Essential attribution', *Journal of Philosophy, LXVII*, 7 (1971). The literature on these topics is now large. The 'metaphysical' modalities are in some respects like Carnap's 'physical' modalities.

48 Quine has not been wholly consistent in his claim that even the status of 'logical truths' is 'open to revision'. In *Philosophy of Logic* (Prentice-Hall, 1970, revised, 1986) he argues that to change the meaning of the logical constants is to 'change the subject'.

49 I exclude predicates formed from sentences with indexical terms like 'here' and 'I' where the indices remain the predicate. Proper names are taken as quasi-indexical, hence as in my paper 'Essentialism in modal logic', being identical to Socrates is a quasi-indexical not a *general* property. In that paper I called such quasi-indexical properties 'referential properties' in that they have components which refer to individuals directly. See note 45.

50 Dagfinn Føllesdal, *Referential Opacity and Modal Logic* (privately distributed, 1966), especially the preface and §§ 19 and 20. The quotes are on p. 102 and p. 120.

51 Dagfinn Føllesdal, 'Essentialism and reference', in L. Hahn and P. Schlipp (eds), *The Philosophy of W. V. Quine* (Open Court, 1986).

25

Quantifying In

David Kaplan

I

Expressions are used in a variety of ways. Two radically different ways in which the expression 'nine' can occur are illustrated by the paradigms:

(1)   Nine is greater than five,
(2)   Canines are larger than felines.

Let us call the kind of occurrence illustrated in (1) a *vulgar* occurrence, and that in (2) an *accidental* occurrence (or, following Quine, an orthographic accident). For present purposes we need not try to define either of these notions; but presumably there are no serious logical or semantical problems connected with occurrences of either kind. The first denotes, is open to substitution and existential generalization, and contributes to the meaning of the sentence which contains it. To the second, all such concerns are inappropriate.

There are other occurrences of the word 'nine', illustrated in

(3)   'Nine is greater than five' is a truth of Arithmetic,
(4)   It is necessary that nine is greater than five,
(5)   Hegel believed that nine is greater than five.

These diverge from the paradigm of vulgar occurrence (they fail the substitution test, the existential

David Kaplan, Quantifying In. *Synthese*, 19 (1968–9): 178–214.

generalization test, and probably others as well), but they are not, at least to the untutored mind, clearly orthographic accidents either: for in them, the meaning of 'nine' seems, somehow, relevant. Let us call them *intermediate occurrences* and their contexts *intermediate contexts*.

These intermediate occurrences have come in for considerable discussion lately. Two kinds of analyses which have been proposed can be conveniently characterized as: (a) assimilating the intermediate occurrences to the accidental occurrences, and (b) assimilating the intermediate occurrences to the vulgar occurrences.

The former view, that the intermediate occurrences are to be thought of like accidental ones, I identify with Quine. Such a charge is slightly inaccurate; I make it chiefly for the sake of dramatic impact. My evidence, carefully selected, is that he has proposed in a few places that quotation contexts, as in (3), be thought of as single words and that 'believes that nine is greater than five' be thought of as a simple predicate. And that after introducing a dichotomous classification of occurrences of names into those which he terms 'purely referential' (our vulgar – his criterion is substitutivity) and those which he terms 'non-referential' (our intermediate and accidental) he writes, "We are not unaccustomed to passing over occurrences that somehow 'do not count' – 'mary' in 'summary', 'can' in 'canary'; and we can allow similarly for all non-referential occurrences of terms, once we know what to look out for." Further, his very terminology: 'opaque' for a context in which names occur non-referentially, seems to suggest an indissoluble whole, unarticulated by semantically relevant components.[1] But be that as it may, I shall put forward this analysis – the assimilation of intermediate occurrence to accidental ones – primarily in order to contrast its defeatist character with the sanguine view of Frege (and his followers) that we can assimilate the intermediate occurrences to vulgar ones.

II

The view that the occurrences of 'nine' in (3), (4), and (5) are accidental may be elaborated, as Quine has done, by contrasting (3), (4), and (5) with:

(6) Nine is such that the result of writing it followed by 'is greater than five' is a theorem of Arithmetic,

(7) Nine is such that necessarily it is greater than five,

(8) Nine is such that Hegel believed it to be greater than five,

in which we put, or attempt to put, 'nine' into purely referential position. Quine would still term the occurrences of 'five' as non-referential; thus, the 'necessarily it is greater than five' in (7) might be thought of as an atomic predicate expressing some property of the number of baseball positions (assuming (7) to be true). And similarly for (6) and (8). I am not trying to say how we would "ordinarily" understand (6)–(8). I merely use these forms, in which the occurrence of 'nine' does not stand within the so-called opaque construction, as a kind of canonical form to express what must be carefully explained, namely that here we attribute a property to a certain number, and that the correctness of this attribution is independent of the manner in which we refer to the number. Thus (6), (7), and (8) are to be understood in such a way that the result of replacing the occurrence of 'nine' by any other expression denoting that number would not affect the truth value of the sentence. This includes replacement by a variable, thus validating existential generalization. In these respects (6)–(8) do indeed resemble (1).

But (3)–(5), which are to be understood in the natural way, are such that the result of substituting 'the number of planets' for the occurrences of 'nine' would lead from truth to falsehood (didn't Hegel "prove" that the number of planets = 5?). Thus, for Quine, these contexts are opaque, and

the result of replacing the occurrences of 'nine' by the variable 'x' and prefixing '$\exists x$' would lead from truth to formulas of, at best, questionable import. In fact, Quine deems such quantification into an opaque context flatly 'improper'.[2] In these respects (3)–(5) resemble (2). Although the impropriety of substituting or quantifying on the occurrence of 'nine' in (2) is gross compared with that involved in applying the corresponding operations to (3)–(5), the view I am here characterizing would make this difference a matter of degree rather than of kind.

I will not expatiate on the contrast between (3)–(5) and (6)–(8), since Quine and others have made familiarity with this contrast a part of the conventional wisdom of our philosophical times. But note that (6)–(8) are not introduced as defined forms whose non-logical apparatus is simply that of (3)–(5), in the way in which

Exactly one thing is greater than five

can be defined in terms of the non-logical apparatus of (1). Instead (6)–(8) are introduced as new primitive forms.

Earlier I said that (3)–(5) should be understood in the natural way, whereas careful explanation was required for (6)–(8). But will careful explanation suffice? Will anything suffice? What we have done, or rather what we have sketched, is this: a certain skeletal language structure has been given, here using fragments of English, so of course an English reading is at once available, and then certain logical transformations have been pronounced valid. Predicate logic was conducted in this way before Gödel and Tarski, and modal logic was so conducted before Carnap and others began to supply semantical foundations. The earlier method, especially as applied to modal logic (we might call it the run-it-up-the-axiom-list-and-see-if-any-one-deduces-a-contradiction method), seems to me to have been stimulated more by a compulsive permutations-and-combinations mentality than by the true philosophical temperament.

Thus, it just is not enough to describe the form (6) and say that the predicate expresses a property of numbers so that both Leibniz' law, and existential generalization apply. What property of numbers is this? It makes no sense to talk of the result of writing a number. We can write numerals and various other names of numbers but such talk as (6), in the absence of a theory of standard names, is surely based on confusion of mention and use.[3]

One is tempted to make the same remark about (7), but in this case an alternative explanation is possible in a metaphysical tradition connected with so-called "Aristotelian essentialism". It is claimed that among the properties of a thing, e.g. being greater than 5, and numbering the planets, some hold of its necessarily, others only contingently. Quine has ably expounded the inevitability of this view of (7).[4]

In contrast to (6) and (7), we can put a strong prima facie case for the sensicalness of (8) by way of illustrative examples which indicate important uses of the form exemplified in (8) as compared with that of the form exemplified in (5). Russell mentions, in a slightly different context, the man who remarked to an acquaintance "I thought that your yacht was longer than it is". The correct rendering here is clearly in the style of (8), viz:

The length of your yacht is such that I thought that your yacht was longer than that.

not in the style of (5);

I thought that your yacht was longer than the length of your yacht.

In 'Quantifiers and Propositional Attitudes', Quine supports the use of (8) as against (5) by an ingenious use of existential quantification. He contrasts:

(9)   Ralph believes that someone is a spy,

in which the quantifier occurs within the opaque construction, as does the term in (5), with:

(10)   Someone is such that Ralph believes that he is a spy,

which is an existential generalization of a formula of the form (8). After pointing out that (9) may be rephrased as:

Ralph believes that there are spies,

Quine remarks, "The difference is vast; indeed, if Ralph is like most of us, [(9)] is true and [(10)] is false." In this connection recall that according to Quine's theory of referential opacity, (10) can not be obtained by existential generalization directly from a formula of the form (5) say,

Ralph believes that Ortcutt is a spy,

since the occurrence of the term to be generalized on is here assimilated to that of the orthographic accident and thus is not immediately open to such a move.

Let me sum up what I have called Quine's elaboration of the view that intermediate occurrences are to be assimilated to accidental ones. For those cases in which it is desired to make connections between what occurs within the opaque construction and what occurs without, a special new primitive form is introduced, parallel to the original, but containing one (or more than one) of the crucial terms in a purely referential position. Quine refers to the new form as expressing the *relational* sense of belief. The possibility of introducing such forms always exists and the style of their introduction seems uniform, but since they are primitive each such introduction must be supplied with an ad hoc justification (to the effect that the predicate or operator being introduced makes sense).

III

Let me turn now to the Fregean view that assimilates intermediate occurrences to vulgar ones. The brilliant simplicity of Frege's leading idea in the treatment of intermediate occurrences has often been obscured by a failure to separate that idea from various turgid details involved in carrying the program through in particular interesting cases. But theory must be served.

Frege's main idea, as I understand it, was just this. There are no *real* intermediate occurrences; the appearance of intermediacy created by apparent failures of substitutivity and the like is due to confusion about what is denoted by the given occurrence. Frege here calls our attention to an implicit assumption made in testing for substitutivity and the like. Namely, that a denoting expression must *always* have its usual denotation, and, *a fortiori*, that two expressions must have the same denotation in a given context if they usually (i.e. in most contexts) have the same denotation.

But we are all familiar with many counter-examples to the assumption that a name always has its usual denotation. Consider:

(11)   Although F.D.R. ran for office many times, F.D.R. ran on television only once.

The natural analysis of (11) involves pointing out that the name 'F.D.R.' is ambiguous, and that in the second clause it denotes a television show rather than a man. Substitutions or any other logical operations based on the assumption that the name has here its usual denotation are pointless and demonstrate nothing. But transformations based on a *correct* analysis of the name's denotation *in this context* will reveal the occurrence to be vulgar. I call this the natural analysis, but it is of course possible for a fanatical mono-denotationalist to insist that his transformations have shown the context:

... ran on television only once

to be opaque, and so to conclude that the second occurrence of 'F.D.R.' in (11) is not purely referential. This view may be expressed moderately, resulting only in an insistence that (11) is improper unless the second clause is rewritten as:

the television show named 'F.D.R.' ran on television only once.

Often when there is a serious possibility of confusion, we conform to the practice (even if not the theory) of the fanatical mono-denotationalist and do introduce a new word, add a subscript, or put the original in bold face, italics, or quotation marks. It is often good practice to continue to so mark the different uses of an expression, even when there is little possibility of confusion. Discovering and marking such ambiguities plays a considerable and useful role in philosophy (some, not I, would say it is the essence of philosophy), and much of what has proved most engaging and at the same time most fruitless in logical theory might have been avoided had the first 25 years of this century not seen a lapse from Frege's standards of mention and use. It would be unwary of us to suppose that we have now caught all such ambiguities. Thus, we should not leap to conclusions of opacity.

I indicated in the case of the fanatical mono-denotationalist how it is possible to trade a finding of opacity for one of ambiguity. Frege attempts his assimilation of intermediate occurrences to vulgar ones by indicating (some would say, postulating) ambiguities where others have seen only opacity. It is not denied that the ambiguities involved in the Fregean analysis are far more subtle than that noted in (11), but on his analysis the difference is seen as a matter of degree rather than of kind.

Frege referred to intermediate occurrences as *ungerade* (indirect, oblique). And the terminology is a natural one, for on his conception such an occurrence does not refer directly to its usual denotation but only, at best, indirectly by way of some intermediate *entity* such as a sense or an expression. I will return to this subject later. For now just notice that occurrences which Quine would call purely referential, Frege might call standardly referential; and those in contexts Quine would call referentially opaque, Frege might call non-standardly referential, but in either case for Frege the occurrences are fully referential. So we require no special non-extensional logic, no restrictions on Leibniz' law, on existential generalization, etc., except those attendant upon consideration of a language containing ambiguous expressions. And even these can be avoided if we follow the practice of the fanatical mono-denotationalist and require linguistic reform so that distinct uses of expressions are marked by some distinction in the expressions themselves. This feature of a development of Frege's doctrine has been especially emphasized by Church.[5]

This then is Frege's treatment of intermediate contexts – obliquity indicates ambiguity. This doctrine accounts in a very natural way for the well-known logical peculiarities of intermediate contexts, such as the failure of substitutivity, existential generalization, etc.

IV

The difficulties in Frege's treatment appear in attempting to work out the details – details of the sort: exactly what *does* 'nine' denote in (3)–(5)? Frege's treatment of oblique contexts is often described as one according to which expressions in such contexts denote their ordinary sense or meaning or intension (I here use these terms interchangeably). But this is a bad way of putting the matter for three reasons. (1) It is, I belive, historically inaccurate. It ignores Frege's remarks about quotation marks (see below) and other special contexts. (2) It conflates two separate principles: (a) expressions in oblique contexts don't have their ordinary denotation (which is true), and (b) expressions in oblique contexts denote their ordinary sense (which is not, in general, true). And (3) in focussing attention too rapidly on the special and separate problems of intensional logic, we lose sight of the beauty and power of Frege's general method of treating oblique contexts. We may thus lose the motivation that that general theory might provide for an attack on the problems of the special theory. My own view is that Frege's explanation, by way of ambiguity, of what appears to be the logically deviant behavior of terms in intermediate contexts is so theoretically satisfying that if we have not yet discovered or satisfactorily grasped the peculiar intermediate objects in question, then we should simply continue looking.

There is, however, a method which may assist in the search. Look for something denoted by a compound, say, a sentence, in the oblique context. (In ordinary contexts sentences are taken to denote their own truth values and to be intersubstitutable on that basis.) And then using the fundamental principle: the denotation of the compound is a function of the denotation of the parts, look for something denoted by the parts. It was the use of this principle which, I believe, led to Carnap's discovery of individual concepts[6], and also led Frege to the view that quotation marks produce an oblique context within which each component expression denotes itself[7] (it is clear in quotation contexts what the whole compound denotes).

Frege's view of quotation contexts would allow for quantification into such contexts, but of course we would have to quantify over expressions (since it is expressions that are denoted in such contexts), and we would have to make some provision to distinguish when a given symbol in such a context is being used as a variable and when it is being used as a constant, i.e. to denote itself. This might be done by taking some distinctive class of symbols to serve as variables.

Let us symbolize Frege's understanding of quotation marks by using forward and backward capital F's. (Typographical limitations have forced elimination of the center horizontal bar of the capital F's.) Then, using Greek letters for variables ranging over expressions we can express such truths as:

(12) $\exists\alpha[\ulcorner\alpha$ is greater than five$\urcorner$ is a truth of arithmetic].[8]

Such is Frege's treatment of quotation marks: it seems to me more interesting and certainly much more fruitful (for the development of any theory in which quotation contexts are at all common) than the usual orthographic accident treatment according to which the quotation marks seal off the context, which is treated as a single indissoluble word. And it is well known that for serious theo-

retical purposes, quotation marks (under the conventional treatment) are of little use.

The ontological status of meanings or senses is less well settled than that of expressions. But we can again illustrate the principle involved in searching for the intermediate entities, and perhaps even engender an illusion of understanding, by introducing some symbolic devices. First, in analogy to the conventional use of quotation marks, I introduce meaning marks. Their use is illustrated in the following:

(13)   The meaning of 'brother' = ^{m}male sibling^m.

Now we can adapt the idea used in producing (12) to meaning marks, so as to produce a Fregean interpretation of them. The context produced by the meaning marks will then not be thought of as referentially opaque but rather such that each expression in such a context will denote its own meaning. Quantification in is permitted, but restricted of course to quantification over meanings. Following the earlier pattern, let us symbolize the new meaning marks with forward and backward capital M's. Using italic letters for variables ranging over meanings, we can express such truths as:

(14) $\exists a\exists b[^M a$ kicked $b^M =\ ^M b$ was *kicked by* $a^M]$

I leave to the reader the problem of making sense of (12)–(14).

This comparison of meaning marks with quotation marks also allows me to make another point relevant to Quine's 'Quantifiers and Propositional Attitudes'. In his section IV, Quine suggests that by a harmless shift in idiom we can replace talk of meanings by talk of expressions, thus achieving ontological security. I agree, but the parallel can be exploited in either direction: as suggested by the introduction of meaning marks, we might also try to replace talk of expressions by talk of meanings, thus achieving ontological insight. These structural parallels are most helpful in constructing a logic of intensions.[9]

V

We have finished comparing the treatments of (3)–(5) with respect to the two main analyses of intermediate occurrences: assimilation to ortho-graphic accident versus assimilation to vulgar occurrence. The forms involved in (6)–(8) were introduced in connection with what I called Quine's elaboration of the first line. Now what can be done in this direction following Frege's line? The purpose of the new forms in (6)–(8) is to get an expression out from an accidental position to a vulgar one; or, in Quine's terminology, to move a term from an opaque context to a purely referen-tial position. There should be no problem here on Frege's theory, because what is opaque for Quine is already fully referential for Frege. Thus the term is in a fully referential position in the first place. But this will not quite satisfy the demands of (6)–(8), because the term in question does not denote the right thing.

At this point it will be useful to reformulate (3)–(8) (or at least (4), (5), (7), and (8)) so as to make explicit what the objects of belief and necessity are. In so doing we take a step along Frege's path, for the non-substitutability of one true sentence for another in such contexts would indicate to Frege an ambiguity in both of them: the sentences lack their usual denotation, a truth value, and instead denote some other entity. Before saying what, note that the necessity symbol will stand for a property – of something or other – and the belief symbol will stand for a two-place relation – between a person and something or other. (This in contrast to treating the necessity symbol simply as a 1-place referentially opaque sentential connective and similarly for belief.) Quine takes the step in Frege's direction in the article under discussion and favors it in the sister article 'Three Grades of Modal Involve-ment'. So I take it here. Now what shall the sentences denote? For my present purposes it will suffice to take the ontologically secure position and let them denote expressions, in particular, themselves.[10] Making this explicit, we rewrite (4) and (5) as:

(15)   N 'nine is greater than five'
(16)   Hegel B 'nine is greater than five'

On the usual reading of quotation marks, (15) and (16) still basically formulate the non-Fregean view, with the referential opacity now charged against the quotes. Keeping in mind that the shift to (7) and (8) was for the purpose of moving 'nine' to a purely referential position, we can rewrite (7) and (8) as:

(17)   Nec ('x is greater than five', nine)

(which may be read: 'x is greater than 5' is neces-sarily true of nine) , and

(18)   Hegel Bel ('x is greater than five', nine).

Here the symbol for necessity becomes a two–place predicate and that for belief a three–place predicate. 'x is greater than five' stands for a compound pre-dicate, with the bold face letter 'x' used only as a *place holder* to indicate subject position. The opacity of quotation marks deny such palce holders a refer-ential position in any Nec or Bel context. 'Nec' and 'Bel' are intended to express Quine's relational sense of necessity and belief.[11]

Frege would reformulate (15) and (16) as:

(19)   N ⌜nine is greater than five⌝.
(20)   Hegel B ⌜nine is greater than five⌝.

Notice that we can use the same predicates as in (15) and (16) since

⌜nine is greater than five⌝ = 'nine is greater than five'

just as

$$(3 \times 10^2) + (6 \times 10^1) + (8 \times 10^0) = 368.$$

It should now be clear that although the occur-rences of 'nine' in (19) and (20) are fully referen-tial, (19) and (20) won't do for the purposes of (17) and (18), because the occurrences of 'nine' in (17) and (18) refer to quite a different entity. Combin-ing (17) with:

(21)   Nine numbers the planets,

we derive:

(22) $\exists y$ [y numbers the planets & Nec ('x is greater than five', y)].

But (19) and (21) seem to yield only:

$\exists y$ [y numbers the planets & N ⌜nine is greater than five⌝],

in which the quantifier binds nothing in the neces-sity context, or:

$\exists \alpha$ [α numbers the planets & N $^\ulcorner \alpha$ is greater than five$^\urcorner$],

which is false because the planets are not numbered by an expression (recall our conventions about Greek variables).

Thus the Fregean formulations appear to lack the kind of recurrence of a variable both within and without the necessity context that is characteristic of quantified modal logic and that appears in (22). But this difficulty can be considerably mitigated by taking note of the fact that though the number nine and the expression 'nine' are distinct entities, there is an important relationship between them. The second denotes the first. We can follow Church[5] by introducing a denotation predicate, 'Δ', into our language, and so restore, at least in an *indirect* way (recall Frege's indirect reference by way of intermediate entities) the connection between occurrences of an expression within and without the modal context, as in:

(23) $\exists y$ [y numbers the planets & $\exists \alpha (\Delta(\alpha, y)$ & N $^\ulcorner \alpha$ is greater than five$^\urcorner$)].

I propose (23), or some variant, as Frege's version of (22); and

(24) $\exists \alpha$ [$\Delta(\alpha, \text{nine})$ & N $^\ulcorner \alpha$ is greater than five$^\urcorner$),

or some variant, as Frege's version of (17). (We shall return later to the variants.) (23) and (24) may not be as exciting as (22) and (17), but neither do they commit us to essentialism. It may well be that (24), and its variants, supply all the connection between occurrences of expressions within and without modal contexts as can sensibly be allowed.

When I summed up Quine's elaboration of the orthographic accident theory of intermediate occurrences I emphasized the fact that to move an expression in an opaque construction to referential position, a new *primitive* predicate (such as 'Nec' and 'Bel' of (17) and (18)) had to be introduced and supplied with an interpretation. In contrast, the same effect is achieved by Frege's method using only the original predicates plus logical signs, including 'Δ', and of course the ontological decomposition involved in the use of the Frege quotes.

Turning now to belief I propose:

(25) $\exists \alpha$ [$\Delta(\alpha, \text{nine})$ & Hegel B $^\ulcorner \alpha$ is greater than five$^\urcorner$],

or some variant, as Frege's version of Quine's (18).

VI

If we accept (25) as the interpretation of Quine's (18), we can justify a crucial form of inference he seems to consider valid and explain certain seemingly paradoxical results which he accepts.

Quine recites the following story. There is a certain man in a brown hat whom Ralph has glimpsed several times under questionable circumstances on which we need not enter here; suffice it to say that Ralph suspects he is a spy. Also there is a gray-haired man, vaguely known to Ralph as rather a pillar of the community, whom Ralph is not aware of having seen except once at the beach. Now Ralph does not know it, but the men are one and the same.

Quine then poses the question, "Can we say of this *man* (Bernard J. Ortcutt, to give him a name) that Ralph believes him to be a spy?" The critical facts of the story are summarized in what we would write as:

(26) Ralph B 'the man in the brown hat is a spy',
(27) Ralph B 'the man seen at the beach is not a spy',
(28) the man in the brown hat = the man seen at the beach = Ortcutt

Quine answers his own query by deriving what we would write as:

(29) Ralph Bel ('x is a spy', the man in the brown hat)

from (26). He says of this move, "The kind of exportation which leads from [(26)] to [(29)] should doubtless be viewed in general as implicative."[12] Now our versions of (26) and (29) are:

(30) Ralph B $^\ulcorner$ the man in the brown hat is a spy$^\urcorner$,
(31) $\exists \alpha$ [$\Delta(\alpha, \text{the man in the brown hat})$ & Ralph B $^\ulcorner \alpha$ is a spy$^\urcorner$].

And (31) certainly is implied by (30) and the nearly analytic truth:

Δ ('the man in the brown hat', the man in the brown hat).[13]

We thus justify exportation.

In discussing a seeming paradox Quine notes that exportation will also lead from (27) to:

Ralph Bel ('x is not a spy', the man seen at the beach)

and hence, by (28). to:

(32)   Ralph Bel('x is not a spy', Ortcutt).

Whereas (29) and (28) yield:

(33)   Ralph Bel('x is a spy', Ortcutt).

Thus, asserts Quine,
[(32)] and [(33)] both count as true. This is not, however, to charge Ralph with contradictory beliefs. Such a charge might reasonably be read into:

[(34) Ralph Bel ('x is a spy and x is not a spy', Ortcutt),]

but this merely goes to show that it is undesirable to look upon [(32)] and [(33)] as implying [(34)].

At first blush it may appear that avoidance of that undesirable course (looking upon (32) and (33) as implying (34)) calls for the most intense kind of concentration and focus of interest. In fact one may be pessimistically inclined to take the easy way out and simply dispose of (32), (33), (34) and any other assertions involving Bel as nonsense. But, as Quine says, "How then to provide for those indispensable relational statements of belief, like 'There is someone whom Ralph believes to be a spy'?"

Fortunately our versions of Bel again conform to Quine's intuitions. (32), (33) and (34) go over respectively into:

(35) $\exists\alpha\ [\Delta(\alpha,\ \text{Ortcutt})$ & Ralph B $\ulcorner\alpha$ is not a spy$\urcorner\ ]$,

(36) $\exists\alpha\ [\Delta(\alpha, \text{Ortcutt})$ & Ralph B $\ulcorner\alpha$ is a spy$\urcorner\ ]$,

(37) $\exists\alpha\ [\Delta(\alpha, \text{Ortcutt})$ & Ralph B $\ulcorner\alpha$ is a spy and α is not a spy$\urcorner\ ]$

which clearly verify Quine's claims, even in the presence of the suppressed premise:

$\forall\alpha\forall\beta$ [Ralph B $\ulcorner\alpha$ is a spy$\urcorner$ & Ralph B $\ulcorner\beta$ is not a spy$\urcorner \rightarrow$ Ralph B $\ulcorner\alpha$ is a spy and β is not a spy$\urcorner\ ]$

VII

So far so good. But further exploration with our version of **Bel** suggests that the rule of exportation fails to mesh with the intuitive ideas that originally led Quine to the introduction of **Bel**. And I believe that our version will also allow us to see more clearly exactly what problems lay before us if we are to supply a notion answering to these motivating intuitions. As I hope later developments will show, there are a number of different kinds of counter-cases which could be posed. I will only develop one at this point.

Suppose that the situation is as stated in (9). We would now express (9) as:

(38)   Ralph B '$\exists y\ y$ is a spy'.

Believing that spies differ widely in height, Ralph believes that one among them is shortest. Thus,

(39)   Ralph B 'the shortest spy is a spy'.

Supposing that there is in fact one shortest spy, by exportation (39) yields:

(40)   Ralph Bel('x is a spy', the shortest spy).

which, under the same supposition, by existential generalization yields:

(41) $\exists y$ Ralph Bel('x is a spy', y).

And (41) currently expresses (10). But (10) was originally intended to express a fact which would interest the F.B.I. (recall Quine's comment that if Ralph is like most of us, (10) is false), and we would not expect the interest of that organization to be piqued by Ralph's conviction that no two spies share a size.

Two details of this case can be slightly improved. First, the near analyticity of Ralph's crucial belief, as expressed in (39), can be eliminated by taking advantage of Ralph's belief that all members of the C.P.U.S.A. (none of which are known to him) are spies. Second, we can weaken the assumption of Ralph's special ideas about spy sizes by using only the well-known fact that two persons can not be born at exactly the same time at exactly the same place (where the place of birth is an interior point of the infant's body). Given any four spatial points a, b, c, d not in a plane, we can use the relations: t_1 is earlier than t_2, and p_1 is closer to $a(b, c, d)$ than p_2 is, to order all space time points. We can then form such names as 'the least spy' with the meaning: ^{m}that spy whose spatio-temporal location at birth precedes that of all other spies^m.

Details aside, the point is that exportation, as represented in our current version of Bel, conflicts with the intention that there be a 'vast' difference between (9) and (10). Still, I am convinced that we are on the right track. That track, roughly speaking, is this: instead of trying to introduce a new primitive relation like Quine's Bel, we focus on trying to define it (or something as close to it as we can sensibly come, remember modal logic) using just the dyadic B plus other logical and semi-logical apparatus such as quantifiers, Δ, etc. and also possibly other seemingly more fundamental epistemological notions.

Some years ago I thought that this task was hopeless and took basically the same attitude toward such quantified belief contexts as Quine takes toward quantified modal logic.[14] At that earlier time I used to argue with my colleague, Montgomery Furth, who shares my attitude toward Frege's theory, about the meaningfulness of such quantifications in as in (10). (This was after noticing the difficulty, indicated above, in our current analysis.[15]) Furth suggested that a solution might lie in somehow picking out certain kinds of names as being required for the exportation. But this just seemed essentialism all over again and we gave up. Although still uncertain that (10) makes sense, I think I can show that it comes to something like what Furth had in mind. Indeed, the analogies between the relational senses of belief and necessity are so strong that I have often wondered why Quine's scepticism with regard to Nec did not extend to Bel.

There is even an inadequacy in our proposed analysis, (24), of Nec parallel to that displayed for our proposed analysis, (25), of Bel. Although our analysis of Nec avoids essentialism, it also avoids rejecting:

(42)   Nec('x = the number of planets', nine),

which comes out true on the understanding:

(43) $\exists \alpha$ ($\Delta(\alpha, \text{nine})$ & N $^\ulcorner\alpha$ = the number of planets$^\urcorner$)

in view of the facts that

N $^\ulcorner$the number of planets = the number of planets$^\urcorner$

and

Δ('the number of planets', nine).

In a sense, we have not avoided essentialism but only inessentialism, since so many of nine's properties become essential. Small consolation to know of our essential rationality if each blunder and error is equally ingrained.

The parallel inadequacies of our versions of Nec and Bel are now apparent. Our analyses credit nine with an excess of essence and put Ralph *en rapport* with an excess of individuals.

VIII

What is wanted is "a frankly inequalitarian attitude toward various ways of specifying the number [nine]".[16] This suggests to me that we should restrict our attention to a smaller class of names; names which are so intimately connected with what they name that they could not but name it. I shall say that such a name *necessarily denotes* its object, and I shall use 'Δ_N' to symbolize this more discriminating form of denotation.

Such a relation is available; based on the notion of a *standard name*. A standard name is one whose denotation is fixed on logical, or perhaps I should say linguistic, grounds alone. Numerals and quotation names are prominent among the standard names.[17] Such names do, in the appropriate sense, necessarily denote their denotations.

Russell and some others who have attempted to treat proper names of persons as standard names have emphasized the purely referential function of such names and their apparent lack of descriptive content. But consideration of the place value system of arabic numerals and our conventions for the construction of quotation names of expressions should convince us that what is at stake is not pure reference in the absence of any descriptive structure, but rather reference freed of *empirical* vicissitudes. Numbers and expressions, like every other kind of entity, can be named by names which are such that empirical investigation is required to determine their denotations. 'The number of planets' and '9' happen to denote the same number. The former might, under other circumstances or at some other time, denote a different number, but so long as we hold constant our conventions of language, '9' will denote the same number under all possible circumstances. To wonder what number is named by the German 'die Zahl der Planeten' may betray astronomical ignorance, but to wonder what number is named by the German 'Neun' can indicate only linguistic incompetence.[18]

$\Delta_N (\alpha, x)$ cannot be analyzed in terms of the analyticity of some sentence of the form $\Delta(---, \ldots)$;
since:

Δ ('the number of planets', the number of planets)

is analytic, but 'the number of planets' is not a standard name of the number of planets (viz: nine), and

Δ ('9', the number of planets)

is not analytic, although '9' is a standard name of that number. We have in Δ_N a relation that holds between the standard name and the number itself, independent of any particular way of specifying the number. Thus there is a certain intimacy between '9' and 9, lacking between 'the number of planets' and the number of planets, which allows '9' to go proxy for 9 in assertions of necessity.

There is a sense in which the finite ordinals (which we can take the entities here under discussion to be) find their essence in their ordering. Thus, names which reflect this ordering in an *a priori* way, as by making true statements of order analytic, capture all that is essential to these numbers. And our careless attitude toward any intrinsic features of these numbers (e.g. whether zero is a set, and if so whether it has any members) suggests that such names may have captured all there is to these numbers.[19] I am less interested in urging an explanation of the special intimacy between 'nine' and nine, than in noting the fact. The phenomenon is widespread, extending to expressions, pure sets of finite rank, and others of their ilk. I would require any adequate explanation to generalize so

as to handle all such cases, and I should hope that such an explanation would also support the limitations which I suggest below on the kinds of entities eligible for standard names.[20]

The foregoing considerations suggest simple variants for our current Fregean versions of (17) and (42). We replace (24) with:

$$\exists \alpha \ (\Delta_N(\alpha, \text{nine}) \ \& \ N \ulcorner \alpha \text{ is greater than five} \urcorner)$$

as our analysis of (17), and we replace (43) with:

$$\exists \alpha \ (\Delta_N(\alpha, \text{nine}) \ \& \ N \ulcorner \alpha = \text{the number of planets} \urcorner)$$

as our analysis of (42). According to the reformed analyses, (17) and (42) come out respectively as true and false, which accords much better with our intuitions and may even satisfy the essentialist.[21] All, it is hoped, without a lapse into irreducible (though questionable) metaphysical assumptions.

There are, however, limitations on the resort to standard names. Only abstract objects can have standard names, since only they (and not all of them) lack that element of contingency which makes the rest of us liable to failures of existence. Thus, Quine can have no standard name, for he might not be. And then what shall his standard name name? Quine's singleton, {Quine}, though abstract, is clearly no better off.

Numerals are reliable; they always pick out the same number. But to suppose a standard name for Quine would presuppose a solution to the more puzzling problem of what features to take into account in determining that an individual of one possible world is "the same person" as that of another. Often when the worlds have a common part, as when we consider alternative futures to the present, the individual(s) can be traced back to the common part by the usual continuity conditions and there compared. But for individuals not extant during an overlap such techniques are unavailing. It seems that such radically disjoint worlds are sometimes contemplated by modal logicians. I am not here passing final judgment but only remarking the relevance of a second difference between Quine and Nine: namely, that he presents a very real problem of transworld identification while it does not.

Thus the device of using standard names, which accounts nicely for my own intuitions regarding the essential properties of numbers, appears to break down when set to discriminating essential properties of persons. I am consoled by the fact that my own intuitions do not assign essential properties to persons in any broad metaphysical sense, which is not to say that quantified modal logic can have no interesting interpretation when trans-world identifications are made from the point of view of a frankly special interest.

IX

All this on Nec was aimed toward analogy with Bel and a charge of inconsistent scepticism against Quine. We have patched our first version of Nec with a more discriminating sense of denotation. The same trick would work for Bel, if Ralph would confine his cogitations to numbers and expressions. If not, we must seek some other form of special intimacy between name and object which allows the former to go proxy for the latter in Ralph's cognitive state.

I believe that the fundamental difficulty with our first version of Bel is that Δ gave us a relation between name and object in which Ralph played no significant role. Supposing all speakers of English to have available approximately the same stock of names (i.e. singular terms), this puts us all *en rapport* with the same persons. But the interesting relational sense of belief, and the one which I suppose Quine to have been getting at with (10), is one which provides Ralph with access to some but not all persons of whom he can frame names. What we are after this time is a three-place relation between Ralph, a name (which I here use in the broad sense of singular term) α, and a person x. For this purpose I will introduce two special notions: that of a name α being *of* x for Ralph, and that of a name being *vivid*, both of which I will compare with the notion of a name *denoting* x.

Let us begin by distinguishing the *descriptive content* of a name from the *genetic character* of the name as used by Ralph. The first goes to user-independent features of the name, the second to features of a particular user's acquisition of certain beliefs involving the name. It is perhaps easiest to make the distinction in terms not of names but of pictures, with consideration limited to pictures which show a single person. Those features of a picture, in virtue of which we say it resembles or is a likeness of a particular person, comprise the picture's descriptive content. The genetic character of a picture is determined by the causal chain of events leading to its production. In the case of

photographs and portraits we say that the picture is *of* the person who was photographed or who sat for the portrait. The same relation presumably holds between a perception and the perceived object.[22] This relation between picture and person clearly depends entirely on the genetic character of the picture. Without attempting a definition, we can say that for a picture to be *of* a person, the person must serve significantly in the causal chain leading to the picture's production and also serve as object for the picture. The second clause is to prevent all of an artist's paintings from being *of* the artist. I will shortly say a bit more about how I understand this relation, which I designate with the italicized '*of*'.

The "user-independence" of the descriptive content of a picture lies in the fact that "identical" pictures, such as two prints made from a single negative, will resemble all the same persons. In this sense, the descriptive content of a picture is a function of what we might call the picture-type rather than the picture-token. The "user-dependent" nature of the genetic character of a picture lies in the fact that "identical" paintings can be such that they are *of* different persons (e.g. twins sitting separately for portraits). Thus the genetic character of a picture is a function only of the picture-token. In order to accommodate genesis, I use 'picture' throughout in the sense of 'picture-token'.

Armed with *resemblance* and *of*-ness, let me recite just a few of the familiar facts of portraiture. First, not all pictures *of* a person resemble that person. Of two recent pictures taken of me, one resembles Steve Allen and the other resembles nothing on earth. Secondly, not all pictures which resemble a person are *of* that person. It is obvious that a picture *of* one twin will, if it resembles the twin it is *of*, also resemble the other twin. What is more interesting is that a picture which resembles a person may not be *of* any person at all. My camera may have had a hallucination due to light leaks in its perceptual system. Similarly, if I have drawn my conception of how the typical man will look in one million years, even if a man looking like that now exists, my picture is not *of* him (unless he sat as a model or played some other such role). Thirdly, a picture may be *of* more than one person, as when, by the split mirror technique, we obtain a composite photograph showing one man's head on another man's body. Indeed, in summary, a single picture may be *of* no one, one person, or many persons, while resembling no one, one person, or many persons, with any degree of overlap between those whom it is *of* and those whom it resembles. Of course, if photographs did not frequently, indeed usually, resemble their subjects, they could not serve many of the purposes for which we use them. Still, on occasion, things can and do go awry, and a bad photograph of one is yet a photograph *of* one.

I turn now to cases in which the causal chain from object to picture is relatively indirect. If one or several witnesses describe the criminal to a police artist who then constructs a picture, I shall say that it is a picture *of* the criminal, even when after such a genesis the resulting picture has quite ceased to resemble the criminal. Similarly, had a photograph of Julius Caesar been xeroxed, and the xerox copy televised to a monastery, where it was copied by a monk, and so was reproduced down through the ages, I would call the resulting copy, no matter how distorted, no matter who, if anyone, it resembled, a picture *of* Julius Caesar.[23]

A police artist's reconstruction of Santa Claus, based on a careful reading of the poem *The Night Before Christmas*, is not a picture *of* anyone no matter how many people make themselves up so that it exactly resembles them, and no matter whether the artist regards the poem as fact or fiction. Even if in combining facial features of known statistical frequencies the artist correctly judges that the resulting picture will resemble someone or other, that person has no special causal efficacy in the production of the picture and so it still will not be a picture *of* anyone. And if the story of Medusa originated in imagination or hallucination (as opposed to misperception or misapprehension), then a rendering based on that legend is *of* no one, notwithstanding the existence of any past, present, or future snake-haired women.

In addition to the link with reality provided by the relation of resemblance the descriptive content of a picture determines its *vividness*. A faded picture showing the back of a man wearing a cloak and lurking in shadow will lack vividness. A clear picture, head on, full length, life size, showing fingerprints, etc. would be counted highly vivid. What is counted as vivid may to some extent depend on special interests. To the clothier, nude portraits may be lacking in detail, while to the foot fetishist a picture showing only the left big toe may leap from the canvas. Though special interests may thus weight detail, I would expect that increase in detail always increases vividness. It should be clear that there are no necessary connections between how vivid a picture is and whether it is *of* anyone or whether it resembles anyone.

Returning now to names, it is their descriptive content that determines what if anything they denote. Thus, denotation is the analogue for names to resemblance for pictures. The genetic character of a name in a given person's usage will account for how he *acquired* the name, that is how he heard of such a thing and, if he believes that such a thing exists, how he came to believe it. It is the genetic character of the name that determines what if anything it is a name *of*. (I here use the same nomenclature, '*of*', for names as for pictures.) The user-dependence of this notion is required by the fact that Ralph and Fred may each have acquired the name 'John Smith', but in such a way that for Ralph it is a name *of* one John Smith while for Fred it is a name *of* another John Smith.

I would suppose that students of rhetoric realize that most of the lines of argument traditionally classified as 'informal fallacies' (*ad hominem, ad vericundiam*, etc.) are commonly considered relevant or even determinative by reasonable men.[24] Cases such as that of the two John Smiths, which emphasize the importance of genetic features in language use, indicate limitations that must be placed on the traditional dichotomy between *what* we believe (assert, desire, etc.) and *how* we came to believe it.

Let us attempt to apply these considerations to the case of proper names. Proper names denote each of the usually many persons so dubbed. Ralph may acquire a proper name in a number of different ways. He may have attended a dubbing with the subject present. I reconstruct such dubbings as consisting of a stipulative association of the name with a perception *of* the subject. Thus, the name becomes a name *of* the subject, and as it passes from Ralph to others retains this feature in the manner of the picture *of* Julius Caesar. We may of course dub on the basis of a hallucination, in which case the name is a name *of* nothing, though it will still denote each actual person, if any, that may be so dubbed. Dubbings sometimes take place with the subject absent, in which case some other name (usually a description) stands in for the perception, and the stipulatively introduced proper name takes its genetic character from the stand-in-name. If the latter only denotes the subject (and is not a name *of* the subject for the user in question), the proper name can do no better. This having a name *of x*, I shall later take to be essential to having a belief about x, and I am unwilling to adopt any theory of proper names which permits me to perform a dubbing in absentia, as by solemnly declaring "I hereby dub the first child to be born in the twenty-second century 'Newman I'", and thus grant myself standing to have beliefs about that as yet unborn child. Another presumably more common way to acquire a proper name is in causal conversation or reading, e.g. from the headline, "Mayor Indicted: B. J. Ortcutt sought by F.B.I.". In such cases we retrace the causal sequence from Ralph back through his immediate source to its immediate source and so on. An especially difficult case of this sort arises when someone other than Ortcutt, say Wyman, is introduced to Ralph as Ortcutt. Suppose that the introduction took place with intent to deceive and that Fred, who made the introduction, acquired the name 'Ortcutt' as a name *of* Ortcutt. Clearly we should count 'Ortcutt' as a name *of* Wyman for Ralph, but also, through Fred, as a name *of* Ortcutt. The situation is analogous to the composite photograph made by the split mirror technique. But here the much greater vividness of the perceptual half of the equation may outweigh the dim reflection of Ortcutt.

I leave to the reader the useful exercise of constructing cases of names (not necessarily proper) which are analogues to each of the cited cases of pictures.

The notion of a vivid name is intended to go to the purely internal aspects of individuation. Consider typical cases in which we would be likely to say that Ralph knows x or is acquainted with x. Then look only at the conglomeration of images, names, and partial descriptions which Ralph employs to bring x before his mind. Such a conglomeration, when suitably arranged and regimented, is what I call a vivid name. As with pictures, there are degrees of vividness and the whole notion is to some degree relative to special interests. The crucial feature of this notion is that it depends only on Ralph's current mental state, and ignores all links whether by resemblence or genesis with the actual world. If the name is such, that on the assumption that there exists some individual x whom it both denotes and resembles we should say that Ralph knows x or is acquainted with x, then the name is vivid.

The vivid names "represent" those persons who fill major roles in that *inner story* which consists of all those sentences which Ralph believes. I have placed 'represent' here in scarequotes to warn that there may not actually exist anything which is so "represented". Ralph may enjoy an inner story totally out of contact with reality, but this is not to deny it a cast of robust and clearly delineated characters. Life is often less plausible than art. Of course a vivid name should make an existence *claim*. If Ralph does not believe that there is a Santa Claus, I would not call any Santa Claus name vivid, no matter how lively it is in other respects.

There are certain features which may contribute strongly to vividness but which I feel we should not accept as absolute requirements. It is certainly too much to require that a vivid name must provide Ralph with a means of recognizing its purported object under all circumstances, for we do not follow the careers of even those we know best that closely. There are always gaps. We sometimes even fail to recognize ourselves in early photographs or recent descriptions, simply because of gaps in our self-concept.[25] It also seems to me too much to require that Ralph believes himself to have at some time perceived the purported object of a vivid name since a scholar may be better acquainted with Julius Caesar than with his own neighbor. Some have also suggested that the appropriate kind of name must provide Ralph with the means of locating its purported object. But parents and police are frequently unable to locate persons well known to them. Also, a vivid biography of a peasant somewhere in Asia, may involve none but the vaguest spatio-temporal references.

One might understand the assertion, 'Ralph has an opinion as to who Ortcutt is' as a claim that Ralph can place Ortcutt among the leading characters of his inner story, thus that Ralph believes some sentence of the form $\ulcorner \alpha = \text{Ortcutt} \urcorner$ with α vivid. This, I believe, is the view of Hintikka. Hintikka institutionalizes the sense of 'represents' with usual quotes by allowing existential generalization on the leading character or inner individual "represented" by a vivid name. Although his symbolism allows him to distinguish between those inner individuals which are actual and those which are not, a central role is assigned to something close to what I call a vivid name.[26] In emphasizing this conceptual separation of vividness, which makes a name a *candidate* for exportation, from those features depending on genesis and resemblence, which determine what actual person, if anyone, the name really represents (without quotes), Hintikka (if I have him right) and I are in agreement.

It is a familiar fact of philosophy that no idea, description, or image can insure itself against non-natural causes. The most vivid of names may have had its origin in imagination or hallucination. Thus, to freely allow exportation a name must not only be vivid but must also be a name *of* someone, and indeed a name *of* the person it denotes. This last is an accuracy requirement which no doubt is rarely satisfied by the most vivid names we use. Our most vivid names can be roughly characterized as those elaborate descriptions containing all we believe about a single person. Such names will almost certainly contain inaccuracies which will prevent them from actually denoting anyone. Also such names are often not *of* a single person but result from conflation of information about several persons (as in Fred's prevaricating introduction of Wyman to Ralph).

One proposal for handling such difficulties would be to apply the method of best fit to our most vivid names, i.e. to seek the individual who comes closest to satisfying the two conditions: that the name denotes him and is *of* him. But it seems that this technique would distort the account of conflations, never allowing us to say that there are two persons whom Ralph believes to be one. There is an alternate method which I favor. Starting with one of our most vivid names, form the largest core, all of which is *of* the same person and which denotes that person. A vivid name resulting from conflation may contain more than one such core name. The question is whether such a core, remaining after excision of inaccuracy, is yet vivid. If so, I will say that the core name *represents* the person whom it both denotes and is *of* to Ralph.

Our task was to characterize a relation between Ralph, a name, and a person, which could replace Δ in a variant analysis of Bel. For this I will use the above notion of representation. To repeat, I will say α *represents x to* Ralph (symbolized: 'R (α, x, Ralph)') if and only if (i) α denotes x, (ii) α is a name of x for Ralph, and (iii) α is (sufficiently) vivid. Our final version of (33) is the following variant of (36):

(44) $\exists \alpha$ [R (α, Ortcutt, Ralph) & Ralph B $^{\ulcorner}\alpha$ is a spy $^{\urcorner}$].

X

Part of our aim was to restrict the range of persons with whom Ralph is *en rapport* (in the sense of

Bel). This was done by means of clauses (ii) and (iii). Clause (ii) excludes all future persons such as Newman[27] and indeed any person past, present, or future who has not left his mark on Ralph. The addition of clause (iii) excludes any person who has not left a vivid mark on Ralph.

The crucial exportation step for the case of the shortest spy is now blocked, because in spite of Ralph's correct belief that such a person exists, 'the shortest spy' is not, for Ralph, a name *of* him.[28]

Clause (iii) takes account of the desire to allow Ralph beliefs *about* (again in the sense of Bel) only those persons he 'has in mind', where the mere acquisition of, say, a proper name *of x* would not suffice to put *x* in mind. Furthermore, if we were to drop clause (iii), and allow any name which both denotes *x* and is a name *of x* to represent *x* to Holmes, then after Holmes observed the victim, 'the murderer' would represent the murderer to him. And thus we would have:

$$\exists y \exists \alpha \ [R(\alpha, y, \text{Holmes}) \ \& \ \text{Holmes B} \ulcorner\alpha = \text{the} = \text{murderer}\urcorner \ ],$$

which is our present analysis of:

$$\exists y \ \text{Holmes Bel ('x} = \text{the murderer'}, y),$$

which is, roughly, Quine's translation of:

There is someone whom Holmes believes to be the murderer.

But this last should presage an arrest and not the mere certification of homicide. Clause (iii) is intended to block such cases. At some point in his investigation, the slow accretion of evidence, all "pointing in a certain direction" may just push Holmes' description over the appropriate vividness threshold so that we *would* say that there is now someone whom Holmes believes to be the murderer.

Clause (iii) could also be used to block exportation of 'the shortest spy'. But that would not eliminate the need for clause (ii) which is still needed to insure that we export to the right individual.

Although I believe that all three clauses are required to block all the anomalies of exportation, I am less interested in a definitive analysis of that particular inference than I am in separating and elucidating certain notions which may be useful in epistemological discussions. According to my analysis, Ralph must have quite a solid conception of x before we can say that Ralph believes x to be a spy. By weakening the accuracy requirements on the notion of representation we obtain in general new relational senses of belief.[29] Any such notion, based on a clearly specified variant of (36), may be worthy of investigation.

XI

A vivid name is a little bit like a standard name, but not much. It can't guarantee existence to its purported object, and although it has a kind of inner reliability by way of Ralph's use of such names to order his inner world, a crucial condition of reliability – the determinateness of standard identities – fails. A standard identity is an identity sentence in which both terms are standard names. It is corollary to the reliability of standard names, that standard identities are either true under all circumstances or false under all circumstances. But not so for identities involving vivid names. We can easily form two vivid names, one describing Bertrand Russell as logician, and another describing Russell as social critic, which are such that the identity sentence simply can not be decided on internal evidence. In the case of the morning star and the evening star, we can even form names which allow us to locate the purported objects (if we are willing to wait for the propitious moment) without the identity sentence being determinate. Of course Ralph may believe the negation of the identity sentence for all distinct pairs of vivid names, but such beliefs may simply be wrong. And the names can remain vivid even after such inaccurate non-identities are excised. It may happen that Ralph comes to change his beliefs so that where he once believed a non-identity between vivid names, he now believes an identity. And at some intermediate stage of wonder he believes neither the identity nor the non-identity. Such Monte Cristo cases may be rare in reality (though rife in fiction)[30] but they are nevertheless clearly possible. They could be ruled out only by demanding an unreasonably high standard of vividness, to wit: no gaps, or else by adding an artificial and ad hoc requirement that all vivid names contain certain format items, e.g. exact place and date of birth. Either course would put us out of *rapport* with most of our closest friends. Thus, two vivid names can represent the same

person to Ralph although Ralph does not believe the identity sentence. He may simply wonder, or he may disbelieve the identity sentence and so believe of one person that he is two. Similarly two vivid names can represent different persons to Ralph although Ralph does not believe the non-identity sentence. Again, Ralph may either suspend judgment or disbelieve the non-identity and so believe of two persons that they are one. Since this last situation is perhaps more plausible than the others, it is important 't see that theoretically the cases are on a par. In fact, a case where Ralph has so conflated two persons and is then disabused by his friend Fred, becomes a case of believing one person to be two simply by assuming that Ralph was right in the first place and that Fred lied.

Quine acknowledge that Ralph can believe of one person that he is two on Quine's own understanding of Bel, when he remarks, as mentioned in VI above, that

(32)   Ralph Bel ('x *is not a spy*', Ortcutt),

and

(33)   Ralph Bel ('x is a spy', Ortcutt),

do not express an inconsistency on Ralph's part and do not imply (34). The background story justifying (32) and (33) involves Ralph twice spotting Ortcutt but under circumstances so different that Ralph was unaware that he was seeing the same man again. Indeed he believed he was not seeing the same man again, since on the one occasion he thought, 'There goes a spy', and on the other, 'Here is no spy'. My point is that though one may quibble about whether each or either of the names of Ortcutt were vivid in the particular cases as described by Quine,[31] and so question whether in those cases exportation should have been permitted, no plausible characterization of appropriate conditions for vividness can prevent analogous cases from arising.

Cases of the foregoing kind, which agree with Quine's intuitions, argue an inadequacy in his regimentation of language. For in the same sense in which (32) and (33) do not express an inconsistency on Ralph's part, neither should (33) and

(45) $\sim$ Ralph Bel ('x is a spy', Ortcutt)

express an inconsistency on ours. Indeed it seems natural to claim that (45) is a consequence of (32).

But the temptation to look upon (33) and (45) as contradictory is extremely difficult to resist. The problem is that since Quine's Bel suppresses mention of the specific name being exported, he can not distinguish between

(46) $\exists \alpha$ [R (α, Ortcutt, Ralph) & $\sim$ Ralph B $\ulcorner \alpha$ is a spy$\urcorner$]

and

(47) $\sim \exists \alpha$ [R (α, Ortcutt, Ralph) & Ralph B $\ulcorner \alpha$ is a spy$\urcorner$]

If (45) is read as (46), there is no inconsistency with (32); in fact, on this interpretation (45) is a consequence of (32) (at least on the assumption that Ralph does not have contradictory beliefs). But if (45) is read as (47) (Quine's intention, I suppose), it is inconsistent with (33) and independent of (32).

So long as Ralph can believe of one person that he is two, as in Quine's story, we should be loath to make either (46) or (47) inexpressible.[32] If (33) is read as (44), we certainly must retain some way of expressing (47) since it expresses the negation of (33). Is it important to retain expression of (46)? In Quine's story, something stronger than (46) holds, namely (32), which we now read as:

(48) $\exists \alpha$ [R (α, Ortcutt, Ralph) & Ralph B $\ulcorner \alpha$ is not a spy$\urcorner$]

But we can continue the story to a later time at which Ralph's suspicions regarding even the man at the beach have begun to grow. Not that Ralph now proclaims that respected citizen to be a spy, but Ralph now suspends judgment as to the man's spyhood. At this time (48) is false, and (46) is true. If we are to have the means to express such suspensions of judgment, something like (46) is required.

I have gone to some trouble here to indicate the source of the notational inadequacy in the possibility of a single person bearing distinct exportable names not believed to name the same thing, and also to argue in favor of maintaining the possibility of such names. I have done this because logicians working in this field have for the most part been in accord with Quine in adopting the simpler language form. In my view the consequence of adopting such a form is either to exclude natural interpretations by setting an impossibly high standard for vividness, and thus for exportation, or else to make such partial expressions of suspended judgment as (46) inexpressible.

XII

When earlier I argued for Frege's method – seek the intermediate entity – it was on the grounds that a clarified view of the problem was worth at least a momentary ontological risk. But now it appears that to give adequate expression to the epistemological situation requires explicit quantificational certification of the status of such entities. I am undismayed and even would urge that the conservative course so far followed of taking expressions as the intermediate entities is clearly inadequate to the task. Many of our beliefs have the form: 'The color of her hair is———', or 'The song he was singing went———', where the blanks are filled with images, sensory impressions, or what have you, but certainly not words. If we cannot even *say* it with words but have to paint it or sing it, we certainly cannot believe it with words.

My picture theory of meaning played heavily on the analogy between names and pictures. I believe that the whole theory of sense and denotation can be extended to apply to pictures as well as words. (How can an identity "sentence" with the components filled by pictures be both true and informative?) If we explicitly include such visual images among names, we gain a new perspective on the claim that we can definitively settle the question of whether Bernard J. Ortcutt is such that Ralph believes him to be a spy by confronting Ralph with Ortcutt and asking 'Is *he* a spy?' Ralph's response will depend on recognition, a comparison of current images with stored ones. And stored images are simply one more form of description, worth perhaps a thousand words, but thoroughly comparable to words. Thus Ralph's answer in such a situation is simply one more piece in the whole jigsaw of his cognitive structure. He might answer 'yes' for some confrontations (compare – 'yes' for some names), 'no' for others, and withhold judgment for still others.

The suggested extension of the intermediate entities poses an interesting problem for the ontologist. Must we posit a realm of special mental entities as values for the variables used in analyzing the relational sense of belief, or will a variant on the trick of taking sentences as the objects of belief also account for beliefs involving visual images, odors, sounds, etc.?[33]

XIII

There are, I believe, two rather different problem areas connected with the analysis of intermediate contexts. The first problem area, which lies squarely within what is usually called the philosophy of language, involves chiefly the more fundamental non-relational interpretation of intermediate contexts. It calls for an explanation of the seemingly logically deviant behavior of expressions in such contexts and perhaps also for a more exact statement of just what inferences, if any, are valid for such contexts. Here I feel that Frege's method outlines a generally acceptable solution. I especially appreciate the fact that for Frege intermediate contexts are not seen as exceptions to a powerful and heretofore general logical theory but rather are seen as fully accessible to that theory with the noted anomalies explained as due to a misreading of "initial conditions" leading to an inappropriate application of the laws. This accounting for seemingly aberrant phenomena in terms of the correct application of a familiar theory is explanation at its most satisfying. By contrast, the view I have associated with Quine – that intermediate contexts are referentially inarticulate – contents itself with a huge and unobvious class of "exceptions to the rules". This is shabby explanation, if explanation at all.

The second problem area specifically concerns the relational interpretation of intermediate contexts. Here I have tried to show how Frege's method, though it may provide a basis for unifying the relational and non-relational interpretation of a given intermediate context and though it immediately provides for some form of quantification in, does not by itself necessarily provide the most interesting (and perhaps indispensible) relational interpretation. Further analysis, often specific to the context in question, may be required in order to produce an appropriately discriminating form of Δ which will yield results in conformity with our intuitive demands. Indeed, such an investigation may well lead far beyond the philosophy of language proper into metaphysics and epistemology. I know of no earlier source than 'Quantifiers and Propositional Attitudes' in which relational uses of intermediate contexts are so clearly identified throughout an area of concern more urgent than modal logic. In that article Quine early expressed his remarkable insights into the pervasiveness of the relational forms and the need for a special analysis of their structure. And in fact following Quine's outlook and attempting to refine the conditions for valid applications of exportation, one might well arrive at the same metaphysical and epistemological insights as those obtained in attempting to refine Δ. What is important is that we should achieve some form of analysis of these contexts without recourse to the very idioms we are attempting to analyze.

The problem of interpreting the most interesting form of quantification in, appears in various guises: as the problem of making trans-world identifications, as the problem of finding favored names, and as the problem of distinguishing 'essential' from 'accidental' properties. The present paper suggests two polar techniques for finding favored names. It is curious and somehow satisfying that they so neatly divide the objects between them, the one applying only to objects capable of being perceived (or at least of initiating causal chains), the other applying only to purely abstract objects. I am well aware of obscurities and difficulties in my formulations of the two central notions – that of a standard name and that of a name being *of* an object for a particular user. Yet both seem to me promising and worthy of further investigation.

Notes

This chapter is intended as a commentary on Quine's 'Quantifiers and Propositional Attitudes'. Quine's article was first published in 1956 and I have been thinking about it ever since. His subsequent writings do not seem to have repudiated any part of 'Quantifiers and Propositional Attitudes' which remains, to my mind, the best brief introduction to the field. The first half of my reflections was read to the Harvard Philosophy Colloquium in January 1966. Its writing was aided by conversations with Montgomery Furth. The present ending has been influenced by a number of different persons, most significantly by Saul Kripke and Charles Chastain. But they should not be held to blame for it. Furth, who also read the penultimate version, is responsible for any remaining deficiencies aside from Section IX about which he is skeptical. My research has been partially supported by N.S.F. Grant GP-7706.

1 The quotation is from *Word and Object*, p. 144, wherein the inspiration for 'opaque' is explicitly given. The assimilation of intermediate occurrences to accidental ones might fairly be said to represent a *tendency* on Quine's part. The further evidence of *Word and Object* belies any simplistic characterization of Quine's attitudes toward intermediate occurrences.

2 In 'Three Grades of Modal Involvement', p. 172 in [20] and other places. An intriguing suggestion for notational efficiency at no loss (or gain) to Quine's theory is to take advantage of the fact that occurrences of variables within opaque contexts which are bindable from without are prohibited, and use the vacated forms as "a way of indicating, selectively and changeably, just what positions in the contained sentence are to shine through as referential on any particular occasion" (*Word and Object*, p. 199). We interpret, 'Hegel believed that x is greater than five' with bindable 'x', as 'x is such that Hegel believed it to be greater than five' which is modeled on (8). Similarly, 'Hegel believed that x is greater than y' is now read as, 'x and y are such that Hegel believed the former to be greater than the latter'. (8) itself could be rendered as, '$\exists x$ [$x =$ nine & Hegel believed that x is greater than five]', and still not be a logical consequence of (5).

3 The reader will recognize that I have incorporated, without reference, many themes upon which Quine has harped, and that I have not attempted to make my agreement with him explicit at each point at which it occurs. Suffice it to say that the agreements far outweigh the disagreements, and that in both the areas of agreement and of disagreement I have benefited greatly from his writings.

4 See especially the end of 'Three Grades of Modal Involvement'. I am informed by scholarly sources that Aristotelian essentialism has its origin in 'Two Dogmas of Empiricism'. It reappears significantly in 'Reply to Professor Marcus', where essential properties of numbers are discussed, and in *Word and Object*, p. 199, where essential properties of persons are discussed. I will later argue that the two cases are unlike.

5 In 'A Formulation of the Logic of Sense and Denotation'.

6 See *Meaning and Necessity*, Section 9, for the discovery of the explicandum, and Section 40 for the discovery of the explicans.

7 See 'On Sense and Reference' pp. 58, 59 in *Translations from the Philosophical Writings of Gottlob Frege*.

8 The acute reader will have discerned a certain similarity in function, though not in foundation, between the Frege quotes and another familiar quotation device.

9 These parallels are exhibited at some length in my dissertation *Foundations of Intensional Logic*.

10 A drawback to this position is that the resulting *correct* applications of Leibniz' Law are rather unexciting. More interesting intermediate entities can be obtained by taking what Carnap, in *Meaning and Necessity* calls 'intensions'. Two expressions have the same intension, in this sense, if they are logically equivalent. Other interesting senses of 'intension' might be obtained by weakening the notion of logical equivalence to logical equivalence within sentential logic, intuitionistic logic, etc. Church suggests alternatives which might be understood along these lines.

11 I have approximately followed the notational devices used by Quine in 'Quantifiers and Propositional Attitudes'. Neither of us recommend the notation for practical purposes, even with the theory as is. An alternative notation is suggested in note 3 above.

12 Also, see *Word and Object*, p. 211, for an implicit use of exportation.

13 The 'nearly' of 'nearly analytic' is accounted for by a small scruple regarding the logic of singular terms. If a language L containing the name '$\imath yFy$' is extended to a metalanguage L' containing the predicate 'Δ' for denotation-in-L and also containing the logical particles, including quotes, in their usual meaning, then I regard

$$[\exists\, x\ x = \imath yFy \rightarrow \Delta\ (\text{'}\imath yFy\text{'},\ \imath yFy)]$$

as fully analytic in L'.

My reasons for thinking so depend, in part, on my treatment of quotation names as standard names. I am being careful, because Quine suggests disagreement in an impatient footnote to 'Notes on the Theory of Reference' (I am grateful to Furth, who recalled the footnote). I do not know whether our disagreement, if a fact, is over quotation or elsewhere. The whole question of analyticity is less than crucial to my line of argument.

14 See *Word and Object*, Section 41.

15 The same difficulty was noticed, independently, by John Wallace and reported in a private communication.

16 Quoted from the end of Quine's 'Reply to Professor Marcus'. I fully agree with Quine's characterization of the case, though not with the misinterpretation of Church's review of 'Notes on Existence and Necessity' from which Quine's characterization springs.

17 See the discussion of what Carnap calls *L-determinate individual expressions* in *Meaning and Necessity*, Section 18, and also Tarski's discussion of what he calls *structural descriptive names* in 'The Concept of Truth in Formalized Languages', Section 1.

18 The latter wonder is not to be confused with an ontological anxiety concerning the nature of nine, which is more appropriately expressed by dropping the word 'number' in the wonder description.

David Kaplan

19 Benacerraf so concludes in 'What Numbers Could Not Be'.

20 The present discussion of standard names is based on that in the more technical environment of my dissertation, pp. 55–7.

21 Given this understanding of Nec, it is interesting to note that on certain natural assumptions '$\Delta_n(\alpha, y)$' is itself expressed by 'Nec ($\ulcorner \alpha = x \urcorner, y$)'.

22 Note that an attempt to identify the object perceived in terms of resemblance with the perception rather than in terms of the causal chain leading to the perception would seriously distort an account of misperception.

23 The corresponding principle for determining who it is that a given proper name, as it is used by some speaker, names, was first brought to my attention by Saul Kripke. Kripke's examples incorporated both the indirect path from person named to person naming and also the possible distortions of associated descriptions.

The existence of a relatively large number of persons with the same proper name gives urgency to this problem even in mundane settings. In theoretical discussions it is usually claimed that such difficulties are settled by "context". I have recently found at least vague recognition of the use of genetic factors to account for the connection between name and named in such diverse sources as Henry Leonard: "Probably for most of us there is little more than a vaguely felt willingness to mean . . . whatever the first assigners of the name intended by it." (*An Introduction to Principles of Right Reason*, section 30.2), and P. F. Strawson: "[T]he identifying description . . . may include a reference to another's reference to that particular . . . So one reference may borrow the credentials . . . from another; and that from another." (*Individuals*, footnote 1, page 182). Though in neither case are genetic and descriptive features clearly distinguished.

Kripke's insights and those of Charles Chastain, who has especially emphasized the role of *knowledge* in order to establish the desired connection between name and named, are in large part responsible for the heavy emphasis I place on genetic factors.

24 Although it is useful for scholarly purposes to have a catalogue of such "fallacies" (such as that provided in Carney and Scheer, *Fundamentals of Logic*), the value of such discussions in improving the practical reasoning of rational beings seems to me somewhat dubious. A sensitive discussion of a related form of argument occurs in Angell, *Reasoning and Logic*, especially pp. 422–3.

25 Such failures may also be due to self-deception, an inaccurate self-concept, but then the purported object does not exist at all.

26 Insofar as I understand Hintikka's 'Individuals, Possible Worlds, and Epistemic Logic', the domain of values of the bound variables fluctuates with the placement of the bound occurrences of the variables. If, in a quantifier's matrix, the occurrences of the variable bound to the quantifier fall only within uniterated epistemological contexts, then the variables range over possible(?) individuals "represented" by vivid names. If, on the other hand, no occurrences of the variable fall within epistemological (or other opaque) contexts, then the variables range over the usual actual individuals. And if the variable occurs both within and without an epistemological context, then the values of the variables are inner individuals which are also actual. Thus if Ralph believes in Santa Claus, and σ is Ralph's vivid Santa Claus description, Hintikka would treat ' $\ulcorner$ Ralph believes that σ = Santa Claus $\urcorner$, as true and as implying '$\exists x$ Ralph believes that x = Santa Claus', but would treat '$\exists x$ [x = Santa Claus & Ralph believes that x = Santa Claus]' and presumably '$\exists x$ [$\exists y = x$ & Ralph believes that x = Santa Claus]' as false, and not as consequences of ' $\ulcorner \sigma$ = Santa Claus & Ralph believes that σ = Santa Claus $\urcorner$.

27 I disregard precognition explained by a reverse causal chain.

28 We might say in such cases that the name *specifies* its denotation, in the sense in which a set of specifications, though not generated by the object specified, is written with the intention that there is or will be an object so described.

29 One such weakened notion of representation is that expressed by 'Ralph Bel ($\ulcorner \alpha = \bar{x} \urcorner, y$)', analyzed as in (44) using our current R, which here, in contrast to the situation for Δ_N (see reference 22 above), is not equivalent to 'R (α, y, Ralph)'. Still this new notion of representation, when used in place of our current R in an analysis of the form of (44), leads to the same relational sense of belief.

30 Note especially the "secret identity" genre of children's literature containing Superman, Batman, etc.

31 At least one author, Hintikka, has seemed unwilling to allow Ralph a belief *about* Ortcutt merely on the basis of Ralph's few glimpses *of* Ortcutt skulking around the missile base. See his 'Individuals, Possible Worlds, and Epistemic Logic', footnote 13.

32 Another way out is to accept the fact that two names may represent the same person to Ralph though Ralph believes the non-identity, but to put an ad hoc restriction on exportation. For example to analyze (33) as: '$\exists \alpha$ [R (α, Ortcutt, Ralph) & Ralph B $\ulcorner \alpha$ is a spy $\urcorner$] & $\sim \exists \alpha$ [R (α, Ortcutt, Ralph) & $\sim$ Ralph B $\ulcorner \alpha$ is a spy $\urcorner$]'. This prevents exportation where contradiction threatens. But again much that we would like to say is inexpressible in Quine's nomenclature.

33 It should be noted that in Church's 'On Carnap's Analysis of Statements of Assertion and Belief' serious objections are raised to even the first step.

Bibliography

R. B. Angell, *Reasoning and Logic*, New York 1963.

P. Benacerraf, 'What Numbers Could Not Be', *Philosophical Review* 74 (1965) 47–73.

R. Carnap, *Meaning and Necessity*, Chicago 1947, 2nd ed., 1956.

D. Carney and K. Scheer, *Fundamentals of Logic*, New York 1964.

A. Church, 'A Formulation of the Logic of Sense and Denotation', in *Structure, Method, and Meaning* (ed. by P. Henle, M. Kallen, and S. K. Langer), New York 1951.

A. Church, 'On Carnap's Analysis of Statements of Assertion and Belief', *Analysis* 10 (1949–50) 97–9.

A. Church, Review of Quine's 'Notes on Existence and Necessity', *Journal of Symbolic Logic* 8 (1943) 45–7.

G. Frege, 'On Sense and Reference', originally published in *Zeitschrift für Philosophie und philosophische Kritik* 100 (1892) 25–50; translated in *Translations from the Philosophical Writings of Gottlob Frege* (ed. by P. Geach and M. Black), Oxford 1960.

K. J. Hintikka, 'Individuals, Possible Worlds, and Epistemic Logic', *Noûs* 1 (1967) 33–62.

D. Kaplan, *Foundations of Intensional Logic* (Dissertation), University Microfilms, Ann Arbor 1964.

H. S. Leonard, *An Introduction to Principles of Right Reason*, New York 1957.

W. V. Quine, 'Notes on Existence and Necessity', *The Journal of Philosophy* 40 (1943) 113–127.

W. V. Quine, 'Two Dogmas of Empiricism', *Philosophical Review* 60 (1951) 20–43; reprinted in [15].

W. V. Quine, 'Notes on the Theory of Reference', in [15].

W. V. Quine, *From a Logical Point of View*, Cambridge, Mass., 1953, 2nd ed., 1961.

W. V. Quine, 'Three Grades of Modal Involvement', in *Proceedings of the XIth International Congress of Philosophy, Brussels, 1953*, Vol. 14, pp. 65–81, Amsterdam; reprinted in [20].

W. V. Quine, 'Quantifiers and Propositional Attitudes', *The Journal of Philosophy* 53 (1956) 177–187; reprinted (minus 15 lines) in [20].

W. V. Quine, *Word and Object*, New York 1960.

W. V. Quine, 'Reply to Professor Marcus', *Syntheses* 13 (1961) 323–330; reprinted in [20].

W. V. Quine, *The Ways of Paradox and Other Essays*, New York 1966.

P. F. Strawson, *Individuals*, London 1959.

A. Tarski, 'The Concept of Truth in Formalized Languages', originally published in Polish in *Prace Towarzystwa Naukowego Warszawskiego, Wydział* III, no. 34 (1933), pp. vii + 116; translated in A. Tarski, *Logic, Semantics, Metamathematics*, Oxford 1956, pp. 152–278.

26

Substitutivity and the Coherence of Quantifying In

Graeme Forbes

Quine's Thesis

This chapter is about the cluster of issues that orbit a well-known thesis of Quine's, as it applies to attitude ascriptions:

> [A] position that resists substitutivity of identity cannot meaningfully be quantified. (Quine 1986, 291).

If this claim – henceforth *Quine's Thesis* ('QT') – is correct, then it generates a puzzle for those who hold that (i) term positions in attitude contexts resist substitutivity, but also (ii) quantifying into them is perfectly meaningful. And these are natural views to hold. For example, taking the Superman fiction as fact, it seems we cannot infer (1c) from (1a) and (1b):

(1a) Lois Lane doubts that Clark Kent can help her.
(1b) Superman = Clark Kent.
(1c) Lois Lane doubts that Superman can help her.

So the position of 'Clark Kent' in (1a) resists substitution, as (i) says. But in accordance with (ii), quantification into this position looks perfectly intelligible. Indeed, if (1a) is true, it could be argued to *follow* that

Graeme Forbes, Substitutivity and the Coherence of Quantifying In. *The Philosophical Review*, 105 (July 1996): 337–72.

(1d) $(\exists x)$(Lois doubts that x\{can help her)

or, in English,

(1e) There is someone who Lois doubts can help her.

There are legitimate questions about the validity of this inference (see later), but there are none about the intelligibility of its conclusion.

For a direct reference theorist who accepts QT, the intelligibility of (1e) is no puzzle at all, just an invitation to *modus tollens*. For a Fregean, the obvious move is to deny QT. But it seems to me that there is a cautious version of QT that merits endorsement, and this version preserves the puzzle. So we should try to find a different solution. A cautious version of QT is required, since there are many "irrelevant" examples of substitution failure where quantification is allowable.[1] Quine was really concerned only with cases in which resistance to substitutivity is a symptom of an underlying deviance in the semantic functioning of a singular term, and it is the deviance of function that is supposed to explain the incoherence of quantifying in. In the standard terminology, such deviance is called "referential opacity," but since the metaphor of opacity is not apt for every account of the mechanism at work in the relevant cases, I shall avoid it. It may even be that the usual range of examples does not embody a unitary phenomenon. But it is enough for my purposes that propositional attitudes constitute a *specific* case of substitution failure for which the correct explanation posits a mechanism that excludes quantifying into the substitution-resisting position. That is, the cautious version of QT claims only that there is a certain range of cases of substitution failure that involve a mechanism incompatible with quantifying in. The puzzle is that although propositional attitudes seem on general grounds to belong to this range – as I will argue – we have the particular example of (1e) to indicate otherwise.

First, let us review two illustrative constructions in which substitution failure *is* coupled with resistance to quantification: (i) pure quotation and (ii) logophor. A pure quotation is one in which the quoted material is simply mentioned, as opposed to being used as well.[2] For instance,

(2a)   'Istanbul' contains eight letters

is a pure quotation. The position surrounded by the quotes resists substitution, as we can see from the truth of

(2b)   Istanbul = Constantinople

and the falsity of

(2c)   'Constantinople' contains eight letters.

And quantification into the quoted position produces the hard-to-interpret

(2d) $(\exists x)(\text{'}x\text{' contains eight letters})$

which appears to consist in a redundant '$(\exists x)$' followed by the falsehood '('x' contains eight letters)'; or, in English,

(2e)   Something is such that 'it' contains eight letters.

There is certainly no compositionally derived meaning for (2d) or (2e) to which each of its parts makes a standard and nonredundant contribution.

There are two main accounts of quotation in the literature, one deriving from Frege (1970) and the other from Tarski (1969). On the Fregean account, in pure quotation the quoted items refer to themselves, and we may conceive of the quotation marks as a kind of punctuation (see further Washingon 1992, 591). Thus, in (2a), the displayed city name refers to that name (we need

not settle whether token or type). On the Tarskian account, surrounding some item i with quotation marks creates a name of which the marks are part and which refers to i. So (2a) contains a name "'Istanbul'" (including the single quotes) that refers to the word 'Istanbul' (see Richard 1986 for a defense of the Tarskian account).

On both the Fregean and Tarskian accounts, quoted material in a sentence does not perform its normal semantic function, and the specific semantic function that *is* performed will depend on what is quoted – thus the resistance to substitution, which alters what is quoted. In addition, since the Fregean account requires the item between the quotes to refer to itself in that context, while the Tarskian account requires the item to be the middle segment of a name of itself that begins and ends with quotes, it is unacceptable to quantify into quotes, as we can see from (2d). The two possible roles for the inner 'x' in (2d), bound variable and the object of a pure quotation, are *inconsistent*: the 'x' cannot be a bound variable and at the same time either (i) a segment of the name "'x'" (for then it is not even a semantic constituent of (2d)) or (ii) an expression referring to itself (for then it refers autonomously and so is not available to receive as its reference whatever is assigned to the 'x' of '$\exists x$'). Thus pure quotation nicely exemplifies the considerations underlying QT: the unsubstitutable singular term functions in a semantically deviant way, and both the Fregean and the Tarskian accounts of the deviance entail that standard quantification into the position of the unsubstitutable term will be unacceptable.[3]

In this example, resistance to substitution is demonstrated by change in truth value, but change in truth value is merely a side-effect of a more fundamental change, a side-effect that need not always be present (consider "'Istanbul' names a city" in place of (2a)). Let us employ a conception of a sentence's truth condition that is *objectual* or *worldly*. In other words, the condition that has to obtain in the world to make a sentence S true (S's "truthmaker") is a complex whose constituents include, at some level, the objects and properties to which the terms and predicates in S refer. On the worldly conception, truth condition is invariant between two sentences with the same structure all of whose corresponding components are coreferential. On this conception, the fundamental change that (non-null) substitution brings about in cases of pure quotation, whether or not there is change of truth value, is change in truth condition.

The phenomenon that I label 'logophor' has a similar structure.[4] The best-known example is due to Quine. Despite the truth of (3a) and (3b),

(3a) Giorgione is so called because of his size
(3b) Giorgione is Barbarelli,

we cannot infer

(3c) Barbarelli is so called because of his size.

Equally, (3a) does not entail

(3d) $(\exists x)$ (x is so called because of x's size),

or, in English,

(3e) Someone is so called because of his size,

which are unacceptable on account of "there being no longer any suitable antecedent for 'so called'" (Quine 1961, 22). Alternatively, we can change truth condition without changing truth value by using 'groundhogs are woodchucks' to substitute in

(4a) Groundhogs, by any other name, would have just as many legs

Though (4a) and

(4b) Woodchucks, by any other name, would have just as many legs

are both true, they have different truth conditions, since substitution alters the semantic value of 'any other name'. Attempted quantification, as in

(4c) There are things which, by any other name, would have just as many legs

is again unacceptable for Quine's reason, lack of a suitable antecedent (for 'other name'). These cases also illustrate the limitations of the opacity metaphor, since the referential functions of 'Giorgione' in (3a) and 'groundhogs' in (4a) are quite standard; it is change in reference of the logophors 'so' and 'other' occasioned by substitution that is responsible for change in truth condition.

'So called' and 'other name' must be linked to positions that contain an expression of the type by which things are called. Our difficulties with (3e) and (4c) indicate that in interpreting a sentence

that contains a logophor, we take the presence in a position of an expression of the wrong sort as sufficient to prevent the logophor from being linked to that position.[5] So if 'so called' or 'other name' functions in a sentence S in a way that allows us to compose the meaning of S from its parts, it is referring to a specific name or name-like phrase (with 'other name' the reference is carried by the implicit demonstrative *that*, as in 'other than *that* name'). Substitution of a different "common currency" name (Kaplan 1990, 108–9) changes truth condition and sometimes truth value. The unacceptability of quantification will follow if it is impossible for an expression to function simultaneously as the anchoring name for a logophor that requires one and also as a bound variable. And this does seem to be impossible. We already have 'e. e. cummings', 'bell hooks', and 'Malcolm X', so there should be no semantic objection to using 'x' as a proper name. But if the second occurrence of 'x' in (3d) is a proper name, then it refers autonomously, and in a recursive evaluation of (3d) it cannot simultaneously take as its value whatever is assigned to the 'x' of the '$(\exists x)$' within whose scope it lies.[6] In sum, logophor supports QT in the same way pure quotation does: the explanation of why substitution changes truth condition involves a mechanism whose presence prevents the substition-resistant position from being occupied by an expression that can function in that position as a bound variable, because any expression in that position has to perform another, incompatible, function.

The puzzle we are going to pursue is based on the view that the same is true of propositional attitude ascriptions. However, there is a much greater range of disagreement about why substitution fails – if indeed it does – in an example like (1a)–(1c) than there is about why it fails in the cases of quotation and logophor, and we can hardly hope to prove that every possible mechanism that would account for the failure excludes quantifying in. Certainly, many mechanisms that have been proposed do predict trouble for quantification. This is obviously so for any quotational semantics for attitude ascriptions, such as that of Carnap 1947, or any semantics that is quotational in spirit, such as that of Davidson 1969.[7] But more general considerations make it plausible that QT is applicable to attitude ascriptions without committing us to any one semantics.

On the face of it, a propositional attitude verb stands for a two-place relation that holds between cognitive agents and propositions, and in a simple attitude ascription, the verb's subject specifies a putative cognitive agent and its clausal complement a proposition. For Frege, the specification of a proposition is made by straightforwardly referring to it with the complement clause, which picks out the proposition by adumbrating its parts in their manner of composition (cf. Richard's notion of an "articulated term" (1993)). Frege's account of substitution failure turns on the idea that the propositional components referred to by the semantically primitive expressions of the complement clause are not the items they ordinarily stand for but, rather, ways of thinking of those items. Specifically, terms that are ordinarily coreferential may, when they occur in the complement clauses of attitude ascriptions, refer to *different* ways of thinking of their ordinary reference (Frege 1970). But then a statement like (1e) or its stilted logician's paraphrase

(5)   There is a person such that Lois doubts that he can help her

should make little sense. For in evaluating (5), the restricted objectual quantifier will be assigned a person who thereby becomes the value of the co-indexed pronoun 'he'. So the semantic value of the complement clause will be an ontological mishmash, since both propositional and nonpropositional components are referred to by the clause's primitive expressions.

Frege's account is too idiosyncratic for it to have broad appeal as a demonstration of the relevance of QT to attitude ascriptions. In particular, the idea that names refer deviantly in attitude ascriptions has little plausibility. If I say

(6a)   Safire believes Hillary Clinton is hiding something

then it seems undeniable that I refer to Mrs. Clinton, not to a way of thinking of her (this objection to Frege has come to be known as the objection from "semantic innocence").[8] However, we can pry the case for the relevance of QT loose from the exact details of Frege's semantics. Let us say that (6a) *describes a state of affairs* whose constituents are Safire, the binary relation of believing, and the proposition that Hillary Clinton is hiding something. Suppose we also agree that it is part of the semantics of (6a) that each semantic primitive in its complement clause *contributes* a propo-

sitional constituent to the proposition that figures in the state of affairs (6a) describes (the manner of contribution need not be reference, as we will see later). A further assumption, the one that does the work in explaining substitution failure, is that coreferential names can make different contributions to the proposition. So the contributions, whatever they may be, are not (simply) the ordinary referents of the names; however, the names may still *refer* as they ordinarily do.

Those who think that substitution failure in attitude ascriptions is a genuine phenomenon but do not endorse a quotational or quasi-quotational explanation of it are likely to find these premises unexceptionable, even if the rough-and-ready notion of "describing a state of affairs" needs refinement. Certainly, Frege-*style* theorists will not object to them. But problems for quantification are not avoided just because we have abandoned Frege's "reference-shift" hypothesis. The ascription

(6b) $(\exists x)$ (Safire believes x is hiding something)

contains a standard quantifier binding a variable in the position of (6a)'s 'Hillary Clinton' only if, when we make an assignment to the 'x' of '$\exists x$', the open sentence

(6c)   Safire believes x is hiding something

describes a state of affairs (relative to that assignment) with the same structure as that described by (6a). In other words, the state of affairs will involve Safire, the believing relation, and a proposition. Since 'Safire' and 'believes' are thereby accounted for, this leaves

(6d) x is hiding something

to contribute a complete proposition relative to the assignment in question.

The contribution of 'is hiding something' is not in question, but what could the contribution of the variable 'x' be? The only evident candidates are (i) the variable's assignment, (ii) the variable itself, or (iii) some entity that includes the variable and its assignment, say, the ordered pair of the two. Whichever option we choose has to be consistent with the proposed explanation of substitution failure, which requires constituents in the subject position that can be many-one related to the thing the proposition is about. This rules out 'x''s assignment as its contribution to the proposition determined by (6d), since the object assigned to the variable cannot be many-one related to itself. Proposal (ii) is barely intelligible; after all, we would expect the contribution of (6d) to be something that would make (6b) true, if Safire believes it. This leaves proposal (iii), that the variable's contribution is the ordered pair of itself and its assignment. This option gives us the bizarre result that the truth value of (6b) could differ from that of the alphabetic variant of (6b) that uses 'y' instead of 'x'. But as language actually is, no real semantic distinction turns on whether we use 'y' instead of 'x' in (6b).

These considerations seem to me to make it plausible that any broadly Frege-style theory of propositions will have trouble with quantifying into attitude ascriptions. As in the cases of pure quotation and logophor, the problems can be dissolved by reconstruing the quantifier in a nonstandard way. But this is not an interesting strategy. For the quantifiers in (1d) and (6b) seem to be perfectly standard, in which case they should be manageable by whatever semantic apparatus suffices to deal with 'something is red'. A solution to the puzzle must either convincingly explain away the appearance of ordinary quantification in (1d) and (6b) – I have no idea how this would go – or else explain how, contrary to appearances, the quantifier can be standard consistent with the explanation of substitution failure. Both Quine's approach and my own are of this second sort.

Quine on Quantifying In

The main idea behind my strategy for resolving the tension between QT and the intelligibility of the likes of (1d) and (6b) is to accept that the quantifier is standard but to deny that the variable that it binds occurs semantically in any expression that contributes constituents to the proposition that fills the second place of the attitude relation. Suppose we distinguish *pseudo-forms* of sentences from their *logical forms*. Pseudo-forms are obtained by straightforward transcription into first-order notation. In uninteresting cases, logical form coincides with pseudo-form; but in more interesting examples, logical forms embody theoretical apparatus imported to account for a range of semantic data about sentences of the kind in

question, particularly data about inferential behavior.[9] The pseudo-forms of (1a) and (1d) are respectively

(7a) Doubts (Lois, that Clark Kent can help her)

(7b) ($\exists x$) (Doubts (Lois, that x can help her)),

where (7b) is inferred from (7a) by a straightforward application of $\exists$I. But even if the meaningfulness of (7b) is in question, it follows that (1d) is problematic only if (7b) is an accurate representation of (1d)'s logical form, at least as regards its locating the variable 'x' in a position where, in the course of evaluating (7b), it must contribute a constituent to the proposition said to be doubted. The way out of our quandary over (1d) is therefore to find an (independently motivated) logical form for it in which the variable is not in such a position.

It is from this perspective that I view Quine's own proposals about the likes of (1d). Quine would say that (1a) contains a potential ambiguity between *notional* and *relational* senses of 'doubts'. The notional sense is the dyadic 'doubts^2' and the relational ones are of higher degree, for example an "irreducibly triadic" 'doubts^3' (Quine 1955, 104). (7a) is an appropriate pseudo-form for the notional sense, but not for a relational one. The triadic relational reading of (1a), as I presume Quine would have it, is

(7c) *Doubts^3* (*Lois*, $\lambda z(z$ can help her), Clark Kent)

and (1d) gets the corresponding logical form

(7d) ($\exists x$)[Doubts^3 (m Lois, λz (z can help her), x)]

in which 'λz (z can help her)' names an attribute (I follow the style of Quine 1955, 104–5). Since it is a term's occurrence *in* a complex term for an intension that accounts for failure of substitution (because ordinary coreference is not intension-preserving), we can make an ordinary term substitutable and quantifiable by moving it out of the term for the intension into "stand-alone" position. In (7c), 'Clark Kent' has been so moved relative to (7a), so that (7c) has the form $Rt_1t_2t_3$, with each t_i substitutable and quantifiable; hence (7d) is correctly inferred from (7c).[10] To the objection that

Quine's account postulates an implausible ambiguity in the English 'doubts' as it occurs in the two readings of (1a), it may be replied that the account merely portrays 'doubts' as *multigrade*, which implies no ambiguity (Quine 1979, 268).

Actually, (7c) and (7d) issue from Quine as "Jewish chef preparing ham for a gentile client" (Quine 1979, 270). Attributes, like all intensions, are creatures of darkness, and something more linguistic is to be preferred: in place of (7c), using a colon for 'such that',

(7e) $Doubts^3$ (Lois, '$z : z$ can help her', Clark Kent)

and so in place of (7d),

(7f) $(\exists x)$ [$Doubts^3$ (Lois, '$z : z$ can help her', x)]

in which again there is no (explicit) quantification into the context created by the quotes.[11]

I think that Quine's official account is unsatisfactory in one way, and the less official account – the one in terms of intensions – in another way. The official (7e) and (7f) explain relational belief in terms of linguistic expressions, but (for the sake of moving on promptly I will just assert that) the strategy cannot accommodate belief ascriptions to foreign speakers or languageless creatures (for more on its difficulties, see Salmon 1995).[12] On the other hand, the less official (7c) and (7d) face at least two difficulties.

First, it is not sufficient to rebut the charge of positing implausible ambiguity to claim that one is using a single predicate of variable degree. For in the present case the *types* of entities to which the predicate applies change as the degree of the predicate changes. Hence there is a significant contrast with standard examples of multigrade predicates, such as 'live together', 'are compatriots', or, as in Morton's analysis of the Goodman–Leonard calculus of individuals, 'made up of (Morton 1975). In Morton's terminology (311), 'Doubts' is being portrayed (in its multigrade part) as both monadic and dyadic, and it is hard not to see the switch from propositions to attributes-and-n-individuals as marking a change in sense as we go from '$Doubts^2$' to '$Doubts^{n+2}$', $n \geq 1$.

Second, and more importantly, the supposedly irreducible '$Doubts^3$' is not irreducible at all – it is easily explicable in terms of '$Doubts^2$'. The triadic relational reading of (1a) can be put this way:

(7g)   Lois doubts, concerning Superman, that he can help her.

However, it is obscure, at least to me, what significant difference there is between this and

(7h)   Lois doubts a proposition concerning Superman to the effect that he can help her.

And in (7h) it is natural to discern the familiar '$Doubts^2$', asserted to hold between Lois and a certain proposition; this proposition is not fully characterized, the relational aspect of the ascription amounting to a statement of who the subject of the proposition is without specifying the mode of presentation of the subject that figures in the proposition. (7h) therefore sits well with the view that all doubt (belief) is fundamentally doubt (belief) towards a complete proposition, relational ascriptions being those which do not specify all the senses that constitute the proposition, but for some give only their references.

Once we have come to doubt the irreducibility of '$Doubts^n$' for $n > 2$, the treatment of notional / relational contrasts as differences in the degree of propositional attitude verbs loses its appeal. So we are still looking for an approach to attitude ascriptions that reconciles the apparent conflict between QT and the evident meaningfulness of (1d) and its ilk. I believe that my own 'logophoric' analysis of attitude attributions can effect such a reconciliation, so I will briefly sketch its basics.

Logophor and Quantifying In

According to the logophoric account, substitution-failure in (1a), 'Lois doubts...', is produced by precisely the same mechanism as in (3a), 'Giorgione is so called...', though the mechanism is hidden: there is a suppressed logophoric 'so' in (1a) whose reference includes 'Clark Kent' and whose reference will therefore change if that name is replaced by 'Superman', accounting for the change in truth condition.[13]

In more detail, attitude attributions are taken to impute psychological relations towards propositions, which in turn I take to be ways of thinking of *situation-types*.[14] There can be different ways of thinking of the same situation-type ('STP'), since the latter are merely complexes of objects and properties, and an unambiguous attitude attribution adverts, *via* the hidden 'so', to a particular one of the ways of thinking of the relevant STP. For example, 'Superman is an extraterrestrial' and 'Clark Kent comes from somewhere other than Earth' refer to the same STP, the same complex of objects and properties. But as complement clauses in attitude ascriptions, they can invoke different ways of thinking of that STP.

According to the analysis, an attribution's complement clause provides a "labeling" by the ascriber of a putative way of thinking employed by the subject of the attribution: the words of the clause are "linguistic counterparts" of the subject's thought constituents (this does not mean the subject uses those same words). Thus we may understand

(8a)   Lois believes that Superman is an extra-terrestrial

to mean

(8b)   The situation-type of Superman's being an extraterrestrial is such that Lois believes her *so-labeled* way of thinking of it.

The logophor 'so' in (8b) refers to the entire phrase 'Superman's being an extraterrestrial', and thus substitution for both 'Superman' and 'extraterrestrial' is blocked, just as substitution for 'Giorgione' is blocked in (3a). So (8a), interpreted as (8b), does not entail that Lois believes that Clark Kent comes from somewhere other than Earth; see Forbes 1990, 1993 for further discussion of the details of this account.

(8b) permits no substitution at all in the complement clause of (8a). A reading of (8a) that permits substitution throughout can be obtained by replacing 'her so-labeled' in (8b) with 'some':

(8c)   The situation-type of Superman's being an extraterrestrial is such that Lois believes some way of thinking of it.

It suffices for the truth of (8c) that Lois believe that Clark Kent comes from somewhere other than Earth.

Intermediate readings of (8a) may be obtained by adjusting what the 'so' refers to (its *extent*). However, explicitly exhibiting the extent of the

'so' requires some notation, which we introduce in a series of steps. According to (8b), at the level of logical form (8a) contains an "articulated term" (Richard 1993) for an STP formed by raising the complement clause out of its surface position and rewording appropriately. I will use square brackets '[' and ']' and the actual wording of the complement clause to form such definite descriptions. Thus in place of "the situation-type of Superman's being an extraterrestrial" I will write '[Superman is an extraterrestrial]'. If we use a colon for 'is such that', then as a first approximation, (8b) becomes

(9a)   [Superman is an extraterrestrial]$_\sigma$: Lois believes her so-labeled way of thinking of it$_\sigma$.

Here 'σ' is a variable to mark the binder of 'it', and in the final formula, (9e) below, it will simply replace the pronoun.

Next, as mentioned a few sentences back, different interpretations of (8a) can be obtained by varying the extent of the 'so', so we need some device for indicating exactly how much of the articulated term for the STP is in its extent. I will use angle brackets for this purpose. Complicated attitude attributions might involve more than one 'so', in which case there would be a need for variable subscripts on the 'so's and on the angle brackets specifying their extents, but in our examples there is only ever one 'so'. To specify the extent of the 'so' in (9a), therefore, we simply write

(9b)   [⟨Superman is an extraterrestrial ⟩]$_\sigma$: Lois believes her so-labeled way of thinking of it$_\sigma$

with no further variable subscripts. It is exactly the material within angle brackets that is in substitution-resisting position.

Finally, although it is not completely necessary for the purposes of this paper, we may standardize a regimentation of such phrases as

(9c)   Lois believes her so-labeled way of thinking of it$_\sigma$

I will not argue the point here, but the treatment of definite descriptions as restricted quantifiers seems to me to be superior to their treatment as singular terms (the square bracket notation for STP terms is a convenient abbreviation of a quantificational form). Russell would have discerned the intermediate form 'Bel (Lois, t)' in (9c), in which t is the singular term 'the ρ such that ρ is a way of thinking of σ so labeled by Lois', using 'ρ' as a variable over propositions. The restricted quantifier form is instead 'the ρ such that $\phi(\rho)$; Bel (Lois, ρ)'; see Neale 1990, 41, for details of the general approach. In our example, the condition ϕ has to say that ρ is so labeled by Lois, for which I write 'so-labeled (Loix$_x$, ρ)'; and also that Lois thinks of the STP σ under ρ, for which I write 'T (she$_x$, σ, ρ)'. In place of (9c), then, we would have

(9d)   the ρ: so-labeled (Lois$_x$, ρ) & T she$_x$, σ, ρ); Bel (she$_x$, ρ).

Putting all this together results in (8b)'s receiving the symbolization

(9e)   [$\langle$ Superman is an extraterrestrial $\rangle]_\sigma$: the ρ: so-labeled (Lois$_x$, ρ) & T (she$_x$, σ, ρ); Bel(she$_x$, ρ).[15]

To get a logical form for (8c), where everything is open to substitution, we simply transform (9e) by deleting the angle brackets and the subformula containing the logophor, and replace 'the' with 'some'. This results in

(9f)   [Superman is an extraterrestrial]$_\sigma$: some ρ : T(Lois$_x$, σ, ρ); Bel(she$_x$, ρ).

Evidently, there would be a bigger disparity with (9e) if we treated descriptions as terms, even if (9e) itself would look more familiar. But if 'the' is a quantifier word like 'some', a parallel is exhibited.

Another possible interpretation of (8a) is

(10a)   Superman is someone whom Lois believes to be an extraterrestrial

in which 'Superman' but not 'is an extraterrestrial' is open to substitution. This is simply

(10b)   [Superman $\langle$is an extraterrestrial $\rangle]_\sigma$: some ρ: so-labeled (Lois$_x$, ρ) & T she$_x$, σ, ρ); Bel (she$_x$, ρ),

in which the positioning of the angle brackets delimits 'so's extent to be 'is an extraterrestrial'.

This indicates, not that Lois believes a "partial proposition" that the ascriber can label 'is an extraterrestrial', but that she believes a (full) proposition specifiable with a complete label that has 'is an extraterrestrial' as a substring. Thus 'some ρ' rather than 'the ρ', since with the labeling restricted to the predicate, there may be more than one such way of thinking of the STP in question that Lois believes. For example, we can imagine a scenario in which Lois comes to believe that Clark, too, is an extraterrestrial, but still without coming to believe that Clark is Superman.

Unproblematic quantifying in is now possible. From (10a) we can infer

(10c)   There is someone whom Lois believes to be an extraterrestrial,

and this is reflected by a straightforward application of $\exists$I to (10b):

(10d)   Some y: [$y\langle$ is an extraterrestrial $\rangle]_\sigma$: some ρ: so-labeled (Lois$_x$, ρ) & T (she$_x$,σ, ρ); Bel (she$_x$, ρ).

(10d) says that for some y, the STP of y's being an extraterrestrial is such that Lois believes some so-labeled way of thinking of it. Here the label is partial, as explained in connection with (10b), and because it concerns only the predicate component of the specification of the STP – the 'so' refers only to what is within the angle brackets – quantification of the name component is unobjectionable: the variable is not part of the extent of the 'so', hence (10d) does not require Lois to believe a proposition that has a constituent of which a free variable is a linguistic counterpart.

The argument in section 1 that a broadly Fregean account of substitution failure in attitude ascriptions will make quantifying in seem impossible goes off the rails at the point where (6b) is introduced. (6b) represents just a pseudo-form. The logophoric account's more complex logical form keeps the quantifier standard while preserving the essentials of Frege's explanation of substitution failure. However, the route by which a name contributes a way of thinking to the relevant proposition is indirect, and the name refers in the ordinary way, like 'Giorgione' in (3a). So the account preserves semantic innocence as well.

345

A Problem with Pronouns

Our original example (1a), 'Lois Lane doubts that Clark Kent can help her', contains a pronoun 'her' in the complement clause that is referentially dependent upon the proper name 'Lois Lane' that occurs outside the clause. (1a) is not synonymous with

(11)   Lois Lane doubts that Clark Kent can help Lois Lane,

since in a case of loss of memory (11) might be true while (1a) is, or permits an interpretation that is, false. Restricting ourselves to this interpretation, the resistance of its 'her' to substitution means that the pronoun is making a specific contribution to determining the proposition at issue, a contribution that is different from the one that would be made by 'Lois Lane'. In the logophoric framework, it follows that 'her' is within the extent of a 'so'. But then it is detached from its referential anchor; so how can it contribute the right propositional constituent? What could be contributed by an unanchored 'her'?

The contrast between (1a) and (11) indicates what the constituent *ought* to be: in (1a), but not in (11), we are attributing to Lois an attitude towards a proposition that contains Lois's *first-person way of thinking* of Lois,[16] and Lois is not employing this way of thinking if she takes an attitude towards the proposition that Clark Kent can help Lois, not realizing that she is Lois. Suppose, then, that Lois *is* employing her first-person way of thinking of herself, as (1a) is most naturally read. A first try at a logical form for (1a), one that illustrates the difficulty about referential dependence, is

(12a)   Lois$_x$: [$\langle$ Clark Kent can help her$_x$)]$_\sigma$: the ρ: so-labeled (she$_x$, ρ) & T (she$_x$, σ, ρ); Doubts (she$_x$, ρ).

Here we have raised the name 'Lois' so that it governs the subsequent 'her'. But the 'x' that marks the coindexing is part of the label, and this puts (12a) on a par with the unacceptable (3d): the bound variable is within the extent of the 'so' but its binder is not, hence there is, adapting Quine, "no longer any suitable antecedent for 'so [-labeled]'."

However, a simple change avoids the difficulty. In (1a), 'Lois doubts that Clark can help her', the

'her' has a double role, fixing a constituent both for the STP, namely Lois, and for the proposition said to be doubted, namely a token of the type of way of thinking *self*.[17] In a logical form for (1a) in which the 'her' is replaced simply by a variable, the second role – provision of a type of way of thinking – disappears. In (12a), the 'her$_x$' goes some way towards making the division of labor explicit: the convention might be that the variable carries the contribution to the STP, while the pronoun fixes the type of way of thinking of the variable's value. But a token way of thinking is determined by the combination of the contributed object and the type (note 17). Thus the correct proposition will be specified even if some of the expressions in the angle brackets only fix types of ways of thinking, so long as some associated expression within the STP term provides an object that, together with the type, fixes a token of that type. This means we can move the variable outside the angle brackets, rendering (1a) as

(12b)   Lois$_x$: [$\langle$ Clark Kent can help *self*$\rangle_x$]$_\sigma$: the ρ: so-labeled (she$_x$, ρ) & T (she$_x$, σ, ρ); Doubts(she$_x$, ρ).

(12b) says that the proposition ρ that Lois doubts is a way of thinking of the STP [Clark Kent can help x], where x = Lois, and has tokens of (i) the 'Clark Kent can help' type[18] and (ii) the *self* type. We may regard the notation of (12b) as the simplest case of a more general construction in which indexical sense-types are mentioned within the extent of a logophor and some device such as a sequence of subscripts immediately following the closing '$\rangle$' associates referents with them, say by order of occurrence.

A nonreflexive use of 'her' in an attitude ascription may or may not invoke a specific propositional constituent. For example, we may understand

(13a)   Lois is in danger, and Lex Luthor doubts that Superman can help her

so that it only requires Luthor to think of Lois in some way or other – for example, demonstratively. So understood, (13a) means the same as 'Lois is in danger, and is someone whom Lex Luthor doubts that Superman can help'. But we can also understand (13a) so that it is true only if the proposition Luthor doubts involves Luthor's specific way of thinking of Lois that is the linguistic counterpart of the ascriber's 'Lois'. There is more than one way of capturing this interpretation, but the simplest is

(13b)   In danger (Lois) & $[\langle$ Superman can help Lois $\rangle]_\sigma$: some ρ: so-labeled Luthor$_y$, ρ) & T (he$_y$, σ, ρ); Doubts he$_y$, ρ)).

Clearly, there is a systematic project waiting here, concerning the rules for writing the logical forms of attitude ascriptions containing pronouns. I hope these examples make it plausible that the logophoric account has the resources to carry such a project through.

Exportation

Neither my approach nor Quine's would be satisfactory to someone who regards the step from (8a) to (10c)

(8a)   Lois believes that Superman is an extraterrestrial

(10c)   There is someone whom Lois believes is an extraterrestrial

as consisting in a single application of standard $\exists$I, like the step from (7a) to (7b), for mere $\exists$I could not get us from (9e) to (10d):

9(e) $[\langle$ Superman is an extraterrestrial $\rangle]_\sigma$: the ρ: so-labeled (Lois$_x$, ρ) & T (she$_x$, σ, ρ); Bel (she$_x$, ρ).

(10d)   Some y : $[y\langle$ is an extraterrestrial $\rangle]_\sigma$: some ρ: so-labeled (Lois$_x$, ρ) & T (she$_x$, σ, ρ); Bel (she$_x$, ρ).

So if semantic innocence demands that (10c) be derivable from (8a) just by $\exists$I, neither Quine's account nor mine is innocent. But I think semantic innocence should not require this. The core idea of innocence is that names in attitude contexts do not cease to refer to what they usually refer to, and the logophoric analysis is innocent in this sense. Moreover, the approach I have outlined certainly *validates* the inference from (8a) to (10c). It is just that it requires us to infer the latter from the former *via* an intermediate step, in which (8a) is first transformed into

(10a)   Superman is someone whom Lois believes to be an extraterrestrial

and only then is $\exists$I used.

The rule used to get from (8a) to (10a) in one step is called "exportation" by Quine, and is somewhat problematic in itself, as Quine's own change of mind about it testifies (compare Quine 1955, 106, with Quine 1979, 272). The difficulty is supposed to be that if a term is exported from (raised out of) the syntactic scope of a psychological verb, it acquires an existential force that it previously lacked. However, purported examples of this phenomenon are a mixed bag. Here are three pairs exemplifying exportation, about which I shall say different things.

(14a)   Keith believes Jacob Horn lived in Pennsylvania.

(14b)   Jacob Horn is someone Keith believes lived in Pennsylvania.

(15a)   Keith is certain Sherlock Holmes could solve the case.

(15b)   Sherlock Holmes is someone Keith is certain could solve the case.

(16a)   Keith suspects the shortest spy is a spy.

(16b)   The shortest spy is someone Keith suspects is a spy.

The background to the three pairs is this: The purported diaries of one Jacob Horn, a Colonial American, were a historical hoax: there was no such person (see Donnellan 1974). For the example, suppose Keith reads the diaries, takes them at face value, and sincerely asserts 'Jacob Horn lived in Pennsylvania'. Regarding (15a), the situation is normal. Keith has read the stories and knows they are fictions. Nevertheless, (15a) could well be a natural way of reporting one of his certainties. And for (16a), suppose that Keith believes there are spies but only finitely many, and suspects that no two have the same height. Then logic alone will lead him to the suspicion reported by (16a) (Sleigh 1968, 397n).

The first pair presents a counterexample to exportation only if (14a) is true and (14b) is not true. I grant that (14b) is not true. But is (14a) true? Many philosophers in both the Fregean and Russellian camps would deny that (14a) is true: because there is no Jacob Horn, there are no propositions that Jacob Horn is thus-and-so to which a thinker could stand in the belief relation; see, for example, Evans 1982, 44–6, Marcus 1993, 246–8; and Braun 1993, 456–65). The logophoric analysis lends plausibility to this view by making it plain that the difference between (14b) and (14a) is less than meets the eye: it is *not* as if the appearance of 'Jacob Horn' within the scope of the 'believes' in the pseudo-form of (14a) could somehow prevent its failure to refer from amplifying into a failure of the ascription to be true. (14a)'s logical form is

(17a) $[\langle$ Jacob Horn lived in Pennsylvania $\rangle]_\sigma$: the ρ: so-labeled (Keith$_x$, ρ) & T (he$_x$, σ, ρ); Bel(he$_x$, ρ).

and (14b)'s,

(17b) Jacob Horn$_y$: $[y\langle$ lived in Pennsylvania $\rangle]_\sigma$: some ρ: so-labeled (Keith$_x$, ρ) & T (he$_x$, σ, ρ); Bel(he$_x$, ρ).

The reason why (17b) is not true is that there is no value for 'Jacob Horn' that when assigned to 'y' produces an STP of y's having lived in Pennsylvania; so the STP-term in (17b) fails to refer (hence there is no such thing as a way of thinking of its reference). But in (17a) the STP-term fails to refer just as clearly. If the reason why (17b) is not true is equally operative in the case of (17a), the pair {(14a), (14b)} is not a counterexample to exportation.

The pair {(15a), (15b)} might be assimilated to the previous case. But there is also another possibility. We can draw a distinction between existence and nonexistence for fictional characters that matches the distinction for ordinary objects. Sherlock Holmes is an existent fictional character, since Conan Doyle actually created him. And if neither Conan Doyle nor anybody else had thought up Sherlock Holmes stories (if anyone else could have) then Sherlock Holmes would not have been an existent fictional character (see further Fine 1984). In this sense, as things actually are, we can refer to Sherlock Holmes, the fictional character. And it is in that sense that (15a) is naturally understood as true or potentially so. But of course, someone seeking a counterexample just to exportation cannot change horses in midstream: if 'Sherlock Holmes' is taken to refer to the fictional character in (15a), the same reference must be maintained in (15b). And then it seems that (15b) is true, not false, particularly as, if the *same* reference is to be maintained, 'Sherlock Holmes is someone...' is not an appropriate phrasing: 'Sherlock Holmes is a character...' would be more accurate. My view, then, is that those who hold {(15a), (15b)} to constitute a counterexample to exportation are interpreting 'Sherlock Holmes' as denoting an actual fictional

character in (15a) and as an empty name, purportedly of a real individual, in (15b). This switch deprives the alleged counterexample of any force.[19]

The pair {(16a), (16b)} is a different matter. The issue is not whether (16a) can be true while (16b) is false (either because there is no shortest spy, or because, even though there is, Keith has no suspicions about *that* person). The pair is certainly a counterexample to *something*. The question is whether it is the same inferential step instantiated in the two previous pairs. To pursue this we must look more closely at descriptive STPs.

Suppose that it is B. J. Ortcutt who is the shortest spy, and that B. J. Ortcutt is American. Then both of these STPs actually obtain:

(18a)   [The shortest spy is an American].
(18b)   [Ortcutt is a spy, is shorter than any other spy, and is American].

But these situation-types should not be identified, since there are possible worlds where (18a) obtains while (18b) does not. It is natural to say that (18a) obtains at the actual world *in virtue of* (18b)'s obtaining there, and obtains at certain other worlds in virtue of the obtaining of other STPs there. (18b) could be said to *underlie* (18a) at the actual world, and to be *singular* relative to (18a), while (18a) could be said to be *general* relative to (18b).[20] (It is this feature of generality that makes the quantifier treatment of 'the' appealing, but a defender of the singular term treatment could hardly quarrel with our observations about (18a)'s relationship to (18b).)

We can now combine these remarks with the logical forms of (16a) and (16b) to get a clear account of what is going wrong in the move from the former to the latter. For (16a) we have

(19a) $[\langle$the shortest spy is a spy $\rangle]_\sigma$: the ρ: so-labeled (Keith$_x$, ρ) & T (he$_x$, σ, ρ); Susp (he$_x$, ρ)

while for (16b) we have

(19b)   the shortest spy$_y$: $[y\langle$ is a spy $\rangle]_\sigma$: some ρ: so-labeled (Keith$_x$, ρ); & T (he$_x$, σ, ρ); Susp (he$_x$, ρ).

Inspection of (19a) and (19b) reveals that raising the definite description replaces the general STP-term '[the shortest spy is a spy]' with the singular '[y is a spy]', in which the variable 'y' is assigned whoever happens to be the shortest spy, if there is such a person, and receives no assignment otherwise. We are therefore in a position to formulate a version of exportation to which {(16a), (16b)} is not a counterexample, not by adding a theoretically unmotivated clause excluding its application to definite descriptions in attitude contexts by *fiat*, but rather by adding a clause excluding transformations that change the reference of the STP in question. Exportation of names will not do this, since names contribute their referents to the STPs for which the sentences they occur in stand.

In sum, then, we have shown why sentences such as

(1e)   There is someone who Lois doubts can help her

are intelligible, despite reason to think that attitude ascriptions cannot be quantified into. According to our analysis, (1d) does not quantify into a substitution-resistant position, the position of 'Clark Kent' in

(1a)   Lois Lane doubts that Clark Kent can help her

interpreted in the substitution-resistant way. We must rather interpret (1a) so that, or infer from it something in which, 'Clark Kent' is in substitutable position; only then can we quantify. Of course, this much is essentially Quine's position in Quine 1955. However, we have also provided a semantic account of the contrast between positions where substitution fails and positions where it does not that uses only binary propositional attitude relations, that proceeds at the level of thought (cf. note 12), and that accommodates the range of interpretations that pronouns in attitude ascriptions can bear. In addition, we have defended the thesis that exportation is necessarily truth-preserving if the noun-phrase-raising by which it is executed does not create an STP-term with a different reference from the one in the premise.

Objectual Attitudes

There is a family of attitude verbs to which the foregoing analysis may seem to have no direct application. And if these cases are intuitively of the same kind as the ones we have been considering, then that would suggest that our theory does not get to the heart of the matter. A *propositional* attitude verb is so called because it expresses a (psychological) attitude to propositions. But there is also a category of verb that we might call *objectual* attitude verbs, because they express (psychological) attitudes to *objects*. Examples include 'worships' (Kaplan 1986, 267, citing Church and Montague), 'admires', and 'is afraid of', as in (20a) and (20b):

(20a)   Lois Lane admires Superman
(20b)   Lex Luthor is afraid of Superman.

There is certainly force to the intuition that substituting 'Clark Kent' for 'Superman' in either of these sentences turns a truth into a falsehood. Hence the position following the verb resists substitution, and a Fregean should expect it to be unquantifiable. That is,

(20c)   Lois Lane admires someone
(20d)   Lex Luthor is afraid of someone

ought to seem semantically anomalous. But both are evidently acceptable; indeed, they are true. Following our previous treatment, we would explain this by saying that (20c) and (20d) are not the results of quantifying (20a) and (20b), but rather the results of applying exportation to (20a) and (20b) and then quantifying. Exportation yields (20e) and (20f) respectively,

(20e)   Superman is someone Lois Lane admires
(20f)   Superman is someone Lex Luthor is afraid of

from which (20c) and (20d) are immediate. Kaplan has pointed out that many accounts of propositional attitude ascriptions that use scope distinctions to account for substitutable versus unsubstitutable occurrences of a term have trouble with such cases, because "without an inner *sentential* context, Russell's distinctions of scope disappear, as do Quine's" (1986, 266). But our apparatus of so-labeled ways of thinking of situation-types is more elaborate, and the absence of an inner sentential context may not prevent us from distinguishing different possible extents for 'so'.

A tempting move for someone who wishes to minimize reengineering in the theory thus far developed is to argue that the class of objectual attitude verbs divides exhaustively into two subclasses, the first containing those objectual attitude verbs that do permit substitution and the second those that are analyzable as disguised *propositional* attitudes. If this view is right, there is no further problem for our theory to face. Indeed, there is an argument that, barring an analysis in terms of propositional attitudes, an objectual attitude verb *cannot* disallow substitution. The argument is that substitutivity must hold without exception for co-referential terms standing for an entity that fills one of the places of the attitude relation. For example, it would be impossible to change truth value by interchanging expressions for the *same proposition* in the scope of a propositional attitude verb: it is only because of disagreement about the identity of propositions, and so about which pairs of *that*-clauses *do* contribute the same proposition, that there is scope for disagreement between Russellians and Fregeans about the soundness of substitutivity for ascriptions of propositional attitudes. But in the case of *objectual* attitude ascriptions that are not propositional attitude ascriptions in disguise, there is no disagreement about the identities of the relevant objects; for instance, it is simply built into the example that Superman is Clark Kent. Hence we must be able to interchange these names in (20a) and (20b), if 'is afraid of' and 'worships' are irreducibly objectual.

An example of an objectual attitude verb that does support substitutivity is 'sees', as for example in Keith's judgment

(21a) I have never seen Degas's *A Cotton Office in New Orleans*.

Suppose it is pointed out to Keith that *A Cotton Office in New Orleans* was the painting everyone was crowded around at a certain exhibition and that he managed to study it briefly (without realizing that it was *A Cotton Office in New Orleans*). Keith certainly saw *that painting*, and that painting was *A Cotton Office in New Orleans*. So Keith has seen Degas's *A Cotton Office in New Orleans*, and he must withdraw (21a). But if Keith also maintains

(21b) I have never believed (until now) that *A Cotton Office in New Orleans* has been exhibited here

then even though he has believed for some time that *that* painting (invoking a perceptual or mem-

ory demonstrative) has been exhibited here, and has just accepted that that painting is *A Cotton Office in New Orleans*, he is under no obligation at all to withdraw (21b) (unless he is in the grip of a Russellian semantics). Thus the difference between seeing and believing.[21]

A likely case of an objectual attitude verb that does admit of a propositional attitude analysis is 'seeks', as in Church's example (1956, 8)

(22a) Schliemann seeks the site of Troy,

which might be rendered, à la Quine (Quine 1955, 102), as

(22b) Schliemann strives that Schliemann finds the site of Troy,

or better,

(22c) Schliemann strives to make it true that he himself finds the site of Troy.[22]

It would be tidy if all objectual attitude verbs could be classified with 'sees' or 'seeks', but I am confident that 'admires' and 'is afraid of' belongs with neither. I have no intuition that substitution fails in the position of the second argument of 'sees', but my intuition that it fails for 'admires' and 'is afraid of' is as strong as my corresponding intuition for propositional attitude verbs.[23] The abstract argument given above about the identities of propositions and objects might be appealed to in order to justify a strategy of explaining away such intuitions of substitution failure in the objectual but not the propositional cases, but we would still owe an explanation of why there are objectual cases where substitution *seems* to fail. And we will see anyway that the abstract argument can be avoided, for it overlooks a way in which substitution failure in objectual attitude ascriptions would be consistent with standard identity conditions for the objects.

As far as assimilating 'admires' and 'is afraid of' to 'seeks' is concerned, explanation is one thing, analysis another. It is quite plausible that we can *explain* the presence of substitution failure in objectual attitude reports of the form $B\phi$'s x in terms of the propositional attitudes of B involving specific ways of thinking of x. It is because of all Lex Luthor's beliefs about Superman, so labeled, that Luthor fears him, and because of all she knows about Superman, so labeled, that Lois admires him. By contrast, there is no difference between seeing Superman and seeing Clark Kent precisely because, the "belief theory of perception" aside, whether or not one sees a thing is not explained by one's beliefs (etc.) towards it.

But to say this is to stop well short of the thesis that 'admires' and 'is afraid of' can be *analyzed* in the same way as 'seeks'. For there may be no single explanatory propositional attitude that is present in *every* case of Superman-admiration, and the explanatory attitudes in a single individual may change with time. In particular, (20a) does not mean 'Lois believes that Superman is admirable', since believing that someone is admirable is one thing, admiring them another ("the devils also believe, and tremble"). So while there is a handful of objectual attitude verbs where analysis as propositional attitudes is possible, this is not the general situation. In the special case, the objectual attitude verb expresses purposeful activity designed to bring about a certain state of affairs, and there is an accomplishment verb analytically related to the objectual attitude verb that can be used to formulate the goal state in a *that*-clause: *seeks/finds*, *looks for/locates*, *hunts/captures* (or *kills*), *wants/gets*, and so on. The activity verb can therefore be replaced by a locution expressing the notion of trying to achieve the goal of realizing the state of affairs that such-and-such. However, verbs like 'admires' and 'is afraid of' do not stand for activities aimed at accomplishing something expressible in a *that*-clause, so this kind of analysis is not available for them.[24]

If the abstract argument covered all the options, then we would be left in the unfortunate position of having to find something for 'Superman' to denote in (20a) and (20b) other than Clark Kent – that is, Superman. A traditional Fregean proposal would be that 'Superman' refers to an individual concept in (20a) and (20b), but this is the sort of view to which Davidsonian incredulity is an entirely appropriate response: it is not a concept that Luthor is afraid of, it is the man himself.[25] However, there is a way of being true to this point and at the same time making it explicit, in ordinary English, that substitution is ruled out. By a quite extraordinary coincidence, the natural locution for achieving this effect is exactly the one on which my general explanation of substitution failure is built. That is, in place of (20a) and (20b), we may assert (23a) and (23b):

(23a) Lois Lane admires Superman, so labeled.

(23b) Lex Luthor is afraid of Superman, so labeled.

In (23a) and (23b), it is clear that 'Superman' refers to Superman, just as it is clear that 'Giorgione' refers to Giorgione in (3a). But the logophoric reference makes the position of 'Superman' substitution resistant. (Another way of getting this effect is to use '*qua*', as in 'Lois Lane admires Superman, *qua* Superman'. The analysis of (23a) and (23b) to follow is a possible explication of this rather mysterious, though undeniably natural, locution.)

The main question about (23a) and (23b) is whether they mean anything (though I used 'so labeled' in the same way without comment three paragraphs back and I suspect the reader did not balk). If it is the man himself whom Luthor fears, what exactly is the 'so labeled' doing in (23b)? We want to answer this question by providing logical forms for (23a) and (23b) that use the same apparatus as our forms for propositional ascriptions, and that entail exported and existentially quantified objectual attitude ascriptions in essentially the same way.

There is, to be sure, a difference between the cases. It is propositions, not situation-types, that are believed, but it is people and things, not ways of thinking of them, that are feared. So the mode of presentation must enter into the objectual attitude ascription in a slightly different way from the way it figures in propositional attitude ascriptions, since in the objectual case, the mode of presentation is not the object of the attitude. One way of achieving this is to make 'admires' in (23a) and 'is afraid of' in (23b) *three*-place rather than two-place (which is not unnatural for (23a) and (23b) anyway – if someone insists that this means the attitudes are not "purely" objectual, so be it). These forms for (23a) and (23b) can then provide (20a) and (20b) with interpretations in which the name resists substitution.

For (23a), I propose 'Superman is such that Lois admires him, so labeled', that is,

(23c) $\langle \text{Superman} \rangle_y$: (the μ: so-labeled (Lois$_x$, μ) & T (she$_x$, him$_y$, μ); Admires (she$_x$, him$_y$, μ)).

The subformula 'Admires (she$_x$, him$_y$, μ)' may be read as 'she admires him under μ', where μ is a way of thinking characterized in (23c) as being of Superman and as being so labeled by Lois. Similarly, for (23b), we have

(23d) $\langle \text{Superman} \rangle_y$: (the μ: so-labeled (Lex_x, μ) & T $(\text{he}_x, \text{him}_y, \mu)$; Is afraid of $(\text{he}_x, \text{him}_y, \mu))$

which says that Lex is afraid of Superman under his (Lex's) so-labeled way of thinking of him (Superman). We then give a logical form for (20e) along the same lines as that of (10b), namely,

(23e) Superman$_y$: (some μ : T $(\text{Lois}_x, \text{him}_y, \mu)$); Admires $(\text{she}_x, \text{him}_y, \mu))$

obtained from (23d) by exportation. Purported counterexamples to exportation on objectual attitude ascriptions can be dealt with in the same way as in (14a)–(16b). Existentially quantify-ing (23e) is unproblematic, since the 'Superman' is not in a substitution-resistant position (not within the extent of 'so'), and hence we can infer

(23f) Some y: (some μ: T $(\text{Lois}_x, \text{him}_y, \mu)$; Admires $(\text{she}_x, \text{him}_y, \mu))$.

These examples make it clear that the account of quantifying in that we have given for propositional attitude ascriptions generalizes in a natural way to objectual attitude ascriptions.[26] Recalling Kaplan's previously quoted remark about the limitations of Russell's "scope" approach, I conclude that to the extent to which the present theory instantiates such an approach, it successfully circumvents the limitations.[27]

Notes

1 For example, "Eve = the mother of Cain, Eve's elder son was Cain, ∴ The mother of Cain's elder son was Cain." This example is one of many to be found in Fine 1989 (see 221), a paper that has heavily influenced my discussion of QT in this section.

2 Someone who says, "Shall we surrender? In the immortal words of Churchill, 'We shall never sur-render!'" both quotes Churchill's words and com-mits to a course of action.

3 The qualifier 'standard' is needed here. Schweizer 1993 presents a semantics for first-order modality that employs "quasi-substitutional" quantification into quotes. But if we regard the substitutional notation as simply shorthand for metalinguistic quantification over expressions, or for infinitary conjunction and disjunction (see Field 1989, 99), then there is no real quantification into quotes in (2d). And I am in agreement with van Inwagen 1981 and Fine 1989, 247, that there is no special "sub-stitutional" sense of the quantifiers. I would argue that substitutional semantics merely *stipulatively associates* a metalinguistic truth condition with the likes of (2d), a truth condition that is not one speak-ers can arrive at by compositional interpretation of the quantified sentences using actual meanings of their constituents (see further note 5).

4 The label is by analogy with 'anaphor', but in logo-phoric dependency the referentially dependent expression refers to the anchoring expression itself instead of the semantic value of the anchoring expression. I thank Jon Oberlander for suggesting this use of the word.

5 (3d) and (3e) are clearly true if their quantifiers are "interpreted substitutionally." The fact that we balk at them is reason to infer that there is no such thing as a special "substitutional" sense of quantifier expres-sions. The objection that substitutional semantics just stipulatively associates a truth condition with a sentence is especially borne out by these cases.

6 Though we can apply "logophor elimination" to (3a) to obtain (i) "Giorgione is called 'Giorgione' because of his size," we cannot similarly eliminate the logophor in (3d) to get the perfectly intelligible (ii) "$(\exists x)$ (x is called 'x' because of x's size)"; a logophor can be eliminated only when it is function-ing correctly. As Fine would emphasize, there are *possible* languages in which (3d) does mean (ii) and is intelligible, and this presents a formidable obstacle to proving any generalized version of QT (Fine 1989, 268). But solutions to puzzles about substitu-tion and quantification are correct only if they iden-tify mechanisms that are at work in our language as it actually is.

7 '$(\exists x)$ (Galileo believed something with the same content as the following: x moves)' appears to require Galileo to have had a belief with the content 'x moves'; the prefix '$(\exists x)$' seems redundant, as in (2d). But see note 11.

8 After Davidson, who wrote, "If we could recover our pre-Fregean semantic innocence...it would seem to us plainly incredible that...words [in atti-tude contexts] mean anything different, or refer to anything else, than is their wont when they come in other environments" (1969, 172).

9 For example, contrast the binary atomic pseudo-form of 'Brutus stabbed Caesar' and the David-sonian logical form. See further Parsons 1990, 22; my 'pseudo' and 'logical' correspond to Parsons' 'atomic' and 'subatomic'.

10 Strictly, the maneuver does not work, for t_2 in (7c) is not substitutable: the 'her' that remains in the intensional term t_2 in (7c) and (7d) cannot be replaced by 'Lois', for reasons illustrated by the familiar kind of case in which Lois loses her memory and does not realize that she is Lois. Yet in (7c) and (7d) the lambda-term '$\lambda z(z$ can help her)' denotes the same attribute as '$\lambda z(z$ can help Lois)'. From the Fregean point of view, Quine has chosen the wrong entities as intensions; it should be a term for a way of thinking of an attribute, not one for an attribute, in second position in 'doubts[3]' atomic formulae.

11 To deal with the problem mentioned in note 7, the Davidsonian can pursue a similar strategy. See Hornsby 1977, 179, and LePore and Loewer 1990, 107–8.

12 Some sophisticated "linguistic" theories in the spirit of Quine's official account have recently been developed; see Haas 1990, Larson and Ludlow 1993, and Seymour 1992. The hardest kind of case for a linguistic account to cope with is one in which there are, intuitively, two or more conceptions or thoughts concerning the same element of reality, but only one linguistic item. Kripke's 'Paderewski' case is the prime example (Kripke 1979). It is not discussed by Haas or Seymour, but Larson and Ludlow suggest "that there actually are two names here, *Paderewski$_1$* and *Paderewski$_2$*" (319). This is implausible; there is only one common currency name, and while we could say that there are two names in Peter's idiolect, it seems more likely that he uses just one, mistakenly thinking there are two, just as he met only one person, mistakenly thinking there are two (Kaplan 1990, 108–9; Richard 1990, 181–2); certainly, Peter did not introduce two names into his idiolect via some private and explicit dubbing, but rather, takes himself to have picked up two names in the usual sort of way. What seems right is that in Peter's mind there are two distinct groupings of information, or two dossiers, his uses of 'Paderewski' sometimes linked to one and sometimes to the other; see Forbes 1990, sec. 4 for an account of Kripke's puzzle that develops this idea at the level of thought instead of at the level of language.

13 Of course, we can also make attitude ascriptions using 'so' explicitly, as in 'Superman can help her – at least, Lois hopes so'.

14 The situations that propositions present must be types – that is, abstract rather than concrete – if false propositions are to present anything. However, unlike the "abstract situation types" of Barwise and Perry 1983 (53), my situation-types are completely specific with respect to all parameters except modality. So distinct concrete situations of the same type must perforce obtain at different worlds.

15 In (9e) we use standard variables to represent the coindexing of pronouns with an antecedent individual constant. In evaluating such a formula, we assign the pronouns the same denotation as the coindexed individual constant that governs them. I will not take the space to make this formally precise here.

16 Frege held that propositions with such constituents are incommunicable (1967, 25–26). In Forbes 1994, I argue that this is based on a misconception about communication.

17 See Peacocke 1983, chaps. 5–6, for this type-token distinction and generally illuminating discussion of first-person modes of presentation. On Peacocke's account, you and I have the same type of way of thinking of ourselves, but each of us employs specific tokens of that type, the tokens being individuated in part by the identities of the persons whom they present (the token rolls up character and content into a single package, if you like).

18 In Forbes 1990 I argue that with a proper name 'NN' we can associate a type of way of thinking that has the cognitive significance 'the subject of this dossier', where the demonstrative refers to a dossier of information labeled 'NN'. Different thinkers who employ 'NN' have numerically different dossiers but think of NN in the same type of way.

19 A similar line might be taken about {(14a), (14b)}. There is presumably a spectrum of cases, with familiar fictions and myths at one end, and at the other, an example where someone simply makes up a name-like word on the spur of the moment. Existential beliefs are a touchstone. 'Keith believes Sherlock Holmes really exists' makes perfect sense, as we would expect if the name denotes a fictional character. If we think 'Keith believes Jacob Horn really existed' is equally acceptable, without construing it metalinguistically, I think we have to say that 'Jacob Horn' also denotes a fictional character or something analogous.

20 See Forbes 1989, chap. 5, for a constructive account of STPs that embodies this account of descriptive STPs.

21 See also Salmon's discussion of seeing in Salmon 1986 (121–25), where it is argued that we can only understand seeing reports as substitution-resistant if we abandon the idea that ordinary perception is of external objects. Other psychological verbs that are like 'sees' include, I think, the objectual 'believes', but not the objectual 'suspects'. However, Mark Crimmins has suggested to me that to the extent that we make sense of 'Lois admires Superman but not Clark', we can also make sense of 'Lois saw Superman yesterday, but not Clark'. Those who agree with this can easily adapt the treatment of admiration I offer in (23c). And *contra* Salmon, perception of external objects need not be abandoned, since the appearances to which the seeings would be relativized could be constituted by perceived objective features of the scene (the red cape, the blue suit, and so on).

22 Contra Kaplan 1986, 267 (see also Loar 1972, 59), I do not think we have to add anything to (22c) about Schliemann recognizing the site of Troy as such, since 'the site of Troy' would be within the extent of the 'so' in a logical form for (22c).

23 And is based on similar considerations: Luthor would deny being afraid of Clark Kent as vehemently as he would deny being afraid that Clark Kent will confront him, and attributing fear of Clark Kent to Luthor would be as useless in explaining his Superman-avoidance behavior as attributing to him fear that Clark Kent is in the vicinity.

24 There is also a group of "trivial" cases where an objectual attitude is derived from a propositional one by nominalization – for example, 'Lois doubts that Luthor is trustworthy' becomes 'Lois doubts the trustworthiness of Luthor'. Obviously, analysis of the objectual as propositional is available here. I thank Kathrin Koslicki for discussion of this issue.

25 Echoing Church, a traditional Fregean could point out that it is no part of her theory that (20b) means the same as 'Lex Luthor is afraid of the concept of Superman', and that "the relation holding between [Luthor] and the concept of [Superman] is not quite that of [being afraid of], or at least it is misleading to call it that – in view of the way the verb [*to be afraid of*] is commonly used in English" (Church 1956, 8 n. 20). The idea is that one fears a person x in virtue of *fearing** a way of thinking of x. But it seems unlikely that changing the primitive notion could lead to a plausible logical form for fear attributions. The posited attitude also seems redundant: surely one's current perceptual beliefs about x can prompt fear of x directly, without a detour through fearing*. Indeed, I doubt that we can *explain* what fearing* a way of thinking of x is except in terms of fearing x. The same objection arises to Montague's approach to objectual attitudes; see Montague 1974, 267.

26 The strategy of discerning a third place is not limited to attitude verbs, but applies to any objectual attitude relation that is underpinned by propositional attitudes involving specific ways of thinking of a thing. Thus "Superman is Lois's hero" is interpretable as "Superman, so labeled, is Lois's hero," in which there is a three-place relation x *is a hero of y under mode of presentation m*. I take it to be just an accident of English that there is no verb *heroize* (like *idolize*). The strategy is the objectual attitude counterpart of a proposal about propositional attitudes made by Schiffer (1987) on behalf of the Russellian (the 'Fido'-Fido theorist, in Schifferese), as a way for the latter to save intuitions about failure of substitutivity. Schiffer then gives a very good reason why the Russellian should resist such blandishments (460–1). But in a later paper, Schiffer objects to discerning a third place on grounds that could include the Fregean in his criticism: the third place is never realized in ordinary language, and when it is purportedly realized in "technical jargon," the result is more suggestive of "a two-place relation with an adverbial qualifier" (1992, 518–19). However, it seems to me that the likes of (23a) and their '*qua*' and 'as such' variants are in ordinary language, not technical jargon (see also Ludlow 1995). Moreover, it is not crucial to my account that it accommodate the 'so labeled' by introducing an extra place. This issue is reminiscent of the question whether a possibilist has to introduce an extra place into predicates to accommodate relativity to worlds (Forbes 1989, 40–41). Nothing fundamental turns on whether we have 'Admires(she_x, him_y, μ)' or 'under μ_y: admires(she_x, him_y)'.

27 I thank David Boonin-Vail, Bruce Brower, Mark Crimmins, Martin Davies, Richard Grandy, Kathrin Koslicki, Genoveva Marti, Norton Nelkin, Mark Richard, Nathan Salmon, Paul Schweizer, Gabriel Segal, Jonathan Sutton, Timothy Williamson, and anonymous referees, for discussion and comments that helped in writing this paper. It is dedicated to the memory of Norton Nelkin.

References

Barwise, Jon, and John Perry. 1983. *Situations and Attitudes*. Cambridge: MIT Press.

Braun, David. 1993. "Empty Names." *Noûs* 27:449–69.

Carnap, Rudolf. 1947. *Meaning and Necessity*. Chicago: University of Chicago Press.

Church, Alonzo. 1956. *Introduction to Mathematical Logic*, vol. 1. Princeton: Princeton University Press.

Davidson, Donald. "On Saying That." 1969. In *Words and Objections: Essays on the Work of W. V. Quine*, ed. Donald Davidson and Jaakko Hintikka, 158–74. Dordrecht: Reidel.

Donnellan, Keith. 1974. "Speaking of Nothing." *Philosophical Review* 83:3–30.

Evans, Gareth. 1982. *The Varieties of Reference*. Oxford: Oxford University Press.

Field, Hartry. 1989. "Is Mathematical Knowledge Just Logical Knowledge?" In *Realism, Mathematics and Modality*, ed. Hartry Field, 79–124. London: Basil Blackwell.

Fine, Kit. 1984. "Critical Review of Terence Parsons' *Non-Existent Objects*." *Philosophical Studies* 45:95–142.

——. 1989. "The Problem of *De Re* Modality." In *Themes from Kaplan*, ed. Joseph Almog, John Perry, and Howard Wettstein, 197–272. Oxford: Oxford University Press.

Forbes, Graeme. 1989. *Languages of Possibility*. Aristotelian Society Monographs, vol. 9, ed. Martin Davies. Oxford: Basil Blackwell.

Forbes, Graeme. 1990. "The Indispensability of *Sinn*." *Philosophical Review* 99:535–63.

——. 1993. "Reply to Marks." *Philosophical Studies* 69:281–95.

——. 1994. "Belief Reports and Speech Reports." In *Direct Reference*, ed. W. Künne, A. Newen, and M. Anduschus. CSLI Lecture Notes Series.

Frege, Gottlob. 1967. "The Thought: A Logical Enquiry." In *Philosophical Logic*, ed. Peter Strawson, 17–38. Oxford: Oxford University Press.

——. 1970. "On Sense and Reference." In *Translations from the Philosophical Writings of Gottlob Frege*, 2d ed., ed. Peter Geach and Max Black. Oxford: Basil Blackwell.

Haas, Andrew R. 1990. "Sentential Semantics for Propositional Attitudes." *Computational Linguistics* 16:203–33.

Hornsby, Jennifer. 1977. "Saying Of." *Analysis* 37:177–85.

Kaplan, David. 1986. "Opacity." In *The Philosophy of W. V. Quine*, ed. Lewis Edward Hahn and Paul Arthur Schilpp, 229–89. LaSalle: Open Court.

——. 1990. "Words." *Proceedings of the Aristotelian Society*, supp. vol. 64:93–117.

Kripke, Saul. 1979. "A Puzzle About Belief." In *Meaning and Use*, ed. Avishai Margalit, 239–83. Dordrecht: Reidel.

Larson, Richard K., and Peter Ludlow. 1993. "Interpreted Logical Forms." *Synthese* 95:305–55.

LePore, Ernest, and Barry Loewer. 1990. "A Study in Comparative Semantics." In *Propositional Attitudes*, ed. C. Anthony Anderson and Joseph Owens, 91–111. Stanford: CSLI.

Loar, Brian. 1972. "Reference and Propositional Attitudes." *Philosophical Review* 81:43–62.

Ludlow, Peter. 1995. "Logical Form and the Hidden Indexical Theory: A Reply to Schiffer." *Journal of Philosophy* 92:102–7.

Marcus, Ruth Barcan. 1993. "Some Revisionary Proposals about Belief and Believing." In *Modalities*, ed. Ruth Barcan Marcus, 233–55. Oxford: Oxford University Press.

Montague, Richard. 1974. "The Proper Treatment of Quantification in Ordinary English." In *Formal Philosophy: Selected Papers of Richard Montague*, ed. Richmond Thomason, 245–70. New Haven: Yale University Press.

Morton, Adam. 1975. "Complex Individuals and Multigrade Relations." *Noûs* 9:309–18.

Neale, Stephen. 1990. *Descriptions*. Cambridge: MIT Press.

Parsons, Terence. 1990. *Events in the Semantics of English*. Cambridge: MIT Press.

Peacocke, Christopher. 1983. *Sense and Content*. Oxford: Oxford University Press.

Quine, W. V. 1955. "Quantifiers and Propositional Attitudes." In *Reference and Modality*, ed. L. Linsky. 101–11. Oxford: Oxford University Press.

——. 1961. "Reference and Modality." In *Reference and Modality*, ed. L. Linsky. 17–34. Oxford: Oxford University Press.

——. 1979. "Intensions Revisited." In *Contemporary Perspectives in the Philosophy of Language*, ed. P. A. French, T. E. Uehling, and H. K. Wettstein, 268–74. Minneapolis: University of Minnesota Press.

——. 1986. "Reply to David Kaplan." In *The Philosophy of W. V. Quine*, ed. Lewis Edward Hahn and Paul Arthur Schilpp, 290–4. LaSalle: Open Court.

Richard, Mark. 1986. "Quotation, Grammar and Opacity." *Linguistics and Philosophy* 9:383–403.

——. 1990. *Propositional Attitudes*. Cambridge: Cambridge University Press.

——. 1993. "Articulated Terms." *Philosophical Perspectives* 7: 207–30.

Salmon, Nathan. 1986. *Frege's Puzzle*. Cambridge: MIT Press.

——. 1995. "Relational Belief." In *On Quine: Proceedings of the University of San Marino International Center for Semiotic and Cognitive Studies 1990 Conference on the Philosophy of W. V. Quine*, ed. Paolo Leonardi and Marco Santambrogio. Cambridge: Cambridge University Press.

Schiffer, Stephen. 1987. "The "Fido"-Fido Theory of Belief." In *Philosophical Perspectives*, vol. 1, ed. James Tomberlin, 455–80. Atascadero: Ridgeview Publishing Company.

——. 1992. "Belief Ascription." *Journal of Philosophy* 89: 499–521.

Schweizer, Paul. 1993. "Quantified Quinean S5." *Journal of Philosophical Logic* 22:589–605.

Seymour, Michel. 1992. "A Sentential Theory of Propositional Attitudes." *Journal of Philosophy* 89:181–201.

Sleigh, R. C. 1968. "On a Proposed System of Epistemic Logic." *Noûs* 2:391–8.

Tarksi, Alfred. 1969. "The Concept of Truth in Formalized Languages." In *Logic, Semantics, Metamathematics*. Oxford: Oxford University Press.

Van Inwagen, Peter. 1981. "Why I Don't Understand Substitutional Quantification." *Philosophical Studies* 39:281–5.

Washington, Corey. 1992. "The Identity Theory of Quotation." *Journal of Philosophy* 89:582–605.

27

The Intensionality of Ontological Commitment

Michael Jubien

The attempt to provide a criterion of ontological commitment is made frequently in the writings of W. V. Quine. His numerous inequivalent formulations have spawned much discussion as to which, if any, provides a satisfactory treatment of the notion. Although Quine's work provides the stimulus for the present discussion, it will not be considered in detail in what follows. The concern here is more general: I try to show that any criterion of commitment which can be interpreted as defining a two-place relation between theories and other things is either inadequate or intensional.

The idea of intensionality has been raised in this connection before. In 1954 Richard L. Cartwright [1] advanced what he considered good reasons to believe that *Quine's* criterion is either inadequate or intensional (in the sense of making unavoidable use of notions from the theory of meaning). This would be a very damaging outcome in view of Quine's well-known antipathy for the theory of meaning and his explicit claims that his criterion is in fact extensional (cf. [2], 130–1 and [4], 15). I will begin by acquainting the reader with Cartwright's position and with a related position put forward by Israel Scheffler and Noam Chomsky.

Cartwright focuses his attention on versions of the criterion which employ the locutions "has to," "must," and so forth. An example of such a version is:

Michael Jubien, The Intensionality of Ontological Commitment. *Noûs*, 51, 4 (1972): 378–87.

The ontology to which an (interpreted) theory is committed comprises all and only the objects over which the bound variables of the theory have to be construed as ranging in order that the statements affirmed in the theory be true. (Quine [4], 11.)

Such versions are to be contrasted with those which seem simply to identify the ontology with the actual range of variables (e.g., Quine [3], 75). An examination of the various formulations will reveal that the "must" versions are able to withstand objections (based on inflating the range) to which the others succumb. Thus the restriction of focus seems a fair one.

Cartwright feels that the use of these key words "strongly suggests that advantage is being taken of notions dealt with in the theory of meaning" ([1], 319). The specific suspicion is that use is being made of the notion of necessity. Cartwright proceeds to construct and examine several candidates for the criterion which do not make any appeal to the theory of meaning. These are found to be objectionable on straightforward grounds. Then he turns to an openly intensional candidate and shows that it has none of the fatal shortcomings of the others. He remarks that this candidate "is presumably equivalent to those formulations [which he] quoted earlier from Quine" ([1], 322). Finally Cartwright concludes that while he has not demonstrated conclusively that an adequate formulation would involve intensional components, he has offered good reasons for accepting that conclusion.

A different approach is adopted by Scheffler and Chomsky [6]. I will briefly indicate their reasoning. First they assume that Quine's criterion is a statement universally quantified with respect to two variables, one of which ranges over theories and the other over the entities presumed.[1] They then argue that strong objections lead one to modify this conception by construing the second variable as ranging over *classes* of entities rather than over the entities themselves. Unfortunately, difficulties are found to arise for this interpretation as well. Without providing further argumentation, the authors venture that the

> source of all these difficulties seems to be the non-extensionality or referential opacity of the relational locution '*x* is assumed by *T*', with respect to '*x*', whether '*x*' is construed as an individual or a class variable ([6], 78).

In what follows I will try to show that while opacity does not account for the difficulties noticed by Scheffler and Chomsky, any adequate relational treatment of the commitment context (that is, any adequate definition of the locution '*T* assumes *a*') would in fact be intensional. This argument will be independent of any of Quine's actual attempts to state a criterion. For the sake of precision and clarity I will proceed under two limitations. First, I will allow only *interpreted theories* to occupy the first position of the defining relation. It is hard to see how an uninterpreted theory could have an ontological commitment; and to consider discourses less well-behaved than theories would introduce unpleasant complications. The second limitation requires a word of background. A review of Quine's various formulations of the criterion leads to the conclusion that there are three fundamentally different kinds of ontological commitment: to entire ontologies, to kinds of entities, and to specific entities. The latter two are suggested at once by theories which contain theorems of the forms '$\exists x P(x)$' and '$\exists x(x = a)$', respectively.[2] As for commitment to entire ontologies, it is tempting to think that this notion collapses into the other two sorts of commitment or into just one of them depending on the nature of the given theory. Quine has remarked in conversation that he would now prefer to distinguish sharply between the *ontology* and the *ontological commitment* of a theory (reserving the former term to apply to those things, if any, which actually exist and are treated by the theory).

This proposal, like the "collapse" approach, would apparently leave two types of commitment to consider. In this paper I will concentrate almost entirely upon the notion of commitment to particulars. It should be clear that neither of these limitations undermines the generality of the thesis I am defending. For any adequate extensional criterion would have to accommodate cases in which an interpreted theory is committed to specific entities.

Let us now ask whether the context is opaque. Here is a familiar[3] and facile argument. If a context is extensional, then quantification into that context is innocent provided it is legitimate by the standards of ordinary logic. Thus let us suppose that the present context is extensional and that a given theory *T* assumes *a*. It follows by existential generalization that

$$\exists x(T \text{ assumes } x).$$

But it is easy to think of cases in which this conclusion is *false* although it is true that *T* assumes *a*. For example, consider the theory of Pegasus, whose only nonlogical axiom is '$\exists x(x = \text{Pegasus})$'. According to our intuition, this theory assumes Pegasus (and only Pegasus). But since Pegasus does not actually exist, it is false that there exists an entity which this theory assumes. It is tempting to conclude immediately that the context is referentially opaque.

But this temptation should be resisted. Closer examination reveals that the problem lies not with opacity but with a careless treatment of the premise '*T* assumes *a*'. When we say that certain theories assume (or are committed to) entities like vampires or Pegasus, we do not use these nouns *designatively*. That is, we do not imply that the words designate anything at all. This must be kept in mind when we render such a remark formally as '*T* assumes *a*'. Since '*a*' may fail to designate, it is in general illegitimate to apply existential generalization and hence the offending inference of the above argument is blocked on ordinary logical grounds. It is clear that this analysis of the difficulty neither presumes nor reveals anything about referential opacity in the ordinary sense of that term. Similar reasoning could be advanced with respect to an obviously extensional context provided "empty" singular terms were permitted to occupy the position in question. (Of course, though the context itself might be extensional, there is a sense in which the broader

Michael Jubien

discourse would be *non*-extensional solely in virtue of admitting non-designating singular terms.) Thus we cannot yet conclude that the commitment relation is opaque.

Scheffler and Chomsky claim to use the term "referential opacity" in "a somewhat extended sense as compared with Quine's usage" ([6], 78n). But unfortunately they provide no clues as to what this broadened usage might be and whether they think the context is also opaque in the narrower, Quinean sense. So we can only proceed by first checking for the usual sort of opacity. The typical way of doing this is to ask whether it is in general legitimate to infer '*T* assumes *b*' from '*T* assumes *a*' and '*a* = *b*'. It is irrelevant whether *a* and *b* are taken as entities, classes of entities, or whatever.

There are two cases to consider. *Case 1*: '*a* = *b*' is a theorem of *T*. Since Quine's criterion is intended for extensional theories, any evidence drawn from *T* that supports '*T* assumes *a*' can be transformed into evidence supporting '*T* assumes *b*' by making substitutions of '*b*' for appropriate occurrences of '*a*' in the relevant sentences of *T*. Since the criterion is meant to assess the commitment of *theories*, pure and simple, it presumably requires reference only to the theory in order to be applied. Hence the inference to '*T* assumes *b*' seems fully warranted in this case. In the event that *T* is not an extensional theory and it proves impossible to make the necessary substitutions, the situation becomes essentially like *case 2* below, in which a justification of the inference is not provided by the theory.

Case 2: '*a* = *b*' is not a theorem of *T*. In this case '*a* = *b*' may merely be a sentence of the metatheory and it is no longer possible to make the substitutions made in *case 1*. We may clearly suppose, then, that the application of the criterion does not yield '*T* assumes *b*' directly, and indeed even that the language of *T* does not contain the symbol '*b*'. Of course it does not follow that the inference is unjustified: it is only that it is not justified by appeal to *T*. So we must look elsewhere. Unfortunately this seems to be a question to which intuition brings no immediate answer since the exact nature of the relation of commitment has been left open to highly diverse interpretations. We should thus try to put the matter more concretely. Consider the following pair of arguments:

(1) *T* assumes Stendhal.
Stendhal is Marie Henri Beyle.
Therefore, *T* assumes Marie Henri Beyle.

(2) Smith assumes that Stendhal wrote
The Red and the Black.
Stendhal is Marie Henri Beyle.
Therefore, Smith assumes that
Marie Henri Beyle wrote *The Red and the Black*.

The question before us is whether we can legitimately interpret '*T* assumes *a*' in such a way that the conclusion of argument (1) does *not* give pause in the way that the conclusion of argument (2) does.

On our assumption that commitment is a relation between theories and other things, to seek an interpretation of '*T* assumes *a*' leads us to consider various ways of filling the second position of the relation. This does not necessarily mean searching for the "true referent" of '*a*', though our first candidate may give that impression. We are trying to find an adequate definition of the phrase subject only to the constraint that it be a relation between *T* and *something else*. This "something else" might prove *not* to be what '*a*' purports to name, and might nevertheless provide a satisfactory analysis of the relation. Thus it is useful to view the process of seeking an interpretation as follows. Ultimately we want to have it that

$$T \text{ assumes } a \text{ iff } R(T, \alpha).$$

The interpretation will consist in saying, first, what sort of thing α might be, and second, what relation is denoted by '*R*'. We shall see in what follows that significant conclusions can be drawn without considering the second component of the interpretation at all. We therefore turn to the first.

Here is an initial attempt: '*T* assumes *a*' means that *R* holds between *T* and *an entity* α, which is in fact named or described by '*a*.' This interpretation makes explicit the initial idea of Scheffler and Chomsky that what is under consideration is a relation between theories and entities of the sorts that they are claimed to presuppose or assume. Under this interpretation the inference to '*T* assumes Marie Henri Beyle' seems completely harmless, for *T* does assume an entity which is in fact named (or described) by 'Marie Henri Beyle', that is, *T* assumes Stendhal. If the *entities themselves* are what are assumed by theories, then the truth of a claim that *T* assumes a particular entity should be wholly independent of the means of referring to that entity. But, as might be expected, this interpretation does not work. For in restricting the second position of the relation to occupancy by entities, it renders it impossible for a theory to assume anything which does not exist (i.e., which is not an entity). In terms of the earlier discussion of existential generalization, this interpretation has the effect of imposing the requirement that in the locution 'T assumes a', 'a' designates. (Equivalently, that 'T assumes a' is to be defined by '$R(T, a)$'.) This interpretation thus makes it impossible for any theory to assume, for example, Pegasus or Count Dracula.

For reasons essentially like those given above, Scheffler and Chomsky abandon the idea that an entity belongs in the second position and consider the possibility that it should instead be filled by a *class*. The idea is that since there is an empty class, the failure (for example) of Pegasus to exist would not prevent the theory of Pegasus from having an ontological commitment. Now if this just means that such theories are committed to the empty class, then it would have the consequence that the theory of Pegasus and the theory of Dracula have the same ontological commitment. But of course they do not.

To make this approach succeed we would have to devise an *intensional* treatment of classes: one which made the class consisting of Pegasus and the class consisting of Dracula *distinct* though their extensions (in this world) are the same.

Scheffler and Chomsky [6] speak (at 74) of a theory's positing "the non-emptiness of a class." Such an interpretation might avoid the above pitfalls and cast light on whether the inference to 'T assumes b' is justified in *case 2*. But what is it to posit the nonemptiness of a class? Presumably it is to posit *that* a certain class is nonempty, which would seem to make R a relation between T and a *sentence*. For example, '$\{x: x = \text{Pegasus}\} \neq \phi$', where '$\phi$' denotes the empty set. Such a sentence, moreover, is one from which reference to classes is readily removed without undue violence to intent. It can be replaced, for example, by '$\exists x(x = \text{Pegasus})$'. Interpretations which treat commitment as a relation between theories and sentences will be considered below.

The difficulties which plague the "entity" and "class" interpretations undoubtedly have their roots in ordinary language, where we find it completely natural to say in the same breath that a theory assumes Pegasus and that Pegasus does not exist. Although there are interpretations which render such language consistent and appropriate, we have seen that they cannot treat 'T assumes a' as

expressing a relation between a theory T and the "entity" a or the class consisting of that supposed entity. After finding similar difficulties for these interpretations, Scheffler and Chomsky surmise that the context is opaque. This overlooks the possibility of other interpretations.

Abandoning the idea of a relation between theories and entities or classes forces us in the direction of intensionality. We seem faced with the following alternative. Either we permit the second position of the context to range over intensional objects, such as concepts or whatever, or else we find a way of interpreting 'T assumes a' which makes a suitable accommodation for the cases in which 'a' fails to designate. Obviously the first route is not inviting to Quine even if it does lead to a successful treatment of commitment. But nor is the second. For Quine himself has observed: "Failure of substitutivity reveals merely that the occurrence to be supplanted is not *purely referential*, that is, that the statement depends not only on the object but on the form of the name" ([5], 140). Having ruled out intensional objects and there being no *other* objects possibly denoted by 'a', we can only conclude that there is nothing *but* the form of the name for the statement to depend on. So we might say that the occurrence of 'a' is entirely nonreferential. In such a situation we should expect substitutivity to fail unless perhaps the *theory* provides the ground for the substitution (viz., '$a = b$'). But recall that we are now considering the more troublesome case: that in which the theory does not yield '$a = b$'. Hence it is to be expected that substitutivity should fail. It is in just this sense that commitment is asserted to be intensional: substitutivity of codesignative expressions in the second position of the locution 'T assumes a' fails.

To recapitulate, we are assuming with Scheffler and Chomsky that 'T assumes a' expresses some binary relation. But there is no object (except perhaps an intensional object) that can stand in the second position and be denoted by the letter 'a'. We can only infer, then, that 'T assumes a' expresses some relation between T and the *expression* 'a' ($R(T, \text{'}a\text{'})$) or between T and a *sentence* in which 'a' occurs essentially (such as '$\exists x(x = a)$'). It is easy to see, however, that a relation between T and such a sentence can readily be reinterpreted as a relation between T and the expression 'a'.

This kind of analysis, given that the aim of the criterion is to reveal the commitment of the *theory*, would be believable only if it depended solely and intimately upon the way in which the expression '*a*' occurred in the theory. But since by hypothesis the expression '*b*' does not occur in T at all, it cannot be that T bears the same relation to '*b*'. (It is sometimes rather difficult in such cases to say just what is meant by the metatheoretical assertion '*a* = *b*'.) Substitutivity must therefore fail, and the context is thus opaque under any plausible interpretation which places an expression (or a sentence) in the second position. Notice that although this shows 'T assumes *a*' to be opaque with respect to the second position, in the defining formula '$R(T, \alpha)$', 'α' denotes the *expression* '*a*', so R *itself* is so far *transparent*. Substitution for 'α' by an expression which designates the expression '*a*' does not disturb the truth-value of '$R(T, \alpha)$'.

The latter of the earlier mentioned alternatives thus should appear no more acceptable to Quine than the first. There is a genuine dilemma for anyone averse to the theory of meaning: in order to establish a criterion of ontological commitment we must either recognize intensional entities or else adopt a referentially opaque definition of 'T assumes *a*'. In this paper it has not been argued that either of these courses would prove satisfactory, but only that the other possibilities do not.

It has been emphasized that the arguments leading to this conclusion make use of the assumption that 'T assumes *a*' is meant to express a relation between the theory T and something else. It is possible to view it instead, for each T, as a predicate (i.e., a unary relation) of the thing that properly occupied the second position on the original

construal (whether this thing proved to be a presumed object, a class of presumed objects, a concept, a sentence, or an expression). It is easy to see that the same reasoning I have given would apply equally if commitment were construed in this rather unnatural way since the first position (now "projected" out of consideration) has played no role in the argument. Of course I have not eliminated the possibility of a totally different treatment of commitment, but I have no idea what such an approach would be like and cannot imagine that it could succeed unless it were in fact translatable into the relational approach.[4]

Scheffler and Chomsky held that certain difficulties that arise for interpretations of Quine's criterion would be accounted for by the opacity of commitment context. The present investigation reveals that these problems result *not* from opacity but rather from the assumption that an entity or class is what belongs in the second position of the relation. Neither Scheffler and Chomsky nor I rely upon opacity in unveiling these difficulties. Indeed, it should be obvious that under either of these interpretations the context is in fact *extensional*: if the truth or falsity of 'T assumes *a*' depends solely upon a specific entity or class, then the occurrence of '*a*' is, in Quine's phrase, *purely referential*, and substitutivity should hold. The difficulties that arise here simply reflect the fact that these interpretations are inadequate. It is when one turns from these to more promising interpretations that intensionality sets in.

Notes

A different version of this paper was read at the University of Illinois at Chicago Circle in January, 1970, and at the Rockefeller University Research Colloquium the following month. I am grateful to John M. Dolan, Edmund L. Gettier, Saul A. Kripke, and Robert A. Schwartz for helpful criticisms.

1 Quine has been criticized for using a host of different terms in connection with the commitment relation. Examples are 'presupposes', 'presumes', 'is committed to', and so forth. Since Quine is seeking to define a precise relation which will square with our intuitions on the matter of commitment, I find this objection without force. The differences of meaning among these expressions in their everyday uses seem in no way to undercut his enterprise. Accordingly I shall use these various terms interchangeably with the understanding that the technical relation is intended.

2 Quine has been unfairly criticized by authors who have utilized examples of commitments of one kind in order to discredit formulations of the criterion appropriate for commitments of the other kind. Of course if there are these different sorts of commitment, then formulations which differ only to this extent should be viewed as coordinate and not as competing versions.

3 Quine ([5], 141, 147–8) argues rightly and in a parallel fashion that the context '——is unaware that . . .' is opaque.

4 John Dolan noticed that the projection could also be taken the other way. That would be to treat commitment as a predicate of theories by having a different sort of commitment for each presumed thing (a "Pegasus-commitment" or a "class-commitment" for example). This approach would again translate into the far more natural relational one.

References

[1] Cartwright, Richard L. "Ontology and the Theory of Meaning", *Philosophy of Science* 21 (1954): 316–25.

[2] Quine, W. V. "Notes on the Theory of Reference", 130–8 in *From a Logical Point of View*, second edition. Cambridge, Mass, 1961.

[3] ——. "On Universals", *Journal of Symbolic Logic* 12 (1947): 74–84.

[4] ——. "Ontology and Ideology", *Philosophical Studies* 2 (1951): 11–15.

[5] ——. "Reference and Modality", 139–59 in *From a Logical Point of View*.

[6] Scheffler, Israel and Chomsky, Noam. "What is Said To Be", *Proceedings of the Aristotelian Society* 59 (1958–9): 71–82.

Index

Index

Index